Introducing Hinduism

Introducing Hinduism describes the array of beliefs and practices of the majority of the people of South Asia, particularly those of India and Nepal.

Introducing Hinduism is the ideal starting point for students wishing to undertake a comprehensive study of this fascinating religion. This lively introduction explores the complexities of Hinduism, including its social structures, especially its caste system, its rituals and many scriptures, its vast mythology and varieties of deities and its religious philosophies. Hillary Rodrigues, an experienced teacher of the Hindu tradition, emphasises the importance of Hindu rituals and practice, subjects of particular interest in contemporary scholarship.

Illustrated throughout, the book also includes text boxes, summary charts, a glossary and a list of further reading to aid students' understanding and revision.

Hillary P. Rodrigues was born in India and has spent many years living, traveling, and studying Eastern religions in South and South-east Asia. He has over a dozen years' experience teaching the Hindu religion to undergraduate students at the University of Lethbridge, where he has been honored with the Distinguished Teaching Award.

World Religions series

Edited by Damien Keown and Charles S. Prebish

This exciting series introduces students to the major world religious traditions. Each religion is explored in a lively and clear fashion by experienced teachers and leading scholars in the field of world religion. Up-to-date scholarship is presented in a student-friendly fashion, covering history, core beliefs, sacred texts, key figures, religious practice and culture, and key contemporary issues. To aid learning and revision, each text includes illustrations, summaries, explanations of key terms, and further reading.

Introducing Buddhism
Charles S. Prebish and Damien Keown

Introducing Hinduism
Hillary P. Rodrigues

Forthcoming:

Introducing Christianity
Introducing Islam

Introducing Hinduism

Hillary P. Rodrigues

Routledge
Taylor & Francis Group
NEW YORK AND LONDON

First published 2006
by Routledge
270 Madison Ave, New York, NY 10016

Simultaneously published in the UK
by Routledge
2 Park Square, Milton Park, Abingdon, Oxon OX14 4RN

Reprinted 2006, 2007 (twice), 2008, 2010

Routledge is an imprint of the Taylor & Francis Group, an informa business

Typeset in Jenson and Tahoma by
HWA Text and Data Management, Tunbridge Wells
Printed and bound in Great Britain by
the MPG Books Group

British Library Cataloguing in Publication Data
A catalogue record for this book is available from the British Library

Library of Congress Cataloging-in-Publication Data
A catalog record for this book has been applied for

ISBN10: 0-415-39268-3 (hbk)
ISBN10: 0-415-39269-1 (pbk)

ISBN13: 978-0-415-39268-6 (hbk)
ISBN13: 978-0-415-39269-3 (pbk)

To my sisters, Ninette and Delyse, who grace everyone with their love, and to my brother, Darryl, whose *darśana* immeasurably enriches my life.

sarvo mamāyaṃ vibhava ityevaṃ parijānataḥ/
viśvātmano vikalpānāṃ prasare 'pi maheśatā//

Contents

Illustrations xi
Acknowledgements xiii
Preface xvi
A note on transliteration xx
Preliminary guidelines on pronunciation xxi

Introduction 1
Preamble 1
"Hinduism," "Hindu," and "India" defined 4
The geographical distribution of Hindus 5
The Indian subcontinent 5
The Indus Valley Civilization 8
Indus Valley religion 10
The Āryans 12
Āryan and non-Āryan influences 14
A brief history of Hinduism 17

1 Vedic religion 24
The Vedic Saṃhitās 25
Vedic deities 26
Ṛta *and cosmic order* 27
The Brāhmaṇas 28
Vedic rituals (yajña) 28
Soma 33
The Āraṇyakas 33
The Upaniṣads 34
Ātman and Brahman 36
Śruti *and* Smṛti 37
Other Vedic literature 38
Astrology 39
Āyurveda 40

2 ***Karma*** **and cosmology** **45**
The Hindu conception of time 45
The Hindu Calendar 47
The Hindu universe 48
Karma, Saṃsāra, *and Reincarnation* 50
Mokṣa 52

3 **Hindu social organization and values** **55**
Dharma *and the Dharma Śāstras* 55
The four classes of Hindu society 57
The caste system 60
The Untouchables 65
Purity and pollution 66
Auspiciousness and inauspiciousness 70

4 ***Dharma*** **and the individual** **76**
Hindu rites of passage (saṃskāra) 77
Investiture with the Sacred Thread (upanayana) 78
Marriage (vivāha) 80
Householder's saṃskāras 84
Final Sacrifice (antyeṣṭi) 86
The four goals/aims and the four stages of life 89
Women in Hinduism 94
Vowed ascetic observances (vrata) *and auspiciousness* (saubhagya) 96
Marriage and pativrata 97
Satī *and the status of widows* 99

5 **The Sanskrit language** **105**
Pāṇinī and the Aṣṭādhyāyī 109
The sphoṭa *theory of language* 109
Structure of the Sanskrit alphabet 110
Mantra *and the theology of sound* 111

6 **Indian philosophical schools** **115**
The wandering philosophers 119
Orthodox versus heterodox schools 120
The heterodox philosophies 121
The six orthodox systems 123

7 **The Epics (Itihāsa)** **136**
The Rāmāyaṇa 137
The Mahābhārata 144

8 The *Bhagavad Gītā* and the rise of *bhakti* **154**
The Bhagavad Gītā *154*
The householder versus the renouncer 157
The Bhagavad Gītā*'s three yogas 158*
Jñāna yoga 158
Karma yoga 160
Bhakti yoga 162
South Indian Hinduism and the rise of devotionalism 165
The Ālvārs and the Nāyanārs 166

9 Major Hindu theistic sects **172**
Śaivism 172
Vaiṣṇavism 177
Śāktism 180

10 Hindu deities and Purāṇic mythology **188**
The Purāṇas 188
The decline of the Vedic deities 190
Śaiva deities: iconography, myths, and festivals 192
Vaiṣṇava deities: iconography, myths, and festivals 199
Śākta deities: iconography, myths, and festivals 205
Other deities 213

11 Hindu art and worship rituals **222**
A note on orthodoxy 225
Domestic worship and pūjā *227*
Darśana *and temple worship 230*
The Hindu temple 234
Some noteworthy temples 236
Sacred specialists 239
Hindu pilgrimage 242

12 Vedānta **249**
Śaṅkara's radical non-dualism 250
Rāmānuja's qualified non-dualism 252
Madhva's dualism 253

13 Tantra **257**
The origins of Tantra 257
Characteristic elements of Hindu Tantra 258
Śaivism in Kashmir 260
Non-dualistic tantric philosophy 261
Kuṇḍalinī yoga 263
The Left Hand Path 265

Goddesses and women in tantra 266
Symbolism of tantric mantras *and* yantras 266

14 Reform and revitalization **273**
Some early critiques of Hinduism and its responses 274
Islam in India (a brief history) 275
Hinduism under Islam 276
Religious syncretism (e.g. bhakti, *Sufism, tantra) in North India* 277
The British in India (A brief history) 280
Hindu responses to Christianity 282
Related developments 285
Hinduism in universalistic religion 286
Hinduism and humanism 288
Hinduism and politics 290

15 Hinduism beyond India **301**
Hinduism in Nepal 306
Hinduism in South-east Asia 308
Hinduism in Indonesia 309

16 Hinduism and the West **314**
Diaspora Hinduism 315
Hinduism for the West 316
Some contemporary teachers of Hinduism to Westerners 323

17 Select themes in Hinduism **329**
Hinduism and ecology 329
Some noteworthy figures in contemporary Hinduism 332
Hinduism and modernity 333

Appendix I **341**
A timeline of Hinduism 341

Appendix II **346**
A: Pronunciation guide and general glossary 346
B: Pronunciation guide and glossary of people's names 361
C: Pronunciation guide and glossary of place names 368
D: Pronunciation guide and glossary of texts 374

Further reading **380**
Index **382**

Illustrations

0.1 A temple lies partly toppled and submerged on the banks of the river Gaṅgā in whose holy waters worshippers bathe (Banāras) 3
0.2 Map of the Indian subcontinent indicating major cities and religious centers 7
0.3 *Liṅga* and *yoni* stones at the edge of a contemporary Hindu temple bathing tank (Nepal) 13
1.1 Brahmins chant Vedic verses and make offerings as a Brahmin patron pours ghee into the flames during this modern *homa* ritual, derived from ancient *yajña* procedures 29
1.2 In the teacher–student image of the Upaniṣads, a father recites from a Sanskrit text teaching his son the value of such learning 35
2.1 A relief depicting the creator god Brahmā emerging seated on a lotus flower growing from the navel of Viṣṇu, who reclines on the endless serpent Ananta (Vijayanagar) 47
3.1 Vagish Shastri, a Brahmin *paṇḍita* and founder of the Vāg-Yoga Institute, at work in his library (Banāras) 63
4.1 A young Brahmin priest performs a *saṃskāra* rite on behalf of a Brahmin family 78
4.2 Newly-wed Hindu couple at a Nāga shrine making offerings in the hope of obtaining children (South India) 85
4.3 A renouncer (*saṃnyāsin*) sits beside an image of Gaṇeśa in the hope of receiving donations from passing worshippers 94
6.1 A Vaiṣṇava renouncer uses prayer beads concealed in a cloth bag as an aid to concentration in his spiritual practice (Nasik) 129
7.1 Lithograph depicting Hanumān setting Laṅkā ablaze with his fiery tail 141
7.2 Lithograph depicting Vālmīki composing the *Rāmāyaṇa* in his *āśrama* with Sītā and her sons Lāva and Kuśa in the background 142
7.3 Lithograph depicting Vyāsa dictating the *Mahābhārata* to Gaṇeśa, the elephant-headed deity who serves as his scribe 144
7.4 Lithograph depicting Duḥśāsana in his attempt to disrobe Draupadī, who is saved by Kṛṣṇa's miraculous intercession 147
8.1 Life-size statue depicting Kṛṣṇa as charioteer delivering the teachings of the Bhagavad Gītā to Arjuna (Rishikesh) 155
9.1 An Aghori Śākta tantric master, Nāgabābā, with disciples, friends, and local village children (Tārāpīṭha Vindhyachal) 182

10.1 Bronze masterpiece depicting Śiva and Pārvatī in classic embrace with rich symbolic significance (Patan Museum, Nepal) 196
10.2 A devotee, with piercings through his tongue and cheek, prepares to carry a decorated *kavaṭi* arch supported by long metal needles inserted in his flesh (Malaysia) 199
10.3 Lithograph depicting Sarasvatī, holding the lute (*vīṇā*), prayer beads, and the Vedas 206
10.4 Lithograph depicting Lakṣmī holding lotus flowers and the jar of plenitude. It also portrays Viṣṇu witnessing Lakṣmī's emergence during the mythic churning of the ocean 208
10.5 Close-up of a tantric practitioner's home shrine image of Kālī, tongue extended, wielding a sword and severed head 210
10.6 Large bas-relief depicting Durgā atop her lion mount battling the buffalo demon Mahiṣa (Mahabalipuram) 212
11.1 Researcher joins singers of devotional hymns (*bhajan*) in the temple courtyard of the goddess Āvarī Mātā where dozens huddle through a night-long vigil in the hope of being cured of their ailments (Rajasthan) 225
11.2 A woman burns honorific flames in her worship at a small shrine to Durgā situated within a large temple complex (Cidambaram) 228
11.3 A woman reverently touches a shrine's entrance in her own rites of devotion within a larger temple complex (Banāras) 232
11.4 The North Indian temple with its soaring spire (*śikhara*) and mountain motif (Khajuraho) 235
11.5 Bṛhadīśvara temple built by the Cola emperor Rājarāja I in honor of Śiva (Thanjavur) 239
11.6 The sensuous form of an *apsaras* graces the walls of a Hindu temple (Khajuraho) 241
13.1 An experienced Bengali ritualist performs an elaborate tantric *pūjā* assisted by a novice *tantradhāraka* 259
13.2 A stone image (*mūrti*) of Śiva's terrifying aspect as Bhairava (Bhaktapur, Nepal) 262
13.3 A copper *yantra* embedded in a temple floor, strewn with flower petals, rice and other offerings (Nepal) 267
15.1 A Hindu ascetic suspended with hooks through his flesh swings from a bamboo scaffold and offers prophesies (Kataragama, Sri Lanka) 306
15.2 Newari Hindu virgin girls (*kumārī*) in Nepal undergo a rite of passage in which they are married to Viṣṇu in the form of a wood-apple fruit 307
15.3 Dance performance in Bali enacting Hindu religious themes 311
16.1 Lifelike image of Swami Bhaktivedanta, founder of ISKCON, at the organization's headquarters in Britain (Watford) [Photo courtesy of Sarah Ginn] 320
17.1 Lithograph depicting the goddess Gaṅgā atop her crocodile mount 330

Acknowledgments

It may seem odd to offer formal thanks to India, the land of my birth, but I cannot dismiss the crucial role that it played in shaping the experiences and sensibilities of my childhood. My father was a forest officer, who sometimes walked a 20 mile daily beat in the jungles of Bombay State, and my mother was a school teacher who studied in Calcutta, where she majored in French language and literature. Our family moved frequently, based on where my father was posted, and so I lived in Dohad, Mandvi, Kolhapur, Poona, and Bandra, a suburb of Bombay, which was home for both my parents. My mother's father was a chief engineer for the Bombay electrical and transport system, and as kids we thus often found ourselves oscillating between my father's work world in the forest, and my mother's world, shaped by vestigial colonial values.

On jungle visits we would stay in forest bungalows and even in huts floored with dried cowdung, or ride in bullock carts. Sometimes we would gather around campfires where villagers wrapped in rough blankets told stories about tigers and local spirits. I particularly remember my father overseeing the construction of a botanical park at the hill-station of Panhala, not far from Kolhapur, where we lived for many years. There, the *mahārāja's* son would come to school in an elegant coach drawn by different pairs of horses. We got to school by horse-drawn *tonga* or the school bus. By contrast, in my mother's father's home we would dine on porcelain dishes set on white linen, and be expected to eat with at least six pieces of silver cutlery. My grandfather would don a solar-topee as he tended to his large garden, teeming with fruit trees and flowers. We would often spend the long holidays with him in Bombay flying kites, going to movies at the Bandra Talkies, or playing by the seaside and eating *bhelpuri* at sunset.

When our family left India, its reality faded as I grew and embraced the culture of our new world and life in Canada. Although I graduated with a degree in chemistry, the counter-culture movement of the 60s and 70s had rekindled my interest in the East. During my year-long travels in Latin America in the mid-70s I heard stories from fellow backpackers who fed the flames of my curiosity about Asian lands and philosophies, and I was soon doing the (mostly) overland route from Montreal to Bali, an ultra low-budget journey of many years in duration. On a sunset ride with my brother on the rooftop of a bus through the Khyber Pass, we entered the subcontinent and into the long-forgotten but unmistakable smell of India. I spent about a year and a half in the region, traveling alone, crisscrossing the country from the Punjab to Sri Lanka to Kashmir and Nepal to Bengal. I flew out of Calcutta to Rangoon on the festival day of Holi, witnessing the joyous pandemonium as millions doused each other with color, realizing even then that India was a place of such tantalizing complexity that I would certainly be drawn back to her.

However, it was more than twenty years before I returned to India in order to conduct fieldwork as part of my doctoral degree work in Religious Studies. Then, too, I spent another 18 months there, mostly in Banāras, where I was affiliated with the History of Art Department at Banāras Hindu University, but did manage to travel extensively for months at a time. In the decade and a half since those years, I have been back to India and Southeast Asia at least a half-dozen times, for weeks or months, with or without my children. Although it may sound clichéd, the lands of my travels and all of the people I have encountered along the way, from con-men, touts, and thieves, to wise travelers, sages, and local inhabitants, have been my teachers. At times, some of them imparted lessons I still value more highly than much of what I have learned through my formal instruction, and so I choose to acknowledge them here.

Of course, I would not have been able to write this book were it not for my formal education in the scholarly study of religion and Hinduism. However, here, too, I recognize that my professors and colleagues taught me as much through the qualities they themselves embodied as through the knowledge they imparted. For instance, from John Arapura and Krishna Shivaraman I learned a love of Indian philosophical traditions, a respect for the profundity of their content, and a realization that sound thinking applied in any particular intellectual context may be easily transposed to other spheres of thought. From Paul Younger I learned to strive to look beyond the obvious appearances of phenomena, such as festival rituals, and to ask courageous questions of my data in order to extract concealed meanings. David Kinsley taught me, through his example, how to teach large audiences of students, and how to mentor with infectious enthusiasm. Ellen Badone, Bill Rodman, and Richard Preston showed me how I might conduct, read, and write ethnography, skills that were subsequently nourished by my colleagues in the Department of Anthropology at the University of Lethbridge, which I chaired for several years. Rosalind Lefeber and Phyllis Granoff guided me deftly through the study of Sanskrit, revitalizing my scientist's delight in rigor, and awakening in me an appreciation for the elegance of grammar.

Om Prakash Sharma, known to virtually every scholar who has conducted fieldwork in Banāras, embodies many of the ambiguities and shifting characterizations of the indigenous research assistant and informant. A master research assistant,

Omji was tutored in his craft as a young man by Jonathan Parry, and has served as such for innumerable scholars. However, as a devout Śākta, to me he was both an informant and mentor, by turns serving as my helper, or my teacher. I am particularly proud to call him my friend. Although Pandits Vagish Shastri and Hemendranath Chakravarty both enhanced my understanding of Sanskrit, my respect, affection, and memories seem hinged to different associations. Vagish Shastri, founder of the Vāg-Yoga Institute, is an icon of orthodox, yet accessible Brahminism, who also provided me with crucial insights into the Hindu teacher–student relationship. Pandit Chakravarty, a student of the renowned scholar Gopinath Kaviraj, taught with a wry humor and open-mindedness that embody attitudes I can no longer disassociate from Tantrism.

There are dozens of people, some formal instructors, others friends, who have nourished my understanding of Hinduism. I cannot list them all here. Similarly, I can but acknowledge my gratitude to the hundreds of fellow scholars who do not know me personally, but from whose labors I continue to learn. Although I have had the benefit of living in India for extended periods of time, and studying Hinduism with an array of teachers from the East and the West, I have also learned through the writings of my colleagues. Thus although it is my hope that this book encourages some to embark upon travels to the East, or to further their studies with living teachers, I would be particularly pleased to know that the novice reader has come away with an enhanced and appreciative understanding of the Hindu tradition. Should this prove true, it would affirm the value of the academic enterprise, which holds the written word as both a crucial medium for the transmission of knowledge, and, despite contrary assertions, an effective catalyst in the expansion of consciousness.

On the practical side, this book would not have reached its timely release were it not for the gentle prodding of Charles Prebish, one of the editors of this series. He, together with Damien Keown, offered enthusiastic support and sound judgment on numerous occasions. I also received unflagging support and guidance from Lesley Riddle and Gemma Dunn, editors at this publishing house. I must also thank my many students over the years at the University of Lethbridge, whose interest in Asian religions continues to inspire me. I extend a special thanks to my student research assistant, J'Lean Lawton, whose keen eye and wide assortment of labors have made this a much better book than it would otherwise have been.

Preface

While introductory texts on Hinduism are not particularly abundant, there are certainly a number of excellent ones available. However, having taught a second-year undergraduate course on the Hindu tradition for over a dozen years, and having evaluated or utilized virtually all of the existing texts, I found myself still yearning for a book that would present Hinduism in a manner that was effective for my students. I teach at the University of Lethbridge in the Western Canadian province of Alberta. Although Canada's multicultural character and the university's foreign student population ensure that my classes have a small percentage of Hindus, some directly from India and several second-generation immigrants, the majority of students enter my courses knowing surprisingly little about Hinduism or Asia. Their background knowledge may derive from some rudimentary exposure to the geography of Asia in elementary school and through occasional interactions with Hindu classmates or friends. They have had virtually no exposure to the history of South Asia. Mostly, they are equipped with caricature images of Hindus through movies and other media representations such as *The Simpsons*. Many, although not all, might have had nominal exposure to Hinduism in an introductory course in World Religions. Conversations with colleagues suggest that such a knowledge profile is not uncommon in most introductory level Western university classroom settings.

This book is therefore crafted for the benefit of anyone wishing to embark upon the study of Hinduism, and whose foundational knowledge is relatively slight. Its material is not presented with the assumption that the reader already knows where Bengal or the Punjab are located, or even that these are states in India. Nor is there the assumption that the reader knows when and how Islam or the British entered the Indian subcontinent. Instead, the book has sections that briefly introduce the geography and history of the subcontinent. It is also equipped with a map and a chronological chart. Efforts are frequently made to clarify whether the item under discussion is a book, a person, a school of thought, a scriptural genre, and so on, since most of these terms are linguistically unfamiliar to students. Furthermore, since the vast majority of students who take up this text are unlikely to continue much further with the formal study of the Hindu tradition, I have refrained from introducing a plethora of unnecessary names, such as those of contemporary scholars, in the body of the text. However, the accessible prose and succinct presentation does not imply a watering down of content, concepts, and the most recent theoretical formulations. Bibliographic references point to more detailed studies in various areas by notable scholars, should readers be interested in writing research essays or otherwise deepening their investigations.

This book attempts to strike a balance between the two extremes that are characteristic of most of the existing Hinduism texts, namely, conveying too much or too little information. Certain introductory studies of Hinduism are so brief as to be useful only for casual readers, while others go into such excessive enumerations of scriptural texts, thinkers, sects, political parties, deities, the research discoveries of particular scholars, and so on, that the novice student is left bewildered. Some of the material within these overly detailed texts reflects needless attempts by the author to demonstrate personal expertise in the field or familiarity with the cutting-edge work of colleagues. A comprehensive university-level introduction to the Hindu tradition should indeed expose students to more texts than the *Ṛg Veda*, the *Bhagavad Gītā*, and the *Rāmāyaṇa*, but it need not discuss the *Yoginīhṛdaya*. And while it should introduce more than Śaṅkara and Mahatma Gandhi, it need not discuss Nimbarka or Utpaladeva. Of course, this does not imply any less worth to these exclusions, but merely reflects a restriction on the depth to which a particular topic is plumbed.

Although it purports to be comprehensive without being pedantic, this textbook does contain more information than may be reasonably covered in a given semester. However, this is due more to its array of topics than to the content within any particular section. Instructors may thus ignore particular portions of the text entirely, while holding students completely responsible for acquiring the knowledge within other sections. There are diverse motivations for embarking on the study of Hinduism, and this text attempts to engage students with a wide assortment of related interests, including history, culture, art and architecture, politics, social organization, language and literature, mythology, ritual, and philosophy. Inevitably, some instructors may wish that particular areas of personal interest (e.g. South Indian Hinduism, women's issues, or contemporary Hinduism in the West – although these are discussed in more detail than in many similar texts) were given more extensive treatment. However, the book is designed pragmatically, and although it can stand on its own as a resource for entering into an understanding of Hinduism, it is intended not to replace but to complement an instructor's capacity to lead their students into more detailed investigations in areas of their specialization, interest, or concern.

While certain religious traditions, such as Buddhism or Islam, readily lend themselves to a presentational structure derived from their origins, historical developments, and spread, the structuring of a Hinduism text presents distinctive challenges. This book might have been organized thematically, divided into such categories as beliefs, practices, scriptures, values, and so on. It could have started with contemporary Hindu practices and then, like peeling an onion-skin, worked to uncover the ancient sources layered in these rites. Other texts have adopted such strategies. However, one has to make a choice, and I have found the semi-historical structuring of material to be particularly effective. After having discussed the early configurations of some religious phenomenon, such as a belief or ritual practice, the text may then proceed, sometimes through a case study, to illustrate its endurance in contemporary Hinduism. For instance, when discussing *jñāna yoga* in the context of the *Bhagavad Gītā,* I offer the case of Ramaṇa Mahāṛṣi, a modern figure who exemplifies this approach.

This structure might be initially frustrating to some, particularly to students from Hindu backgrounds, for instance, who might assume that vegetarianism was always part of Hindu practice, or who do not "recognize" the face of "their religion" in early Vedic or Tantric rites. Of course, the historical study of anyone's own religious tradition is often surprising and instructive. As the text progresses, these students will likely be pleased to find many of their questions answered, and indeed recognize and better understand their brand of Hinduism. Often, the "burden" of their familiarity with aspects of the tradition eventually becomes an asset. For the majority of students, "unburdened" by experience and belief (in Hinduism), the semi-historical approach can be reassuring. It provides them with a structure, like a symbolic raft, with which to navigate the turbulent waters of the Hindu tradition, from the various tributaries of its ancient sources, which repeatedly merge and divide, to its surge into the future.

If reader-friendliness is so fundamental to this text, one might wonder why I have insisted on the use of diacritic marks when transliterating foreign language terms. One compelling rationale is that every scholar who is seriously engaged in the study of Hinduism uses them. Sanskrit, the foreign language most encountered in this book, is a phonetic language. Thus if one knows its rules of pronunciation, words may be uttered exactly as they should be. Scholars have agreed upon a standardized method of transliterating Sanskrit into English. Phonetic spellings, without the use of diacritics, may appear less intimidating, but tend to perpetuate errors. When students who understand the rules of Sanskrit pronunciation see "Śiva," they immediately know how it is pronounced. However, when rendered as "Shiva" for the reader's convenience, instead of the correct "SHIV-uh," it tends to be mispronounced as "SHEE-vaa," with lengthened "i" and "a" sounds. Also, without diacritics, there is no way of distinguishing between the male god Śiva and the goddess Śivā, or between the goddess Kālī and the Kali Yuga. Most importantly, an appreciation of the vital role played by the Sanskrit language in the Hindu tradition (as discussed in Chapter 5) is greatly diminished when one shies away from diacritics.

The potential for progress in the study in Hinduism may also be impeded when diacritics are not used. A formally transcribed word such as "*saṃskāra*" may be informally rendered as "*samskara*," "*sanskara*," "*samskar*" or "*sanskar*" in various formulations, based on whether one opts for Sanskritic or Hindi-based pronunciation schemes. A student who has been taught "*sanskar*" would later find it difficult to recognize that "*saṃskāra*" in other textbooks refers to the same concept. It is true that words such as Viṣṇu or Kṛṣṇa appear unusual when compared to the commonly rendered Vishnu and Krishna. However, the pronunciation guide that is provided will enable students to pronounce such frequently occurring terms correctly. Presenting Sanskrit terms without their diacritics would be like rendering French words, such as "*garçon*" or "*élève*," without their distinctive accents.

As technology and the forces of globalization help to dissolve the boundaries that isolated cultures from each other, we begin to see more examples of foreign words entering the English language. One no longer resists using the word "sushi," or stumbles with the name of one's friend, Māyā. Thus this text has not shied away from introducing key Sanskrit terms. These generally serve a purpose and are not included to make the subject needlessly challenging. Incidentally, all translations in this text, often rendered as paraphrases, are my own. When translating a verse or phrase from a scripture, I have occasionally indicated key terms in the original language, sometimes to justify my rendition. However, most of the foreign terms that appear in this text are crucial for understanding the Hindu tradition. They are intended to provide readers with a solid foundation, leaving them poised for further formal or informal studies.

The imaginary scenarios are provided to animate the subject material. While presented to draw students into the world of Hinduism through the proven powers of narrative, creative visualization, humor, and mystery, the scenarios are not completely fabricated fictions. Their fiction lies in what they do not tell as much as in the distortion inherent in any kind of telling. Although this book is written for the scholarly study of a religious tradition, I felt it was worth conveying the slightest sense of the lived experience of Hindus, or at least of someone engaged in discovering what that might be. There is no intention in these scenarios to be comprehensive, to avoid Orientalism or Occidentalism, to provide a balanced treatment of gendered, class, regional, or topical perspectives. They are fragmentary vignettes, theoretically grounded in a variety of postmodern sensibilities. As much as it is also related to social, cultural, political, and economic factors, religion is very much about an engagement with the sacred, which is "set apart" from this-worldly values and realities. Thus although there is little justification for accepting the "reality" of a *sui generis* "sacred" in the scholarly study of religion, it is crucial that the scholar acknowledge the acceptance of such a reality among adherents of particular religious worldviews. The scenarios are thus also intended to evoke a sense of that encounter with the "other" (natural and supernatural), which is intrinsic to any such study.

A note on transliteration

Sanskrit diacritics are used for Sanskrit words, which are also used where a choice exists between Sanskrit and Hindi or Tamil equivalents. Hindi words, if used, are transliterated phonetically. Thus one finds the Sanskrit "*dharmaśālā*" instead of the Hindi phonetic "*dharamsālā*" and the Sanskrit Śiva and Saṅgham instead of the Tamil Civaṉ and Caṅkam, although Tamil and Hindi equivalents are provided on occasion. The compromise is to facilitate the students' learning experience without impeding their ability to engage in advanced studies.

The transliteration choices of the names of people, places, or organization may appear arbitrary, and to some extent they are. Place names are written as they commonly appear on maps, unless they figure significantly in religious or scholarly literature. Thus one finds Maharashtra, not Mahārāṣṭra, and Sri Lanka, not Śrī Laṅkā, but Kāśī, not Kashi, and Gaṅgā, not Ganga or the Ganges. The names of some persons or organizations, especially contemporary ones, which are routinely rendered in familiar ways, are reproduced in their commonly known forms. Thus one encounters Ramakrishna and Gangaji, instead of Rāmakṛṣṇa and Gaṅgājī.

The illustrative lithographs used in this book are from my personal collection, and all photographs are my own unless otherwise acknowledged. I have included lithographs not only because they convey aspects of contemporary Hindu aesthetics, but also because, when framed and used for worship by Hindus, which they often are, they may actually be regarded as images that embody a divine presence. At the end of each chapter, this book also presents brief sections on Further Readings. More extensive bibliographies for instructors and self-directed students who wish to kick-start further investigations, research essays, and so on, may be found at <http://www.mahavidya.ca/>. This website also provides links to translated scriptures, as well as to some in Sanskrit and Tamil for instructors who have facility with these primary languages. Audio-visual resources listed there not only provide general information on pertinent titles, but wherever possible, connect also directly to a supplier site.

Preliminary guidelines on pronunciation

The Glossaries in Appendix II provide phonetic pronunciations for significant Sanskrit words and other terms. A more extensive pronunciation guide and glossaries of all the Sanskrit terms used in this text may be found at <http:// www.mahavidya.ca/>. Other pertinent comments on pronunciation are also found in the section on the Sanskrit language in Chapter 5. The following general guidelines will enable the reader to pronounce many of the foreign terms mostly correctly, from the outset.

The short "a" in Sanskrit words is always pronounced like the "uh" in "huh," and the letter "c" is always pronounced like the "ch" in "chat." Thus *cakra* is not pronounced "SHAK-raa," but "CHUK-ruh," and Cola is not "KO-laa," but "CHO-luh." The long "ā" is pronounced like the "a" in "art," while "ś" and "ṣ" are mostly pronounced like the "s" in "sugar." Thus *āsana* is pronounced "AA-suh-nuh," while *āśrama* is not pronounced "ASH-rama," but "AA-shruh-muh." The short "u" and long "ū" are pronounced, respectively, like the "oo" in "loot" and a somewhat lengthened "oo" in "ooze." The so-called retroflex consonants, such as "ṭ" "ḍ" and "ṇ" and the vowel "ṛ" are sounded with the tongue at the roof of the mouth, as in the words "frond" or "front."

Particularly difficult to indicate are the Sanskrit dental "t" and "d" pronounced sounds. In the English alphabet, "t" and "d," when pronounced, actually sound closer to the Sanskrit "ṭ" and "ḍ" sounds. Thus *aṣṭa* and *maṇḍala* are pronounced like "UHSH-tuh" and "MUHN-duh-luh" respectively. By contrast, the Sanskrit "t" should be pronounced more like the "th" in "this" or "these." So *satya* does not sound like "SUT-yuh," but is pronounced "SUTH-yuh." It is somewhat more problematic to indicate the dental "d" in words such as *darśana*, which is somewhere between "DHUHR-shuh-nuh," and "THUHR-shuh-nuh." In the Glossary's pronunciation guide, such mixed consonant sounds will, for example, be indicated as "D/THUHR-shuh-nuh." Thus the word Hindu, which is commonly mispronounced as "HIN-doo," actually sounds somewhat closer to "HIN-d/thoo." So too, Hindi and Hinduism sound more like "HIN-d/thee" and "HIN-d/thoo-ism," respectively.

Long vowels provide an indication as to which syllable is emphasized. Unlike English, in polysyllabic words Sanskrit will place the emphasis, by default, on the third-from-last rather than on the second-last syllable. So *Rāmāyaṇa* is not "Raa-maa-YAA-naa," but something like "raa-MAA-yuh-nuh," and *Mahābhārata* is not pronounced "ma-haa-bha-RAA-taa," but "muh-HAA-BHAA-ruh-thuh". Students may take heart to know that many reputable and renowned scholars of Hinduism, including those who have made outstanding contributions in the area of Sanskrit translations, routinely mispronounce Sanskrit words. This is because the emphasis in Western scholarship has been on appropriating the language's challenging grammar, and learning to read and translate written material. Ironically, the religious significance of Sanskrit, particularly in the Hindu tradition, has been centrally based on its oral and sonic dimensions. This text thus seeks to orient the novice towards an appreciation of those crucial aspects of the sacred language even if they continue to struggle with appropriate pronunciation.

Introduction

In this chapter

This chapter is written to orient the reader to the study of Hinduism *writ large*. It discusses the problems involved in defining Hinduism and the tradition's inherent complexities. It provides an overview of the geography of the Indian subcontinent and the worldwide distribution of Hindus. Since the text is mostly structured along the lines of Hinduism's historical development, the Indus Valley Civilization and speculations on its religion serve as a starting point. Scholarly controversies concerning the nature of the Āryans are explored, as is the Āryan relationship to non-Āryan cultures. Foreshadowing the topical content and organizational layout of the book, the chapter ends with a succinct summary of the history of Hinduism.

Main topics covered

- Preamble
- "Hinduism," "Hindu," and "India" defined
- The geographical distribution of Hindus
- The Indian subcontinent
- The Indus Valley Civilization
- Indus Valley religion
- The Āryans
- Āryan and non-Āryan influences
- A brief history of Hinduism

Preamble

"Hinduism" is a loosely defined term used to designate the broad array of beliefs and practices of the majority of the people of South Asia, particularly those of India and Nepal. Practitioners of Hinduism are known as Hindus. If you walked along the banks of the Gaṅgā (Ganges) River in Vārāṇasī (Banāras), one of Hindu India's holiest cities, you would almost certainly begin to appreciate the wide diversity of Hinduism.

Imagine, if you will, this scenario

As the sun rises above the eastern horizon, it bathes the Gaṅgā and its western riverbank with a golden light, suggestive of one of Banāras's other names, Kāśī, the "luminous." The river Gaṅgā is believed to be a living goddess, and is thus deeply revered by most Hindus. At Banāras, the river's western bank is lined with old palaces, temples, and even the occasional hotel. Stone steps lead down to the river where hundreds of persons perform ritual baths believed to be spiritually purifying. Here, a man clad only in a loincloth stands in the river and performs oblations facing the rising sun. He fills a copper pot with river water and then, while uttering a Sanskrit prayer, pours it back in a slow stream. A loop of string is draped over his left shoulder and around his torso. There, an elderly widow who has finished her bath and donned a clean dry white *sārī*, carries away a jar of Gaṅgā water as she walks to the temple of the smallpox goddess, Śītalā, to perform her morning worship. You might pass wandering cows, venerated by Hindus, and even large bulls, sacred to the god Śiva. A group of men squats on a stone platform by the river. Their hair is wild and matted, and they have long beards and mustaches. Their bodies are smeared in ash. Their foreheads and upper arms are marked with three horizontal lines and two of the men appear to be holding tridents. They pass around a clay pipe filled with hashish, calling out in praise some of the many names of the great god Śiva, and then draw deeply of the intoxicating smoke. Nearby, tourist-pilgrims from the urban metropolis of Mumbai (Bombay), dressed in blue jeans and T-shirts click photos of these scenes from a large weathered rowboat, oared by one of the city's many boatmen. As part of their pilgrimage, they will make offerings to the black stone phallic emblem (*liṅga*) of Śiva as Lord of the Universe (Viśvanātha) in his golden-roofed temple located within a honeycomb of narrow, congested alleys in the heart of the old city.

Further along on your walk you come upon a cluster of large bonfires. You note that the flames lick at human corpses atop the wood pyres and realize that you have reached the city's cremation grounds. "Those men who burn the dead bodies are Doms," intones a distinguished elderly gentleman, wearing a long white shirt (*kurtā*) over drawstring pants (*pāyajāmā*), hoping to engage you in conversation. "They are Dalits." Through the ensuing discussion you learn more about the Hindu caste system and some of its complexities. For instance, even Brahmins, the highest class in the Hindu social hierarchy, who would acquire ritual pollution through contact with a Dalit (hence the term "Untouchable" is often used for members of that group), might nevertheless be cremated by an "Untouchable" Dom. You learn that your informant, himself a Brahmin, is a professor at Banāras Hindu University. You express to him

Figure 0.1 A temple lies partly toppled and submerged on the banks of the river Gaṅgā in whose holy waters worshippers bathe (Banāras)

your sense of wonder, yet confusion, about the many castes in Hindu society, the numerous deities, and so on. "All that exists is Śiva," he replies. "You, me, that Dom, those burning bodies, the Gaṅgā, the sand on its banks, the earth, the heavens, and all the gods and goddesses in those temples – they are all part of one great whole, and that is Śiva," he continues. "Does that mean everyone is a Hindu?", you ask. "No," he replies, "but everyone is Śiva, at least according to the philosophy that I follow." You leave with enhanced clarity about some issues, but with new questions about the relationship between religion and philosophy, about what it means to be a Hindu, and about how you and a grain of sand can both be God. As you leave the riverbank and meander with a group of pilgrims through the city's alleys towards the temple of Śiva Viśvanātha, you hope for a glimpse of its sacred stone liṅga. Unfortunately, your appearance alerts the priests to your non-Hindu status, and you are prevented from entering the temple.

The complexities of Hinduism are visible everywhere: in its social structure, its rituals, its vast mythology, its many scriptures, its variety of deities, and its religious philosophies. It is unreasonable to expect this book to plumb these complexities in the detail that they deserve. However, I hope to offer the reader an inroad into several of the most salient dimensions of the Hindu tradition. In tandem with material found at <http://www.mahavidya.ca/> which provides a window into a large assortment of resources, this book provides one of the most effective starting points for a comprehensive study of Hinduism.

"Hinduism," "Hindu," and "India" defined

"Hinduism" is actually a term that has been coined fairly recently. The words "Hindu" and "India" are derived from the Sanskrit word Sindhu (literally, "ocean"), used to name the great river, now known as the Indus, which flows from the Himalaya Mountains in Tibet, through modern-day Pakistan, into the Arabian Sea. The Sanskrit word for "place" is *sthāna*, and thus the region around and beyond the Indus River was known as Sindh or Hindusthāna. One of the great river valley civilizations, the Indus Valley Civilization flourished there from about 2500 BCE to 1500 BCE. The Greeks, after Alexander the Great's encounter with the territory in the fourth century BCE, named the region India. India itself is still often called Hindustan. However, since the term "Hindu" now refers to a religious orientation, many consider Hindustan inappropriate for the religiously plural country of India. The use of the term "Hindu," as a religious designation, developed with the spread of Islam into the Indian subcontinent. Muslims from neighboring Persia originally used "Hindu" to refer to the people of Sind/India, but eventually "Hindu" became a term to differentiate Muslims from non-Muslims. When the British ruled India from the eighteenth century, they continued to use "Hinduism" as a blanket term to refer to the religion of the Indian people, unless they belonged to religions with readily identifiable designations, such as Islam, Christianity, and Jainism. It is only in the last two centuries that the terms "Hinduism" and "Hindu" have gained widespread usage.

Despite the common use of the terms "Hinduism," and "Hindu," it is difficult to define with precision what Hinduism is, and what makes one a Hindu. Most attempts fall short because they tend to exclude the beliefs, practices, or philosophical orientations of sizeable segments of the Hindu world. For instance, some definitions attempt to give pre-eminence to a particular set of scriptures, notably the Vedas. Others might offer the terms *dharma* or *sanātana dharma* (eternal faith) as better designations than Hinduism, since they are at least indigenous categories, rather than a word of foreign extraction. However, in spite of the important place of the Vedas in much of Hinduism, not all Hindus hold them, in particular, as pre-eminent. Some prefer the scriptures of their own sectarian traditions. Others disregard the importance of any scripture. As for the term *dharma*, its meaning may vary from duty, righteousness and legal prescriptions, to social responsibility and obligation, and even to the specific religious teachings of a particular sect. Moreover, Hindu practices may actually encompass much more than the notions covered by the term. The term *sanātana dharma* is charged with universalistic, upper class, and orthodox connotations, which diminishes the authenticity of a wide range of regional beliefs and popular practices that are clearly part of Hinduism. This is because Hinduism includes elements that many of the mainstream world religions would not deem centrally religious. For instance, Hindu scriptural texts include works on astrology, medicine, prosody, and even logic and grammar. There is even a resilient tendency in Hinduism to locate all of reality, and certainly all human endeavors, especially those pertaining to knowledge and creativity, within the compass of the sacred. Thus although the word Hinduism has intrinsic weaknesses, its nebulousness is workably appropriate for its object of study, which is an equally expansive and loosely defined constellation of constituents.

The geographical distribution of Hindus

The vast majority of Hindus live on the Indian subcontinent. However, immigration to other countries, particularly in the last few centuries, has created a worldwide Hindu diaspora. A reasonable estimate of the global population of Hindus is about 850 million; most of these (over 98 per cent) live in South Asia. Between 85 and 90 per cent of the people of Nepal are Hindus, and in the 2001 census of India, 80.5 per cent (or 828 million) declared themselves to be Hindu. There are many Hindus in Bangladesh and Sri Lanka. Hindus also constitute substantial percentages (25–48 per cent) of the populations of Fiji, Mauritius, Guyana, and Trinidad and Tobago. The North American population of Hindus has been growing but is still below one million. About one per cent of the population of Great Britain is Hindu.

The Indian subcontinent

The Indian subcontinent is roughly shaped like a diamond whose upper half is embedded in the continent of Asia, while the lower half extends as a peninsula into the Indian Ocean. The state of Jammu and Kashmir is located at the northern tip of the diamond, and the states of Kerala and Tamil Nadu occupy its southern tip. The island of Sri Lanka is located just off India's southernmost point, known as Kanyā Kumārī (Cape Comorin). The eastern corner of the subcontinent contains a collection of isolated and protected states, such as Assam and Nagaland, as well as the nation of Bangladesh, while the western corner is occupied by the state of Gujarat. India is bordered by Pakistan on its upper western side, along which runs the Thar Desert. The states of Rajasthan and Punjab are also located there. The subcontinent's upper eastern side is flanked by the country of Nepal and the massive wall of the Himalaya Mountains, beyond which lies the Tibetan high plateau and China. India's lower eastern side is bordered by the Bay of Bengal, and the lower

A note about statistics

All numerical data provided on populations in this text, such as national percentages, should be understood as approximations. The difficulties inherent in gathering statistical data on populations can be enhanced in remote regions and where the population is illiterate or suspicious of government questionnaires. Furthermore, questionnaires sometimes restrict a person's choices to particular religions, caste affiliations, and so on, and responses to these may not accurately reflect the social and cultural reality of the populace. Such factors contribute to inaccuracies in such counting procedures. Nevertheless, like maps, they provide variously useful indications of the territory represented and the concerns of the map-makers. They are presented in this book to address the curiosity of the reader.

western side faces the Arabian Sea. The oceans, mountains, rivers and deserts that bound the subcontinent have inhibited terrestrial travel into India, providing it with natural defenses against invasion.

The subcontinent is roughly divided into North and South India by the Narmadā River and the Vindhya mountain range. The Gaṅgā River flows through the northern portion of the country, through the highly populated states of Uttar Pradesh, Bihar, and Bengal. The country's capital, New Delhi, is also located in the northern half. Central Indian states include Madhya Pradesh and Orissa. Andhra Pradesh, Maharashtra, and Karnataka are among the states in the south. Between early June and mid-July, India's major monsoon sweeps northwest from the Bay of Bengal. The monsoon ushers in a four-month rainy season, which is vital for India's agricultural food base. Rivers swell and transportation is hindered. From the alpine conditions of the Himalayas, the highest mountains in the world, to the tropical rain forests in its eastern and southern regions, India possesses the full spectrum of geographic terrains. In terms of biodiversity, more than 7 per cent of the world's various animal species and over 10 per cent of its floral species are represented on the subcontinent. Among its unique animal species is the Asian lion, found in the Gir Forest in Gujarat. India's national tree is the banyan, which puts down aerial roots from its branches, sometimes creating a small grove from a single massive parent. Alexander the Great is said to have camped with several thousand soldiers under a single banyan. The sacred Bodhi tree, under which the Buddha is believed to have attained *nirvāṇa* is a banyan species.

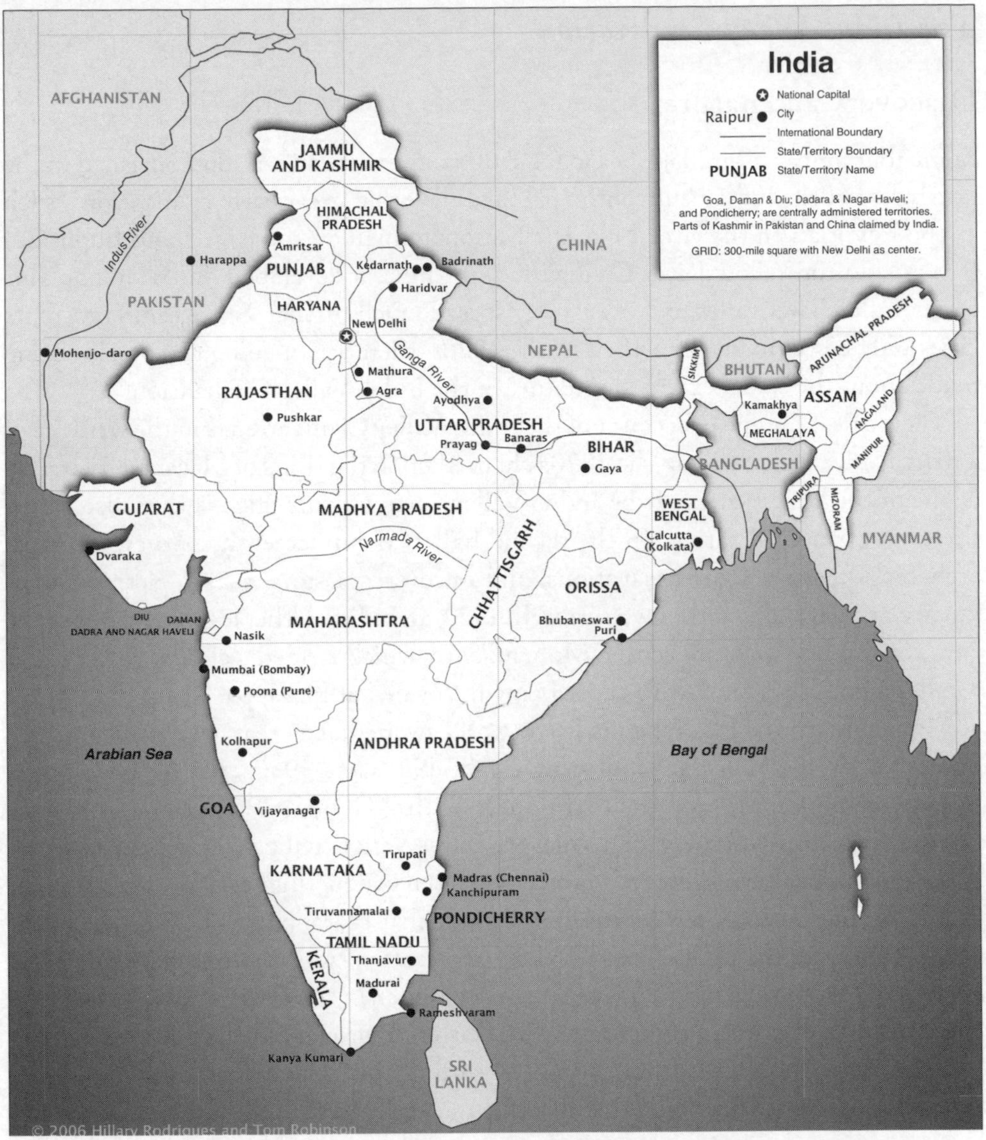

Figure 0.2 Map of the Indian subcontinent indicating major cities and religious centers

The Indus Valley Civilization

Discovery and nature

Some four and a half millennia ago (c. 2500 BCE) a vast civilization flourished in the northwest of the Indian subcontinent. Like the other great early civilizations, such as the Egyptian on the river Nile, the Mesopotamian on the Tigris and Euphrates Rivers, and the Yellow River Civilization in China, it developed on the floodplains of the Indus River valley, but eventually spread much further. Since remnants of its cities only began to be unearthed in the 1920s, there are ongoing discoveries being made about the actual extent and nature of the Indus Valley Civilization.

The earliest European account of the Indus Valley Civilization is in the writings of a British adventurer, who in the 1820s chanced upon the ruins of Harappa. Harappa is one of the largest cities of the Indus Valley Civilization, which is thus also called the Harappan Civilization. In the second half of the nineteenth century, a British archeologist began some excavations, and uncovered a stone seal depicting a one-horned animal and an unknown script. In 1922, an Indian archeologist discovered the ruins of another large city center, Mohenjodaro, which yielded weights, pottery, and a collection of seals similar to those being uncovered at Harappa. These discoveries at Mohenjodaro and Harappa made the world aware that a great urban culture once flourished on the Indian subcontinent. In the 1920s and 1930s, the Archaeological Survey of India uncovered such structures as the "Granary," now thought to be a "Great Hall." In 1946, the remains of a pre-Indus Valley civilization were discovered. A current archeological research project has been conducting regular excavations at Harappa since 1986. Their discoveries suggest that Harappa, which was the major urban center in the upper Indus Valley Civilization, was continuously inhabited since 3300 BCE. Mohenjodaro was the major center in the lower Indus Valley, and there were other cities of comparable size scattered throughout the cultural region.

The Indus Valley Tradition began as early as 6000 BCE when inhabitants of the region began to develop a distinct cultural style. In about 2600 BCE city-states began to emerge with common, standardized, and shared elements, such as writing, pottery styles, bricks, and stone weights. There was internal trade throughout the civilization, consisting of beads, lumber, pottery, and cotton, transported by bullock carts and boat, as well as far-flung trade with surrounding cultures to the east and west. Certain Mesopotamian sites, such as the ancient city of Ur, have yielded materials of Harappan origin. By 1900 BCE there appear signs of distinct regional developments. Local languages and writing began to develop and long-distance trade diminished. However, a broader-based, more fluid cultural tradition emerged, stretching from the Indus to the flood plains of the Gaṅgā in north India.

The Indus Valley Civilization covered a region much larger than most scholars imagined, even a few decades ago. From the Himalayas and upper Afghanistan to the north as far as Mumbai (Bombay) to the south, there is evidence of the Indus Valley Tradition, along with a substantial coastal network in the state of Gujarat. Settlements also stretch over a thousand miles from Delhi in the east, westward to the border of Iran. Apart from the major cities such as Mohenjodaro and Harappa, which at their peak may have each had over 40,000 inhabitants, the people lived in small towns and villages. These were located not just along the Indus River, but also along the Ghaggar-Hakra River which lay to the east of the Indus and ran parallel to it. The ancient Vedic scriptures referred to the Sarasvatī River, whose existence is thought by some scholars to be a myth, while others regard the Ghaggar-Hakra to be the Sarasvatī. Satellite imaging reveals the location of the dried up river bed of the Ghaggar-Hakra and provides a rationale for the position of the old settlements. The demise of the Ghaggar-Hakra likely contributed to the demise of the Indus Valley Civilization, whose inhabitants appear to have migrated farther to the south and east over the centuries. In time, the Indus River, too, changed its route. The absence of access to the river, combined with unexpected seasonal floods, led to the abandonment of many settlements and a decline in the highly uniform characteristics of the civilization. Subsequent to the Indus Valley Civilization (also now referred to as the Sarasvatī-Sindhu Civilization by some scholars), the region was occupied by cultures named after the ceramic production with which they are associated. The Painted Grey Ware culture flourished from 1200 to 800 BCE, the time of the early Iron Age in India, followed by the Northern Black Polished Ware culture from about 700 to 300 BCE.

Indus Valley urban planning was sophisticated. Each city was built on a mud brick platform, providing it with a protective elevation against rainy season flooding. Mohenjodaro had a large paved water tank used for public or ritual bathing, as well as a citadel and a Great Hall. The roads were paved, and drains were covered. Homes were often two storied and constructed of uniformly cast baked or sun-dried mud bricks that were used throughout the civilization. Homes were equipped with bathrooms, with drainage systems that funneled water to communal sewer systems. The standardization of the bricks, and other elements, such as weights and measures, used over such a large territorial area of hundreds of thousands of square miles and through a period of many hundreds of years, suggest a strong centralized government.

Artisans fabricated jewelry and implements of stone, ceramics, bone, shell, ivory, and soft metals such as bronze, copper, gold and silver. One finds cookware, mirrors, toys, tools, and game pieces. Among the most intriguing objects excavated are an abundance of small square seals fashioned from stone or clay. They mostly depict animals; particularly, a one-horned creature designated a unicorn.

These seals are also engraved with symbols of the Indus Valley script. Unfortunately, due to the short strings of characters found on the seals, and the absence of bilingual inscriptions, the script has not yet been deciphered. A shard of pottery, dated to about 3500 BCE, has been discovered with a few symbols that appear to be rudimentary forms of the Indus Valley script, and may be the earliest evidence of writing, older than Egyptian hieroglyphs and Mesopotamian cuneiform. Unfortunately with the demise of the Indus Valley Civilization, evidence of writing appears to have vanished from the Indian subcontinent by about 1700 BCE. After that, the next evidence of writing, with different scripts from the Indus Valley, only emerges in the fourth century BCE during the reign of the Mauryan Dynasty. Certain scholars doubt that an evolved written language ever existed among the Harappans. They suggest that the sophisticated symbol system evident on the seals dovetails with a certain disdain for writing and the primacy given to oral transmission in the elite orthodox Hinduism of a later period.

A small population of Brahui people lives near Mohenjodaro, which is about a hundred miles from their home in Kalat, Baluchistan. Samples of pottery and script from other early settlements in Baluchistan, such as Mehrgarh, closely resemble Harappan findings. The Brahui are an isolated group of Dravidian language speakers, numbering about a million, in the Indus Valley region. These observations have contributed to scholarly speculation that the people of the Indus Valley Civilization may have spoken a Dravidian language and originally come from Baluchistan.

Indus Valley religion

It is difficult to know with certainty what the religious practices of the Indus Valley people were since we do not have any decipherable written information available. The archeological record provides us with the material basis for reasoned speculations,

A note on dates

One of the earliest histories of India was written in the fourteenth century. So historians of India have had to rely on epigraphic (i.e. inscriptional) evidence, linguistic analysis, textual references, and so on, to ascertain dates for the compositions of various texts, or the periods in which particular people lived. When dates cannot be established with certainty, there are cultural, political, and religious agendas that may play roles in the attribution of dates. For instance, a person who reads scriptures literally may choose to believe that certain events took place long before historians would place these events based on the evidence at their disposal. Variations of a few centuries, or even a few decades, may carry implications as to who influenced whom. Unless expressed with precision, the dates provided in this book are conservative approximations derived from contemporary scholarly literature.

but most of these ideas are open to debate. The dead, for instance, were buried in wooden coffins, and were accompanied with jars that probably contained food. Both the food provision and the burial suggest a belief in some form of afterlife. There have been no examples of royal tombs and elaborate burials with expensive ornaments, such as of gold and silver.

Simple terracotta images of men, women, and animals have been unearthed. A particularly well crafted image is of a man who sports a beard and a disc forehead ornament, as well as a decorated cloak draped over his left shoulder. The eyes seem half shut, as if in meditation. The royal demeanor and garb of this figure have led archeologists to dub it the "Priest-King," although whether such functionaries as "priests" or "kings" even existed in the Indus Valley Civilization, and what their roles might have been, is unknown.

The large number of terracotta female figurines suggests a cult of the feminine, and have prompted scholarly speculation that goddesses were widely worshipped. Many female images appear to have headdresses that could be filled with oil and burned as lamps in rituals.

The seals and molded tablets sometimes depict narrative scenes. For instance, one tablet shows a figure with a foot pressing down upon the head of a water buffalo, which it is simultaneously spearing. A figure with a horned headdress seated in a yogic posture, with the soles of the feet pressed together looks on. The reverse of this tablet shows a female figure throttling two tigers. An elephant stands below. Such images suggest certain continuities with myths and beliefs in modern Hinduism. For instance, certain Hindu deities (such as Skanda and Durgā) are associated with the slaying of a buffalo demon, and modern representations of Hindu deities are still portrayed accompanied by animals such as tigers and elephants. Certain Indus Valley seals portray female figures entwined in or fused with trees and plants, which resonates with the association Hindus still draw between women, goddesses, fertility, and vegetation.

The figure in the yogic posture mentioned above is particularly intriguing. There are several seals depicting such a figure, some with different details than others. In one seal the figure appears to have a horned headdress and three faces. The soles of his feet are pressed together in what is sometimes called *mūla-bandha-āsana,* a classic yogic posture, and he wears a number of bracelets on his arms. The figure appears to possess an erect penis. Animals, including a water-buffalo or bull, rhinoceros, elephant, and tiger are also depicted around the figure, which has come to be referred to as the "ithyphallic proto-Śiva." This is because the seal contains many characteristics similar to those associated with the Hindu god Śiva, and have led some to suggest that this is an early depiction of that deity. Śiva is regarded as the *yogi* par excellence, and is often worshipped in the form of an erect phallus (*liṅga*). His animal mount is the bull, and he is also called Paśupati (Lord of Animals). Despite such compelling connections, the evidence that these seals actually depict an early form of Śiva is inconclusive.

Another potential continuity between Indus Valley religion and modern Hinduism is the emphasis on ritual bathing and personal hygiene. The bathing tank at Mohenjodaro suggests a connection with the bathing tanks found at many Hindu temple sites. Similarly, smooth oval and doughnut-shaped stones at Indus Valley sites have led to speculations that these are evidence of early worship of the symbols of male and female generative principles, the *liṅga* and *yoni*, respectively, which are widespread in Hinduism today. However, these may merely have been grinding or tethering stones. We shall have to await the accumulation of much more data before we can comfortably assert knowledge about the nature of Indus Valley religion.

The Āryans

From about 1500 BCE, a pastoral, cattle-herding people known as the Āryans (Noble Ones), appeared on the Indian subcontinent. The prevailing view among scholars is that they originated from the area of central Asia near the Caucasus Mountains and migrated westward into Europe, and eastward into the Indian subcontinent. However, there is also a view held by a minority of scholars that the Āryans originated in or close to the Indus Valley. This Cultural Diffusion Hypothesis derives from a number of uncertainties inherent in the Indo-European (i.e. Āryan) Migration Thesis. It is also bolstered by orthodox Hindu political ideologies. In this regard it suspects the Āryan Migration Thesis of being based on a white-supremacist ideology and a colonialist paradigm. These theses will continue to be hotly debated until new evidence, particularly from archeological excavations, provides a compelling answer.

The Indo-European (Āryan) Migration Thesis

According to this dominant thesis, the Āryans were a light-skinned, Indo-European people who migrated into the Indian subcontinent in waves. They carried with them a set of sacred oral scriptures, known as the Vedas, which tell us much about their beliefs and practices. They were warrior-nomads who had the horse-drawn war chariot, which enabled them to conquer many of the cultures they encountered. The Vedas tell of the Āryans conquering the darker skinned Dāsas and Dasyus, and scholars originally speculated that this referred to a conquest of the people of the Indus Valley. However, archeological evidence now suggests that the Indus Valley Civilization had already declined before the arrival of the Āryans. There is scarce evidence of the horse or a violent overthrow at the excavated Indus Valley sites. The Āryans thus moved beyond the Indus, pushing east and south into the subcontinent. The people that they encountered in the south may have been the descendants of the displaced Indus Valley inhabitants. In the nineteenth century, the term Dravidian

Figure 0.3 *Liṅga* and *yoni* stones at the edge of a contemporary Hindu temple bathing tank (Nepal)

(Southern) was coined to refer to the family of the non-Sanskritic based languages spoken mainly in South India, and to the shared "Dravidian" culture of the speakers of these tongues. According to the migration thesis, a mingling of Āryan and "Dravidian" cultures took place. Āryan cultural elements, such as their sacred language, Sanskrit, and derivative forms, eventually became dominant, particularly in the north. However, "Dravidian" cultural elements endured with more resilience in the south.

In support of this thesis, one notes that North Indian languages are based on Sanskrit and belong to the Indo-European family of languages, which includes English. By contrast, South Indian languages belong to the family of Dravidian languages, probably based on an ancient form of Tamil, a language with a rich literature and tradition, as ancient as Sanskrit, but linguistically quite different from it. Furthermore, the Brahui language, spoken by the Brahui people who are relatively isolated in the vicinity of the Indus Valley sites, is a Dravidian language. Since Brahui is now surrounded by Sanskritic-based languages in North India, it suggests that Dravidian languages and "Dravidian" culture originally inhabited the Indus Valley, and were at that time much more widespread on the subcontinent. These languages were eventually superceded in the north by the Indo-European languages such as Sanskrit.

In further support of this thesis, the Vedas describe a civilization that does not seem particularly urban. It refers to a pastoral culture, with practices such as the herding of cows, and does not refer to temples, bathing tanks, and so on.

The Cultural Diffusion Hypothesis

This hypothesis proposes that Āryan civilization, whose sacred language was Sanskrit, and where the Vedas originated, developed close to the Harappan Civilization, and may well have been one and the same with it. As an advanced civilization, with great social and political stability, the complex Vedic/Āryan culture that developed in the Indus Valley diffused into neighboring lands. Although the use of scriptures as historical documents is fraught with problems, proponents of both the Indo-European Migration Thesis, and the Cultural Diffusion Hypothesis often use the content of the Vedas to substantiate their arguments. This is because, in the absence of datable inscriptions or other evidence from the archeological record, these ancient scriptures offer the only other source of potentially historical information. Thus Cultural Diffusion theorists note, for instance, that the Vedas contain many references to the ocean, which casts doubt on the proposition that they were composed in landlocked central Asia. And references to astronomical phenomena, such as the positions of particular constellations, suggest that the Vedas were composed far earlier than the Indo-European Migration thesis would suggest. Furthermore, there is very little archeological evidence of the Indo-European Migration.

Āryan and non-Āryan influences

The prevailing scholarly view is that Vedic literature can tell us much about the early religious culture of the Āryans. This is because we have that ancient scriptural record of their beliefs and practices. By contrast, we do not have any written testimony of ancient non-Āryan religion. The Āryans strove to maintain an elite status, distinguishing themselves from non-Āryans through such measures as the class (*varṇa*) system and the privileged status granted to knowledge of the Sanskrit language and its literature. Nevertheless, over the centuries Āryan and non-Āryan cultures mingled and influenced each other and aspects of these changes were progressively reflected in the content of Sanskritic scripture itself. We may thus infer something about the nature of ancient non-Āryan religions through the changes that took place in the Āryan/Vedic/Sanskritic corpus of scriptural writings over the course of time. For instance, there is no mention of the god Śiva in the earliest Vedic (i.e. Āryan) scriptures (e.g. the *Ṛg Veda Saṃhitā*). This suggests that his worship originates from a non-Āryan religious tradition on the subcontinent. Some scholars propose, based on such evidence as the "ithyphallic proto-Śiva" seals, that Śiva's worship derives from the Indus Valley Civilization. However, by the time of the composition of later

Vedic scriptures, such as the *Śvetāśvatara Upaniṣad*, we find mention of Śiva, and later still, when the Epics and Purāṇas were composed, he is one of the great gods of Hinduism. Similar processes hold true for a number of other Hindu deities, such as the elephant-headed god Gaṇeśa, the monkey god, Hanumān, and a large number of goddesses, all of whom were progressively assimilated into the Vedic pantheon.

This process, designated by some social scientists as "universalization," in which the elite, dominant classes (i.e. the "Great Tradition") adopt the practices of the lower classes (i.e. the "Little Tradition"), and legitimize them by incorporating them into the cultural forms of the upper classes (e.g. incorporating them into Sanskrit scriptural texts), is still under way. However, nowadays, we see it more at work between upper class and popular (i.e. that of the masses) culture, between orthodox and unorthodox (e.g. tantric) Hindu beliefs, and between mainstream priestly and low class/tribal practices, than between Vedic and non-Vedic high cultures, which initially took place. The upper classes portray their value system as normative, that is, the authoritative standard which pertains to everyone (i.e. universal). Furthermore, since they dominate political and legal systems, the term "universalization" also refers to their advancement of these values throughout their spheres of influence.

A corollary of this trend is a process known as "Sanskritization," in which the lower classes, in order to enhance their social status, adopt the values and practices of the upper dominant classes, such as notions of purity (e.g. adopting vegetarianism) and pollution (e.g. renouncing animal sacrifice), and holding similar things (e.g. the Vedas), to be sacrosanct. For instance, quite early in the process of contact between the Āryans and non-Āryans, we note that local, non-Āryan rulers (*rājan*) allowed Brahmin priests to perform various rites of consecration, and adopted some of the Brahmin notions of religious righteousness (*dharma*). In so doing these rulers enhanced their status and that of their subjects. As more rulers accepted this form of status-enhancement, Hinduism spread throughout the Indian subcontinent and into parts of Southeast Asia, such as Thailand, Cambodia, and Indonesia.

The concepts of "universalization" and "Sanskritization" have often been used interchangeably, and somewhat loosely, in the context of South Asian studies. To a large extent, the development of what we today call Hinduism could be imagined as an ongoing interaction between the religious culture of the Āryan priestly elite (i.e. the Brahmins) and other religious cultures through such processes as "Sanskritization" and "universalization." However, orthodox values (i.e. those of the Brahmin elite) were imposed on a broader body of peoples with varying degrees of success. Moreover, various forms of non-Āryan religious traditions persisted, and select dimensions of these influenced Brahminic tradition, until they were adopted after undergoing adaptations into forms acceptable to the orthodoxy.

In order to simplify the complex dynamic of socio-cultural interactions that have been taking place on the Indian subcontinent for millennia, we might say that Hinduism is thus a blend of three main components. The first is what one might loosely term Āryan religion, also known as Vedic religion, the Sanskritic, or orthodox tradition, or Brahmanism (after the priestly Brahmin class). As these terms suggest, it is characterized by the high regard it has for the Vedas and other Vedic scriptures and their religious teachings, which are upheld as authoritative. It also firmly upholds the hierarchy of the class (*varṇa*) system, which grants a privileged status to the upper three classes of Priests (Brahmins, *brāhmaṇa*), Warriors (*kṣatriya*), and Merchants (*vaiśya*), over the Servant (*śūdra*) class, with Brahmins at the top of the pyramid.

The second component may be, somewhat problematically, termed "Dravidian religion," which refers to the non-Āryan high cultures on the Indian subcontinent. They may include the Indus Valley Civilization religious traditions and, after its demise, those that followed in the Gaṅgā River valley and further south, as well as those that may have developed independently in those regions. These religious cultures are also loosely linked to the peoples who speak the Dravidian family of languages such as Tamil and Telugu. The term "Dravidian" for this culture and religion is problematic because medieval myths, held to be true by people who believe those religious texts to be accurate historical documents, speak of Vedic, Āryan origins of the Dravidian (Southern) peoples and languages. Also, because invasions and colonial rule ravaged Hindu culture in North India, South Indian traditions often preserve better instances of Vedic religion. Furthermore, drawing "racial" distinctions between North and South India is sometimes seen as the vestige of a British colonial strategy to divide the nation. The notion of "Dravidian identity" has spearheaded separatist political movements in the last century. In this book, Dravidian will be used to refer to the category of non-Sanskritic languages related to Tamil, while "Dravidian" will be used to indicate the non-Sanskritic, non-Āryan, people, societies, and high cultures that do not include aboriginal, tribal societies indigenous to the Indian subcontinent.

The third component contributing to the formation of Hinduism derives from the assortment of disparate religious beliefs and practices of aboriginal tribal groups throughout the subcontinent. Living in remote areas or thick jungles, these groups did not belong to the non-Vedic (i.e. "Dravidian") high-cultural traditions. In general terms, one associates animistic beliefs (i.e. that spirits inhabit rocks, trees, lakes, and other natural phenomena), concerns with the fertility of the community and the natural world, and the presence of shamanic religious specialists with such tribal societies. Because the Sanskritic/Āryan tradition developed hegemony (i.e. preponderant influence and authority) over much of the non-Āryan traditions, it has been the dominant "voice" in the articulation of Hinduism. And because the "Dravidian" and aboriginal religious traditions left no historical (i.e. written) record of their early beliefs and practices, the written record of the Hindu tradition has been strongly shaped by Sanskritic oral literature and writings. Thus it is difficult to separate out which non-Āryan components in the composition of Hinduism derive from "Dravidian" traditions, and which derive from tribal religions.

A brief history of Hinduism

Our knowledge of the early phases of Hinduism derives from the sacred literature of the Āryans. The earliest of these are four Vedas, collections of hymns, and in particular, the *Ṛg Veda Saṃhitā*, which is the oldest. The *Ṛg Veda Saṃhitā* (or for convenience, simply the *Ṛg Veda*) itself was composed over several centuries, and may have achieved its final form by about 1000 BCE. The remaining three Vedas (i.e. *Sāma, Yajur,* and *Atharva*) took their final form a few centuries later. Other Vedic texts, such as the Brāhmaṇas, Āraṇyakas, and Upaniṣads followed, and tell us more about the religious traditions of the period. Although we refer to this literature as "text" or "scripture," it must be remembered that we have no written records from this period (and no evidence that there even was writing). These texts appear to have been composed orally, and were transmitted from teacher to disciple through rigorous memorization. Although with the advent of writing, oral scripture was eventually committed to the page, this has generally been regarded as a diminution of its sacred character, and the tradition of oral chanting, memorization, and transmission continues right to the present day.

By the sixth century BCE we note the rise of the *śramaṇa* movement in India. The *śramaṇas* were wandering philosophers, who were intent on discovering the meaning of existence. Many practiced rigorous forms of asceticism, and some gathered schools of disciples. This period reflects a time when the views of the Brahmin priesthood, who derived their authority from Vedic scriptures, were being challenged. Of the innumerable *śramaṇa* schools that formed, certain ones, such as the Ājīvikas, grew into large movements that flourished for many centuries before dying out. Others grew into religions or philosophical schools that still exist today. Two such notable *śramaṇa* based religions are Buddhism and Jainism. Buddhism developed from the teachings of Siddhārtha Gautama, who became the Buddha (the Awakened One), while Jainism derives from the teachings of Vardhamāna, also known as Mahāvīra or the Jina (the Conqueror). Orthodox Hinduism classified Buddhism and Jainism as heterodox religious philosophies because they rejected the divinely revealed status of the Vedas, and questioned the validity of the class system, especially since it granted spiritual supremacy to Brahmins merely on the basis of birth.

Alexander the Great's army crossed into northwest India in 326 BCE. At the Battle of Hydaspes (now known as the Jhelum River) he waged a fierce battle with the army of King Puruṣottama (Porus), claimed victory, but did not progress much beyond what is modern Pakistan. Alexander died a few years later. In 322 BCE another great empire developed on the Indian subcontinent. Founded by Candragupta Maurya, this Mauryan (Peacock) Dynasty developed from the kingdom of Magadha in northeast India, and had its capital at Pataliputra (now Patna). Candragupta's grandson, Aśoka (ruled 265–238 BCE) expanded the empire to its maximum size covering most of the subcontinent, except for some southern kingdoms, and westward into Baluchistan and Afghanistan. Aśoka's conversion to Buddhism lent substantial support and led to the expansion of that religious philosophy throughout his empire. However, he is known to have also supported other *śramaṇa* movements as well as orthodox Hinduism. Aśoka erected large stone columns with inscriptions and other stone edicts throughout his empire, which are among the earliest evidence of post-Indus Valley Civilization writing on the subcontinent.

In 187 BCE the Mauryan Empire fell to the Śuṅga Dynasty, and eventually broke up into smaller kingdoms. There was a revival of orthodox Hinduism, which had, however, undergone a number of changes. Cults emerged that were centered on the god Vāsudeva, later identified with the Vedic god Viṣṇu. The value of non-harming (*ahiṃsa*), and the critique of animal sacrifices for worship, which were voiced in several heterodox movements, began to be embraced by orthodox Hinduism, particularly among these Viṣṇu-centered groups. Worship of the god Śiva in the form of the *liṅga* (phallus) is also evident on coins, as are stone carvings of male and female nature sprites (*yakṣa/yakṣī*). Between the second century BCE and the second century CE we note the emergence of the *Rāmāyaṇa* and the *Mahābhārata*, the two major Hindu epics. They reveal the importance of the worship of Viṣṇu through two of his *avatāras* (incarnations), Rāma and Kṛṣṇa.

In the following few centuries northwest India was invaded several times by such people as the Śāka-Parthians and the Kuṣāṇas, and opened itself to trade and contact with the expansive Roman Empire. This was also true of the three major southern kingdoms that had evaded amalgamation into the Mauryan Empire. These were the Cera (around modern Kerala), the Cola and the Pāṇḍya, whose maritime trade included Rome and Southeast Asia. In fact, Chinese accounts refer to a Hindu kingdom in Vietnam in about the second century CE, and Sanskrit inscriptions dated to the fourth century CE tell of Brahmin priests conducting rites for local chieftains in Borneo. Elements of Hindu religion spread further east, to China and Japan, primarily via Buddhism. It is difficult to know with certainty to what extent Hindu ideas influenced western thought. Certainly, the Indian numeric and decimal system made its way to the West, but it is not clear whether notions such as reincarnation and cyclical creation as found in the writings of Pythagoras (fifth century BCE), or even meditative intuition as evident in the works of Plotinus (third century CE) have Indian roots.

From 320 to 550 CE, the Gupta Dynasty, also centered at Pataliputra, dominated north India. The Gupta period is seen as the classical or "golden" age of Hinduism, because of its social stability and great cultural achievements. Among these achievements were the development of Sanskrit literature and temple architecture. One of the greatest of Indian playwrights, Kalidāsa, lived and produced his works during this period. While early Indian temples were made of wood (none of which survive), brick and stone temples began to emerge. The Gupta emperors were supporters of Viṣṇu, particularly in his wild boar (Varāha) and Kṛṣṇa incarnations.

Theistic cults to the sun god, Sūrya, as well as to Śiva and several goddesses, were also in evidence. The war god Skanda (or Kārttikeya) was already being worshipped by the second century CE. There is, however, no evidence of the worship of the elephant-headed god Gaṇeśa until the fifth century CE. It is only in the seventh century CE (at Mahabalipuram, south of Madras (Chennai)), in a region ruled by the Pallava Dynasty, that one sees the first evidence of Hindu cave temples.

Devotional worship (*bhakti*) of a personal god, although first mentioned before the first century CE, began a major revival in the seventh century CE in South India. We associate this movement in particular with the devotional hymns of the Ālvārs, who were worshippers of Viṣṇu, and the Nāyanārs, who were dedicated to Śiva. Characterized by evoking strong emotional responses through singing and chanting, the *bhakti* movement spread northward, growing in popularity among the grassroots of Indian society. In the process, it spearheaded a Hindu revival which weakened Buddhism, while simultaneously being influenced by it. The Hindu philosopher Śaṅkara, for instance, promulgated a philosophy that parallels major strands of Buddhist thought, and he is even reputed to have begun a monastic system for Hindu renouncers. Buddhists monks had belonged to such communities for over a thousand years.

Islam first entered India in the late seventh century CE, but only began to make major inroads into the subcontinent in the eleventh century when Mahmud of Ghazni conducted highly effective cavalry attacks leading to the annexation of the Punjab. This paved the way for subsequent invasions and soon much of India, particularly the north, was subsequently ruled from the thirteenth to the sixteenth centuries CE by a series of Turko-Afghan dynasties referred to as the Delhi Sultanate. Muslim rule continued its hold on India during the period of the Mughals from the sixteenth to the nineteenth centuries CE. The Mughals, who were descendants of the Mongol emperor Genghis Khan, had long been converts to Islam, and were influenced by Persian culture, which they brought to India. It was in this period that an architectural style developed that is so strongly associated with India, the best known example of which is the Taj Mahal.

During the entire period of Muslim overrule in various regions of India, from the eleventh to the nineteenth centuries CE, Hinduism continued to adapt and evolve. Hindu rulers governed as well, under the umbrella of Muslim emperors. At times Hinduism suffered severe persecution, as under the rule of the Mughal emperor Aurangzeb, who ruled from 1658 to 1707 CE. Many Hindu temples, particularly in North India, were destroyed, and all non-Muslims were required to pay special taxes. However other Muslim leaders, such as the Mughal emperor Akbar, who ruled from 1556 to 1605 CE, supported Hinduism. Conversion to Islam took place in large numbers in certain areas, such as the northern and northwest regions of Kashmir and modern-day Pakistan, as well as in West Bengal (now Bangladesh). The Mughal arrival in India was accompanied by a global colonizing effort by the

Europeans. Portugal established a colony on the Indian southwest coast by the early sixteenth century CE, and the British and the French had established outposts by the seventeenth century CE. The British East India Company became the dominant colonial power, and as Mughal power declined, it came to rule most of India by the nineteenth century.

New syncretic religions, such as Sikhism developed, although Hindu society grew progressively more segregated. Marriage restrictions were strictly enforced to inhibit the intermarriage of Hindus with non-Hindus and even among Hindus of differing castes. Hindu sects with various theistic philosophies emerged during these centuries. They include the Viṣṇu-centered (i.e. Vaiṣṇava) groups founded by Rāmānuja, Madhva, and Śrī Caitanya. There were Śiva-centered (i.e. Śaiva) groups, such as the Śaiva-siddhānta school in South India, and the sophisticated philosophies of Kashmir Śaivism.

Although Christianity had reached India as early as the sixth century CE (or even earlier, by local tradition), the arrival of the Portuguese in the sixteenth century marks the notable effect of Christian missionaries in India, which developed as the British grew in power and began to dominate the subcontinent. There were numerous Hindu reform movements that emerged in response to the effects of European rule, culture, and religion. Among these was the Brāhmo Samāj, which sought a syncretism between certain Christian and Hindu ideals. Another such organization was the Ārya Samāj, which emphasized the divine sanctity of the Vedas as the basis of religious doctrine.

By the twentieth century CE a vibrant movement for independence from foreign rule had developed in India. Hinduism and various selections of its values were often co-opted to establish a sense of national identity and garner support. Mahatma Gandhi is the most well known of the leaders who drew upon traditional Hindu values, such as asceticism and non-harming (*ahiṃsā*), interpreted in distinct ways, to fashion an ideology that worked effectively in the struggle for independence.

India achieved independence in 1947. However, the departing British had legally authorized the division of the country into the two nations of India and Pakistan. This led to a mass migration of millions of people as Hindus left their homes in Pakistan, and Muslims left India for Pakistan. Hundreds of thousands died in the slaughter that ensued during that migration. India, led by the Congress Party and its first prime minister, Jawaharlal Nehru, insisted on a secular democratic state. The Congress Party dominated Indian government for almost forty years. However, this ideal has been deteriorating in the direction of a government shaped by Hindu values. In the late 1990s, the Bharatiya Janata Party swept into power on a platform that was markedly pro-Hindu. Interestingly, in the elections of 2004, the Congress Party was returned to power with a minority government, which is currently led by a Sikh prime minister.

Although the traditional structures of Hinduism are undergoing transformations, especially in the more cosmopolitan urban centers, other aspects of the religion continue to flourish. For instance, television productions of Hindu epics, such as the *Rāmāyaṇa*, still garner enormous audiences. Religious teachers of long established Hindu religious disciplines such as *yoga* continue to attract disciples from outside India, while others have successfully taken modified or syncretized aspects of Hinduism abroad. Hinduism appears to have the capacity to adapt to the forces of modernity, such as the hi-tech revolution, Western influences, and globalization.

Key points in this chapter

- Due to its many complexities, it is difficult to define Hinduism, which is a term referring to the wide range of beliefs and practices of the majority of the people of South Asia.
- The term "Hindu," as a religious designation for practitioners of Hinduism, developed with the spread of Islam into the Indian subcontinent in order to differentiate Muslims from non-Muslims.
- Hinduism includes elements that many of the mainstream world religions would not deem centrally religious.
- The vast majority of Hindus live on the Indian subcontinent. However, immigration to other countries, particularly in the last few centuries, has created a worldwide Hindu diaspora.
- From about 2500 BCE, the vast Indus Valley Civilization flourished in the northwest of the Indian subcontinent. It is still unclear as to what extent, if any, Hinduism is related to the Indus Valley religion.
- From about 1500 BCE, a pastoral, cattle-herding people known as the Āryans (Noble Ones) appeared on the Indian subcontinent. Both the Cultural Diffusion Hypothesis and the Indo-European (i.e. Āryan) Migration Thesis speculate on their origins.
- Processes such as "universalization" and "Sanskritization," allow us to note the transformations underway in Hinduism, and to make inferences regarding the religious beliefs and practices of ancient peoples of whom we have no written record.
- Hinduism is a blend of three components: Āryan religion, "Dravidian" religion, and the tribal religions of the subcontinent.
- Hindu religious and cultural elements spread throughout the East and eventually across the globe due to invasions of the subcontinent, India's involvement in trade, and the immigration of Hindus abroad.

- In the late seventh century CE, Islam entered India and began to spread in the eleventh century. This ushered in a period of colonialism and persecution until Hinduism experienced a revival in the late eighteenth century.
- In response to European colonialism, Hindu movements emerged seeking independence for the people of the subcontinent. This independence was achieved in 1947 with the country divided into two nations, India and Pakistan.
- Hinduism has adapted to the various influences it has encountered over time, and will likely continue its transformation as it encounters future challenges.

Discussion questions

1. What difficulties arise when attempting to define "Hinduism?" Do you think that these complexities will continue as Hinduism evolves over time?
2. Why might the discovery of the seal depicting the "ithyphallic-proto Śiva" be important to Hinduism?
3. Discuss both the Cultural Diffusion Hypothesis and the Indo-European Migration Thesis. Which of these theses do you think is stronger, and why?
4. What are some of the potential continuities between Indus Valley religion and modern Hinduism?

Further reading

On the Indus Valley Civilization and the Āryans

Allchin, B. and R. Allchin (1982) *The Rise of Civilization in India and Pakistan.* Cambridge: Cambridge University Press.

Kenoyer, J.M. (1998) *Ancient Cities of the Indus Valley Civilization.* (American Institute of Pakistan Studies). Karachi: Oxford University Press.

Marshall, J. (1931) *Mohenjo Daro and the Indus Civilization,* 3 vols. London: University of Oxford Press.

Parpola, A. (1994) *Deciphering the Indus Script.* Cambridge University Press: New York.

Poliakov, L. (1974) *The Aryan Myth.* New York: Basic Books.

Possehl, G.C. (ed.) (1982) *Harappan Civilisation: A Contemporary Perspective.* Warminster: Aris & Philips.

Thapar, R. (1993) *Interpreting Early India.* Delhi: Oxford University Press.

Wheeler, M. (1953) *The Indus Civiliation.* Cambridge: Cambridge University Press.

On Indian history and culture

Basham, A.L. (1959) *The Wonder that Was India.* New York: Grove Press.

Basham, A.L. (1984) *A Cultural History of India.* Reprint. Delhi: Oxford University Press.

Metcalf, Barbara D. & Metcalf, Thomas R. (2002) *A Concise History of India.* Cambridge: University Press.

Singer, Milton (1972) *When a Great Tradition Modernizes: Text and Context in the Study of Hinduism.* New York: Praeger Publishers.

Thapar, R. (1966) *A History of India,* 2 vols. Baltimore: Penguin.

Wolpert, Stanley A. (2003) *A New History of India.* New York: Oxford University Press.

1 *Vedic religion*

In this chapter

The Āryan religious heritage leaves an indelible imprint on the character of Hinduism. Its character is most evident in Vedic religious literature, beliefs, and practices, which are explored here. The various genres of Vedic religious texts, such as their hymn collections, ritual manuals, and works of speculative philosophy are characterized, as are works on health and astrology. The chapter presents close examinations of certain Vedic rituals, some of which are humanity's oldest enduring rites, and discusses the nature of important Vedic deities. The crucially significant conception of the Vedic Absolute, or the One, is also introduced here, as is its relationship to the pervasive notion of sacrifice.

Main topics covered

- The Vedic Saṃhitās
- Vedic deities
- *Ṛta* and cosmic order
- The Brāhmaṇas
- Vedic rituals (*yajña*)
- Soma
- The Āraṇyakas
- The Upaniṣads
- Ātman and Brahman
- *Śruti* and *Smṛti*
- Other Vedic literature
- Astrology
- Āyurveda

The Vedic Saṃhitās

The most highly regarded literary works of the Āryans are hymns in praise (*ṛg*) of various deities. Many of these hymns were chanted during a New Year festival centered on a ritual to prepare, offer, and imbibe a sacred beverage, Soma. The oldest collection (*saṃhitā*) is the *Ṛg Veda Saṃhitā*, which consists of over 1000 hymns arranged in ten books known as *maṇḍalas*. Scholars who have scrutinized this collection surmise that the first and last of these *maṇḍalas* were among the last to be added to the collection. So, despite the antiquity of the *Ṛg Veda Saṃhitā*, there appear to be discernable stages in its compilation. The exact dates of its composition are still debated, with some proponents postulating dates as early as 5000 BCE or even earlier, while more conservative scholarly estimates suggest that the *Ṛg Veda Saṃhitā* reached its final form by about 300 BCE. A prevailing number of estimates suggest a date of about 1000 BCE. There are Hittite-Mitanni treaty tablets from the region of modern Iraq, dated at about 1400 BCE, which mention the Vedic gods Indra, Mitra, and Varuṇa, suggesting that portions of the *Ṛg Veda Saṃhitā* were composed at about the same time. In the ensuing centuries two other Saṃhitās were produced. These were the *Sāma Veda Saṃhitā* and the *Yajur Veda Saṃhitā*, which together with the *Ṛg Veda* constituted early orthodox Āryan scripture. The *Sāma Veda* mostly contains verses from the *Ṛg Veda* and presents these in a form to be chanted (*sāman*) by *udgātṛs*, a special class of priests, during the sacrificial offerings of Soma (a sacred plant) in Vedic rituals. The *Yajur Veda* consists of verse prayers (*yajus*), also mostly drawn from the *Ṛg Veda*, to be learned by *adhvaryus*, priests who performed the main elements of Vedic rituals, such as the construction of the fire-altars, and so on. It also contains prose instructions on how to perform rituals such as the horse sacrifice. The *Yajur Veda Saṃhitā* exists in two recensions, popularly known as the *Black* and the *White Yajur Vedas*. The *Black Yajur Veda* or *Taittirīya Saṃhitā* is challenging to decipher because of the arrangement of its contents. By contrast, the *White Yajur Veda* or *Vājasaneyi Saṃhitā*, which contains essentially the same material, is more accessible in its structure.

An examination of these three Vedic Saṃhitās reveals a progressive development in Vedic ritual art, with greater specialization on the part of priests (e.g. *udgātṛ*, *adhvaryu*) entrusted with particular duties in the performance of rites. Geographical references suggest a movement from the regions around the Indus to the Gaṅgā river basin, leading to postulations that the Āryans migrated from the northwest of the Indian peninsula to the east and south. These movements resulted in interactions with the local cultures whose religious beliefs and styles were partially assimilated into the compositions of the Saṃhitās and the rituals that accompanied them. The Saṃhitās are composed in verse in an archaic language known as Vedic Sanskrit to distinguish it from subsequent forms of the Sanskrit language that comply with more accessible grammatical structures.

The fourth Vedic Saṃhitā, the *Atharva Veda*, was accepted into the orthodox Āryan canon several centuries later. There is no mention of it in certain early authoritative textual sources, such as the *Laws of Manu*, or the Buddhist Jātakas, which refer to the triad of the *Ṛg*, *Sama*, and *Yajur Vedas*. The *Atharva Veda* is markedly different from this triad. Although about a sixth of its hymns are common to the *Ṛg Veda Saṃhitā*, the *Atharva Veda* contains hundreds of original hymns dealing with different themes, which are often categorized as benevolent or malevolent. Within the beneficial class are spells and chants for the cure of illnesses, for the acquisition and retention of fertility and virility, and even for success in securing a lover. Within the malevolent category are incantations and formulae to bring harm to others. The *Atharva Veda Saṃhitā* reveals ancient techniques of medicinal practice, warfare, and ritual, as well as astrological knowledge and philosophical speculation. Indeed, many of its prayers and accompanying rites may derive from non-Āryan and pre-Āryan sources, and it appears that the astrological and medicinal concerns of the *Atharva Veda* priestly lineages were initially not regarded favorably by the Āryan priesthood. Thus the *Atharva Veda* may have been initially resisted, and only included as the fourth canonical Saṃhitā later in time. However, many of its hymns suggest an origin as early, if not earlier, than the other three hymn collections. Contemporary scholarly studies are beginning to note compelling continuities between the religious concerns voiced in the *Atharva Veda* and the beliefs and practices of Tantra, whose literature emerges more than a thousand years later.

Vedic deities

Of the various deities to whom hymns are addressed in the *Ṛg Veda Saṃhitā*, Agni (Fire) and Indra (God of Storms and Lightning) each receive about 200 hymns, suggesting their high status among the gods of the Āryan pantheon. There are hymns to Sūrya (the Sun), Dyaus-pitṛ (God of the Heavens), Vāyu (the Wind), and Varuṇa (God of the Waters), and even to Soma (a sacred plant and the intoxicating drink prepared from it). The pantheon of Vedic deities is mostly populated by male gods, but there are a few hymns to such goddesses as Uṣas (the Dawn), Rātrī (the Night), and Pṛthivī (the Earth). Scholars conjecture that the prevalence of male deities, some of whom, like Indra, have warrior natures, reveals a patriarchal social structure among the Āryans. Others suggest that since goddesses come to command a sizeable part of Hindu worship, quite in contrast to their representation in the Saṃhitās and other early Āryan literature, these feminine deities may have figured significantly in non-Āryan worship traditions, which progressively influenced the dominating Āryan culture.

Through a study of the deities in the Vedic pantheon, early influential Indologists, such as Max Müller, speculated on the origin of religion itself. The close relationship between the Vedic deities and natural elements led Müller to suggest that human beings, in awe at natural phenomena such as the sun and lightning, and even such purely abstract qualities as "brilliance," began to attribute anthropomorphic qualities to these, and subsequently to envision a divine actor behind the manifestation of these powers. So the Ṛg Vedic linguistic term "*dyaus*," rendered by Müller as "shining" or "radiant," was eventually identified with a particular deity, Dyaus-Pitṛ. In fact, Müller suggested that the cognate words in Indo-European languages, such as *deva*, *deus*, *theos*, general terms for "god," eventually became particularized into specific gods such as Zeus, Dyaus-Pitṛ, and Jupiter. Thus Müller argued it was a "disease of language" that led human beings to mistake words originally used for abstract principles and reify them into imagined realities. Most scholars acknowledge the close linguistic relationship between the names for Vedic deities such as Dyaus-Pitṛ and those of the western Indo-European gods, such as Zeus and Jupiter, or between Varuṇa and Uranus, which suggest common socio-cultural origins. However, theorizing on the origin of religion has fallen out of favor in the last century, because there is little evidence available to evaluate the truth behind such speculations.

Ṛta and cosmic order

Among the concepts encountered in Vedic literature is *ṛta*, which may be translated as "the right way," and is often rendered as "the cosmic order." It reveals that Āryan civilization was aware of an overarching orderliness to the workings of the cosmos, evident in the movement of the heavenly bodies, the seasonal changes, and the course of human life. One discerns a sense of acceptance of an inexorable principle, akin to "Fate" in its controlling power, but different in that it was not necessarily capricious, but orderly. *Ṛta* controlled the way plants grew, rivers flowed, and persons developed. In time, it becomes apparent that alignment with this cosmic order is regarded as beneficial, while to be in discord with it is harmful.

The concept of *ṛta* eventually disappears from usage, and is taken up by the term *dharma*. *Dharma* develops into a notion of individual human and social actions in relationship with the overarching cosmic order. Dharmic action is in accord with *ṛta*; undharmic action is not. Religious authorities, regarded as having intuited the nature of this orderly "course of things," which was now seen as encapsulating a divine, moral order, began to prescribe how individuals should behave through the course of their lives in order to follow the way of religious righteousness.

The Brāhmaṇas

A genre of texts next emerged that primarily deal with the power (*brahman*) within the recitation of sacred verses (*mantra*), and with the ritual practices of the priestly class (*brāhmaṇa*, or Brahmin in this text to minimize confusion). The Brāhmaṇas, as these texts are called, are composed in Vedic Sanskrit prose, and extol the virtues of sacrificial rites known as *yajña*. They contain commentaries on hymns from the Vedic Saṃhitās, and describe a variety of rituals in detail. They also offer interpretations, and explanations for the origins, of aspects of ritual practice. Their interpretations often strive to demonstrate parallels between three realms: the macrocosm, which is the abode of the gods, the mesocosm of society, and the microcosm of individual human life and ritual action. Hence, the fire sticks that are rubbed together to kindle the sacrificial fire are equated with the sexual union between a Vedic god and goddess, and the clarified butter used to stoke the fire is likened to the rain, to semen, and to the divine child produced by their sexual union. The content of these texts, although once dismissed as being of little merit, are attracting renewed attention by some scholars engaged in ritual studies.

Vedic rituals (yajña)

The term that was originally used for Vedic sacrifices is *yajña*, and the patron who commissioned such a rite is the *yajamāna*. Nowadays, it is much more common to hear the term *homa* used for such Vedic-styled rituals of offerings into the fire. The Brāhmaṇa literature begins to emphasize *yajña* even more than the gods to whom the offerings are made, insinuating that it is *yajña* that gives the gods their powers, or that it is because they themselves performed *yajña* that the gods gained prestige. Thus the Vedic gods are seen as dependent on the performance of *yajña*, and in turn on the ritual acts of the priests who are capable of conducting the rites. The Vedic deity Bṛhaspati, regarded as the high priest and wise spiritual preceptor to the gods themselves, served as a divine model for the earthly members of the priestly class, who presided at *yajñas*. The performance of *yajñas* was deemed vital for anyone desiring entry into heaven. *Yajñas* were thought to maintain the very order of the cosmos by providing nourishment for the gods. The gods consumed the essence of the offerings that were made into the fire, requiring these offerings as their sustenance. What are left behind are the empowering consecrated remnants of the offered food that the gods have tasted. Although the term "sacrifice" often conjures up the image of the offering of animals, Vedic *yajñas*, and certainly contemporary *homa* rites, rarely involve offerings of flesh and blood. Milk, clarified butter or ghee, yogurt, rice or other grains and pulses, and even parts of sacred plants such the *datura* fruit, wood-apple leaves (*bilva patra*), or Soma, might be offered.

Figure 1.1 Brahmins chant Vedic verses and make offerings as a Brahmin patron pours ghee into the flames during this modern *homa* ritual, derived from ancient *yajña* procedures

The most ancient types of *yajña* were rituals performed for the benefit of the social or cosmic good. Collectively known as *śrauta* rites, they involved the use of three sacred fires. The patron (*yajamāna*) of these rites was typically a king, to whom particular benefits of the ritual would accrue. However, *śrauta* rites were supposed to be performed in accord with the rhythms of the natural world, for instance, during seasonal changes, in accord with lunar cycles, or even at junctures of the day. By commissioning priests and staging these *śrauta* rites, some of which were on an exceptionally grandiose scale, the ruler demonstrated his own largesse, secured the harmonious workings of the cosmos, and obtained the beneficial fruits of the sacrifice. These fruits might include prosperity of the kingdom, fertility of his lineage and of the land, and revitalization of his own power.

While the earlier pattern of *yajña*, as suggested in the hymns of the Vedic Saṃhitās, appeared to reiterate events of a cosmic battle between gods and titans, order and chaos, as exemplified by the warrior-god Indra's defeat of Vṛtra, the Brāhmaṇas emphasize the science of ritual itself. The timely performance of these *yajñas*, with exactitude in adhering to the system of rules of ritual action, was eventually perceived as essential for the proper functioning of the cosmos. Thus human beings, through the indispensable mediation of the Brahmin priests, were thought to have substantial control over their world.

Yajñas that were prescribed for individuals, which involved the use of a single sacred fire, were known as *gṛhya* or household rites. The simplest of these could be performed by the householders of the upper classes themselves. In time, the number of prescribed rituals increased, as did the belief that erroneous performance could result in dangerous consequences for the *yajamāna*. The responsibility for the correct performance of *yajñas* flowed in the direction of the priestly classes, as did those offering materials from the rite that were not consumed in the sacrificial fire. It became commonly understood that without the *dakṣiṇā*, the monetary or material payment for services provided, even the spiritual benefit would go to the priest(s) who performed the rite, rather than to the patron. *Dakṣiṇā* was regarded as the "spouse" of *yajñā*, and an indispensable payment to bring about the transfer of spiritual merit from the ritualist to the patron.

Case Study: The *aśvamedha*

One of the grandest of all *śrauta yajñas* was the *aśvamedha* or horse sacrifice. Only the most wealthy and powerful of kings could afford to commission this *yajña* since it was financially costly and politically provocative. The ritual was designed primarily to extend and consolidate a king's dominion, as well as to obtain offspring. In the *Rāmāyaṇa*, a Hindu epic of a later period, King Daśaratha performs an *aśvamedha* that leads to the birth of Rāma, the hero of the tale. The horse sacrifice would begin with the selection from the king's stable of his finest stallion, which would undergo a three-day rite of purification and consecration. Marked with an insignia of the king, the stallion would then be released to roam freely for an entire year. It would be followed by an entourage of the king's warriors. If the horse wandered into a neighboring monarch's territory it set the stage for potential conflict. If that ruler allowed the horse free access to his lands, he essentially submitted to the stallion's owner. However, if he seized the animal for himself, he would initiate a battle for sovereignty over his own land. If the horse's wandering progressed smoothly, the stallion of the victorious emperor would return to the capital at the end of the year.

In accord with its concerns for fertility, the chief queen or *mahiśī* played a central role in the concluding rites, over which several priests presided. The king would cleanse himself by gargling, and shaving his beard and head. Together with the chief queen, he would perform an all-night vigil before a sacred fire on the night of the new moon. The next day, the horse would be adorned and anointed, while a variety of animals were sacrificed. Among these was the dog, a symbolic antagonist of the horse, and thus a symbol of the king's enemies. The chief officiating priest, the horse, and the king would be identified with the Vedic creator deity, Brahmā Prajāpati. Rice, representing the stallion's virile semen, would also be cooked in the rite. It was equated with the gold given to the priests by the king, who was the patron of the rite. Finally the horse would be "quieted," although its vital breaths would be "restored." Some scholars suggest that this meant the animal was suffocated. In keeping with the rite's concerns with fertility, the chief queen would lie beside the horse, who symbolized the king, be covered with a cloth, and enact a mock copulation. The horse would subsequently be dismembered, offered into the sacrificial fire, and portions of its flesh would be consumed by the participants. The consumption of the cooked rice was believed to distribute the stallion's virility among Prajāpati, the priests, and the king. In a description of the horse sacrifice in a version of the *Rāmāyaṇa* epic, portions of the rice are consumed by the chief queen and King Daśaratha's next two chief wives, all of whom subsequently bear children.

The performance of one hundred *aśvamedhas* was reputed to grant to a human ruler the throne of Indra, king of the gods. However, since the rite took over a year to perform, this was hardly possible. There are mythic tales of gods themselves, such as Brahmā, and kings, such as Yudhiṣṭhira of the *Mahābhārata* epic, having performed the *aśvamedha*. Several historical kings are also known to have performed the rite. Among these was Samudragupta of the Gupta dynasty, who cast coins commemorating the event. In the city of Banāras, a renowned spot (*ghāt*) on the banks of the river Gaṅgā bears the name Daśāśvamedha Ghat, because a local royal dynasty reputedly performed ten (*daśa*) *aśvamedhas* there. A recent performance of the rite was by Sawai Jai Singh II, a king of Jaipur in the eighteenth century.

A repeating motif in Hindu sacrifice is based on the notion that the creation is the result of the dismemberment of the creator deity Prajāpati. By building the sacrificial altar and making offerings into it, Prajāpati, and the creation itself is temporarily reconstituted and restored.

Case Study: The *agnicayana*

Another example of Vedic *yajña* is the *agnicayana*, perhaps humanity's oldest surviving religious ritual. The Nambudiri Brahmin community from the state of Kerala has maintained knowledge of ancient Vedic traditions with little change. However, since the *agnicayana* was a costly rite it was rarely performed by them, and even if conducted, had not been witnessed by outsiders. A detailed study of this ritual was conducted by renowned Indologists who commissioned the rite in 1975. It was filmed by a visual anthropologist, photographed, and studied, providing us with a remarkable record of the procedure. Since the 1975 performance, a few others have been commissioned, suggesting a revival and endurance of this ancient rite. An elaborate twelve-day ritual, the *agnicayana* is typically commissioned by a patron in order to attain vitality, offspring, or even immortality. It requires the ministrations of seventeen priests and many months of preparation. It is performed in the fortnight between the new and full moon in spring.

The ritual takes place in a temporary enclosure built according to prescribed specifications where measurements are related to various dimensions of the human body. The ritual enclosure is typically a thatched roof supported by wooden posts. A stick, measuring from the toes to the tips of the middle fingers of the patron's upstretched arms, raised as if in prayer, serves as the main length against which all other measurements are made. The ritual site is a reconstruction of the cosmos itself, whose dimensions are mirrored in that of the human microcosm. One sees, in this ancient rite, early applications of the astronomical sciences in the necessary timings of each event, of mathematics, in its computations and structural geometries, and of the physical sciences in the casting of bricks, the making of fire, and the offering of oblations. One sees applications of culinary art in the production of the Soma sacrifice and other oblations into the fire, as well as sonic science in the recitation of Vedic chants with their varied metrical forms. The *agnicayana* weaves together an elaborate tapestry, with threads of technological knowledge transmitted from antiquity, in the service of a vision of the world that integrates human beings (e.g. the patron) with the broader cosmic reality, through the agency of indispensable priestly functionaries who are custodians of that arcane knowledge.

The center piece of the *agnicayana* is an elaborate brick altar (*vedi*) fashioned from over a thousand bricks placed in five layers and laid out in the shape of a bird. It is located in the Great Altar (*mahāvedi*) section of the sacred enclosure while the other section holds the domestic altars and fire pits. This domestic section represents the home of the patron (*yajamāna*) who must preside over the ritual with his wife, who holds a parasol to keep her partially concealed from the view of onlookers. Only a Brahmin who has maintained the tradition of keeping three domestic fires burning in his household is entitled to commission the *agnicayana*, the "piling up of fire" rite.

The ritual process in summary is as follows. On the first day of the rite, the patron and priests enter the enclosure carrying three fires. Clay pots are constructed, an animal sacrifice is traditionally performed for the god Vāyu (the Wind), and fire, generated through churning a wooden shaft in a wood receptacle, is placed in one of the pots. The patron undergoes some purification rites and takes a vow of silence for the duration of the ritual, except for the utterance of various prayers. A sacrificial pole is prepared in the domestic section, while the dimensions and placement of the Great Altar are laid out in their appropriate place. Construction of the bird-shaped Great Altar begins on the fourth day, with the second, third and fourth layers of bricks laid on successive days. The patron voices a prayer that each of the bricks be transformed to cattle to enhance his wealth. The construction of the altar reiterates the reconstitution of the divided creator deity Prajāpati. The fifth and final layer is positioned on the eighth day. Appropriate Vedic hymns are chanted throughout the ritual by the priests specialized for the task.

Oblations of water and ghee are made and one of the old domestic altars is replaced with a new one. An animal sacrifice is performed. Continuous rites follow from

Soma

The identity of the sacred Soma plant, and the Soma beverage prepared from it, continues to puzzle scholars. Vedic descriptions of its preparation and properties suggest that it had intoxicating and possibly even hallucinogenic capacities, and differed from mere alcoholic beverages. The golden-hued liquid was obtained by pressing Soma between stones. There are over a hundred Vedic hymns in praise of Soma, and they tell that the gods Indra and Agni drink it in large quantities. The mycologist R. Gordon Wasson made a compelling case that Soma was likely the "fly agaric" mushroom, *Amanita Muscaria*. This fungus has been used by Siberian shamans in various cultures to induce altered states of consciousness. Recent discoveries of ephedra, and other plant substances, in jars at sites of the ancient Zoroastrian *haoma* ritual, which parallels the Vedic Soma rite, have led other scholars to consider that these plants might have been Soma. However, in both India and Persia, a variety of plants have been substituted for whatever might have been the original Soma/*haoma*.

the tenth to the twelfth day. These include the pressing of the stalks of the sacred Soma plant to produce a hallucinatory beverage. Hymns are chanted in honor of the divine plant. At various points in the ritual, the Soma is consumed by the priests and patron, or offered into the fire. The gods, including Indra, are invited to participate in the oblations. Eleven more animals are sacrificed. In the 1975 enactment of the ritual, non-animal substitutes were used for what would typically have been goat sacrifices. At the conclusion of the rite, the patron and his wife take a purifying bath and don new clothes. Another animal is sacrificed and the ritual enclosure is set ablaze. The patron departs with fire to install in his domestic altars which have been rejuvenated in the process. Thereafter, he will be expected to perform the domestic *agnihotra* ritual daily, for the remainder of his life. The *agnihotra* is a simple ritual to be performed at sunrise and sunset in which offerings of rice and ghee are made into a fire fuelled by dried cow dung. Prayers to Sūrya (the Sun), Prajāpati, and Agni (Fire) are uttered during the rite.

The Āraṇyakas

The Āraṇyakas are a loosely defined genre of texts that bridge the concerns of the Brāhmaṇas and those of the Upaniṣads. They are even sometimes classified within those categories. Thus the *Bṛhadāraṇyaka,* which is attached to the *Śatapatha Brāhmaṇa,* is regarded as an Upaniṣad. Like the Brāhmaṇas, the Āraṇyakas, or wilderness (*āraṇya*) texts, concern themselves with sacrificial rituals of offerings into sacred fires, and like the Upaniṣads, endorse the value of meditative practices. The *Aitareya Āraṇyaka* even designates itself as an Upaniṣad. As their name suggests, the Āraṇyakas uphold the value of retreating beyond the outskirts of the village to study their teachings. In fact, their content is held to be dangerous and to be studied in secret while adhering to an ascetic lifestyle. As such, they are eventually associated with the forest-dweller (*vanaprastha*) stage of life prescribed by orthodoxy. However, the concerns of the texts may actually derive from the ritual practices of nomadic warriors who herded cattle and dwelt apart from village communities. The Āraṇyakas emphasize symbolic speculation on the nature of rituals rather than exclusive attention to the performance of the rite itself, and thus, although they are primarily concerned with Brāhmaṇa-like ritual action, are clear forerunners of the speculative spirit encountered in the Upaniṣads.

The Upaniṣads

The oldest Upaniṣads, which may have been composed as early as the eighth century CE, are appended to the Āraṇyakas or partially embedded within them. There are as many as eighteen principal Upaniṣads, "principal" because they are appended to the previously mentioned genres of Vedic literature, namely the Vedic Saṃhitās, the Brāhmaṇas, and the Araṇyakas. Of these eighteen, the *Bṛhadāraṇyaka Upaṇisad* (attached to the *White Yajur Veda*) and the *Chāndogya Upaniṣad* (attached to the *Sāma Veda*) are the earliest, and composed in Vedic Sanskrit prose. The expression Vedānta is often used when referring to the Upaniṣads and their teachings, since they form "the end or concluding sections (*anta*) of revealed Vedic literature." Other principal Upaniṣads include the *Īśa, Śvetāśvatara, Kena, Kaṭha, Jābāla,* and *Māṇḍukya Upaniṣads*. They appear to have been composed in subsequent centuries, some in verse, and others in classical Sanskrit prose. There are over a hundred other "lesser Upaniṣads," some of which were composed only a few hundred years ago. These reflect the concerns of specific philosophical schools, such as those of Sāṅkhya or Yoga, or have sectarian orientations towards particular deities, such as Śiva or Viṣṇu.

Actually, tradition holds that any text with secret teachings is an Upaniṣad, but scholars classify them according to their style and thematic content. The term "*upaniṣad*" is said to derive from the classic image of a student sitting (*ṣad*) down (*ni*) beside (*upa*) a spiritual mentor. The format of many of the Upaniṣads reflects this terminology since they are framed as conversations between a disciple (*śiṣya*) and teacher (*guru*). Although there are considerable variations in the content of the Upaniṣads, they are generally classified as texts of speculative philosophy, and become a cornerstone of the Indian philosophical tradition that subsequently develops.

The primary concern of the Upaniṣads is with the nature of Absolute Reality (Brahman), the true nature of the individual self (*ātman*), and the relationship between

Figure 1.2 In the teacher–student image of the Upaniṣads, a father recites from a Sanskrit text teaching his son the value of such learning

Brahman and Ātman. This focus reflects a trend prefigured in the Āraṇyakas, to uncover an underlying principle of coherence that unifies the apparent diversity of the created world. The *Bṛhadāraṇyaka Upaniṣad,* which bridges the two genres of Āraṇyaka and Upaniṣad, exemplifies this in its cosmological interpretation of the Vedic horse sacrifice (*aśvamedha*). What is significant is not the performance of the rite, but an intuitive grasp of the relationships that connect particulars from the realm of human ritual action to the fullness of the universe. So, the Upaniṣadic sage proclaims that Dawn itself, both the goddess in Vedic myth and the natural phenomenon, is the head of the sacrificial horse. So, too, the Sun is the horse's eye; the wind, his breath; the sacrificial fire, his open mouth; the seasons, his limbs; the stars, his bones; plants and trees, his hair, and so on. When the horse shakes himself, there is thunder; when he urinates, it rains; and Speech itself is his voice (*Bṛhadāranyaka Upaniṣad* I.1.1). Thus the pantheon of Vedic deities, and their corresponding natural phenomena, are united and symbolically interpreted as parts of a unity. In this case that unity is the sacrifice, again understood as a whole, comprising both the sacrificial offering (i.e. the horse and his faculties) and the sacrificial fire (I.2.7). The implication is that what appears to untutored eyes as merely the immolation of an animal, to those who have the insight to recognize it, is "verily" (*vai*) the revelation of a mystery. A hidden power, the veritable source of all "selves" in creation, took up form in the particular manifestation of the sacrificial animal. In the act of sacrifice, the particular form of the hidden power is released, and reunited with itself. Those who realize this truth become one with that power and transcend the realms of life and death. Generally, the Upaniṣadic sages refer to that unseen power, principle, or reality as Brahman or the Self (*ātman*).

Ātman and Brahman

The word "*brahman*" originally referred to a hallowed power within the sacred utterances (*mantra*) of the Vedic *ṛṣis*, but by the time of the Upaniṣads was used to signify ultimate reality itself. This is not to say that the Upaniṣads as a whole are consistent in the way they depict Brahman. Vedānta philosophy, for instance, which is rooted in interpreting the teachings of the Upaniṣads, has produced an assortment of schools that reflect the variations in Upaniṣadic depictions of the nature of Brahman. Brahman can represent the underlying essence of the material world. Brahman is mostly unseen, hidden to the senses, and even to rational thought. The Upaniṣads depict Brahman as supreme (*parā-brahman*), and it is also designated as Nirguṇa Brahman (Brahman beyond attributes) and as Saguṇa Brahman (Brahman that can be characterized).

Brahman is consistently identified as intrinsically connected to the innermost being of all things in existence, including our selves. Thus the Self (*ātman*) is often used as a synonym for Brahman, with which it is identified. In the *Katha Upaniṣad*, for example, the youth Naciketas consults the Lord of Death, Yama, on the question of whether anything endures beyond the death of one's body. Yama delivers a teaching on Brahman and Atman, pointing out that the Supreme Lord is the innermost Self (*ātman*) of all beings, who although one, appears to have manifold forms. Only the wise, who recognize the Supreme Lord (i.e. Brahman) within themselves, attain eternal joy (*Katha Upaniṣad* II. ii. 12). The *Bṛhadāraṇyaka Upaniṣad* (I.4.10) also presents this perspective when it points out that whoever knows "I am Brahman" (*aham brahmāsmi*) becomes all of reality. Not even the gods can prevent it, for that person is then the very Self (*ātman*) of the gods. However, the gods are displeased with this for such an individual is freed from serving them. Just as animals serve human beings, so too those who do not know the Self, serve the gods.

In the *Chāndogya Upaniṣad*, a young man named Śvetaketu is instructed by his father Uddālaka Āruṇi in the knowledge that he did not receive despite twelve years of conventional Vedic education. Although he was proud and arrogant, thinking himself to be well educated, Śvetaketu was surprised to discover that he did not learn how that which is unperceived may be perceived, and how the unknowable may be known. Uddālaka explains to his son that just as a close examination of a pair of nail scissors can lead one to discover that it is actually made of iron, discovering the underlying essence of seemingly diverse particular things is a vital beginning. By knowing iron, one may then know the nature of all things made of iron, since the

does not differentiate between man + being able to be aware of Brahman within →

particular form that it takes is simply linked to a word that names it. Although this verbal designation appears to give it a distinct existence, in fact it is really still just iron. So too, when the underlying essence of all things is known, all things that derive from that underlying essence may be known. That underlying essence, Uddālaka calls Being, only one reality, without any other. All the various manifestations of the cosmos, Uddālaka explains, from fire to water to plant life and the myriad creatures in existence, from a lion to a mosquito, have their root in Being, have Being as their abode, and Being as their support. The whole world has this subtle essence as its Self. His father exclaims, "That is the True. That is the Self (*ātman*). That is You (*tat tvam asi*), Śvetaketu."

Uddālaka further explains that just as rivers appear to be different even though their source and destination is the ocean, so too creatures imagine themselves to be separate beings, unaware of their true source in Being. Just as a tree does not die when one of its branches is cut, the Self does not die, he explains, when the body dies. Asking Śvetaketu to break apart the tiny seed of a fig (*nyagrodha*) tree, Uddālaka demonstrates that there is virtually nothing visible remaining, and yet the majestic tree exists precisely because of that subtle essence within the seed. Asking Śvetaketu to sip salt water from a glass repeatedly, his father illustrates how, although the salt is invisible, it permeates the water thoroughly. So too, he explains, the Self is not perceived, although it is everywhere. Uddālaka emphasizes that finding a spiritual teacher enables persons to recognize their predicament of bondage to ignorance until they fully realize the Self.

Śruti *and* Smṛti

The four genres of Vedic literature that are appended to each other, namely the Saṃhitās, Brāhmanas, Āraṇyakas, and Upaniṣads, are collectively regarded as *śruti*. The term *śruti*, derives from the Sanskrit verbal root "*śru*," to hear. It is intended to evoke the idea that the contents of these texts were divinely perceived (i.e. heard) or revealed to the *ṛṣis*. Thus the authorship of this literature is purported to be some greater unseen power, channeled through the semi-divine perceivers (*ṛṣi*) with whom their teachings are associated. All other religious literature is classified as *smṛti*, which derives from the Sanskrit verbal root "*smṛ*," to remember. Thus *smṛti* is literature that is held to have been composed by human beings and passed down as tradition through the generations. *Śruti* and *smṛti* set up a dichotomy between "revealed" and "traditional" religious literature, granting a special status and authority to what are loosely called the Vedas, the Veda, or Vedic scripture.

Despite the distinction between *śruti* and *smṛti*, the categories are somewhat permeable. For instance, we note that for certain orthodox groups, only the *Ṛg*, *Sāma*, and *Yajur Vedas* were originally regarded as *śruti*, with the *Atharva Veda* only becoming a later addition to the category. Similarly, subsequent religious literature often strives to be included in the sacrosanct, revealed category. The *Mahābharata* epic, for instance, lays claim to being a fifth Veda, although this claim is not taken very seriously. However, the *Bhagavad Gītā*, which is part of the *Mahābhārata*, enjoys a remarkable authority and sanctity among contemporary Hindus, giving it the status of *śruti* in all but its official designation. Some Hindus would like to deem it an Upaniṣad to include it within the category of *śruti*.

And while the Brāhmaṇas and Āraṇyakas enjoy the prestige of being *śruti*, their content is little understood by most Hindus and has marginal impact on their religious lives. The so-called "lesser Upaniṣads" could arguably be categorized as either *śruti* or *smṛti*. The influence and authority of some of these "lesser Upanisads" is greater on particular Hindu sects than the so-called "principal Upaniṣads." An early classification scheme, found in a Dharma Sūtra text, claims that there are both Vedic and Tantric (or Āgamic) *śrutis*. This would appear to be reasonable, since the Tantras and Āgamas have been arguably even more influential in the fabric of Hinduism than the Vedas. However, orthodoxy does not accept Āgamic scripture as *śruti*. Thus while the conventional designation of *śruti* is a telling hallmark of orthodoxy, *smṛti* literature plays no less of a role in shaping the religious lives of Hindus.

A significant feature of sacredness relates to whether or not a text is transmitted orally or in writing. Although we now tend to think of "texts" as written objects, prior to the advent of writing texts were memorized and transmitted orally. *Śruti* literature continues to be transmitted orally because committing it to writing is regarded as diminishing its sacredness. This does not mean that the Vedas were never written down. The Brahmin scholar Sāyaṇa wrote valuable commentaries on the Vedic Saṃhitās and other Vedic literature in the fourteenth century, and many scholars think that written versions of the Vedas may have existed by the third century BCE. However, despite being part of the written tradition for centuries, particular families of Brahmins have maintained the tradition of memorizing and reciting the Vedas. The Upaniṣads were only rendered into written Latin in the early nineteenth century from seventeenth-century Persian translations.

Other Vedic literature

By the fifth century BCE, a variety of texts had developed that were classified as primary and secondary appendages (*aṅga*) to the Vedas. The primary appendages are called the Vedāṅgas and the secondary ones are the Upāṅgas. These appendages developed as adjuncts to the knowledge (*veda*) deemed necessary for the priestly class, or were aids for the performance of priestly duties. They are often composed in the form of *sūtras* (aphoristic verses). There are six categories of Vedāṅgas. These are: 1) Śikṣā, literally, "instruction," in the rules for proper pronunciation of the Veda; 2) Vyākaraṇa, or "grammatical analysis," such as the works of Pāṇini; 3) Chandas or "prosody," which explain the various meters used in Vedic recitation; 4) Nirukta, or "lexicon" of the meanings of Vedic terms, such as that by Yākṣa; 5) Jyotiṣa, or "astrology"; and 6) Kalpa, or explanations of ritual action. The Kalpa literature, or Kalpa Sūtras, followed the divisional scheme of the four Vedas and were appended to them. Thus the Kalpa Sūtras attached to the *Sāma Veda* would be studied by *Sāma Veda* Brahmins. Each Kalpa Sūtra has four parts: 1) Śrauta Sūtras, which dealt with elaborate public rites; 2) Gṛhya Sūtras, dealing with life cycle rites (*saṃskāra*) and household rituals; 3) Dharma Sūtras, on moral prescriptions for householders; and 4) Śulva Sūtras, concerning the measurement and construction of ritual spaces, demonstrating aspects of early mathematical sciences.

The Upāṅgas are traditionally grouped as follows: 1) Purāṇa, or "antiquities," which are mythological texts with pseudo-historical content; 2) Nyāya, or treatises on "logic"; 3) Mīmāṃsā, which refers to textual interpretation or "investigation" of the Vedas; and 4) Dharma Śāstra, or the codices on behavior regarded as appropriate and aligned with the cosmic order (i.e. dharmic).

Astrology

Astrology has played a significant role in Hindu life from Vedic times, when its study was regarded as supplementary to the Vedas themselves. The study of luminaries (*jyotiṣa*) in the heavens was deemed vital for determining the appropriate times for conducting rituals. The celestial forces are known as *graha,* literally "graspers," semi-divine forces that affect human activities. The nine *grahas* or *nava-graha* are: Sūrya (the Sun), Candra (the Moon), Maṅgala (Mars), Budha (Mercury), Guru or Bṛhaspati (Jupiter), Śukra (Venus), Śani (Saturn), and Rāhu and Ketu (North and South nodes of the moon, related to the points where the lunar orbit intersects the solar ecliptic). Rāhu and Ketu are thus not "planets" or even heavenly bodies like the Sun and Moon, but astronomical points in space. When the Sun and the Moon simultaneously fall on Rāhu and Ketu a solar or lunar eclipse occurs. This exemplifies the grasping power of these celestial phenomena, which periodically "swallow" the Sun or the Moon. Like Western astrology, Hindu astrology recognizes the same twelve signs of the Zodiac. However, it adds a system of twenty-four lunar mansions (*nakṣatra*), which enriches the sophistication of its interpretations.

A Hindu myth, widespread across many parts of Asia, tells how the gods and demons co-operated briefly to churn the ocean of milk and extract "nectar of immortality." The gods were the first to drink of this nectar, but a demon disguised himself as a god and sat among them. Just as he sipped the nectar, the Sun and the Moon, between whom he was seated discovered his disguise. Viṣṇu immediately hurled his discus and severed the demon in two. Unfortunately, it was too late, for he had tasted the elixir of immortality. His fierce, four-armed upper part is Rāhu, and his dragon-tailed lower half is Ketu. Burning with anger and thirsting for vengeance, Rāhu and Ketu try to devour the Sun and Moon whenever they come near, leading to partial or total eclipses. During eclipses, it is still a tradition to shriek at the heavens to repel the demon from his act of revenge.

Rāhu and Ketu stand as an example that challenges the simplistic application of scholarly categories in the study of religious phenomena. Hinduism is replete with such phenomena. For one, Rāhu and Ketu belong to a branch of Hinduism, astrology, which many would not classify as traditionally "religious." But the *grahas* form a vibrant component of Hindu religion. Many Hindu temples have *nava-graha* shrines, which receive regular attention, particularly on Tuesdays and Saturdays. Tuesday is said to be ruled by Mars, and Saturday by Saturn, both of which, like Rāhu and Ketu, are pernicious *grahas*. Offerings are made to the *grahas*, and other deities may also be worshipped to solicit their aid in warding off inauspicious planetary influences. Auspiciousness and inauspiciousness are weighty categories in many spheres of Hindu belief. Astrological considerations play an important role in determining the appropriate periods in the year for weddings and times in the day that are most auspicious for the performance of religious rituals. Astrological charts are routinely consulted when determining whether marriageable partners are suitable. Hindu astrology is also closely paired with gemology, the fabrication of jewelry, and the bodily sciences. For instance, an astrologer might prescribe wearing a necklace made of crystal beads or a ruby set in a silver ring placed on a particular finger of a particular hand in order to circumvent inauspicious influences.

Rāhu and Ketu also demonstrate that *jyotiṣa* includes the science of astronomy, for their "positions" are not based on visible heavenly bodies, but on mathematical calculations grounded in astronomical observations. Furthermore, the tales of the demons reflect a juxtaposition of astronomical science and mythic creativity. It is naïve to suggest that the mythic tale of Rāhu and Ketu reflects a pre-scientific explanation of a natural phenomenon, which should disappear with the "real" understanding of what was "actually" occurring during an eclipse. It is evident that the "scientific" understanding of the phenomenon is ancient, and coexists with its mythic exposition. Immature studies by outsiders have often failed to penetrate the complex layers and multiplicity of meanings embedded in the symbols of the Hindu tradition. It is instructive to remind ourselves of this in our exploration of Hinduism.

Āyurveda

The traditional Hindu knowledge (*veda*) of life (*āyus*), forms a body of literature sometimes classified as an Upaveda, a supplement to the Vedas. Other Upavedas include treatises on the fine arts and music, on politics, and warcraft. Āyurvedic medicine is still widely practiced in India today, alongside modern Western-styled medicine. The three most highly regarded classical texts of Āyurveda are the *Caraka Saṃhitā*, the *Suśruta Saṃhitā*, and the *Vāgbhaṭa Saṃhitā*, each named after the physician-sages who codified the teachings of ancient *ṛṣis* that are believed to have been originally transmitted from the gods. The works themselves date from the first to the seventh centuries CE, but certainly are based on medical knowledge from preceding centuries.

Āyurveda differs from the host of other regional and folk healing methods because it is grounded in a complex philosophy and theory of bodily science. Illness (*roga, vyādhi*) is typically believed to be caused by an imbalance of humors of the body. There are three humors (*tri-doṣa*): phlegm (*kapha*), bile (*pitta*), and wind (*vāta*), associated with the water, fire, and air elements respectively. The Āyurvedic approach to healing consists in diagnosing which of the humors are out of balance and then prescribing primarily herbal medicine or dietary changes to restore the balance. The study of Āyurveda therefore requires an understanding of the various qualities (*guṇa*) inherent in substances in the body (e.g. blood, bone, fat) and the created world. While there are three fundamental *guṇas*, there are twenty subcategories of these. The fundamental *guṇas* are the *sattva* (pure, luminous), *rajas* (energetic), and *tamas* (dark, heavy). Among the subcategories are heat-producing, cooling, slimy, and rough substances. The three *guṇas* are associated with the Sāṅkhya school of Indian philosophy. In its theories of matter and atoms, Āyurveda also draws upon concepts derived from Vaiśeṣika philosophy.

A person's bodily constitution is primarily categorized according to the *doṣa* that is dominant, although most people's constitutions are combinations of all three. Since the *vāta* or *vāyu doṣa* (the air/wind humor) is believed to control breathing, expulsion of wastes, and the movement of thoughts, an imbalance can lead to worries and insomnia, or constipation. And because the *kapha doṣa* (the water/phlegm humor) is associated with bodily fluids, an excess can produce congestion, or laziness. The *pitta dosa* (the fire/bile humor) is believed responsible for digestion; thus imbalances can produce indigestion and ulcers.

Internal imbalances are believed to be triggered by external causes, and Āyurveda also incorporates diagnoses based on pernicious agents such as poisons (e.g. snake bites), injury, and affliction by a wide range of spirits (*bhūta*), particularly for psychological illnesses. Besides dietary modifications, treatments include surgical procedures, massage, fumigation, enemas, baths and sweating. The preparation and wearing of amulets, recitation of sacred phrases, and the performance of special rituals are also among its therapeutic prescriptions.

Physicians and patients who are exploring approaches to healing beyond those conventionally associated with modern Western medicine have been turning to some aspects of Āyurveda. A well-known current exemplar is Deepak Chopra, whose teachings on psycho-physical health combine non-dualistic Vedānta philosophical perspectives with Āyurveda and Western medicine. Various Indian institutions such as Banāras Hindu University have been offering accredited degrees in Āyurveda.

Key points in this chapter

- The Vedic Saṃhitās are the most esteemed literary works of the Āryans.
- The *Atharva Veda* contains hundreds of original hymns dealing with an assortment of topics with differing concerns from the other three Saṃhitās.
- Some scholars speculate that most Vedic deities are male due to an Āryan patriarchal social structure. Indologist Max Müller speculated on the origin of religion. However, such speculation is currently unpopular due to lack of evidence to support such theorizing.
- The "cosmic order" was important to Āryan civilization, as was the degree to which all aspects of life were aligned with it.
- Sacrificial rites (*yajña*) were elevated in the Brāhmaṇas to an importance that surpassed the gods, for it was believed that *yajña* itself maintained the cosmic order.
- Tradition holds that any text with secret teachings is an Upaniṣad. The Āraṇyakas, forerunners of the Upaniṣads, have similar associations with secrecy and philosophical speculation.
- The Upaniṣads are concerned primarily with the nature of Absolute Reality (Brahman), the true nature of the individual Self (*ātman*), and the relationship between the two.
- The four genres of Vedic literature that are appended to each other (namely, the Saṃhitās, Brāhmaṇas, Āraṇyakas, and Upaniṣads) are regarded as *śruti* (divinely revealed), whereas all other religious literature is regarded as *smṛti* (traditional).
- By the fifth century BCE, texts developed that were classified as primary and secondary appendages (*aṅga*) to the Vedas, namely the Vedāṅgas and the Upāṅgas.
- Since ancient Vedic times, astrology has been regarded as a vital supplement to the study of the Vedas themselves.
- Āyurveda is considered supplemental to the Vedas, and this status ensures that Āyurvedic styles of medicine are well regarded and still widely practiced in India today.

Discussion questions

1. Āyurveda is widely practiced today. Discuss possible reasons for its continued success.
2. What appear to be similar motifs in the *aśvamedha* and *agnicayana* rituals?
3. Discuss the nature of Brahman and Ātman, and the relationship between them.

4. Explain what is included in the categories of *śruti* and *smṛti*. Discuss the differences, and the various complexities that arise from such designations.
5. What do the types of literature that are included in the "limbs" of Vedic literature tell us about the values of Āryan society?

Further reading

On Hindu religious literature

Farquhar, J.N. (1967) *An Outline of the Religious Literature of India*. Reprint. Varanasi: Motilal Banarsidass.

Macdonell, A.A. (1961) *A History of Sanskrit Literature*. Reprint. Delhi: Motilal Banarsidass.

Santucci, J.A. (1977) *An Outline of Vedic Literature*. Missoula: Scholars Press.

Winternitz, M. (1927–67) *A History of Indian Literature*. S. Ketkar and H. Kohn (trans.) 3 vols. Reprint. Calcutta: University of Calcutta.

On the Vedic Saṃhitas, Brāhmaṇas, and Āraṇyakas

Gonda, Jan. (1963) *The Vision of the Vedic Poets*. The Hague: Mouton & Co.

— (1975) *Vedic Literature (Saṃhitās and Brāhmaṇas)*. A History of Indian Literature, vol. 1. fasc. 1. Wiesbaden: Otto Harrasowitz.

Griffith, R.T.H. (1957) *Hymns of the Yajurveda*. Reprint. Benares: Chowkhamba.

— (1957) *The Texts of the White Yajurveda*. Reprint. Benares: Chowkhamba.

— (1963) *Sāmaveda*. Reprint. Varanasi: Chowkhamba.

— (trans.) (1963) *Hymns of the Ṛgveda*, 2 vols. Reprint. Benares: Chowkhamba.

Macdonell, Arthur A. (1898) *Vedic Mythology*. Reprint. New Delhi: Motilal Banarsidass, 1995.

O'Flaherty, Wendy Doniger (1981) *The Rig Veda: An Anthology*. Harmondsworth: Penguin Books.

On the Upanisads

Deussen, Paul (1906) *The Philosophy of the Upanisads*. Reprint. New York: Dover, 1966.

Hume, R. (trans.) (1921) *The Thirteen Principal Upaniṣads*. Oxford: Oxford University Press.

Olivelle, Patrick (1996) *Upaniṣads: A New Translation*. New York: Oxford University Press.

Radhakrishnam, S. (1967) *The Principal Upanisads*. London: Allen & Unwin.

On Vedic religion and ritual

Elizarenkova, Tatyana J. (1995) *Language and Style of the Vedic Ṛṣis*. Albany, NY: State University of New York Press.

Gonda, Jan (1990) *Vedic Ritual: The Non-Solemn Rites*. Leiden: E. J. Brill.

Heesterman, Jan (1985) *The Inner Conflict of Tradition: Essays in Indian Ritual, Kingship, and Society*. Chicago, IL: University of Chicago Press.

Macdonell, A.A. (1954) "Vedic Religion." In *Encyclopedia of Religion and Ethics*. E. Hastings (ed.) (3rd edn), vol. 12, pp. 601–18.

Neufeldt, R.F. (1980) *Max Müller and the Ṛg-Veda: A Study of its Role in his Work and Thought*. Columbia, Mo.: South Asia Books.

Staal, J. F. (1983) Agni: *The Vedic Ritual of the Fire Altar*, 2 vols. Berkeley, CA: University of California Press.

Wasson, R. Gordon (1968) *Soma, the Divine Mushroom of Immortality*. Ethno-Mycological Studies I. New York: Harcourt, Brace and World.

On Vedic sciences

Chatterjee, S. K. (1998) *Indian Calendric System*. New Delhi: Ministry of Information and Broadcasting.

Filliozat, Jean (1964) *The Classical Doctrine of Indian Medicine*. New Delhi: Munshiram Manoharlal.

Kakar, Sudhir (1982) *Shamans, Mystics, and Doctors: A Psychological Inquiry into India and its Healing Traditions*. New York: Alfred A. Knopf.

Khanna, Madhu (2004) *The Cosmic Order*. New Delhi: D.K. Printworld.

Kutumbiah, P. (1962) *Ancient Indian Medicine*. Reprint. Bombay: Orient Longman, 1999.

Pingree, D. (1981) *Jyotiḥśāstra: Astral and Mathematical Literature*. A History of Indian Literature Vol. 6, fasc. 4. Wiesbaden: Otto Harrassowitz.

Wujastyk, Dominik (2003) *The Roots of Ayurveda: Selections from Sanskrit Medical Writings*. London: Penguin Books.

Audio-visual resources

Altar of Fire (1994) Robert Gardiner and Frits Staal, producers. Berkeley: University of California. Extension Center for Media and Independent Learning.

2 Karma *and cosmology*

In this chapter

Since antiquity, the Hindus conceived of time and space as vast in scale, and formulated effective symbol systems through which to describe them. Time was viewed as cyclical, undergoing repetitive processes of various orders, from the daily and annual cycles to those of much longer duration. The Hindu universe was also imagined as being geometrically harmonious, following an evident sacred symmetry. Human lives were viewed as consonant with this cosmic order, and subject to the cycles of birth, death, and rebirth through the various realms of existence. The only way to free oneself from this endless series of incarnations was through a profound intuitive realization about one's true nature. This was liberation.

Main topics covered

- The Hindu conception of time
- The Hindu Calendar
- The Hindu universe
- *Karma, saṃsāra,* and reincarnation
- Mokṣa

The Hindu conception of time

Hindus accept the notion that time and creation move in repetitive cycles. The origin of this idea may derive from observations of the yearly cycle of repetitive seasonal change. The Dharma Śāstras describe various divisions of the cycles of time, such as a *muhūrta* (about 48 minutes) and a *yuga.* A *muhūrta* is traditionally composed of thirty *kalās,* each of which is made up of thirty *kāṣṭhās,* each of which is the time it takes to blink fifteen times. By the time the Purāṇas were being composed an elaborate conception of cyclical time had developed.

There are four main *yugas* (ages), each progressively shorter in duration. They are the Satya or Kṛta Yuga (lasting 4800 god (*deva*) years), the Tretā Yuga (3600 *deva* years), the Dvāpara Yuga (2400), and the Kali Yuga (1200). The total, known as a *mahāyuga* (great age) is 12,000 god years. Since one human year of 360 days is but a day in the life of the gods, one *deva* (god) year is 360 human years. Thus the actual duration of the Kṛta Yuga is 1,728,000 human years. A *mahāyuga* is thus 4,320,000 years. Seventy-one *mahāyugas* make a *manvantara*, an age of humanity, presided over by a divine being known as a Manu. We are in the twenty-eighth *mahāyuga* of the seventy-one that make up our particular *manvantara*. A thousand *mahāyugas* constitute a *kalpa*. There are fourteen *manvantaras* within a *kalpa*. We are in the Vaivasvata *manvantara*, the seventh of the fourteen within our particular *kalpa*. Two *kalpas* constitute a day and a night of the creator god Brahmā, whose life span is a 100 years. This figure, which describes the duration of a single cycle of creation of the universe, is about 311 trillion solar or human years. We are believed to be roughly in the middle of this vast cosmic time cycle and a few thousand years into the Kali Yuga in our particular *mahāyuga*.

When the cosmos is first created, it is renewed, but undergoes degeneration through time. This progressive decline is mirrored within a *mahāyuga*, where the Kṛta Yuga is marked by human life-spans of 400 years, and where beings adhere to *dharma* or righteousness. Likened to an animal standing firmly on four feet, with each passing *yuga* a supporting foot is removed. Life-spans diminish by one quarter and *dharma* decays. The destructive nature of time is symbolized and personified (or deified) by the goddess Kālī, whose name may be translated as "time" or "black." Since the current age in which we live, the Kali Yuga, when *dharma* stands precariously balanced on one leg, is the most degenerate and ultimately heading for destruction, people sometimes think of it as the Kālī Yuga. However, the *yugas* are named after various throws in an ancient Indian game of dice. "Kali" is the most unfavorable throw.

At the end of a life cycle of Brahmā, the cosmos enters a period of dissolution known as the *pralaya*. The symbolic representation of the *pralaya* is the deity Viṣṇu asleep on the cosmic serpent, Anānta, whose name means "without end." Viṣṇu represents a subtle, yet powerful principle that endures beyond the seeming end to a cosmic cycle of creation. Some estimate the duration of the *pralaya* to be as long as a life span of Brahmā, but it may well transcend the categories of time and space. From this state, because the principle of repeated cyclical creations, symbolized by Viṣṇu, still endures, the creation re-emerges once again. This activity is symbolized by a lotus flower with a long stalk growing like an umbilical cord from Viṣṇu's navel. Seated atop the lotus flower is the creator god Brahmā, who brings forth a new creation through his contemplation. There have been, and will be, countless Brahmās, as universes are produced again and again.

Figure 2.1 A relief depicting the creator god Brahmā emerging seated on a lotus flower growing from the navel of Viṣṇu, who reclines on the endless serpent Ananta (Vijayanagar)

The Hindu Calendar

Hindus follow both the solar calendar, consisting of a seven-day week, and a monthly lunar calendar based on cycles of waxing and waning fortnights followed by the full and new moon, respectively. A lunar day is known as a *tithi*. The waning or dark fortnight is favored by deceased spirits, while the waxing or bright fortnight is the more auspicious of the two. Hindus use the solar calendar for birthdays and sectarian activities, but religious rituals often follow the lunar system. So the Hindu festival of Navarātra, in honor of the Great Goddess, takes place on the first nine nights of the waxing fortnight of the lunar month of Āśvina. Because of the discrepancy between the solar and lunar systems (a lunar month is a little over twenty-nine days), this festival could occur in either September or October.

In 1957, in order to standardize the calendrical system, the Government of India initiated the use of a National Calendar, which is sometimes called the Hindu Calendar. It is based on an authoritative version of an ancient astrological compendium, or *pañcāṅga*. Beginning with the Śaka Era (78 CE), it consists of 365 days, with months of fixed durations. Its first month is Caitra, which falls on March 22 or March 21 on leap years. This marks the beginning of spring, the first of the six traditional seasons. Spring is followed by summer, the rainy season, autumn, winter, and the cool season prior to the spring. Despite this effort at standardization, Hindus actually continue to follow a number of different calendar schemes, making the process of establishing the exact timings of religious rituals particularly challenging. It is therefore common to consult religious specialists, who work with various *pañcāṅgas*, to determine the relationships between solar days and lunar *tithis*, and discern when inauspicious influences of *grahas* may make the performance of a rite unsuitable.

The Hindu universe

Hinduism does not have a single authoritative cosmology. There is an assortment of descriptions about the origin and nature of the universe. The Vedic Saṃhitās present a fundamental dualism, mirrored in early Chinese thought, between heaven and earth. Heaven is regarded as male and paternal, while Earth is female and maternal. In the *Ṛg Veda*, we encounter hymns to the sky god Dyaus-Pitṛ and the earth goddess, Pṛthivī. In a portion of the *Ṛg Veda* (10.90) believed to have been composed rather late, there is the *Puruṣa-Sūkta*, a hymn that describes the cosmos as a giant being/person (*puruṣa*), mostly transcendent, only a quarter of whom is the manifest universe. He has a thousand heads, eyes, and feet. Puruṣa begets Virāj (the Widespread), a feminine principle, who in turn is said to beget Puruṣa. It is unclear if this refers to a mutual creation or if a second Puruṣa, a "son," is created from Virāj. Puruṣa is sacrificed by the gods and sages, along with everything, as an offering to himself. From that sacrifice, Puruṣa created the cosmos, including the gods. In a paradoxical fashion, typical of many Vedic hymns, where sacrifice is the paradigm of creation, the divided portions of Puruṣa become the cosmos. The moon arose from his mind, the sun from his eye, the sky from his head, Indra and Agni from his mouth, and the Wind from his vital breath. The sacrificial beast, which in this case is the cosmic being Puruṣa, through the act of sacrifice, which in this case involves the offering of totality, is thus offered to himself. Out of the sacrifice, the manifold cosmos emerges, poised to make sacrifices to itself. Through the act of sacrifice, the cosmos is kept in order.

A *Ṛg Veda* hymn (10.121) tells of a Golden Embryo (*hiraṇya-garbha*), associated with primeval waters, who generated both sky and earth. There are numerous other qualities accorded to the various principles or powers that seem to be associated with creation. For instance, *Ṛg Veda* 10.81–2 praises the One, the Maker of All (Viśvakarman), who, like a supreme designer, shaped and implemented the cosmic order. Likened to the processes of Vedic sacrifice, he is both sacrificial priest (10.81.1) and the sacrifice (10.81.5), who sacrifices the worlds of his cosmic creations as offerings (10.81.1). The orderly arrangement of the cosmos is like the ritual construction of the sacrificial altar, which subsequently re-enacts the creation. This creator, likely identified with the Golden Embryo (10.82.5) of *Ṛg Veda* 10.121, is vastly powerful, profoundly wise (10.82.2), conceals what has passed, and enters into what is yet to come (10.81.1). All our wonder and speculation is directed to this power (10.82.3). And yet he is concealed, even from those who merely chant the hymns of praise (i.e. priests), since they are described as shrouded in ignorance, babbling nonsense, and being intoxicated with worldly pleasures (10.82.7). *Ṛg Veda* 10.72 tells of the mother goddess Aditi, and Dakṣa, the male creative principle, born from each other (10.72.4), after manifest existence emerged from the unmanifest (10.72.3). With legs spread, suggestive of childbirth, Aditi gave birth to the earth, the sky (10.72.4), and eight gods (10.72.9).

Many of the Vedic hymns utter such statements about the nature of the gods, the creation, or aspects of reality. However statements are also often framed as questions, such as: To whom should the sacrifice be offered? What was the source and substance of the creation? One of the most intriguing and influential of the cosmological hymns is the *Nāsadīya Sūkta* (*Ṛg Veda* 10.129), which gives us a remarkable insight into the sophistication of philosophical speculation already evident in the earliest collection of Hindu scriptural literature. The hymn typifies the aforementioned juxtaposition of speculative assertions and questions. It begins by asking: "Then, before the presence of Being, and non-Being, what was there? Where was it? Overseen by whom?" (10.129.1). The poem continues with a number of descriptive cosmological declarations. "Before the existence of death, or of deathlessness, before a sign of day and night, The One breathed, breathless, and self-sustained" (10.129.2). "Desire (*kāma*), which arose in The One, was the primal seed of mind. Poets, who have looked wisely within their hearts, know the connection between that which is manifest and the unmanifest" (10.129.4). However, these declarations are quickly juxtaposed with a number of questions. "Who indeed knows to say how, from what and where this creation has emerged?" (10.129.6). Asserting that since the gods came after the creation (10.129.6), it asks: "Who really knows its origin?" (10.129.6). And the hymn concludes with a striking speculative note: "Whether or not it formed itself, maybe that One, who looks down from the highest heaven knows, or perhaps even He does not know!" (10.129.7).

As part of the tenth book (*maṇḍala*), the *Nāsadīya Sūkta* is a relatively late addition to the collection of hymns in the *Ṛg Veda Saṃhitā*. It is evident that the *ṛṣi*(s) who composed this hymn was aware of a host of cosmogonic ideas in circulation. It appears to suggest that there is a type of intuitive understanding, which poets (i.e. seers, sages) are capable of achieving through meditative introspection. As such, the hymn prefigures the teachings of the Upaniṣads and the Hindu philosophical traditions that subsequently develop.

By the time of the Upaniṣads, the notion of a triple world system or Tri-loka was well established. These were typically: 1) the world of the gods, known as heaven (*svar*) or the *deva-loka*; 2) the world of the ancestors, known as the atmosphere (*bhuvaḥ*) or the *pitṛ-loka*; and 3) the human world, known as the earth (*bhūr*) or *manuṣya-loka*. By the Puranic period, the system was greatly elaborated, with many variations. The *Viṣṇu Purāṇa* describes the world egg (*brahmāṇḍa*) made up of seven *lokas*, with four other worlds above the aforementioned three. Some sectarian scriptures might place Viṣṇu's heaven, Vaikuṇṭha, or Śiva's mountain abode, Kailāsa, at the very top. In addition to these *lokas*, there are the seven netherworlds (*tala*). The lowest is Pātāla, the serpent kingdom of the Nāgas, and the highest, Atala, the realm of the Yakṣas. Below the Talas are as many as twenty-eight or more hells (*naraka*), although seven major ones are typically listed. It is also common for the term Tri-loka to refer to the upper worlds, the earthly world, and the underworlds.

By the Puranic period an elaborate spatial model had developed which linked the geography of the Hindu world with an idealized vision of the cosmos. It consists of a series of concentric islands. The innermost island is Jambu-dvipa (The Island of the Jambu (Wood-apple) Trees), at the center of which towers the Golden Mountain, Mount Meru or Sumeru, an *axis mundi*, or cosmic pivot. Jambudvipa is further divided into nine regions (*varṣa*), of which the southernmost is Bhāratavarṣa, or India, which is to this day known in Hindi as Bhārat. Jambudvipa is surrounded by the salt ocean. Six other ring-shaped islands surround Jambudvipa, each progressively larger and each separated by an ocean of similar size. The entire system of worlds and islands is enveloped by the Brahmā Egg (*brahmāṇḍa*). Hindu emperors, such as the Khmer ruler Suryavarman II, modeled the great temple tomb of Angkor Wat on such a cosmograph. However, due to the complexity of the system, and its many variations in Purāṇic accounts, there is no particular model that is known or universally shared by most Hindus. But, there is a general belief in multiple worlds, including heavens and hells, populated by a range of beings, human and spirit, semi-divine, divine, and demonic, who, if not indifferent, may be benevolently or malevolently disposed towards human beings.

Karma, saṃsāra, *and reincarnation*

The word *karma* derives from the Sanskrit verbal root "*kṛ*" and simply means "to do," or "to act." Thus *karma* originally referred to activity of any kind. However, as early as the Upaniṣads, the idea had developed that one's actions have consequences both for this lifetime and future ones. The notion of birth in other worlds is prefigured in the Vedic Samhitās, which indicate a fear of re-death (*punar-mṛtyu*). By the Upaniṣadic period the concept of repeated reincarnations, or *punar-janman* (birth-again), unless one attained Self-realization, is clearly articulated. *Karma* thus developed into the notion of a moral principle of causality, in which no deed is without its consequences. Good deeds are meritorious (*puṇya*), while evil or sinful deeds (*pāpa*) have painful effects.

According to the *Bṛhadāraṇyaka Upaniṣad* (VI.2. 15, 16) and *Chāndogya Upaniṣad* (IV.15), upon death, persons' *karma* can lead them either via the path of the gods (*deva-yāna*) or the path of the ancestors (*pitṛ-yāna*). Those who have faithfully meditated and have attained Self-realization, whether or not their funerary rites are performed, go to the light, via daylight, to the bright fortnight of the moon, and from there via the bright half of the annual cycle (the so-called northern circuit, when the sun ascends through the Zodiac), to the sun, the moon, to lightning, and finally merge with Brahman. For those ones there is no rebirth. However, those who have followed the path of sacrificial offerings, charitable deeds, or asceticism enter the *pitṛ-yāna*. From the smoke of the cremation pyre, they enter the night, and then move through the dark fortnight of the moon, to the dark half of the solar cycle, to the world of the ancestors (*pitṛ-loka*). From there they journey to the moon, where they are fed upon by the gods. They then move into space (*ākāśa*) and finally make their way back into the earthly realm, taking birth either as human beings or other life forms.

Thus the belief in repeated rebirths in various realms, as various types of beings, became, and still is, commonplace in Hinduism. The term *saṃsāra* literally means "to flow together," or "to wander," and thus refers to this cycle of repeated rebirths. Beings wander through the various realms, taking up birth and ultimately dying again and again. *Saṃsāra* is thus often rendered as "the cycle of rebirth." This cycle is virtually endless, and is generally regarded as having no beginning. Eventually, the term *saṃsāra* is also applied broadly to worldly existence itself and reality as it is experienced by those ignorant of the nature of the true Self (*ātman*). The individual soul (*jīva*) carries with it a subtle body that is the vehicle for *karma*. As the *jīva* transmigrates from one rebirth to the next, it brings along its karmic residue.

The mechanics of *karma* are consistently described as akin to other processes observed in the natural world. Acts are spoken of as seeds (*bīja*), which although they may lay dormant for long periods of time, will germinate and bear fruit (*phala*) under the appropriate conditions. The fruits of *karma* may be produced in this lifetime or in any future incarnation. The notion of rewards for actions performed is related to the relationship thought to exist between Vedic ritual action and its purported fruits. If a ritual that was commissioned was performed by a priest with exactitude, it was believed to render results with certainty. However, certain rites were believed not to produce results immediately, but at some later point in time. Vedic ritual was grounded on manipulating cosmic powers, deities, and laws, compelling particular responses on behalf of the performer and patron. Vedic ritualists are to this day called *karmakaṇḍi*. So ritual action, or *karman*, may have played a role in the subsequent development of the notion that all actions, not just ritual ones, had consequences for the actor. The principle thus holds that if one accumulates good *karma*, through the performance of good deeds, this may result in more fortunate rebirths, perhaps as a *gandharva* (celestial musicians known for lives of pleasure), or even as a god (*deva*). In fact, the inexplicable causes for the present circumstances of one's life are also attributed to *karma*. If one is beautiful or intelligent, born into a wealthy home, or gifted with talents, these are regarded as the fruits produced from previously sown karmic seeds. Similarly, *karma* is also regarded as responsible for misfortune. The ramifications of this principle are that all acts are either *karma*-producing seeds, or the fruit of previous *karma*. Essentially, beings are in the thrall of *karma*, which rules their lives with the unerring certainty of other laws of nature.

Mokṣa

Mokṣa, derived from the Sanskrit root *"muc,"* meaning "to release," is related to its synonym *"mukti"* and refers to freedom from *saṃsāra.* The idea of liberation arises in conjunction with the *śramaṇa* (ascetic wandering philosopher) movements that began in the Upaniṣadic period, and reflects a pivotal shift in values from the preceding period. The religious goals of the Vedic Saṃhitās and Brāhmaṇas are often centered on ritual performance and karmic action to secure wealth, longevity, and other such worldly ends. Their trans-worldly concerns are at best concerned with better rebirths in heavenly realms. However, the Upaniṣads, and such *śramaṇa* movements as Buddhism and Jainism, promote shedding one's pursuit of those goals. *Mokṣa* or *mukti* is contrasted with *bhukti,* the enjoyment of worldly pleasures. The cycle of rebirth, or existence in *saṃsāra,* is viewed as painful. One is in bondage to the karmic laws of causality, and enmeshed in ignorance about the true nature of the Self. Thus *mokṣa* becomes synonymous with freedom from *saṃsāra* and freedom from *karma. Mokṣa* is release from worldly existence. It is freedom from the bondage of ignorance into the liberation that comes with knowledge of the Self (*ātman*) or Absolute Reality (Brahman).

Various Hindu philosophical systems vary in the terms they use to designate the concept of *mokṣa.* In Saṅkhya philosophy, for instance, one encounters the term *kaivalya* (aloneness), a term also used in Yoga texts. The word *yoga* itself may be understood as meaning *mokṣa,* because *yoga* refers to both a spiritual path to Self-realization and its goal. The Buddhist notion of *nirvāṇa* is akin to *mokṣa,* since both refer to the goal of emancipation or freedom from *karma* and *saṃsāra,* and insight into the true nature of reality and the Self. However, Buddhism and Hindu systems can differ, quite fundamentally, in their descriptions of what constitutes the ultimate realization. Nevertheless, they value the ultimate attainment of *mokṣa/nirvāṇa* above all other achievements.

Despite its initial emphasis on ritual action, orthodox (i.e. Vedic) Hinduism eventually promoted four goals or aims of life, in which *mokṣa* is regarded as the supreme and most valuable pursuit. Significantly, *mokṣa* cannot be achieved merely through the pursuit of good karmic acts, such as routine ritual performance, and the avoidance of pernicious *karma.* These latter activities might only result in desirable karmic fruits, such as better rebirths, still within saṃsāric reality. Since *mokṣa* is the complete transcendence of *karma,* karmic action alone cannot free one from *karma. Mokṣa* requires attainment of liberating wisdom, a penetrating insight into Truth, into the Self, or Absolute Reality. And it is held to be possible and necessary to achieve such a realization while one is alive. Thus *mokṣa* is not a state that is typically achieved in the afterlife, like a heavenly reward for a good life. Rather, it is an understanding that grants immortality before one physically dies. Such a Self-realized being is veritably Brahman, and is known as a *jīvanmukti* (liberated while alive). Such sages or saints are highly sought after for teachings and blessings.

Key points in this chapter

- Hindus believe that both time and creation move in repetitive cycles.
- According to Hindu cosmology, when the cosmos is first created, it is renewed, but undergoes degeneration through time.
- Hindus follow both the solar calendar and a monthly lunar calendar, often creating challenges for non-specialists regarding the exact timing of various religious rituals.
- Hinduism does not have a single authoritative cosmology, but a variety of descriptions concerning the origin and nature of the universe.
- Many of the Vedic hymns utter assertions concerning the nature of the gods, the creation, or aspects of reality, but such statements are often framed as questions.
- For most Hindus, there is a general belief in multiple worlds, populated by an assortment of beings.
- *Karma* developed into the idea of a moral principle of causality, in which good deeds are meritorious (*puṇya*), while evil or sinful deeds (*pāpa*) have painful effects.
- The belief in repeated rebirths in various realms, as various types of beings, was and still is commonplace in Hinduism.
- *Saṃsāra* is the cycle of repeated rebirths, but it can also refer to worldly existence itself and reality as perceived by one ignorant of the nature of the Self (*ātman*).
- *Mokṣa* refers to freedom from *saṃsāra* and is contrasted with *bhukti*, the enjoyment of worldly pleasures.
- Buddhist and Hindu concepts of ultimate realization can differ greatly; however, both value the attainment of *mokṣa/nirvāṇa* over all other achievements.

Discussion questions

1. Why do you think Hinduism does not have a single authoritative cosmology? And, do you think this has had a positive or negative impact on the tradition?
2. Many of the Vedic hymns make assertions about the nature of the gods, the creation, or aspects of reality, but such statements are often framed as questions. Why do you think this is so?

3. There are a few general beliefs regarding cosmology that Hindus agree upon. What are some of these general beliefs, and why do you think they are agreed upon while other beliefs are contested?
4. Hindus have an elaborate conception of time. Give a detailed description of this concept, explaining where humanity is currently located within this notion of time.
5. Hinduism offers an assortment of explanations regarding the origin and nature of the universe. What are some of these explanations?
6. Define *karma, saṃsāra,* and reincarnation. Then discuss the concept of *mokṣa* giving a detailed explanation of its relationship to the three aforementioned concepts.

Further reading

Fort, Andrew O., and Patricia Y. Mumme (eds) (1996) *Living Liberation in Hindu Thought*. Albany, NY: State University of New York Press.

Gombrich, Richard F. (1975) "Ancient Indian Cosmology." In *Ancient Cosmologies*, Carmen Blacker and M. Loewe (eds) London: George Allen and Unwin, pp. 110–42.

Keyes, Charles F. and E. Valentine Daniel (eds) (1983) *Karma: An Anthropological Inquiry*. Berkeley, CA: University of California Press.

Kuiper, F.B.J. (1983) *Ancient Indian Cosmogony*. New Delhi: Vikas Publishing House.

Neufeldt, R.N. (ed.) (1986) *Karma and Rebirth: Post-Classical Developments*. New York: State University of New York Press.

O'Flaherty, Wendy Doniger (ed.) (1980) *Karma and Rebirth in Classical Indian Traditions*. Berkeley, CA: University of California Press.

Tull, Herman W. (1989) *The Vedic Origins of Karma: Cosmos as Man in Ancient Indian Myth and Ritual*. Albany, NY: State University of New York Press.

Welborn, G.R. and G.E. Yocum (eds) (1985) *Religious Festivals in South India and Sri Lanka*. Delhi: Manohar.

3 *Hindu social organization and values*

In this chapter

The concept of alignment with the divine cosmic order was expanded upon and articulated in semi-authoritative texts, which prescribed righteous actions. Here we examine the contents of these codices and their notions of *dharma*. Injunctions on *dharma* were closely related to the stratification of Hindu society into its class and caste systems. These, in turn, were knitted with ideas of purity and impurity, as well as those dealing with propitiousness, with the intention of weaving together cosmic, social, and personal orders to provide for a harmonious existence.

Main topics covered

- *Dharma* and the Dharma Śāstras
- The four classes of Hindu society
- The caste system
- The Untouchables
- Purity and pollution
- Auspiciousness and inauspiciousness

Dharma *and the Dharma Śāstras*

Dharma derives from the Sanskrit root *dhṛ* (to support or uphold), and appears to develop in relationship to the Vedic conception of *ṛta*. Whereas *ṛta* affirmed the existence of an orderly creation, subject to patterns and orderly cycles, *dharma* developed into a notion of the way things should be if harmoniously aligned with *ṛta*. As such, *dharma* both articulates the way things are and prescribes how one should behave in relation to the cosmic order. In the *Ṛg Veda, dharma* refers to actions that should be undertaken to uphold the cosmic order. There is a sense that the gods are themselves dharmic, placing things in their proper place, such as the sun in its orderly movement through the sky, and making the seasons change, the rain fall, and so on. Through self regulation and the regular performance of sacrifice the gods sustain the cosmic order. By the period of the Brāhmaṇas, priestly ritual action was promoted as the support of the cosmic order, and thus it became the cornerstone of *dharma*.

In time, *dharma* became closely aligned with *karma*, both as ritual action and as personal and social behavior in harmony with the cosmic order. Since the effects of *karma* are being experienced at all times, one is faced with the disturbing prospect of experiencing unpleasant effects from previous actions in previous lives, despite living a righteous life. The confusion that might result from such misfortunes could be disorienting. *Dharma* offers individuals a guide for righteous behavior in the midst of life's caprices. For instance, in the Hindu epic, the *Rāmāyaṇa*, the hero and heroine, Rāma and Sītā, are faced with unforeseen predicaments, such as exile and abduction. They are renowned for their strict adherence to *dharma*, which leads Rāma to slay the demon Rāvaṇa, who abducted Sītā, and thus restore a cosmic balance in favor of righteousness.

The Kalpa Sūtras, one of the genres of literature classified as the Vedāṅgas (Limbs of the Veda), were the first to articulate the prescriptions for self-controlled and orderly behavior. Within these were prescriptions on household rituals and rites of passage (Gṛhya Sūtras), on small to large scale public rites (Śrauta Sūtras), on geometrical principles for building ritual altars (Śulva Sūtras), and on the rules for proper social behavior (Dharma Sūtras). These Kalpa Sūtras are attributed to sages such as Gautama and Āpastamba. In the centuries around the beginning of the Common Era, another genre of literature emerged. These are the Dharma Śāstras, which as their name suggests are treatises (*śāstra*) that deal specifically with *dharma*. There are several of these compendiums, but the most well known are the *Yājñavalkya Smṛti* and the *Mānava Dharmaśāstra* (*Laws of Manu*). These texts do not have the sacrosanct status of *śrūti* (revealed) literature, because they belong to the category of *smṛti* (remembered, traditional). In fact although *smṛti* typically includes the Vedāṅgas, the Epics, and the Purāṇas, it is often the Dharma Śāstras alone that are thought of as synonymous with the term. The *Laws of Manu* is thus sometimes called the *Manu Smṛti*. Despite their secondary status in the *śrūti/smṛti* distinction, the Dharma Śāstras have been enormously influential in shaping the values and behavior of Hindus. The Dharma Śāstras come to be regarded as legal codices or Law Books. However, because individual texts are at times contradictory in their content and there are variations in the prescriptions from one Śāstra to the next, interpretations of their rulings still rest in the hands of groups of Vedic scholars (*paṇḍita*).

The Dharma Śāstras lay out the specifics of social obligations for Hindus in a system known as *varṇāśramadharma*. *Varṇa* refers to the various classes into which Hindu society is traditionally divided, while *aśrama* refers to the stages that demarcate a person's journey through life. These injunctions are complex because the system attempts to incorporate variations based on gender, socio-economic circumstances, and so on in relationship to a conception of the cosmic reality within which human beings are located. The *Laws of Manu*, for instance, covers such topics as the creation, cosmic geography, the divisions of the Vedas, and the class system. It tells how to choose a wife, and how to perform post-cremation rituals. It discusses issues of purity and pollution, and what foods are fit to eat and what should be avoided. It prescribes rules for kings, and how they should conduct themselves in war. It has prescriptions for dealing with boundary disputes, loans, and punishing thieves. It deals with relationships between master and servant, husband and wife, king and subject, and one *varṇa* toward another. It discusses the duties of the *varṇas*, injunctions for women, and even discusses the law of *karma*.

It is evident that the rise of this literature was a response to tensions that had developed on the Indian subcontinent during that period. The *śramaṇa* movements had begun to challenge the authority of the Vedic world view, which was grounded in concerns about attaining fortunate rebirths by sustaining the cosmic order through sacrificial ritual. Furthermore, interactions with "outsiders" provoked concerns on issues such as intermarriage and differences in values. The Dharma Śāstras provide a codified attempt to articulate standards of conduct, to protect the status of the upper classes, and to effect compromises that incorporate newer religious values, such as renunciation, along with the traditional ones, such as social involvement.

The four classes of Hindu society

Hindu society is divided into four main classes (*varṇa*). The *Puruṣa Sūkta* hymn of the *Ṛg Veda* (X.90) tells of a giant cosmic being or person (*puruṣa*) who is sacrificed by the gods. From his head/mouth emerged the Brahmin (*brāhmaṇa*), from his arms the *rājanya*, from his thighs, the *vaiśya*, and from his feet the *śūdra*. This hymn thus provides a religious sanction for a purported divinely ordained distinction between the four main classes of Hindu society. The designated selections of body parts insinuate a hierarchy among the classes, placing the Brahmins or priestly *varṇa* at the top and the *śūdra* or servant *varṇa* at the bottom. The *rājanya*, or ruling class, are later on mostly referred to as the *kṣatriya*.

The stratification of Hindu society, already evident by the time of the Vedic Saṃhitās, is one of its most distinctive features. The divisions extend far beyond the four classes or *varṇas*, and consist of thousands of smaller groups, known as *jātis*. This social structure is generally referred to as "the caste system" believed to derive from the term "*casta*" (breed, stock) used by the Portuguese. I am among those scholars who prefer to use the term "class" to designate *varṇa*, and "caste" for *jāti*. However, people also routinely talk about "the four castes" of Hindu society in reference to the *varṇa* system, and almost everyone refers to "the caste system" when discussing both *varṇa* and *jāti*. Furthermore, the term "class" is often used by social scientists to designate socio-economic status, as in the "middle class," and so on. There is no firm correlation between socio-economic class and *varṇa* (class). Although many members of the lowest ranked *varṇas*, such as the *śūdras*, and those who are outside the *varṇa* classification system, such as Untouchables, often are low on the socio-economic class scale, there may be wealthy members of these groups. Similarly, members of the *vaiśya varṇa* may be very wealthy and wield political power, while certain groups of Brahmins may be relatively poor.

The word *varṇa* means "color," leading some scholars to speculate that the original division of the classes was related to a distinction based on skin complexion. The upper three *varṇas*, namely the Brahmin, *kṣatriya*, and *vaiśya*, are known as *dvija* or "twice-born," and enjoy privileges not available to the fourth and lowest class, the *śūdra*. The skin-complexion theory proposes that *dvija* classes were possibly the light-skinned Āryan colonizers of the subcontinent who subordinated the darker skinned "Dravidians," relegating them into the servant class. The *Laws of Manu* firmly promotes marriage within one's own *varṇa*, suggestive of efforts to prevent racial mixture. This is also evident much earlier in Āryan attitudes to the dark-skinned Dasyus and Dāsas mentioned in the Vedic Saṃhitās. However, intermingling of the groups had evidently already become commonplace by the Upaniṣadic period, and warriors (*kṣatriya*) such as Kṛṣṇa, and *ṛṣis* such as Vyāsa, who enjoy extremely high status even among orthodox Brahmins of the period, are described as having dark complexions. Nevertheless, there is to this day a cultural preference among many Hindus for lighter over darker skin.

The nature of the four *varṇas* of Hindu society and their social duties were progressively defined and codified through subsequent centuries and especially through the Dharma Śāstra literature. The *Laws of Manu*, for instance, lays down detailed prescriptions for the appropriate behavior for each of the *varṇas* at various stages of their lives. It places Brahmins at the uppermost position of the social structure and defines the duties of the other classes in relationship to the Brahmins. It even states that it is better to follow one's own *dharma* (*svadharma*) inadequately, than to do the *dharma* of another *varṇa* thoroughly, for this immediately disenfranchises persons from their own *varṇa*. According to *Manu*, Brahmins are the veritable embodiment of *dharma* itself, and worthy of attaining realization of Brahman. They are the highest class and have the protection and support of *dharma* as their fundamental duty. Originally, the term *brāhmaṇa* (Brahmin, in this book, to avoid confusion with similar terms) was applied to a specific class of priests who presided over Vedic rituals, but it eventually applied to all members of the priestly class. This is not to say that all Brahmins, even in the past, worked as priests, but that priestly functions could be performed only by members of that class. Brahmins were supposed to recite the Vedas and promulgate Vedic teachings, conduct rituals for themselves and on behalf of others, give and receive gifts, and generally embody a dharmic life style. The Dharma Śāstras hold Brahmins to a high code of ethical and moral behavior. As such, regardless of what occupation they actually followed, members of the class were associated with a superior spiritual status.

According to *Manu*, *kṣatriyas* were expected to offer protection to people (especially Brahmins), to give gifts (especially to Brahmins), to commission sacrificial rituals (with the aid of Brahmin priests), to study the Veda (from Brahmin teachers), and to avoid attachments to sensual indulgences. They had the right to bear arms. *Vaiśyas* should tend cattle and cultivate land, trade, lend money, bestow gifts, offer sacrifices, and study the Vedas. *Śūdras* had but one prescribed duty, according to *Manu*, and that was to serve the upper three classes. In times of duress, if one could not maintain one's livelihood, Brahmins, *kṣatriyas*, and *vaiśyas* were permitted to take up the occupations of lower classes temporarily. However, there were certain caveats. For instance, Brahmins could not till the soil, lest they injure small creatures. If *śūdras* could not be gainfully employed by members of the twice-born classes, and were faced with the starvation of their families, they could produce handicrafts, and adopt such technical occupations through which the upper classes would best be served. If persons of low class nonetheless coveted and adopted the occupation of a higher class, *Manu* instructs that it was the king's duty to deprive them of their possessions and banish them from the land.

Manu describes the duties of a king in some detail. The king is very much designated as the enforcer of punishments should social dharmic prescriptions be breached. The king must himself embody a dharmic lifestyle to ensure the prosperity of his kingdom, because if he is seen as lax and adharmic the land will fall into ruin. He should be lenient towards Brahmins but severe with his enemies. He should worship Brahmins daily, upon awakening, and heed their advice. Of the various ministers that a king appoints, the senior-most should be a learned Brahmin with whom he consults on the most important issues of state. Gifts to others are meritorious, but gifts to Brahmins, especially to those most learned in the Vedas, are many times more beneficial.

It is worth recognizing that the extreme prescriptions in the Dharma Śāstra texts, such as the *Laws of Manu*, were not followed by all groups of Hindus. Only at particular periods of time, among particular communities, in particular regions, and on particular issues, would a particular Śāstra be treated as authoritative. Typically, groups of Brahmin scholars would gather to pronounce judgment on a situation and would cite the standards from the Śāstric literature with which they were familiar. However, although the Śāstric literature conveys an idealized notion that the four *varṇas* existed in a harmonious balance, with the Brahmins at the top, presiding over personal, familial, and social righteousness, offering political guidance, conferring rulership on kings, and so on, there are many regions of India, even today, where there were few, if any, Brahmins, or *kṣatriyas*. Hindu social reality did not and does not always conform to the idealized presentations in its scriptural literature.

Although the Brahmin class has mostly wielded power over the other *varṇas*, its authority has been consistently challenged by various segments of society. The heterodox *śramaṇa* movements, such as Buddhism and Jainism, questioned the spiritual status of Brahmins, whose only claim to religious authority was their family lineage. The founders of Buddhism and Jainism were reputedly princes and thus from the *kṣatriya* class. Yet, they were eventually accorded a status higher than any Brahmin, and even attracted members of the Brahmin *varṇa* as disciples. They did not endorse the class system, but actually allowed members from all classes to join their religious orders, and were thus subsequently categorized as promulgators of heterodox religions. Their teachings were particularly attractive to members of the merchant class, the *vaiśyas*, who were relegated to the sidelines in most of the preceding religious literature. The *kṣatriya* class also voiced dissent on other grounds. Kings did not always concede that their power to rule should be sanctioned by Brahmins. The tension between these two classes, in particular, is evident throughout Hindu literature and history. It reflects a perennial tension found in societies where "church" and "state" are separated. Recent scholarship has also begun to question the extent to which the lower classes in the past actually shared the orthodox perspective and values. Despite these dissents and tensions, the *varṇa* system is a crucial feature of the religiously supported structuring of Hindu society, evidently upheld to sustain the supremacy of the upper-classes and, in particular, the Brahmin *varṇa*.

The caste system

The true complexity of the Hindu caste system derives from the category of *jāti*, a word which translates as "birth group." Hindus often identify themselves according to family lineage (*gotra*), their village of origin (*grāma*), or their *jāti*. The *gotra* is a generally fictitious lineage association connected to semi-divine clan ancestors. There are thousands of *jātis*. *Jātis* most often designate an occupational category, such as a barber (Nai), or a potter (Kumhar), or farmer, but are far more subdivided than merely such designations. For instance, there are hundreds of agricultural (farmer) *jātis*. Small tribal groups may also be regarded as particular *jātis*, while larger tribal societies may be composed of subdivisions which are designated as *jātis*.

The system of *jātis* and *varṇas* coexist and overlap to a certain degree. For instance, certain *jātis* may claim to belong to particular *varṇas* although a particular *jāti*'s claim may not be supported by other groups. The *kāyastha* caste, for instance, which has numerous sub-*jātis*, such as the *khattri* (who are found in North India) and the *cheṭṭiār* (in South India), lays claim to Brahmin or to *kṣatriya varṇa* status, but are often classified as *vaiśyas* or even as *śūdras*, by other *jātis*. Actually, because of the elite status granted to the Brahmin, as well as to the *kṣatriya varṇas*, a status promoted by orthodox religious values, members of the vast majority of *jātis* would like to belong to those higher classes. Within a ten-year period in the early twentieth century the Census of India reported that many *jātis* that had originally claimed to belong to the *kṣatriya* or *vaiśya varṇas* had subsequently claimed to belong to the Brahmin *varṇa*. Thus it is not easy or even desirable for scholars to assign the many thousands of Hindu *jātis* to the system of four *varṇas*. The claims for a certain status by a particular *jāti*, and the contestation of those claims by other *jātis*, can reveal much about the social, political, economic, and religious dynamics at work within that social group. Furthermore, there are *jātis*, such as leather workers (Camār) and those who cremate the dead (Dom), who are regarded by orthodox Brahmins as so "polluting" that they are not accepted as belonging to the four-fold *varṇa* system at all. They are *caṇḍālas*, belonging to a fifth category, also known as Untouchables.

An illustrative example of a *jāti* that has mostly managed to change its *varṇa* designation is the case of the Marathas. The Marathas were primarily agricultural workers in the region of what is now Maharashtra State. They were conventionally designated by the upper classes as belonging to very low *varṇas*, namely the *vaiśya* and *śūdra* classes. During the Mughal period in India the Marathas led a successful armed insurgency movement, carving out a large kingdom in central and north India. The famous Maratha leader, Shivaji Bhonsle, and subsequent Maratha rulers, who wished to be acknowledged as legitimate "kings," struggled with Brahmin authorities who would only consecrate members of a *kṣatriya varṇa* to such a position. The Peshwas, from Brahmin *jātis*, became the chief ministers and eventually rulers of the Maratha Empire. In the modern period, however, most Hindus know of the Maratha role in Indian history through their military exploits. This has led many Maratha *jātis* to make successful claims to *kṣatriya varṇa* status, based on the warrior profession of their ancestry. Thus *jāti* mobility within the *varṇa* system is possible. However, it is not individuals who can move between *jātis* or *varṇas* within a single lifetime. Entire *jātis* may move to different hierarchical rankings within a particular *varṇa*, or even move to different *varṇa* categories over periods of time spanning many generations.

Manu attempts to explain the origin of various *jātis* through successions of offspring resulting from inappropriate intermarriage between various *varṇas*. While unconvincing, it confirms the existence of a diversity of tribes, regions, and occupational divisions on the Indian subcontinent at the time that the Śāstra was composed, as well as evident intermingling among the *varṇas* for centuries.

Jātis are circumscribed in particular ways. Most typically, *jāti* refers to the group into which a Hindu is born, and from which he or she should traditionally choose a marriage partner. Hindu marriages are typically exogamous, meaning that one should marry a partner outside of one's close family lineage (*gotra*). Thus *jātis* typically include a number of family lineages (*gotra*) with whom marriage is permissible. Thus the *jāti* is a closed endogamous group. Hypergamous marriages, where a female weds a male from a *jāti* of higher rank, are permissible although discouraged. *Jāti* is almost akin to a self-imposed designation as a particular "species" or "kind," insinuating that such activities as having sexual relations, eating the same foods together, or participating in particular religious rites with persons outside of one's *jāti* are not just undesirable, but actually go against the natural order. Members of the same *jāti* often share a common "family name," and speak the same language. *Jātis* may also live in a particular region, composed of hundreds of small villages. It is quite common for members of particular *jātis* to live in extended families, and cluster together in particular quarters of heterogeneously composed towns or villages. If one gazes at the city of Jodhpur, in Rajasthan, from the Mehrangarh fortress which overlooks it, one will see homes in sections of the city painted with a blue wash, traditionally used to designate the homes of the Brahmin *jātis*. However, nowadays other *varṇas* also use the same color.

Jātis are relatively closed communities, and thus define themselves in relationship to the "other" *jātis* with which they must interact, and interact often they must, particularly if their communal definition is based on a particular occupation, rather than on regional or tribal connections. In villages made up of members of a variety of *jātis*, there is often a general consensus reached on the hierarchical ranking among them, although even this is subject to contestation and disagreement. Typical villages may have from twenty to forty *jātis* represented. Any seemingly well established ranking in a particular village may, however, not hold for villages in different regions of the country with similar *jātis* represented. Thus *jāti* ranking is thoroughly situational. There may be villages with no Brahmins present, or where members of agricultural *jātis* dominate. Some villages may be dominated by a Brahmin *jāti* with virtually no representatives from the *kṣatriya* or *vaiśya varṇas*, while most of the other members of the village are regarded as belonging to the *śūdra varṇa* or are even classified as *caṇḍalas*. At village gatherings, where members of various *jātis* must interact and perhaps eat together, caste divisions are most evident. Efforts are made to separate the various groups or acknowledge their hierarchical status. Higher caste members may be seated on platforms or high chairs, while lower caste members may be seated on the ground. Food may be served at different times, and so on, in order to accommodate the concerns the upper castes, in particular, may have with issues of ritual purity and pollution.

Jāti divisions are far more telling about actual social distinctions among Hindus than the category of *varṇa*. For instance, there are hundreds of Brahmin *jātis*, each considering itself to be the purest. If one counts subdivisions of these *jātis* they number over a thousand. A brief examination of *jāti* among Brahmins may enable us to appreciate the complexity of the *jāti* system as a whole. Tradition has it that all Brahmins originate from about seven or eight families or lineages of *ṛṣis*. The actual names of these lineages (*gotra*) vary in different scriptural accounts, but they include the names of *ṛṣis* such as Bhṛgu, Atri, Vaṣiṣṭha, and Kaśyapa, credited with composing the Vedic Saṃhitās. Many *jātis* from the other twice-born *varṇas* also claim to belong to the same lineages. Other non-Brahmin *jātis* often trace the origin

Figure 3.1 Vagish Shastri, a Brahmin *paṇḍita* and founder of the Vāg-Yoga Institute, at work in his library (Banāras)

of their group to some legendary hero or mythic semi-divine or divine figure. Most Brahmins also identify themselves through different categories than their *gotras*. For instance, Brahmins may be classified according to the particular Vedic Samhitā to which they ascribe (e.g. *Ṛg Veda* or *Sama Veda* Brahmins). There are also groups of North and South Indian Brahmins with narrower regional affiliations. Among the North Indian Brahmins are the Kanya-kubja, who originated in Kanauj (modern-day Kanpur), and the Maithilā from Mithilā. Among the South Indian Brahmins are the Maharashtra and Malabar. These are further subdivided. For instance, the Chitpāvans and Sarasvata are subsets of Maharashtra Brahmins, and the Vārendras of Bengal derive from the Kanyākubja. Other Brahmins, such as those from Kashmir do not easily lend themselves to these categories. Furthermore, the recent political situation in Kashmir has led to the death, or migration of most of the Kashmiri

Brahmin priestly community to other regions, so their regional designation as Kashmiri Brahmins no longer corresponds to their actual place of residence. Such movements due to war or famine are very much a part of the history of India, and affected not just the Brahmin *jātis*.

Moreover, even among Brahmins who continue to work in their traditional roles as religious functionaries, there are wide variations. Some Brahmins memorize and recite Vedic scriptures at rituals. Others teach Sanskrit language and grammar, translate texts, and so on. Some specialize in the Vedic sciences that constitute the Vedāṅgas, such as astrology and medicine. Some Brahmins live as renouncers, shunning traditional religious establishments. Other Brahmin renouncers may belong to hermitages (*āśrama*) and teach philosophies of renunciation. Yet others work as temple priests or serve as functionaries at death rituals. Although all of these various Brahmin *jātis* belong to the same *varṇa*, there is a considerable amount of hierarchical jostling among them, which is particularly evident when marriage arrangements are concerned. Certain Brahmin *jātis* are generally agreed upon as being low in rank. For instance, temple and pilgrim priests, who have constant interactions with people from a wide range of *jātis*, are subject to constant ritual pollution through these contacts. They also accept gifts for their services, which further diminishes their purity. The Brahmins who study and teach the Vedas to members of the twice-born classes, and who do not exchange services for gifts, but only accept alms, hold themselves to have the highest rank. For these Brahmins, it would be highly inappropriate to allow their daughters to marry men from the lower Brahmin *jātis*. In fact, some scholars have noted that the *mahābrāhmaṇas*, the priests who preside over death rituals and thus accrue ritual pollution, are virtually treated like Untouchables by the upper *jātis*, although they belong to the Brahmin *varṇa*.

It would appear that those most closely related to the transcendent source of creation, such as liberated persons, who are regarded as having attained unity with it, enjoy the highest status. Slightly lower in the hierarchy are those who hold occupations closest to the source, such as Brahmins who recite the Vedas, which are believed to be sonic vibratory manifestations from the Absolute. One's status is related to where on the spectrum of the cycles of creation one's occupational activities are located. Thus those Brahmin *jātis* engaged in the performance of sacrificial rituals are ranked yet lower in the hierarchy, while the lowest are those who deal with the polluted remnants of life, decay and death, such as priests who preside over certain rites of passage, especially birth rituals, and, of course, funeral priests.

This stratification, which bases one's status in relation to a religious ontology (i.e. the nature of being or existence), extends to other non-Brahmin *jātis* as well, placing the latrine cleaner and leather worker at the bottom of the hierarchy. This ontic stratification, supported by Brahmin orthodoxy, overlaps with another stratification based on socio-economic power, which is supported by those, such as rulers and wealthy landowners, who wield it in particular social groups. While there are ongoing tensions between these two status systems, they also mutually interact and support each other. Rulers commission rituals to enhance their authority and cohere the society governed, while religious specialists articulate the metaphysics and perform the appropriate rites that maintain the social structure and confer legitimacy on the rulers.

Even in the past, certain family members from a particular *jāti* may have taken up occupations that were different from their *jāti*'s traditional occupational designation. Such occupational diversification has become more common in modern times, and is supported by India's secular democracy. However, the centuries-old tradition of identifying persons with and through their *jāti* still leads many Hindus to regard a soldier who is from a washerman's *jāti* or a politician from an Untouchable *jāti* as inherently unfit for their jobs. A change in occupation does not change one's *jāti*, so it is misleading to define *jāti* exclusively along occupational lines. However, such occupational *jāti* designations are appropriate because particular members within that *jāti* probably still engage in those activities. Also, the *jāti* system does not remain exclusive to Hinduism in India. It is found among other religions on the subcontinent and even in places where Hinduism and these religions have migrated. Hierarchical rankings among *jātis*, exclusivity in approved marriages, and the like, are found within Christian, Jain, Buddhist, Sikh, and Muslim communities in India, despite the egalitarian and "anti-caste" sentiments voiced within these religions.

The Untouchables

The word *caṇḍāla*, which means "fierce," is found in early scriptural references such as the Upaniṣads and Buddhist texts, where it refers to members of aboriginal tribes who dressed in animal skins and tree leaves that gave them a frightening appearance. *Caṇḍālas* were designated as outside the system of the four *varṇas*. Sometimes this group is known as *avarṇa* (without caste) or *pañcama* (the fifth [category]). Foreigners (*mleccha*), and the offspring from illegitimate inter-caste unions (e.g. a *śūdra* male and Brahmin female), who were banished from their caste groups, were also included in this category. The term "Untouchable" was eventually used to designate these people, who were "outside" the *varṇa* system, as well as members of a number of *jātis* that engaged in occupations regarded as the most ritually polluting. These include the Bhangis, who clean out the excrement from toilets, and the Camārs, who are leather workers. The ritual pollution associated with these groups is believed to transfer temporarily to the higher castes through contact. The highest Brahmin castes needed to maintain the highest level of ritual purity in order to perform worship rites to the gods. Contact with members of the polluting group would immediately diminish one's purity, requiring a series of actions to restore purity. Hence members of the highest castes tried to avoid contact with *caṇḍālas* entirely, leading *caṇḍālas* to have the designation of "Untouchable."

In certain regions *caṇḍalas* were required to live outside of towns and villages, and to signal their arrival within the town. *Manu* stipulates that they should dress in the clothes of the deceased, wear iron ornaments, and eat from broken dishes. The extent to which they were to be avoided went to extremes in various regions. For some high caste Hindus, touching the shadow or merely the sight of an Untouchable, or even contact with the wind wafting from their direction was deemed polluting and requiring ritual purification. Reform movements spurred by critiques from Muslims, Christians, and a modernizing Hindu population have led to efforts to restore the highly diminished status of these *jātis*. Mahatma Gandhi referred to them as Harijans (Children of God), although many now simply prefer the term Dalit, which means "oppressed." The Government of India, which has officially abolished Untouchability, uses the term "Scheduled Castes" and "Scheduled Tribes" in reference to them. They constituted more than a fifth of India's population. When combined with members of the *śūdra varṇa* and others who converted to non-Hindu religions, from 50–70 per cent of Indians are socially and economically underprivileged. Indian citizens found guilty of discrimination against members of these groups may now be prosecuted. Nevertheless, the stigmatization of the Dalit is deeply rooted in Hindu culture, supported by scriptural injunctions and religious practices that have endured for millennia.

Purity and pollution

Notions of ritual purity and ritual pollution play an extremely important role in Hinduism. Despite their shortcomings, the terms "ritual purity" and "ritual pollution/impurity" are used to differentiate these concepts from conventional ideas of the pure and the polluted. For instance, we might tend to think of ecosystems as polluted by toxic wastes or garbage, and uncontaminated water as pure, and so on. However, the notions of ritual pollution and purity relevant to our study of Hinduism are religious categories, and are not necessarily related to secular or scientific conceptions of clean and unclean, or hygienic and unhygienic. Thus while defecation does increase one's ritual pollution, and this can be rectified by washing, bathing, and donning clean clothes, it is also possible to enhance one's ritual purity by bathing in or sipping the waters of the river Gaṅgā in Banāras, which might, by all conventional scientific measures, be regarded as unhygienic and polluting.

Members of the uppermost castes assert their status by strictly adhering to various daily regimens to ensure purity and avoid pollution. Other castes adopt such behaviors as well to declare their own elevated status. For instance, upon arising in the morning, one is already in a state of moderate ritual pollution brought about by having been asleep. Bodily outflows are traditionally regarded as causes of ritual pollution. The outflows of urine, feces, snot, pus, saliva, semen, blood (especially menstrual), sweat, or tears are all sources of ritual pollution. So are hair- and nail-clippings. The morning toilet thus further affects one's state of purity. However, a bath in flowing water and putting on clean clothes will restore one's state of purity. It is in this state that one is ready to worship the gods either at one's home shrine or in a temple. Eating breakfast will again decrease purity, but this can be restored by washing one's hands and gargling after the meal. There are pure (*śuddha*) and impure (*aśuddha*) foods and naturally the latter should be avoided. Meals should only be prepared in the proper manner, by equally pure persons, and only served by such. For many castes, the consumption of meat is terribly polluting and should be avoided at all costs. For others, certain types of meat are permissible. Beef is shunned by virtually all Hindus, since the cow is regarded as sacred. Alcohol is acceptable to certain groups and not to others. Since the day's activities can bring one in contact with members of lesser and thus more impure castes, another bath at midday is prescribed. Again, one should bath at sunset, don clean clothes, worship the gods and only then proceed to the evening meal. Flowing water, Gaṅgā water, and the products of the cow (e.g. milk, ghee, cow urine, and cow dung) are generally regarded as purifying. The degrees to which such prescriptions are followed, even by the uppermost castes, vary widely, because modern urban lifestyles do not easily permit individuals to bathe or eat home-cooked meals at noon. Nevertheless, these are only modifications based on necessity, which have not undermined the enduring importance of the categories of purity and pollution.

Case study: The Havik Brahmins of Mysore

Since ritual purity and impurity is also contingent on human interactions, examining a particular case study in some detail illustrates how it can actually play out. Because ritual purity and pollution derives from religious values, in which Brahmins have been the main arbiters, a Brahmin community's attitudes are especially instructive. Pollution is transmitted through contact with the more impure. Purity is not transmitted, but is maintained or achieved. The Havik Brahmins of the region of Sagar in the Malnad part of South India are a high caste consisting of about 200,000 members. Villages consist mainly of Havik Brahmins and members of lower classes, designated as *śūdras* or as Untouchables, with virtually no representatives from the *kṣatriya* and *vaiśya varṇas*. The *śūdra jātis* are themselves hierarchically ranked, as are the Untouchables. Havik Brahmins must inevitably interact with members of all *jātis*, including the Untouchables on certain occasions, and regularly with the *śūdra jātis*. Members of highly ranked *śūdra jātis* may work in Havik Brahmin homes as servants, causing nominal pollution through such interactions. Contact with Untouchables, however, can lead to greater degrees of impurity. The highly polarized divisions between upper and lower castes in this social group provide a simplified model through which one may appreciate purity/pollution relationships in Hindu society.

The Haviks have three general terms to designate categories of pure and polluted. *Maḍi* is "ritually pure," *muṭṭucheṭṭu* is "ritually impure," and *mailige* is one's everyday ritual status, which is neither the highest purity nor impure. Defiling acts can move the Havik Brahmin male from *mailige* to *muṭṭucheṭṭu,* and it takes special purifying acts to move him from either the *muṭṭucheṭṭu* or *mailige* states to *maḍi,* the state of highest purity. The gods may only be worshipped by a Havik Brahmin male in the purest state of *maḍi. Maḍi* can be achieved by taking a ritually cleansing bath, which will move him up from his normal condition of *mailige.* However, sleeping, eating, or touching another Havik Brahmin who is in the *mailige* state will automatically eliminate the state of *maḍi* and return him to *mailige.* Contact with any item touched by a menstruating woman or an Untouchable can place him in *muṭṭucheṭṭu.* There are various levels of *muṭṭucheṭṭu,* some so severe that they cannot be eliminated. There are levels of *maḍi* and *mailige* as well.

Ideally, the Havik Brahmin should bathe three times daily, in cold water, although a daily bath in warm water is more the norm. To enter the state of *maḍi,* the water should be drawn by another Brahmin who is not in *muṭṭucheṭṭu,* the full body should be washed, including the hair, and the cotton clothes subsequently worn should have been washed by a Brahmin in the *maḍi* state. The clothes should have made no contact with anyone else. *Maḍi* cotton holds its purity for three days if untouched, while silk is believed to be more impervious to pollution. The Havik Brahmin male in this state of purity can lose it if he even speaks to a *śūdra* en route to his place of worship.

Havik Brahmins only accept cooked food from members of their own caste, typically Havik women. The main meal, eaten in late morning or early afternoon, must be cooked and served by someone in *maḍi.* Since saliva is polluting, the food cannot be tasted by the cook, because a portion of it serves as the food offering to the gods conducted in worship rites before the main meal. A major worship rite is performed by one male member of the household, while the other male members perform minor rites. Food is eaten with the right hand, and served on a fresh banana leaf, which serves as a disposable plate. Eating places one in *mailige,* so Havik women typically wait until the men and children have eaten, and then, since they are still in *maḍi,* serve themselves but once. A husband should leave a little food on his plate as a sign of affection, and although in most other circumstances this would be highly polluting, the Havik wife eats off the same plate as her husband after he leaves.

Menstruating women are highly polluting, even more so than Untouchables, who are almost in a permanent state of *muṭṭucheṭṭu.* During their menstrual period which officially lasts five days, women are expected to reside "outside" the home, such as on the verandah or back porch. The woman is in temporary *muṭṭucheṭṭu.* She should not change clothes or comb her hair. She has a first bath after a few days, which restores her to *mailige,* but is only fully pure after the ritual bath on the last day. During her period she is freed from her household duties, and may spend most of her time in conversation with other women in the household or neighborhood. She should avoid contact with any abodes of deities, not just temples and household shrines, but any sacred locale. Naked children do not transmit pollution, and so they may have contact with their mothers if necessary. Dried cow dung is often used to purify clothing and the polluted spaces inhabited by the menstruating woman. Contact with a menstruating woman puts the Havik Brahmin male into *muṭṭucheṭṭu,* and purification requires a ritual bath, pure clothes, and consuming the *pañcagavya,* a preparation made from the five products of the cow: milk, ghee, bile/yogurt, urine, and dung. The male's Sacred Thread also needs to be replaced by commissioning the appropriate ritualist.

Death brings pollution, primarily to all close relatives of the deceased, whose statuses become akin to that of an Untouchable. This pollution lasts until the completion of the death rites, which take about twelve days. The polluted members should avoid contact with deities and participation in sacred rituals. Necessary rites are postponed. Contact with these persons would put other Haviks into the state of *muṭṭucheṭṭu,* requiring bathing and pure clothes. The polluted members need to do the same, consume *pañcagavya,* and the males should change their sacred thread. The household shrine and gods need to be purified, and all clothing in the home needs to be washed. Birth brings a similar pollution to the mother and the members of the household which lasts about eleven days. The husband is in a *muṭṭucheṭṭu* state similar to an Untouchable and must observe practices, such as residing "outside" the home, similar to those of a menstruating woman.

Urine splashed on the feet is polluting, encouraging the practice of squatting while urinating. Water is necessary for purification after defecating, and the left hand is used for this and other contacts with polluting agents, rendering it unsuitable for eating. The left hand and left side are generally regarded as less pure than the right hand and right side. The use of toilet paper is considered impure. Leather is impure. Sexual relations with members of one's own caste put one into the state of *mailige,* but a lower than normal *mailige,* which requires a cleansing bath. Solar or lunar eclipses bring pollution, as do haircuts and clipping one's fingernails.

If Haviks take food from or have sexual relations with an Untouchable, they can be cast out of the *jāti.* The same acts with *śūdras* lead to a temporary isolation. These are rare occurrences, because they would also bring pollution to bear upon the perpetrator's family members. Furthermore, food sharing is uncommon because of the social norms that separate upper and lower castes, and sexual liaisons are difficult to prove. If a Havik widow has a child from someone other than her husband she would traditionally be cast out in a process initiated by her husband's family, whom she has defiled. Her child would belong to the fairly high-ranking Maleru caste, composed entirely of the illegitimate offspring of Havik widows.

Although Havik women can and must attain the pure state of *maḍi* to prepare food for their husbands and the gods, they are not regarded as pure enough to perform the ritual worship of the high gods themselves. By touching her husband's arm or shoulder, a woman may derive the meritorious benefits from the rite. So the Havik male's state of *maḍi* is higher than that of Havik women. Despite this high standard of purity, Haviks may subordinate themselves to world-renouncers by touching or bathing their feet and eating from their plates, thus ascribing the renouncers with a divine status.

The hierarchies of purity and pollution extend even to the gods and other supernatural beings. Gods can be made *muṭṭuchеṭṭu* in circumstances where they are worshipped by someone in such a state, or, for instance, if a menstruating woman should enter a temple compound. Defiled gods need to be purified through bathing, and the recitation of prayers or sacred verses (*mantra*). If defiled or ignored, or if they are simply hungry, deities may also become angry and cause trouble to human beings. And since *śūdras* are more often in impure states than Brahmins, it is often the indiscreet action of such lower caste individuals that are believed to incur divine wrath. If one is in an impure state, one is even more susceptible to an attack from an angry deity. Ritual purity acts as a kind of protective armor against the attacks of lesser spirits, who are mostly malevolent. Livestock, children and women are particularly susceptible to these attacks, and *śūdra* men more so than Brahmin males. The lower gods and goddesses, who might accept blood sacrifices, are more easily given over to anger than the higher, "Sanskritic" deities, who generally accept only vegetarian offerings. The high gods enjoy an aura of purity, and like Brahmin males cannot be easily defiled. However, should it happen, they are quickly restored to states of purity by priestly ministrations and will then act benevolently for the benefit of persons.

The preceding example of the Havik Brahmin villages highlights many of the features of the notions of purity and pollution. Similar ideas are held by other Brahmin *jātis* as well as by non-Brahmin *jātis*. Since all *jātis* strive for high hierarchical rank within their social milieus, one means of attaining such status is to emulate the standards of the highest castes of Brahmins. Of course, this is impossible in certain occupations, for a person who cremates the dead or makes leather sandals or washes polluted clothing or cleans out latrines is constantly encountering ritual impurity. However, members of certain other castes, particularly those typically designated as belonging to the *kṣatriya* or *vaiśya varṇas*, may well take up a lifestyle that mirrors that of a high-caste Brahmin. Nevertheless, since members of non-Brahmin *jātis* are intrinsically forbidden from performing the ritual worship of the high gods, their states of purity are never as high as that of the purest Brahmin male.

Auspiciousness and inauspiciousness

Another telling dimension of Hinduism is its concern with the categories of auspiciousness (*maṅgala, śubha, bhadra*) and inauspiciousness (*durmaṅgalya, aśubha*).

They derive from fundamental ideas of cosmology, and permeate all aspects of religious behavior and social interactions. One notes that the cosmological cycles of creation, the span of a human life, the seasonal changes in a year, and even the progress of a day are marked by periods of growth and creation, and periods of decay and destruction. Thus portions of time, in its daily, weekly, monthly, and annual cycles are categorized as auspicious or inauspicious. The night is generally more inauspicious than the day. Particular days of the week, such as Tuesday, ruled by the inauspicious heavenly power, Mars (Maṅgala), and Saturday ruled by Saturn (Śani), are less favorable than Monday and Thursday, ruled respectively by the Moon and Jupiter. The dark fortnight is less favorable than the bright or waxing half of the lunar month, just as the southern route of the sun determines the less auspicious half of the yearly cycle than its northern route (from the winter to the summer solstices) when the days grow longer. The so-called "bright half" of the year is like daytime for the gods, and the "dark half" (from the summer to the winter solstice) is like their night-time. Additionally, the effects of Rāhu and Ketu during eclipses are obvious inauspicious influences, and they, along with the other pernicious "planets" (*graha*), can even make particular phases within the normally auspicious periods problematic. The great god Viṣṇu is believed to sleep during the months of the rainy season, which is generally regarded as inauspicious for the celebration of marriages.

During inauspicious times, pernicious powers, such as the *graha* Śani (Saturn), have an enhanced capacity to inflict damage. These are also periods when ghosts, spirits, and other dangerous supernatural beings wander the earthly realms. However, inauspicious times do not absolutely indicate that one should refrain from any undertaking. On inauspicious days, such as Tuesday and Saturday, Hindus often visit temples, or make offerings at the shrines of the Navagrahas (Nine Heavenly Powers). These acts of worship are intended to override or limit the dangerous influences associated with those particular days. If there are alternative possibilities, it is considered undesirable, if not foolhardy, to begin a major undertaking, such as a long journey or an important religious ritual, or conduct a wedding during an inauspicious time of year or time of the day. Should some calamity befall a person, their disregard for some aspect of inauspiciousness may well be identified as a contributing factor.

Auspiciousness and inauspiciousness are somewhat malleable categories. While the general features that dictate favorable or unfavorable phases are built into the cyclical cadences of time itself, there are actions and events that nuance, or even invert, the implications of these periods. For instance, there is the intersection of favorable days with unfavorable influences by Rāhu and Ketu. Or there are unfavorable days during the favorable fortnight of the lunar cycle. Or there are favorable days, during a favorable fortnight, but in the inauspicious half of the annual cycle. In the course of one's life, one's horoscope might reveal an inauspicious period of years when Saturn or Mars runs through significant lunar mansions, although these influences may be moderated by the activities of other auspicious planetary effects.

A telling illustration of the interplay of these categories is found in the well-known myth of the prince Rāma who needed the help of the Goddess Durgā before undertaking a war with the demon Rāvaṇa. However, the Goddess was routinely worshipped during an auspicious month in the spring, and was believed to sleep during the inauspicious autumn months, when Rāma had to wage war. Rāma, because of his great purity of spirit, in what is popularly known as an untimely awakening (*akāla bodhana*) decided to proceed with the worship. Durgā tested Rāma's piety, and when assured that he was sincere, granted his wish.

The autumn celebrations of Navarātra (Nine Nights) and the Durgā Pūjā, which re-enact Rāma's and other mythic victories, are enormously popular festivals throughout the Hindu world. They involve worship activities during the nights of the waxing fortnight in the month of Āśvina (September–October), near the autumn equinox, almost the middle of the "dark half" of the year, and virtually midnight in a god's day. Thus it is a period that is conventionally regarded as particularly dangerous because of the presence of evil spirits and demonic forces. By propitiating Durgā at this time of year, worshippers gain access to her strength and protection, because according to mythic accounts, she embodies a power capable of vanquishing all demonic forces. So the Navarātra has become an auspicious festival period within an inauspicious cycle of time, and recollects the power of the divine to vanquish the demonic. Even so, priests who perform the rites of Durgā worship will take care not to conduct crucial portions of the ritual during inauspicious periods during the nine-night cycle.

It is not just time and its cycles that dictate auspiciousness. People and places may be auspicious or inauspicious. Birth during an inauspicious planetary configuration, it is believed, may indeed lead a person to be the victim of unfortunate events throughout their lives. However, continual contact with impurity may also lead persons to be regarded as inauspicious. Thus, by extension, even the sight of an Untouchable may be regarded by high caste Brahmins as inauspicious. Since a wedding ceremony celebrates and hopes for marital happiness for a husband and wife in years to come, some Hindus consider a widow's presence at such rites as inauspicious. Even the Brahmin priests, the *mahābrāhmaṇas*, who preside over death rituals in Banāras are regarded as inauspicious. The dharmic behavior of a king (or in the modern context a political leader) is believed to be essential for the auspiciousness of the realm. If natural disasters, such as drought, famine, or disease, which are marks of inauspiciousness, befall a kingdom or nation, it would not be unusual to suspect the dharmic status of its rulers.

Key points in this chapter

- *Dharma* is an expression of how one should behave in rectitude with the cosmic order.
- The Dharma Śāstras are treatises dealing specifically with *dharma.*
- Hindu society is divided into four main classes (*varṇa*).
- Hindu society consists of thousands of smaller groups, known as *jātis.*
- The *Laws of Manu* contain prescriptions of appropriate behavior for each of the *varṇas.*
- Hindus often identify themselves according to family lineage (*gotra*), their village of origin (*grāma*), or their *jāti.*
- The term "Untouchable" refers to one who is outside the *varṇa* system.
- Notions of ritual purity and ritual pollution play an extremely important role in Hinduism.
- The Havik Brahmins illustrate how pollution is transmitted and purity maintained or achieved.
- Notions of auspiciousness and inauspiciousness permeate all aspects of Hindu society.

Discussion questions

1. What impact do you think the *Puruṣa Sūkta* hymn of the *Ṛg Veda* has had on Hindu religion and society?
2. How is status determined in Hindu society, and how do notions of status affect Hindu religion?
3. According to the Havik Brahmins, even the gods are susceptible to the hierarchies of purity and pollution. Why do you think this is so?
4. Discuss the hierarchical stratification of Hindu society and the content of the texts associated with it.
5. Discuss the role that notions of ritual purity and ritual pollution play in Hindu society. How do these notions relate to the *varṇa* system?
6. Hinduism is concerned with the categories of auspiciousness and inauspiciousness. Explain these categories, where they derived from, and the dimensions of society that they impact.

Further reading

On Dharma

Banerjea, S. C. (1962) *Dharma Sutras: A Study of their Origin and Development.* Calcutta: Punthi Pustak.

Derrett, John Duncan M. (1973) *Dharmasutras and Juridical Literature.* History of Indian Literatures, fasc. 1. Wiesbaden: Otto Harrassowitz.

Doniger, Wendy (trans.) (1991) *The Laws of Manu.* Harmondsworth: Penguin Books.

Gonda, Jan (1969) *Ancient Indian Kingship from the Religious Point of View.* Leiden: E. J. Brill.

Kane, P. V. (1930–62) *History of Dharmaśāstra*, 5 vols. Poona: Bhandarkar Oriental Research Institute.

Olivelle, Patrick (1999). *Dharmasūtras: The Law Codes of Ancient India.* Oxford: Oxford University Press.

— (2004) *The Law Code of Manu.* Oxford: Oxford University Press.

On class and caste

Beteille, A. (1965) *Caste, Class and Power: Changing Patterns of Stratification in a Tanjore Village.* Berkeley, CA: University of California Press.

— (1969) *Castes, Old and New.* New York: Asia Publishing House.

Bhattacharya, Jogendra Nath (1986) *Hindu Castes and Sects.* Calcutta: Thacker, Spink & Co.

Carstairs, G. Morris (1958) *The Twice-Born: A Study of a Community of High-Caste Hindus.* Bloomington, IN: Indiana University Press.

Das, Veena (1977) *Structure and Cognition: Aspects of Hindu Caste and Ritual.* Delhi: Oxford University Press.

Deliége, R. (1999) *The Untouchables of India.* Nora Scott (trans.). Oxford: Oxford International Publishers.

Dumont, Louis (1980) *Homo Hierarchicus: The Caste System and its Implications.* Mark Sainsbury, Louis Dumont, and Basia Gulati (trans.). Chicago, IL: University of Chicago Press.

Klass, Morton (1980) *Caste: The Emergence of a South Asian Social System.* Philadelphia, PA: Institute for the Study of Human Issues.

Kolenda, Pauline M. (1985) *Caste in Contemporary India: Beyond Organic Solidarity.* Prospect Heights, IL: Waveland Press.

Mendelsohn, Oliver, and Marika Vicziany (1998) *The Untouchables: Subordination, Poverty and State in Modern India.* Cambridge: Cambridge University Press.

Quigley, Declan (1993) *The Interpretation of Caste*. New York: Oxford University Press.

Raheja, Gloria G. (1988) *The Poison in the Gift: Ritual, Prestation, and the Dominant Caste in a North Indian Village*. Chicago, IL: University of Chicago Press.

Smith, Brian K. (1994) *Classifying the Universe: The Ancient Indian Varṇa System and the Origins of Caste*. Oxford: Oxford University Press.

On purity and auspiciousness

Carman, J.B. and A. Marglin (eds) (1985) *Purity and Auspiciousness in Indian Society*. Leiden: E. J. Brill.

Douglas, Mary (1966) *Purity and Danger: An Analysis of the Concepts of Pollution and Taboo*. New York: Praeger.

Dumont, Louis, and David Pocock (1959). "Pure and Impure." *Contributions to Indian Sociology* 3:9–39.

Harper, Edward B. "Ritual Pollution as an Integrator of Caste and Religions," *Journal of Asian Studies*, XXII (June 1964), 151–97.

4 Dharma *and the individual*

In this chapter

Orthodox elaborations on the nature of *dharma* extended beyond generalized schemes about how society should be structured (e.g. through the *varṇa* system). They pertained to perceived distinctions between men and women, and articulated how individual members of each sex should best live their lives. Here we explore orthodox Hindu prescriptions on the rituals that should accompany the stages of life (i.e. rites of passage). These prescribed duties for twice-born men and women formed the cornerstone of the householder's way of life, which was the backbone of orthodox society. While prescribing these householder obligations the Dharma Śāstras simultaneously established long-enduring values that continue to give Hinduism much of its characteristic cultural forms.

Main topics covered

- Hindu rites of passage (*saṃskāra*)
- Investiture with the Sacred Thread (*upanayana*)
- Marriage (*vivāha*)
- Householder's *saṃskāras*
- Final Sacrifice (*antyeṣṭi*)
- The four goals/aims and the four stages of life
- Women in Hinduism
- Vowed ascetic observances (*vrata*) and auspiciousness (*saubhagya*)
- Marriage and *pativrata*
- *Satī* and the status of widows

From the time of the Āraṇyakas one notes attempts to mediate between the orthodox expectation to perform Vedic sacrificial rituals in order to ensure the orderly functioning of the cosmos, and attitudes favoring the renunciation of all such external religious practices through the performance of meditative visualizations. By the

Upaniṣadic period, in conjunction with *śramaṇa* movements such as Buddhism and Jainism, the prospect of attaining *mokṣa*, and the liberation it promised to grant from the malaise of saṃsāric existence, was apparently gaining in popularity. In Buddhist literature we get a sense of the turmoil such a culture of renunciation began to cause, as rulers began to watch their heirs give up their thrones, and young men gave up their family trades and inheritances. Orthodox Hinduism responded by striking a compromise between what becomes a perennial tension in many Asian religious philosophies, namely, the quest for liberation (*mokṣa*) through renunciation versus righteous social engagement (*dharma*) with the world through the householder's way of life. One response to this tension is the promotion of both *dharma* and *mokṣa* as worthy goals. Another is found in the promotion of appropriate stages in life, during which particular goals are best pursued.

Hindu rites of passage (saṃskāra)

Hindu orthodoxy prescribes that the whole of life be lived in an orderly manner, passing through sequential stages in accord with one's *varṇa* and gender. Each stage should be marked with an appropriate life-cycle ritual or *saṃskāra*. The term *saṃskāra* literally means "constructed," and thus conveys the sense of something put together correctly. In the yogic sense, our thoughts (*citta*) are shaped or constructed by latent effects from previous thoughts, known as *saṃskāras*. Upon first glance, *saṃskāra*, as a rite of passage, may seem quite different from the term in its yogic usage. However, rites of passage bring together or connect two chapters of an individual's life, as the previous state of being is brought to a conclusion, and a new phase is generated out of the ashes of the old. Thus *saṃskāras* sequentially "construct" the person, putting them together, through sacrificial rites, in progressively more refined ways until their final return to the source of existence.

Saṃskāras are vitally important in orthodox Hindu life, and participation in them effectively certifies that one is a member of the Hindu tradition. There are as many as forty *saṃskāras* prescribed, but only about a dozen that are commonly discussed in any detail in the Dharma and Gṛhya Sūtras. The most important of the *saṃskāras* are the Investiture with the Sacred Thread, known as *upanayana*, Marriage or *vivāha*, and Cremation or *antyeṣṭi*. *Saṃskāras* require the mediation of a Brahmin priest, and one cannot qualify to have certain ones performed without having first undergone others. As such, *saṃskāras* belong to the broader category of *dīkṣā*, or initiation rituals, which can demarcate graded progress through worldly and spiritual life. Just as particular *dīkṣās* may entitle a student to higher levels of spiritual teachings from a master (*guru*), by accepting to have *saṃskāra* rites performed, a Hindu affirms the religious authority of the Brahmin priest to confer on him (or her) a particular status, or to construct for him (or her) a particular configuration of personhood.

Figure 4.1 A young Brahmin priest performs a *saṃskāra* rite on behalf of a Brahmin family

Investiture with the Sacred Thread (upanayana)

Certain Dharma Śāstras actually claim that until the *upanayana* is performed, every Hindu is merely a *śūdra*. *Upanayana* means "leading one to [oneself]," and is prescribed for male adolescents from the Brahmin, *kṣatriya*, and *vaiśya varṇas*. As we have noted, since *varṇa* claims are under constant negotiation by various *jātis*, requests to have the *upanayana* rite (and other such rituals) performed grant to the Brahmin priest an authoritative dispensation as to who may be permitted to undergo this *saṃskāra*. The *upanayana* is said to grant the person a second birth. The Brahmin preceptor embodies the Veda itself, and serves as the womb within which the initiate is said to be carried like an embryo, until he is born again as the offspring of the Veda. In contrast to birth from his mother's womb, this second birth is an initiation into the world of the sacred knowledge (*veda*) of sacrifice. It is initiation into the knowledge of the deathless Self (Brahman), who through sacrifice became the mortal embodied self (the initiate), who in turn, through participation in sacrificial action may ultimately acquire the liberating knowledge to reintegrate mortal self with the immortal Self. Thus *upanayana* leads the initiate through the threshold that separates those that do not know from those that do. Only those who have crossed this threshold will have access to the study of the Veda. The *upanayana* ritual itself includes the symbolism of parturition, renunciation, Vedic learning, and sacrificial oblations. Within these elements one also notes how the imperatives of renunciation are balanced with expectations to preserve the domestic and social order.

Tradition prescribes that the *upanayana* be performed on Brahmin boys at the age of eight, eleven for *kṣatriyas,* and twelve for *vaiśyas,* keeping in mind that age is counted from the time of conception. Thus a person is already regarded as being a year old when they are born. These prescriptions may be modified, and a boy may undergo the *saṃskāra* earlier or later. One risks social isolation if the ritual is not performed before a reasonable age. Since such rituals entail a fair amount of expense, families may group together and perform the rite for several boys at the same time. Because a Hindu boy cannot be married by a Brahmin priest without first having undergone the *upanayana,* nowadays it is not uncommon for families to commission the rite immediately prior to the marriage of their sons.

The *upanayana* rite requires appropriate preparation. Astrological considerations determine a suitable time for the ritual to be performed. A Vedic altar consisting of a square fire pit is ritually constructed. At some point, whatever his age, the boy is seated on his mother's lap and is fed by her like a small child. This is expected to be the final time he will receive food into his mouth from her hands. At an auspicious juncture of time the boy has his head shaven, leaving only a tuft of hair at the back known as the *śikhā,* a sign of the twice-born *varṇas.* The naked boy, clad only in a loincloth, may be rubbed down with turmeric paste by his sisters. The symbolic progressive separation of the child from his maternal connections as he joins the male world of Vedic truth is evident. Through the tonsure, the turmeric rub, and the feeding on his mother's lap, the boy is returned to a state that resembles a newborn, and evokes the pivotal transition from his former condition as a human child to his new state as a child of the Veda.

Next, the boy is given a staff, a belt, and an antelope skin, all symbolic of the ascetic's few acceptable possessions. At this point he is also given the sacred thread, known as the *yajñopavita* (*janëu* in Hindi), which is the item that gives this rite its popular name. The *yajñopavita* is a loop of thread that is made to ritual specifications and should be draped across the torso, over the left shoulder and under the right arm. It is made of three threads, each of which is made of three threads, each in turn fashioned from three threads. The origin of the *yajñopavita* is unclear, since it is not mentioned in the earliest Gṛhya Sūtras. It is likely a ritual substitute for a piece of cloth that the twice born were supposed to wear on their left shoulder. The sacred thread has become the most pervasive symbol of twice-born (*dvija*) *varṇa* status.

As fires burn in the sacrificial altars, Vedic verses are chanted, and the boy requests that he be accepted as a student. He asks to enter into the way of Brahman (*brahmacarya*) and is accepted. The presiding priest separates the boy from the rest of the group by taking him behind a screen or covering himself and the boy with a blanket. He then whispers the Gāyatrī *mantra* in the boy's ear. The transmission of a sacred verse (*mantra*) is a common mode of spiritual initiation (*dīkṣā*). In this case, it is a hallmark of the boy's rebirth as the offspring of the sacred sound from which all creation emerges. The Gāyatrī is believed to be the condensed essence of the Vedas, and so even if the initiate does not undertake further Vedic study, the periodic repetition of this verse is regarded as sufficient. He also makes an offering of wood into the sacred fire, affirming his membership in a career of sacrificial worship, and the world of the householder who maintains the social order. In an apparent contrast to this, the boy also begs for his first meal and for gifts for his teacher. He embodies a fusion of the renouncer's way of life with the values of the householder, implying that he will live an austere life while engaged in his Vedic learning, yet support the goals of marriage, raising a family, and so forth. The completion of the *upanayana* rite traditionally marked the boy's entry into the student stage of life, the first of four prescribed stages known as the *catur-aśrama*.

There are *saṃskāras* that developed later to mark the phases of learning. For instance, some treatises prescribe a rite known as the Vidyārambha (Beginning of Study) to mark the start of learning, prior to the student stage in life, when the child begins to learn the alphabet and to read. This is prescribed for the age of five. The Vedārambha (Beginning of Vedic Knowledge) is prescribed for after the *upanayana*, and before commencing to study the Vedas. Keśānta is the first shave, to be performed at the age of fifteen, and marked a sexual maturation on the part of the student. He is expected to renew his vows of sexual continence during the remainder of his formal studies. The Samāvartana (Returning [Home]) *saṃskāra* marked the end of the student stage in life, and the end of formal Vedic education. Its central feature was a purifying bath (*snāna*), leading the newly graduated student to be known and respected as a *snātka* (the bathed one). Bathing (*snāna*) is a ubiquitous component of Hindu rituals, often marking the termination of initiatory rites. It both purifies and consecrates. In the terminology of anthropological theory, Samāvartana is a clear example of an aggregation rite, in which the student who was separated from householder society, and who abided to the ascetic disciplinary rules of the student stage of life, now sheds his student garments, puts on new clothes, and re-enters social life with a transformed status. The majority of these educational rites are seldom performed by most Hindus these days, or their meanings are said to be incorporated into other *saṃskāras*.

Marriage (vivāha)

In crucial ways, marriage forms the cornerstone of Hindu religious life. While the *upanayana* rite is deemed vital for boys of the *dvija* classes, for girls marriage serves as the equivalent of that rite of passage, since they do not undertake any major initiatory rite earlier in their lives. A male may not be married by a Brahmin priest without having undergone the *upanayana saṃskāra*. Marriage marks a girl's entrance into spiritual life, and for both partners it marks the beginning of the householder stage in life. Householders are responsible for the regular performance of religious rites, and thus constitute the matrix that supports most other institutional religious forms. Most Hindu marriages were, and still are, arranged by the fathers of the bride and groom, and are generally initiated by the bride's family. Caste, age, education, personality, and even skin color are important features in the decision-making process. Typically, the prospective couple meets a few times, in the presence of their family members, in order to get acquainted with each other. Astrological charts are consulted. This is an extremely important feature of the arrangements. Horoscopic incompatibility would almost certainly lead to an annulment of the arrangement. Incompatible horoscopes may also be used as an excuse to avoid a match thought to be undesirable for other reasons, without causing the families of the potential bride or groom any offense.

Polygamous marriages were not uncommon in Hindu society. Ancient texts speak of both polygyny (multiple wives) and polyandry (multiple husbands). In the *Rāmāyaṇa* epic, King Daśaratha fathers four children through his three wives. In the *Mahābhārata* epic, Princess Draupadī married the five sons of King Paṇḍu, and bore their children. Certain Himalayan tribes still practice polyandry today. In efforts to unify the wide variations in marriage practices throughout the many regions of India, the post-Independence Government of India introduced The Hindu Marriage Act in 1955, which by 1976 became the official marriage law after undergoing various amendments. It promotes monogamous marriage and allows for divorce under reasonable circumstances. However, the cultural norm is to disapprove of divorce, although a woman may return to her own family if she finds married life unbearable. A man may remarry if the couple is unable to produce offspring. Remarriage for women, particularly among the upper *varṇas,* is rare. Grooms must be over twenty-one years of age and brides over eighteen. A ceremony may follow local regional traditions, but if the rite of taking seven steps (*saptapadī*) is performed, a common feature in most Hindu weddings, completion of the seventh step legally confirms the marriage.

The Dharma Śāstras prescribe advice for men when selecting a bride. The *Laws of Manu* (3.5–10) exhorts one not to choose a wife with reddish hair or with too little or too much bodily hair. She should not be quarrelsome nor named after a constellation, a tree or a snake, or with a name that inspires terror. She should have an agreeable name, be free from bodily defects, have delicate limbs and small teeth, and have a gait like a swan or elephant. *Manu* (3.12–15) also states that a Brahmin man should marry a Brahmin woman, a *kṣatriya* man a *kṣatriya* woman, and so on, for their first marriage. However, should desire arise, men from the twice-born classes may subsequently take on wives from classes lower than their own.

Manu (3.20–50) also provides eight categories of marriage available to the four *varṇas*. These are the Brāhma, Daiva, Ārṣa, Prājāpatya, Āsura, Gāndharva, Rākṣasa, and Paiśāca types of marriage. The Brāhma (i.e. pertaining to the god Brahmā, or to Brahman) rite, in which a daughter, adorned and honored, is given to a man learned in the Vedas, whom the father has approached, is regarded as the best type of marriage. In the Daiva (i.e. pertaining to the gods (*deva*)) rite, which is similar to the Brāhma, the daughter is given to a priest while he is engaged in the performance of the sacrifice. The Ārṣa (i.e. pertaining to the seers (*ṛṣi*)) rite is similar, but the father of the bride receives at least a bull and a cow. In the Prājāpatya (i.e. pertaining to the creator god Prajāpati) rite, the bride and groom are blessed and the groom's wishes are honored. The adorning of the bride with expensive clothes and jewelry, in these first four types of marriage, loosely supports a dowry system in which the bride brings wealth and gifts with her. In the Āsura (i.e. pertaining to the demons (*asura*)) rite, a wife is obtained after the groom provides the bride and her family with all the wealth he can afford. This type of marriage involves the concept of a bride-price, and is associated with the ancient practices of *vaiśyas* and *śūdras*. The Gāndharva (i.e. pertaining to the heavenly pleasure enjoying spirits (*gandharva*)) rite is a "love marriage," undertaken by a man and a woman on mutual consent derived primarily from desire and for the purpose of sexual union. In the Rākṣasa (i.e. pertaining to the devils (*rākṣasa*)) rite, the groom attains the bride by forcibly abducting her from her home, while she weeps and resists, after he has slain or beaten her kinsmen. This marriage, which at the more acceptable end of its spectrum depicts the taking of women as "booty" after warfare, is approved for *kṣatriyas*. For instance, in the *Mahābhārata* epic, the *kṣatriya* hero Arjuna, on the advice of the incarnate god Kṛṣṇa, Subhadrā's own brother, abducts and weds the princess in this manner. Also, the warrior Bhiṣma abducts three princess sisters, Ambā, Ambālikā, and Ambikā as brides for the king of Hastinapur. The last type of marriage rite is the Paiśāca (i.e. pertaining to the flesh-devouring ghoul (*piśāca*)), which deals with the seduction of a girl who is sleeping, intoxicated, or mentally disturbed. This is the most depraved type of marriage, and should be avoided by all. It is clear that *Manu* only approves of the first four types for Brahmins.

Hindu marriage is evidently not primarily the joining together of a man and a woman due to their mutual love for each other. The so-called "love marriage," classified by *Manu* as the Gāndharva style, is regarded as the practice of foreigners, and often forms the theme of Indian films. More often than not, such "love-based" attractions are portrayed as having unpleasant results for all concerned. Hindu marriages are not intended merely to link individuals. They connect family lineages. They both bind and separate. The firm injunctions to marry within the permissible lineages of one's *jāti* further demonstrate the role marriage plays in maintaining social cohesion among particular groups, while simultaneously demarcating distinctions between groups. A cardinal function of marriage is to produce offspring, particularly a male heir, in order to continue the lineage. Only then is a man regarded as complete. *Manu* recommends that one should not choose a bride from a family that has no male heir, or where the bride has no brother. This emphasis on male offspring continues to place enormous pressure on Hindu married couples. The eldest son is designated to preside over the death rituals of his parents, and orthodox Hindus fear that their soul's trajectory in the afterlife will be misguided without his ministrations.

The Hindu wedding ritual itself varies considerably from region to region, but most variations share certain features. Weddings are costly affairs, often putting the families of the bride and groom into onerous debt. They can be particularly expensive for the family of the bride if the dowry tradition is followed. Despite governmental efforts to inhibit it, the dowry tradition is still widely practiced, particularly in North India. Wedding rituals mirror the central role played by the king in the organization of Hindu society. Each wedded couple forms the core of a family unit and embarks on the householder's stage in life. The king is the paradigmatic householder, who produces heirs to propagate his lineage, and thus maintains the dynasty. He patronizes religious rituals which are presided over by Brahmin priests, and invites the participation of various members of his kingdom to attend and participate in public rites. In doing so, he affirms his power and garners new prestige. He binds the kingdom together, legitimates the value of religious rites and the functionary role of the priesthood. Each wedded couple emulates the kingly paradigm to the degree that it can. Just as families might bestow their daughters as wives to the king, so too, the daughter is gifted to the groom, in a rite known as the *kanyā-dāna* (gift of a virgin). The father of the bride pours water out of a jar to symbolize this gift. There is an implicit hypergamy (i.e. marrying up) here, because the daughter's family is by this act subordinated to the groom's family. The groom's acceptance of the bride forges an alliance between the two family lineages, although to some extent, because of the patrifocal (i.e. father-centered) nature of most Hindu social groups, the bride becomes part of the groom's family and leaves her own.

On the main day of the marriage rite, the groom rides up to the wedding site, generally at the bride's home, on a white mare, an elephant, or nowadays, in an automobile. He is accompanied by musicians and the dancing and parading members of his household. Previously, both bride and groom have taken ritual baths, been anointed with consecrated oils, and are dressed in wedding finery. The bride's *sārī* may be extremely expensive; for those who can afford it, it may be made of the finest Banāras silk with gold brocade. Her hands are decorated with henna, or red lacquer, and she is adorned with her best jewelry. A corner of the bride and groom's garments are knotted to each other, and a sacred fire is lit in a Vedic-styled fire pit. This will constitute their new household fire. The presiding priest is honored and offerings of sandalwood, clarified butter, and other materials are made into the fire. The groom then takes the bride's hand. They then recite wishes for happiness, offspring, and the well-being of each other, and their relatives. The groom leads the bride around the sacred fire, saying, "Let us marry. Let us have sons and daughters. Let us be kind and loving to each other, well-intentioned, may we live long lives." After each round the bride steps on a stone while the groom says, "Step on this stone. Be firm like this stone. Resist enemies. Overcome adversaries." This is followed by the *saptapadī* rite, in which the groom leads the bride to take seven steps in a northerly direction. It is the highpoint of the marriage ceremony. The groom says, "Take one step for sap, the second for juice, the third for prosperity, the fourth for refuge, the fifth for offspring, the sixth for enduring change. May you be my friend with the seventh step. May you be faithful to me. May we have many sons, who grow old." There are numerous variations and elaborations on what is said during the *saptapadī*. This rite legally sanctions the completion of the marriage.

The groom ties the *maṅgala sūtra*, a thread necklace symbolizing auspiciousness, around the neck of the bride. He also applies *tilaka*, a bright red powder (*sindūra*), to her forehead between the part in her hair, which symbolizes her married status. Some hold that for women the *maṅgala sūtra* is like the *yajñopavita* for men, since both are threads that symbolize their initiation into the world of Vedic values. The tradition of exchanging rings is becoming common, although this may be done long before the wedding ceremony as part of the engagement procedures. After the wedding ritual, the bride leaves her parents' home for the home of her husband. The couple is expected to remain chaste for three days, the bride under the care of an unwidowed Brahmin mother. The household fire is rekindled in the new home, and after appropriate oblations the marriage is consummated. Sexual relations are an integral expectation in Hindu marriage, since having children is vital for the continuation of the family lineage.

Householder's saṃskāras

There are a large number of *saṃskāras* prescribed for householders. These concern the rites that precede conception and that follow the birth of a child. However, most Hindus follow only a few of these rites, while the most orthodox try to incorporate as many as they can afford. In order to conceive a child successfully a ritual known as Garbhādhāna (Impregnation) is prescribed and should be performed between the fourth and sixteenth day following the onset of the wife's menstrual period. By the fourth month of a successful pregnancy, the Puṃsavana (Quickening of a Male Child) is to be performed to inhibit the possibility of miscarriage and ensure the birth of a male child. Later in the pregnancy, prior to birth, the Sīmantonnayana (Dividing of the Hair) rite is prescribed. It involves the parting of the pregnant woman's hair, perhaps a symbolic prefiguring and facilitating of the upcoming delivery. *Smṛti* texts say that women in their first pregnancy are particularly vulnerable to evil spirits, who seek to devour the fetus. This prenatal rite, which need not be performed for

Figure 4.2 Newly-wed Hindu couple at a Nāga shrine making offerings in the hope of begetting children (South India)

subsequent pregnancies according to certain Śāstras, honors the expectant mother and invokes the Goddess of Prosperity, Śrī, on her behalf.

The moment of birth is naturally noted for horoscopic reasons, and the Jātakarman (Birth Rites) is the *saṃskāra* to be performed then or shortly afterwards. These rites are meant to ensure the development of intelligence, strength, and longevity in the child. At some point before the end of the child's first year, although preferably on the tenth or twelfth day after birth, following the period of ritual impurity that accompanies childbirth, the Nāmakaraṇa (Name Giving) *saṃskāra* is prescribed. The father speaks the name and astrological sign into the child's ear. Blessings for the child are provided by Brahmins, who are invited to the rite and offered food. The Gṛhya Sūtras attempt to prescribe advice on the composition of a name, suggesting the number of syllables it should contain, such as two or four for boys and three for girls. However, their prescriptions are inconsistent. The *Laws of Manu* suggests that a girl's name be easy to pronounce, pleasant sounding, auspicious, end with a vowel, and convey a blessing. Typically, Hindus tend to give girls names that end in a long "i" or "a" and denote femininity, while boys' names denote masculinity and tend to end in short vowels or consonants. Children may often be named after family deities, or deities that preside over the astrological sign under which the child was born. They often convey *varṇa* or *jāti* status.

The Niṣkramaṇā (Exit from the Birth Room) *saṃskāra* should take place between the twelfth day and the fourth month after birth. The child is taken out into the sunlight, and may now have more interactions with other family members. The Annaprāśana *saṃskāra* celebrates the baby's first eating of solid food (*anna*). This first feeding begins the process of weaning the infant from the mother's breast. The Karṇavedha (Ear Piercing) *saṃskāra* should be performed between the twelfth day and fifth year following birth, although it is now sometimes done along with the *upanayana* rite. Suśruta, an Ayurvedic authority, claims that it has health benefits, preventing the later development of diseases, and provides adornment. The Cūḍākaraṇa (Hair Cutting) *saṃskāra* is prescribed for the first or third year of life. It may be symbolically understood as furthering the process of maturation, as the hair with which one was born is removed. In the *cūḍākaraṇa* rite, the head is shaved completely, except for the *śikhā* or tuft of hair that follows family tradition and designates twice-born status. The ritual is said to be auspicious, granting both health and beauty. If families have prayed to a particular deity to give them a child, the tonsure rite may be performed at a temple of that deity, as an offering of thanks. Tonsure is an integral part of many Hindu rites, including the *upanayana*, and *śrāddha*. The Śāstras enjoin the performers of all the aforementioned rites to invite Brahmins, receive their blessings, and offer them food.

Final Sacrifice (antyeṣṭi)

The *antyeṣṭi* (Final Sacrifice) is a person's last *saṃskāra*. In compelling ways, one could understand it as the final sacrifice in the Vedic career of a twice-born Hindu, in which the final oblation is oneself. Although death is regarded as polluting, the corpse, when properly prepared for cremation, is regarded as a pure offering into the sacred fire. In a world view that sees existence as cyclical, death marks a transition to another state of existence, and as such needs to be commemorated and guided through ritual action. Upon death, the person becomes a *preta*, a being who has "departed" from this life. As we have noted, the Vedic ideology of diversified creation through sacrificial dismemberment of the primordial One, and return to the unitive source through sacrificial oblations, is repeated here. Human beings are embodiments of that dis-integrated unity, and it is only through the inner sacrifice of Self-realization or through participation in the rites of external sacrifice that re-integration can occur. As the Upaniṣads maintain, the path of external sacrificial rites can lead to rebirth in the realm of the ancestors, and *antyeṣṭi* initiates this process of orchestrated rebirth.

Immediately prior to death, the dying person may be fed Gaṅgā water while verses from the *Bhagavad Gītā* or *Rāmāyaṇa* are chanted. This is precisely the procedure at various death hospices in Banāras, the sacred city where many Hindus yearn to die. Death within the sacred perimeter of Banāras is believed to grant liberation to the deceased, and it has thus, for centuries, attracted ageing and ailing Hindus, who wish to spend their last days there. Upon death, the body is washed, its hair and nails are cut, and it is wrapped in an unbleached, uncut shroud. The body is laid on a bamboo stretcher and carried above the shoulders, feet first, towards the cremation grounds on the outskirts of the city. In Banāras, a city sacred to the god Śiva, the cremation grounds are on the banks of the Gaṇgā but, in an inversion of normative notions of purity and pollution, located in the center of the city's sacred perimeter. There is rarely a time when a cremation pyre is not burning at one of the cremation grounds in Banāras. The eldest son should lead the procession, and the male relatives, who follow behind the stretcher, chant the *mantra*: *Rāma nāma satya hai* (Rāma's name is Truth).

A wood pyre is constructed and the corpse is placed atop it. In Banāras, the lower half of the body and stretcher are first submerged in the Gaṅgā. In a vestige of the custom of *satī*, some Śāstras prescribe that the wife of a deceased man lie down on the pyre with the corpse, indicating her willingness to be cremated with him. The deceased's younger brother is then expected to call her off the pyre. This prescription is no longer practiced. The body is smeared with ghee, and with the appropriate Vedic prayers the pyre is set alight. At some point during the cremation, a length of bamboo is used to split the skull of the corpse, to release its soul (*jīva*), which is believed to escape through the region of the *śikhā*, and begin its journey to the next realm. Just as the *upanayana* rite was a second birth for the twice-born *varṇas*, some texts liken the cremation rite to a third birth, into the realm of the ancestors (*pitṛ*). Relatives are expected to refrain from crying during the ritual, to avoid polluting the corpse. The eldest son (or the senior male who heads the funerary rites) bathes and performs a final honorific circumambulation of the corpse. He does so three times while holding a clay pot filled with Gaṅgā water at his left shoulder, and lets it drop and smash behind him as he and the relatives leave the cremation grounds without looking back. The bits of bone and ashes that remain from the cremation are disposed of into the Gaṅgā, or some other local body of water regarded as homologically equivalent to the Gaṅgā. Some families, who do not reside near the Gaṅgā, may collect and carry these bone fragments and ashes on later pilgrimage to cities such as Banāras or Gāyā to deliver them into the sacred river. Electric crematoriums are growing in popularity, particularly in large urban centers, because they are more economical and environmentally conservational than wood pyres.

Visible grieving may occur within the confines of the home as the closest relatives of the deceased enter a state of ritual pollution equivalent to that of an Untouchable for about twelve days. The relatives are expected to shave their heads at some point during that period. The cracking of the corpse's skull marks the beginning of the period of ritual pollution, of mourning, and of the post-mortem rites for the soul of the deceased. Collectively, these rituals are known as *śrāddha*, and priests from particular *jātis* specialize in their performance. The purpose of the *śrāddha* rites is to reconstruct a body for the deceased spirit, the *preta*, so it may journey to the *pitṛ-loka*, or realm of the ancestors. The soul is believed to linger close to the cremation pyre or a body of water. The *śrāddha* rites were supposed to span a year, and the twelve-day period is seen as a condensation of that original prescription.

The *preta* is regarded as needing a bodily vehicle. These are ritually constructed in the form of small cakes or balls, known as *piṇḍas*, made of barley or rice flour, and parallel what was believed to be the sequence through which an embryo developed during its months in the womb. Although the prescription is to prepare a *piṇḍa* on each of the ten days following the cremation, the ritual is often performed on the tenth day. The first *piṇḍa* houses the head of the *preta*, the second, the nose, ears, and eyes; the third, the chest and neck; the fourth, the arms and sexual organs; the fifth, the legs and feet; the sixth, the vital organs; the seventh, the bones, marrow, arteries, and veins; the eighth, the teeth, nails, and hair; the ninth, semen; and the tenth houses the sensations of hunger and thirst. Some Hindus consider this rite to transform the departed *jīva* into a *preta*. On the eleventh day a bull or cow may be released, believed to help the soul cross the Vaitarni River, which flows with pus, excrement, and blood, and separates the realm of the god of death, Yama, from the earthly realm. On the eleventh day, another set of *piṇḍas* may be offered to the gods and the *preta*. *Piṇḍas* are disposed of in a sacred river or body of water, and left for the crows to eat. If crows eat the *piṇḍas*, the rites are believed to be proceeding favorably. A member of the special *jāti* of funerary priests, the Mahābrāhmaṇa, may be invited to consume food containing a bit of the ashes or ground-up bones of the deceased. In doing so, the priest takes on and transmutes any of the sinfulness that remained in the dead person. For this reason, due to their intimate contact with the sins of the deceased, the Mahābrāhmaṇa priests are regarded by other Brahmin *jātis* as akin to Untouchables in ritual impurity.

On the twelfth day, another *śrāddha* rite known as the *sapiṇḍikaraṇa* takes place. *Sapiṇḍikaraṇa* elevates the *preta* to the status of an ancestor, while moving the senior-most ancestor beyond the ancestral realm. Four *piṇḍas* are prepared. Three represent the father, the grandfather, and great-grandfather of the dead person, respectively. The fourth represents the deceased, the *preta*, in his newly constructed body. This *piṇḍa* is divided into three parts and joined with the other three ancestral *piṇḍas*. Thus the *preta* is ritually merged with and transformed into an ancestor (*pitṛ*). As an ancestor, the individual may now continue to receive worship and guide the lives of living descendants. Ancestors may be worshipped at regular intervals, typically at yearly anniversaries of their death, and more generally during specific times of the year, such as at Pitṛ-pakṣa, a dark fortnight in the month of Āśvina (September–October). These ancestral rites are also known as *śrāddha*. If *śrāddha* rites are not performed many Hindus fear that the deceased will remain a spirit (*bhūta*), forced to wander aimlessly in the world, haunting the living, or worse, eventually fall into a lower or hellish realm and take up rebirth in some demonic form.

The Upaniṣads prescribe cremation for both the Self-realized and those destined for rebirth, although the former are not in need of it since for them there is no rebirth. Many *saṃnyāsins* are therefore not cremated, but entombed in structures known as *samādhis*, or their bodies are delivered to a sacred river, such as the Gaṅgā. Certain *Smṛti* texts prescribe that certain groups do not need or do not qualify for the cremation rite. These variously include boys who have not undergone the *upanayana* and girls before marriage, or babies, or thieves, and those who are the offspring of inappropriate mixed *varṇas*. On rare occasions one may still see uncremated bodies of persons who were likely deemed as belonging to such categories set afloat in the Gaṅgā.

The four goals/aims and the four stages of life

The development of Hinduism reveals a progressive tension, by the period of the Āraṇyakas, between sacrificial religion to obtain a more fortunate rebirth and renunciation in order to secure liberation from rebirth. The growing popularity of the latter, fuelled by the teachings of the Upaniṣads and many of the *śramaṇa* movements, resulted in a variety of responses by Brahmin orthodoxy, which forged a compromise between these seemingly contrasting goals. One compromise is articulated in the orthodox prescription to pursue the four goals (*puruṣārtha*) of life, and to do so in four distinct stages (*āśrama*).

The four goals recognized as attractive to human beings, and which were deemed worthy of pursuit were: 1) *dharma*, 2) *artha*, 3) *kāma*, and 4) *mokṣa*. The four stages of life, prescribed primarily for male members of the twice-born *varṇas*, were: 1) *śiṣya* or *brahmacarya*, 2) *gṛhastha*, 3) *vānaprastha*, and 4) *saṃnyāsa*. These divisional categories are interconnected with each other and with the *saṃskāra* system, providing a rather encompassing framework for the lives of orthodox Hindus.

In essence, a boy born into a family of the twice-born *varṇas* would be expected to undergo various rites of passage (*saṃskāra*) until his *upanayana* rite. In this religious childhood, he would begin to be exposed to the proprieties of a dharmic upbringing through the influence of his family members, their moral sensibilities, and their regular performance of appropriate rituals. He would experience *dharma* (i.e. righteousness, duty) in the milieu of the householder's way of life, although as a child would be free from many of the responsibilities incumbent on adults in that stage of life. Traditionally, the *upanayana saṃskāra* would mark the boy's entry into the first *āśrama* or stage of life, namely that of his formal Vedic education. This is known as the *śiṣya* (student) stage, a term often paired with the term *guru*, the teacher of spiritual truths. The *guru–śiṣya* relationship is upheld in virtually all Hindu religious texts as the pre-eminent of human relationships, for it transmits the knowledge that grants spiritual maturity and may even lead to liberation. However, it was believed that when the *śiṣya* entered formal Vedic education, his Brahmin teacher who taught him the dharmic duties appropriate to his *varṇa,* such as the performance of sacrificial rites and support of the social order, was not necessarily the teacher (*guru*) of the ultimate knowledge. In the Upanisadic tale of Śvetaketu, who returns to his home after twelve years of Vedic learning, the boy still requested to be taught the highest truth by his father, who served as his spiritual *guru.* Thus Hindu tradition uses the term *guru* to designate teachers of both conventional Vedic knowledge as well as liberative understanding. Nowadays, the term is often also used to designate any kind of teacher.

The *śiṣya* stage required the boy to take up residence with his instructor in a hermitage (*āśrama*), and lead an austere life of formal study of at least one Veda for a certain period of time, traditionally listed as between nine to thirty-six years. Vedic study would free him of the first of three debts that all people are born with, namely, his debt to the seers (*ṛṣi*). Upon completion of those studies he could then decide if he wanted to remain as a student in the *guru-kula* (teacher's household or lineage), or return to the householder's way of life. Another term for this student stage is *brahmacarya,* which means "progressing within Brahman" and suggests that the boy, known as a *brahmacārin,* who was born through the *upanayana* as a child of the Veda, is now growing within Brahman. It is here that he would receive formal instruction in the Vedic teachings on *dharma,* and the responsibilities incumbent on members of his *varṇa. Dharma,* one of the four valid goals of life, points him in the direction of righteousness, and what is required to maintain the social order.

The term *brahmacarya* has also come to be synonymous with chastity, more specifically with sexual continence, and, least euphemistically, with living without the spilling of semen. The *śiṣya* stage foreshadows the *saṃnyāsa* stage in life, which is also typically characterized by austerity and chastity. The maintenance of chastity is undoubtedly particularly challenging for adolescent males. The spilling of semen is regarded as ritually polluting, while the retention of semen is believed to build up a purifying inner heat (*tapas*) and confer great spiritual potency. Semen, capable of engendering life, connotes the process of creation when spilled, and the *brahmacarya* stage is seen as a period of abiding in the undifferentiated Brahman, prior to creation. Furthermore, sexual license could complicate this period of resident education with the Brahmin *guru,* whose wife and daughters might attract the attentions of his male students.

Nowadays, there are only a few groups of Hindus who follow modified versions of the ancient Vedic system of schooling. They may send their sons to *guru-kulas,* modeled on the traditional system for a few years. Others may visit and reside at *āśramas* for spiritual instruction for a few days, weeks, or months at any point in their lives. Public schooling is the norm for both boys and girls in India, and it begins well before the prescribed age for the *upanayana* rite. Nevertheless, sexual chastity during one's education is still a highly regarded value, and premarital sex is frowned upon in traditional Hinduism.

The second prescribed stage in life, which is that of the *gṛhastha* or householder, begins with marriage or the *vivāha saṃskāra*. Traditionally, this would occur shortly after the *brahmacarya* stage. It is still conventional for children from wealthier families to marry after the completion of their formal education. In poorer families, children are often unable to attend school, and begin working at a young age. Marriage then takes place when they are regarded as being old enough, and when a suitable partner has been found. With the exception of a small percentage of modern families who typically come from large urban centers, most Hindu marriages are arranged by the parents of the prospective bride and groom. It is generally expected that marriage has procreation, rather than merely sexual pleasure, as its goal, and Hindu married couples are encouraged to have children, at the very least one male child, to carry on the lineage. In so doing, the male householder removes the second of the three debts that all people are said to be born with, namely, the debt to his ancestors (*pitṛ*).

The *gṛhastha* stage in life, connected as it is with sexuality and reproduction, from an orthodox Vedic perspective, embodies the creative expression of the Self or Absolute. The once celibate *brahmacārin* may now release his pent up semen to create life. His wife is likened to a field that he is to plough and seed. It is during this stage in life that both husband and wife, who have chosen to enter into the social world that embodies the sacrificed and differentiated Brahman, must sustain that process through their own sacrificial actions. Sacrificial offerings remove the last of the three debts one has in life, namely, that owing to the gods (*deva*). Thus it is traditionally incumbent on householders to perform the prescribed cyclical rituals, ensure that their children undergo the appropriate *saṃskāras*, and generally put into practice the dharmic teachings they have learned from their families and through their formal education. So, the *gṛhastha* stage in life is the cornerstone that supports and upholds *dharma*. Naturally, the Dharma Śāstras regard the householder's life as the best of all four *āśramas*. Such valorization suggests that the *āśramas* were not originally stages, but lifestyle options, and placing them in a sequence removed a tension inherent in having to choose among them.

Unlike the renouncer and the celibate student, whose lives are characterized by austerity and the generation of potent inner heat (*tapas*), the householder is expected to pursue the legitimate goal of *kāma* or sensory pleasure. *Kāma* entails the experience of pleasure or the fulfillment of desires, and particularly deals with love and sexual gratification. Orthodox Hinduism encourages the pursuit of this goal during the householder stage in life. After marriage both partners are linked to each other's families, and thus it is important to nurture the qualities of love that extend beyond the simple confines of one's immediate family. Sexual and other shared sensory pleasures enhance life and relationships, and bind husband and wife to each other, providing the family unit with cohesion. Kāma Śāstra literature extols the nature of these pursuits, which still form the substance of many popular songs, films, and contemporary literature. *Kāma* is a crucial interest of human beings and is sanctified within the Hindu tradition. So is the other goal, *artha*, which is skill, attainment, power, or wealth. While the *brahmacārin* and renouncer have no need for wealth and the knowledge that enables them to prosper in society, it is the householder who needs to pursue these goals. Thus both *kāma* and *artha* are primarily the concerns of the householder. The unrestrained pursuit of *kāma* and *artha* can lead to excess, and thus *dharma* is viewed as the regulator of these two goals.

The most well known texts in the Kāma Śāstra literature are the *Kāma Sūtra* of Vatsyāyana and the *Anaṅga Raṅga*, both of which deal mainly with human sexuality and sexual relationships. Innumerable versions of portions of the *Kāma Sūtra* are produced throughout the world, often with illustrations detailing varieties of positions for sexual union. However, the *Kāma Sūtra* also contains classifications of human beings based on their sexual constitution, instructions on seduction, and so on. Moreover, the treatise encourages women to learn the sixty-four arts, which more broadly constitute *kāma*. These arts include singing, dancing, and playing musical instruments, adorning the body, worshipping divine images, learning culinary art and mixing drinks, knowing magic, tailoring, reading and reasoning, gardening and carpentry, as well as knowing the arts of warfare, and learning languages.

Such arts of *kāma* dovetail with the goal of *artha*, which is centrally about effective personal growth and empowerment. Householders are expected to develop their professional skills, through which they may secure more wealth and more effectively provide for the well-being of their families. A potter should learn to make better pots, a merchant to do better business, and so on. Wives, who traditionally preside over domestic affairs, are expected to learn frugality, to live within their means, spending wealth wisely for the benefit of their family members. The best known treatise on *artha* is the *Artha Śāstra*, whose authorship is attributed to the political strategist Kautilya, minister of the emperor Candragupta Maurya. It concerns the *artha* of a *kṣatriya* destined to become king and fulfill that *dharma* properly. It contains instructions on how one should organize a kingdom and its economics, select and test ministers of the realm, operate a network of spies, tax the citizenry, implement and enforce laws, protect one's subjects, wage war, negotiate peace, and maintain the harem.

Although the bulk of its advice is not particularly relevant to most people, the *Artha Śāstra* highlights the many complexities involved in the pursuit and maintenance of material success for that paradigmatic of all householders, the king. The king seeks and exercises power, accrues wealth, and enjoys pleasures (*kāma*), but must manage his affairs successfully for the benefit of his kingdom. It is his *dharma* to embody righteousness, for by so doing he inculcates righteousness in the realm. Thus he should commission the performance of grand scale public sacrificial rituals (*śrauta yajña*), and duly look after the well-being of the priestly and other classes. The pursuit of *artha*, namely, wealth, power, and glory, renders him auspicious, and generates auspiciousness for the kingdom. These are precisely the kinds of values that are incumbent on all householders, who need to integrate the goals of *dharma*, *kāma*, and *artha* to render their lives and that of their families auspicious.

When the householder's children have children of their own and, as some texts indicate, there are grey hairs appearing in his beard, tradition recommends entering a period of retirement. This is the *vanaprastha* stage in life, so called because it proposes that one take up residence (*prastha*) in the forest (*vana*). The elderly male *dvija* is encouraged to pass most of his wealth and possessions to his wife and children, who have greater material needs, and to live in a hut in the forest, perhaps reading scriptural texts and learning from sagely renouncers. He may be accompanied by his wife, and does not need to abandon the household fire. Thus they may prepare meals, enjoy social and conjugal relationships, and even engage in moderate sacrificial rituals, but the general tenor of the stage is transitional, winding down one's preoccupations with *kāma* and *artha*, as one begins to turn to the pursuit of *mokṣa*. It is not common for Hindus to enter this stage, and most elderly Hindus simply continue to live in their family homes with their children. However, there are a number who retire to the hermitage (*āśrama*) of a well-regarded religious teacher, or move to a town with some religious renown. Banāras, once known as the Forest of Bliss, although it is now mostly urban, still is a favorite retirement site for the pious. Retired Hindu men and women may go on frequent pilgrimages to various religious sites, taking up abode in *āśramas* in places such as Haridvar or Rishikesh, Tiruvannamalai, or Pondicheri, for weeks or months at a time.

It is even rarer for Hindus to enter the final recommended stage of life, namely *saṃnyāsa*. The *saṃnyāsin*, or renouncer, is generally respected for the courage required to embark on this stage. *Saṃnyāsins* are expected to bid their spouses and others goodbye, perform their death rites, burn their sacred threads, abandon the household fire, and wander the world in pursuit of the final and highest goal, namely liberation or *mokṣa*. Having renounced virtually all their material possessions, renouncers are expected to don rag robes, traditionally dyed in a saffron hue to conceal stains, take up a staff for support in their old age, and carry a bowl into which householders may place food and other offerings. Unconcerned with social norms and even with formal religious proprieties, renouncers are expected to avoid remaining too long in one site so that they do not develop attachments to particular places or to the companionship and generosity of particular persons. For some, the path of renunciation takes the form of severe asceticism.

Although it should lend itself to highly individualistic forms of seeking, *saṃnyāsa* often manifests in normative forms. Many renouncers join particular communities, following the norms and practices of their groups. Thus there still exist various types of Śaiva renouncers, who worship Śiva as the supreme form of divinity and understand *mokṣa* to be unitive identification with him. Similarly, there are Vaiṣṇava renouncers who hold Viṣṇu as the supreme divinity. Such groups appear to have emerged along with the earliest worship of these deities. The Vedānta philosopher Śaṅkara (or his

Figure 4.3 A renouncer (*saṃnyāsin*) sits beside an image of Gaṇeśa in the hope of receiving donations from passing worshippers

disciples), many centuries later, is also reputed to have organized renunciation by establishing a monastic system, complete with monasteries (*maṭha*) with leadership lineages, and traditions for appropriate renunciation and deportment. Jainism and Buddhism had initiated such monasticism as a form of organized renunciation almost a thousand years earlier, and, whether or not Śaṅkara was its true founder, monasticism certainly had become part of the configuration of Hindu *saṃnyāsa* since Śaṅkara's time.

Women in Hinduism

The overwhelming majority of Hindu writings was produced by males, and thus tend to ignore discussion of the lives and concerns of women. So there is ongoing scholarly effort to try to understand the lives of Hindu women in ancient India, often by reading through these limited and often untextured textual portrayals of women. For instance, there are relatively few hymns to female deities in the *Ṛg Veda*, suggesting the patrifocal, male-centered nature of Āryan society. The goddess Rātrī, the Night, is depicted as fearsome, yet alluring, while Uṣas, the Dawn, is beautiful, and Pṛthivī, the Earth, is nurturing. The qualities of these divinities are associated with women in later literature. Wives played crucial roles in Vedic rituals, and were expected to participate with their patron husbands in the performance of certain *yajñas*. In the Upaniṣadic story of the sage Yajñavalkya, we encounter his wife Maitreyī, who seeks after *mokṣa*. When Yajñavalkya decides to depart for the forest-dweller stage in life, he summons his two wives to divide his property between them. Maitreyī is not content with merely receiving her share of their material possessions, and quests after the same liberating knowledge that he seeks. In other stories Maitreyī is a spiritual teacher in her own right, indicating that in the ancient Vedic period, Hindu women were deemed suitable to take up renunciation, regarded as capable of attaining the highest realization (*mokṣa*), and respected for acting as spiritual teachers (*guru*), transmitting wisdom to disciples. Even today, there are women, such as the Bengali saint, Ānandamayī Mā, who enjoy such acclaim. However, males far outnumber women in taking up *saṃnyāsa*, and as being among those widely acclaimed to have reached the ultimate goal. Furthermore, it is also evident that by the Upaniṣadic period, the status of women had declined in orthodox Hinduism. Women were mostly regarded as incapable of attaining liberation.

Religious figures such as Ānandamayī Mā and Maitreyī, because of both their accomplishments and their rarity, illustrate that women have had to struggle, and some have done so successfully, against a Hindu cultural backdrop of inequality and male prejudice. Tantric religious literature is somewhat exceptional in this regard. It generally upholds women as divine, and to be worshipped as such, because they embody Śakti, the power that animates the cosmos. However, in some Hindu scriptures that are quite influential among orthodox Hindus, women are equated with *śūdras* and animals. Women were prohibited from learning the Vedas. They are portrayed as fickle and childish, easily changing their mind, irrational, and lustful. The Dharma Śāstras recommend that they be under the protection of their fathers when they are young, their husbands when they are married, and their sons when they are widowed. Protection came to mean "control" and Hindu women are expected to be obedient and demure, deferring to their hierarchically superior male relations, at least in public, and in final matters of judgment.

Thus Hindu women may have to negotiate a challenging journey through life precisely because they are women. This life may be marked and influenced by cadences of veneration and worry by her relatives. When born, a baby girl may be greeted with less than joy by parents who would have preferred a son. Prior to her first menstruation, a young girl, known as a little princess (*kumārī*), may be treated with love and affection and even periodically venerated as a goddess. However, once her menstrual periods begin, and she is capable of bearing children, she may be viewed as a burden. Her strong, unpredictable, teenage emotions present grave uncertainties to orthodox Hindu parents, particularly concerning her sexuality. When of marriageable age, she will be wedded to a man she hardly knows, appropriately selected according to caste eligibility and related factors, and will have to leave her home to live with her husband and his family. There, she might live under the less than favorable scrutiny of her husband's mother, who must yield some of her son's attention to his new wife.

Pregnancy and the birth of a child, particularly a son, elevate her status considerably. She then becomes a wife and mother, nurturer of the male lineage-holder.

While young girls may be treated like little princesses, young boys are treated like little deities, and the Hindu wife and mother is an active agent in this process of cultural valorization. The mother–son relationship is a powerful female–male relationship in Hindu culture, different in nature, although arguably as strong as that between husband and wife. A Hindu mother generally surrenders her daughter to her husband's family after marriage, while her son remains with her for the duration of her life. Should her husband die, leaving her a widow, the Hindu woman enters another ambivalent state, marked by some inauspiciousness. However, after menopause, her status is again elevated as she enters a state of ongoing ritual purity, freed from the periodic impurity caused by menstruation.

Vowed ascetic observances (vrata) *and auspiciousness* (saubhagya)

It is a cultural obligation for Hindu wives to cultivate *saubhagya*. *Saubhagya* is auspiciousness as it relates to married women and their concerns. The term derives from a woman's sexuality and fertility, her erotic nature and vitality, but extends to her domestic duties and household, and particularly to the well-being of her husband and children. The Hindu goals of *kāma* and *artha*, as they pertain to women's domestic lives, relate to the development of *saubhagya*. By nurturing the various arts of pleasure and the skills of material success, a wife enhances the quality of her household and the experiences of those living within it. Women may worship the gods in their household shrines, draw auspicious diagrams at the entrance of their homes, visit temples to ask for divine favors and ward off dangerous planetary effects, and introduce special foods into their cuisine for the well-being and health of the family.

A particularly common assortment of practices performed by both men and women, but particularly by Hindu women, is the *vrata*. A *vrata* is a vowed ascetic observance voluntarily chosen in order to enhance one's personal spiritual power, or *śakti*. It is a vowed observance in the sense that one commits to a particular observance for a fixed period of time. The duration could, for instance, be between sunrise and sunset, or the *vrata* may last for several days, weeks, or even months. It is ascetic in that it always involves some kind of personal deprivation or austerity, typically some form of fasting or food restriction. Discussion of the varieties of formal *vratas*, how they are to be performed, and what their benefits are, are found in the Purāṇic literature and in the Nibandhas, but are also mostly transmitted orally from religious teachers to women, and among women.

The Karva Chauth Vrata, for instance, is to be performed for the welfare and longevity of husbands. It is done on the fourth (Hindi: *chauth*) of the dark fortnight of the autumn month of Kartika (October–November), just after harvest. There are regional variations of the *vrata*, but women typically awaken before sunrise and eat a special meal provided by their mothers-in-law. They bathe and pray to Śiva, Pārvatī, Gaṇeśa, Kārttikeya, and the moon, and then refrain from any food or drink until moonrise. In the evening they dress and adorn themselves in their wedding finery, having spent the day decorating their hands and feet with henna, and exchange presents with their mothers-in-law. Mothers may also send their daughters gifts. They may gather in groups to perform a *pūjā* to the goddess Gaurī (or Pārvatī), the wife of Śiva, often in the form of a lump of earth or cow dung, although images are now also common, by sprinkling the image of the goddess with water from a clay pitcher (*karva*). These jars may be filled with bangles, ribbons, and other ornamental items and exchanged with other women. The story of the *vrata* is recited, and the women await the rising of the moon, which is also worshipped, before breaking their fast with a feast.

During the spring and autumn Navarātras, nine-night festivals in honor of the Great Goddess, women (and men) may adopt a *vrata* during the first and last days, or for all of the nine days. Some refrain from all food and drink from sunrise to sunset. Others eat only fruits and yogurt, and drink only water and juice. Some may eat only specific kinds of uncooked foods, such as a type of water chestnut, flavored with a reddish-hued rock salt. These Navarātra *vratas* are not directed towards the welfare of family members, and are concerned with the acquisition of personal power through communion with Śakti, the Goddess herself, who embodies all cosmic power. Hence, the *vrata* appeals to both men and women.

Both of the types of *vrata* exemplified above, whether done for the benefit of specific family members or for personal empowerment, play a role in the enhancement of a woman's *saubhagya*, her auspiciousness during her stage in life as a married householder. The dietary specifics or restraints are believed to develop discipline, build fortitude in dealing with the hardships of life, and are also thought to have medicinal benefits. Ayurveda has long upheld the benefit of periodic fasting to flush the body of impurities, invigorate the digestive system, and restore a balance to the psycho-physical system. Thus Hindu women derive a variety of benefits from the *vrata* tradition, which allows them to interact socially with other women, to prepare special foods, to engage in the creation of ritual art, to resolve problems, to enhance personal purity and power, as well as to demonstrate piety and religious devotion.

Marriage and pativrata

The practice of *vrata*, which emanates from ancient Hindu ideas of asceticism as intrinsic to spiritual attainment, meshes with the obligatory duties of married women in the *pativrata* ideal. Since Hindu women do not undergo an equivalent of the *upanayana* (sacred thread ceremony), marriage serves as their rite of entry into spiritual life after their years of childhood. Although bride and groom are fairly close in age these days, the *Laws of Manu* prescribed that men should marry women much younger than they were. Fears about the inappropriate mixing of the *varṇas* led orthodox Hindus to arrange the marriage of their daughters at a very young age, well before puberty, and on occasion even shortly after birth. The sexual consummation of those child-marriages would take place after the girl was sexually mature. So marriage, which often occurred shortly before a woman reached puberty, initiated her into her *śiṣya* (student), *gṛhastha* (householder), *vanaprastha* (forest-dweller) and *saṃnyāsa* (renouncer) stages of life, all rolled into one, and all of which constituted her ongoing education in *strī-dharma* (woman/wife's *dharma*). Of course, she would have begun to learn these duties informally with her parents prior to marriage, but through marriage she would become part of her husband's family line, and thus needed to be inculcated into those norms and values. Since Hindu women now have access to formal education this scenario is modified, but marriages of young girls still take place in parts of India.

Through marriage a woman would be ushered into her husband's family and there begin her life of austere service and learning. This would parallel her husband's *śiṣya* stage in life in its ascetic orientation. A wife's great and ongoing *vrata* is thus the *pativrata*, the ascetic dedication to her husband (*pati*). He and his parents, particularly his mother, would serve as her primary teachers in her new life of dedicated service to her family. It is believed that if he were her first and only sexual partner, her affection and attraction would more likely remain towards him. Orthodox texts encourage Hindu wives to regard their husbands as gods. He, too, should regard her as a form of the goddess of fertility and good fortune, Śrī, within the household. Her contentment with married life brings auspiciousness to the home, while her dissatisfaction brings calamity and ruin. So men are encouraged to honor their wives with gifts of jewelry, and so on, on a regular basis. A Hindu wife is expected to be modest in public, perhaps covering her head and concealing her face with her *sārī*, and should avoid intimate contact with other men.

Within *dvija* families, the husband is expected to adhere to his *dharma* in order to maintain a ritual purity necessary to worship the family deities, while wives should maintain the ritual purity necessary to worship their husbands. He would be pure enough to offer food to the gods; she would be ritually pure enough to offer food to him. He would eat the leftovers from offerings to the gods, while she would eat the leftovers of food prepared for and consumed by him. He is like Śiva; she is like Pārvatī or Gaurī. He is like Viṣṇu or Kṛṣṇa and she is like Lakṣmī. Together, they are expected to raise a family, continue the lineage, strive for material success and enjoyment, the fruits of their sacrifices, and worship the gods through appropriate rituals. The wife may accompany her husband into his *vanaprastha* (forest-dweller) stage in life, and may return to reside with her eldest son if her husband should take up *saṃnyāsa* or die before she did, a highly likely possibility if she was much younger than him.

Satī and the status of widows

The *pativrata* ideal is closely related to the concept of *śakti*, or power. Asceticism of any type is believed to generate an inner heat (*tapas*), and give rise to personal spiritual power (*śakti*). A wife is expected to use this power to enhance *saubhagya*, which includes the well-being and longevity of her husband and children. To some degree the married couple is thought to be like complementary halves of a single unit, and traditionally, while the husband offers the protection, earns the income, and generally provides the structural framework for social life, the wife embodies the power that sustains their existence. Just as the Vedic gods depend on humans for their nourishment, the husband's survival and strength is dependent on his wife's *śakti* or power.

A Hindu myth recounted by the *ṛṣi* Mārkaṇḍeya in the *Mahābhārata* tells the story of Sāvitrī, who won her husband, Prince Satyavan, back from Yama, the Lord of Death, through her absolute dedication. After Sāvitrī had chosen Satyavan as her husband, she was made aware of a curse that would cause him to die in a year. Nevertheless, she chose to wed him. True to the prediction, Satyavan dropped dead at the prescribed time, despite Sāvitrī's intense prayers and austerities in a three-night *vrata* on the preceding days. The empowerment from this *vrata* enabled her to see and converse with Yama, dark-skinned and red-eyed, dreadful in appearance, and carrying a noose, when he came to usher the soul of Satyavan back to the realm of the departed. Binding Satyavan's soul, no bigger than a thumb, in his noose, Yama began his southern journey back, but Sāvitrī too began to follow. Yama noticed and warned her to desist in her effort, but she insisted that a wife's place is with her husband, even after death. Yama, impressed, granted her a wish in order to stop her from following, and with this she restored her father's lost kingdom and eyesight. However, she kept on following the red-robed God of Death, and her dead husband's spirit. Yama granted her another wish to stop her from following, through which her father was graced with more children. Sāvitrī continued to speak words of such dharmic sweetness, which were like cool water to the parched senses of Yama, that he granted her one last wish, provided it was not the life of Satyavan. Sāvitrī accepted and asked that she may have a hundred children, all fathered by Satyavan. Realizing he was bested by her dedication and intelligence, Yama left, restoring Satyavan back to life and granted both of them extended life-spans. He placed Satyavan, awakening as if from a long bad dream, in the arms of his beloved wife.

Hindu scripture abounds with tales of such wifely loyalty, extending even beyond death's door. The Hindu practice of *satī* was reinforced by such idealism. *Satī* is the act in which a wife allows herself to be immolated, while alive, atop the cremation pyre of her dead husband. Reiterating the sacrificial motif that runs throughout Vedic Hinduism, the woman, also known as a *satī* (good, true), "goes together" with her husband in his final sacrificial offering. Their household fire is extinguished together. Had he taken up *saṃnyāsa* earlier, or had she died before him, she might have been spared the burden of this choice. Through *satī*, a woman is said to avoid entry into widowhood and is believed to cleanse her husband of the consequences of his karmic misdeeds, thus guaranteeing him a favorable rebirth. In the *Mahābhārata*, the two wives of the mythic king Pāṇḍu face this choice when he dies. Mādrī decides to undertake *satī*, while Kuntī, who plays an important and respected role in the remainder of the epic, does not. In fact, there is far more ancient literature favorably portraying women who made the choice of widowhood over *satī*. In the *Rāmāyaṇa*, the three wives of King Daśaratha, Kausalyā, Kaikeyī, and Sumitrā, do not perform *satī* when he dies. *Satī* was always more of an extreme ideal than the normal fate of Hindu widows. Fifth century inscriptions do testify to its actual practice, and by the period of Islamic rule in North India, from the twelfth century, we find hundreds of *satī* and *jauhar* stone markers. *Jauhar* was a related practice initially associated with *kṣatriya* women, who would perform a mass suicide, through immolation, to avoid falling into the clutches of a marauding army that had slain their men on the battlefield.

The Muslim Mughal rulers of India tried to outlaw the practice, but the British, in the early nineteenth century, still yearly encountered hundreds of cases, which they began to document. In 1818, there were well over 700 cases in Bengal alone. This was not representative of the situation in all of India, because certain regions, such as Bengal and Rajasthan, endorsed the practice at particular points in history much more than other parts of the country, where it was hardly practiced at all. The British finally passed a bill in 1829 in Bengal prohibiting its practice and designating it as culpable homicide, punishable by death for those complicit in its performance. By 1846 it was prohibited in Rajasthan. It continued to be permitted until the early twentieth century in Nepal. In a celebrated case in 1988, a young bride named Roop Kanwar performed *satī* in the village of Deorala, Rajasthan. It generated much outrage from virtually all quarters in India, leading to the arrest but eventual acquittal of those who were charged with complicity in the act. Yet, in a stark revelation that such extreme orthodox values still endure and can be revived, however onerous to women they may appear from modern Hindu and western cultural perspectives, thousands of women joined protest marches upholding their right to commit *satī*. Sporadic cases of *satī* still occur in Nepal.

The alternative to *satī* was widowhood, generally viewed by orthodox Śāstric texts as an inauspicious condition. When men who married women much younger than themselves died, or when warriors were slain in battle, they often left behind young widows, who were still capable of bearing children. The presence of these sexually available, fertile females disturbed orthodox Hindu sentiments, which were deeply concerned with the purity of family lineages, issues of inheritance, social stability, and so on. Thus orthodox prescriptions forbade remarriage for widows in all but exceptional cases. When conjoined with practices of child-marriage, this could be an exceptionally heavy burden, for there were often mere girls and very young women thrust into widowhood. These unfortunate women were obliged to spend most of their lives without any other marital relationship. Among poor families, the young widow might be regarded as a financial burden in the home of her deceased husband, whose in-laws might have little loyalty or concern for her. Furthermore, a widow was expected to dress in non-flamboyant colors, such as a white *sārī*, without embellished borders, and spend most of her time in prayer, meditation, and other religious pursuits. Although widow remarriage was legally permitted through the Hindu Widows Act in 1856, the old values still endure, and remarriage is not met with great approval.

Having lost their husbands, widows are still regarded as inauspicious, and are generally prohibited from certain rituals such as weddings, and fertility enhancing rites. Widows should generally avoid adornment, such as bangles, and the forehead *tilaka*, which is the mark of a *sumaṅgalī*, a woman with a living husband. However, a post-menopausal widow, who continues her austere religious regimen, may be held in high regard. Freed from the periodic ritual pollutions of menstruation, incapable of producing offspring, and generating high levels of spiritual merit through her practices, she poses no threat to the social order. If she has received special initiations, she may be called upon to preside at particular religious rites, or prepare sanctified offerings for certain deities. In Bengali communities, such post-menopausal, initiated widows prepare cooked food offerings for the goddess Durgā. They may even be regarded as wise, possessing high levels of spiritual attainment, and capable of imparting religious teachings to others.

Discussion questions

1. Do you think that the *saṃskāras* prescribed by orthodox Hindus are still relevant for modern times? Why or why not?
2. Why you think ancestors play such an integral role in Hindu beliefs in the religious affairs of those still living?
3. What are *saṃskāras*, and why are they important to the orthodox Hindu tradition? List the most important *saṃskāras*, describing them in detail and the reasons for their importance.
4. In what ways does marriage form the cornerstone of Hindu religious life? Describe the marriage process, the texts, rites, and requirements associated with it.
5. What is known about the Hindu women of ancient India? What is expected of women in Hindu society, and how are they regarded during the various stages of their life?

Key points in this chapter

- Hinduism regards both *dharma* and *mokṣa* as worthy goals.
- Hindu orthodoxy prescribes that the whole of life be lived in an orderly manner, passing through sequential stages in accord with one's *varṇa* and gender, and with each stage demarcated by an appropriate life-cycle ritual or *saṃskāra*.
- The sacred thread has become the most pervasive symbol of the twice-born (*dvija*).
- Marriage forms the cornerstone of Hindu religious life.
- Emphasis on male offspring places pressure on Hindu couples.
- Cremation is a person's last *saṃskāra* and may be understood as the final sacrifice in the Vedic career of a twice-born Hindu, in which the final oblation is oneself.
- Orthodox Hindus prescribe four life-stages and four goals deemed worthy of pursuit.
- Most Hindu writings were produced by males, and mostly disregard issues concerning women.
- *Vrata*s are vowed ascetic practices performed mostly by women for personal and familial well-being.
- The *pativrata* ideal is related to the concept of auspicious power and a wife's ascetic dedication to her husband.

Further reading

On childhood, rites of passage, goals of life, and death

Bloch, Maurice and Jonathan Parry (eds) (1982) *Death and the Regeneration of Life.* Cambridge: Cambridge University Press.

Filippi, Gian Giuseppe (1996) *Mṛtyu: Concept of Death in Indian Tradition.* New Delhi: D. K. Printworld.

Justice, Christopher (1997) *Dying the Good Death: The Pilgrimage to Die in India's Holy City.* Albany, NY: State University of New York Press.

Kakar, Sudhir (1978) *The Inner World: A Psycho-analytic Study of Childhood and Society in India.* Delhi: Oxford University Press.

— (1979) *Indian Childhood: Cultural Ideals and Social Reality.* Delhi: Oxford University Press.

Kangle, R. P. (ed. and trans.) (1960–1) *Kautilīya's Ārthaśāstra.* Bombay: University of Bombay.

Knipe, David M. (1977) "*Sapiṇḍikāraṇa*: The Hindu Rite of Entry into Heaven." In F. E. Reynolds and E. H. Waugh (eds) *Religious Encounters with Death: Insights from the History and Anthropology of Religions*. University Park, PA: Pennsylvania State University Press, pp. 111–24.

Madan, T. N. (ed.) (1982) *Way of Life. King, Householder, Renouncer. Essays in Honor of Louis Dumont*. Delhi: Vikas Publishing House.

— (1987) *Non-renunciation*. Delhi: Oxford University Press.

Olivelle, Patrick (1993) *The Āśrama System: The History and Hermeneutics of a Religious Institution*. New York: Oxford University Press.

Pandey, Raj Bali (1969) *Hindu Saṃskāras: Socio-Religious Study of the Sacraments*. New Delhi: Motilal Banarsidass.

Parry, Jonathan (1994) *Death in Banaras*. Cambridge: Cambridge University Press.

Rangarajan, L. N. (1992) *The Arthashāstra: Edited, Rearranged, Translated and Introduced*. Delhi: Penguin.

Sharma, Arvind (1982) *The Puruṣārthas: A Study in Hindu Axiology*. East Lansing, MI: Michigan State University.

On marriage, women, and family

Allen, Michael and S. N. Mukherjee (eds) (1982) *Women in India and Nepal*. Canberra: Australian National University Publications.

Altekar, A. S. (1956) *Position of Women in Hindu Civilization*. New Delhi: Motilal Banarsidass.

Apffel-Marglin, Frédérique (1984) "Types of Sexual Union and their Implicit Meanings." In John Hawley and Donna M. Wulff (eds) *The Divine Consort: Rādhā and the Goddesses of India*. Delhi: Motilal Banarsidass.

Bennett, Lynn (1983) *Dangerous Wives and Sacred Sisters: Social and Symbolic Roles of High-Caste Women in Nepal*. New York: Columbia University Press.

Gatwood, Lynn E. (1985) *Devī and the Spouse Goddess: Women, Sexuality, and Marriage in India*. Delhi: Manohar.

Ghadially, Rehana (ed.) (1988) *Women in Indian Society: A Reader*. New Delhi: Sage Publications.

Gold, Ann G., and Gloria G. Raheja (1994) *Listen to the Heron's Words: Reimagining Gender and Kinship in North India*. Berkeley, CA: University of California Press.

Harlan, Lindsey, and Paul B. Courtright (eds) (1995) *From the Margins of Hindu Marriage: Essays on Gender, Religion, and Culture*. New York: Oxford University Press.

Hawley, J. S. (ed.) (1994) *Satī, the Blessing and the Curse: The Burning of Wives in India*. New York: Oxford University Press.

Jacobson, Dorane, and Susan Wadley (eds) (1977) *Women in India: Two Perspectives*. Columbus, MO: South Asia Books.

Jamison, S. W. (1995) *Sacrificed Wife/Sacrificer's Wife: Women, Ritual, and Hospitality in Ancient India*. New York: Oxford University Press.

Kumar, Nita (ed.) (1994) *Women as Subjects: South Asian Histories*. Charlottesville, VA: University Press of Virginia.

Leslie, Julia (1989) *The Perfect Wife: The Orthodox Hindu Woman According to the Strīdharmapaddhati of Tryambakayajvan*. Delhi: Oxford University Press.

— (ed.) (1991) *Roles and Rituals for Hindu Women*. London: Pinter Publishers.

McDaniel, June (2003) *Making Virtuous Daughters and Wives: An Introduction to Women's Brata Rituals in Bengali Folk Religion*. Albany, NY: State University of New York Press.

Pearson, Anne M. (1996) *"Because It Gives Me Peace of Mind": Ritual Fasts in the Religious Lives of Hindu Women*. Albany, NY: State University of New York Press.

Uberoi, Patricia (ed.) (1993) *Family, Kinship and Marriage in India*. Delhi: Oxford University Press.

Wadley, Susan S. (ed.) (1976) *The Powers of Tamil Women*. Syracuse, NY: Syracuse University.

Weinberger-Thomas, C. (1999) *Ashes of Immortality: Widow-Burning in India*. J. Mehlman and D. G. White (trans.). Chicago, IL: University of Chicago Press.

5 *The Sanskrit language*

In this chapter

We here turn to the sacred language of Hinduism, Sanskrit, offering a brief survey of its origins before discussing the work of its most brilliant grammarian. The structure of the Sanskrit alphabet, along with further pronunciation guidelines, forms the foundation for a discussion of some Hindu linguistic theories. This provides a necessary framework for an exploration of the crucially important role that *mantra* plays in virtually all dimensions of Hindu practice.

Main topics covered

- Pāṇinī and the *Aṣṭādhyāyī*
- The *sphoṭa* theory of language
- Structure of the Sanskrit alphabet
- *Mantra* and the theology of sound

Imagine, if you will, the following scenario

You have arrived in Vārāṇasī (Banāras) to conduct research. A fellow scholar tells you about a learned man (*paṇḍita*) who is accepting students to study Sanskrit. You have already studied Sanskrit for several years with some of North America's best instructors, and have fared very well in their evaluations. However, your knowledge is a bit rusty. Although your field-research is primarily conducted in Hindi, the vernacular language of the city, you decide to approach the pundit for instruction. You bicycle to the Śivāla quarter of the city to his home, painted with a pale blue wash, and climb the stairs to the first floor. His son first greets and then directs you to the upper terrace, where the pundit is catching some of the cool evening breezes. The sun is low on the horizon, and the sky is alive with hawks, crows, high circling vultures, and paper kites.

He is a short, stocky man, bespectacled and balding, with graying hair and a warm smile. He is clothed in a *dhoti*, a finely woven white cotton garment which is wound around the waist and between the legs. His upper body is bare except for a loop of thread draped over a shoulder and across his torso. You introduce yourself and express the reason for your visit. "So you say you know some Sanskrit," he says, and instantly proceeds to speak to you in that language. You are somewhat dumbfounded. All your previous training has emphasized studying Sanskrit in its written form. Although your teachers had required you to read out aloud, and enunciate the sounds of the language, instruction was never approached in the oral style as one might, for instance, take up the study of Spanish before venturing on some travels in Guatemala. The Sanskrit that emanates from the pundit's mouth is at once familiar and alien. It sounds something like the Hindi that is spoken all around you in the city, and you are able to discern the sounds of some of the endings of verbal conjugations and noun declensions which you had spent years memorizing; but it is otherwise incomprehensible. You continue to stare at him in wide-eyed silence. In a sharp twist from his disarming greeting, he bluntly says, "You do not know Sanskrit. We will start at the very beginning, with a teaching system that I have developed. It is called the Yoga of Speech. Be here tomorrow at 7 a.m." He now appears strangely aloof and distant.

The next morning you arrive at the pundit's home and are directed to his library, where the classes are held. A student is already leaving the premises, having finished an earlier class. You remove your sandals at the door, and follow the behavior of the two or three other students, Westerners and Indians, who have arrived just before you. You learn that one of these students is an Indian Catholic priest who is interested in learning about Hindu religion and culture, and its ancient language. You respectfully touch the pundit's feet as you enter the room and seat yourself on a cushion on the cool marble floor. He is seated cross-legged upon a wooden bed, behind which is a chalkboard used for instruction. Built-in stone shelves along the walls of the library are crammed with his published books, notebooks, and stacks of yellowing papers. Large, framed lithographs of the elephant-headed god Gaṇeśa, the goddess Sarasvatī, four-armed and playing a musical instrument, and Śiva are hung high overhead. They are draped with garlands of fresh flowers. Guru-jī, as you begin to call the *paṇḍita*, is dressed in a similar garb as the previous evening, except that each of his upper arms is smeared with three stripes of paste, and his forehead is anointed with a yellow dot within which is placed a red dot. Instruction begins, and you soon discover that you indeed have much to learn in this milieu, not only about Sanskrit, but about the teacher–student relationship in the home of a Brahmin scholar where Sanskrit is one of the family's spoken languages.

Over the course of a year and a half, you find that Guru-jī is a man of enormous intellectual vigor. He bathes daily in the Gaṅgā River, which flows nearby, and performs rites of worship in his home before classes begin. He sleeps little, and mostly teaches and writes, by his admission, having authored or edited nearly a hundred books and articles. His students study a range of literature from the ancient Vedic hymn collections, treatises on grammar and philosophy, and the narratives of the Hindu Epics, to the devotional literature of the Purāṇas. "I decided to learn Russian so I could translate," he once said. "Have you actually translated anything into Russian?" you ask, somewhat impressed by his interests. "No. I like Tolstoy," he remarked. "I think that good literature should be available in all the great languages. So I decided to translate some portions of Tolstoy into Sanskrit." Your mind reels. While your attitude about Sanskrit has been to regard it as an ancient, near-dead language, Guru-jī's experience of it is quite the reverse. "My three sons do not know how to speak Sanskrit well," Guru-jī later confides to you. "They do not think it is necessary to learn it anymore." However, his granddaughter, a curious three-year-old, frequently wanders into the library and listens to his Sanskrit teachings. A decade and a half later you will see her grown into a vivacious young woman whose voice can move you to tears as she sings hymns of devotion in flawless Sanskrit.

The earliest evidence of writing on the Indian subcontinent is the Indus Valley Civilization script found on its unearthed seals. Unfortunately, the language has not been deciphered, but could quite likely be some form of early Dravidian. When the Indus Valley Civilization ended, for reasons yet unknown, writing seems to have also stopped. The last evidence of writing from those sites dates to about 1700 BCE, and puzzlingly, evidence of writing does not emerge until the fourth century BCE, possibly the result of Alexander the Great's invasion of the subcontinent. Researchers wonder why the tribes that formed from the dispersal of the Indus Valley Civilization did not take some forms of writing with them. It is conceivable that the Indus Valley script does not reflect a fully developed written language, but a sophisticated symbol system that was closely tied to an oral language, whose non-written character was culturally valued. However, it is equally unusual that the Āryan tribes that entered the subcontinent, according to the Āryan migration thesis, did not bring writing with them, for they would surely have been exposed to Sumerian cuneiform and other Mesopotamian scripts. And yet, without any apparent written language for over a thousand years, Indian civilizations produced some of the most complex linguistic systems, elaborate ritual procedures, and profound philosophical teachings. They maintained vast armies and managed large domains.

When Indian empires did resume the use of writing, they adopted forms of Aramaic script used by Alexander's Macedonian scribes. One of the earliest such scripts was Kharoṣṭhī, in which early Buddhist manuscripts from north-western India are written. The Brāhmī script developed from Kharoṣṭhī and spread widely since it was used by the Mauryan emperor Aśoka, whose inscribed edicts are found throughout his vast empire. By the twelfth century, Brāhmī had developed into

Devanāgarī ([Writing of the] Divine Abode), the script in which Sanskrit is still currently written. The scripts of many north Indian languages, such as Gujarati and Bengali, are related to the Devanāgarī script. Brāhmī script was also introduced to the South Indians, who adopted it for their Dravidian-based languages. Thus the host of South Indian Dravidian languages, such as Tamil and Telugu, and the North Indian Sanskritic languages, such as Hindi, all share Brāhmī as a common ancestral script, even though the Dravidian and Sanskritic languages themselves have different ancestral sources.

Despite the differences in North and South Indian languages, Sanskrit holds a privileged place in Hinduism, since one of its early forms, Vedic Sanskrit, or simply Vedic, is the language in which the Vedas are composed. Moreover, much of the finest and influential religious literature of Hinduism is composed in Sanskrit, which became a marker of the elite, educated upper classes. The English word "Sanskrit" derives from the Sanskrit word *saṃskṛta*, which means "refined" or "purified," and stands in contrast to all other languages which were regarded as *prākṛta* (Prākrits) or "unrefined/vulgar." The story of the development of Sanskrit on the Indian subcontinent involves its interactions with these other vernacular languages or Prākrits, such as Ardhamāgadhī and Pālī. Many of the early Buddhist and Jain scriptures are composed in Prākrits. Aśokan inscriptions in Brāhmī script are in Pālī and other Prākrit languages, suggesting that while Brahmin orthodoxy promoted the use of Sanskrit, Prākrit languages may have been more in use among the ruling and other classes.

Sanskrit belongs to the Indo-European family of languages, whose modern offspring include English, German, French, Spanish, Greek, Welsh, Russian, Farsi (Persian) and Hindi. Early Indologists postulated that Vedic Sanskrit might be the mother of all Indo-European languages, but it is now surmised by the majority of linguists that Vedic Sanskrit, along with ancient Iranian languages such as Avestan, probably had a hypothetical common ancestor, designated Proto Indo-Iranian. Vedic Sanskrit is among the oldest within the Indo-Iranian branch of Indo-European languages. The Indo-Iranian branch, along with other branches such as the Anatolian languages of the Hittites, are extrapolated back to a hypothetical common ancestor known as Proto Indo-European, which may have originated in Anatolia or in the steppes north of the Caucasus Mountains, somewhere between 7000 and 4000 BCE.

Vedic Sanskrit yielded to Classical Sanskrit, the language of the *Mahābhārata* and *Rāmāyaṇa*, and the literary works of Kalidāsa and Bāna, when grammarians such as Pāṇinī codified and composed structural rules that kept the written language from rapid mutation. Classical Sanskrit began to diminish in use as a spoken language from the first century CE, and experienced a rapid decline after the fifth century CE, when Apabrahmśa languages, precursors to the modern vernaculars such as Hindi began to grow dominant. Sanskrit prayers are still recited during religious rituals, and some Hindus continue to compose literature, classical vocals, and even produce television shows in the language. Sanskrit is designated as one of the eighteen official languages of India, and is often offered as a course in public secondary schools in India. While less than seven thousand identified it as their first language in India's 1981 census, and fewer than two hundred thousand claimed it as a second language in the 1960s, through efforts to sustain the language and promote its use, some sources claim that about four million people are now able to speak Sanskrit.

Pāṇinī and the Aṣṭādhyāyī

Pāṇinī, who composed his extraordinarily sophisticated work of grammar known as the *Aṣṭādhyāyī* (*Eight Chapters*), is reputed to have lived in north-west India sometime between the seventh and third centuries BCE. His references to Vedic Sanskrit suggest that spoken forms of it were already in decline. Pāṇinī mentions other grammarians before him; however their works do not survive, making the *Aṣṭādhyāyī* the oldest extant Sanskrit grammar. It is actually one of the oldest works of linguistics and is of such remarkable elegance that it has not been surpassed. In fewer than 4000 *sūtras* (aphoristic verses) Pāṇinī lays down the entire structure of the grammar of Sanskrit, a language to whose grace and complexity its students repeatedly, even tearfully, testify. Pāṇinī's morphology, that is, his explanation of the forms of Sanskrit words, virtually unchanged since its composition, constitutes the basis of classical Sanskrit down to the present day. Building from about 800 verbal roots, together with various affixes (prefixes, infixes, suffixes, and so on) applied in accord with its system of rules, the morphology is able to generate all of its words. In recognition of this extraordinary achievement, and in keeping with the ancient tradition that acknowledges the sacred structure of grammar (*vyakāraṇa*), which is a Vedāṅga, or disciplinary appendage of Vedic knowledge, when explaining concepts, such as *karma* or *dharma*, teachers often begin by pointing out the verbal root, such as "*kṛ*" or "*dhṛ*" from which the word develops. Some have seen similarities between Pāṇinī's treatise and highly sophisticated computer programming languages. It is all the more remarkable that he might have produced this monument of erudition without the use of writing.

The sphoṭa *theory of language*

The grammarian Patañjali (second–first century BCE) sometimes identified with the author of the *Yoga Sūtra*, who was likely a different person, wrote the *Mahābhāṣya*, a commentary (*bhāṣya*) on Pāṇinī's work. Patañjali is credited with presenting a substantive introduction to the *sphoṭa* theory of language. *Sphoṭa* means "bursting forth" and refers to how meaning is conveyed through sound. Although sounds in language may vary with regional accents, or even in the speed with which they are

Structure of the Sanskrit alphabet

Sanskrit is made up of 49 phonemes. The vowels, that is, sounds that can be voiced on their own, are: a (as in hut), ā (as in father), i (as in tin), ī (as in seen), u (as in put), ū (as in loot), ṛ (as in riff), and ḷ (as in sickle). There are also long forms of ṛ and ḷ. The diphthongs, that is, combined vowel sounds, are: e (as in play), ai (as in smile), o (as in home), and au (as in town). Sanskrit consonants are arranged in groups according to where they are produced, beginning from the throat and moving forward towards the lips. The Gutturals, produced in the throat, are k, kh, g, gh, and ṅ. The first (k) is a hard guttural. The second (kh) is aspirated, because it pushes out air as it is sounded. The third (g) is a softened guttural. The fourth (gh) is soft and aspirated. And the fifth (ṅ) is a nasal guttural that sounds like the ng in rung. This pattern is followed for the subsequent groups. The Palatals are produced at the rear of the mouth, by the palate. They are c (pronounced like the ch in chip), ch (aspirated), j, jh, and ñ (pronounced as ny in canyon). The Retroflex consonants are produced by curling the tongue to touch the roof of the mouth. These are ṭ, ṭh, ḍ, ḍh, and the nasal, ṇ. The Dentals are produced by having the tongue touch the back of the teeth. These are t, th, d, dh, and n. The Labials are sounded with the lips. These are p, ph (as the p-h in cup-handle), b, bh, and the dental nasal, m. There are four semi-vowels: y, r, l, and v. There are also three sibilants: ś, pronounced like sh in shoe, ṣ which sounds similar to ś but that is a retroflex produced by placing the tongue at the roof of the mouth, and s. Finally there is a voiced aspirate, h, an unvoiced aspirate, ḥ, known as the *visarga*, which echoes the preceding vowel, and ṃ, known as the *anusvāra*, which nasalizes the preceding vowel.

voiced, to those who know the language, meaning is still transmitted. So *sphoṭa* is the invisible and inaudible vehicle through which meaning bursts forth the instant a word is voiced and heard by a listener.

Bhartṛhari (c. fifth century CE), another Sanskrit grammarian, also known for his poetry, elaborates extensively on the *sphoṭa* theory in his *Vākyapadīya* (*On Sentence and Word*). He bases his ideas on the Vedic concept of the unitary Brahman, which undergoes differentiation. *Sphoṭa* first arises in the mind of the speaker, who conveys it through words (*pada*) or sentences (*vākya*). The instant those auditory vibrations are adequately received by the listener, the meaning bursts or shines forth in the mind of the listener. Thus the speaker who wishes to convey something is first gripped by an impulse to express. The idea he or she wishes to express is the *sphoṭa*, which is already a movement away from the primary unity of the Absolute. This movement consists of both the particular meaning to be expressed, and the specific sounds and words that will be used to convey that meaning. *Sphoṭa* is both components of this movement. The sounds in a particular word, or the words in a particular sentence, which are uttered, convey *sphoṭa,* but meaning intuitively bursts forth to the listener, apart from the separate and sequential bits of the sounds. These sounds may be examined by the listener after the meaning has been attained. So, in essence, there is a unitary whole that is perceived, as in viewing a painting, apart from its individual colors and brushstrokes. However, the sounds are necessary components of the movement of *sphoṭa,* which does not stand apart from them. Meditation on the sounds may also allow meaning to blossom. Sacred utterances, such as *mantras,* when repeated, may thus serve as auditory vehicles through which their profound meanings may be revealed.

Mantra *and the theology of sound*

Novice students to Hinduism might wonder why one should attend to the structure of the Sanskrit language. Not only is Sanskrit the language of much of Hindu sacred literature, but its sounds also play important roles in Hindu philosophy and ritual. The Sanskrit alphabet, as well as the language, is regarded as sacred. The sacred utterance, *Aum* or *Om,* is said to be Brahman as sound. In the terminology of the *sphoṭa* theory described above, meditatively voicing or hearing the sound *Aum* could actually reveal the nature of Brahman. Thus, the entire Sanskrit syllabary is said to derive from *Aum,* which is the beginning and end of all speech. Hindu religious teachers sometimes point out that *Aum* is formed by the opening and closing of the mouth, beginning with the first vowel, a, and ending with the final *anusvāra,* ṃ. Thus all vowels and consonants are contained within it. *Aum* is not merely a symbol of Brahman, but is often regarded as Brahman itself, manifest in the form of sound. In the *Yoga Sūtra, Aum* encapsulates Īśvara, the Lord of Yoga, and sustained contemplation on *Aum,* known as the *pranava* (vibratory hum), will reveal its meaning by purifying consciousness of its defilements.

In some Hindu formulations, the Absolute Unity, Brahman, is conceived of as composed of two complementary polarities called Śiva and Śakti, the quiescent male and active female principles. The vowels of the Sanskrit alphabet, self-empowered since they can be sounded on their own, are said to be Śakti. Consonants, however, as the term suggests, need to be empowered by vowels, "sounded in concert" with them, and thus are likened to the male Śiva principle. Through their union, language is generated.

Mantras (thought instruments) are utterances believed to derive from the single source, the Absolute Brahman. Just as the single syllable, *Aum,* is regarded as encapsulating all of the Vedas and thus all sacred knowledge, so every Vedic syllable is an elaboration upon or expansion on *Aum*. Every Vedic sound and verse is thus a *mantra*, an instrument through which Brahman sacrificially differentiates itself, and the instrument, through whose contemplation the multiplicity may be sacrificially reintegrated. A *mantra* is primarily a mental vibration, a thought (*man*), intuitively perceived by *ṛṣis* (the seers), and closest to the undifferentiated Source when it is not uttered, yet a powerful instrument of differentiated manifestation as it takes on progressively grosser forms (as audible sound) and more complex articulations (as lengthy prayers and other formulations), which constitute the divinely heard *śrūti*. Words are thoughts made apprehensible to the other senses. Therefore in Vedic philosophy, through *mantra* the world is made manifest, and through *mantra* the world is reabsorbed. Thus *mantras* play a central role in virtually all features of Hindu ritual activity. They may be used to invoke the presence of a specific deity, to worship that deity, and finally to dismiss it. And they may also be used as contemplative aids in internal embodied yogic sacrificial rituals aimed at liberation.

The *Maitrī Upaniṣad* (6.22) states that Brahman should be meditated upon as both sound (*Aum*) and non-sound, but only through the former is the latter revealed. However, the sound that is Brahman is also characterized in other ways than *Aum*. Like the sound of the space within the heart when the ears are closed with the thumbs, it is also compared to the sound of a river, a bell, rain, and speech in stillness. By moving beyond these forms of "Brahman as sound" one merges into Brahman beyond sound. In the Mīmāṃsā school of philosophy, Vedic mantric sounds are not arbitrary and idiosyncratic signifiers chosen to convey meaning (the signified). They are the sonic manifestations of the intrinsic features of Ultimate Reality as it is differentiated. They have been discerned or "seen" by the *ṛṣis*, or been intuitively heard, and then uttered as Veda. Thus every sound in the Veda, every verse, is an actual vibratory manifestation of the thing signified. There is no deity different from the Vedic *mantra* that sounds out its name, for the sounded name is merely a grosser vibratory manifestation of its nature. Extrapolating this thinking, all mantric sounds, intuitively derived from Vedic Sanskrit, are both signifiers and the signified. The word *is* the thing, at least in some degree of that thing's intrinsic expression.

Discussion questions

1. Do you think Hindu notions of purity and impurity enter into the realm of Indian language?
2. Sanskrit language is created through the union of consonants and vowels, likened to the union of Śiva and Śakti. What do you think this says about the Sanskrit language?
3. Explain the concept of *sphoṭa* and how it relates to *mantra*.
4. What is *Aum* or *Om*, and why is it so important to the Sanskrit language?

Key points in this chapter

- The earliest evidence of writing on the Indian subcontinent is the Indus Valley script.
- When the Indus Valley Civilization ended, writing appears to have stopped, and emerged again in the fourth century BCE.
- Devanāgarī is the script in which Sanskrit is most commonly currently written.
- Sanskrit, which belongs to the Indo-European family of languages, is revered in Hinduism, since Vedic Sanskrit was used to compose the Vedas.
- Pāṇinī composed the *Aṣṭādhyāyī* (*Eight Chapters*), the oldest extant Sanskrit grammar.
- *Sphoṭa* means "bursting forth" and refers to how meaning is conveyed through sound.
- The Sanskrit alphabet, as well as the language, is regarded as sacred.
- Since every Vedic syllable is an expansion on *Aum*, every Vedic sound is a *mantra*.
- In Vedic philosophy, the world is both made manifest and reabsorbed through *mantra*.
- According to Mīmāṃsā philosophy, every Vedic sound is a vibratory manifestation of the thing signified.

5. Philosophically, what role does Brahman play in relation to the Sanskrit language?

Further reading

On Sanskrit language and grammar

Coulson, Michael (1976) *Sanskrit: An Introduction to the Classical Language* (Teach Yourself Books). New York: David McKay Company, Inc.

Goldman, Robert P. and Sally J. Sutherland (1980) *Devavāṇīpraveśikā: An Introduction to the Sanskrit Language*. Berkeley, CA: University of California Press.

Lanman, Charles (1971) *A Sanskrit Reader: Text and Vocabulary and Notes.* Cambridge, MA: Harvard University Press.

Perry, Edward (1936) *A Sanskrit Primer.* Reprint. Delhi: Motilal Banarsidass, 1986.
Whitney, William Dwight (1889) *Sanskrit Grammar: Including both the Classical Language, and the Older Dialects, of Veda and Brahmana.* Reprint. Cambridge, MA: Harvard University Press, 1981.

Sanskrit dictionaries

Apte, V. S. (2004) *The Practical Sanskrit–English Dictionary: Containing Appendices on Sanskrit Prosody and Important Literary and Geographical Names of Ancient India.* Reprint. Delhi: Motilal Banarasidass.
Monier-Williams, Sir Monier (1899). *A Sanskrit–English Dictionary: Etymologically and Philologically Arranged with Speical Reference to Cognate Indo-European Languages.* Oxford: Clarendon Press.

On mantras, sonic theology and language

Alper, Harvey P. (1989) *Understanding Mantras.* Albany, New York: State University of New York Press.
Beck, Guy L. (1993) *Sonic Theology: Hinduism and Sacred Sound.* Columbia, SC: University of South Carolina Press.
Coward, Harold G. (1976) *Bhartṛhari.* Boston, MA: Twayne Publishers.
— (1986) *The Sphoṭa Theory of Language.* Delhi: Motilal Banarsidass.
Coward, H. G., and K. K. Raja (1990) *The Philosophy of the Grammarians.* Princeton, NJ: Princeton University Press.
Gonda, Jan (1963) "The Indian Mantra." *Oriens* 16: pp. 244–97.
Killingly, D. (1987) "Om: The sacred syllable in the Veda." In Julius Lipner (ed.) *A Net Cast Wide.* Newcastle upon Tyne: Grevatt and Grevatt, pp. 14–31.
Matilal, B. K. (1990) *The Word and the World: India's Contribution to the Study of Language.* Delhi: Oxford University Press.
Padoux, A. (1990) *Vāc: The Concept of the Word in Seleced Hindu Tantras.* Albany, NY: State University of New York Press.
Renfrew, Colin (1987) *Archaeology and Language: The Puzzle of Indo-European Origins.* London: Jonathan Cape.
Sastri, G. (1981) *A Study in the Dialectics of Sphoṭa.* Delhi: Motilal Banarsidass.
Staal, F. (ed.) (1973) *A Reader on the Sanskrit Grammarians.* Cambridge, MA: Massachusetts Institute of Technology Press.
Vasu, Sirisa Candra (ed. and trans.) *Pāṇini's Aṣṭādhyāyī*, 2 vols. Reprint. Delhi: Motilal Banarsidass.

6 *Indian philosophical schools*

In this chapter

We now turn our attention to the rise of philosophical systems that had emerged during the Upaniṣadic period. Orthodoxy began to classify the most vibrant of these, broadly dividing them into those that could be included within its parameters and those that could not. The latter, heterodox, category included Buddhism and Jainism, while the former included Sāṅkhya and Yoga. We briefly examine the salient elements of some of the major heterodox philosophical systems, before turning to more detailed examinations of the orthodox ones. Sāṅkhya and Yoga are discussed most thoroughly with special attention to Patañjali's *Yoga Sūtra* and its teachings. A separate chapter is dedicated to Vedānta philosophy and its schools.

Main topics covered

- The wandering philosophers
- Orthodox versus heterodox systems
- The heterodox philosophies
- The six orthodox systems

Imagine, if you will, this scenario

You travel through the "valley of the gods" in a local bus jammed with chickens and goats, baskets of fruit and vegetables, and an assortment of people from the towns along the way. Arriving in Manali in the Himalayan foothills, you seek out accommodation among the residents, and soon find yourself staying on the ground floor of a home in a forested hillside, where the room next door houses the family's buffalo. The scenery around you is bucolic. Meandering trails lead to wood and stone bridges spanning gurgling streams, and through welcoming forests to villages where groups of children play while their parents attend to harvest tasks or gathering firewood. Time itself appears to move at a slower speed here. As you inhale the crisp, cool air, with its scent of pine needles and the comforting odor of fireplace smoke, you repeatedly remind yourself that this alpine terrain is still India, so different from its more commonly encountered dry jungles, deserts, tropical forests, or bustling cities.

One day during your stay here you walk for a few hours to a larger village, located midway up the opposite hillside. You notice a few Westerners there, some of whom are wanderers like you, while others, drawn by the valley's natural beauty, have become longer term residents. Hearing of a temple built on the site of nearby hot springs, and dedicated to a renowned sage after whom the village is named, you make your way there. The temple looks ancient, with eroded wood and stone carvings. The pools of hot water there, although not particularly inviting at first glimpse, do provide an invigorating soak. There is virtually nobody around. As you dry off in the afternoon sun, you notice that there are two men in neighboring sections of the pilgrims' rest-quarters (*dharmaśālā*). They appear to be *sādhus*, holy men who have renounced the world. You have seen such people throughout your travels in India and, despite their often frightening yet intriguing appearance, have developed the courage to converse with them. You make eye contact with the first of the men, who smiles and beckons you to join him.

"Namaste Baba," you say in polite greeting. Baba knows only a few words of English, some Hindi, and you cannot decipher the language he normally speaks. He motions you to sit beside him. Seated on a simple grass mat, Baba appears to have few possessions. He owns a rustic staff, a few items bundled in a cloth, and a brownish-yellow bowl fashioned of some unknown material, perhaps bone, which appears to be well used. Opening a simple tin box, he extracts a silver rod, about as long as a knitting needle, but somewhat thinner, one end of which is beaten into the shape of a cobra's flared hood. Baba breaks off a lump of blackish brown substance, also stored in a smaller container within his box, and skewers the lump on the needle. "*Charas*," he says, which is the term for hashish, and you nod knowingly. In a mixture of sign language, gesturing to the mountains, and with broken bits of English and Hindi, he conveys to you that he has collected this substance from plants in these neighboring mountains, and you begin to realize that the ensuing ritual is altogether different in tone, attitude, and purpose from what you have observed with your friends of college-day escapades at "getting high." There is an aura of profound sanctity that accompanies every aspect of Baba's actions.

He strikes a wooden match, applies the flames to the *charas*, crumbles it into tiny pieces and mixes it with tobacco. He stuffs it into a chillum, a simple tube of clay, wide at one end and narrower at the other. A fluted stone placed midway in the chillum creates an upper bowl, and prevents the *charas* mixture from falling through the tube, while allowing smoke to flow through. Baba dampens a small rag with water from the sacred springs collected in his bone bowl, and places it around the narrow base of the chillum. He grips the chillum with both hands in a manner that creates a funnel allowing him to draw air through it without his lips touching its surface. He motions you to strike a few matches simultaneously, while he raises the pipe to his forehead and calls out in reverence, "Śiva! Śankara! Śambhu! Baba Bholanātha!" and other phrases you cannot understand. You hold the flames to the mixture in the bowl, and then, by taking a number of deep, but rapid tugs on the pipe, Baba sets it ablaze. You are amazed at the volume of smoke that Baba expels from his lungs, as he passes you the pipe to share in this sacred rite of worship.

Your body first responds to the effect of the smoke with a sort of quickening, and you feel a "rush" of energy within your consciousness. Shortly thereafter, reappraising your surroundings in your newly altered state of perception, you feel a strong sense of presence and an unusual bond with Baba, whose smiling eyes seem to suggest that he knows exactly what you are experiencing. "Is it not extraordinary to experience this world with one's senses renewed?" he seems to say. You now notice that his chillum is extremely simple, an unadorned black cone, and learn that he has made it himself, from clay gathered by some apparently renowned river bank.

After sitting in silent contemplation for a time, you think that you would like to preserve a memory of this moment. With some embarrassment, motioning to your camera, you ask Baba if you might take his photograph. Baba bursts out into laughter. "Ha, ha. Many many people take Baba-ji's picture. Switzerland, Germany, America," he says. "Wait, wait," he motions for you to hold off from snapping the shot, as he prepares himself. Removing the tattered blackish-red robe that he has been wearing, and loosening the bundle of his hair that was wound into a top-knot, he reveals a body that is lean, muscular, and extremely dark. You wonder if he is South Indian. And then, taking the needle that he had used to prepare the *charas*, he bends forward, and skewers it through his tongue, as you gaze in wide-eyed surprise. He assumes the full-lotus yogic position; his hands adopt a special gesture by his knees, and his long black hair falls in snarled dreadlocks over his shoulders. With the silver needle through his pink outstretched tongue, visible in sharp relief pressed against his lips, dark face, and beard, he lisps these words: "Now take Baba's picture!" He looks like an iconic martyred saint, unforgettable, as you frame and snap the photo, somewhat disappointed by his vanity, yet thoroughly pleased at the image you have captured. "This one I'll blow up and frame one day," you think to yourself. Baba removes the needle, applies ashes from the pipe to his tongue, which shows little sign of blood, collects his belongings, smilingly nods farewell, and departs into the mountains.

After some time spent wandering around the temple courtyard, as you begin to depart, you pass the roofed enclosure where the other renouncer is staying. Emboldened by your previous encounter, you decide to approach him to say hello. "Namaste Baba." "Namaste," he replies, also with a warm and serene smile, and then continues, "It's lovely here, isn't it?" in perfect English. Your surprise leads you to look at him more closely, and you notice how much he differs from the *sādhu* with whom you had just shared the pipe. This Baba's skin is light brown. He wears a white garment draped around his waist and, although he has a shawl draped around his neck, you note that his torso is toned and muscular. His long white hair and beard give him a dignity of appearance that resembles a cross between Walt Whitman and Tagore. Quite significantly, among his possessions he has thick books.

"Yes, it's very beautiful," you agree. "And so peaceful." As the conversation unfolds, you realize that like you, he too is a wanderer, although not quite like your cohort of Western travelers. "There are a lot of Tibetans in Kullu and here too," he remarks. "Yes," you agree, but in that innocent exchange, you have an instant insight. You realize that your observation was a response affirming a piece of information that you had read about. As the bus passed through Kullu, you noticed the many Tibetans that your guidebook had mentioned resided there. Baba's observations seemed to derive directly from his perceptions of the world. "How did you get here?" you ask. "Oh, I walked," he replies. "From where?" you inquire. "South India," he replies. "I've been wandering throughout the country." Having yourself traveled here from South India, albeit by bus and train, you are duly impressed by his long pilgrimage on foot.

But Baba continues to astonish you with each of his ensuing sentences. "I left home when I was seventeen to find God. Now, I am fifty-five." You think that fifty-five is really quite old, and are impressed by the *sādhu's* physical, mental, and emotional state. He seems strong, alert, and with such an intelligent bearing about him. Reflecting on the appearance of so many of the adults in your homeland, whose obese bodies house hearts and minds that are equally burdened with the stresses of city life, you think, "I would be quite content to be like him when I am fifty-five." As a low-budget traveler, who dispenses money with a careful discipline that would even make a renouncer envious, you are particularly interested in how this Baba survives. You have encountered travelers who have been "on the road" for years. In fact, after years of travel, you yourself are now one of them, no longer "on a trip" with the intention of returning home, but interested in being "at home in the world," wherever you happen to be. "You mean you have been wandering around India for almost forty years! What do you do for money? How do you survive?"

"God provides everything," he answers, so matter-of-factly that it takes you by surprise. "Do not think for a minute that your survival depends entirely on your own actions. It is mostly in God's hands. Do any other living things, plants or animals, worry about the future? And yet they survive. Point yourself in the direction of your desires and leave the rest to God. Whatever is God's will for you – that will unfold. Eventually, you will not know the difference between your will and God's!" While you have encountered innumerable touts and hustlers in your travels who have always wanted something from you, this Baba seems disinterested in "selling" you anything. He appears to speak from his experience of the world, only sharing his understanding with honesty in response to your questions. You leave the temple and village wondering if it is really possible to live in this world with such trust in a divine providence and without a safety net.

Nearly two years later, upon developing the film from your travels, you discover to your dismay that of the hundreds of photographs you have taken, only one roll is damaged. It appears to be overexposed, perhaps because of excessive X-raying by airport security machines. While you can clearly discern the content of all the mostly ruined, overexposed photographs on that roll, it is only the image of the chillum Baba that is an utterly obliterated blaze of light. In years to come, when you tell this story to your Hindu friends, they nod knowingly. "This is a very common experience in India," many say. "It is a demonstration of yogic power." Some suggest that you had encountered a *siddha*, a great yogic adept, or Babajī, a mythic master who appears periodically in the Himalayas, or even Śiva himself.

The wandering philosophers

By the sixth century BCE historians note the rise of philosophical movements that challenged the values upheld by Brahmin orthodoxy, values that were grounded on maintaining the cosmic order through the regular performance of sacrificial rites, and held the Vedas to be divinely revealed teachings of unquestionable authority. The impetus for these dissenting philosophies was likely aided by changes in the socio-economic conditions of the period, which was marked by a growth in new urban centers along the Gaṅgā River valley. Expanding trade and the urban social interactions between groups of people who had formerly lived in rural and more isolated intellectual environments catalyzed a free-spirited attitude of exploration and inquiry. Wandering ascetic philosophers, or *śramaṇas*, took up itinerant lifestyles often characterized by a rejection of the direction in which social life was then heading. For instance, they questioned the pre-eminent status granted to Brahmins based solely on birth, and had misgivings about the performance of animal sacrifices, not to mention the growing costs of staging large-scale rites. There is evidence that various types of ascetics, often naked or clad in rags, and typically portrayed as having wild, disheveled hair, were even around from the time of the composition of the Vedic Saṃhitās. They were also often associated with mortification of the body, the consumption of consciousness-altering substances, and were believed to possess supernormal powers. Although some were solitary mendicants, others belonged to sectarian groups dedicated to Śiva or other deities. The roots of Tantra also lie in the religious beliefs and practices of these figures.

Orthodox versus heterodox schools

Dharma Śāstra texts composed many centuries after the rise of the *śramaṇa* movements attempt to prescribe the forms that renunciation should take, attempting to bring it under the purview of Brahminic traditions, but it seems that the earliest configurations of these renouncers and their religious ideas had not posed a substantial challenge to orthodoxy. However, by 600 BCE certain influential *śramaṇas* had begun to gather disciples, organize themselves with their own codes of conduct, and voice concerted challenges to orthodox teachings. They attracted support from rulers and wealthy patrons. They especially gained membership from the *kṣatriya* and *vaiśya varṇas,* since people in both these classes probably felt disenfranchised from power and spiritual status by the priestly class. In time, Hindu orthodoxy began to define itself in distinction to certain groups, which they labeled as heterodox (*nāstika*). Although the actual implications of some *śramaṇa* philosophies are quite inconsistent with the values of orthodoxy, these were still classified as orthodox (*āstika*) if they did not overtly dispute that the revelatory status of the Vedas was unimpeachable, or that the configuration of the *varṇa* system was sacrosanct. The term *darśana,* which means "viewpoint" or "perspective," is used to designate these religio-philosophical systems, which are neither exclusively religions nor philosophies by western standards of classification.

Although there were undoubtedly numerous heterodox *darśanas,* Jainism, Buddhism, and the Cārvāka philosophies are normally listed in this category. Buddhism and Jainism developed into distinct religions that still endure to the present day. There are six conventionally listed orthodox *darśanas,* often grouped in pairs because of certain intrinsic relationships. These are Sāṅkhya and Yoga, which share a common metaphysics in their earliest writings, Nyāya and Vaiśeṣika, which deal with logic and proto-science, and Mīmāṃsā and Vedānta, which are based on interpretation of Vedic *śrūti* literature. It is worth noting that the orthodox classification is not a comprehensive categorization of the full sweep of religious activity on the subcontinent. Many *śramaṇa* philosophies are not included. For instance, the Ājīvikas are an example of a once vigorous *śramaṇa* movement, which, although it no longer survives, could also be classified as heterodox. In addition, there was a wide assortment of regional, tribal, and popular religious practices. In the emerging Buddhist and Jain literature, for example, we learn about the existence of Nāga (snake) and Yakṣa (nature spirits) cults, whose centers of worship focused on their abodes in sacred trees, lakes, rocks, and other natural settings.

The heterodox philosophies

Jainism

Scholars attribute the foundation of Jainism to Vardhamāna Mahāvīra, a prince from a north Indian kingdom. However, Jains regard Mahāvīra as the twenty-fourth in a lineage of teachers known as Tīrthāṅkaras (Ford Makers). Mahāvīra reputedly took up renunciation with intense ardor and reached the highest state of realization, known to Jains as *nirvāṇa*. Thus he was known as the Jina (Conqueror), and his followers are Jainas (or Jains). He is believed to have lived sometime between 599 BCE and 467 BCE. The Jains were likely the founders of the first organized monastic system for renouncers. They began to gain royal patronage in the centuries that followed, and their communities spread to South India. Mahāvīra and his followers espoused nudity for all renouncers, since clothing was a sign of vanity, shame, or material attachments. A branch which developed later, and whose membership now far outnumbers the naked sect, promotes the wearing of a simple white garment. Since there is no missionary imperative in Jainism, their growth has been relatively slow, and they number about four million in India today.

Jainism is characterized by its strong emphasis on non-violence, and has influenced Hindu moral values in this area. Jains even take special care to avoid the accidental killing of small creatures. Renouncers may wear masks so that small insects are not inhaled, and may sweep the ground in front of them to reduce the likelihood of stepping on insects. Jains believe that each being possesses an eternal, omniscient soul (*jīva*), whose immaculate qualities are obscured by the effects of *karma*. *Karma* is not merely a moral principle of cause and effect, but a fine material substance that adheres to the *jīva*, impairing it. Since *karma* handicaps the *jīva*, Jains do not promote any doctrine purporting to be the absolute truth, for knowledge can only be partial and subject to uncertainty. Virtually any action sows karmic seeds, whose effects may only be nullified through the inner heat generated by asceticism. Thus one of the highest practices in Jainism is a religious death brought about by remaining motionless, without food or drink, until all *karma* is destroyed and the body perishes, liberating the *jīva*.

Buddhism

Buddhism begins with the teachings of Siddhārtha Gautama, a prince from the Śakya kingdom in the Himalayan foothills of modern Nepal who lived a century or more prior to the reign (c. 265–238 BCE) of the Mauryan emperor Aśoka. Claiming to have attained the highest state of realization, known as *nirvāṇa*, Gautama was called the Buddha (The Awakened). The Buddha began to teach and gather disciples in the region of Magadha around the city of Banāras. He formed a monastic organization of renouncers who wished to follow his teachings with intensity, and they received some land grants and support from local kings and wealthy merchants. This paved the way in subsequent centuries for the development of Buddhist monasteries, permanent residences for the once wandering renouncers. When the emperor Aśoka converted to Buddhism he promoted it throughout his vast empire and sent missionaries to neighboring lands, such as modern day Sri Lanka and Burma/Myanmar. After the collapse of the Mauryan Empire, Hindu orthodoxy experienced a revival under the support of different dynasties, although by then it too had undergone a transformation through the rise of cults dedicated to the worship of Śiva, Viṣṇu and Devī. By the sixteenth century CE Buddhism had virtually disappeared from India. It began a revival in India in the early twentieth century through the archeological discoveries of ancient Buddhist sites. It has continued to grow through the mass conversion of hundreds of thousands of Untouchables to Buddhism under the influence of B. R. Ambedkar, and the exile of the Buddhist leader, the fourteenth Dalai Lama, from Tibet into India.

Buddhism differed from orthodox Hinduism in a variety of ways. It encouraged renunciation, which poached at the householder support base of sacrificial ritual. It accepted members of all *varṇas* into its fold, including Untouchables, and even permitted women to take up formal renunciation as nuns. It taught that a true "Brahmin" was not necessarily one who was born into a Brahmin *varṇa*, nor one who appeared to have the outward look of a matted-haired *śramaṇa*, but one whose life-style embraced a rigorous dispassion, and whose understanding displayed penetrating wisdom. It did not support unquestioning faith in any scripture. Furthermore, Buddhism also promulgated the Anātman doctrine, which held that there was no convincing ground on which to base a belief in an eternal, unchanging Absolute Self or Reality, such as Brahman or Ātman.

Cārvāka

The Cārvāka (Sweet-Voiced) philosophy is also known as the Lokāyata or the Way of the Masses. Its earliest extant systematic writings are only a few centuries old, but its ideas may be inferred through criticisms voiced by rival *śramaṇa* philosophies. The Cārvāka promotes a materialistic outlook on life, rejecting a belief in *karma*, reincarnation, deities, or any permanent soul that endures into some form of after-life. The nature of the self is precisely as one is currently experiencing it, and the reasonable goal of existence is to maximize happiness and minimize sorrow. Its critics portray it as an outlook that is narrowly focused, providing little if any larger meaning to human existence, and conducive to an exploitative hedonism. In turn, the Cārvāka dishes out substantial criticisms of the religious exploitation perpetrated by self-serving priests and the needless mortification endured by muddled-brained renouncers. The Cārvāka promotes a life-style grounded in a discerning, aesthetic engagement with the best this life has to offer. In compelling ways, the orthodox Hindu goals of *kāma* and *artha* acknowledge these dimensions of Cārvāka values. However, orthodoxy weaves them into a grander scheme that provides a place for dharmic concerns sustained through the actions of priestly functionaries and for *mokṣa* that may be attained through renunciation.

The six orthodox systems

Sāṅkhya

The word *sāṅkhya* may be translated as "calculation" or "enumeration" and refers to the philosophy's attempt to list the various components that make up reality. It also refers to the tradition of writing commentaries on its foundational treatises. Sāṅkhya is one of the oldest systematic *darśanas,* whose origins are attributed to the semi-legendary sage Kapila. We find references to Sāṅkhya-like terms in the Epics, particularly in the *Bhagavad Gītā,* in the Upaniṣads, and even in Buddhist and Jain writings. A crucial point of departure for Sāṅkhya's philosophical speculations, as for many of the *śramaṇa darśanas,* was to understand the cause of and solution to suffering (*duḥkha*). Īśvarakṛṣṇa's *Sāṅkhya Kārikā,* composed in about 400 CE, is the earliest extant systematic treatment of the philosophy. However, it is certain that Sāṅkhya had a well-developed structure much earlier. For instance, Patañjali's *Yoga Sūtra,* often dated at about 200 CE is grounded in a coherent Sāṅkhya metaphysics.

Sāṅkhya is a dualistic philosophy, positing that reality is composed of two types of entities. The first is Puruṣa, which may be understood as pure, or supreme consciousness, or as the true Self, and the second is Prakṛti, often translated as nature or materiality. Both are real, but transcendent, in that they are not readily apprehensible to the senses. Prakṛti is composed of three qualities, or *guṇas.* These are the *sattva guṇa* of luminosity, clarity, or purity, the *rajas guṇa* of passion and activity, and the *tamas guṇa* of inertia, dullness, or opacity. Puruṣa, or supreme consciousness, is the impassive observer of all phenomena. Prakṛti, however, in response to Puruṣa's presence, has its *guṇas* thrown out of equilibrium. It moves from transcendence to immanence and undergoes a series of transformations through which the multiform world comes into being. Sāṅkhya then enumerates twenty-three *tattvas,* components or elements of Prakṛti's evolutionary manifestation, from *buddhi,* the most subtle element, to the *mahābhūtas,* the grossest elements. Every *tattva* contains the three *guṇas,* but in various proportions. The *guṇa* concept is still pervasive in many aspects of Hinduism beyond the Sāṅkhya system. For instance, pure foods such as ghee may be classified as *sattvic,* while stimulating foods such as alcohol might be regarded as *rajasic,* and disagreeable or ritually polluting foods, such as rotting flesh, are *tamasic.*

There are five *mahābhūtas* (gross elements), which are earth, water, air, fire, and ether/space. It is useful to imagine these as aspects of solidity, liquidity, gaseousness, energetic interactions, and inter-material dimensionality. The *tamas guṇa* is at its highest proportion in these elements. Progressively less gross are the five subtle elements, namely, odor, flavor, shape/color, texture, and sound, which mediate between the gross elements and the five senses or organs of knowledge. These senses are: smelling, tasting, seeing, touching, and hearing. Less dense than the senses, but grosser than the subtle elements, are the action senses, which are: reproduction, excretion, locomotion, appropriation, and communication.

Even more subtle than these twenty *tattvas* are three elements that constitute mind or thought and are collectively called *citta*. They may also be thought of as material consciousness in contrast to Puruṣa, which is supreme consciousness. Most dense among the interior *tattvas* is *manas*, the heart-mind, which refers to the faculties of thinking and feeling, and the inner sense organ that makes us aware of these interior processes. Still more subtle is *ahaṅkara*, the I-maker, or ego, an element that generates the sense of self. The *ahaṅkara* generally identifies self, the "I" or the "me," with an assemblage of constituents drawn from the grosser *tattvas*. Thus we think of ourselves as possessing particular thoughts, feelings, sensations, bodily forms, and so on. The most subtle of Prakṛti's manifest elements is *buddhi*, the capacity to discriminate between things, particularly between the false and the true, the Self and the non-Self. Thus *buddhi* is called intelligence, or *mahat*, the great. In *buddhi*, the *sattva guṇa* is at its highest proportion.

According to Sāṅkhya teachings, particularly as articulated in the practical teachings of Yoga, it is vital for intelligence, that is, the discriminating intellect (*buddhi*), to function at its highest or purest capacity. As it does so, it begins to discern the workings of *ahaṅkara*, and its mistaken identifications. Figuratively, the grosser *tattvas* then get progressively enfolded into their subtler elements. *Ahaṅkara* ceases its erroneous activities, and *buddhi* too recognizes that it is not the true observer, and stops it functioning. Thus Prakṛti returns to its unmanifest state, and Puruṣa, unobscured by the dynamic activities of manifest Prakṛti, knows itself as pure consciousness, the true Self, isolated from any delusions. This is known as "onlyness (onliness)" or *kaivalya*, and is akin to *mokṣa* in the Sāṅkhya system. There are only Puruṣa and Prakṛti, two real but transcendent principles. Puruṣa, the true Self, was never really in bondage, or enmeshed with Prakṛti. It had been a conditional self, produced through Prakṛti's manifestations, which was burdened with suffering through misapprehensions and false identifications.

It is noteworthy that in many South Asian *darśanas*, the created world begins with the existence of pure, potent, and generally transcendent supreme consciousness. From supreme consciousness, creation emerges in a subtle form and grows progressively more substantial. In Sāṅkhya, this varies slightly because creation emerges from Prakṛti, not Puruṣa. Nevetheless, supreme consciousness is still frequently the substratum, agent, or observer of the manifest and empirically observable reality. This is just the reverse of modern western scientific conceptions of the universe, in which life and consciousness are viewed as the end-products of an initially lifeless and unconscious material creation. The western perspective is consistent with a linear view of time that comes into existence with creation, and progresses steadily forward. Evolutionary changes, not in the Darwinian sense but as the mutable diversification of the creation, thus occur as singular unintended sequential events as time unfolds. However, in the cyclical conception of creation that is accepted by many South Asian *darśanas*, life and consciousness are not the incidental or accidental outcomes of creation. Just as the trunk, branches, flowers and fruit of an apple tree are the intrinsic objectives of an apple seed, so too, the multiform creation is a purposeful manifestation of supreme consciousness, which is both its source and its end.

Yoga

The *darśana* classified as Yoga is often grouped together with Sāṅkhya, because the early articulations of Yoga philosophy are based on the metaphysical system of the *tattvas* associated with Sāṅkhya. The earliest systematic presentation of Yoga, and still one of its most authoritative treatises, is Patañjali's *Yoga Sūtra* (*Aphorisms on Yoga*). Researchers generally date its composition to about the second century CE, and consider its author to be different from the grammarian of the same name. Those who regard them as the same person date the text a few centuries earlier. The *Yoga Sūtra* was later commented on by Vyāsa, a different person from the sage credited with the authorship of the *Mahābhārata*. Others, like Vyāsa, have continued to comment and elaborate on the philosophy of Yoga with an intrinsically Sāṅkhya perspective right up to the present day. However, Yoga, which emphasizes practice, has also been adopted by other *darśanas*, and even the language of Patañjali's *Yoga Sūtra* has been adapted to suit their metaphysical systems. One finds, for instance, Vedānta commentaries on the *Yoga Sūtra*, which equate Puruṣa with Ātman/Brahman, and Prakṛti with Māyā.

Yogic techniques have also been used by Buddhists, Jains, and virtually all *darśanas* that emphasize meditative practice. The word *yoga* derives from the Sanskrit root, *yuj*, "to unite," and means "union." It is cognate with the English word "yoke." From the perspective of Sāṅkhya metaphysics one might understand that through *yoga* one unites or integrates the various components of Prakṛti until Puruṣa is revealed. Others describe *yoga* as uniting the seemingly separate and incorrectly conceived self with its true nature. The origins of Yoga are unknown, but certainly ancient. Its focus on the interior exploration of consciousness gives it a distinctly South Asian stamp, suggesting that its origins may be traced to the Indus Valley Civilization. The so-called "ithyphallic proto-Śiva" seals found at Indus Valley Civilization sites appear to depict a figure seated in a yogic posture known as *mūla-bandha-āsana*. The horned figure, surrounded by animals, and possibly possessing an erection (ithyphallic), has many attributes associated with the Hindu god Śiva, who is renowned as the supreme practitioner of *yoga* (*mahā-yogin*). However, such assertions remain speculative.

There are many types of *yoga*. The *Bhagavad Gītā's* teachings on liberation, which predate Patañjali's text, are regarded as *yogas*. Tantrism is associated with Kuṇḍalinī Yoga. Various schools of religious philosophy have presented their own yogic systems, such as Nāda yoga, based on sound, Lāya yoga, the path of absorption, Kriyā yoga, with a focus on purification, and, more recently, Sri Aurobindo's Integral yoga. Patañjali's yoga is also known as Rāja (Royal) yoga.

Patañjali's *Yoga Sūtra*

The earliest extant systematic treatise on Yoga is Patañjali's *Yoga Sūtra*, which infers in its opening aphorism that it is a presentation of an existing *darśana*. Although his work is enormously influential, Patañjali is therefore not credited with the creation of Yoga. What is often surprising to students in the West, where *yoga* has been growing in popularity as a form of exercise for physical health and stress reduction, is Patañjali's second aphorism, which provides a succinct definition of *yoga*. There, Patañjali states that *yoga* is the ending (*nirodha*) of the whirling (*vṛtti*) of thought (*citta*). Since Sāṅkhya regards *citta* as composed of *manas* (heart-mind), *ahaṅkara* (ego), and *buddhi* (intelligence), it is their activities that need to stop in order to achieve *yoga*, which is used to designate both the practice and the goal. By bringing the activities of the interior faculties, *citta*, here translated as "thought," to a halt, *mokṣa*, or *kaivalya* (aloneness) is achieved.

Some prefer to translate *citta* as "consciousness." Each English equivalent has shortcomings, and this is a fine illustration of the challenges faced by translators. "Consciousness" is problematic because it implies that the other twenty *tattvas*, such as the five knowledge senses, are not part of consciousness, which they clearly are. This is particularly evident in certain other Hindu philosophical systems such as Kashmir Śaivism, which draw upon Sāṅkhya categories, and in which everything is consciousness. "Thought" is also problematic for rendering "*citta*" because one might argue that thought only circumscribes one aspect of the function of *manas*, namely "thinking" and does not even include "feeling." *Ahaṅkara* and *buddhi*, one might posit, are not thinking, per se, but activities linked to thought. *Ahaṅkara* identifies such thoughts as "I," "me," or "mine," with various other thoughts, while *buddhi* discriminates between the nature of thoughts, their referents, and relationships. However, like a cloud-chamber that leaves behind tracks of subatomic particles, the actions of *ahaṅkara* and *buddhi* leave traces of thought. Thus their activities are *citta-vṛtti*, the spinning of thought. Students determined to probe deeply into the study of Asian *darśanas* are therefore advised to attempt to penetrate beyond the words to the intended referents. Since it is often more helpful to retain the original signifiers (e.g. *citta, ātman,* and *puruṣa*) than to use misleading English equivalents, scholarly studies are replete with Sanskrit terms. Patañjali's elegant, and somewhat terse presentation, consists of about two hundred *sūtras,* which delineate how one should go about ending *citta-vṛttis.*

The *Yoga Sūtra* also discusses various supernormal powers, known as *vibhūtis* or *siddhis,* which can be obtained through the practice of *yoga.* These include the ability to see into the past and future, understand the languages of all beings, remember previous rebirths, have enormous strength, and become invisible. Although Patañjali cautions practitioners against getting too caught up in the acquisition and exercise of *siddhis,* which could divert them from their goal of final liberation, it is evident that such powers were an attractive feature of ascetic disciplines. In Tantra, the attainment and mastery of *siddhis* is encouraged.

Rāja yoga is fundamentally non-theistic. It asserts the existence of Īśvara, the Lord, a unique *puruṣa* (supreme consciousness) that has never experienced the cognitive play of Prakṛti's manifestation. Unbound by time, it has been venerable since antiquity. Īśvara is embodied by the cosmic vibration, the *pranava* (*Aum/Om*), whose repetition leads to the comprehension of its meaning. However, in other yogic formulations, that are not strictly Rāja yoga, Īśvara begins to take on a theistic flavor. Śiva, known as the supreme *yogi,* is also known as Maheśvara (Great Lord), and is thus identified by his devotees with the Lord of Rāja yoga. Vedānta philosophers, who identify Brahman with the *pranava,* tacitly identify Rāja yoga's Īśvara with some mode of Brahman.

The eight limbs of *yoga*

A handy summary of the essential components of yogic practice is found in Patañjali's list of the eight limbs (*aṣṭānga*) of *yoga,* which are elaborated upon by later commentators. These are: 1) *yama,* 2) *niyama,* 3) *āsana,* 4) *prāṇāyāma,* 5) *pratyahara,* 6) *dhāraṇa,* 7) *dhyāna,* and 8) *samādhi. Yama* (restraints) refers to practices that should be avoided for the effective attainment of liberation. These restraints are: not-harming (*ahiṃsā*), not lying, not stealing, chastity (*brahmacarya*), and not being acquisitive. *Niyama* (observances) refers to practices that should be cultivated. These are: self-purification, contentment, austerity (*tapas*), self-study (*svadhyaya*), and a sincere commitment to the endeavor. According to Patañjali, *āsana,* or posture, should be steady and relaxed, transcending the dualities of effort and lassitude. The varied postures, which most observers associate with *yoga* practice, derive from prescriptions in other texts, such as the *Haṭha Yoga Pradīpika.* Posture-work is merely foundational to the goal of Rāja yoga, and not an end in itself. *Prāṇāyāma* entails regulation of the vital energy (*prāṇa*), which is all around us. It is believed that *prāṇa* moves through us and within us, and air is one of its vehicles. Yoga regards mastery of regulated breathing, in combination with the control of the movement of "air" through the body, aided by opening and closing various prāṇic valves (*bandha*), necessary to maintain vitality and enhance concentration.

Sense withdrawal (*pratyahara*) enables the practitioner, known as a *yogi* or *yogin* (feminine: *yoginī*), to detach any and all of the five senses from their engagement with external objects. This allows the *yogi* to be freed from sensory distractions and focus on interior processes (*antaḥ-karaṇa*). Mastery of the capacity to disengage the senses permits the development of *dhāraṇa* or concentration. The *yogi* should strive to develop *ekagratā*, one-pointedness, which is the ability to pay singular attention to a phenomenon, particularly mental ones. As *dhāraṇa* intensifies in duration, and has the capacity to attend with unbroken awareness to the dynamic interplay of mental phenomena, it becomes meditation (*dhyāna*). Some interpreters see this as akin to the slow unbroken stream of honey poured from one container to another. Contemplative absorption (*samādhi*) arises as the apparent emptiness of phenomena (*svarūpa śūnyam iva*) shines forth.

Rāja yoga distinguishes between two types of *samādhi*: *sabīja* (with seed) and *nirbīja* (without seed). *Sabīja samādhi* is a unitive absorption with an "object" in material consciousness. In all *samādhi* states, the boundary between an observing consciousness and the observed phenomenon vanishes. In this sense, it is *samādhi* (literally, "coming together" or "absorption"). However, the existence of an "object," even though it may be a subtle mental phenomenon that is observed, and even though it is no longer "objectified" since in the state of *samādhi* it has ceased to be different from the observing consciousness, still sows a karmic seed (*bīja*), which will bear fruit as a ripple in thought (*citta-vṛtti*). In Sāṅkhya terminology, Prakṛti is thus still manifest although extremely subtle. *Buddhi* (intelligence) needs to exercise its highest act of discrimination (*viveka*). Recognizing the intrinsic emptiness of all manifest phenomena, including itself, which is one of the most subtle "objects" of material consciousness, *buddhi* then ceases its manifestation. Prakṛti figuratively returns to its transcendent state and Puruṣa (supreme consciousness) shines forth, no longer with any Prakṛti-produced "object" with which to be absorbed. This is seedless or *nirbīja samādhi*, the perfection of *yoga*, and the attainment of *mokṣa*. Patañjali ends the *Yoga Sūtra* (IV.34) by saying that pure perceptual power (*cit-śakti*), the purpose of supreme consciousness, abides alone, in its true nature, when the qualities of material phenomena (*guṇa*), recognized as intrinsically empty (*śunya*), are aborted. The activities of a liberated *yogi* are beyond categorization as good or bad.

Nyāya and Vaiśeṣika

These two *darśanas*, which are often grouped together, have received sparse attention since the ascendancy of western logic, mathematics, and science. Gautama Akṣapāda, author of the *Nyāya-sūtra* (*Aphorisms on Inquiry*) is credited with the founding of

Figure 6.1 A Vaiṣṇava renouncer uses prayer beads concealed in a cloth bag as an aid to concentration in his spiritual practice (Nasik)

Nyāya *darśana* somewhat earlier than the second century CE. Although Nyāya is characterized as a school of logic, it is also concerned with rhetoric and debate. Nyāya explores the notion of *pramāṇa*, the means through which we obtain valid knowledge. Most *darśanas* explored six categories of *pramāṇas*: Perception, Inference, Testimony, Analogy, Implication, and Negation. Consider the following example. Western (i.e. Aristotelian) syllogistic reasoning might present something such as: A) Where there is smoke there is fire; B) There is smoke on the mountain; C) Therefore, there is fire on the mountain. The two premises A and B, lead to C, the conclusion. Nyāya, by contrast, promotes a five-part syllogism, as for instance: A) There is a fire on the mountain; B) Because there is smoke there; C) As in a cooking fire; D) The mountain fire is similar; E) Therefore there is a fire there. A distinguishing feature of Nyāya's presentation, besides its use of five instead of three statements, is the use of an empirical example for comparison through analogy. The mountain smoke, which can be seen, is like the smoke from a cooking fire, in which the relationship between smoke and fire has been or could be seen and verified. Therefore, one can infer the existence of fire on the mountain by analogous comparison to the cooking fire.

Whatever the shortcomings of this approach may be, including its bulkier form in comparison to the elegant Aristotelian model, it points to the importance placed on experience in validating a truth claim. This emphasis on experience also gives primacy not only to empirical observations (i.e. those made with the five senses) but also to intuitive liberative insights (*yoga-jñāta*) gained through meditative practices, which are ranked as superior sources of valid knowledge than may be obtained through the mere application of logic. These insights, for the recipient, fall under the category of perception. Unfortunately, the subjective nature of such experiences does not lend them to ready comparison or verification, and they thus, for others, fall into the category of testimony. A person may claim or testify to have attained to a particular realization, or such so-called revealed truths are often presented in scripture. This obliges others to make judgments about the truth claims of such testimony, which require one to make inferences about the character of the person making such claims, and the motivations behind testimonial assertions.

Vaiśeṣika philosophy was first described systematically in the *Vaiśeṣika Sūtra* (*Aphorisms on Particularities*), likely composed before the second century CE and attributed to Kaṇāda. Vaiśeṣika is viewed as a sort of proto-science and concerns itself with the study of seven component categories of reality. These are: 1) Substance (*dravya*), 2) Quality (*guṇa*), 3) Action (*karma*), 4) Generality, 5) Particularity (*viśeṣa*), from which it derives its name, 6) Relation, and 7) Non-existence. Substances (*dravya*) are subcategorized into earth, water, air, light, ether, time, space, soul, and mind. Vaiśeṣika introduces the notion of an atom (*paramāṇu*), an eternal and indivisibly small unit of substance. The concept of particularity (*viśeṣa*) addresses the differences between similar things, such as two atoms of light, which are intrinsically similar, yet different. Another valuable contribution made by later developments in Vaiśeṣika philosophy is its exploration of the category of non-existence. For instance, certain things have a quasi-existence through the words that designate them. Both a house that will be built or a jar that was broken are non-existent. However, the house has an incipient existence in the bricks that will be used to construct it, and the pot a subsidiary existence in its shards. One may refer to both the house and the pot with words, as if they are existing realities, when in truth they have no existence. Thus Vaiśeṣika draws our attention to the potentially problematic nature of concepts in the quest for truth, and how they may not correspond to existing realities.

Mīmāṃsā and Vedānta

The Mīmāṃsā (Interpretation) *darśana* concerns itself with investigating and reflecting upon the meanings within Vedic scripture. As such, it has a particularly strong affiliation with orthodoxy. It is traditionally divided into two parts: Pūrva-Mīmāṃsā (Investigation of the Primary), and Uttara-Mīmāṃsā (Investigation of the Latter). Uttara-Mīmāṃsā is better known as Vedānta since it deals with the latter (*anta*) portion of the Vedas, namely the Upaniṣads. By default, Pūrva-Mīmāṃsā, dealing with the interpretation of the other sections of the Veda, comes to be known simply as Mīmāṃsā. Its foundational texts are Jaimini's *Pūrvā Mīmāṃsā Sūtra*, dated at about the second century BCE, and subsequent commentaries. Since the Vedas are sometimes said to address two major subjects, action and knowledge, Mīmāṃsā is regarded as dealing with the former, while Vedānta deals with the latter. Vedānta has, by far, captivated the interests of students of Indian philosophy in the West, and novices often think of it simply as *the* philosophy of Hinduism, unaware of the other *darśanas*. A more extensive treatment of Vedānta will follow in a separate chapter. Mīmāṃsā, by contrast, focused as it is on ritual action, has a distinctly theological flavor, and has been generally marginalized by students and scholars. However, as ritual studies and scholarly interest in Hindu theology have begun to gain in momentum, the ruminations of Mīmāṃsā are receiving renewed attention.

Mīmāṃsā's main aim is Vedic apologetics, the defense and justification of Vedic ritualism. In order to do this Mīmāṃsā strives to establish its parameters for valid sources of knowledge, essentially arguing that sufficient conditions provide valid knowledge. When our senses are healthily functioning and objects present themselves, we perceive. When we have enough data, we infer. And we accept the existence of distant lands, and so on, on the testimony of the authoritative texts we have read. So too, it claims that the testimony of the Vedas, which are *apauruṣeya*, not the result of human authorship, are not subject to human error. When read, the truth within the Vedas becomes self-evident, and the purpose of Mīmāṃsā is to remove any doubts that may arise due to misunderstanding.

Since the Vedas are believed to constitute unquestionable truth, the Mīmāṃsā seeks to explain the value of ritual and *dharma* explained within them. Although rites may be performed to please particular deities, and achieve various goals, such as giving birth to sons or bringing the rains, some Vedic rituals do not appear to have any stated objective. Mīmāṃsā contends that the rationale for performing such rites is merely because the Vedas say they should be done. This is *dharma*, duty performed for its own sake. In fact, the focus in much of Mīmāṃsā thought turns to the details of the actions themselves, and the deities begin to be marginal to the performance of sacrifice. Sacrifice is to be done because it is said that it should be done. *Dharma* is obedience to these injunctions. The potent benefits (*apurva*) of each dharmic action accrue to the soul of the patron of the rite, and ultimately result in the attainment of heaven (*svarga*), which was the goal in early Vedic sacrificial religion.

Early semblances of Mīmāṃsā thought are found in Vedic literature itself, such as in the Brāhmaṇas and the Kalpa Sūtras, where the analysis of the actions of ritual by priestly functionaries begins to take center stage over the deities involved and the immediate rewards promised. Mīmāṃsā's emphasis on the irreproachable truth in the Vedas becomes a hallmark of orthodoxy, and disallows the possibility of extrapolative development. So, although women and *śūdras* could learn to perform a Vedic ritual, and execute it exactly, it would still generate no *apurva*, because the Vedas simply exclude them from the scheme. Mīmāṃsā thought has played an instrumental role in maintaining the Vedas as a cornerstone of Hinduism and the widely pronounced sentiment by certain segments of orthodoxy that for anything to be regarded as genuinely Hindu, its origins should be traceable back to the Vedas.

Key points in this chapter

- By the sixth century BCE philosophical movements emerged that challenged Brahmin orthodoxy.
- Hindu orthodoxy began defining itself in distinction to groups they labeled as heterodox (*nāstika*).
- Jainism, Buddhism, and the Cārvāka philosophies are categorized as heterodox *darśanas*.
- There are six conventionally listed orthodox *darśanas*, which are often grouped in pairs.
- The Sāṅkhya philosophy attempts to list the various components that make up reality.
- The metaphysics of many Asian philosophies invert modern western scientific conceptions about the origins of consciousness in the universe.
- The word *yoga* derives from the Sanskrit root, *yuj*, "to unite," and means "union."
- The earliest extant systematic treatise on *yoga* is Patañjali's *Yoga Sūtra*.
- Nyāya places importance on experience, sensory or supersensory, in validating a truth claim.
- Vaiśeṣika is a proto-science concerning itself with the study of seven categories of reality.
- The Mīmāṃsā *darśana* investigates and reflects upon the meanings within the Vedas, having as its main aim the defense and justification of Vedic ritualism.

Discussion questions

1. Patañjali states that Yoga is the ending (*nirodha*) of the whirling (*vṛtti*) of thought (*citta*). If Yoga means "union," how might ending the turnings of thought be regarded as "union"?
2. Discuss Vaiśeṣika's category of non-existence, and come up with some examples of things that contain a quasi-existence through the words that designate them.
3. Discuss why you think the Nyāya and Vaiśeṣika *darśanas* have received sparse attention since the ascendancy of western logic, mathematics, and science.
4. Explain what Hindu orthodoxy meant by heterodox, and then compare and contrast the heterodox *darśanas* of Jainism, Buddhism, and the Cārvāka.
5. Describe in detail the Sāṅkhya *darśana*. What is the Sāṅkhya view of reality, and of suffering (*duḥkha*)?
6. Describe the Yoga *darśana* in detail. Make sure to include the origins of *yoga*, the various types of *yoga*, and the important people and texts associated with it.

Further reading

General studies on Indian philosophy

Chatterji, S. and D. M. Datta (1968) *An Introduction to Indian Philosophy*. Calcutta: University of Calcutta.

Dasgupta, Surendranath (1922) *History of Indian Philosophy*, 5 vols. Reprint. Delhi: Motilal Banarsidass, 1988.

Frauwallner, E. (1983–1984) *History of Indian Philosophy*, 2 vols. V. M. Bedekar (trans.). Delhi: Motilal Banarsidass.

Potter, K. (1963) *Presuppositions of India's Philosophies*. Englewood Cliffs, NJ: Prentice-Hall.

— (ed.) (2004) *Encyclopedia of Indian Philosophies*, 11 vols. (28 vols. projected). Delhi: Motilal Banarsidass.

Radhakrishnan, Sarvepalli and Charles A. Moore (1957) *A Source Book in Indian Philosophy*. Princeton, NJ: Princeton University Press.

Smart, Ninian (1964) *Doctrine and Argument in Indian Philosophy*. London: Allen and Unwin.

On the heterodox philosophical systems

Barua, B. M. (1921) *History of Pre-Buddhistic Indian Philosophy*. Calcutta: University of Calcutta.

Basham, A. L. (1981) *History and Doctrines of the Ājīvikas*. Delhi: Motilal Banarsidass.

Chattopadhyaya, D. (1959) *Lokāyata*. New Delhi: People's Publishing House.

Dundas, Paul (1992) *The Jains*. London: Routledge and Kegan Paul.

Prebish, Charles and D. Keown (2005) *Buddhism – the eBook*. The Journal of Buddhist Ethics Books.

Shastri, D. R. (1930) *Short History of Indian Materialism*. Calcutta: The Book Company.

On yoga

Aranya, Swami Hariharananda (1983) *Yoga Philosophy of Patañjali*. Albany, NY: State University of New York Press.

Connolly, Peter (2006) *A Student's Guide to the History and Philosophy of Yoga*. London: Equinox.

Eliade, Mircea (1973) *Yoga: Immortality and Freedom*. Princeton, NJ: Princeton University Press.

Feuerstein, Georg (1979) *The Yoga-sutra of Patanjali*. Reprint. Rochester: Inner Traditions International, 1989.

Miller, Barbara S. (trans.) (1996) *Yoga, Discipline of Freedom: The Yoga Sutra Attributed to Patanjali*. Berkeley, CA: University of California Press.

Varenne, Jean (1976) *Yoga and the Hindu Tradition*. Derek Coltman (trans.) Chicago, IL: University of Chicago Press.

Woods, J. H. (1914) *The Yoga-System of Patañjali*. Cambridge, MA. Harvard Oriental Series XVIII.

On the other orthodox systems

Chatterjee, S. (1965) *The Nyāya Theory of Knowledge*. Calcutta: University of Calcutta.

Halbfass, W. (1992) *On Being and What There Is. Classical Vaisesika and the History of Indian Ontology*. Albany, NY: State University of New York Press.

Hulin, M. (1978) *Sāṃkhya Literature*. History of Indian Literature 6 fasc. 3. Wiesbaden: Otto Harrassowitz.

Larson, Gerald J. (1969) *Classical Sāṃkhya*. Delhi: Motilal Banarsidass.

Larson, G., and R. S. Bhattacharya (1987) *Sāṃkhya: A Dualist Tradition in Indian Philosophy*. Delhi: Motilal Banarsidass.

Matilal, B. K. (1985) *Logic, Language and Reality*. Delhi: Motilal Banarsidass.

Mishra, V. (1983) *The Conception of Matter According to the Nyāya-Vaiśeṣika*. Reprint. Delhi: Gyan Publishers.

On Hindu renouncers and ascetics

Bhagat, M. G. (1976) *Ancient Indian Asceticism*. Delhi: Munshiram Manoharlal.

Bharati, Agehananda (1961) *The Ochre Robe*. London: Rider.

Bronkhorst, J. (1993) *The Two Sources of Indian Asceticism*. Bern: Peter Lang.

Denton, Lynn Teskey (2004) *Female Ascetics in Hinduism*. Albany, NY: State University of New York Press.

Ghurye, G. S. (1964) *Indian Sādhus*. Bombay: Popular Prakashan.

Gross, Robert (1979) *Hindu Asceticism: A Study of the Sadhus of North India*. Berkeley, CA: University of California Press.

Hartsuiker, D. (1993) *Sādhus: The Holy Men of India*. London: Thames and Hudson.

Oman, J. C. (1973) *The Mystics, Ascetics and Saints of India*. Reprint. Delhi: Oriental Publishers.

Sinha, S., and B. Saraswati (1978) *Ascetics of Kashi*. Varanasi: N. K. Bose Memorial Foundation.

Tripathi, B. D. (1978) *Sadhus of India*. Bombay: Popular Prakashan.

Zysk, Kenneth (1991) *Asceticism and Healing in Ancient India*. Delhi: Oxford University Press.

7 The Epics (Itihāsa)

In this chapter

While the genres of literature discussed thus far, such as the Vedic hymn collections, the ritual treatises, and the philosophical and ethical prescriptive texts, do tell us much about early religious beliefs and practice, the narrative texts that begin to emerge at the end of the Vedic period, provide many more details on social values and structures. The most influential of these narratives are two Epics, whose characters and their adventures are very well known to most Hindus. This chapter therefore recounts these stories in some detail, since familiarity with their content is vital to a fuller understanding of the Hindu tradition.

Main topics covered

- The *Rāmāyaṇa*
- The *Mahābhārata*

A highly influential genre of Hindu literature emerged at the end of the Vedic period, which was marked by the composition of the principal Upaniṣads. These works are the Epics, known as Itihāsa ("thus indeed it was"), of which the two main representatives are the *Mahābhārata* (*The Great [Story of the] Descendants of Bharata*), and the *Rāmāyaṇa* (*Rāma's Circuit*). The Epics are long narratives, which probably grew out of tales of heroic exploits of warriors, knitted together for courtly recitations to particularly receptive *kṣatriya* audiences. As writing came into vogue, the Epics were likely given a written textual form by Brahmin sages, whose embellishments to the tales augmented their hegemony over the social order. Thus *dharma* is a central feature of the Epics, and *kṣatriya dharma*, in particular, is articulated in the form of explicit teachings on the topic, and also illustrated through the lives and adventures of the stories' characters. Tensions between Brahmins and *kṣatriyas* are evident, although rarely explicitly, and the nature of true *dharma* is explored in a wide variety of situational contexts. The Epics are useful because, unlike the philosophical works, the ritual texts, and the Vedic hymns that precede them, they describe social and courtly life in vivid detail. We read about the relationships between family members, their feelings and motivations, and their day to day activities. Hindus, and even non-Hindus in South and South-east Asia where the Epics have circulated, are intimately familiar with these narratives, which they have learned since childhood, and which continue to be retold in popular media from comic books to film.

The Epics contain useful geographical references to places both fictive and actual, which fuel sectarian imaginations and scholarly research. For instance, the birthplace of Rāma, the hero of the *Rāmāyaṇa*, is Ayodhyā, still a city in North India. Although the events of the *Rāmāyaṇa* are said to have taken place in the Tretā Yuga, hundreds of thousands of years ago, some Hindus believe that a Mughal mosque was built atop a razed temple that marked his actual birthplace in that city. In 1992, groups of believers tore down the mosque, and have been pressuring the Government of India to permit the rebuilding of the Hindu temple on the site. Scholars are less dismissive of speculations that the land of Laṅkā, the abode of the *Rāmāyaṇa's* demon king Rāvaṇa, might refer to the island of Sri Lanka. Although the Epics also purport to convey historical information, they are of limited usefulness in extracting much beyond mythic genealogies. The texts reflect a transitional period in Hinduism. Vedic gods such as Indra and Agni are prominent, but other deities who are marginal in the Vedas, such as Viṣṇu and Brahmā, as well as Śiva, are also significant in the Epics. Quite notably, the notion of deities manifesting on the earth in human form is commonplace. Both Rāma and Kṛṣṇa are incarnate forms of the god Viṣṇu.

The Rāmāyaṇa

The *Rāmāyaṇa* circulates throughout South Asia in many versions. The oldest authoritative version is attributed to the sage Vālmīki, who plays a role in the story itself, a common motif in Hindu literature. Researchers sense that, stylistically, Vālmīki's *Rāmāyaṇa* was mostly composed by one person, although there were certainly additions to it over the centuries, through the insertion or deletion of words, verses, or episodes in the body of the text. The epic is made up of eight books known as *kāṇḍas,* totaling over 20,000 verses. The final book, the Uttara Kaṇḍa, in particular, appears to have been an addition. The metrical style of the *Rāmāyaṇa's* verses is the *śloka,* which becomes so widely used in literary compositions, that the term *śloka* is often used subsequently as a synonym for a Sanskrit couplet, although the language has a rich assortment of metrical verse forms. Narrative traditions transmitted by wandering bards are characteristically malleable, and often adapt themselves to the situation of each telling. Thus there are numerous variations on the story, even in its written forms. Vālmīki's *Rāmāyaṇa* took shape between 400 BCE and 400 CE, although the events of the story are said to have taken place in the Tretā Yuga.

The story begins in the north Indian kingdom of Ayodhyā ruled by king Daśaratha. Although blessed with an auspicious kingdom, and with three wives, Daśaratha had no children, and thus commissioned an *aśvamedha*, the Vedic horse-sacrifice, to rectify the problem. The sanctified rice dish produced from this *yajña* was fed to his three queens, Kausalyā, Kaikeyī, and Sumitrā, who in time gave birth to four extraordinary sons. The senior-most wife, Kausalyā, gave birth to Rāma, legitimate heir to the throne. Kaịkeyī's son was Bharata. And Sumitrā gave birth to the twins Lakṣmana and Śatrughna. The boys grew up to be fine princes, skilled in the *kṣatriya* arts, and were much loved by all of the king's wives. Rāma and Lakṣmana were inseparably close.

One day, a *ṛṣi* named Viśvāmitra came to Daśaratha's court and demanded that Rāma accompany him on a journey to destroy a troublesome *rākṣasī* (demoness). Although Rāma was not quite a young man, Daśaratha despondently conceded to the sage's demands. Lakṣmana accompanied Rāma on his initiatory journey into manhood with Viśvāmitra. The sage, who was once a *kṣatriya* himself, but who had through intense austerities transformed himself into a Brahmin-like *ṛṣi*, taught the boys secrets of weaponry, and related many tales on the sacred histories of the various places and people they encountered. After successfully slaying the demoness, Tāṭakā, and other demons, who were defiling the *yajñas* of forest-dwelling ascetics, the princes journeyed home, but stopped en route to attend the *svayaṃvara* of the princess Sītā in the kingdom of Mithilā. A *svayaṃvara* ("one's own choice") is a ceremony through which a *kṣatriya* princess might select her husband, often through a skill-testing contest. Sītā's father, King Janaka, challenged her suitors to lift up and string a great bow, said to belong to the god Śiva himself. Few of the competing kings and princes could even lift the bow, much less string it, and when all had failed, Rāma was urged to attempt the task. Not only did he effortlessly pick up and string the bow, but also, when he drew it to its full length, the bow snapped in two, to the amazement of all the onlookers. He had overwhelmingly demonstrated his right to Sītā's hand in marriage, much to the pleasure of the royal family of Mithilā.

Rāma and Sītā enjoyed some marital bliss in Ayodhyā until Daśaratha decided to cede the throne to Rāma, whom he felt was now competent to assume rulership of the kingdom. Everyone rejoiced at the prospect of the forthcoming coronation, including Queen Kaikeyī, who loved Rāma like her own son, Bharata. However, her maidservant, the hunchback Mantharā, quickly succeeded in poisoning Kaikeyī's mind. She made Kaikeyī worry about the upcoming change in her own status, from Daśaratha's favorite queen to merely mother of the new king's brother. And she was led to worry about Bharata's fate once Rāma became king. Swayed from her love and trust of Rāma by her needless fears, Kaikeyī confronted Daśaratha, asking to redeem two boons he had once granted her for saving his life on the battlefield. She asked that Bharata be crowned king, and that Rāma be sent into forest exile for fourteen years. Daśaratha was devastated by her requests. Lakṣmana and other members of the court were angered by this turn of events, but Rāma was not disturbed. He pointed out that it was a king's *dharma* to keep his word, and that Bharata would make a competent ruler. So saying, he set out on his exile.

Lakṣmana decided to accompany him, and so did Sītā, against many protests. As a princess, who enjoyed a pampered upbringing in palaces, she would find the hardships of the forest unbearable. But Sītā insisted, saying that a wife's *dharma* was to be with her husband, even in situations of extreme duress. So Sītā, Lakṣmana, and Rāma set out for the forest and their departure eventually took its toll on Daśaratha, who died of heartache.

Meanwhile, Bharata, who had not heard the news of Rāma's departure until much later, was shocked and angry at his mother for her actions. He gathered a small army to follow and find Rāma to persuade him to return. From their tiny forest hermitage in Citrakūṭa, by the river Mandākinī, Lakṣmana spotted Bharata's army and suspected it was intent on hunting down and killing Rāma. But Rāma calmed Lakṣmana's fears, and warmly greeted Bharata, who despite his efforts was unable to convince Rāma to return. Respectfully touching Rāma's sandals with his head, Bharata carried back the sandals to place on the throne of Ayodhyā, as symbolic representatives of Rāma himself, vowing to yield the rule to Rāma at the end of his exile.

As the years went by, the exiled trio traveled deeper into the forests to the south, meeting and learning from various sages, slaying demons, and finally building a hermitage at Pañcavaṭī. They were beginning to appreciate the joys of what was a premature entry into the forest-dweller stage of life and the beauty of living close to nature. However, one day a shape-shifting demoness named Śūrpaṇakhā spotted Rāma and was attracted to him. Assuming a charming shape she made sexual advances, but he resisted, pointing out that he was married. Seeing Sītā, Śūrpaṇakhā threatened to devour her, at which point Lakṣmana mutilated the demoness by chopping off her nose and ears. She fled, bleeding, to her demon relative, Khara, who attacked them in vengeance, but Rāma destroyed both him and his armies. Still seeking vengeance, Śūrpaṇakhā traveled to Laṅkā to beseech help from her brother, one of the greatest of all demons, the ten-headed *rākṣasa* Rāvaṇa.

At first Rāvaṇa was reluctant to comply with his sister's request, but when he heard about Sītā's beauty, he was determined to possess her. Devising a plan with his minister Mārīca, he flew to Rāma's hermitage in his flying chariot, Puṣpaka, setting it nearby yet out of sight. The demon Mārīca then took the form of a deer, with an extraordinary golden hue, which so enthralled Sītā when she spotted it, that she urged Rāma to fetch her its skin. Rāma set off, asking Lakṣmana to watch over Sītā. Some distance into the deep forest, Rāma, an archer of peerless skill, spotted the deer and loosed his dart. The arrow found its mark, but as the demon Mārīca collapsed dying, he called out to Lakṣmana for help, mimicking Rāma's voice. Sītā, hearing the cry, ordered Lakṣmana to seek out and help Rāma, and he reluctantly obeyed. While

Sītā was alone, Rāvaṇa, assuming the guise of a sagely Brahmin ascetic and chanting Vedic scriptures, approached, and she thought it proper to offer him food. But when he was close enough, Rāvaṇa revealed his true form and expressing that he was love-struck with her, dragged Sītā into Puṣpaka and took flight for Laṅkā. Jaṭāyu, the vulture king and ally of Rāma, who was soaring nearby, spotted the abduction and gave chase, but Rāvaṇa dealt him lethal wounds and he fell to the ground dying.

When Rāma and Lakṣmana returned to the hermitage, realizing they had been deceived, they discovered that Sītā was missing and set out in search of her. They came upon Jaṭāyu, their valiant friend, who died in their arms as he told them of Sītā's abduction at the hands of Rāvaṇa. Determined to find and rescue her, they set out yet deeper into the forests to the south.

Meanwhile, back in his kingdom of Laṅkā, Rāvaṇa, who was wed to the beautiful Mandodarī, and who had previously possessed other women by force, now sought to win Sītā's love. When Sītā refused his advances, he placed her in a forest grove within his palace walls, and hoped that her demoness attendants would wear down her resistance. Sītā did not know if Rāma was still alive, or if anyone was still looking for her. And Rāvaṇa, who enjoyed great power, wealth, and prestige, had promised her his world. Still, she remained dharmically steadfast to her husband.

As Rāma and Lakṣmana neared Kiṣkindhā, the southern kingdom of the monkey people, they were spotted by Hanumān, the general of the monkey armies. He approached and soon befriended them. Hanumān then pledged them his loyalty if they would help his king, Sugrīva, regain his kingdom from his brother Vālin (or Vāli). They agreed, and later, Rāma slew Vālin as he fought with Sugrīva. In fulfillment of his agreement, Sugrīva sent groups of monkeys in various directions to seek out Rāvaṇa's kingdom of Laṅkā. One of these special forces, which chose to explore further south, was headed by Hanumān. Arriving at the very end of land, the group encountered the ocean and was almost about to give up the search. However, Hanumān did not lose heart and leapt across the waters to the island kingdom of Laṅkā, where he set about searching for the palace.

After stealing into the palace grounds and observing many attractive women there, he finally reached the forest grove where Sītā was being held prisoner. He instantly realized from her extraordinary beauty, only enhanced by her psychological ordeal, that he had found her. He showed her a ring belonging to Rāma to certify his identity, and asked her to flee Laṅkā with him. But Sītā said that it was not dharmically appropriate for her to touch another man, even a friend and ally of Rāma's, and that *dharma* dictated that Rāma rescue her himself. Somewhat perplexed by the dharmic proprieties involved, Hanumān set off to inform Rāma of his success in finding Sītā, but before doing so, allowed himself to be captured by the palace guards and taken into Rāvaṇa's presence. The demons bound Hanumān and set his tail on fire, but he freed himself from his bonds, escaped from the palace, and set portions of Laṅkā

Figure 7.1 Lithograph depicting Hanumān setting Laṅkā ablaze with his fiery tail

ablaze with his still-burning tail before leaping across the ocean and heading home to Kiṣkindhā.

Rāma and Lakṣmana, joined by their monkey allies, mobilized a vast army at the ocean's edge. They then constructed a bridge spanning the waters to Laṅkā, there to meet Rāvaṇa's forces in battle. Many a hero from the monkey army fell, and valiant demon warriors, including Rāvaṇa's own sons, and his giant brother Kumbhakarṇa also died in the ensuing carnage. The demons unleashed horrific magical weapons, and at one point both Rāma and Lakṣmana lay dying on the battlefield. Only certain herbs found in the Himalayas could serve as a remedy. Again, Hanumān came to the rescue. Leaping to the north, he carried back an entire mountain with its healing herbs which revived the princes. Vibhīṣaṇa, a dharmic brother of Rāvaṇa, aided Rāma and the monkey armies in defeating Rāvaṇa. Eventually, Rāma confronted

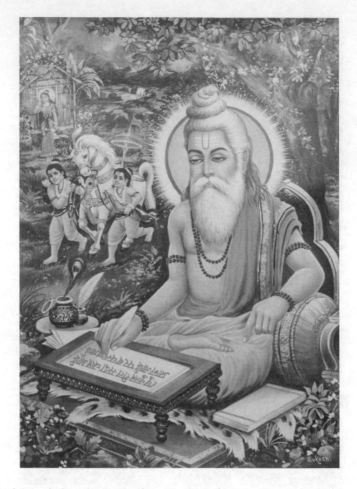

Figure 7.2 Lithograph depicting Vālmīki composing the *Rāmāyaṇa* in his *āśrama* with Sītā and her sons Lāva and Kuśa in the background

Rāvaṇa, and the blue-skinned incarnation of the great god Viṣṇu soon unleashed a potent arrow that felled the ten-headed demon king.

While Sītā expected Rāma to rush to see her, he asked that she bathe, adorn herself and be brought before him. There he explained that he had fulfilled his *dharma* by slaying Rāvaṇa and rescuing her. However, since her chastity was in question since she had been touched by Rāvaṇa and had spent a year in captivity with him, she should be banished. Shocked and dismayed, Sītā pledged to prove her fidelity and chastity by surviving a fire ordeal. Entering the flames, she was delivered from them, unburned, by Agni himself. The god of fire told Rāma that Sītā was pure and that he should not treat her harshly. The heroes all returned to Ayodhyā triumphantly, and Rāma was restored to his rightful kingship.

Unfortunately, after returning to Ayodhyā, the citizenry still did not fully accept Sītā's purity, and Rāma's capacity to rule effectively was being jeopardized. Unaware that she was pregnant, Rāma got rid of her and, abandoned in the forest, she eventually made her way to the hermitage of the sage Vālmīki, the author of the epic. There she gave birth to twin sons Lāva and Kuśa, who learned the epic from Vālmīki. When they had grown up, Lāva and Kuśa visited Ayodhyā and recited Vālmīki's *Rāmāyaṇa* to Rāma. As the tale reached the end, Rāma realized that Sītā had not perished, and that the bards in front of him were his own sons. He sent for Sītā, hoping to restore her to her rightful place as queen, but she no longer wanted any part of that life. She beseeched the Earth to receive her if she was truly pure. Instantly, the ground opened and Sītā was swallowed up by the Earth, from whence she had originally come. King Janaka's daughter had not been born in the conventional manner, but was discovered in a furrow (*sītā*) of the Earth as it was ploughed in a sacrificial rite.

The *Rāmāyaṇa* leads us to wonder about innumerable issues, but the answers proposed to most of the questions that it raises remain speculative. For instance, does the myth contain at its core a story of events that actually transpired? If so, who were the demons and monkeys described in the narrative? Do Rāma and Sītā come from northern Āryan kingdoms that progressively spread and dominated kingdoms to the south of the subcontinent? Was Rāvaṇa the king of one of these great southern (i.e. "Dravidian") kingdoms? Were the monkeys (the term *vānara*, could merely mean "of the forest") actually forest-dwelling tribes that allied with the northern Āryans in the conquest of the south? If demons such as Vibhīṣaṇa could be dharmic, in what sense are they demons? If Rāma epitomizes *dharma*, then why are his actions on occasion seemingly so adharmic? For instance, in the final book of the epic, Rāma, based on the complaints of Brahmin priests, beheads a *śūdra* for performing religious rites that were only permissible to *dvija varṇas*. He slays Vālin with an arrow released from a place of hiding, inflicting on Vālin, as he lies dying, to a long tirade about Rāma's breach of *kṣatriya dharma*. Others see Rāma's treatment of Sītā as misogynistic. Despite the critiques of those who see the epic as entrenching anachronistic values, the *Rāmāyaṇa* continues to serve as a vehicle for the transmission of dharmic ideals. Rāma is seen as the ideal man, whose adherence to *dharma* overrides his personal desires and interests. Sītā is the ideal wife, loyal to her husband under all sorts of duress.

The Mahābhārata

The *Mahābhārata* is said to consist of 100,000 verses and as such is a contender for the world's longest book. The Tibetan *Epic of King Gesar* is certainly longer, but still belongs to the oral bardic tradition. The *Mahābhārata* is more than five times longer than the great western epics, Homer's *Iliad* and the *Odyssey*, combined. Scholars place its composition between 200 BCE and 200 CE, although its events are said to usher in the juncture of the transition from the Dvāpara to the Kali Yuga, the most degenerate of all ages, in which family members wage war on each other. Like the *Rāmāyaṇa*, its story centers on a forest exile by princes, followed by a war, and thus is clearly a story of *kṣatriya* concerns. Unlike the *Rāmāyaṇa*, the *Mahābhārata* is a sprawling tale, varying in compositional style and full of interpolations, although its authorship is credited to the sage Vyāsa, who is himself a character in the story. Vyāsa is said to have composed the entire story in his head over a period of several

Figure 7.3 Lithograph depicting Vyāsa dictating the *Mahābhārata* to Gaṇeśa, the elephant-headed deity who serves as his scribe

years, and was encouraged by the god Brahmā to commit it to writing. The elephant-headed god Gaṇeśa served as his scribe on the condition that Vyāsa would not cease his recitation. Vyāsa agreed, provided that Gaṇeśa did not write down anything without thoroughly understanding it. Vyāsa, whose name means "the separator," is sometimes credited with dividing up the four Vedas, so that their size would be manageably accessible to human beings. The *Mahābhārata*, like other Hindu scriptures, makes claim to being a "fifth Veda." Although no one really takes this claim seriously, inserted within the epic's eighteen books, known as *parvans*, is the *Bhagavad Gītā*, which enjoys such status in Hinduism that it is *śruti* in all but name.

Vyāsa, the *Mahābhārata*'s author, surrogately fathered the princes Dhṛtarāṣṭra and Pāṇḍu for the king Vicitravīrya, who had died prematurely, leaving his queens, Ambikā and Ambālikā, childless. Dhṛtarāṣṭra was born blind, and Pāṇḍu was pale skinned. Their kingdom of Hastināpura was presided over by Bhīṣma, a powerful warrior who should have been king, but who ceded to and supported his father Śantanu's decision that only the descendants of Śantanu's second wife should inherit the throne. Bhīṣma took a vow of celibacy to avoid conflicts of inheritance, and actually secured the wives, Ambikā and Ambālikā, for Vicitravīrya. Because of his celibacy and unflinching dharmic character, Bhīṣma had grown enormously powerful, having the boon that he could only die when he chose to do so.

Because Dhṛtarāṣṭra, the eldest, was blind, Pāṇḍu ruled in his stead. One day, while hunting, Pāṇḍu shot a deer while it was copulating. For taking its life while it was engaged in an act of pleasure, the deer cursed Pāṇḍu that he would die the next time he made love to either of his two wives, Kuntī or Mādrī. Pāṇḍu thus renounced the throne and retired to the Himalayas with his wives, where he lived in celibate austerity. There, he discovered that his wife Kuntī had received a special *mantra* that allowed her to have a child with any god she chose to call upon, and Pāṇḍu encouraged her to do so, so that they might have heirs. Unbeknown to anyone, Kuntī had once used the *mantra* in her youth to summon the sun god, Sūrya, through whom she had given birth to the brilliant, golden-armored Karṇa. But fearing reprimands for her condition of unmarried motherhood she set Karṇa afloat on a river, where he was discovered and raised by a charioteer in the armies of Hastināpura.

On Pāṇḍu's bequest, Kuntī now summoned the god Dharma (or Yama, also known as Dharma-rāja), and gave birth to Yudhiṣṭhira (Firm in Battle), a son of impeccable dharmic character. She next summoned Vāyu, the Wind god, and gave birth to Bhīma, a son of vast proportions, appetite, and strength. From the thunder god, Indra, she produced Arjuna, a peerless warrior. Mādrī, too, desiring children, used the *mantra* and produced twins, Nakula and Sahadeva, by calling down the Aśvins, god-twins. One day, overwhelmed by Mādrī's beauty, Pandu approached her sexually despite her efforts to ward him off, and true to the curse he died instantly. Mādrī performed *satī* on his funeral pyre, and Kuntī returned to Hastinapura with the five "sons of Pāṇḍu," the Pāṇḍava princes, in her care.

Meanwhile Dhṛtarāṣṭra had married the princess Gāndhārī, who upon discovering that her husband was blind, herself put on a blindfold, vowing never to remove it. They eventually gave birth to one daughter, and a hundred sons, the eldest of which was Duryodhana. These princes were known as the Kauravas, after their lineage ancestor, the king Kuru. On Kuntī's return to the kingdom, the Kauravas were in constant rivalry and conflict with their cousins, the Pāṇḍavas. They trained in the arts of warfare with Droṇa, a master warrior, who sensed that Arjuna would be the greatest warrior. However, once, during an exhibition of their skills, the golden-armored warrior Karṇa arrived and gave challenge. He bested the princes, matching all of Arjuna's feats. The Pāṇḍavas, recognizing his prowess, jealously sought to deny him due honor on account of his low status. However, Duryodhana, recognizing in him a powerful ally, instantly made him king of the region of Aṅga, upon which Karṇa swore to him undying loyalty. Kuntī, witnessing the event, recognized Karṇa, and saw the sad turn of events in which her own first son would now be pitted against his own brothers.

Duryodhana's hatred of the Pāṇḍavas increased as he sensed that people wished Yudhiṣṭhira and the Pāṇḍava lineage would inherit the throne after Dhṛtarāṣṭra's death. He thus hatched a plot to have them killed. He had the Pāṇḍavas housed in a highly inflammable palace while they, together with Kuntī, were visiting Vanavrata to attend a Śiva festival. However, the Pāṇḍavas got wind of the plot, tunneled out of the house, leaving corpses in their beds, and escaped the death-trap as the house was engulfed in flames. They fled into the forest and wandered until they were given a home by a kind Brahmin. One day Bhīma killed a demon that had been terrorizing a nearby village. This led people to suspect that the Pāṇḍavas were still alive and in hiding.

One such person was King Drupada, whose daughter Draupadī, was holding her *svayaṃvara*. The Pāṇḍavas, in Brahmin ascetic disguise, attended, and after all the *kṣatriyas* who were present failed the test, the Brahmins were invited to compete. The contest involved stringing a bow, and hitting a revolving overhead target while gazing at its reflection in a pool of water. To everyone's amazement, Arjuna, in disguise, handily struck the target, winning the hand of Draupadī. Upon returning home, Kuntī realized that all the brothers desired her, and Draupadī agreed to wed all five of them. The Pāṇḍavas then presented themselves to Dhṛtarāṣṭra's court, and were given the territory of Indraprastha in order to avoid the tensions growing between them and the Kauravas.

With the aid of an *asura* architect, the Pāṇḍavas built a sumptuous palace and transformed the harsh land of Indraprastha into a wealthy kingdom. Yudhiṣṭhira even performed the *rājasūya yajña*, a glorious imperial coronation rite that demanded the attendance of other kings whose presence indicated allegiance or subservience. However, Duryodhana was envious of the Pāṇḍavas' success. He was determined to destroy them after being humiliated during a visit, when the water and glass whimsies throughout their palace got the better of him. With the aid of his uncle Śakuni, he challenged Yudhiṣṭhira to a game of dice, knowing that gambling, although it is a worthy pursuit for *kṣatriyas*, was also Yudhiṣṭhira's weakness. Yudhiṣṭhira accepted the invitation and, not very skilled in the game of dice, progressively wagered and lost his kingdom and all of his possessions. He even gambled and lost himself and his brothers. Finally, desperate and taunted by the Kauravas, he wagered Draupadī on a roll of the dice, and lost. Duḥśāsana, Duryodana's younger brother, then dragged Draupadī by her hair out of her private chambers, where she had modestly retreated since she was in her menstrual period, and into the Great Hall. Her humiliation

Figure 7.4 Lithograph depicting Duḥśāsana in his attempt to disrobe Draupadī, who is saved by Kṛṣṇa's miraculous intercession

continued while everyone watched as he tried to strip her naked. However, she prayed to Kṛṣṇa for help. As Duḥśāsana pulled off her clothing, Draupadī's layers of garments miraculously appeared to be endless, and he finally gave up in frustration. Dishonored and enraged, Draupadī chastised her husbands for allowing such a fate to befall a princess. Bhīma vowed to rip open Duḥśāsana's breast in battle and drink his blood.

To ameliorate an already dismal turn of events a final wager was agreed upon. The losers would surrender their kingdom and enter into a forest exile for thirteen years. If, during the last year, they were discovered, they would have to repeat the terms of their exile. Once again Yudhiṣṭhira lost, and the Pāṇḍavas, with Draupadī, began their long exile. The epic heroes had many adventures during their exile. Their children grew up. Bhīma fathered the giant, Ghaṭotkaca, with the demoness Hiḍimbā. Arjuna collected celestial weapons. They were periodically visited by Kṛṣṇa, who had a particularly close friendship with Arjuna. Arjuna had fathered the child, Abhimanyu, with Kṛṣṇa's sister Subhadrā. During the thirteenth year, the Pāṇḍavas hid in the palace of King Virāṭa in clever disguises. Yudhiṣṭhira, who had finally mastered the game of dice, disguised himself as a Brahmin and instructed the king. Arjuna, who was experiencing a year-long curse that had stripped him of his virility, instructed the women of Virāṭa's harem in the arts of music and dance. Draupadī served as the queen's maidservant. As the year approached its end, Kīcaka, Virāṭa's general, made aggressive sexual advances towards Draupadī, and she was forced to call upon Bhīma for help. Disguising himself as Draupadī, Bhīma lured Kīcaka for a rendezvous and pummeled him to death. Meanwhile Arjuna aided Virāṭa's son in repelling Duryodhana's raid on their kingdom. Their disguises were thus uncovered, but the year had successfully ended.

Having fulfilled the terms of their exile, the Pāṇḍavas expected the return of their half of the kingdom, but Duryodhana denied them even five small villages. The stage was thus set for a war of succession, and both the Kauravas and the Pāṇḍavas tried to mobilize their allies. Both Duryodhana and Arjuna approached Kṛṣṇa in his home kingdom of Dvāraka for help. As a family friend he pledged to offer himself to one side as a non-combatant adviser, and grant to the other side all of his armies. Although the Pāṇḍavas were outnumbered, Arjuna chose Kṛṣṇa, who then served as his charioteer. Unfortunately, on the eve of the battle, as the armies were fully arrayed, Arjuna was faced with a crisis of conscience. He asked Kṛṣṇa to drive his chariot between the two armies facing each other. Within the ranks of his enemies, Arjuna saw teachers, relatives, and other loved ones, many of whom he would be forced to slay in the ensuing battle. His bow slid from his hand and he slumped into his chariot. There ensued a conversation of profound import. Kṛṣṇa, who was the god Viṣṇu incarnate, began to convince Arjuna to fight. Only by so doing might the forces of *dharma* stand a chance of being victorious over *adharma*. Whenever *adharma* seriously threatens to overtake *dharma*, he explained, the great god Viṣṇu periodically incarnates to rectify the cosmic balance. The conversation, through which Kṛṣṇa successfully convinced Arjuna to fight, both by instructing him in various modes of Self-realization, and through a theophany in which Kṛṣṇa partially revealed to Arjuna his divine form, is known as the *Bhagavad Gītā* (*Song of the Lord*).

With Arjuna ready to fight, the great war began, and the *Mahābhārata* dedicates most of its chapters to the details of warfare. Many heroes fell on both sides during the fray, including Ghaṭotkaca, Bhīma's giant demon son. Kṛṣṇa often prescribed seemingly unscrupulous advice to the Pāṇḍavas to enable them to overcome various adversaries. Droṇa, their formidable instructor in the arts of warfare, for instance, was made to believe that his son had died in battle. Yudhiṣṭhira, who was known never to tell a lie, whispered to Droṇa that half-truth, causing Droṇa to lay down his weapons and be slain. Bhīṣma was skewered with arrows when refusing to fight against Śikhaṇḍin, a trans-gendered woman whose life he had once ruined. Refusing to die, Bhīṣma presented Yudhiṣṭhira extensive teachings on kingly *dharma*, while suspended on his bed of arrows. When Karṇa's chariot wheel got stuck, leaving him vulnerable, Arjuna slew him on Kṛṣṇa's insistence. Finally, as the war turned in favor of the Pāṇḍavas, and when Bhīma confronted Duryodhana in a battle with maces, Kṛṣṇa advised Bhīma to break the Kaurava king's thighs, a non-dharmic target in the conventions of battle. Draupadī, who had left her hair unbound and disheveled since the day of her humiliation, bathed it in Kaurava blood.

Although they finally won the war, on one grim night nearly all of the Pāṇḍavas' children were massacred in vengeance by Droṇa's son while they slept. Only Parikṣit, Abhimanyu's son survived. The frame story of the *Mahābhārata* is set around a sacrificial rite that was being performed by King Janamejaya, Parikṣit's son. Vyāsa attended the ritual, and asked his disciple to recite to the king the *Great Bhārata*, the story Vyāsa had recently composed in order to tell the story of Janamejaya's glorious ancestors, descendants of the ancestral king Bharata. The epic ends with the Pāṇḍavas' victory and their subsequent righteous rule under Yudhiṣṭhira, who continues to display his perfect dharmic nature into the very doors of heaven. Another text, the *Harivaṃśa* (*Dynasty of Viṣṇu/Hari [i.e. Kṛṣṇa]*), sometimes seen as an appendix to the *Mahābhārata*, further develops the story of Kṛṣṇa's childhood and life, progressively intensifying affirmations of his divinity.

Both the *Rāmāyaṇa* and the *Mahābhārata* are influential texts in the transmission of Hindu religious values. The narrative genre is highly engaging, and the stories are easily remembered and readily retold. Metaphoric and symbolic dimensions within the Epics have provided fertile soil for interpretations by scholars and religious teachers for the two thousand years since their composition. For instance, one might note in the wanderings of Rāma, a resonance with the stallion of the Vedic horse sacrifice. As the horse lays claim to the lands and territories where it roams, Rāma, too, claims an empire for his northern kingdom of Ayodhyā. Sītā's abduction by Rāvaṇa is akin to a challenge to Rāma's sovereign right to move freely through his sphere of political influence. Similarly, Kṛṣṇa, as Arjuna's charioteer, may be understood symbolically as the divine power that drives the lives of all persons. The Pāṇḍavas may represent the internal virtues latent within each of us, while the Kauravas are the innumerable psychological obstructions, such as anger and vengeance, with which we must constantly struggle. Thus the *Mahābharata* war may be interpreted as a symbolic representation of the inner battle between our quest to live dharmically and the forces that draw us towards adharmic deeds.

Despite criticisms that characters such as Rāma and Sītā are one-dimensional paragons of goodness, a close reading of the *Rāmāyaṇa* illustrates that they are more complexly drawn. The teachings of both epics oblige Hindus to explore the nature of *dharma* further, either to justify or challenge the actions of the portrayed characters. Was it indeed dharmic for Rāma to shoot Vālin as he did? Was Lakṣmana's treatment of Śūrpaṇakhā justified? Should Arjuna have killed Karṇa as he did, or Bhīma, Duryodhana? Do the ends justify the means in a war believed to be righteous? Who is the better role model for women, the devoted, uncomplaining wife, Sītā, who, despite her fidelity, gets poorly treated by Rāma, or the passionate Draupadī, who spurs her husbands to action, and extracts vengeance on those who violated her dignity?

The stories contained in the Epics continue to be retold in other types of texts. Viṣṇu-centered Purāṇas provide many more details about Kṛṣṇa's life, and other versions of the *Rāmāyaṇa* were written in subsequent centuries. Philosophical versions, such as the *Adhyātma Rāmāyaṇa*, are replete with portrayals of Rāma as a Self-realized being, often with a Vedāntic emphasis. The *Rāmacaritamanas* (*Ocean of the Deeds of Rāma*), a sixteenth-century telling by Tulsidās, written in an appealing versified form of old Hindi, is one of India's most popular versions. Written from within a growing tradition of devotional worship, Rāma's divine nature is emphasized far more than in Vālmīki's Sanskrit version. The Epics continue to captivate Hindu hearts and minds. Recent serialized television productions, which spanned many months of weekly airings, drew record audiences in India.

The Epics are known throughout South and South-east Asia. There are even Buddhist and Jain versions of the stories. *Rāmāyaṇa* bas-reliefs are carved on the walls of Buddhist temples in Thailand, Laos, and Cambodia. Kings of the current dynasty in Thailand are each named Rāma, and their ancient capital was named Ayutthaya, after Rāma's capital, Ayodhyā. Classical dance forms of the *Rāmāyaṇa* and episodes of the *Mahābhārata* are still enacted in Java and Bali.

Key points in this chapter

- The Epics, which centrally feature dharmic and *kṣatriya* concerns, emerged at the end of the Vedic period.
- The Epics mark a period when "deity as human" identifications become common.
- The Epics introduce and develop the mythologies of an array of deities that were insignificant or absent in Vedic *śruti* literature.
- The numerous variations in the stories of the *Rāṃāyaṇa* and the *Mahābhārata* reflect the interests of the social groups among which they circulated.
- The *Rāmāyaṇa* is renowned as a tale whose main characters, Rāma, Sītā, and Hanumān, serve as models of virtue for others to emulate.
- Inserted within the *Mahābhārata* is the *Bhagavad-Gītā*, a text that is *śruti* in all but name.
- The *Bhagavad-Gītā*'s pivotal location in the *Mahābhārata* contributes to its enduring renown in Hindu religious literature.
- Episodes and characters in the Epics are well known to most Hindus and these narratives are frequently used to illustrate religious teachings and values.

Discussion questions

1. In what ways are the *Rāmāyaṇa* and *Mahābhārata* similar, and how are they different from each other?
2. Why might the Epics also appeal to non-Hindus in South and South-east Asia?
3. In what ways is *dharma* a central feature in the *Rāmāyaṇa* and *Mahābhārata* epics?
4. Why are the Epics effective means of transmitting dharmic values?
5. The Epics emerged at the end of the Vedic period. In what ways might this have shaped the stories that were told, and why?

Further reading

General

Brockington, John (1998) *The Sanskrit Epics*. Leiden: E. J. Brill.

The Rāmāyaṇa

Buck, William (1976) *Rāmāyana*. Berkeley, CA: University of California Press.

Dharma, Krishna (aka Kenneth Anderson) (2000) *Rāmāyana: India's Immortal Tale of Adventure, Love, and Wisdom*. Badger, CA: Torchlight Publishing, Inc.

Goldman, Robert P. (gen. ed.) *The Rāmāyaṇa of Vālmīki: An Epic of Ancient India*. Vol. I: *Bālakāṇḍa*. Robert P. Goldman (ed. and trans.) 1984; Sheldon Pollock (ed. and trans.) Vol. II: *Ayodhyākāṇḍa*. 1986; Sheldon Pollock (ed. and trans.) Vol. III: *Āraṇyakāṇḍa*. 1991; Rosalind Lefeber (ed. and trans.) Vol. IV: *Kiṣkindhākāṇḍa*. 1996; Robert P. Goldman and Sally Sutherland Goldman (ed. and trans.). Vol. V: *Sundarakāṇḍa*. 1996. All, Princeton, NJ: Princeton University Press.

Hill. W. D. P. (1952)*The Holy Lake of the Acts of Rama: An English translation of Tulsi Das's Ramacaritmanasa*. Calcutta: Oxford University Press.

Menon, Ramesh (2001) *The Rāmāyana*. New York: North Point Press.

Narayan, R. K. (1996)*The Rāmāyana*. New Delhi: Vision Books Pvt. Ltd.

Prasad, R. C. (ed. and trans.) (1988) *Tulasidasa's Shriramacharitamanasa: The Holy Lake of the Acts of Rama*. Delhi: Motilal Banarsidass.

Rajagopalachari, C. (1962) *Rāmāyaṇa*. Bombay: Bharatiya Vidya Bhavan.

Sundaram, P. S. (2002) *Kamba Rāmāyana*. N.S. Jagannatha (ed.). New Delhi: Penguin.

Tapasyananda, Swami (1985) *The Adhyatma Rāmāyana: The Spiritual Version of the Rāma Saga*. Mylapore, Madras: Sri Ramakrishna Math.

Vālmīki (1996) *The Rāmāyaṇa*, abridged. Arshia Sattar (trans.) New Delhi: Penguin.

Venkatesananada, Swami (1988) *The Concise Rāmāyana of Valmiki*. Albany, NY: State University of New York Press.

On the Rāmāyaṇa and its tradition

Blank, Jonah (1992) *Arrow of the Blue-Skinned God, Retracing the Rāmāyana Through India*. Boston, MA: Houghton Mifflin Company.

Dehejia, Vidya, (ed.) (1994) *The Legend of Rama – Artistic Visions*. Bombay: Marg Publications.

Lutgendorf, Philip (1992) *The Life of a Text: Performing the Rāmcaritmānas of Tulsidas*. Berkeley, CA: University of California Press.

Richman, Paula (ed.) (1991) *Many Rāmāyanas: The Diversity of a Narrative Tradition in South Asia*. Berkeley, CA: University of California Press.
— (ed.) (2001) *Questioning Rāmāyanas: A South Asian Tradition*. Berkeley, CA: University of California Press.
Whaling, F. (1980) *The Rise of the Religious Significance of Rāma*. Delhi: Motilal Banarsidass.

The Mahābhārata

Buck, William (1973) *Mahābhārata*. Berkeley, CA: University of California Press.
Buitenen, J. A. B. (1973–8)*The Mahābhārata*, 3 vols. Chicago, IL: University of Chicago Press
Fitzgerald, James L. (2004) *The Mahābhārata*, Vol. 7. Chicago, IL: University of Chicago Press.
(1933–78) *Mahābhārata, Critical Edition*, 22 vols. Poona: Bhandarkar Oriental Research Institute.
Narayan, R. K. (1978) *The Mahabharata*. New York: Viking.
Rajagopalachari, C. (trans.) (1958) *Mahābhārata*. Bombay: Bharatiya Vidya Bhavan.

On the Mahābhārata and its tradition

Hiltebeitel, Alf (1988) *The Cult of Draupadi*, Vol. I. *Mythologies: From Gingee to Kuruksetra*. Chicago, IL: University of Chicago Press.
— (1991) *The Cult of Draupadi*, Vol. II. *On Hindu Ritual and the Goddess*. Chicago, IL: University of Chicago Press.
— (1999) *Rethinking India's Oral and Classical Epics: Draupadi among Rajputs, Muslims, and Dalits*. Chicago, IL: University of Chicago Press.
— (2001) *Rethinking the Mahābhārata: A Reader's Guide to the Education of the Dharma-King*. Chicago, IL: University of Chicago Press.
Sullivan, Bruce (1990) *Kṛṣṇa Dvaipayana Vyāsa and the Mahābhārata: A New Interpretation*. Leiden: E. J. Brill.
Sukthankar, V. S. (1957) *On the Meaning of the Mahābhārata*. Bombay: Asiatic Society.

8 *The* Bhagavad Gītā *and the rise of* bhakti

In this chapter

We now turn to key elements in the teachings of the *Bhagavad Gītā*, illustrating how it syncretized many of the values within varied religio-philosophical streams that predated it, and how it successfully reconciled key tensions among many of them. Through case studies, the three paths to *mokṣa* articulated in the *Gītā* are shown to have had enduring relevance through to the present day. The *Gītā*'s pivotal role in the rise of *bhakti* (loving devotion) is highlighted among the Śiva and Viṣṇu worshipping poet-saints of South India.

Main topics covered

- The *Bhagavad Gītā*
- The householder versus the renouncer
- The *Bhagavad Gītā*'s three *yogas*
- Jñāna yoga
- Karma yoga
- Bhakti yoga
- South Indian Hinduism and the rise of devotionalism
- The Ālvārs and the Nāyanārs

The Bhagavad Gītā

The enormous influence of the *Bhagavad Gītā* makes it worth special consideration. Researchers wonder whether it circulated as an independent Upaniṣad-like scripture, which it resembles in its student-teacher dialogical format, prior to its insertion into the *Mahābhārata*. Its location within the epic is pivotal, book-ended by the captivating story that leads to the onset of a terrible conflict, and the dreadful events of the ensuing battles. The existential plight that Arjuna faces is poignant: to fight or to yield, to renounce his kingly inheritance for the sake of peace, but

Figure 8.1 Life-size statue depicting Kṛṣṇa as charioteer delivering the teachings of the Bhagavad Gītā to Arjuna (Rishikesh)

by so doing to allow unrighteousness to prevail. Arjuna's dilemma has a symbolic resonance with challenges faced by each of us at critical junctures in life, when the course of appropriate action is not always clear. Kṛṣṇa's teachings to Arjuna offer him a resolution to his paralytic indecision, and in the centuries since the *Gītā*'s composition Hindu religious teachers and philosophers have tirelessly mined its contents.

A particularly effective aspect of the *Gītā* is that it does not present a simple, unified philosophy. Kṛṣṇa makes reference to religious and philosophical ideas that were in circulation at the time of its composition, skillfully fusing them into a conglomerate that suits the sensibilities of a wide variety of religious orientations. Within it one finds resonances with Buddhist notions of transcending dualistic extremes, treatment of the doctrines of *karma* and rebirth, affirmation of the *varṇa* system and the value of doing one's prescribed duties, Upaniṣadic teachings on the absolute Brahman, and terminology associated with Sāṅkhya philosophy.

At first Kṛṣṇa attempts, unsuccessfully, to convince Arjuna to fight based on an appeal to his dharmic duty as a *kṣatriya*. It is interesting that both Buddhism and Jainism were founded by *kṣatriya* princes in the centuries during or just prior to the *Gītā*'s composition, who renounced their kingly inheritances for spiritual paths emphasizing non-violence and involving a hermit's life in the forest. In both the *Rāmāyaṇa* and the *Mahābhārata*, we encounter tales of princes who end up in the hermit's forest lifestyle, albeit more due to circumstances beyond their control.

Nevertheless Rāma's contentment with life in his hermitage prior to Sītā's abduction, and Arjuna's crisis of conscience on the eve of battle, offer us more evidence of existing tensions in that era between the seemingly burdensome obligations to uphold the social order by fulfilling one's dharmic duty and the prospect of giving it all up for a life of peaceful contemplation. For warriors, dharmic duty can be particularly onerous. The Hindu Epics manage to resolve the dilemma in favor of upholding the social order. Unlike the Buddha and the Jina, Rāma and the Pāṇḍavas go into the forest with their wives, and ultimately return to resume their social responsibilities with their spouses. The outcome of this choice is not portrayed in naively glowing terms. Rāma banishes Sītā, and for many years does not know of his own children, while the Pāṇḍavas have to face the death of their children at the hands of their enemies. Thus Self-realization, or *mokṣa*, is still implicitly upheld as the preferred goal, for only it offers the promise of freedom from the sufferings that accompany embodied existence.

It is within this context that the *Bhagavad Gītā*'s teachings play such a pivotal role, for they offer paths that reconcile the quandary between choosing life in society or away from its demands. Kṛṣṇa teaches Arjuna three paths to Self-realization. These are the Jñāna Marga (The Path of Transcendental Knowledge), the Karma Marga (The Path of Action), and the Bhakti Marga (The Path of Loving Devotion). The three paths are also known as Yogas, methods leading to a unitive condition. The *Gītā* is one of the earliest texts to introduce the *bhakti* approach, and identifies Kṣṛṇa as the ideal and supreme object of devotion.

With stirring eloquence Kṛṣṇa described his divine nature to Arjuna, who had tacitly accepted, but did not fully realize Kṛṣṇa's divinity. Arjuna, enthralled by this description, asked to see Kṛṣṇa's divine form. Kṛṣṇa conceded, granting Arjuna supernatural vision, and then displayed a partial revelation of his universal form (*viśvarūpa*) that was terrifying in both its immensity and power. Kṛṣṇa's body shone like a thousand suns, and contained within it all of the gods. With innumerable heads, eyes, and arms, it encompassed all the creatures in creation, and yet also stood in the form of the four-armed Viṣṇu with his club and discus. Arjuna then glimpsed within Kṛṣṇa's form the imminent future in which the warriors on both sides of the impending fray were devoured by his many mouths. In like fashion, he saw the worlds themselves meet their end in Kṛṣṇa's all-destroying being. Fully convinced of Kṛṣṇa's divinity, but unable to bear the awesome nature of the unfolding vision, Arjuna asked for it to cease, and Kṛṣṇa resumed his normal human form. Kṛṣṇa commented that only a select few are graced with such a theophany, and that even the gods long for it.

The teachings of the *Bhagavad Gītā* became foundational for Vedānta philosophy. The text also provided crucial scriptural justifications for an array of Hindu religious practices that began to displace aspects of Vedic religion, such as its emphasis on sacrificial ritual. The *Gītā* marks the rise in what is sometimes called the period of

Classical Hinduism, characterized by the ascendancy of deities such as Śiva, Viṣṇu, and Devī, who are celebrated in Purāṇic scriptures. Classical Hinduism is also marked by the building of Hindu temples, and the *bhakti*-oriented performance of *pūjā*. All of these innovations were progressively incorporated by and accepted into what constituted a newer Brahmin-sanctioned orthodoxy.

The householder versus the renouncer

The period of the Epics marked a pivotal shift in the nature of Hinduism, and in the features of Hindu orthodoxy. The worship of older Vedic gods, such as Prajāpati, Indra, and Agni through *yajña* was beginning to yield to the worship of other deities, as well as to a questioning of the metaphysics that valorized Vedic-styled ritual religion. *Śramaṇa* philosophies of the late Vedic period had already begun to challenge the authority of the Vedas, and to prescribe renunciation and the practice of meditation as more beneficial than sacrifice. Renunciation in the quest for Self-realization and the ending of suffering stood in sharp tension with the conventional practices associated with the householder's way of life and the sacrificial rites that accompanied it. Brahminic orthodoxy had evolved in accord with these conflicting imperatives through the inclusion of the Upaniṣads, which articulated philosophies of Self-realization by means other than sacrifice, into the Vedic corpus. The *varṇāśrama dharma* prescriptions offered yet another compromise by orthodoxy, by recommending that one could be both a householder and a renouncer, merely by taking up each stage in its proper sequence at appropriate points in one's life. The goals of *dharma*, *artha*, *kāma*, and *mokṣa* could each be pursued and attained. Nevertheless, many could not abide with enduring the formalities of the social order before pursuing the goal held in highest regard, namely *mokṣa*. Moreover, there was certainly mounting pressure from other disenfranchised groups for fuller participation in religious life, and for authorization of their capacity to engage with it in a meaningful way. They were undoubtedly already engaged in their own forms of worship, some of which may have mimicked, while others may have sharply deviated from orthodox styles. The Buddhist response was to permit women, *śūdras*, and Untouchables to join their renunciant order. It is from within this milieu of contrasting spiritual values and demands for religious inclusion and empowerment that the *Bhagavad Gītā* presented its teachings.

The Bhagavad Gītā's *three* yogas

The *Bhagavad Gītā*'s teachings markedly widen the parameters of what constitutes legitimate Hinduism. It is difficult to say whether it actually ushered in these practices, or effectively expressed what was already burgeoning at the time. However, it clearly becomes the scriptural point of reference for the vision of Hindu religious belief and practice that it promotes. No other scripture articulates the centrally defining features of Hinduism as succinctly and effectively as the *Bhagavad Gītā*. Highly syncretic, and at times even contradictory, the *Gītā* has become mandatory reading for Hindu, particularly Vedānta, philosophers over the centuries. Although divided into eighteen chapters, each of which is called a teaching on a particular *yoga* or discipline, its teachings are conventionally grouped into three major approaches (*marga, yoga*) to liberation. These are the paths of Jñāna ([Transcendental] Knowledge), Karma (Action), and Bhakti ([Loving] Devotion). While the paths of knowledge (*jñāna*) and action (*karma*) had been discussed in other scriptures, the *Gītā* reconfigures them, particularly the path of action. Quite notably, the *Gītā* describes the path of loving devotion (*bhakti*), of which almost nothing is said in the scriptural literature that precedes it. The *Gītā* effectively strikes a compromise between the concerns of orthodoxy and the needs of the masses. Its masterful accomplishment of this feat is evident in its endurance to the present day, and its continual invocation by the holders of hegemony and the disenfranchised alike.

Jñāna yoga

The *Bhagavad Gītā* offers relatively conventional Upaniṣadic teachings on the nature of the knowledge that leads to the realization of Brahman. Arjuna is confounded by the apparent contradictions between the demands of his *dharma* and the world-view that he has been taught. As a warrior he is supposed to fight and kill, but in his current predicament, this would mean the destruction of teachers, his *gurus*, and even his family members. War, he argues, destroys family lineages, leading to the corruption of its women and, by leaving behind no one to venerate the lineage ancestors, will cause them too to descend into lower realms. He grieves that *kṣatriya dharma* requires him to perform actions that damage all that he has been taught is good. Kṛṣṇa responded by first explaining that although it may appear that Arjuna is killing or that he himself may be killed, the true Self endures beyond death. The wise grieve for neither the living nor the dead, because they know of the existence of the deathless Self beyond the body. Arjuna, Kṛṣṇa, and all the warriors arrayed before them have always existed, explains Kṛṣṇa, and they always will exist. The true Self changes bodies with each incarnation, as a person changes clothes. The liberated person knows this truth about one's immortal nature, but the deluded do not. Therefore, Arjuna should attend to his duty, for nothing is better for a warrior than to fight in a righteous war. If killed, he would attain heaven. If victorious, he would gain earthly glory. But fleeing from the fight would lead to sin and infamy. Still confused, Arjuna persists in his inquiry, providing Kṛṣṇa the opportunity to expand his teachings.

Kṛṣṇa explains that, unlike Arjuna, he is a realized being, knowing himself as the supreme source of all of reality. Although unborn and deathless in his essential being, he has taken up rebirth repeatedly through his delusive power. Kṛṣṇa equates himself with Brahman, the absolute source and substance of all reality. He teaches Arjuna many of the conventional methods of attaining the highest knowledge (*jñāna*), as are more systematically expressed in the Upaniṣads, and the writings of Sāṅkhya and Rāja yoga. Self-restraint, concentration of mind, and regarding a Brahmin and an Untouchable with an equal eye, are among the qualities that characterize this path. The *Gītā* also discusses aspects of this approach in the language of "the field" and "the knower of the field" (*kṣetra-jña*). To know both the field and the knower of the field is true knowledge (*jñāna*). When one discerns (*anupaśyati*) that the differentiated identities of beings abide as The One (*eka-stham*), which has diversified, then one unites with Brahman. Without a beginning and beyond qualification, this supreme Self (*ātman*), although it performs no actions, is all-pervading, and abides within each body. The "knower of the field" illuminates "the field," and those knowers who, with the eye of *jñāna* understand the difference between the field and its knower, and are [simultaneously] freed from the materiality of things (*bhūta-prakṛti-mokṣam*), they attain the Supreme (13.35).

Jñāna yoga is held in especially high regard by followers of radical non-dualistic Vedānta philosophy. By others, this path has also been interpreted as involving the study of religious teachings on liberation. However, although the word *jñāna* may be used to mean "knowledge," in the context of Jñāna yoga, it refers not merely to mundane intellectual knowledge, but to a transcendental "knowing" of the Absolute, which is a deeply experienced truth, and which provides meaning to the facts and data that constitute our gathered information about the world.

Case study: Ramaṇa Mahārṣi

The Hindu saint, Ramaṇa Mahārṣi (1879–1950) is an ideal exemplar of the Jñāna yoga approach. Born in South India, Ramaṇa's family moved to the temple city of Madurai after the death of his father. Religiously inclined, he was inspired by the stories of the Nāyanārs, South Indian saints who were devotees of Śiva, and whose stories are recounted in the *Periya Purāṇa*. Then at the age of seventeen, he underwent an experience that radically changed his life. As he later explained, while seated alone in his room, he was overtaken by an intense fear of death. Rather than distract himself by seeking out the company of others, Ramaṇa decided to delve more deeply into his fear. He lay on the ground, stretching out as if a corpse, accepting his death, and progressively yielding to the conditions of death. Entering into a state akin to the deepest yogic meditative states of *samādhi*, where all thought, including that of the "I" had stopped, he received a vivid realization. He found himself absorbed into the deathless Self, a condition that instantly removed his fear of death. Thereafter, thoughts began to move again, like notes of music, but the unbroken absorption in the Self continued for the remainder of his life, providing as it were the fundamental vibration underlying and influencing all other notes.

Shortly thereafter, he left home, abandoned most of his possessions, and took up abode in a small secluded shrine at Arunachala, a hill sacred to Śiva, near Tiruvannamalai. Carried like a tiny speck in a vast flood, he found himself disoriented in the world. His hair grew matted, and his body was sore and bleeding from infected insect bites, but he did not notice or care about what was occurring, and fortunately had his basic physical needs attended to by other residents of the main temple. He began to attract devotees, and slowly began to regain his sense of orientation with the world. He gathered disciples, and treated all with equanimity. He refused to accept gifts, and although his fame spread widely he refused invitations to move to more luxurious accommodation. He actually lived in still silence in a cave for sixteen years. In a few short books, Ramaṇa presents the essence of his religious philosophy that may be characterized as a form of non-dualistic Vedānta. One's true Self (*ātman*) is Brahman.

Ramaṇa's approach may be appropriately classified as Jñāna yoga, because when questioned by disciples on how they might attain Self-realization, he offered the technique of *vicāra*, or inquiry. The relentless pursuit of the question, "Who am I?" will lead to realization. By recognizing what one is not, and observing the nature of the responses provided by the mind, the mind will begin to cease its activities and its mistaken identifications, leaving behind only the presence of the Self.

Karma yoga

Prior to the teachings of the *Bhagavad Gītā*, the path of *karma* (action) meant the performance of deeds that maintained the cosmic order. For orthodoxy, this was the performance of one's caste-ordained *dharma*, which entailed the regular performance of public and domestic rituals. These would accumulate benefits and result in a better rebirth, possibly even in heaven (*svarga*). This reward was not very appealing to those who sought *mokṣa*, for heaven, too, was envisioned as an impermanent abode. The *Gītā*'s teachings prescribe that one perform one's ordained duty, but that one should renounce attachment to fruits, that is, the success or failure of those actions. This it calls *yoga*. Arjuna is instructed that Kṛṣṇa himself, Supreme Divinity, performs actions without attachment, and so persons should do the same. Kṛṣṇa also cautions against indecisiveness and inaction, which is a form of "doing" and carries with it karmic consequences. Attachment (*kāma*) to the outcomes of actions,

Kṛṣṇa instructs, binds individuals to the laws of causality, while renunciation of such attachment, can result in the highest attainment. This attitude to activity, known as *niṣ-kāma karma* (action without attachment), reorients the performance of deeds in the direction of *mokṣa*.

Certain lines of interpretation emphasize the *Gītā*'s support of the performance of traditional dharmic actions, such as sacrificial rites, *varṇa*-appropriate behavior, and so on, without attachment. However, the *Gītā* also sets Karma yoga in relationship with devotion, insisting that devotional acts should be performed in the spirit of non-attachment to their results. Through such devotion one may also obtain *mokṣa*. Furthermore, "action" need not only be the performance of prescribed sacrificial rituals. By offering up all of one's thoughts, words, and deeds to Kṛṣṇa, with devotion, while renouncing attachment to their fruits, one engages in the supreme sacrifice and can obtain liberation. This teaching, while not contradicting the benefits of traditional Vedic ritual, redefined the meaning of sacrifice. The notion of an inner sacrifice, conducted through meditative practice in the context of renunciation, was already incipient in the teachings of the Āraṇyakas and Upaniṣads, but the *Gītā* fused renunciation with the householder's way of life. One may continue to live in the world, it teaches, performing one's regular activities. Without renouncing the everyday activities that sustain the social order, but armed with an attitude of renunciation of attachment to the outcomes of these actions, one may actually gain *mokṣa*. One may thus be both a student and a renouncer, or a householder and a renouncer. True *saṃnyāsa*, by implication, is not the external abandoning of material possessions and one's engagement with social life, but an inward spirit of detachment.

The practice of Karma yoga developed many conventional forms in the subsequent millennia. Action without attachment is regarded as action without self-concern, and self-less action is action for the benefit of others. Thus sweeping up in a temple, cooking food for priests and pilgrims in a hermitage (*āśrama*), or any kind of work that is done on behalf of others, is often called Karma yoga. Hindu religious organizations, such as the Ramakrishna Missions, which run clinics and hospitals, orphanages and leprosariums, embody this ideal. The religious sentiment behind all Hindu philanthropy and the work of its charitable institutions may be placed within the rubric of Karma yoga.

Case study: Mahātma Gandhi

Mohandas Karamchand Gandhi (1869–1948), was born in the north-eastern state of Gujarat. He studied law for three years in London and then took up legal work in South Africa, where an event of pivotal consequence took place. Although he held a first class ticket, on a winter trip to Pretoria Gandhi was ejected from the train when he refused to give up his seat to a white man who boarded mid-journey. Humiliated, as he stood on the icy platform, he was made painfully aware of the reality of social injustice, and this set him on his life's struggle to bring about change. Gandhi spent twenty-one years in South Africa, mostly engaged in efforts for equal rights for Indians who were experiencing discrimination as inferiors under the system of apartheid, and being victimized by unjust laws. It was here that he developed many of the strategies of political activism that he subsequently applied in India. Gandhi coined the term *satyagraha* ("holding fast to truth"), which conveys a sense of the power inherent in just causes. *Satyagraha* involved active resistance to injustice and oppression, but through non-violent civil disobedience. After some successes in South Africa, Gandhi returned to India, where he became involved in the struggle for Indian independence.

Gandhi and his freedom-fighters, known as *satyagrahis*, were frequently imprisoned for breaking the law. To subvert an unfair tax on salt, the production of which was turned into a government monopoly, Gandhi led a protest march to the seashore to collect natural salt, thus breaking the law. He and his followers were arrested, but his actions brought attention to the plight of the poor under this unjust law.

Gandhi explained that the *Bhagavad Gītā*'s teachings were very influential in his life. Although he was a married man with four children, and came from a *vaiśya varṇa*, Gandhi saw that the *Gītā*'s teachings were inspirational to his life's interests. Gandhi interpreted the notion of *niṣkāma karma* as a call to just and selfless action. One ought to do what is right, and not be preoccupied with the effects that such action might incur to oneself. It took extraordinary courage to practice *satyagraha*, because it required more than a moral indignation and intensity when encountering unrighteousness; it demanded action. Moreover, that action needed to be conducted without harming anyone, for Gandhi interpreted Kṛṣṇa's teachings to Arjuna as fundamentally non-violent. It was a call to conquer the enemy within, to engage in an internal struggle against one's fears of failure, pain, and even death, as well as one's desires for success, pleasure, and fame. To Gandhi, the way to keep God first and foremost in mind, and to be totally dedicated to God, was through service to humanity. Gandhi, who was given the title Mahātma (Great Soul), embodies the path of Karma yoga, since his life was characterized by unselfish action on behalf of others, without attachment to the fruits of those deeds.

Bhakti yoga

Although the word *bhakti* appears in earlier texts such as the *Śvetāśvatara Upaniṣad*, dedicated to Śiva, the *Bhagavad Gītā* is the first scripture to elaborate upon its meaning. *Bhakti*, as explained by the *Gītā*, dramatically democratizes access to worship and to *mokṣa*. Although it upholds the status of Brahmins and *kṣatriyas*, the *Gītā* states that all those of unfortunate birth, such as women, *vaiśyas*, and even *śūdras*, can reach the highest goal if devoted to Kṛṣṇa (9.32). Even someone who may have committed the most heinous act is rendered a saint through devotion (9.30). Not only does the

Gītā open up worship to everyone, and uplift sincere devotees to the highest status, it democratizes modes of devotion and the envisaged forms of divinity. Kṛṣṇa teaches that even those who worship other deities with sincerity actually worship him, no matter how unorthodox their rites may be (9.23). Thus Kṛṣṇa identifies himself with every deity that is the object of genuine devotion. This teaching is crucial in comprehending Hinduism's characteristic tolerant polytheism. A sincere love for and devotion to the divine, however divinity may be conceived, and in whatever manner that worship might take, is regarded as leading the devotee to the Absolute, as it truly is, and to liberation. Although the *Gītā*'s teachings promote Kṛṣṇa as the supreme deity, they also pave the way for any conception of divinity to be "substitutes for" or "superimposed onto" the Absolute. For instance, in his interpretation of the *Gītā*, the influential eleventh-century philosopher Abhinavagupta points out how Kṛṣṇa offers guidance for a liberation (*mokṣa*) that is "absorption in Lord Śiva."

Kṛṣṇa also identifies himself with the Upaniṣadic Brahman/Ātman, with Sāṅkhya philosophy's Puruṣa, and with the traditionally imagined four-armed Viṣṇu. He points out how many do not recognize his divinity in the human form in which he presents himself. He is everywhere. He is the sacrificer, the sacrifice, the sacred fire, and the deity who receives the offering. He is in the most subtle of phenomena. Whatever is awesome, splendid and glorious has its existence in a shard of his being (10.41). These teachings of the *Bhagavad Gītā* inform our understanding of the Hindu propensity to worship both natural phenomena and images crafted by human hands as abodes of divinity. Many strands within the Abrahamic religious traditions (i.e. Judaism, Christianity, and Islam), have strong sentiments against depictions of God, whose transcendence ought not to be compromised through such portrayals. Furthermore, their theological doctrines do not proclaim God to be embodied within the creation. The *Gītā*'s teachings allow for this type of understanding, but their syncretic character actually permits a panentheistic formulation. While pantheism is the belief that God is identical with the creation, found in all things, and that everything taken together is God, panentheism is the belief that God interpenetrates the universe, encompasses it, and yet is greater than it, being both within but nevertheless transcending the creation. Thus a river, a rock, a lump of cow dung, a flower, or a graven image may represent the Absolute, as well as embody it. And yet, the Absolute is beyond all such manifestations. Whoever offers a leaf, a flower, fruit, or water, with purity of spirit, will have that offering accepted, says the *Gītā* (9.26), thus providing a rationale for the traditional forms that *pūjā*, Hindu devotional worship, takes.

Although it presents a variety of acceptable paths to both God and liberation, which it essentially equates, the *Bhagavad Gītā* makes its most compelling case for Bhakti yoga. The Rāja yoga path of ascetic disciplinary control of body–mind is endorsed, but the most accomplished *yogis* are those who, with their minds absorbed in the divine, worship God in full faith (6.47). Similarly, while Jñāna yoga is effective, the highest *jñāna* is knowledge of God, most effectively attained through loving devotion. And Karma yoga's detached and selfless action is best applied to devotion to God, without attachment to the desired fruits of worship. By fixing one's mind on God, being lovingly devoted, sacrificing, rendering homage, and making God one's cardinal interest, one's Self, so thoroughly absorbed in God, will surely come to God (9.34).

Case study: Śrī Caitanya

An excellent exemplar of the Bhakti yoga approach is Śrī Caitanya (1486–1533), who revitalized the worship of Kṛṣṇa and Viṣṇu in Bengal. Our knowledge of Caitanya's life is derived from hagiographies, embellished biographies, often of saints, written to promote their divine and extraordinary nature. Caitanya was born in Navadip, Bengal, and the hagiographies portray him as Kṛṣṇa-like in his youthful beauty and playfulness. Educated, married, and working as a schoolteacher, he appears to have been initially content with his householder's life. However, at the age of twenty-two a visit to the city of Gāyā, where he had gone to perform *śrāddha* rites for his father, led to an encounter with a Kṛṣṇa worshipper named Īśvara Puri who changed his life.

Having heard about Kṛṣṇa, Caitanya soon grew more absorbed in Kṛṣṇa devotion and gave up his teaching career. He soon began to lead the city's Vaiṣṇava (Viṣṇu-dedicated) community and thus shape the character of Kṛṣṇa worship in Bengal. In particular, he introduced the tradition of public *kīrtana,* namely, singing, dancing, and chanting out the name of Kṛṣṇa, to the clash of cymbals and drums, while parading the city streets. The intention was to proclaim that devotion should not always be a private affair, but could be playful and ecstatic, mirroring the dalliance of the milkmaids with Kṛṣṇa in the mythic tales of his boyhood in Vṛndāvana. Caitanya took up *saṃnyāsa,* official renunciation, in 1510, and although he longed to go to Vṛndāvana left his home for the holy city of Puri, and later journeyed through South India. There, he debated renouncers from various schools, converted many to Kṛṣṇa *bhakti,* and returned to Puri as a living saint.

Caitanya began to emphasize that the attitude of devotion should be akin to that displayed by Kṛṣṇa's mythic lover Rādhā. Rādhā can think of nothing other than Kṛṣṇa when separated from him, and enjoys the greatest joy when united with him. The devotee should be like Rādhā, continuously engaged in an ecstatic loving devotion to Kṛṣṇa. Eventually, Caitanya left for Vṛndāvana in a state of progressively intensifying God-intoxication. Everything he saw in Vṛndāvana reminded him of Kṛṣṇa and Rādhā, and plunged him into states of rapture.

Caitanya clearly embodies the Bhakti yoga path centered on Kṛṣṇa devotion, the character of which he actually shaped for Bengali Vaiṣṇavas. Kṛṣṇa increasingly became the center of Caitanya's life, and Caitanya's ardent love induced him to see signs of Kṛṣṇa and Rādhā everywhere. In appearance and lifestyle he was a renouncer, but unlike the unemotional states that seem to characterize *saṃnyāsa*, Caitanya's inner world was a passionate love affair with God. His devotees now regard Caitanya as an incarnation of Kṛṣṇa himself, who in his divine playfulness, took up embodiment as a human being in order to experience the ecstasy of his own devotees' all-consuming love for their Beloved.

South Indian Hinduism and the rise of devotionalism

The emotionally charged *bhakti* that we associate with Śrī Caitanya is only vaguely prefigured in the *Bhagavad Gītā*. The earliest evidence of *bhakti*'s association with a sort of mystical love appears in South India, within the poetry of the "Tamil saints." The major early kingdoms of South India, from where we derive the core of our historical understanding of the region, were the Cola, Pāṇḍya, and Cera. The people of these kingdoms spoke Dravidian languages, such as Tamil, and prior to the fourth century BCE had been negligibly influenced by the North Indian, Sanskritic tradition. They had even resisted annexation into Aśoka's vast empire. From about the second century BCE to the third century CE, the South Indians composed literary works that reflect distinct cultural styles and values, which have endured even after almost two thousand years of Sankritic influence. The literary works of this period are collectively known as the Saṅgham literature, which lays mythic claims to having been composed during cultural expositions (*saṅgham*), stretching back for thousands of years.

Vedic traditions entered into South India through the patronage of rulers who promoted orthodoxy, which through Brahminic consecration rites, conferred upon them special status and powers. Some rulers claimed lineage association with the heroes of the Epics, or even claimed participation in the *Mahābhārata* war. The *Tolkāppiyam*, an early grammar text of literary Tamil named after its author, was composed in about the first century CE, and shows evidence of Sanskritic (i.e. Āryan, Brahmin) linguistic and cultural influences. Other Saṅgham literature consists of eight anthologies of poetry, which primarily deal with secular themes such as love, classified as an interior (*akam*) sentiment, and heroism, classified as an exterior (*puram*) one. The *Tolkāppiyam* describes a compelling series of associations between landscapes and the cadences of romantic love as evidenced in this poetry. The verdant hills are associated with attraction and union, the desert's arid land with separation, the forests with expectation and waiting, the seashore with sorrow and despair, and cultivated landscape with sulking anger. The vibrant Tamil tradition of poetic composition, with its propensity towards themes of love, foreshadows the rise of devotional *bhakti* poetry that would develop in subsequent centuries.

As the Saṅgham period ended, Buddhism and Jainism, which had spread from North India, became established in the south. Their ascetic ideals of renunciation contrasted with the style of indigenous folk cults in which ecstatic possession of devotees by a deity was commonplace. One of the most revered gods in South India, Murugan (Murukaṇ) was worshipped in this way. The god himself was an irresistibly handsome young man, associated with love and war, neither of which resonated well with the dispassionate character of the renouncer traditions. It is not surprising that as the North Indian theistic traditions, recounting stories of the god Kṛṣṇa and his romantic life in Vṛndāvana, permeated the south, they were soon embraced. Two main groups of Tamil *bhakti*-poets emerged from the sixth to the eleventh centuries CE. These were the Ālvārs and the Nāyanārs, whose *bhakti* compositions and sentiments actually inspired philosophical and theological developments, and eventually influenced a resurgence of *bhakti* in both North and South India. As *bhakti* traditions grew and gained royal patronage, they undermined the strength of Jainism and Buddhism.

The Ālvārs and the Nāyanārs

The Ālvārs ("submerged [in the divine]") were itinerant bards, who sang hymns to Viṣṇu, while the Nāyanārs ("leaders") expressed their devotion to Śiva. The poetry of these South Indian *bhakti* saints is marked by intense emotion, conveying the gamut of emotions experienced in relationships of romantic love (Tamil: *anbu*). However, while the object of love in earlier Tamil poetry was another human being, in these works the beloved is God, and the lover is the love-sick devotee. Thus the poets sing of the sorrow of being separated from the Divine, when God was hidden, but mostly of the ecstatic joy felt in the company and presence of God revealed. Unlike the proponents of Upaniṣadic Hinduism, the *bhakti* saints did not yearn for an immediate dissolving into the Divine, but for a prolonged interactive relationship in which the distinction between the lover and the Beloved would generate the blissful pleasures that are only dimly mirrored in human relationships.

There were twelve Ālvārs. Āṇṭāḷ, the only woman among them, was the daughter of Maturakavi, a Brahmin priest and also an Ālvār. In one set of Āṇṭāḷ's poetry she assumes the role of a cowgirl (*gopī*), who, like her mythic models, longs for the love of Kṛṣṇa. Between the sixth and the tenth centuries, the Ālvārs roamed from temples to other pilgrimage sites, singing their songs of devotion to Viṣṇu. One of the most renowned was Nammālvār (early 10th century), whose *Tiruvāymoli* (*Venerable Ten*) contains a thousand hymns to Māyon, Viṣṇu as the Dark Lord, the Lord of Illusion. Sometimes referred to as the Tamil Veda, the *Tiruvāymoli* is all the more remarkable because Nammālvār was from the *vellala* agricultural *jāti*, identified by some as a *śūdra* caste. In the tenth century, Nāthamuni collated the poems of the Ālvārs into a text called the *Nālāyira Divyaprabandham* (*Four Thousand Divine Literary Works*). In time, the Ālvārs were themselves regarded as manifestations of aspects of Viṣṇu, and Āṇṭāḷ as the goddess Śrī, his consort.

The Nāyanārs (or Nāyanmārs) were sixty-three Tamil saints, mostly from the twice-born classes, but including even an Untouchable, who sang devotional hymns to Śiva. Their poems, which date from the sixth to the eighth centuries CE, are compiled in a collection of eleven books, known as the *Tirumurai*. One of its books, the *Tēvāram*, contains the writings of three of the most renowned Nāyanārs, namely, Sambandar (Campantar), Appar, and Sundarar (Cuntarar). The poetry of Māṇikkavācakar, who enjoys a status akin to these three, and who is sometimes regarded as a sixty-fourth Nāyanār, constitutes the *Tiruvācakam*, another book in the *Tirumurai*. The first three Nāyanārs visited over 250 Śiva shrines in South India. The wanderings of these poet saints heightened the reputation of the temples and other sites where they temporarily resided, and enhanced the *bhakti* oriented worship of Śiva in these places. A hagiography of their lives, known as the *Periya Purāṇam*, was written in the twelfth century. The Nāyanārs also influenced the development of Śaiva Siddhānta philosophy, and *bhakti*'s intrinsic praise of the power of emotions and its implicit critique of formal worship fuelled other developments, such as the anti-orthodox Liṅgayat movement that began in the twelfth century.

Key points in this chapter

- An effective aspect of the *Gītā* is that it does not present a simple, unified philosophy.
- The *Gītā* reconciles the dilemma between choosing a religious path in or away from society.
- In the *Bhagavad Gītā,* Kṛṣṇa teaches Arjuna three paths (*yogas*) to Self-realization.
- The *Gītā* is one of the earliest texts to introduce the *bhakti* approach, for which it makes its most compelling case.
- The *Gītā* identifies Kṣṛṇa as the ideal and supreme object of devotion.
- The teachings of the *Bhagavad Gītā* became foundational for Vedānta philosophy.
- The period of the Epics marked a pivotal shift in Hinduism, and Hindu orthodoxy, by widening the parameters of what constitutes legitimate Hinduism.
- The *Gītā* articulates the centrally defining features of Hinduism succinctly, and effectively compromises between the concerns of orthodoxy and those of the masses.
- Two main groups of Tamil *bhakti*-poets, the Ālvārs and the Nāyanārs, emerged from the sixth to the eleventh centuries CE.
- As *bhakti* traditions grew, they undermined the strength of Jainism and Buddhism in South India.

Discussion questions

1. Discuss why you think it is effective that the *Gītā* does not present a simple, unified philosophy.
2. What is the *Gītā*'s notion of the supreme sacrifice as mentioned, and what might the consequences of such a notion of sacrifice be?
3. Karma yoga involves action without attachment. Discuss whether you think attachment might ever be considered helpful in the quest for enlightenment.
4. What are the paths laid out in the *Bhagavad Gītā* and how do they solve the dilemma of choosing a life in society or away from it?
5. In what ways did Hinduism, and Hindu orthodoxy change during the period of the Epics?
6. Why do you think the *Bhagavad Gītā* makes its most compelling case for Bhakti yoga?

Further reading

On bhakti

Eck, Diana L., and F. Mallison (eds) (1991) *Devotion Divine from the Regions of India: Studies in Honor of Charlotte Vaudeville*. Groningen: Egbert Forsten.

Haberman, D. L. (1988) *Acting as a Way of Salvation: A Study of Rāgānuga Bhakti*. New York: Oxford University Press.

Hardy, E. T. (1983) *Viraha Bhakti: The Early History of Kṛṣṇa Devotion in South India*. Delhi: Oxford University Press.

Narayanan, Vasudha (1987) *The Way and the Goal: Expression of Devotion in the Early Śrī Vaishṇava Tradition*. Washington, DC: Institute for Vaishnava Studies.

Tyagisananda, Swami (trans.) (1955) *Nārada Bhakti Sūtras: Aphorisms on the Gospel of Divine Love*. Mylapore, Madras: Ramakrishna Math.

Werner, Karel (1993) *Love Divine: Studies in Bhakti and Devotional Mysticism*. Richmond: Curzon Press.

The Bhagavad Gītā

Bhaktivedanta, A. C., Swami (1968) *Bhagavad Gītā: As It Is*. New York: Macmillan.

Buitenen, J. A. B. (trans.) (1981) *The Bhagavadgītā in the Mahābhārata*. Chicago, IL: University of Chicago Press.

Chidbhavananda, Swami (trans.) (1986) *The Bhagavad Gita*. Tirupparaitturai: Sri Ramakrishna Tapovanam.

Easwaran, Eknath (trans.) (1985) *The Bhagavad Gita*. Tomales, CA: Nilgiri Press.

Edgerton, F. (trans.) (1944) *Bhagavadgītā*. Cambridge, MA: Harvard University Press.
Minor, R. (1982) *Bhagavad-Gītā: An Exegetical Commentary*. Columbia, MO: South Asia Books.
Radhakrishnan, S. (trans.) (1956) *Bhagavadgītā*. London: Allen & Unwin.
Stoller-Miller, B. (trans.) (1986) *The Bhagavad-Gita: Krishna's Counsel in Time of War*. New York: Bantam Books.
Zaehner, R. C. (trans.) (1969) *Bhagavadgītā*. Oxford: Oxford University Press.

On the Bhagavad Gītā's teachings

De Nicolás, A. T. (1976) *Avatāra: The Humanization of Philosophy through the Bhagavad Gītā*. New York: Nicholas Hays.
Minor, Robert (ed.) (1986) *Modern Indian Interpreters of the Bhagavadgītā*. Albany, NY: State University of New York Press.
Sharpe, Eric J. (1985) *The Universal Gītā: Western Images of the Bhagavadgītā*. La Salle: Open Court, 1985.

On Ramaṇa Mahārṣi

Brunton, Paul (1952) *Maharṣi and His Message*. London: Rider & Co.
Godman, D. (ed.) (1985) *Be as you are: The Teachings of Ramana Maharsi*. Boston, MA: Arkana.
Mahadevan, T. M. P. (1951) *Ramaṇa Maharṣi and His Philosophy of Existence*. Annamalai: Annamalai University.
Miller, J. and G. Miller (eds) (1972) *The Spiritual Teaching of Ramana Maharishi*. Boulder, CO: Shambala.
Nagamma, Suri (1974) *My Life at Sri Ramanasrama*. Tiruvannamalai: Sri Ramanasram.
Osborne, A. (1962) *Ramana Maharshi and the Path of Self-Knowledge*. Bombay: Jaico.
— (1959) *The Collected Works of Ramana Maharshi*. New York: Samuel Weiser.

On Mahātma Gandhi

Chatterjee, M. (1983) *Gandhi's Religious Thought*. South Bend, IN: University of Notre Dame Press.
Desai, Mahadev (1946) *The Gita According to Gandhi*. Amhedabad: Navajivan.
Erikson, E. H. (1970) *Gandhi's Truth*. New York: W. W. Norton.

On Śrī Caitanya

Bhaktivedanta, A. C., Swami (1968) *The Teachings of Lord Chaitanya*. New York: International Society for Krishna Consciousness.

Chaudhuri, S. K. (trans.) (1959) *Sri Caitanyacaritāmṛtam*, 3 vols. Calcutta: Gauḍia-Math.

Kennedy, M. T. (1925) *The Chaitanya Movement*. Calcutta: Association Press.

Majumdar, A. K. (1969) *Caitanya: His Life and Doctrine*. Bombay: Bharatiya Vidya Bhavan.

On South Indian Hinduism

Balasundaram, T. S. (1959–60) *The Golden Anthology of Ancient Tamil Literature*, 3 vols. Madras: South Indian Saiva Siddhanta Book Publishing Society.

Buck, Harry M. and Glenn E. Yocum (eds) (1974) *Structural Approaches to South Indian Studies*. Chambersburg: Wilson Books.

Carman, J. B., and V. Narayanan (1989) *The Tamil Veda: Piḷḷān's Interpretation of the Tiruvāymoli*. Chicago, IL: University of Chicago Press.

Dehejia, Vidya (1988) *Slaves of the Lord: The Path of the Tamil Saints*. Delhi: Munshiram Manoharlal.

— (1991) *Āntāl and her Path of Love: Poems of a Woman Saint of South India*. Albany, NY: State University of New York Press.

Diksitar, V. R. (1930) *Studies in Tamil Literature and History*. London: Lusac.

Govindacharya, Alkondavilli (1902) *The Divine Wisdom of the Draviḍa Saints*. Madras: C. N. Press.

Hart, G. (1976) *The Relationship between Tamil and Classical Sanskrit Literature*. History of Indian Literature 10, fasc. 2. Wiesbaden: Otto Harrassowitz.

Hooper, J. S. M. (1929) *Hymns of the Ālvārs*. Calcutta: Association Press.

Jesudason, C. S. H. (1961) *A History of Tamil Literature*. Heritage of India Series. Calcutta: Y.M.C.A. Publishing House.

Kailaspathy, K. (1968) *Tamil Heroic Poetry*. Oxford: Oxford University Press.

Kingsbury, F. and G. E. Philips (trans.) (1921) *Hymns of the Tamil Śaivite Saints*. Calcutta: Association Press.

Mainckam, V. S. (1962) *The Tamil Concept of Love*. Madras: South Indian Saiva Siddhanta Works Publishing Society.

Navaratnam, R. (trans.) (1963) *Tiruvācakam*. Bombay: Bharatiya Vidya Bhavan.

Peterson, I. (1989) *Poems to Śiva, The Hymns of the Tamil Saints*. Princeton, NJ: Princeton University Press.

Pillai, K. K. (1973) *A Social History of the Tamils*, Vol. 1. Madras: University of Madras.

Pope, G. U. (ed. and trans.) (1970) *Tiruvācagam*. Reprint. Madras: University of Madras.
Pope, G. U., W. H. Drew, J. Lazarus, and F. W. Ellis (trans.) (1962) *The Tirukkural*. Tinnelvelly: South India Saiva Siddhanta Works Publishing Society.
Ramanujan, A. K. (1981) *Hymns for the Drowning*. Princeton, NJ: Princeton University Press.
Ramaswamy, Vijaya (1997) *Walking Naked: Women, Society, Spirituality in South India*. Shimla: Indian Institute of Advanced Study.
Sastri, K. A. N. (1935) *The Colas*, 3 vols. Madras: University of Madras.
— (1955) *History of South India*. Madras: Oxford University Press.
— (1964) *The Culture and History of the Tamils*. Calcutta: Firma K. L. Mukhopadhyay.
Shulman, David D. (1985) *The King and the Clown in South Indian Myth and Poetry*. Princeton, NJ: Princeton University Press.
Yocum, Glen E. (1982) *Hymns to the Dancing Śiva: A Study of Manikkavācakar's Tiruvācakam*. Columbia, MO: South Asia Books.
Zvelebil, K. (1973) *The Smile of Murugan*. Leiden: Brill.

9 *Major Hindu theistic sects*

In this chapter

The emerging *bhakti* traditions reflect the growing influence of theistic sects devoted to a variety of gods and goddesses. However, the sectarian dimensions of Hinduism were not solely evident through *bhakti*. Philosophical schools advanced sophisticated metaphysical systems, while other groups were characterized by distinctive ritual practices. There were also trends to amalgamate minor cults under the rubric of a particular, all-encompassing divine figure. Here we examine the histories of the three major theistic sectarian traditions within Hinduism, namely, the Śaivas, the Vaiṣṇavas, and the Śāktas. We also explore the metaphysical systems of some of the most influential schools within these sects.

Main topics covered

- Śaivism
- Vaiṣṇavism
- Śāktism

Śaivism

The origins of Śiva worship are traced by some to the Indus Valley Civilization, where a few stone seals depict a figure often referred to as the "ithyphallic proto-Śiva." However, it is not completely clear if the figure represented on these seals is ithyphallic, or even if it is anthropomorphic. Similarly, claims that rounded elongated stones found at Indus Valley sites are evidence of *liṅga* worship, are unconvincing. *Ṛg Veda* hymns to Rudra ("Howler") first mention the word *śiva*, which means "auspicious." Rudra is portrayed as clad in animal skins, a terrifying god of storms, both destructive of cattle and human beings, and yet offering protection from disease if propitiated. Shaggy-haired, he wields a sharp weapon and fast arrows. In the *Śatarudriya* (*One Hundred [verses] concerning Rudra*) hymn of the *Yajur Veda*, which is still frequently chanted in Śiva temples, he is described as blue-throated, mountain-dwelling, red-complexioned, the lord of thieves, bull-mounted, and a hunter, who presides over and abides within the forest. He is Paśupati, the Lord of Beasts. By the time of the *Śvetāśvatara* (*Having White Mules*) *Upaniṣad*, composed perhaps earlier than the fourth century BCE, we have the first evidence of a *bhakti*-like sentiment developing. The text reflects a shifting emphasis from the monism (i.e. centered on the One, Absolute Reality) of the earlier Upaniṣads, such as the *Chāndogya*, to a qualified, theistic monism or dualism. Rudra, also called Śiva and Maheśvara (Great Lord), is referred to in a monistic manner, as the *eka deva* (One God), who is both transcendent and within the hearts of all created beings. He is equated with Brahman, the origin of all things, and is said to be a magician who generates and upholds the cosmos through his power (*śakti*). Through a combination of yogic practice and divine grace, the devoted soul may gain union with the Lord.

Although we find these early *śruti*-based references to Śiva, which elicit a continuity between him and Rudra, researchers generally associate Śiva's origins with the non-Āryan component of Hinduism. The Vedic occurrences are slight and of relatively late origin, suggesting a progressive incorporation of the deity into the orthodox pantheon, although not without tensions. Contrasting with the Vedic evidence, there are plenty of references to Śiva and his deeds in the *Mahābhārata* (10.18; 12.274), where the myth of Śiva's destruction of Dakṣa's *yajña* hints at these processes of conflict and orthodox assimilation. We also note the existence of Śaivite sects, such as the Pāśupatas, formed in about the second century CE, who gave rise to the Kālāmukhas. The rise of Śiva-*bhakti* is evident in South India in the poems of the Tamil saints, the Nāyanārs (early sixth to eighth centuries). The influence of these sects was enormous on the kingdoms of South India, which began to patronize Śaivism as the official religion, and led to the weakening of Buddhism and Jainism in the region. From the preceding influences, two other Śaiva sects of consequence developed in the south. These were the Śaiva Siddhānta and the Vīraśaiva movements, the latter founded by Basava in the twelfth century. The mythology of Śiva and the divine members of his "family," such as the goddesses Satī, Pārvati, the elephant-headed god Gaṇeśa, and the war god Kārttikeya, were elaborated upon in Purāṇic literature.

Meanwhile, in North India, Kashmiri Śaivism, influenced by both Buddhist and Tantric philosophical ideas, began to develop from the late eighth century, reaching a pinnacle in the works of Abhinavagupta and Kṣemarāja. Gorakhnātha founded a Śaivite sect known as the Nāths, who emphasize Haṭha yoga practice for the attainment of supernormal powers (*siddhi*).

Śiva is widely worshipped among Hindus today, perhaps equaling, if not outnumbering the percentage of Vaiṣṇavas. However, such sectarian designations are poor indicators of actual practice, since Hindus who might label themselves as Vaiṣṇavas are still likely to visit Śiva temples and celebrate some Śaiva holy days.

Smārta Brahmins, who are a mainstay of Hindu orthodoxy, include Śiva among the five deities they hold worthy of worship. Thus Śaivism has moved from its marginal, anti-Āryan status during the early Vedic period into the very core of Hindu orthodoxy.

Some noteworthy Śaiva schools

We encounter a reference to the earliest known Śaivite sect, the Pāśupatas, in the *Mahābhārata*. However, much earlier in composition than the Epics, the *Atharva Veda* (15.5.1–7) refers to a group of ascetic warriors known as *vrātyas* in connection with a group of seven gods, including Mahādeva, Pāśupati, Rudra, and Īśāna, each associated with different regions, and each of whom are later identified with Śiva. It is possible that the *vrātyas*, who were marginalized by Āryan society, and who practiced yogic-like rites of breath control, and tantric-like ritual sexual intercourse, may have been a source, or one of the early configurations of Śaivite, or proto-Śaivite sects.

The Pāśupatas, the earliest known of the Śaiva sects, were founded in about the second century CE by the semi-legendary Lakulīśa (Lord of the Club), who was later regarded as an incarnation of Śiva himself. Their practices involved a sequence of stages, beginning with a relatively traditional period of moral development with their *guru* in a temple. During this phase they were expected to smear their bodies in a bath of ashes thrice daily. This was followed by a period of antinomian public behavior, such as speaking gibberish and lewdly gesturing to women. Those who scorned them would end up absorbing the Pāśupata's bad *karma*, and relinquish their own merit to the practitioner. The next stages were ones of seclusion accompanied by intense meditation, and they would ultimately resort to the cremation grounds, surviving as they could, until their death and final union with Rudra. The Pāśupatas gave rise to the Kālāmukhas, whose name simultaneously evokes a crescent moon forehead ornament, a dark, ash-smeared face or forehead, and the ending of time, all features associated with Śiva. The Kālāmukhas smeared themselves in the ashes of corpses. Both groups flourished in South India between the seventh and fourteenth centuries, and the Kālāmukhas even had their own temples.

Another sect, the Kāpālikas, is less well understood. They took on the appearance of Śiva, ash-smeared, with matted hair, and carried a skull-topped staff, known as a *khaṭvaṅga*. In a Purāṇic version of the myth of Śiva's decapitation of Brahmā's fifth head, the act makes Śiva guilty of the crime of killing a Brahmin. To expiate the *karma* of this deed, Śiva is forced to wander penitently for twelve years in what is known as the Great Ascetic Observance (*mahāvrata*), until Brahmā's skull (*kapāla*), which has adhered to his hand, is released. The myth resonates with the practices of Śaivite ascetics, such as the Lākulas and Kāpālikas, who wore ornaments of bone and carried a renouncer's bowl, fashioned from a human skull. These groups disappeared as coherent sects, but still endure in the practices of less clearly categorized Śaivite ascetics.

The Nāyanārs, the Tamil *bhakti* poets, who lived from the sixth to the eighth centuries CE, were known for their ecstatic expressions of love for Śiva. Their songs were passionate and promoted egalitarianism that challenged orthodox hierarchies based on caste. They were also known for their extreme devotion. Legend has it that one of the Nāyanārs, Kaṇṇapar, once noticed that the eyes on the Śiva *liṅga* he was worshipping were bleeding, and plucked out his own eyes to replace them. Similarly, Ciruttoṇṭar was once asked by a wandering Śaivite to cook up and serve his own son as a food offering. He did so immediately in a display of absolute obedience and devotion. In both cases, Śiva appeared, praised his devotees, and restored their losses.

An influential sect of philosophical Śaivism, the Śaiva Siddhānta (Ultimate Goal of Śaivism), developed through influences from the Nāyanārs, whose poems, contained in the *Tirumurai*, are included in their canon of authoritative texts. Although it originated in the north, the philosophy migrated to the south where it gradually incorporated Tamil *bhakti* into its ritual-centered style. Śaiva Siddhānta distinguishes three real and eternal entities. These are: the Lord (*pati*), souls (*paśu*, literally, "beast"), and that which binds them (*pāśa*, literally, "noose"). The Lord (Śiva) is both transcendent, yet immanent in all aspects of creation. As Sadāśiva, out of pure playfulness, he emits the world, maintains it, reabsorbs the world, conceals himself, and reveals himself through grace. Souls (*paśu*), which are different from the Lord, become entrapped in the creation through ignorance, *karma*, and *māyā*, which constitute the three impurities (*mala*). *Māyā* is the substratum or matrix within which the soul's bondage is played out. The soul must be freed from all three impurities to be liberated. This is achieved through three practices: 1) proper conduct (*cārya*), which is mostly orthodox worship of the Smārta Brahmin style, 2) ritual worship (*kriyā*), which follows tantric styles of *pūjā*, and 3) meditative disciplines (*yoga*), all performed in the spirit of deep loving devotion (*bhakti*).

These practices should be overseen by a Śivaguru, an initiated master, who ideally is himself liberated. He (for women are prohibited from involvement in this path) moves the practitioner through a series of graded initiations. As the soul frees itself from its fetters, it recognizes its complete dependence on the power of the Lord. Śiva's grace (*śāktipat*) is ultimately the only source of liberation to souls, either directly, or through the *guru*. Upon liberation, Śiva reveals himself, and the soul eventually realizes its pure state as equal to Śiva, although it does not become Śiva, the Lord. Unlike the non-dual Śaiva philosophies of Kashmir, where it originated, Śaiva Siddhānta is a dualistic system that maintains a distinction between the Lord and his creation, even upon liberation. Śaiva Siddhānta still flourishes in the state of Tamil Nadu. Specially initiated priests known as Śivācāryas or Ādiśaivas, believed to belong to the lineage of five Brahmin *ṛṣis* are primarily qualified to perform the worship rites in Śaiva Siddhānta temples.

The Vīraśaiva (Heroic Followers of Śiva) sect was formed by Basava, also known as Basavanna (1106–1167), mainly in Kannada-speaking regions of South India. Followers of this Śaiva sect were decidedly anti-orthodox, rejecting temple worship, pilgrimages, sacrifices, and the caste system, although they themselves have come to be regarded as a caste within the Hindu fold. Basavanna promoted a passionate devotion to Śiva, whom he worshipped as the "Lord of the Meeting Rivers." This intense love for Śiva should result in the direct experience of Śiva, unmediated by rites, customs, and beliefs, most of which are regarded as obstacles to that realization. The Vīraśaivas do not promote image worship, since they believe that Śiva is everywhere, making no particular abode more sacred than another. However, as an insignia of their beliefs, they do wear a *liṅga* on a necklace, which they worship daily. Thus they are also known as Liṅgayats. Over the centuries, they have developed an institution of hereditary priests, and some rituals. The Vīraśaivas hold that devotion is its own reward, and that one should not perform good deeds with the expectation of finding God. A female Vīraśaiva saint, Mahādevyakka became a naked ascetic, forsaking her human marriage for her divine husband, Śiva. The Vīrāśaivas' criticism of the caste system, which led them to promote marriages even between Brahmin women and Untouchables, attracted members of the lower, disenfranchised classes to their ranks, but unleashed waves of persecution by orthodox Hindus. Nevertheless, they have endured, and now claim a sizeable and influential community of about six million followers in the state of Karnataka. Their religious literature includes the emotionally stirring, impassioned poems of Basavanna, Mahādevyakka, and other Vīrāśaiva saints.

Gorakṣanātha (Hindi: Gorakhnāth) is traditionally attributed with the authorship of the first treatise on Haṭha yoga, and is one of the great teachers within the ancient Nāth sect of Śaivism. There are widely varying claims about his place and date of birth, which was in North India perhaps before the thirteenth century. Important Haṭha yoga texts, such as the *Siddhasiddhānta-paddhati* (*Manual on the Ultimate Goal of the Siddhas*) and the *Gorakṣa-śataka* (*Hundred Verses by Gorakṣa*) are said to have been composed by him. These outline the relationship between the macrocosmic creation and the microcosm of the human body, which mirrors or parallels it. Through the practice of various yogic techniques centered on bodily discipline, one can move energy through the body and induce a fusion between macrocosm and microcosm, leading to liberation. Followers of his sect worship Śiva as Bhairava, and are known as Nāths, Gorakhnāthis, or Kānphaṭā (Split Ear) Yogis, because of the large earring that is placed during an initiation ceremony through the central hollow of their ears. Some carry a trident, a symbol of Śiva. The sect is regarded as being in decline, although they are widespread throughout India.

Vaiṣṇavism

Viṣṇu is praised in five *Ṛg Veda* hymns, and mentioned in a few others, where he is called the supporter of heaven and earth. He is also referred to as *trivikrama* (the three-stepping), which initially identifies him with the Sun's movement through the skies. Later references to his three steps connect them with saving the gods by defeating demons. In the Brāhmaṇas, Viṣṇu is also linked to Puruṣa, the primal sacrificer and sacrificial victim, from whom the whole creation emerges. There are a few occurrences in the principal Upaniṣads linking him to the supreme Brahman. Unlike many scholars, Vaiṣṇavas do not consider the relatively thin references in the Vedic *śruti* literature to be an indication of Viṣṇu's minor status at the time of their composition. However, it is evident that Viṣṇu's mythology is primarily developed within the Epics and Purāṇas.

Vālmiki's *Rāmāyaṇa* generally portrays Rāma as a human hero, but later interpolations appear to highlight his divinity and identifications with Viṣṇu. The *Mahābhārata*, by contrast, clearly has a Vaiṣṇava orientation through the person of Kṛṣṇa. The Epics and Purāṇas typically pick up Vedic themes but rework them in ways that forge connections with stories and deities of regional and contemporary importance at the time of their composition. Viṣṇu as the sacrificial victim disappears, and the salvific act by the three-stepping Viṣṇu is reported as but one in a series of such deeds that he performs through his various incarnations.

Inscriptions from a column near Sanchi, in the state of Madhya Pradesh, dated at about the first century BCE indicate the existence of the worship of the god Vāsudeva by Heliodorus, a Greek ambassador, who is called a Bhāgavata, worshipper of the Lord (Bhagavat). These and other epigraphs point to the existence of an early cult which scholars refer to as Bhāgavatism, centered on the deities Vāsudeva, Nārāyaṇa, and Saṅkarṣaṇa (Balarāma), all of whom are later associated with Viṣṇu. Kṛṣṇa, who was probably a deified hero or ruler of the Yādavas, eventually was identified with Vāsudeva, who was the deity of the Vṛṣṇi tribe, which is identified with the Yādavas. In the *Bhagavad Gītā*, Vāsudeva-Kṛṣṇa is identified with Viṣṇu.

Bhakti-based approaches as promoted in the *Bhagavad Gītā*, led to the development of theistic worship of Viṣṇu and Kṛṣṇa after the first century CE. The *Harivaṃśa*, a *Mahābhārata* supplement, develops Kṛṣṇa's mythology which is further elaborated upon in the *Bhāgavata* and *Viṣṇu Purāṇas*. The title, *paramabhāgavata* (supreme worshippers of the Lord), was adopted by rulers in the Gupta period (fourth to sixth centuries CE), who patronized the worship of Viṣṇu through the construction of temples to him, and by commissioning rituals in his honor. Bhāgavatas were also priests who worshipped Viṣṇu through Vedic-styled sacrificial offerings into fire. Besides the Bhāgavata sect, other Vaiṣṇava traditions with distinctive rituals or theological and philosophical doctrines also developed. Among these were the Pañcarātra, a tantric system, and the orthodox Vaikhānasa tradition.

The concept of Viṣṇu's descents (*avatāra*) or incarnations also developed during this period, amalgamating the cults of numerous deities under the rubric of Vaiṣṇavism. Although it is now conventional to enumerate ten *avatāras*, this was a late development. Early lists of Viṣṇu's *avatāras* vary in their count from as few as four to almost forty. The South Indian *bhakti* movement, exemplified by the Ālvārs (sixth to ninth centuries), further promoted the worship of Viṣṇu. They influenced the development of a variety of Vedānta schools such as the Śrī Vaiṣṇava, and others founded by Madhva and Vallabha. These will be discussed in the chapter dedicated to Vedānta. The Śrī Vaiṣṇava tradition influenced the development of Gauḍīya Vaiṣṇavaism in Bengal, which was centered on devotion to Kṛṣṇa and Rādhā. The devotional hymns of saints such as Jñāneśvara (thirteenth century) and Tukārām (*c.* 1568–1650), in the state of Mahārashtra, furthered the development of the Vārkarī sect in Central India. In North India, Rāma became the focus of *bhakti*, and is typified by the Rāmānandi sect.

Some noteworthy Vaiṣṇava schools

The Bhāgavatas, the earliest mentioned Vaiṣṇava sect, appear to have been a rather broadly defined group of Viṣṇu worshippers whose deities may have included Kṛṣṇa, Vāsudeva, Bhagavan, Nārāyaṇa, and Saṅkārṣaṇa. The *Bhagavad Gītā*, the scripture with which they are associated, reflects a tolerant and encompassing theology.

The Pañcarātra sect perhaps derives its name from a five (*pañca*) night (*rātra*) sacrifice to Nārāyaṇa mentioned in the *Śatapatha Brāhmaṇa*. Their main texts emerge in the seventh century, and are known as the Pañcarātra Saṃhitās. Included among these are the *Ahirbudhnya Saṃhitā* and the *Lakṣmī Tantra*. Pañcarātra doctrines appear to have permeated South-east Asia as early as the seventh century, and literature was still being produced in the seventeenth century. The Pañcarātra develops a complex doctrine of emanations or *vyūhas*. Essentially, the highest principle or the Lord (Bhagavan, Vāsudeva) possesses six qualities (*guṇa*): omniscience (*jñāna*), power (*śakti*), majesty (*aiśvarya*), strength (*bala*), vigor (*vīrya*), and splendor (*tejas*). The *vyūha* that is Saṅkarṣaṇa (the name of Kṛṣṇa's elder brother, also known as Balarāma) emanates from *jñāna* and *śakti*. Saṅkarṣaṇa emanates Pradyumna (the name of Kṛṣṇa's son), in whom *aiśvarya* and *bala* are more prominent. From Pradyumna comes Aniruddha (the name of Kṛṣṇa's grandson), in whom the divine qualities of *vīrya* and *tejas* are most significant. These four *vyūhas* in turn generate more emanations, but these first four are the highest, and should be the object of worship for those seeking liberation. They constitute the pure realm. The Lord is always associated with Śrī or Lakṣmī, his Śakti. The impure, material creation is generated from a constellation of intermediary emanations. Upon liberation, individual souls (*jīva*) enter into God, a state figuratively described as sharing an existence with him in his abode of Vaikuṇṭha. However, they do not become the Lord, but maintain an independent existence.

The Vaikhānasas are a small sect of Vaiṣṇavas, whose main temple center is Tirupati in the state of Andhra Pradesh. They follow their own scriptures, known collectively as the Vaikhānasa Saṃhitās, within which the earliest, the *Vaikhānasa Sūtra*, is dated to about the fourth century CE. Adherents of the sect claim to derive directly from the lineages of Vedic ritualists of the *Black Yajur Veda* School, and their temple rites now replace Vedic fire sacrifices.

The Vedānta traditions centered on Viṣṇu, as exemplified by Rāmānuja (in Tamil Nadu) and Madhva (in Karnataka), which arose after the eleventh century, were characterized by sophisticated theologies and temple worship. They influenced subsequent developments in Viṣṇu worship in Bengal and Maharashtra, although in these the emphasis returned to the emotional fervor associated with the poetry of the Ālvārs.

In Maharashtra, a brilliant young man named Jñāneśvara (*c.* 1275–1296 CE) (also known as Jñānadeva), influenced by the Vedāntic philosophy of Madhva, and the teachings of the Naths, wrote a commentary on the *Bhagavad Gītā*, known as the *Jñāneśvarī*, along with other devotional poetry. He is reputed to have composed nine thousand verses of the *Jñāneśvarī* at the age of fifteen. His concept of the divine transcends simple categorization as centered on Viṣṇu, because he uses Śaiva symbols and points to the transcendence of God beyond all humanly constructed categories. Jñāneśvara emphasizes the role of one's spiritual preceptor, the *guru*, as an object of devotion almost equal to the divine, since through the *guru* one may be led to God. His disciple, Nāmdev (1270–1350 CE), began to compose poetry in Marathi, the vernacular language of Maharashtra, and carried his teachings to the Punjab. Namdev accentuated the focus of *bhakti* on Viṭhobā, a pastoral deity whose main temple was located at Pandharpur, in Maharashtra. Viṭhobā was assimilated with Kṛṣṇa, and his shrine became the focus of a popular pilgrimage. The followers of this tradition are known as Vārkarīs (Pilgrims), and their annual pilgrimages to Pandharpur are characterized by singing and the ideology of caste-free equality, although in reality upper-caste distinctions still endure. Other saints such as Eknāth (sixteenth century), and the most highly revered, Tukārām (seventeenth century), a *śūdra*, continued to enhance the tradition of devotional worship to God. Collectively these Maharashtrian saints belong to the Sant (holy person) tradition, which through figures like Eknāth extended to Punjab and North India, where the transcendent, non-sectarian nature of God was highlighted over the southern Vaiṣṇava tradition. The Northern Sants include figures such as Kabīr and the female mystic saint, Mīrabai.

The Gauḍīya Vaiṣṇava traditions developed in Bengal, and are characterized by a passionate love for the divine. Kṛṣṇa, who is identified with Viṣṇu takes center stage, so much so that some would prefer to refer to this tradition as a Kṛṣṇaite, rather than a Vaiṣṇavite one. Early contributors to the tradition include Jayadeva, who wrote an influential twelfth century lyric poem, the *Gītāgovinda*. Composed in the style of classical Sanskrit verse (*kāvya*), it explores, through the emotional states of the divine lovers, Rādhā and Kṛṣṇa, the cadences of the soul's relationship with the Divine. Caṇḍidāsa and Vidyāpati, both poets of that north-eastern region, continued the tradition of Kṛṣṇa-Rādhā romantic poetry in subsequent centuries. However, the most influential architect of Gauḍīya Vaiṣṇavism was Kṛṣṇa Caitanya (1486–1533), better known as Śrī Caitanya, who emphasized an almost erotic sentiment and ecstatic devotion to the Divine. The relationship between the devotee and God, likened to the love between Rādhā and Kṛṣṇa is intimately connected yet distinct, and has been characterized as *acintya-bhedābheda* (unimaginable separation in union). The International Society for Kṛṣṇa Consciousness (ISKCON), a North American-originated offshoot of this tradition, has widely popularized its teachings worldwide in the last few decades.

Śāktism

Quite early in Hindu scriptures one notes the tendency to identify deities with each other, placing them all under the rubric of the Upaniṣadic Absolute, The One, or Supreme Reality, Brahman. The Purāṇas also typify the trend of forging connections between non-Vedic and Vedic deities. These movements dovetail in the formulation of the concept of a Hindu Great Goddess, known as Mahādevī, or simply as Devī, who is equated with Brahman. At times a particular goddess, such as Lakṣmī or Pārvatī, may be regarded as the Mahādevī. Typically, such associations suggest sectarian preferences towards a particular goddess, who is perhaps linked to Vaiṣṇava or Śaiva theologies. However, the Mahādevī develops as an independent goddess, unattached to any male sectarian tradition, and becomes the basis of a goddess-based sectarian tradition with its own theologies. She is Śakti, the power that animates the cosmos, and those worshippers who hold her as the highest conception of divinity are known as Śāktas.

In comparison to the number of hymns to male deities, there are relatively few hymns to goddesses in the *Ṛg Veda*. This contrasts with the large numbers of terracotta female figurines found at Indus Valley Civilization sites, which suggest, albeit inconclusively, the existence of some form of worship of the feminine there. Some of the Indus Valley stone seals show female figures intertwined with trees, suggestively prefiguring the contemporary association of goddesses with plants, flowers, trees and fruit. A number of goddesses, such as Koṛṛavai, worshipped among the non-Sanskritic Tamils, were eventually subsumed into Vedic deities, such as Durgā. To this day, villagers on the subcontinent worship innumerable good-natured or malevolent local spirits, many of which are female. The tradition of worshipping such village and forest goddesses may also have contributed to the development of the Śākta tradition in Hinduism. Among the few goddesses in the Vedic sources, some such as Sarasvatī, Uṣas (Dawn), and Pṛthivī (Earth) are benign and nurturing. Others, such as Rātrī (Night) and Nirṛti are dangerous and feared. The goddess Aditi is praised as the mother of the gods, of Indra, and of the Ādityas, a cluster of deities including Mitra, Varuṇa, and Dakṣa. The *Devī Sūkta* hymn in the *Ṛg Veda*, sung by the goddess Vāc to herself, presents a number of characteristics with which the Devī will eventually be associated. These include her as being a power that is everywhere, and having an immanent presence in all beings.

Philosophically, the concepts of Prakṛti, associated with manifest creation in Sāṅkhya philosophy, Śakti, the creative energy that animates the entire creation, and Māyā, the principle that obscures consciousness from directly perceiving its true nature, are fused into the persona of the Great Goddess. The comparison of Vedic material with evidence from the non-Vedic record leads many scholars to surmise that the impetus for placing the feminine at the religious center may derive from non-Vedic attitudes, but that there is an ongoing Vedicization (i.e. absorption into orthodoxy) of the goddess worshipping cults of South Asia.

Some noteworthy modes of Śāktism

It is evident from both literature and observations of Hindu religious practices that goddess worship is more widespread than previously thought. It is rare to find a village that does not have a local goddess who serves as a protector, or whose temperamental nature may require periodic propitiation to keep her from inflicting harm. Among the pantheon of goddesses found in the Epics and Purāṇas, many, such as Pārvatī and Lakṣmī, are worshipped in conjunction with their male consorts or spouses. However, other deities, such as Gaṅgā, or the small-pox goddess Śītalā, receive veneration in their own right, and are not primarily associated with other male deities. Thus even Hindus who would designate themselves as Vaiṣṇavas and Śaivas may worship a number of female deities as part of their religious activities. However, those who would designate themselves as Śāktas, that is, those who worship Śakti, the Great Goddess, as their principle conception of Absolute Divinity, form a smaller segment of the Hindu population than either Śaivas or Vaiṣṇavas.

Some hymns to the Devī in the *Mahābhārata* appear to connect her with Śiva and with Viṣṇu. However, the concept of a single Goddess who encompasses all other goddesses appeared to gain prominence by about the sixth century CE. The *Devī Māhātmya* (or *Durgā Saptaśatī*), dated at about the sixth or seventh century CE, reflecting the sentiments of a Śākta tradition of the period and because of its enormous subsequent influence, articulates and establishes the conception of a Great Goddess who is independent and not attached to any male deity. In this regard the *Devī Māhātmya* resembles the *Bhagavad Gītā*, which it parallels in many other ways. For instance, the text mirrors the *Gītā*'s length, and the Devī reveals that, like Viṣṇu, she will incarnate periodically to rectify the cosmic imbalance and restore *dharma*. Most importantly, the *Devī Māhātmya* conveys the message that all goddesses are indeed just aspects or forms of one supreme goddess, also referred to as Durgā (Formidable). Furthermore, she incorporates the energies and powers of all the male gods, making her the supreme deity, and is also equated with Brahman, the Absolute. Purāṇic works that are Devī-centered emerged by the seventh century CE, but most were composed several centuries later. They continue to develop a Śakti-based philosophy and mythology that reiterates the pre-eminence of the Devī.

The Devī is also the pre-eminent conception of divinity in much tantric literature. Since the Goddess is associated with power, and since the acquisition and mastery of powers is an intrinsic component of Tantra, the worship of Śakti is equally intrinsic to Tantra. Śākta Tantrism flourished in Kashmir, Assam, Bengal, and South India. Furthermore, the feminine component of reality plays such an important role in Tantra that many erroneously consider all Śāktas to be tantric. This is further complicated because Tantra is itself a somewhat vaguely defined and encompassing category. However, even though there may be many tantric elements in their ritual practices, not all Śāktas would consider themselves to be Tantrics, preferring to be regarded as *bhāktas* (those engaged in devotional worship (*bhakti*)), or following Vedic procedures.

Goddess worship appears to have certain phenomena routinely associated with it that often conflict with orthodox values. For instance, the independent goddesses such as Kālī and Durgā may accept offerings of liquor and blood. Possession by a goddess is also a common feature utilized by healers and others to channel the deity's powers for some goal. In tantric rites, ritual engagement with traditionally polluting activities may also be practiced. Such characteristics have led orthodoxy either to

Figure 9.1 An Aghori Śākta tantric master, Nāgabābā, with disciples, friends, and local village children (Tārāpīṭha Vindhyachal)

keep goddess cults at arm's length, or to exercise creative means of incorporating them within its purview. For instance, orthodox Hindus who worship at a goddess temple, and who witness a blood sacrifice taking place there, might claim that the sacrifice is not being offered to the main deity (for this would pollute her in their eyes, diminishing her sattvic status), but is in fact directed to a lesser, tamasic aspect of the goddess.

Śākta traditions tend to center themselves on particular goddesses or sacred sites, which likely developed their reputations as a result of royal patronage, or because of renowned religious figures who worshipped there. The myth of the goddess Satī's dismemberment, in which her body parts fell to earth sacralizing the spots where they landed, evokes the Hindu tendency to connect places with deities. Features of the land, lakes, rivers, trees, rocks, mountains, and so on may be abodes of the divine, and especially abodes or seats (*pīṭha*) of Śakti. The southernmost tip of the Indian sub-continent is Kanyā Kumārī, named after the Virgin Goddess worshipped there for at least two millennia. Another such place that is particularly renowned is at Kāmarūpa in Assam, a center of goddess worship from at least the fourth century, and where worship of the goddess Kāmākhyā was promoted by the Ahom kings of Assam from the seventeenth century. The worship of Kālī and Durgā have gained renewed prominence from the seventeenth century. The eighteenth century Bengali poet Rāmprasād Sen wrote devotional songs to the goddess Kālī, and exemplifies the *bhakti* Śākta tradition, although he is also clearly associated with tantric practice. The nineteenth century Hindu saint Ramakrishna Paramahamsa enhanced the prestige of Dakshineswar temple, near Calcutta, where he worshipped. His teachings, as presented by his disciple Swami Vivekānanda, take on a distinctly orthodox Vedantic aura, although he too is known to have engaged in Tantrism throughout his life.

Just as myths tell how Śiva's marriage tames his wild and independent nature, so too, myths relate how independent and thus potentially dangerous goddesses are domesticated through marriage. So the goddess Mīnākṣī (Fish Eyed Goddess), whose great temple at Madurai indicates the prominence of Devī worship there, was transformed from a powerful warrior queen into a shy and modest woman when she encountered Śiva, whom she eventually married. In another similar myth told at the South Indian temple of Cidambaram, when the goddess Kālī disturbed Śiva's meditation he challenged and defeated her in a dance contest. She then became his wife and began to worship him. The interplay of sectarian rivalries between Śaivite and Śākta traditions is evident in these myths. The myths also reflect the "socialization" of deities through their participation in orthodox rites (e.g. the marriage *saṃskāra*), and by extension the control of untamed, independent women through the presence of a male (husband).

Key points in this chapter

- Researchers generally associate Śiva's origins with the non-Āryan component of Hinduism.
- The *vrātyas*, who practiced yogic and tantric-like rites, may have been an early configuration of Śaivite, or proto-Śaivite sects.
- The Pāśupatas, the earliest known of the Śaiva sects, were founded in about the second century CE by the semi-legendary Lakulīśa.
- The Nāyanārs, Tamil *bhakti* poets (sixth to eighth centuries CE), were known for their ecstatic expressions of love for Śiva.
- Śaiva Siddhānta philosophy migrated from its origins in the north to the south where it gradually incorporated Tamil *bhakti* into its ritual-centered style.
- Śaiva Siddhānta is a dualistic philosophy that maintains a distinction between the Lord and his creation, even upon liberation.
- The Vīraśaivas, or Lingayats, founded by Basavanna, are unorthodox in their beliefs, and do not promote image worship, since they believe that Śiva is everywhere.
- Although present in the Vedas, Viṣṇu's mythology is primarily developed within the Epics and Purāṇas.
- The early cult of Bhāgavatism, centered on the deities Vāsudeva, Nārāyaṇa, and Saṃkarṣaṇa (Balarāma) who are later associated with Viṣṇu.
- Pañcarātra doctrines produced from the seventh to the seventeenth century develop a complex system of divine emanations or *vyūhas*.
- The Gauḍīya Vaiṣṇava traditions developed in Bengal, and are characterized by a passionate love for the divine, especially envisioned as Kṛṣṇa.
- In comparison to the number of hymns to male deities, there are relatively few hymns to goddesses in the *Ṛg Veda*.
- The concepts of Prakṛti, Śakti, and Māyā are fused into the persona of the Great Goddess, Mahādevī, a supreme divinity not typically associated with a divine male consort.

Discussion questions

1. Does Śiva's polar associations with eroticism and asceticism reveal something fundamental about human tensions?
2. Is it possible to distinguish characteristics that make Śaivism, Vaiṣṇavism, or Śaktism more appealing than their other two counterparts?
3. Are Hindu goddesses, more typically than gods, associated with blood and with features of the landscape? If so, why?

4. Explain the metaphysics of Śaiva Siddhānta philosophy.
5. Explain the metaphysics of Pañcarātra philosophy.
6. Explain the characteristics of Śāktism.

Further reading

The rise of Hindu theism in general

Bhandarkar, R. G. (1965) *Vaiṣṇavism, Śaivism and Minor Religious Systems*. Reprint. Varanasi: Indological Book House.

Carpenter, J. E. (1921) *Theism in Mediaeval India*. London: Constable and Co.

Chattopadyaya, S. (1963) *The Evolution of Theistic Sects in Ancient India*. Calcutta: Progressive Publishers.

Gayal, S. R. (1967) *A History of the Imperial Guptas*. Allahabad: Kitab Mahal.

Klostermaier, Klaus (1984) *Mythologies and Philosophies of Salvation in the Theistic Traditions of India*. Waterloo, ON: Wilfrid Laurier University Press.

— (2000) *Hindu Writings: A Short Introduction to the Major Sources*. Oxford: Oneworld.

— (2000) *Hinduism: A Short History*. Oxford: Oneworld.

North-Indian teachers and saints

Abbot, J. E. (ed. and trans.) (1926–1941) *The Poet Saints of Mahārāṣṭra*, 12 vols. Poona: Scottish Mission Industries.

Bhattacharya, D. (1963) *Love Songs of Vidyāpati*. London: Allen and Unwin.

— (1967) *Love Songs of Chandidās*. London: Allen and Unwin.

Hawley, J. S. (1985) *Sūrdās: Poet, Singer, Saint*. Seattle, WA: University of Washington Press.

Kuppuswamy, G. and M. Hariharan (eds.) *Jayadeva and Gītāgovinda: A Study*. Trivandrum: College Book House.

Macnicol, N. (1919) *Psalms of the Maratha Saints*. Heritage of India Series. Calcutta: Association Press.

Raghavan, V. (1966) *The Great Integrators: The Saint Singers of India*. Delhi: Ministry of Information and Broadcasting.

Ranade, R. C. (1982) *Mysticism in India: the Poet Saints of Maharashtra*. Albany, NY: State University of New York Press.

Siegel, L. (1978) *Sacred and Profane Dimension of Love in Indian Traditions as Exemplified in the Gītāgoviṇda of Jayadeva*. Oxford: Oxford University Press.

Śaivism

Ayyar, C. V. Narayana (1936) *Origin and Early History of Śaivism in South India*. Madras: University of Madras.

Banerjea, A. K. (1962) *Philosophy of Gorakhnāth*. Gorakhpur: Mahant Dig Vijai Nath Trust.

Briggs, G. W. (1938) *Gorakhanātha and Kānphaṭa Yogis*. Calcutta: Association Press.

Chekki, D. A. (1997) *Religion and Social System of the Vīraśāiva Community*. Westport, CT: Greenwood Press.

Dhavamony, M. (1971) *Love of God according to Śaiva Siddhānta: A Study in the Mysticism and Theology of Śaivism*. Oxford: Clarendon Press.

Dunuwila, R. A. (1985) *Śaiva Siddhānta Theology*. Delhi: Motilal Banarsidass.

Hunashal, S. M. (1957) *The Vīraśaiva Social Philosophy*. Raichur: Amaravani Printing Press.

Lorenzen, D. N. (1972) *The Kāpālika and Kālamukhas: Two Lost Śaivite Sects*. Berkeley: University of California Press.

Nandimath, S. C. (1941) *Handbook of Vīraśaivism*. Dharwar: L. E. Association.

Paranjoti, V. (1954) *Śaiva Siddhānta*. London: Luzac.

Pillai, G. S. (1948) *Introduction and History of Śaiva Siddhānta*. Annamalai: Annamalai University.

Rao, V. N. R. (1990) *Śiva's Warriors: The Basava Purāṇa of Palkuriki Somanātha*. Princeton, NJ: Princeton University Press.

Sakhare, M. R. (1942) *History and Philosophy of the Lingayat Religion*. Belgaum: Sakhara.

Sivaraman, Krishna (1973) *Śaivism in Philosophical Perspective*. Delhi: Motilal Banarsidass.

Vaiṣṇavism

De, S. K. (1961) *Early History of the Vaiṣṇava Faith and Movement in Bengal*. Calcutta: Firma K. L. Mukhopadhyay.

Dimock, E. C. (1966) *The Place of the Hidden Moon: Erotic Mysticism in the Vaiṣṇava-sahajiyā Cult of Bengal*. Chicago, IL: University of Chicago Press.

Gonda, Jan (1965) *Aspects of Early Viṣṇuism*. Reprint. Delhi: Motilal Banarsidass.

Rosen, S. (ed.) (1992) *Vaishnavism: Contemporary Scholars Discuss the Gaudiya Tradition*. New York: Folk Books.

Schrader, O. (1916) *Introduction to the Pāñcarātra and Ahirbudhnya Saṃhitā*. Reprint. Madras: Adyar Library and Research Centre, 1973.

Śāktism

Agrawala, P. K. (1983) *Goddesses in Ancient India*. Atlantic Highlands, NJ: Humanities Press.

Bhattacharyya, N. N. (1974) *History of Śākta Religion*. Delhi: Munshiram Manoharlal.

Biardeau, Madeleine (2004) *Stories about Posts: Vedic Variations around the Hindu Goddess*. J. Walker, A. Hiltebeitel, and Marie-Louise Reniche (trans.). Chicago, IL: University of Chicago Press.

Brooks, D. R. (1990) *The Secret of the Three Cities: An Introduction to Śākta Hinduism*. Chicago, IL: University of Chicago Press.

Coburn, Thomas B. (1984) *Devī Mahātmya: the Crystallization of the Goddess Tradition*. Delhi: Motilal Banarsidass.

— (1991) *Encountering the Goddess: A Translation of the Devī Mahātmya and a Study of its Interpretation*. Albany, NY: State University of New York Press.

Kumar, Pushpendra (1974) *Sakti Cult in Ancient India (with special reference to the Puranic Literature)*. Varanasi: Bharatiya Publishing House.

Payne, A. A. (1933) *The Śāktas*. Calcutta: YMCA Publishing House.

Pintchman, Tracy (1994) *The Rise of the Goddess in the Hindu Tradition*. Albany, NY: State University of New York Press.

Sirkar, D. C. (1948) *The Śākta Pīṭhas*. Delhi: Motilal Banarsidass.

10 *Hindu deities and Purāṇic mythology*

In this chapter

The Epics are followed by the Purāṇas, a genre of literature that develops the concerns of orthodoxy in relationship to the growing prominence of *bhakti* approaches to worship. Deities from the Vedic pantheon begin to fade in importance, while an assortment of gods and goddesses, often encountered in the Epic literature, become the focus of attention. Sectarian scriptures developed in tandem with the Śaiva, Vaiṣṇava, and Śākta sects discussed in the previous chapter. These texts elaborate upon mythic exploits of Śiva, Viṣṇu, the Devī as well as the worship traditions of various related gods and goddesses. Here, we touch upon the myths, iconographic representations, and main festivals to these deities, which still find expression among Hindus today.

Main topics covered

- The Purāṇas
- The decline of the Vedic deities
- Śaiva deities: Iconography, myths, and festivals
- Vaiṣṇava deities: Iconography, myths, and festivals
- Śākta deities: Iconography, myths, and festivals
- Other deities

The Purāṇas

As a genre of Hindu scripture, the Purāṇas constitute a vast body of literature. There are about eighteen or nineteen major or Mahāpurāṇas, but the numbers of other, so-called lesser Purāṇas (*upapurāṇa*) are much greater. The Purāṇas derive from the oral tradition of lengthy recitations in temples or royal courts subsidized by wealthy patrons. They are often categorized along with the Epics as *itihāsa-purāṇa* and, as the term *purāṇa* ("tales of old") suggests, purport to convey historical information, although such content is blended with pseudo-history and myth. The Purāṇas mimic the Epics in many ways. For instance, both genres are composed in the *śloka* meter, and the Purāṇas claim to be compiled by Vyāsa, the reputed author of the *Mahābhārata*. However, while the Epics seem concerned primarily with the elucidation of *dharma*, the Purāṇas are centrally expositions on *bhakti*. It is difficult to date the composition of these texts because they are quite malleable, not being subject to the Vedic *śrūti*-like expectations that they be accurately memorized and repeated verbatim. Furthermore, particular stories contained within any given Purāṇa may have circulated independently for centuries earlier than the compiled texts themselves. The earliest Purāṇas were probably produced by about the fourth century CE.

The Purāṇas claim to deal with five signature subjects: creation, renewal, genealogies, *manvantara* periods of time, and tales of the genealogical figures. However, their subject matter is actually much broader. The Purāṇas are also classified along sectarian lines. Some, such as the *Śiva* and *Liṅga Purāṇas* are clearly Śaiva in orientation, the *Bhāgavata* and *Viṣṇu Purāṇas* are Vaiṣṇava, and the *Devī-Bhāgavata*, an *upa-purāṇa*, is a goddess-centered, or Śākta *purāṇa*. However, other Purāṇas, such as the *Vāmana* and *Mārkaṇḍeya*, do not lend themselves to such simplified sectarian classifications. The Purāṇas are texts that primarily attempt to convey a view of reality that supports Vedic orthodoxy, while including the host of non-Vedic deities first encountered in the Epics, as well as emerging gods and goddesses, demigods, and legendary heroes that derive from folk and regional traditions. The Purāṇas are the source books for much of Hinduism's rich mythology. It is here that we encounter stories of the churning of the ocean, of Devī's battle with the Buffalo Demon, of Viṣṇu and his incarnations (*avatāra*), Śiva's marriage to Satī, and how Gaṇeśa got his elephant head. Descriptions of the Hindu cosmos with its cyclical creation scheme of time subdivided into *yugas*, *manvantaras*, and so on, as well as its spatial layout of islands and concentric oceans, are also found in these texts. The Purāṇas extol the virtues of holy cities (e.g. the *Kāśi Khaṇḍa* of the *Skanda Purāṇa* is dedicated to Banāras), and of the value of pilgrimages to these places. The methods of devotional worship (*pūjā*), ascetic observances (*vrata*), and the calendrical cycles of holy days are other topics of discussion.

The foremost concern of the Purāṇas is to align the world-view of Vedic Hinduism with rapidly expanding *bhakti* theism. In these texts we again encounter Hinduism's remarkable malleability and adaptability. In the voices of the *ṛṣis* who are depicted as recounting the tales and teachings, we note the processes of Sanskritization and universalization at work in which the democratizing features of the *bhakti* path are progressively incorporated, granted legitimacy, and systematically defined by orthodoxy. *Bhakti* was opening, to women and all classes, the right to and capacity for ritual worship. By formulating the appropriate methods of such worship, through *pūjā*, pilgrimage, and so on, the Purāṇas distinguish these practices from Vedic *yajña*, while yet locating them within a newly configured, broader orthodox universe. Śrauta Brahmins were those who persisted in adhering to the most orthodox of practices, namely that described in the *śruti* literature. However, Smārta Brahmins began to follow the teachings in the *smṛti* literature, namely the Dharma Śāstras, the Epics and Purāṇas.

Bhakti was also forging a relationship between theistic devotion and the attainment of *mokṣa*. The Purāṇas describe and expand upon the lives and lineages of gods and human beings, attempting to connect the particulars of regional cults into an overarching scheme of a cosmos pervaded by a particular deity, identified as the Vedic One, the Absolute. Thus various deities are strung together in the scheme of Viṣṇu's *avatāras* (e.g. *Bhāgavata Purāṇa*), and multiple goddesses are fused together into the persona of the Great Goddess, the Mahādevī (e.g. *Mārkaṇḍeya Purāṇa*). Śiva's family incorporates deities such as Skanda, Gaṇeśa, and certain goddesses, such as Pārvatī, and Satī. Three deities emerged as most important in this process: Viṣṇu, Śiva, and Devī/Śakti. Smārta Brahmins reflect this transitional shift for they worship at the shrines of five main deities: Śiva, Viṣṇu, Gaṇeśa, Sūrya (the Vedic Sun god), and Devī. Regional, non-Sanskritic deities, such as the South Indian Murugan and Koṟṟāvai are subsumed into more widely accepted Sanskritic ones, such as Skanda and Durgā, respectively. The Purāṇic tradition is still alive. They continue to be studied and recited, cited by devotees and the learned as authoritative sources, and new renditions continue to be composed. By drawing on threads from the tales of old, the Purāṇas weave these together with the places, beliefs, and practices of current sacredness, producing a fabric of devotional Hinduism to clothe Brahmin and *śūdra* alike.

The decline of the Vedic deities

The *śramaṇa* movements ushered in the decline of most of the Vedic deities, such as Indra, Varuṇa, and Soma, as renunciation and meditative practices began to compete with sacrificial religion. The Epics and Purāṇas exalt a newer assortment of deities, further marginalizing the gods of the Vedic Saṃhitās, although the worship of Vedic deities does not disappear entirely from Hinduism. Epic and Purāṇic myths reduce their significance. In one myth, Kṛṣṇa holds the mountain Govardhana overhead, defying the efforts of Indra to disrupt the inhabitants of Vṛndāvana with a torrential thunderstorm. In an episode in the *Mahābhārata*, Kṛṣṇa and Arjuna set fire to a forest to feed the malnourished god Agni. Śiva, hardly mentioned in any Vedic literature, also rises to prominence in this period. Viṣṇu, who is a relatively minor Vedic god, grows in stature, and through his incarnations (*avatāra*) incorporates other deities, such as Rāma and Kṛṣṇa who have their own developing cults. The Vedic god Sūrya enjoyed a robust expansion of his cult in the classical period, but is not worshipped much any more.

Case study: Brahmā/Prajāpati

Brahmā is primarily a Purāṇic deity who appears in innumerable myths. Brahmā is occasionally cited as part of the *trimūrti*, or three forms of a supreme divinity, Brahman, in which Brahmā is the creator, Viṣṇu is the preserver, and Śiva is the destroyer. However, this configuration, often used in oversimplified presentations of Hinduism, is not widespread. Brahmā derives some eminence from his association with Brahman, the Vedic One, or Absolute, which is sometimes grammatically rendered as Brahma, without the long "a". More often, his Vedic association is with the god Prajāpatī (Lord of Offspring), or Brahma Prajāpati, who is propitiated in the *aśvamedha* and other Vedic rites. Brahmā is regarded as having produced the creation, although the accounts of how this was done vary considerably. According to the *Laws of Manu*, the self-existent Lord (i.e. Brahmā/Brahman?) emerged from the void, and created the cosmic waters into which he placed his seed. This seed grew into a luminous golden egg, from which he himself was born as Brahmā. In the *Matsya Purāṇa* account, he produced a beautiful female, named Sāvitrī, Sarasvatī, or Brāhmanī, drawn out from his own form, and smitten with desire for her, produced four heads in the cardinal directions, and a fifth above in order to gaze at her as she moved around and above him. Through intercourse they produced all the creatures in existence, including human beings, gods, and demons. Brahmā often grants boons to those who propitiate him.

Brahmā is depicted with four bearded faces. He is red in color and has four arms. He may be portrayed holding a water-pot, the Vedas, a bow (or scepter), a rosary (*mālā*), a ladle for sacrificial offerings, and a lotus. His mount or *vāhana* is the goose (*haṃsa*). Mythic accounts (e.g. *Mahābhārata*) relate how Śiva decapitated Brahmā's fifth head, some providing the rationale that Śiva was angered at Brahmā's incestuous intercourse with his "daughter" to produce the cosmos. Another version (*Padma Purāṇa*) holds that Śiva cut off Brahmā's upper head because it grew inflated with self-glorification at its own creation. In Vaiṣṇava myths, at the beginning of each cycle of creation, Brahmā appears atop a lotus flower that emerges like an umbilical cord from Viṣṇu's navel. In the preceding myths Brahmā is made subordinate to Viṣṇu and Śiva. Although Brahmā is mythically accorded the power of creation, and often listed with Viṣṇu and Śiva as constituting a kind of Hindu trinity, in terms of actual prominence, the Devī is much more significant than Brahmā, and through her associations with cosmic power (Śakti) actually presides over many of Brahmā's creative functions.

There are only a few temples and renowned sites dedicated to Brahmā throughout India. The most celebrated of these is at the holy lake of Pushkar, in Rajasthan, where during an annual festival in the month of Kartika (November), hundreds of thousands of pilgrims gather to bathe in its waters and visit the Brahmā temple there. Now surrounded by dozens of whitewashed temples and stone stairways leading to bathing points along its perimeter, the small circular lake is believed to have formed from a lotus flower that fell from Brahmā's hand. Various explanations circulate about the virtual absence of Brahmā worship. According to certain accounts, since the initial work of creation is completed, it is only the gods who preside over preservation, namely Viṣṇu, and destruction, namely Śiva, that now need to be worshipped. In a Śaivite mythic tale, Viṣṇu and Brahmā asked Śiva if they could discern the limits of his vast power, and so they set off in opposite directions to search for the beginning and end of his effulgent *liṅga*. Viṣṇu soon discovered that the task was impossible, and returned humbled. However, Brahmā encountered the *ketaka* (Latin: *pandanus*) flower along the way, and encouraged it to substantiate his lie that he had indeed reached the tip of Śiva's *liṅga*. Omniscient Śiva, knowing that Brahmā had lied, and angered at his egotism, pronounced a curse that Brahmā should never be worshipped again. Śiva also cursed the *ketaka* flower that it should never be used in devotional offerings.

The case of Brahmā demonstrates how the Purāṇas recount myths of deities that were not significant in the Vedic pantheon. Brahmā may have had some measure of a devotional following in regions of North India, judging from evidence of his cult in such places as Pushkar and Gāyā, and frequent references to him in Buddhist and Jain literature. In the Purāṇas, he is fused with deities from the Vedic pantheon, such as Brahman and Prajāpati, and his mythology is elaborated upon in relation to these and the other deities of the burgeoning Purāṇic *bhakti* pantheon. However, due to the sectarian orientations of other Purāṇas, he is generally portrayed as subordinate to Viṣṇu and Śiva, whose popularity surpasses him.

Śaiva deities: iconography, myths, and festivals

Śiva

Śiva's name, which is generally translated as "auspicious," likely derives from the Dravidian term for "red," the color with which he (and Rudra) was frequently associated in early textual references. In modern depictions he is often shown with an ash-colored skin, clad in animal skins. His hair is long and matted, tied into a top-knot. He has snakes (*nāga*) as belts and bracelets, and wields a trident. The river goddess Gaṅgā is often shown entrapped within his locks, or spouting out from his hair. His mount is the bull, Nandi, a symbol of his virility.

The application of structural theory to the Purāṇic myths of Śiva reveals that his persona embodies a bipolar character. He is the supreme *yogi*, given to such fierce asceticism that not blood, but ash flows within him. He has generated immense inner heat (*tapas*) through his austerities and can release it through his wisdom or third eye, located on his forehead. He will annihilate the cosmos at the end of time, and thus when categorized in a triad with Brahmā and Viṣṇu, he is regarded as the

Destroyer. However, Śiva is also highly erotic in nature. His asceticism is associated with the accumulation of enormous creative power, symbolized by his erect phallus. This is the sign (*liṅga*) of Śiva, and is the icon with which he is most often worshipped in temples and shrines. For Śaivites, Śiva embodies the full spectrum of creative, preservative, and destructive dimensions of the divine. The erect *liṅga* represents his erotic power, his associations with fertility and creative potential, and his destructive capacities. The erect phallus has not spilt its seed, and thus symbolizes how Śiva restrains creation from emerging.

Although at first glance he gives off an appearance of being unkempt, Śiva embodies a savage beauty and an irresistible attraction. In Purāṇic myths, he seduces the wives of the *ṛṣis* of the Pine Forest, to punish their husbands for their arrogance. Śiva is said to have a disdain for social niceties, preferring the wilderness as his habitat, and even resides at cremation grounds. His heavenly abode is Mount Kailāsa in the Himalayas. It is often said that one must become Śiva to worship Śiva, and devotees thus may take up the appearance and behavior of Śiva in order to please him and become one with him. He is generally regarded as easy to please, being satisfied with sincerity in worship more so than elaborate rites. Śiva is often associated with an easygoing, dreamy, intoxicated state (Hindi: *masti*). Thus some devotees use and offer him intoxicants and other powerful, consciousness altering substances, such as liquor or the hallucinogenic *datura* plant. Cannabis leaves (Hindi: *gañja, bhāng*) or resin (Hindi: *charas*) are consumed in food or drink preparations, or smoked, to be in communion with and to worship Śiva.

One of Śiva's most celebrated festivals is Mahāśivarātri (Great Night of Śiva), when devotees perform fasts, stay up all night long visiting important Śiva temples, and even make offerings at obscure or neglected *liṅgas*. Music and dance programs may be held to celebrate the night vigils. One of Śiva's most engaging iconic forms is as Naṭarāja (Lord of the Dance), in which he is depicted encircled by flames with his matted locks wildly flying. He is engaged in the *tāṇḍava* dance, which brings about the destruction of the cosmos. This is the form in which he is worshipped at Cidambaram, a vast Śiva temple in South India. Perhaps the most revered Śiva temple is located in Banāras or Kāśī, where he presides as Viśvanātha (Lord of the Universe) in the form of a small, black stone *liṅga*. The *liṅga* barely protrudes above the fluids in the *yoni kuṇḍa*, the rectangular tank in which it sits, which is filled with Gaṅgā water, milk and flower offerings. The temple, which is topped with a gold spire, is located within a honeycomb of narrow alleys, and has been rebuilt beside a mosque that was constructed upon the ruins of the previous temple.

Satī/Pārvatī

The myths of Satī and Pārvatī are so closely interconnected that they are often regarded as the same goddess. Typically Pārvatī is viewed as an incarnation of Satī.

The earliest references to Satī/Pārvatī occur in the *Mahābhārata* (13.140.43–44), where Pārvatī is described as dallying with Śiva in the Himalaya Mountains. Later Purānic traditions link Pārvatī, whose name means "She of the Mountain (*parvata*)" with the Vedic goddess Umā Haimavatī (Umā, She of Himavat (i.e. the Himalayas)), mentioned in the *Kena Upaniṣad* (3.12). It is in the Purāṇas and in literary works after the fourth century CE that the distinct mythologies of Satī and Pārvatī develop.

Satī is portrayed as having intensely desired to be the spouse of Śiva, and who, through her ascetic practices and deep devotion, eventually wins his attention. They are duly wed and retire to the mountains for love play. However, Satī's father, Dakṣa, does not like Śiva's unconventional appearance and habits. When Dakṣa plans a great *yajña*, he invites all the divine beings, but deliberately does not invite his daughter and Śiva. Emotionally agitated by the snub, Satī attends the sacrifice only to be further humiliated, at which point she commits suicide, in some versions by casting herself into the sacrificial fire. Śiva, enraged by what has transpired, generates terrible beings, which defeat the celestial hosts, destroy Dakṣa's sacrifice, and kill him. Eventually, Dakṣa is resuscitated, the sacrifice is restored, and Śiva is included among the guests. In certain versions of this myth, the deeply grieving Śiva then carries the body of Satī with him across the universe, disrupting the cosmic order. To restore normalcy, Viṣṇu slices off parts of Satī's body which fall to the earth transforming each of those locations into a sacred site, known as a *pīṭha*, a "seat" of the goddess. The myth of Satī's dismemberment relates to the Hindu conception of the intrinsic sacrality of the creation. The presence of divinity may thus be discerned in features of the natural world, such as trees, rock, lakes, and so on, by those who have the spiritual acumen to do so, or through divine grace. There are more than fifty sites that lay claim to being *śakti pīṭhas*, such as at Kāmarūpa in Assam, where Satī's *yoni* is believed to have fallen. Realizing that he was no longer carrying Satī, Śiva stopped his grieving, and resumed his normal role.

The foregoing myths, which exist in numerous variations, suggest a sectarian, and cultural, tension between Brahmā worshippers (i.e. orthodox, Āryan, Brahmin, Vedic) and Śaivas (i.e. unorthodox, non-Vedic). Dakṣa is sometimes associated with Prajāpati, or regarded as a son of Brahmā. Śiva, who is unconventional, and uninterested in Vedic sacrificial rituals, the householder's social life, and so on, is brought into the social order through his marriage to Satī. However, there is a tense relationship between the households of the bride and groom. Some see a relationship between Satī's suicide and the Hindu tradition of widow immolation that bears the same name. However, this is tenuous at best because Satī's husband, Śiva, is neither dead nor in need of salvation. Śiva, who embodies the wandering ascetic's lifestyle, is shown to be greater than the Vedic deities, whom he defeats, and his destruction of the *yajña* is clear evidence of a disdain for sacrificial religion. In the restoration myth we see Śiva once again brought back into social order by being incorporated into the orthodox pantheon in which the sacrifice is reinstituted.

The myths partly cast Śiva's marriage to Satī into the framework of an arranged marriage, designed to bring the celibate ascetic into the social order. Śiva's austerities threaten to destroy the cosmos prematurely, and he thus needs to be induced to release his seed in order to fertilize and invigorate the creation. However, the myths also emphasize that Satī yearns for Śiva. She wins his heart. Śiva feels desire (*kāma*) for Satī, prior to their marriage. Theirs is also something of a love marriage, not fully endorsed by her side of the family. He grieves when losing her.

Pārvatī's worship may originate among non-Āryan mountain-dwelling tribes. Almost all her myths cast her in relationship with Śiva as his wife. If one weaves together her story based on various Purāṇic accounts, Satī reincarnated as Pārvatī and was born to Himavat, the deified Himalaya Mountains, and his wife, Mena. Extremely beautiful, and dark-skinned in complexion, Pārvatī is attracted to Śiva from an early age. Since a demon named Tāraka had received a boon of invincibility against all but a son of Śiva, and threatened the cosmic balance, the gods enlisted the aid of Kāma, the god of love. A splendidly handsome youth, Kāma shot Śiva with flowery arrows of love, fired from his bow fashioned out of sugar cane and strung with honey bees. Enraged by the awakening of desire that had disrupted his meditative calm, Śiva destroyed Kāma with fire from his third eye. However, he was already smitten by Pārvatī, who, like Satī, had already been engaged in intense devotion and ascetic practice to attract Śiva's attention. Śiva eventually restored Kāma to life.

While Satī's marriage to Śiva was dysfunctional due to family disapproval, with disastrous consequences, Pārvatī's parents endorse and support her marriage. She becomes a domesticating influence on her antisocial husband, whose appearance, interests, and behavior are outside the margins of orthodox notions of propriety. She mediates both his erotic and his ascetic dimensions, channeling them into dharmically appropriate manifestations of sexuality within marriage.

Pārvatī is implicitly present in every *yoni* stone upon which a Śiva *liṅga* is placed. She is also often depicted in iconography along with Śiva, seated on his lap or in close embrace. This image resonates with a common setting in tantric scriptures, in which Pārvatī asks questions of Śiva, who teaches her tantric truths. In certain tantric texts, he asks the questions and she provides the answers. Pārvatī is often said to embody Śiva's *śakti*, or power. Thus she is implicitly linked with Śakti in tantric Śiva-Śakti formulations. In Śaiva Siddhānta philosophy, she embodies the power of devotion which, when awakened within devotees, impels them towards Śiva. She is simultaneously Śiva's grace (Tamil: *arul*), which leads devotees to liberation. There are relatively few temples dedicated exclusively to Pārvatī. An exquisite life-sized image sculpted in black stone is found in her temple at Baijnāth in the Kumaon Himalayas. She is sometimes equated with the Hindu Great Goddess (Mahādevī), and thus is shown with a lion as her mount. Certain images fuse Śiva and Pārvatī together into a form of the divine known as Ardhanarīśvara (The Lord who is Half Woman). One half of these images is the feminine Pārvatī, recognizable through its

Figure 10.1 Bronze masterpiece depicting Śiva and Pārvatī in classic embrace with rich symbolic significance (Patan Museum, Nepal)

prominent breast and delicate features, while the other half is the masculine Śiva, perhaps shown wielding his trident. A particularly beautiful Ardhanarīśvara image is found at the Elephanta Caves on an island not far off the coast of Mumbai.

Gaṇeśa

The elephant-headed god, Gaṇeśa is one of the most memorable deities in the Hindu pantheon. Gaṇeśa does not appear in the Vedic *śruti* literature, but the Hindu fascination with and respect for elephants has ancient roots. Elephants, whose large grey shapes resembled thunderclouds, were associated with the celestial waters and the fecundity of the rains. Just as the god Indra rode his elephant mount Airāvata, elephants were and continue to be symbols of royalty, the vehicle of kings. Gaṇeśa derives from non-Āryan worship traditions, and his cult was progressively incorporated into the orthodox pantheon. He is one of the five deities worshipped by orthodox Smārta Brahmins. Early iconography, from the fifth century CE, shows him associated with groups of goddesses known as the Mātṛkās (the Mothers).

A well-known myth provides one version of his origins. One day, when Śiva was away, Pārvatī, wishing a child of her own, fashioned Gaṇeśa out of the rubbings from her body. She asked him to serve as a guardian, preventing anyone from entering and disturbing her. When Śiva returned and wanted to see Pārvatī he was stopped by Gaṇeśa. Angered by the boy's resistance, Śiva decapitated Gaṇeśa. Pārvatī, outraged by Śiva's act, demanded that he be restored to life. The first creature encountered was an elephant, and its head was used as a replacement. Since Śiva was impressed by the boy's courage, he made him the chief (*pati, īśa*) of the *gaṇas*, Śiva's cohort of spirits and demigods. Hence he derives his name Gaṇeśa or Gaṇapati. His staunch defense of Pārvatī's entryway reflects Gaṇeśa's identity as a guardian deity, and he is often depicted on the lintels or pillars of doorways to homes and temples.

In one myth Gaṇeśa competes with his "brother" Kārttikeya to race around the universe three times. Knowing that he would never catch up with Kārttikeya, who had already sped off, Gaṇeśa calmly circumambulated his parents, Śiva and Pārvatī, three times, knowing that they embodied the entire cosmos. Thus he won the race, demonstrating the value of wisdom and measured action over impetuosity. Another of Gaṇeśa's names is Vināyaka (Remover), relating to his capacity to remove obstacles if propitiated. In rituals to other deities, Gaṇeśa traditionally receives worship first to insure that he might remove unforeseen obstacles to the successful performance of the rite. Hindus propitiate him before unpredictable undertakings, such as journeys or examinations.

In modern iconography Gaṇeśa is portrayed with large ears, a curved trunk, a large belly, and a broken tusk. He wears a serpent as a belt or as his sacred thread, and often holds an elephant goad, a noose, and sweets in his four or more hands. His mount is the mouse (*mūśika*), which may symbolize Gaṇeśa's subtle movements and resourceful qualities. The goad prods devotees along the path of righteousness, while the noose symbolizes the bondage brought about by ignorance. A myth tells how when he ran out of ink, Gaṇeśa, serving as a scribe for Vyāsa who was dictating the *Mahābhārata*, snapped off his own tusk to serve as a pen to maintain his promise to not stop writing (See Figure 7.3). Some Hindus regard him as celibate, while others pair him with two wives, Buddhī and Siddhī (or Ṛddhi), representing his associations with wisdom and supernormal attainments. Gaṇeśa has a huge following in the state of Maharashtra, and during a ten-day festival in August, colorful clay images are fabricated, installed in temporary shrines, worshipped, and finally delivered into the ocean or some body of water.

Skanda/Kārttikeya

Skanda/Kārttikeya is typically regarded as the son of Śiva. His origins may derive from a divinized warrior chieftain, and he has Vedic associations with warfare. In the *Mahābhārata,* he is the son of Agni. North-west Indian coins from about the second century CE appear to depict him. According to the *Śiva Purāṇa*'s account, after marrying Pārvatī Śiva retired with her to Mount Kailāsa for sexual dalliance lasting a thousand *deva* years. Beseeched by the gods, who had been defeated by the demon Tāraka, Śiva let his semen fall to the ground. No one, except Pārvatī, was able to hold Śiva's hot seed, but it was first picked up by Agni, and finally passed into the goddess Gaṅgā, who deposited it in a reed grass forest. There it turned into a splendid boy, delighting the gods. The six heavenly women known as the Kṛttikās (i.e. the Pleiades constellation) spotted him and each longed to suckle him. He thus developed six faces to drink from their breasts. Thus he comes to be known as Kārttikeya, as well as Skanda, since he was produced from the "oozing/spurting" of Śiva's semen. Kārttikeya is regarded as the god of war, alluded to in his mythic birthplace, since arrows are fashioned from reeds. Tāraka had received a boon that he could only be slain by a son of Śiva, and so the gods had striven, with the aid of Kāma, the god of love, to induce Śiva to marry Pārvatī, and finally produce a son. Skanda, who is also known as Kumāra (Prince), eventually slew Tāraka, and restored the gods to their proper abode.

In modern lithographs Skanda is typically portrayed as a handsome young man, wielding a bow and arrow, or the *śakti* weapon (or Tamil: *vēl,* a spear), and with a peacock mount. In South India, the deity Murugan has been worshipped since antiquity. He was a war god, associated with the peacock and worshipped with an ecstatic trance-inducing dance, known as the *veriyadāl,* performed by the Vēlan, the priests of his cult. Murugan embodied youthful male virility. Eventually Murugan was absorbed into the North Indian pantheon, and identified with Skanda/Kārttikeya. His two wives Valli and Teyvayanai, at times contentious with each other in mythic accounts, evoke some of the tensions between Sanskritic and Tamil culture. Devasenā (Teyvayanai) is Murugan's wife, in compliance with northern-styled orthodoxy, while Valli is the local tribal chieftain's daughter that he loves and marries.

There are numerous temples to Skanda throughout the Hindu world. The temple of Palani, near Madurai in South India is visited by thousands of pilgrims yearly. During the festival of Thaipusam, more than a million pilgrims visit his temple at the Batu Caves in Malaysia. A distinctive aspect of Murugan's worship may feature devotees dancing while carrying bamboo or wooden structures decorated with peacock feathers, known in Tamil as a *kāvaṭi.* Some may pierce themselves with long needles or hooks, performing extraordinary feats of bodily mortification in a demonstration of their piety.

Figure 10.2 A devotee, with piercings through his tongue and cheek, prepares to carry a decorated *kavaṭi* arch supported by long metal needles inserted in his flesh (Malaysia) [Photo courtesy of Natasha Elder]

Vaiṣṇava deities: iconography, myths, and festivals

Viṣṇu

Viṣṇu (The Pervader) is typically portrayed in contemporary religious prints with benign features and four arms. His name may derive from the Dravidian term *viñ* (blue sky), which supports his enduring representations with a blue skin color. He holds a discus (*cakra*), a club (*gada*), a conch (*śaṅkha*), and a lotus flower (*padma*). The club and discus are the means with which he destroys demons and re-establishes or preserves the cosmic order since he is most frequently regarded as being the "Preserver" in the Hindu trinity, which designates Brahmā as the Creator, and

Śiva as the Destroyer. He has a mark known as the *śrīvatsa* on his breast. Viṣṇu is often depicted seated like a monarch on a throne, accompanied by his queenly wife Śrī Lakṣmī, or reclining in slumber upon the endless serpent Śeṣa or Ānanta (Without End). From his navel, a lotus flower like an umbilical cord snakes upward, upon which is seated the creator god, Brahmā. Viṣṇu's feet are massaged by the goddesses Śrī Lakṣmī and Bhu Devī. In this he represents the condition of supreme absorption, in which all of creation has been re-absorbed, having moved into a state of transcendence, during a phase known as the *pralāya,* before and after the next cycle of manifestation. As the "Preserver" he is also the principle of continuity of cyclical creation, enduring beyond what might otherwise be an *eschaton,* an "end of times."

Badrinath is a famous temple dedicated to Viṣṇu, who presides there as Badri Nārāyaṇa. The temple is located in the Himalayas at one of the sources of the Gaṅgā. *Śālagrāma* stones found in the Himalayas, typically from the river bed of the Gandaki River, are spherical ammonite fossils which are believed to be forms of Viṣṇu. They should be worshipped in home shrines, not temples, They should be neither bought nor sold, and are regarded to convey to the worshipper the most beneficence if intact, without having been cracked open to reveal the spiral features within. The Śrīraṅgam temple in Tamil Nādu is the largest temple complex in all of India. It houses a large image of Viṣṇu as Raṅganātha, reclining on the endless serpent. Viṣṇu's mount is Garuda, the king of birds, who is sometimes portrayed as a winged human being. Garuda is widely depicted in Nepal and South-east Asia.

Viṣṇu's Avatāras

It is now traditional to regard Viṣṇu as having ten main descents (*avatāra*) or incarnations. These are: 1) Fish (*matsya*), 2) Tortoise (*kūrma*), 3) Boar (*varāha*), 4) Man-Lion (*narasiṃha*), 5) Dwarf (*vāmana*), 6) Rāma with Axe (*paraśu-rāma*), 7) Rāma (hero of the *Rāmāyaṇa*), 8) Kṛṣṇa (of the *Mahābhārata*), 9) Balarāma or the Buddha, and 10) Kalki. Of these *avatāras,* Rāma and Kṛṣṇa are the most celebrated. *Avatāras* of Viṣṇu that belong to other lists include Kapila, the legendary sage attributed with founding Sāṅkhya philosophy, and Hāyagriva, a horse-necked incarnation. In the *Bhagavad Gītā,* Kṛṣṇa explains that when chaos (*adharma*) threatens to tip the cosmic balance, through the powers of *māyā* and nature, the transcendent Lord periodically manifests to destroy evil and restore order and righteousness (*dharma*). Accounts of the rationales behind the incarnations vary in Purāṇic accounts. The versions that follow are composites of textual and popular beliefs.

The Fish *avatāra* manifested and rescued the sage Manu from a great deluge. Manu had rescued the fish by nurturing it in progressively larger containers and finally releasing it into the ocean. The fish warned him of an impending flood and advised him to build a large boat, and to take with him a combination of seeds and beasts.

It is Viṣṇu himself who dictates the *Matsya Purāṇa* while in his Fish incarnation, as he towed the boat to a high mountain peak. Manu then became the forefather of all human beings.

The Tortoise *avatāra* manifested when the gods and demons decided to churn the Milk Ocean to produce *amṛta* (Nectar of Immortality). At this time both groups were mortal. The Tortoise's shell served as the pivot upon which Mount Mandara was placed to serve as the churning rod. The serpent Vāsuki was the churning rope, and the gods (*sura, deva*) and the demons (*asura*) struck a truce and toiled together, finally producing the desired ambrosia. Several items emerged from the churning, including Kāmadhenu (or Surabhi) the wish-granting cow, and a deadly poison that threatened the entire creation. Śiva drank this poison which lodged in his throat turning it blue. In certain Śākta versions of this myth, the Devī suckles him back to life. Viṣṇu then assumed the female form of Mohinī, whose captivating beauty distracted the demons. The gods drank the *amṛta*, granting them immortality. Only the demon Rāhu's head received immortality, since he disguised himself as a god before being discovered. He was beheaded by Viṣṇu's discus.

The demon Hiraṇyākṣa (Golden Eye) had sunk the earth into the bottom of the cosmic ocean to prevent the gods from being worshipped. Viṣṇu took up the Boar incarnation, dove to the ocean bottom, and dug up the earth with his tusks. As he swam upwards the demon engaged him in a battle of cosmic proportions. Viṣṇu placed the earth, personified as the Earth Goddess, on his lap, and slew Hiranyākṣa. The kings of the Gupta Dynasty were patrons of the Boar incarnation of Viṣṇu. An impressive sculpture of the Boar *avatāra* is also found in a temple site built by the Chandella Dynasty at Khajuraho in Northern India.

Hiranyākṣa's brother Hiraṇyakaśipu (Golden Garment) despised Viṣṇu. When his own son, Prahlāda became a devotee of his enemy, the demon attempted to kill the pious boy. However Viṣṇu intervened on several occasions. The demon was fearless because he had performed intense austerities through which he had attained a boon from Brahmā. He had asked for immortality, which could not be granted, and so requested that he should die neither by day nor by night, neither indoors nor outdoors, not on land, in the air, or in water, nor should he be killed by man or beast, or by any weapon. Brahmā granted the boon, and the demon grew arrogant and unafraid of any divine retribution. One day, exasperated at his son's devotion, Hiraṇyakaśipu readied to kill Prahlāda on the spot, arrogantly challenging Viṣṇu to appear and face his death. At that moment, at dusk (neither night nor day), Viṣṇu appeared from a pillar in the doorway (neither indoors nor outdoors), in the dreadful form of Narasiṃha (Nṛsiṅgha) the Man-Lion (neither man nor beast). He raised Hiraṇyakaśipu onto his lap (neither on the ground nor in the air), and disemboweled him with his claws (not a weapon). A massive granite sculpture of Narasiṃha is located at a ruined temple site in Hampi, the ancient capital of the South Indian kingdom of Vijayanagara.

The Dwarf *avatāra* appeared to restore a balance when the demon Bali, a grandson of Prahlāda, had conquered the three worlds. Although he was a dharmic demon, it was still necessary to restore the heavens to the gods, and so Viṣṇu appeared before Bali in the guise of a dwarf (or a young Brahmin boy). Bali was pleased by the Dwarf's pious behavior and granted him whatever he wished for. The Dwarf asked for whatever he could cover in three steps. Surprised at the meager request, Bali granted it, at which point Viṣṇu grew to enormous proportions. In his three steps he took back the triple world sending Bali down into the underworld realm, Pātāla, with his third step. The three steps of the Dwarf *avatāra* resonate with Viṣṇu's three-stepping (*trivikrama*) feat alluded to in early Vedic literature. An excellently rendered image of the Dwarf *avatāra* is found in the Vāmana temple at Khajuraho in Madhya Pradesh.

Paraśurāma was a human incarnation of Viṣṇu. He manifested as a warrior Brahmin, who rectified the cosmic balance by restoring power to the Brahmin class by slaying an entire lineage of arrogant *kṣatriyas* who stole his father's wish-granting cow and eventually killed his father. He wielded an axe given to him by Śiva. In other myths, he beheads his own mother Renuka.

There is an interesting confrontation between Viṣṇu's next incarnation, Rāma, and Paraśurāma. When Rāma strung and broke the bow of Śiva to win Sītā's hand, his feat elicited the attention of Paraśurāma, who challenged him to battle. Paraśurāma offered Rāma the bow of Viṣṇu, claiming it to be more powerful. Rāma quickly strung that bow as well, inserted one of Paraśurāma's own deadly arrows into it, but desisted from slaying him since he was a Brahmin. Instead he destroyed all of Paraśurāma's sacred abodes. This episode is a revealing confrontation between sectarian and *varṇa*-based streams of discourse, in which the *kṣatriya* hero, Rāma, whose dharmic nature surpasses most Brahmins, gains supremacy over the Brahmin warrior, Paraśurāma, regaining status for the *kṣatriya varṇa*. However, both are accommodated as divine manifestations of Viṣṇu, and the *kṣatriya* Rāma affirms deference to the Brahmin Paraśurāma, whom he refuses to harm. Paraśurāma is still worshipped in Kerala, and his mythic deeds are believed to have produced the land of Kerala itself.

Rāma's divinization appears to occur after Kṛṣṇa's, because he stands out most as a human hero in Vālmīki's *Rāmāyaṇa*. However, his divine nature was accentuated through subsequent versions of the epic. A particularly influential version is the *Rāmacaritamānasa*, composed in Banāras by Tulsidās (1532–1623), which is a crucial scripture for the Rāmānandi sect headquartered in Ayodhyā, Rāma's legendary birthplace. Unlike the erotically charged relationship of Rādhā and Kṛṣṇa, this sect has an ascetic character, and its Rāma *bhakti* emphasizes the Hanumān–Rāma relationship. Hanumān, who belongs to the Vaiṣṇava sectarian tradition, is regarded as the perfect servant of Rāma, and becomes the model for all devotees. Hanumān, who is also viewed as a guardian deity, has enormous appeal among the lower classes. The Rāmlīlas are popular festivals staged in North India. In Banāras, many communities stage these celebrations, which may involve re-enactments of episodes from the *Rāmāyaṇa*. The largest of these, which spans several weeks, is patronized by the Mahārāja of Banāras in Rāmnagar, the site of his palace, across the Gaṅgā River. In 1992, mobs of Hindus descended on the Babari Masjid, a mosque built by the Mughal emperor Babar/Babur on what they believed to be the site of a razed Hindu temple commemorating Rāma's birthplace in Ayodhyā. They destroyed the mosque, and there are constant efforts to initiate the reconstruction of the Rām Janma Bhumi (Site of Rāma's Birth) temple in its place. Rāma has thus proved to be a particularly potent political symbol for Hindus, managing to unite various sectarian strands under the emblem of an idealized governance, one which upholds traditional religious values, while remaining free from moral corruption.

Viṣṇu's ninth *avatāra* is Balarāma in some accounts and the Buddha in others. Balarāma is regarded as Kṛṣṇa's older brother and in iconographic depictions wields a plough and a mace. Fond of alcohol and impetuous in nature, he is light-skinned and is often identified with Viṣṇu's endless serpent Śeṣa. He is said to have remained neutral in the *Mahābhārata* war, when Kṛṣṇa sided with the Pāṇḍavas. The Buddha *avatāra* is a problematic inclusion in the series, because his teachings against the *varṇa* system and Vedic authority are regarded as heterodox. It likely derives from a period when Buddhism had grown in popularity and efforts were being made to come to terms with it. However, in some Purāṇic sources, the orthodox explanation is that Viṣṇu incarnated as the Buddha to teach a false doctrine and thus lead the demons astray. Naturally Buddhists do not regard the Buddha as an incarnation of Viṣṇu. The final incarnation of Viṣṇu is the Kalki *avatāra*, who has yet to come. He will either be or ride a white horse and wield a weapon of immense destruction. He will destroy the unrighteous at the end of the Kali Yuga, and usher in an era of *dharma*.

Many observers have noted a sort of evolutionary scheme in the system of *avatāras*, which begin with an aquatic creature (fish), and then move from a reptile (tortoise) towards more normal human life forms (man-lion, dwarf). The *avatāras* then progress to more spiritually evolved human forms (Rāma, Kṛṣna, etc.). What is evident, however, is that the *avatāra* scheme has enabled a wide array of deities to be incorporated under the rubric of Vaiṣṇavism. The concept of *avatāras* continues to be advanced by various sects. Thus Śrī Caitanya is often regarded as an *avatāra* of Kṛṣṇa, and Swami Bhaktivedanta is held by many of his disciples to be an incarnation of Caitanya.

Kṛṣṇa

The Kṛṣṇa *avatāra* is immensely popular in Hinduism, undoubtedly due to the influence of the *Bhagavad Gītā*. Kṛṣṇa's mythology, which was developed in the

Harivaṃśa, and subsequently in Purānic accounts, proved to be highly captivating. His cult and life story is an amalgam of a number of components fusing the worship of Vāsudeva, Viṣṇu, Govinda, and other deities, with *bhakti* and tantric elements. In the *Bhāgavata Purāṇa*, although Kṛṣṇa is portrayed as an *avatāra* of Viṣṇu, the text's tone is centrally devoted to Kṛṣṇa who is for all intents and purposes the supreme form of divinity. The centrality of Kṛṣṇa is a defining feature of Gauḍiya (i.e. Bengali) Vaiṣṇavism. Kṛṣṇa's mythic life offers human beings a divine persona that lends itself to affection. He is not a remote deity, abstract and devoid of character, but an irresistibly attractive human being. The account that follows is culled from Purāṇic and popular accounts.

Kaṃsa, the king of Mathurā, had heard a prophesy that the eighth child of his sister Devakī would kill him. He thus imprisoned Devakī and her husband Vasudeva and began to kill each child that was born to them. Viṣṇu had the fetus of Devakī's seventh child transferred into the womb of Vasudeva's other wife, Rohiṇī, and he grew up to be Balarāma (or Saṅkārṣaṇa). When Devakī gave birth to her eighth child, the infant was smuggled across the Yamunā River to the village of Gokul, where he was exchanged for the newborn daughter of the cowherds Yaśodā and Nanda. They named him Kṛṣṇa (Black) because of his dark skin. When Kaṃsa tried to kill the baby girl, she flew up into the air, revealed herself as a form of the Goddess (Devī), and informed Kaṃsa that Devakī's eighth child was already born and would slay him as predicted. Kaṃsa attempted to slay all the young boys of the kingdom, but Kṛṣṇa managed to avoid the murderers, and to kill others. For instance, the she-demon Pūtanā smeared her breasts with poison and suckled Kṛṣṇa, but he managed to suck the very life out of her.

His mother Yaśodā had a stunning glimpse of his divinity when one day she noticed that the baby Kṛṣṇa had been eating dirt. When she raced over to remove the mud and stones, she was awestruck by a vision of the entire cosmos within his mouth. Kṛṣṇa grew up to be a mischievous, but lovable, child who charmed all the cowherd women (*gopī*) of Gokul. He would play pranks on them and loved to find, steal, and eat butter no matter where his mother or the *gopīs* tried to hide it. As Kṛṣṇa grew, his adventures unfolded in the region of Vṛndāvana, a nearby forest, where he lived the life of a humble cowherd (*go-pala*). Once, when the serpent Kāliya had poisoned the waters of the Yamunā, Kṛṣṇa dove into the water, wrestled with the snake and overpowered it. He was seen playing his flute as he danced upon its hood.

Kṛṣṇa had developed into an extremely attractive young man, and all of the *gopīs* were in love with him. In one incident, while they bathed, he gathered up their clothes and made each of them appear naked before him before he passed their garments back. When he played his flute in the forests of Vṛndāvana, the *gopīs* found themselves unable to resist its call and longed to go out to meet him for a love tryst. Kṛṣṇa's love play with the *gopīs* is celebrated as the *rāsa-līlā* (tumultuous play).

Each of the many *gopīs* felt that they had a special relationship with Kṛṣṇa, although he loved them all. However, Kṛṣṇa's favorite *gopī* is Rādhā, and their relationship becomes the basis of much devotional poetry.

On another occasion, when the god Indra threatened the people of Vṛndāvana with torrential rains and a terrible flood, Kṛṣṇa supported Mount Govardhana with his finger, providing dry protection for his people. He enjoined them to worship the mountain that provided them with sustenance and protection, rather than perform Vedic sacrificial rites to Indra. Eventually Kṛṣṇa was invited to a wrestling match at Kaṃsa's palace, where he confronted his evil uncle and finally killed him. Kṛṣṇa's myths move from Vṛndāvana to his capital at Dvāraka, where he ruled. The myths associate him with many wives, including Rukmiṇī, with whom he fathered Pradyumna. He aided the Pāṇḍavas in their victory over the Kauravas, and delivered the *Bhagavad Gītā*'s teachings to his friend Arjuna. Kṛṣṇa was finally killed by a hunter's misguided arrow, which struck him in the foot.

Kṛṣṇa's popularity is undoubtedly related to the many accessible images of divinity in which he presents himself. The baby Kṛṣṇa is the apple of every mother's eye, a lively young boy, on whom one can shower maternal love. Devotees may imagine themselves as loving parents, envisioning God as their child. As a teenager, Kṛṣṇa is the ideal friend, protecting his companions from danger. As a young man, he is the irresistibly attractive lover. When older, he is a spiritual adviser and political strategist, friend, and ally. *Bhakti* offers devotees a variety of modes through which they may approach devotion to a deity. Some choose to imagine themselves as servants of the Lord. Even the idea of an antagonistic relationship, including bickering, arguing, and even fighting as an enemy with God, is regarded as a form of relationship. Kṛṣṇa offers these and many more personal styles of relationship with him. Devotees may envision themselves as doting parents, friends, lovers, loyal subjects, or spiritual disciples.

Kṛṣṇa Janmāṣṭamī (The Eighth [in celebration] of Kṛṣṇa's Birth) is a popular festival in honor of Kṛṣṇa's birth. It occurs in August or September. People visit shrines to view decorated and adorned images of Kṣṛṇa, gather to sing devotional songs and listen to recitations of Kṛṣṇa's exploits, and participate in communal meals.

Śākta deities: iconography, myths, and festivals

Sarasvatī

Unlike most Hindu goddesses, the worship of Sarasvatī (She who is Full of Juice) can be traced back to the Vedic Saṃhitās. In the *Ṛg Veda* she is worshipped as a river goddess. The Indus Valley Civilization is also known to researchers as the Sarasvatī-Sindhu Civilization, after the two major rivers of that period that flowed through that region of North-west India, although the Sarasvatī has since dried up. Sarasvatī's riverine associations have been taken up by the goddess Gaṇgā, undoubtedly reflecting the migratory shift of the cultural centers of Hinduism to the Ganges river basin. By the time of the Brāhmaṇas, Sarasvatī was identified with the goddess of speech, Vāc, or Vāgdevī. Since Vedic revelation is expressed in mantric sound, Sarasvatī has an extremely high status in orthodox ideology, because she embodies the creative power of Brahman. As such she later becomes associated with the creator god Brahmā, as his consort. In certain Purāṇic accounts she is produced from him, and then unites with him to produce the creation. She is eventually associated with all of the creative and intellectual arts, such as music, poetry, and education. As Mahāsarasvatī, she is either equated with the supreme Śakti or seen as the power that presides over creation within the triad that includes Mahālakṣmī, who presides over preservation, and Mahākālī, who is associated with destruction.

Iconographically, Sarasvatī is generally depicted with four arms, holding a rosary (*mālā*), the Vedas, a water pot, and a *vīṇā* (lute), a stringed instrument resembling a *sitār*. She is fair in complexion and often clad in white, symbols of her purity. Her mount, like Brahmā's, is the swan. In North India, her festival of Sarasvatī Pūjā is celebrated in the spring. At that time, temporary images of Sarasvatī are ritually installed in homes, offices, and educational institutions, and offered worship. It

Figure 10.3 Lithograph depicting Sarasvatī, holding the lute (*vīṇā*), prayer beads, and the Vedas

is also customary for other items, such as books and musical instruments to be worshipped on that day. Some traditions consider every institution of learning to be an abode of Sarasvatī. As with Brahmā, it is rare to find temples dedicated centrally to her. One such temple, dating from the twelfth century, is located at Kuthanur in Tamil Nadu.

Śrī Lakṣmī

The goddess Lakṣmī (Grace) is generally identified with the Vedic goddess Śrī (Glory), who is associated with glory, prosperity, royalty, and fame in the *Śrī Sūkta*, a hymn within a late appendix to the *Ṛg Veda*. There, Śrī is also associated with soil and agricultural fertility, and one of her abodes is said to be cow dung. Lakṣmī and Śrī were combined into the persona of a single goddess in the Upaniṣads, and Śrī Lakṣmī's mythology was then developed in the Purāṇas. In certain Purāṇic accounts she originates when the gods (*sura*) team up with the demons (*asura*) to churn the Milk Ocean to extract the nectar of immortality. Among the items that emerge are the goddess Lakṣmī, who embodies good-fortune, and her sister Alakṣmī, who brings ill-fortune. Ancient iconography often portrays Lakṣmī flanked by elephants that are showering her with water from their trunks. These Gaja-Lakṣmī (Lakṣmī with Elephants) images emphasize her association with royal consecrations, in which kings have auspicious waters poured onto them.

In modern lithographs Śrī Lakṣmī is often shown clad in a pink or red *sārī*, standing or seated on a lotus flower, holding a jar in one hand while gold coins flow from the other hand. The brimming jar, known as a *pūrṇa-kalaśa*, filled with water, leaves and topped with a coconut is a sort of cornucopia, symbolizing fertility and abundance. It holds the waters of life, the sap that flows through all living things, and the fruits of plenty. The lotus, too, is a symbol pregnant with meaning in Hinduism and Buddhism. It, too, represents royalty and spiritual authority, and Hindu deities, as well as Buddhas and Buddhist saints (*bodhisattvas*) are often portrayed seated upon lotus thrones. The lotus emerges pure and undefiled from the mucky earth within which it grows. The lotus also represents the blossoming of all desires. Reality blossoms from the desire of The One, which in the language of the *Ṛg Veda*'s creation hymn was the first seed of mind. The simile of seed and flower, or seed and fruit is pervasive in Hinduism, and the lotus represents the flowering of all karmic seeds. The creator god Brahmā is thus also depicted seated atop a lotus flower that emanates from Viṣṇu's navel, and it is through Brahmā's *karma* (action) that each particular cosmic cycle blossoms.

By the fifth century CE Śrī Lakṣmī is associated with Viṣṇu as his wife and consort, typically portrayed as a royal couple in Viṣṇu's heavenly abode of Vaikuṇṭha. On other occasions she is depicted with Viṣṇu's other consort, Bhū Devī (Goddess Earth), with whom she is also identified. They are both shown massaging Viṣṇu's

Figure 10.4 Lithograph depicting Lakṣmī holding lotus flowers and the jar of plenitude. It also portrays Viṣṇu witnessing Lakṣmī's emergence during the mythic churning of the ocean

feet as he sleeps atop the endless serpent Ānanta (See Figure 2.1). As other deities are incorporated into the Vaiṣṇava pantheon, through the scheme of the *avatāras*, each of their consorts is identified as an incarnation of Lakṣmī. Thus Rāma's wife, Sītā, who is associated with the earth, from which she was born and into which she was absorbed, and Kṛṣṇa's lover, the cowherd girl, Rādhā, are both regarded as forms of Lakṣmī. In Pañcarātra philosophy, Lakṣmī is regarded as the *śakti* of Viṣṇu, who is essentially passive. It is through Lakṣmī that the universe is created and destroyed, and thus she dominates the entire manifest creation. In Śrī Vaiṣṇava philosophy, Śrī Lakṣmī is the grace of Viṣṇu that grants liberation to devotees. In Śākta philosophy, she may be identified with the supreme Śakti, or seen as the preserving aspect within the triad that includes Mahāsarasvatī, and Mahākālī. A renowned Mahālakṣmī temple is located in Kolhapur in Maharashtra State.

Śrī Lakṣmī is widely worshipped throughout India, appealing to agricultural workers who hope for a bountiful harvest, to soldiers, who hope for good fortune in dangerous conflicts, and to merchants, who seek wealth through successful business transactions. Her connection with fertility, riches, and good luck make Lakṣmī enormously appealing, for she is propitiated by all who seek the benediction of her grace. She is worshipped on many occasions through the year, and often with special vowed ascetic observances (*vrata*) in the hope of accessing boons of well-being. She is especially worshipped during the festival of Dipāvalī or Dīvālī (Row of Lights), which occurs in late autumn. People light lamps throughout their homes, and set off fireworks to invite good fortune and to frighten off evil spirits and bad fortune. For some, Dīvālī marks a New Year's celebration, and thus merchants open new account books. Simple clay images of the goddess that were placed in the home are discarded and replaced with new ones for the year ahead.

Kālī

The dark skinned goddess Kālī (Dark Time) has riveting imagery. There are no references to her in the Vedas, although in later writings she is occasionally linked with such Vedic goddesses as Rātrī (Night). Kālī's name is a feminine form of the Sanskrit word *kāla,* which means both "black" and "time." Appropriately, Kālī is associated with the destruction that Time brings to all created things, and she is mostly portrayed with black or dark skin. In the *Devī Māhātmya* section of the *Mārkaṇḍeya Purāṇa,* dating from about the sixth or seventh century CE, Kālī's mythic origins are explained. During a fierce battle with demons, the Great Goddess (Devī) grows angry and her complexion turns dark. Kālī emerges from the Devī's forehead and is gruesome in appearance. She is black, withered, with a gaping mouth and lolling tongue. She wears a garland of human heads. She destroys demons on the battlefield by ripping them apart, devouring them in her jaws, or beheading them with her sword. Later in this tale, she is summoned to confront the demon Raktabījā, whose every drop of blood on contact with the earth spawns a demon clone, making him virtually impossible to defeat. Kālī's gaping mouth devours the demons that have already been produced, and as a host of goddesses unleash their weapons on Raktabījā, Kālī laps up every drop of his blood before it touches the ground, destroying him.

Kālī's dark, destructive nature naturally leads her to be paired with Śiva, and she is sometimes regarded as his consort. In Śākta ideology, as Mahākālī, she is identified with the supreme Śakti, or embodies the destructive dimension of the triad composed with Mahāsarasvatī and Mahālakṣmī.

Contemporary lithographs of Kālī portray her naked, with black or dark blue skin, and with disheveled hair. She wields a bloody cleaver in one hand, and holds a severed human head in another. She wears a garland of human heads or skulls, and a skirt or belt made of severed human arms. Her bloody tongue protrudes from her mouth, and she stands atop the body of a supine, quiescent Śiva. Once, to bring an end to an unstoppable rampage that threatened to destroy the world prematurely, Śiva prostrated himself like a corpse on the ground before her. Devotees explain that only when she stepped upon his breast did she realize what she had done, and calmed

Figure 10.5 Close-up of a tantric practitioner's home shrine image of Kālī, tongue extended, wielding a sword and severed head

down. In a reversal of the myth in which Pārvatī domesticates the wild and wayward Śiva, it is Śiva that pacifies the uncontrollable Kālī. More ancient imagery sometimes depicts her with fangs, a sunken belly and withered breasts. She sometimes squats atop Śiva, in sexual intercourse with him. This imagery relates to Kālī's association with tantric Hinduism, where she is regarded as the active dynamic pole of reality, Śakti, while Śiva represents the passive, static principle. The sexual symbolism also references particular tantric rites that include ritual intercourse. Within certain schools of tantric Hinduism, Kālī also begins to take center stage as the highest divinity and becomes the main object of spiritual practice (*sādhana*).

In modern images Kālī is depicted as beautiful with full breasts and a more benign appearance. This, too, derives from her identification as the highest reality in tantric Hinduism. The trend continued with Śākta devotional movements, particularly those that arose in Bengal after the seventeenth century, where she is approached, not as a hideous goddess of destruction, but as a loving mother. Although she may bring death and heartbreak in her wake, she crushes desires and attachment to worldly things, thrusting her devotees into the realization of their complete dependence on her power and grace. Bengalis celebrate Kālī Pūjā during Dīpāvalī by constructing colorful clay images of her and rendering them devotional worship. One of her most renowned temples in India, the Kālīghat temple in Kolkata (Calcutta) daily witnesses numerous blood sacrifices of goats in her honor.

Mahādevī Durgā

One of the earliest and still one of the most influential scriptures to articulate the theology of the Hindu Great Goddess, Mahādevī (or simply Devī) is the *Devī Māhātmya (Glorification of the Great Goddess)*, which perhaps dates from the sixth or seventh centuries CE. It describes her mythic origins when the gods are defeated by the Buffalo Demon, Mahiṣa, who had driven them from heaven. The myth is retold with elaborations in other texts, such as the *Devī Bhāgavata Purāṇa*. Mahiṣa had received a boon making him invulnerable to all except women, whom he was sure would be incapable of defeating him. Pooling together their collective effulgence (*tejas*), the gods produced a mass of light that coalesced into the form of an irresistibly beautiful young woman, whom they equipped with weapons drawn from their own armaments. Paralleling Viṣṇu's characteristic involvement in the preservation of order by overthrowing the forces that threaten the cosmic balance, the Mahādevī sets out to destroy the Buffalo Demon. Wielding the trident of Śiva, Viṣṇu's discus, and other weapons in her many arms she rode out on her mount, the great lion Mahāsiṅgha, and lured Mahiṣa into battle. After slaying many members of his demon cohort, she finally faced him in battle. Quaffing nectar from her cup, Devī leapt upon the demon, crushed him with her foot and impaled him with her spear. As he crawled out of his own buffalo mouth, she beheaded him with her great sword. The gods sang her praises. One of Mahādevī's most widespread images is as Mahiṣamardinī (Crusher of the Buffalo [Demon]).

Despite her warrior-like persona in many myths, Devī is typically invoked as Mā (Mother). To her devotees she is the cosmic mother, like a lioness with her cubs, powerfully protective of her children and capable of overcoming all dangers that may confront them. Unlike other spouse goddesses, such as Sītā and Pārvatī, she is not typically seen as the wife, consort, or *śakti* of particular male gods, but is regarded by her devotees as utterly independent, and embodying the powers of all the gods combined. Durgā is also seen as incorporating all goddesses, each of whom is a particular manifestation of her. Thus she embodies the powers of creation, preservation, and destruction, which in certain formulations may be represented by Mahāsarasvatī, Mahālakṣmī, and Mahākālī. When given a name, the Great Goddess is most often known as Durgā (She who is Formidable), or Caṇḍī (She who is Fierce). The *Devī Māhātmya* is therefore often referred to as the *Durgā Saptaśatī (Seven Hundred [Verses] to Durgā)*. Philosophically, Devī incorporates the principles of supreme cosmic power, Śakti, manifest creation or nature, Prakṛti, and the great matrix of phantasmal reality, Mahāmāyā.

Figure 10.6 Large bas-relief depicting Durgā atop her lion mount battling the buffalo demon Mahiṣa (Mahabalipuram)

Two particularly important festivals for Mahādevī Durgā occur during nine-day periods known as Navarātras or Navarātrīs (literally, "nine nights"), which take place in the spring month of Caitra (March/April) and in the autumn month of Aśvina (September/October). During the spring celebrations, Devī's associations with fertility are particularly evident. She is installed in a clay jar set atop an earthen altar, and worshipped with recitations of the *Devī Māhātmya*. The autumn celebrations add a martial dimension. Communities patronize the fabrication of large, colorful, unbaked clay images of Durgā and her lion in the act of slaying Mahiṣa. She is flanked by Lakṣmī and Sarasvatī, as well as Gaṇeśa and Kārttikeya (Kumāra). Priests are commissioned to conduct an elaborate worship ritual, known as the Durgā Pūjā, on her behalf. Goats and even buffaloes may be sacrificed in her honor. Prepubescent girls are worshipped as human embodiments of the Devī. At the end of the festival, the images are carried with great fanfare and thrown into a body of water, such as the Gaṅgā River. One of her most highly regarded temples is located in Banāras, by the site of a water tank known as Durgā Kuṇḍa, from which the temple derives its name. It is one of nine temples to Durgā in Banāras that are visited in an annual pilgrimage during Navarātra.

The mythic accounts contained in the Purāṇas also reveal various tensions, such as those between theistic *bhakti*, and yogic renunciation. For instance, many of the demons who have attained boons have done so through the practice of fierce austerities. It is often a god, such as Brahmā, who grants them their boons, which still subordinates the fruits of their ascetic disciplines to theistic grace, rather than as the outcome of personal effort. The result of these ascetic activities often leads to great sovereign power wielded over the lesser (i.e. Vedic) gods, but also to pride and arrogance. Demons often do not appear to "know their place" in the social order, and infringe upon the realms of the gods. The great Purāṇic deities, Śiva, Viṣṇu, or Devī, must therefore intervene to destroy the demons. The sectarian nature of certain Purāṇic accounts is also evident in episodes that subordinate rival deities to the one being promoted. Thus Viṣṇu's bow is promoted as superior to Śiva's, the Devī wields the power of all the male gods, and Mīnākṣī is subdued by Śiva. The nature of "demons" raises many questions, for it is not simply a matter of adharmic conduct that makes one a demon. Prahlāda and Bali are dharmic demons. Is there a historical and socio-cultural undercurrent to these tales? Does "demon" refer to groups of people who had different religious beliefs and practices from the Purāṇic authors? Or were there overlapping belief systems, but social and cultural differences? While some researchers struggle to decipher ancient social and political realities embedded within these Purāṇic accounts, others emphasize their nature primarily as literary compositions, which evoke emotions and induce reflection, and thus convey religious values through the vehicle of narrative exposition.

Other deities

In the *Bṛhadāraṇyaka Upaniṣad* (III.9.1), a student named Śākalya asked the sage Yājñavalkya to tell him how many gods there really were. Answering in accord with a traditional hymn of praise to the gods of the universe, Yājñavalkya replied that there were three hundred and three, and three thousand and three. His student was unsatisfied and pressed him with the same question. "But how many gods are there, Yājñavalkya?" "Thirty-three," the sage now replied. Śākalya acknowledged his answer by saying "Aum," but kept pressing Yājñavalkya further, repeatedly asking him the same question. "Six," "three," "one and a half," came the answers, and the sage finally answered, "one." "That is Brahman. They call him That" (III.9.9).

This dramatic conversation is instructive, for it demonstrates the late Vedic (i.e. Upaniṣadic) conception that the profuse numbers of deities are in truth just The One (*tad ekam*), the Absolute, Brahman. In the Epics and Purāṇas the great deities, such as Śiva, Viṣṇu, and the Devī, are each equated with Brahman. The host of other deities and divine beings are identified with or connected to these great deities, either as family members (e.g. Skanda as Śiva's son), or incarnations (e.g. Paraśurāma as Viṣṇu), or manifest forms or aspects (e.g. Kālī as Devī). While the orthodox Vedic perspective may appear to be inclusive, drawing in all conceptions of divinity and all modes of worship under its umbrella, there are also pressures within orthodoxy to remain exclusive and maintain distinctions. For instance, while Smārta Brahmins might, in principle, agree that all their five deities are indeed aspects of The One, Brahman, they prefer to engage in the actual worship of five divine manifestations, one of whom is Durgā. And although in principle they might agree that Kālī is but an aspect of Durgā, some might find it problematic to worship Kālī, whose purity is diminished by her acceptance of "impure" offerings such as blood, flesh, or alcohol. Thus exclusion and distinctions allow individuals or particular *jātis* to worship deities of their choice in the forms that they prefer, without intruding on the purity/pollution sensibilities of other groups.

It is also necessary to note that not all Hindus share the opinion voiced by Yājñavalkya above. If pressed with the question about how many gods there really are, some might defer to local scholars (*paṇḍita*) or Brahmin priests for the "proper answer." However, in practical terms, for most, their perception of the various deities that they worship, or propitiate, is that they are different divine beings, each with distinctive names, abodes, characteristics, and spheres of influence. It is thus a facile oversimplification to subsume all the diversity of Hindu polytheism under the monistic rubric of Brahman, or some monotheistic configuration. Such efforts may also reflect theological agendas by their proponents, both Hindu and non-Hindu. Yet it is equally naïve to designate Hinduism as merely polytheistic, for this would overlook its monistic and monotheistic features. The problem of categorization is, of course, mostly a scholarly concern for religionists, anthropologists, and others engaged in the study of Hinduism. The difficulty arises from efforts to generalize about something that is in actuality many things. Some scholars have therefore preferred to speak of "Hinduisms," rather than Hinduism. While some have referred to Hinduism as an impenetrable jungle, they seem to have missed the mark. Perhaps because of my childhood experiences I am fond of regarding Hinduism with the pervasive Hindu symbol of the forest, teeming with a vast array of life forms, each existing in a competitive, yet mutually dependent dynamic interaction. The innumerable deities encountered in the Hindu world may each be likened to a particular tree, vine, animal, or insect that lives within that great forest, receiving its nourishment from other inhabitants, providing food for some, shelter for others, and struggling for survival or flourishing amid the ranks of its neighbors.

The small assortment of deities discussed in the following section is intended primarily to illustrate in the most rudimentary way Hinduism's extraordinary diversity. The selection is arbitrary and in no way indicates that these deities form the next strata of "importance" after the major gods and goddesses discussed earlier.

In 1975, a film entitled *Jai Santoshi Mā* (*Hail Mother [who grants] Satisfaction*) was released, and proved to be so popular that it raised the profile of its goddess and her worship throughout India. Researchers were surprised to discover that the cult of this goddess did not extend much earlier than the 1960s, but as a result of the film her temples were springing up everywhere. The Santoshi Mā *vrata*, performed to receive her favor, requires a simple rite of devotional worship (*pūjā*), and offering her roasted gram and jaggery (i.e. unrefined cane sugar), a traditional sweet among the poor. The story (*kathā*) recounting a renowned performance of her *vrata* should be recited or heard, and only one meal a day is permitted. The film was an elaboration upon Santoshi Mā's rather sketchy *vrata kathā*, and locates her within the orthodox pantheon by portraying her as a daughter of Gaṇeśa. No sour or bitter foods should be eaten or fed to anyone on the day of her *vrata*, which may last from a single day to sixteen weeks. The film achieved such notoriety that many people began to approach its viewing in a manner similar to visiting a temple. They would remove their shoes at the theatre entrance, and throw coins and flowers at the screen when the goddess appeared.

Among the many things that can be learned from the case of Santoshi Mā is the evident ability for a goddess with little or no previous renown to emerge from relative obscurity to pan-Hindu status within a generation. Although the speed of her ascendancy must be attributed to the power of technology and film as a communication medium, her acceptance reveals Hinduism's remarkable capacity for inclusiveness. While the tradition of performing *vratas* is ancient, particular *vratas* belong to the oral tradition, much of which was originally in the custody of women. The film's annexation of Santoshi Mā to Gaṇeśa exemplifies the trend to include marginal deities within the "family" of the mainstream gods and goddesses. While Western sensibilities might think of film as a profane medium, indicative of popular culture, modern, and therefore unworthy of representations of divinity, to the vast majority of Hindus there was little such concern. Santoshi Mā was not merely portrayed in the film, but, for many, the presence of divinity, which may be discerned anywhere, was actually manifest there on the screen, a luminous projection of light through celluloid.

Another deity that many non-Hindus find intriguing is Śītalā (She who is Cool), the goddess associated with smallpox and cholera. When depicted anthropomorphically, Śītalā is naked, with wild, disheveled hair, riding a donkey and wielding a broom. Her name is actually a synonym for smallpox and may refer to the shivering experienced by feverish patients suffering from the disease. The South Indian goddess Mariyamman is also associated with smallpox. When disease strikes, it is not uncommon for Hindus to consider it the agency of some local goddess. Sometimes, as in the case of Śītalā, the disease and the goddess may have the same name. The identification of smallpox with the goddess Śītalā, appears around the sixteenth century CE, even though the disease was long known about and is even testified to in Ayurvedic treatises from about the fourth century CE.

Religionists (i.e. Religious Studies scholars) sometimes distinguish between the terms "propitiate" and "worship." Goddesses such as Śītalā, they might say, are propitiated or appeased to keep them from bringing sickness and death. This is certainly true, for a Śītalā image is often brought into the home, given offerings, frequently with a blood sacrifice, and then taken to the base of a tree, such as the Nīm, one of her traditional abodes, and left there, in the hope that having been satisfied she will not revisit the home. However, such distinctions as between "propitiate" and "worship" do not always hold true, particularly in the case of a goddess such as Śītalā, who may have emerged as a local malevolent spirit, but whose cult is now widespread throughout North-east India. While the power of communications media propelled Santoshi Mā to widespread fame, it may well have been the epidemic spread of disease that gave Śītalā her status. She is not merely propitiated any more, and receives her share of devotional worship like any other deity. She is mentioned in the *Skanda Purāṇa* as a goddess worthy of worship. However, the priests who preside at her temples are generally from non-Brahmin *jātis* and she is mostly patronized by the poor, tribals, and members of low-status *jātis*. Some even see disease as the "grace" of the goddess; others view it as her play or sport. In all cases, the goddess is seen as "visiting" the afflicted person, who has become her abode. The symptoms of the ailment may be seen as the goddess inflicting her wrath upon a person, or engaged in a battle with destructive forces. Since the goddess is believed to still have her abode there, it was often the case that the bodies of those who died from such diseases were not cremated but placed in a sacred body of water, such as the Gaṅgā, which itself is a riverine goddess of enormous importance (see Figure 17.1). Despite the connotations of her name, Śītalā may be classified as a "hot" goddess, who transfers the heat of her anger to the person afflicted, although with her passion unaroused, she better befits her epithet as the Cool One.

Nāgas are serpents who have a long tradition of worship in Hinduism, and are often associated with fertility (see Figure 4.2). Their abode is the water and the netherworld, where they are custodians of wealth and knowledge. Segments of their cults are incorporated into Vaiṣṇavism through Ānanta, and in Śaivism through Śiva's association with snakes (e.g. as his ornaments). In Bengal the snake goddess Manasā is still widely worshipped. She is regarded as the sister of Vāsuki, the Nāga king who served as the rope when the Ocean of Milk was mythically churned by the gods and demons. The Nāgas are among a number of classes of divine beings that derive from local religious traditions of the early inhabitants of the Indian subcontinent. These beings include Yakṣas ("worshipped ones") and their female counterparts, Yakṣīs, Mātṛkās (Mothers), Bhūtas (Spirit beings), Pretas (Ghosts), Apsaras (Nymphs), and Gandharvas (heavenly musicians). They are often associated with the sky, water, forests, trees, caves, and other natural features, and may be either malevolent or benevolent. Some regard them as belonging to an animistic strand in Hinduism in which elements of the natural world are imbued with spirit or life (*anima*). Others note the autochthonous nature of these beings, since they appear to have emerged from the very places where they may still be encountered. Kubera (The Deformed One), for instance, is sometimes regarded as the lord of all evil spirits. In the *Rāmāyaṇa* he is the half-brother of the *rākṣasa* Rāvaṇa. He presides over all the precious metals and jewels of the earth. He is sometimes seen as the king of the Yakṣas, and one of his wives is named Yakṣī. He is depicted as pot-bellied, and since his other wife's name is Ṛddhi, one notes the amalgamation of his cult with Gaṇeśa, who presides over many of Kubera's functions.

The Mātṛkās are a grouping of typically seven, eight, or more feminine deities. Their names vary, and although portrayed as malevolent in early literature, they are "domesticated" by the time of the Purāṇas. In the *Devī Māhātmya*, the Mātṛkās are the feminine counterparts (*śakti*) of several major male gods, including Brahmāṇī (from Brahmā), Vaiṣṇavī (from Viṣṇu), Māheśvarī (from Śiva Maheśvara), and Aindrī (from Indra). Bhūtas are generic spirits who are ever present and are routinely appeased with some offerings during the performance of *pūjās*, to keep them away from the offerings to the deities being venerated. The Apsaras are nymphs of inordinate grace, possessing youthful beauty, produced in vast numbers during the churning of the Milky Ocean. Since neither gods nor demons would wed them, they offer pleasure to the host of heaven, and frequently visit the earth for amorous adventures. Heroes, who have fallen in battle, or those who have won heaven through their spiritual practices, enjoy the company of the Apsaras in Indra's heaven. Sometimes, the Gandharvas, or heavenly musicians are said to be their spouses, but these sons of Brahmā are also regarded as liberal with their affection.

Discussion questions

1. Prahlāda and Bali are considered to be dharmic demons. Discuss the meaning of *dharma*, and the ways in which it might be possible for a demon to be dharmic.
2. Do you think that there are ancient socio-political realities embedded within the Purāṇic accounts, or do you think it is more likely that they are primarily literary compositions?
3. Why do you think there is a tendency in Hinduism to include marginal deities within the "family" of the mainstream gods and goddesses?
4. What are the Purāṇas, and why and how is *bhakti* such an important part of them?

5. Describe the scheme of Kṛṣṇa's *avatāras*, and briefly outline the central myth associated with each of them.
6. What brought about the decline of the Vedic deities, and which deities emerged to take their place? Describe each of these "newer" deities from the Purāṇic literature in detail.

Key points in this chapter

- The Purāṇas constitute a vast body of literature, and are source books for much of Hinduism's rich mythology.
- The Purāṇas mimic the Epics in many ways and are concerned with aligning the world-view of Vedic Hinduism with *bhakti* theism.
- The *śramaṇa* movements ushered in the decline of most of the Vedic deities.
- Śiva embodies a bipolar nature. He is the supreme ascetic and yet is associated with eroticism and fertility.
- The myths of Sati and Pārvatī often overlap with each other.
- Gaṇeśa and Skanda are associated with the Śaiva sectarian tradition.
- Viṣṇu is traditionally regarded as having ten main descents (*avatāra*) or incarnations, among which Kṛṣṇa is likely the most popular.
- The categorization of Hinduism is problematic when using general terms such as polytheistic or monistic.
- The case of the goddess Santoshi Mā demonstrates the ability of deities to emerge from relative obscurity to pan-Hindu status within a generation.

Further reading

Relating to the Purāṇas and Hindu mythology

Ali, S. M. (1966) *The Geography of the Purāṇas*. New Delhi: People's Publishing House.

Bhāgavata-Purāṇa (1952–1960), 2 vols. text and translation. Gorakhpur: Gītā Press.

Bhattacharji, Sukumari (1970) *The India Theogony: A Comparative Study of Indian Mythology from the Vedas to the Purāṇas*. Cambridge: Cambridge University Press.

Devī Bhāgavata Purāṇa, The Śrimad. Swami Vijnananda (ed. and trans.) Allahabad: Panini Office. Reprint. Oriental (1986).

Dimmit, C., and J. A. B. van Buitenen (eds and trans.) (1978) *Classical Hindu Mythology: A Reader in the Sanskrit Puranas*. Philadelphia, PA: Temple University Press.

Dowson, J. A. (1961) *Classical Dictionary of Hindu Mythology and Religion, Geography, History and Literature*. London: Routledge & Kegan Paul.

Gangadharan, N. (1980) *Liṅgapurāṇa: A Study*. Delhi: Ajanta Books International.

Gyani, S. J. (1966) *Agni Purāṇa: A Study*. Benares: Chowkhamba.

Hazra, R. C. (1958–1963) *Studies in the Upapurāṇas*, 2 vols. Calcutta: Sanskrit College.

O'Flaherty, Wendy D. (1975) *Hindu Myths*. Harmondsworth: Penguin Books.

— (1976) *The Origins of Evil in Hindu Mythology*. Berkeley, CA: University of California Press.

Pargiter, F. E. (1962) *The Purāṇa Text of the Dynasties of the Kaliage*. Oxford: Oxford University Press.

Prakash, Om (1977) *Political Ideas in the Puranas*. Allahabad: Panchanda Publications.

Pulasker, A. D. (1955) *Studies in the Epics and Purāṇas of India*. Bombay: Bharatiya Vidya Bhavan.

Rocher, Ludo (1986) *The Purānas*. History of Indian Literature, Vol. 2 Fasc. 3. Jan Gonda (gen. ed.) Wiesbaden: Otto Harrassowitz.

Shastri, J. L. (trans.) (1970–1971) *Śiva Purāṇa*, 4 vols. Delhi: Motilal Banarsidass.

Wilson, H. H. (1961) *Viṣṇu Purāṇa*. Reprint. Calcutta: Punthi Pustak.

Śaiva deities

Clothey, F. (1978) *The Many Faces of Murukan: The History and Meaning of a South Indian God*. Religion and Society, No. 6. The Hague: Mouton.

Clothey, F. and J. B. Long (eds) (1983) *Experiencing Śiva*. Columbia, MO: South Asia Books.

Courtright, Paul B. (1985) *Gaṇeśa: Lord of Obstacles, Lord of Beginnings*. New York: Oxford University Press.

Getty, A. (1936) *Gaṇeśa*. Oxford: Oxford University Press.

Grimes, John A. (1995) *Gaṇapati: Song of the Self*. Albany, NY: State University of New York Press.

Kramrisch, S. (1981) *The Presence of Śiva*. Princeton, NJ: Princeton University Press.

Meister, M. W. (ed.) (1984) *Discourses on Śiva*. Philadelphia, PA: University of Pennsylvania Press.

O'Flaherty, W. D. (1973) *Asceticism and Eroticism in the Mythology of Śiva*. London: Oxford University Press.

— (1981) *Śiva: The Erotic Ascetic*. New York: Oxford University Press.

Ramanujan, A. K. (trans.) *Speaking of Śiva*. Harmondsworth: Penguin Books, 1973.
Shulman, D. D. (1980) *Tamil Temple Myths: Sacrifice and Divine Marriage in the South Indian Śaiva Tradition*. Princeton, NJ: Princeton University Press.
Zvelebil, K. (1982) *Tiru Murugan*. Madras: International Institute of Tamil Studies.

Vaiṣṇava deities

Archer, W. G. (1957) *The Loves of Krishna in Indian Painting and Poetry*. London: Allen & Unwin.
Das, Bhagawan (1962) *Kṛṣṇa: A Study in the Theory of Avatāras*. Bombay: Bharatiya Vidya Bhavan.
DeLeury, G. A. (1960) *The Cult of Vithoba*. Poona: Deccan College Postgraduate and Research Institute.
Dhal, Upendra N. (1978) *Goddess Lakṣmī: Origin and Development*. New Delhi: Oriental Publishers.
Dimock, E. C. (trans.) (1963) *The Thief of Love: Bengali Tales*. Chicago, IL: University of Chicago Press.
Hawley, J. S. (1983) *Kṛṣṇa the Butter Thief*. Princeton,NJ: Princeton University Press.
— (1981) *At Play with Krishna: Pilgrimage Dramas from Brindavan*. Princeton, NJ: Princeton University Press.
Hein, N. (1972) *The Miracle Plays of Mathura*. New Haven, CT: Yale University Press.
Klostermaier, Klaus (1971) *In the Paradise of Kṛṣṇa*. Philadelphia, PA: Westminster Press.
Sheth, Noel (1984) *The Divinity of Krishna*. Delhi: Munshiram Manoharlal.
Singer, M. (ed.) (1969) *Krishna: Myths, Rites and Attitudes*. Chicago, IL: University of Chicago Press.
Stoller-Miller, B. (1977) *Love Song of the Dark Lord*. New York: Columbia University Press.
Vaidyanatha, K. R. (1992) *Śri Krishna: the Lord of Guruvayur*. Bombay: Bharatiya Vidya Bhavan.

Śākta deities

Beane, W. C. (1977) *Myth, Cult and Symbols in Śākta Hinduism: A Study of the Indian Mother Goddess*. Leiden: E. J. Brill.
Brown, C. M. (1974) *God as Mother: A Feminine Theology in India: An Historical and Theological Study of the Brahmavaivarta Purāṇa*. Hartford, VT: Claude Stark.

— (1990) *The Triumph of the Goddess: The Canonical Models and Theological Visions of the Devī-Bhāgavata Purāṇa*. Albany, NY: State University of New York Press.

Goldberg, Ellen (2002) *The Lord who is Half-Woman: Ardhanarisvara in Feminist Perspective*. Albany, NY: State University of New York Press.

Harding, E. (1993) *Kali: The Black Goddess of Dakshineswar*. York Beach, ME: Nicholas-Hays.

Hawley, J. S., and D. M. Wulff (eds) (1982) *The Divine Consort: Rādhā and the Goddesses of India*. Berkeley, CA: University of California Press.

— (1996) *Devī: Goddesses of India*. Berkeley,CA: University of California Press.

Kakati, B. K. (1948) *The Mother Goddess Kāmākhyā*. Gauhati: Lawyers' Book Stall.

Kinsley, David (1975) *The Sword and the Flute: Kālī and Kṛṣṇa: Dark Visions of the Terrible and the Sublime in Hindu Mythology*. Berkeley, CA: University of California Press.

— (1986) *Hindu Goddesses*. Berkeley, CA: University of California Press.

Srivastava, M. C. P. (1979) *Mother Goddess in Indian Art, Archaeology and Literature*. Delhi: Agam Kala Pakashan.

Woodroffe, J. (Arthur Avalon) (1964) (trans.) *Hymns to the Goddess*. Reprint. Madras: Ganesh & Co.

— (1978) *Shakti and Shakta*. Reprint. New York: Dover Publications.

On other Hindu deities and sects

Bailey, G. M. "*Notes on the Worship of Brahmā in Ancient India*," Annali del' Istituto Orientale de Napoli 39 (1979): pp. 1–170.

Coomaraswamy, Ananda (1971) *Yakṣas*. 2 parts. Delhi: Munshiram Mahoharlal.

Dasgupta S. H. (1962) *Obscure Religious Cults*. Calcutta: Firma K. L. Mukhopadhyay.

Elmore, Wilber T. (1915) *Dravidian Gods in Modern Hinduism: A Study of Local and Village Deities of Southern India*. Hamilton, NY: Pub. by Author.

Fergusson, J. (1868) *Tree and Serpent Worship*. London: W. H. Allen.

Hiltebeitel, Alf (ed.) *Criminal Gods and Demon Devotees: Essays on the Guardians of Popular Hinduism*. Albany, NY: State University of New York Press.

Sontheimer, G. D. (1993) *Pastoral Deities in Western India*. Anne Feldhaus (trans.). Delhi: Oxford University Press.

Vogel, J. P. (1926) *Indian Serpent Lore*. London: Probsthain.

Whitehead, H. (1921) *The Village Gods of South India*. Calcutta: Association Press.

11 *Hindu art and worship rituals*

In this chapter

A defining characteristic of Hinduism is its pervasive concern with ritual activity. While the rise of *bhakti* may have weakened the hegemony of the Vedic sacrificial ritualism, the devotional approach soon developed its own ritual forms. After a brief discussion on the concept of "orthodoxy," this chapter explores modes of *bhakti* rituals from *pūjā* in homes and temples to pilgrimage. The styles and symbolism of the Hindu temple, aspects of temple worship, and the temple traditions of some specialists are also examined. Through these, the reader is introduced to facets of Hinduism's artistic forms and some of its extraordinary temples.

Main topics covered

- A note on orthodoxy
- Domestic worship and *pūjā*
- *Darśana* and temple worship
- The Hindu temple
- Some noteworthy temples
- Sacred specialists
- Hindu pilgrimage

Imagine, if you will, this scenario

You have been horse-back riding in the countryside of the state of Rajasthan and return late to your lodge on the outskirts of the city of Udaipur. As you deliver your horse to the stable attendant, you hear a voice ask, "Did you enjoy the ride?" You turn to see an elderly gentleman sitting in a nearby gazebo. He has a distinguished demeanor, wears a small, tightly-wrapped turban, and sports a dramatic grey handlebar moustache. "Very much!" you reply enthusiastically. "Although I wish I was a better rider and could venture further. The landscape is magical." "Have you visited the palace yet?" he asks. "Oh yes. This isn't my first time in Udaipur. I've been there several times. I'm always amazed. It's quite incredible." "I grew up in that palace. I used to play in those rooms," he surprises you with his comment. "My nephew, who owns this lodge, is also a member of the royal family. We used to have hundreds of horses, camels, and elephants." As the gentleman continues to speak you begin to realize that the era of the Indian *mahārājās* is not at all ancient, and you are actually conversing with a man whose memories include those days of imperial pomp and splendor. He learns that you have an interest in Hinduism, and directs you to query his nephew about a remarkable goddess shrine associated with his family.

"My uncle is a dreamer," the lodge owner says, shaking his head when you tell him about your conversation the previous evening. "We will never see any of those *lakhs* of rupees that the Indian government promised the royal families. It was part of their strategy to dissolve the power of the ruling families and acquire their properties. That is why I am running this lodge. Many former *mahārājas* have turned their palaces into hotels or museums. However, regarding the goddess temple, here are directions to the village, and this letter will instruct the caretaker to put you up in a room in a building our family maintains for our visits."

You travel for several hours by local bus into the Rajasthan interior, and arrive at the village and temple of Āvarī Mātā. The caretaker is delighted with your visit, and shows you to your room in this village, which is little more than a street, devoid of tourists, and with almost nothing for a traveler to eat. The village appears to exist for the small temple, which has a paved walled courtyard adjacent to a natural bathing water tank. A distinctive feature of this temple is a hole in a wall of the sanctum. The caretaker explains that Āvarī Mātā is known for her healing powers. He encourages you to take *darśana* of the goddess, and to make a wish to be healed. "Those who come for healing enter to see the *devī* through that hole," he instructs. "I'm not here to be healed," you try to explain, but he insists that you make a request. At first unable to think of what to ask, you recall that you have had a nagging cough since your arrival in India three months earlier. Undoubtedly exacerbated by the dusty, dry weather, by city pollution, and by your smoking of *bīdīs*, a type of Indian cigarette made of tobacco flakes wrapped in forest leaves, your cough persisted, and you had subsequently tried everything to shake off the ailment. Antibiotics, Āyurvedic medications, sipping lots of fluids, and even temporarily quitting smoking had all failed, and so you had resigned yourself to the periodic ritual of exhausting coughing, particularly in the mornings. "Āvarī Mātā, please cure my cough," you mentally make the request, mostly skeptically, but with some small hope that it might actually work and rid you of your horrible cough. The caretaker smiles and shakes his head approvingly in a characteristically Indian way.

The pilgrims who arrive at Āvarī Mātā's temple are mainly from local villages, and you are surprised to see that unlike the temples in large urban centers, this goddess is sometimes offered bottles of liquor, whose contents the devotees themselves subsequently drink. "Tonight you must not stay in your room, but must spend the night here in the courtyard," the caretaker further instructs, and gives you a blanket to keep yourself warm. Pilgrims, devotees, and wandering musicians arrive through the course of the evening. As dusk falls, the priest performs the last formal worship rite, waving a flame before the goddess. You are huddled with a mass of blanketed bodies in the courtyard as the musician groups begin to sing. The harmonium emits a mesmerizing tune, while another musician bows a stringed instrument in an ear-catching rhythm. Then, a tall man with a large yellow turban, a *dhoti* around his waist, and wearing the upward curling, pointy-toed Rajasthani shoes, evoking an image out of the *Arabian Nights*, begins to sing. You cannot understand his words, but the sound of his voice is warm, raw but deep, and yearning. You feel instantly at home in the welcoming atmosphere of this gathering, and the songs move you through such moods as celebration, longing, and gratitude. They are not sung to the people there, but to Āvarī Mātā. Then, to your genuine surprise, a young Rajasthani woman begins to dance with sensuous movements before the door of the inner sanctum. "Is she a *devadāsī*?" you wonder, one of those women who were associated with temples, and who danced for the deity. You have often seen men dressed as women dance at temples. And you have seen female dancers who have been commissioned to dance at temple theatrical performances. However, here at Āvarī Mātā, you are told, the musicians have come voluntarily to play for the goddess, and the dancer's performance is also spontaneous.

Armed with a few cassette tapes of Āvarī Mātā *bhajans*, devotional hymns, that you have purchased at one of the stalls outside the temple, you leave the village the following morning. It seems that the royal bedroom was unnecessary, since you had spent the entire night in the temple courtyard drifting between sleep and wakefulness, amid the dozens of pilgrim villagers who were mostly doing the same. You wished you could speak and understand all of India's many languages, so you could get clearer answers to the questions that reeled through your mind as a result of the previous night's experience. What was the origin of this temple? Who was Āvarī Mātā, and what was her story? What were those songs really about? Clouds of dust flow through the open windows of the bus as it rattles on the unpaved road back towards Udaipur. Two Rajasthani men, who were also leaving the village, light up *bīdīs* in the back of the bus. Recognizing you as a fellow pilgrim, they offer you a smoke. As you draw deeply on the little cigarette, and its unmistakable odor mixes with the dust and the equally unforgettable morning smell of the smoke of India's cow dung fires, you suddenly realize that your relentless cough has been quite completely cured.

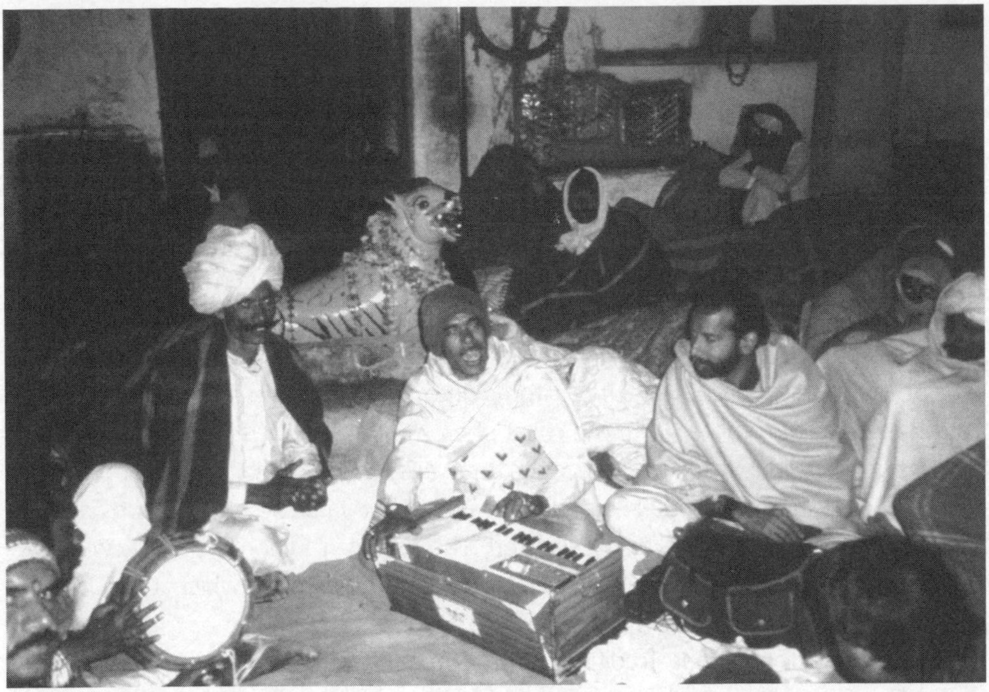

Figure 11.1 Researcher joins singers of devotional hymns (*bhajan*) in the temple courtyard of the goddess Āvarī Mātā where dozens huddle through a night-long vigil in the hope of being cured of their ailments (Rajasthan)

A note on orthodoxy

Several of the male authors in Vaiṣṇava and Śaiva traditions persist in promulgating stereotypical portrayals of women as embodiments of the power that lures men away from their focus on transcendence. However, the developing *bhakti* ideology embraced women and lower-caste participation. It is necessary to recognize that the segments of South Asian society that promulgated and espoused *bhakti* did not suddenly begin to become religious at this time. They were very likely engaged in their own religious practices, beliefs, and modes of conduct throughout the history of Hinduism that we have traced thus far. However, the "voices" of these groups were marginalized, or not represented, in the earlier Sanskritic tradition known through the Sanskrit literature that we have available. The progressive penetration of *bhakti* into orthodoxy reflects the mutual interaction between the so-called "Great Tradition" (i.e. in the context of Hindu culture, it is generally characterized as Sanskritic, Āryan, Brahmin male-dominated, northern, elite culture) and the "Little Tradition" (i.e. generally characterized as non-Sanskritic, non-Āryan (i.e, "Dravidian," village, tribal), non-Brahmin, southern, popular culture).

The terms "Great Tradition" and "Little Tradition" can, of course, be misleading if misunderstood, for the "Little Tradition" is often made up of the broader masses, and may wield considerable power in its own areas of influence. The "Great Tradition" generally articulates itself as such, and by virtue of its access to knowledge management and influence over political authorities, it orchestrates hegemonic discourse. In other words, the topics that it discusses (e.g. Vedic deities), the activities that it considers valuable (e.g. sacrificial ritual (*yajña*), or rites of passage (*saṃskāra*) presided over by the priestly class), the texts that it values (e.g. the Vedas), the social structure that it endorses (e.g. the *varṇa* system, Untouchability), the moral and ethical values that it promotes (e.g. the roles of women and *śūdras*, *dharma*, *karma*, purity, auspiciousness), are the ones that are deemed worthy, appropriate, and acceptable, while other "discourses" (i.e. other value systems, worldviews, etc.) may be ignored or even persecuted. The "Great Tradition" generally wields political influence, and thus has the legal instrument through which it can have its world views and value systems imposed upon others.

However, the "Great Tradition" is in constant interaction with the "Little Tradition," each mutually influencing the other, so much so that upon very close examination, the boundaries separating these categories disappear altogether. Sacrifice-centered Vedism melded with a renouncer-centered, *mokṣa*-seeking value system to form a new definition of "orthodoxy" at the time of the Upaniṣads. This "orthodoxy" which promoted renunciation at the end of one's life, while maintaining the value of Vedic study and sacrifice during the householder's stage, was one salient example of the "Great Tradition" redefining itself through the influences of the "Little Tradition." By the period of the Epics, yet another discernable configuration of "orthodoxy" appeared. Sacrifice and renunciation were not discarded, for through *niṣkāma karma*, one could simultaneously be a householder and a renouncer. Furthermore, *bhakti* reinstated theism, now focused on non-Vedic gods, such as Gaṇeśa and Kṛṣṇa. *Bhakti*-styled worship was open to women and men not only of the twice-born classes. The Tamil poet-saints spearheaded a style of religious sentiment and activity, whose broad appeal likely reflected an ethos which had long been simmering among the masses with whom their approach resonated. This mode of the *bhakti* movement ultimately reconfigured "orthodoxy," allowing both for the acceptance of non-Sanskritic languages, and for passion as a permissible emotion for religious expression.

Domestic worship and pūjā

The *Bhagavad Gītā* (9.26) makes it clear that whatever is offered with a pure heart, be it a leaf, a flower, a fruit, or water, that act of devotion will be accepted. This articulates the essential feature of *bhakti* offerings, where the sincerity of the sentiment is more important than the items being offered, or the ritualized manner in which those offerings are made. However, the prescriptive ritualization of the processes of *bhakti* worship which developed may reflect the hand of priestly functionaries in securing a niche for their craft. *Pūjā* is this ritualized form of devotional worship. The origins of the word are unclear. Some trace it to the Tamil "*pūcu*" (to smear), while others relate it to the Sanskrit root "*pūj*" (to honor). The formal rites appear to parallel the procedures used to welcome a guest found in Vedic literature. However, the characteristic style of *pūjā* is personal and interactive, which does not have precedents in Vedic modes of worship. *Pūjā* does not typically need the ministration of priests. However, it entails three main components: invocation of the deity, devotional worship of that deity, and dismissal of the deity. Priests have come to play an indispensable role in all three of these processes particularly to deities in temple settings, and during the performance of elaborate *pūjās*. However, Hindu men and women of all classes routinely perform *pūjā* in domestic settings without the aid of priests.

Pūjā is grounded in achieving an intimate interaction with divinity. Thus it begins with invoking the god or goddess into a form that is apprehensible to the devotee's sensibilities. One may merely call upon the name of the deity and render a prayer of homage. However, most Hindus offer *pūjā* to a deity that is already embodied in some material form, known as a *mūrti*. A *mūrti* may be a simple lithograph or some kind of pictorial depiction of the deity in question. It may be a symbolic icon, such as a phallic emblem (*liṅga*) for Śiva or a cosmological diagram (*yantra*). Quite often it is a statue of the deity in one of its characteristic representations. Although Hinduism's panentheistic tendencies would likely acknowledge the presence of the divine in anything, the thrust of *pūjā*'s invocation is to "experience" the presence of the deity in the form that has been chosen. Thus any statue or picture of a god or goddess is not regarded as an abode unless and until the deity has been perceived to be present there, or has been duly invited to take up its presence in that particular *mūrti*. Shrines and temples may grow up around some natural abode of a deity, whose presence there has been acknowledged by worshippers. However, *mūrtis* may also be installed in temples. Here ritualists, typically Brahmin priests, who are acclaimed to have the knowledge to invoke and establish a deity's presence within a *mūrti* are called upon to perform the installation rites. These rites generally involve elaborate purifications of the sacred space, repeated ablutions and anointings of the image, all accompanied by the appropriate prayers. In the humblest of settings, a devotee may merely acquire an image, place it in the home shrine, and through repeated acts of worship and devotional service experience the sacred presence of the deity

Figure 11.2 A woman burns honorific flames in her worship at a small shrine to Durgā situated within a large temple complex (Cidambaram)

there. Of course, in homes and temples, deities are not dismissed after the acts of devotional service have been completed. They are regarded as continuously abiding in the abodes where they have been installed.

Most Hindus have a picture, a shelf, or a corner of a room set off as a shrine. Wealthy families may have a shrine room, while others may even maintain small temples on the premises of their homes. Certain wealthy families actually commission Brahmin priests to visit their homes daily to perform regular *pūjās* to the deities installed in their home shrines. More typically, the devotees themselves perform the acts of worship. The technical term for these acts of devotional worship is *upacāra,* which most people equate with the performance of *pūjā.* The simplest form of *upacāra* consists of five offerings, and thus is sometimes called a five-part *pūjā*. In it, the devotee first anoints the *mūrti* with a fragrant paste (*gandha*). This is often sandalwood, ground into a powder and mixed with water. Then the deity is offered fresh flowers (*puṣpa*) or the image is draped with a garland. Incense (*dhūpa*) is waved before the image, producing a fragrant smoke and aroma. A flame (*dīpa*), generally from a bit of ignited camphor or a lamp fuelled by ghee, is also passed before the image. And the fifth item is an offering of something edible (*naivedya*) to the deity. This is typically a sweet or a piece of fruit. The worshipper then may utter a simple honorific exclamation, such as "Homage to Śiva," while bowing slightly and making a gesture of reverence (*praṇāma*) such as an *añjali*, a widely used Hindu form of greeting, made by pressing the palms and fingertips of the hands together. The devotee may perform a partial or full prostration. The food offering is regarded as having been consumed or transformed by the deity, and is therefore rendered immaculate (*prasāda*) or blessed. This consecrated edible is then eaten by the devotee, and portions distributed to the family members who were attending the rite.

The hierarchy between the devotee and the deity in the feeding rite is sometimes likened to the relationship between husband and wife. The wife eats from her husband's plate, partaking in the "impurity" of his leftovers, and demonstrating her subordination. Devotees similarly place themselves in a hierarchically subordinate position to the deity by eating the food the deity has already consumed. However, a deity's "consumption" of the food renders it sacred. Thus it is less an act of consumption than of consecration and transmutation. When devotees consume the *prasāda* they ingest pure or blessed substance, elevating themselves in the process to a state that is closer to divinity.

Pūjās performed on special occasions may be much more elaborate. For instance, during domestic celebrations of the Durgā Pūjā, a rite that spans several days, the priest invokes and installs the Great Goddess Durgā in a variety of different material forms including a clay jar, a cluster of plants, and an anthropomorphic clay image. He then renders devotional service (*upacāra*) to her with dozens of offerings, including water to wash her feet, water for gargling, extensive bathing, offerings of clothing, and so on. These replicate the sort of procedures that would be used to honor a respected guest who has entered the home. Just as *pūjās* may be elaborate, they may also be abbreviated. It is quite common for a shopkeeper or auto-rickshaw driver to simply wave the smoke from a few sticks of incense in front of the deity's image in his store or scooter-taxi, offer it a flower, and utter a brief prayer. The crucial element in *pūjā* is intimate relationship with the divine. The degree to which this intimacy is conceived or realized depends on the experience of the devotee. Some, with monistic worldviews, strive for the deepest connection leading to absolute integration, becoming one with the deity. Others, and this is quite characteristic of many *bhakti* world views, strive for the greatest closeness that still retains the separate identities of the divine and the devotee. "I want to taste sugar, not become sugar," is a commonly voiced dualistic *bhakti* sentiment.

Darśana and temple worship

A Hindu temple is regarded as the abode of a deity. Although there are hundreds of Śiva temples in the city of Banāras, each temple is the residence of a particular manifestation of Śiva. Thus Śiva is Viśvanātha (Lord of the Universe) in his renowned temple in the city's center, and he presides in his fierce form as Kāla Bhairava in another temple in the city. Worshippers often remark that they are going to a particular temple for *darśana* or for *āratī*. The term *darśana*, which means "seeing" or "viewing," is akin to having an audience with the deity, who presides in its temple like a monarch in a palace. Temples come in many shapes and sizes, and while the majestic analogy is not apparent in a small shrine, it is certainly evident in large sanctuaries, where the scale of the temple may evoke the feeling of entering a grand palace, and the many priests who serve the deity are like a ruler's servants and attendants.

A chief priest closely attends to the needs of the deity. He may awaken early, perform his daily personal purification rituals, and then proceed to "awaken" the god or goddess, who is located in the inner sanctum of the temple. The *mūrti* is often bathed, and the bathwater, which has been consecrated by contact with the divine form, is used as a *prasāda* for worshippers who will later visit the temple for *darśana*. The *mūrti* may then be anointed with fragrant pastes, dressed in fine clothing, adorned with a garland of fresh flowers, and offered food. This is essentially part of the devotional service portion of *pūjā*, here performed for the awakened deity. The doors of the inner sanctum are then opened so that devotees who have gathered get their first glimpse of the deity. During the Nine Night (Navarātra) festival to the Great Goddess, this first glimpse of the goddess Durgā, which takes place quite early in the morning, is known as *maṅgala darśana*, since it is particularly auspicious (*maṅgala*). The priest typically continues his ministrations to the deity, offering flowers and so on. The high point of the worship rite occurs when the priest ignites a flaming torch or lamp and passes it before the deity. This flame (*dīpa*) offering is no different from the type conducted in a home *pūjā*. However, in temples the scale may be dramatically different. On special festival days, a priest may set ablaze simultaneously a hundred and eight flames on a brass lamp, no ordinary feat of ritual technical accomplishment, and wave this before the deity. This segment of the rite is known in Hindi as *āratī/ārti* (Sanskrit: *ārātrika*, honoring), and is often used as a synonym by worshippers for the worship procedure as a whole. During *āratī*, while the priest waves the flaming lamp, devotees may ring the temple bells, beat drums, and clash cymbals, producing a clamor of honorific noise that can be heard well beyond the temple premises. People throughout the neighborhood are aware that the *āratī* of a particular local god or goddess is taking place by the sound of the bells and drums. The flame, now consecrated, is often passed to the gathered devotees, who pass their hands over the fire and smoke and then wave their hands over their faces and bodies, an action explained as cleansing them of all sins.

When the *āratī* is finished, a priest typically takes up position at the portal of the inner sanctum and attends to the devotees who approach to make offerings. When visiting a Hindu temple it is customary to buy some offerings from the vendors who line the entrance. Typically one purchases a few flowers or a flower garland in a leaf container, washes one's hands, removes one's shoes and walks barefoot through the entrance. On special occasions, such as festival days, one may bring more elaborate offerings. At goddess temples in North India, devotees may include a red scarf and a coconut as gifts. Votaries ring a bell strung above the temple doorway, announcing their arrival to the deity. They rarely approach the inner sanctum directly, and generally circulate around the temple in a clockwise direction before making their way to the main *mūrti*. At the entrance to the inner sanctum they may pass their offerings to the priest. He will anoint their forehead with a mark (Sanskrit: *tilaka*; Hindi: *tika*) typically made of red powder, although sandalwood paste or ash may also be used. The priest sometimes touches their offering not to the image itself, but to a symbol of the divine, such as footprints (*pāduka*) close to the entrance of the sanctum, where he is located. Elaborate offerings, such as a fine garland of flowers may actually be placed on the deity, if deemed pure. An offered coconut may be smashed and part of it placed in the inner sanctum, while the other half is returned to the devotee. The coconut water may be drunk as *prasāda*. The priest dispenses some of the consecrated water from the deity's morning bath into the cupped right hand of worshippers, who sip it and dispense of the rest by passing it over the hair on their head. Devotees, making a reverential gesture (*praṇāma*) and uttering a prayer of homage, then gaze at the deity, taking *darśana*, hoping that the gaze is reciprocated and that the deity simultaneously looks back, acknowledging their presence and devotion, and hopefully attending to their needs. The eyes of *mūrtis*, particularly of goddesses, are often distinctively rendered to be "eye-catching" and thus facilitate the process of *darśana*.

The doors to the inner sanctum of a temple may be closed in the afternoon, while the deity takes a nap. In certain temples, a portable surrogate image of the main deity may be carried and "put to bed" in the shrine with its spouse deity. Formal devotional service (i.e. *āratī*) may be performed several times a day, although around sunrise and sunset is most common. It is customary for whoever is within the vicinity of the temple or shrine while the *āratī* is being conducted, to attend it. However, unlike congregational worship in typical Christian celebrations of the Mass in a church, where people might gather together and in hushed unison perform ritual acts such as hymn-singing, kneeling, standing, sitting and so on, the Hindu temple is mostly a place where people may choose their mode of worship. It is not essential that they attend to the ministrations of the priest. They may occupy themselves with their own forms of worship. They may be performing devotional services (*upacāra*)

Figure 11.3 A woman reverently touches a shrine's entrance in her own rites of devotion within a larger temple complex (Banāras)

to deities in other subsidiary shrines. Some may be engaged in private spiritual practices (*sādhana*) with the intention of developing powers or achieving liberation. Others may be chatting with each other in the shade of a pavilion, and pilgrims may be preparing a meal in some rest areas (*dharmaśālā*) on the temple premises, provided for their shelter. Besides the traditional rationale for visiting a temple, namely, to show devotion to the deity abiding there, worshippers may also be performing *pūjā* as part of a *vrata*, a vowed ascetic practice in order to attain some measure of personal power and auspiciousness. Others may be engaged in requesting a favor, or fulfilling a promise (Hindi: *manauti*) to a deity. Although requesting favors from a deity is regarded as in somewhat poor taste, it is extremely common. Quite often devotees may pledge some act of service to the deity if a particular request is fulfilled. If newlyweds prayed to a deity to grant them a child, they might promise that the child's tonsure ceremony will be conducted in the temple. There can be a fair amount of anxiety generated if a deity is believed to have granted a favor, and devotees have not acted on their promise. The emotional tension is further heightened if the deity's personality is fierce, and prone to anger and harsh punishment.

When one examines the dynamics and intentional thrust of *pūjā*, it is evident that it provides a conduit (*marga*) between devotee and deity, each of whom travel from opposite ends to meet somewhere along the path's trajectory. The actions of *pūjā* parallel the yogic reintegration of the gross, subtle, and mental elements of created reality. Material substances are offered, the senses are activated, and in the vibratory utterance of prayers and the self-abnegating sentiment of loving devotion, worshippers may potentially offer themselves up completely to the deity. They indicate their willingness, if not the capacity, to travel the entire route from their embodied material condition to meet the divine in its transcendent state. In similar fashion, their (or the priest's) ministrations have simultaneously moved the deity from its transcendent abode into a material form within the devotee's mundane reality, where it may be encountered and interacted with as one would another human being.

Darśana is therefore potentially much more than just mutual seeing. The word refers to the profoundly intimate union between devotee and divinity that is possible through the act of *bhakti*. *Darśana* is direct, unmediated perception of the divine. The word "perception" elicits the image of "seeing," but Indian metaphysical systems routinely refer to a direct and complete apprehension of absolute reality, with all of the senses, but also with faculties that transcend the senses. *Darśana* evokes the notion of theophany. The *Bhagavad Gītā* (BG) is especially instructive in this regard. Arjuna, the typical devotee, although aware of Kṛṇṣa's divinity, was unable to perceive him in his divine form. Kṛṣṇa then granted Arjuna a divine eye with which to see his universal form. "This form, as you have seen it (*dṛṣtvan asi*), is very difficult to see (*sudurdarśam*); the *devas* too aspire to perceive it (*darśana-kaṅkṣinaḥ*)" (11.52), says Kṛṣṇa. In two separate verses, which reiterate similar ideas, he states that not through the Vedas, sacrificial offerings, study, charitable deeds, ritual acts, or severe asceticism, may one see him in the form that was revealed (11.48, 53). Kṛṣṇa then states emphatically, "O Arjuna, by *bhakti* alone may I, in such a manner, be known and seen in very truth and entered into (11.54).

Although the devotees' modes of relationship to the divine are akin to the closest human relationships, it is the deity who condescends to grace the worshipper with this level of familiarity. Incapable of bearing the vision of divinity in its supreme form, Arjuna begged Kṛṣṇa to assume his four-armed form, with the discus and club (BG 11.46). Kṛṣṇa complied, and eventually assumed his human form (BG 11.50, 51). Arjuna pleaded with Kṛṣṇa to grace him by enduring being worshipped as the Lord, as a parent with a child, a friend with a friend, and a lover with their beloved (BG 11.44). Within most theologies of *bhakti*, the deity is not in need of any ministrations. The divine is not dependent on the devotee. Perennially pure, the deity does not need to be cleansed. It does not need to be fed. Devotion displayed towards the deity brings the devotee into relationship with the divine, and the actions and sentiments of love and care, such as washing, clothing, feeding, and honoring, actually purify and consecrate the worshipper. Devotees drink the consecrated water that washed the deity. They eat the blessed *prasāda*, and purify themselves with the honorific *āratī* flame that passed before the deity. *Bhakti* cleanses *bhāktas* of the karmic defilements that separate them from their Beloved, and progressively deepens the levels of intimacy that they may enjoy in their relationship with the Divine.

The Hindu temple

Early Vedic religion was centered on sacrificial rituals of offerings into fire in temporarily constructed altars in the open air or under temporary shelters (e.g. the *agnicayana* rite). However, it is evident from literary sources that for at least several centuries before the Common Era, Hindus had been building temples. These early temples were probably wood constructions, none of which survive today. Excellent examples of wooden Hindu temples are found in the South Indian state of Kerala, and in the Himalayan kingdom of Nepal. However these, which are at most a few centuries old, are reconstructions of earlier temples that were destroyed by fire, earthquakes, or age. The Buddhists and Jains made extensive use of rock cut cave temples which sometimes mimic the style of more ancient wood constructions. Hindu cave temples, which were far less common, likely derived their inspiration from these sources. The emergence of free-standing stone temples may have been the result of Hellenic and Roman influences.

It was during the rule of the Gupta Dynasty (fourth to sixth centuries CE), in what is often known as the Classical Period of Hinduism, that temple design and construction expanded dramatically. Although there are numerous variations, Hindu temples are classified into two main types: the Northern or Nāgara style, and the Southern or Draviḍa style. The Nāgara style is characterized by its soaring spire, known as a *śikhara*, which surmounts the inner sanctum. The Draviḍa style is characterized by a series of rectangular walled enclosures that surround the inner sanctum, each of which possesses impressive gateways, known as *gopuras*. Even the most rudimentary temples often incorporate the dual symbolism of the male and female principles, for the inner sanctum is located within a dark, cave-like space evoking the female reproductive organ (*yoni*) and is surmounted by a mountain-like structure, evoking the male reproductive organ (*liṅga*).

The Nāgara temple's *śikhara* resonates with many of Hinduism's mountain symbols, such as Mount Mandara, used as the rod in the mythic churning of the Milk Ocean, Mount Meru, the cosmic mountain at the center of the world, and Mount Kailāsa, Śiva's abode. It suggests the motif of ascent, commonly found in spiritual literature, in which the individual's journey to encounter the Divine is likened to an arduous climb upward from the lower realms toward the heavens. The temple itself is configured according to a sacred diagram known as the *vāstu-puruṣa-maṇḍala*, a cosmograph that maps the primordial being (*puruṣa*) to the temple's ground plan (*vāstu*). Since the creation emerges from the sacrificial division of *puruṣa*, the treatises on temple architecture define the ideal locations for the shrines of various deities in

Figure 11.4 The North Indian temple with its soaring spire (*śikhara*) and mountain motif (Khajuraho)

the temple's layout. Of course, the deity to whom the temple is dedicated is housed in the inner sanctum.

The Draviḍa temple evokes the motif of the spiritual journey as a return to the source of all creation. When approaching a Draviḍa temple one is typically struck by its towering *gopuras*, which are often profusely adorned with sculptures of deities. The *gopuras* are portals into the rectangular enclosures that surround the inner sanctum. The journey to the center should ideally be a spiral, in which one circumambulates the inner sanctum in a clockwise direction, moving progressively closer to the center. Enormous Draviḍa temples, such as the Mīnākṣī temple in Madurai, have *gopuras* that tower over ten storeys in height. They may have numerous shrines and structures within their walled enclosures. The Mīnākṣī temple's Thousand-Pillared Pavilion has over 980 pillars, each with sculptural adornment. Both northern and southern styled temples often have bathing tanks or pools on the premises, where devotees may take a purifying dip and don clean clothes before entering the site.

The inner sanctum of a Hindu temple is known as the *garbha-gṛha*, which literally means "home (*gṛha*) of the embryo (*garbha*)," or "womb." The *garbha-gṛha* is often a dimly lit, cool, dark space. When one finishes the circumambulatory approach to the center, and gazes upon the *mūrti* of the deity housed within the *garbha-gṛha*, the imagery of a womb is even more compelling. After moving through the ornate *gopuras*, or viewing the sculptural decorations on the exterior of the *śikharas*, of southern or northern styled temples, one leaves behind the mundane world of multiplicity and sensory stimulus, and nears the source of all creation.

Some noteworthy temples

Many examples of Nāgara temple architecture were destroyed during the period of Islamic rule in North India. Some of the best surviving examples are found in the state of Orissa, and among the temples of Khajuraho in the state of Madhya Pradesh. The Khajuraho temples were built by the Chandella Dynasty over a period from about the tenth to the late twelfth centuries. There were about eighty temples located at the site, most of them built of sandstone, and only one of which is currently still a "living" temple, regularly visited by members of the local community. One of the finest among Khajuraho's temples is the Kandāriya Mahādeva (Great God of the Crag Cave), dedicated to Śiva. Facing east, it stands atop a ten foot high platform, and is approached by stairs leading up to it from that direction. The temple demonstrates an advanced state of artistic and architectural development in the Nāgara style of construction, since it possesses a series of roofed enclosures leading to the *śikhara*-topped inner sanctum. These enclosures are an outer entrance hall, an assembly hall, and an inner assembly hall, each of whose roofs rise higher. The temple is decorated on its exterior and interior with over eight hundred exquisitely carved sculptures, each between two and three feet in height. An oft-repeated motif among the Khajuraho temples is the *śārdula*, a sort of leogryph, which is depicted in battle with a warrior of much smaller proportions. Some have speculated that it represents Māyā or Śakti, the invincible force against which one heroically struggles. Others think it to be a heraldic symbol of the Chandella kings. There are thousands of *apsaras* (nymphs) or *sura-sundarīs* (divine beauties) represented in Khajuraho's sculptural art. Bare-breasted, they are depicted engaged in a variety of acts, from sensuously disrobing, or applying cosmetics, to writing letters or dislodging a thorn. The temples are particularly well-known for their profuse representations of *mithuna* (loving couples) and *maithuna* (coitus) images.

Sexual imagery on Hindu temples is still puzzling to many, and was disturbing to the sensibilities of Muslim armies and Christian missionaries who encountered them in the past. This has led many Hindus themselves to be uncomfortable with having to provide justifications for such depictions on their most sacred edifices. There are many rationales for such images, some of which derive from Hindu culture's acknowledgement of the significant role played by pleasure in life. Unlike religious traditions that have attempted to suppress the pursuit of pleasure, seeing it as antithetical to spiritual attainment, orthodox Hinduism admitted *kāma* as one of the reasonable goals of life. Sexual intimacy and sexual union are highly appealing forms of pleasure, and thus circumscribe a sacred dimension of existence. Furthermore, temples depict abodes of the deities, who are surrounded by heavenly nymphs, and who are enjoying royal sexual pleasures with wives, consorts, and concubines, to degrees far surpassing that of worldly monarchs. Sexual images also convey the bliss of communion with the divine. Tantric approaches to Self-realization embraced the use of sexual passion, sexual symbolism, and sexual union in their religious practices. The erotic imagery suggests associations with fertility, reproduction, and bounty, all of which were important concerns to worshippers seeking children, successful harvests, and wealth.

One of the extraordinary examples of the Nāgara style is the great temple, sometimes known as the Black Pagoda, to the sun god Sūrya located at Konārka (Konarak) in the state of Orissa. Constructed of sandstone in the thirteenth CE, the temple is fashioned as the chariot of the sun god. Supported by 24 wheels, each nearly twice the height of a human being, and pulled by seven sculpted stone horses, the temple is intricately carved and abounds with erotic imagery. The horses are reined in by Aruṇa, the Lord of the Dawn. All that now remains is the assembly hall of the temple, which is so impressive in scale that one can scarcely imagine what the temple must have looked like with its soaring *śikhara* rising over two hundred feet above the sanctum.

The Jagannātha temple, built in the twelfth century CE at the sea-coast town of Puri in Orissa is famous for its annual chariot festival or Rātha Yātra. At 214 feet (taller than the Leaning Tower of Pisa), it is the tallest of Orissan temples, and was probably modeled on the Liṅgarāja temple in the Orissan city of Bhubaneshwar, which although smaller, surpasses Jagannātha in ornamental magnificence. An interesting feature of the Jagannātha temple is that its *garbha-gṛha* houses three painted images, carved out of *nimba* wood. These are of Viṣṇu/Kṛṣṇa as Jagannātha (Lord of the World), Balabhadra, identified as Kṛṣṇa's brother, and the goddess Subhadrā, identified as his sister. Unlike *mūrtis* carved in accord with rules laid out in the official treatises, the Śilpa Śāstras, these images have a folk, tribal, and totemic appearance, suggestive of the deities' pre-Āryan origins. During the Rātha Yātra, which attracts hundreds of thousands of pilgrims, the images are placed on massive wooden chariots attached with large ropes and pulled by hundreds of devotees in a procession around the city. Apparently, the sight of persons falling before and being crushed by the enormous wheels of the chariots led British travelers to coin the word "juggernaut" for a powerful, moving, unstoppable object or force. Such chariot processions take place at numerous temples across India.

The chariot motif also figures in another extraordinary temple located at Ellora in Maharashtra State. This is Kailāsanātha (Lord of Kailāsa), a massive temple dedicated to Śiva and hewn entirely out of a single rock. Built by the Rashtrakuta Dynasty in the late eighth century CE, Kailāsanātha is one of over thirty temples carved into the Ellora cliff face. However, while the other temples are rock-cut caves, Kailāsanātha was carved from the top down to form a temple located within a courtyard, whose front wall is the stone face of the cliff. Inspired by the architectural styles prefigured in the seventh century Pallava stone hewn temples at Mahabalipuram, Kailāsanātha is easily the world's greatest rock-cut shrine. The temple stands ninety feet high, and it is estimated that about 85,000 cubic meters of rock were methodically chipped away to reveal the immense temple within the interior of the cliff. It covers twice the area of the Parthenon in Athens. Estimates suggest that it would have taken at least five thousand laborers more than a hundred years to complete. Built mostly in the Draviḍa architectural style, it is fashioned to resemble Mount Kailāsa, Śiva's mythic abode. However it also mimics the chariot (*rātha, vimāna*) motif, being supported not on wheels but on the back of elephants, whose restless movement lends the entire temple grace and dynamism.

Śrīraṅgam's Raṅganāthaswami, built in the classic Draviḍa style, is the largest temple in all India. It was praised by the Ālvārs, Tamil *bhakti* poets, as the foremost of Viṣṇu's shrines. Located on an island in the sacred Kaveri River, in the state of Tamil Nadu, the main temple is surrounded by seven concentric walled rectangles totaling over six miles in length and enclosing an area of over 150 acres. Like a small city, about 50,000 people live within its enclosures, all occupied with some aspect of temple life. At the southernmost entrance, a recently constructed *gopura* (gateway), the tallest of some twenty such towers, soars 244 feet upwards. The seven enclosures are believed to represent the sheaths of the human being, which are symbolically penetrated as devotees progress towards the center of the temple, where the true Self, the Ātman, here represented as Viṣṇu, resides. The central image in the *garbha-gṛha* is a large image, in polished black stone, of Viṣṇu reclining on the cosmic serpent, Ānanta. According to myth, during a visit to Rāma's kingdom of Ayodhyā, Vibhīṣaṇa, the demon Rāvaṇa's dharmic brother was given the gold *vimāna* (chariot) with the image of Raṅganātha, to take back to establish and worship in Laṅkā. Vibhīṣaṇa had been appointed the newly established ruler of Laṅkā, after Rāvaṇa's death. Although he was instructed not to allow the image to touch the ground, it grew heavier on his journey south, and Vibhīṣaṇa was obliged to place it down at Śrīraṅgam, from where it could no longer be dislodged. Hence, against the convention of facing east, the image faces south.

Other remarkable temples include the Bṛhadīśvara Temple and Angkor Wat. Angkor Wat, the largest religious monument in the world, was a temple dedicated to Viṣṇu. Located in Cambodia, it forms the backbone of that nation's burgeoning tourist industry. The Bṛhadīśvara (Great Lord) temple was built in the eleventh century at Thanjavur (Tanjore) by Rājarāja I, the greatest of the kings of the Cola Dynasty. It is constructed out of granite and soars to a height of over 200 feet. The capstone crowning the structure, constructed of two pieces, weighs over eighty tons. Housed in its own shrine, which faces the main temple, sits a twenty-foot long, monolithic statue of Nandi, Śiva's bull mount, which weighs about twenty-five tons.

Figure 11.5 Bṛhadīśvara temple built by the Cola emperor Rājarāja I in honor of Śiva (Thanjavur)

The form of Śiva in the *garbha-gṛha* is thought to be the largest Śiva *liṅga* in India, standing over twenty-five feet high.

Sacred specialists

Religious institutions, such as temples and monasteries, served as the primary centers of learning and culture in ancient India. Royal patronage meant that architects, sculptors, artisans, and a host of laborer *jātis* were employed in the construction of these edifices. When in use, temples served as centers for the study of religious texts, the composition of philosophical and theological writings, and for instruction in sacred music, dance, and theatre performance. Since temples attracted pilgrims, they were economic centers, providing a livelihood for merchants and tradespersons within their catchment areas. An important dimension of religious cultural learning was ritual art, and the *pūjāri* and *devadāsī* are but two exemplars of these traditions.

The *pūjāri*

The *pūjāri* is a priest who conducts the rites of worship at a temple. Sometimes known as a *purohita*, he may also perform worship at household shrines. The *pūjāri* is typically a Brahmin male, who is qualified to perform *pūjā* to various deities. Unlike renouncers, for whom celibacy is often normative, Hindu priests are typically married householders. The vast majority of *pūjāris* have learned their trade through association with a temple where a parent or relative worked, and after a period of apprenticeship have been entrusted with more responsibility. The *pūjāri* may not be very skilled in Sanskrit, having learned particular prayers from his mentors that enable him to serve as a functionary at particular rites. Due to their contact with votaries of many lower castes, and their acceptance of monetary gifts for services rendered, temple priests are often ranked lower on the purity hierarchy among Brahmin *jātis*.

However, *rāja-purohitas*, who are associated with royal families, command greater respect. Also large and renowned temple centers, whose deities require elaborate ministrations, are sometimes served by priests from particular Brahmin *jātis*, or those who have special training. Thus, only Ādiśaiva Brahmins, who have studied the appropriate rituals and scriptures in Āgamic schools, taught to them by other Ādiśaiva instructors, are entitled to worship the goddess Mīnākṣī at her temple in Madurai. The Dīkṣitar priests of the Śaiva temple of Cidambaram (Clad in Consciousness) worship Śiva there with Vedic rites. They partially shave their heads in a distinctive fashion allowing the unshaved sections to grow long. Some claim that in appearance this conveys the dual-gendered nature of the Absolute, that is both Śiva and Śakti. Such priests enjoy higher status due to their specialized training or associations.

This is also true for the performance of particular rites, in which the *pūjāri* must have appropriate initiation. For instance, in the Bengali style of Durgā Pūjā, the priest must have a special Śākta initiation, which enables him to worship certain high goddesses. The worship rites are extremely complex, requiring him to recite hundreds of prayers, construct cosmograms, and perform sacred gestures. Errors in the performance are believed to endanger both him and the rite's patrons. Typically, such a highly qualified *purohita* is accompanied by an assistant, known as a *tantradhāraka* (holder of the schema) who guides him through the performance with the aid of a ritual manual. For experienced *purohitas*, the assistant is an apprentice, while for novice *purohitas*, the *tantradhāraka* is likely his mentor.

The *devadāsī*

Devadāsīs ("servants of God") were women, particularly associated with large temple complexes such as Jagannātha, in Puri, who rendered service to the deity. They were the custodians of a wide range of arts, especially sacred dance and music, which were utilized to please the deity. *Devadāsīs* also made offerings of food and flowers to the temple's main god or goddess. Many temples are equipped with dance-halls located in front of the inner sanctum, where performances could be staged for the deity's pleasure. According to the accounts of Muslim invaders, who sacked it in the eleventh century, the temple of Somnāth in the state of Gujarat had a thousand priests and five hundred *devadāsīs*. Since the king was often regarded as the embodiment of his patron deity on earth, *devadāsīs* were sometimes initiated into "marriage" with the deity through sexual intercourse with the king. In this manner the *devadāsī* was identified with the goddess, and remained perennially auspicious. Since the temple was regarded as a palatial heavenly abode of the deity, *devadāsīs* were also akin

Figure 11.6 The sensuous form of an *apsaras* graces the walls of a Hindu temple (Khajuraho)

to the *apsaras* and *sura-sundarīs* whose images grace many temple walls. As such they also rendered pleasure to those who visited the divine abode. In time, secular interests permeated the *devadāsī* tradition, and temple priests, who sexually enjoyed the women, became guilty of prostituting them to visiting devotees. Appropriate concerns about the exploitation of these women under religious pretexts were skewed by puritanical attitudes and a misunderstanding of Hindu religious values. The tradition of *devadāsī* dedication to temples was legally outlawed by the middle of the twentieth century. Unfortunately, it led to the demise of the one existing class of Hinduism's female temple ritualists, and with it their knowledge of sacred dance and other such specialized rites.

Hindu pilgrimage

Pilgrimage (*yātra*) is mostly an optional, although highly popular type of religious practice, since it fuses a religious quest with the adventure of travel and the pleasure of tourism. Hindus may undertake a *yātra* as part of a vowed ascetic observance (*vrata*), or to eliminate sins. Others travel to perform particular rites, such as going to Gāyā for postmortem rituals, or to celebrate particular festivals, such as attending the Kumbha Melas. Each such holy site is known as a *tīrtha* (ford or crossing place), so called because it provides a passage across the perilous waters of samsāric reality to the far shore of liberation. Although one might conceivably traverse between worldly and divine spheres anywhere, *tīrthas* are locations where it is believed to be easier to cross from profane to sacred realms. When sacred chronology intersects with sacred geography the *tīrtha* is particularly charged, and pilgrims flock to avail themselves of these purifying and liberating portals in the divine time–space continuum. For instance, the Kumbha Melas occur every three years rotating between four locations. The one that takes place every twelve years at Prayāg (Allahabad) is the world's largest festival gathering. It attracts well over fifteen million worshippers who clamor to bathe in the confluence of the Gaṅgā and Yamunā Rivers during an auspicious astrological conjunction.

There are literally thousands of pilgrimages available to Hindus. Some might undertake the Pañcakroṣi Yātra that circumambulates the sacred city of Banāras. Others may travel to various holy cities along the Gaṅgā River such as Haridvāra (Hardwar), where the river descending from the mountains meets the plains, or higher up in the Himalayas at Kedarnāth or Badrināth, close to the sacred river's sources. Sectarian affiliations especially draw pilgrims to sites associated with their *iṣṭa-devatas*, their personally favored deities. Kṛṣṇa-*bhāktas* might visit Mathurā or Dvāraka, and Rāma-*bhāktas* may visit Ayodhyā. Śaivas are attracted to the sites of renowned Śiva *liṅgas*. The temple of Śrī Veṅkaṭeśvara, a form of Viṣṇu, located on the town of Tirupati's Tirumala Hill in the state of Andhra Pradesh, is believed to be the wealthiest temple in India. It attracts between five to ten thousand pilgrims daily, and is estimated to earn about two billion Indian rupees annually. Śākta Hindus are drawn to Vaiṣṇo Devī, in the northern state of Jammu and Kashmir, where the Devī is located in a mountain cave temple in the form of three round stones, respectively representing Mahālakṣmī, Mahāsarasvatī, and Mahākālī. There are pilgrimages around Mount Kailāsa, or around the Gaṅgā River. There is even a highly auspicious pilgrimage to four important sites at the "edges" of the Indian subcontinent. These are Dvāraka on the west, Badrināth to the north, Puri on the East, and Rāmeśvaram, located near India's southernmost tip, where Rāma is said to have worshipped Śiva before launching his attack on Rāvaṇa.

Despite the touristic dimension of pilgrimages, whose sites are quite commonly visited by honeymooning Hindu couples, if characterized by ordeal their value is often substantially enhanced. The Himalayan pilgrimages, which holy men (*sādhu*) generally perform on foot, involve arduous journeys to high mountain caves and glaciers. A particularly vigorous pilgrimage, which has dramatically grown in scale over the last half century, takes place at Sabarimalai, in the state of Kerala, during December and early January. For each of forty-one or fifty-one days, about 175,000 men undertake a pilgrimage to the mountain shrine of Lord Aiyappan. Aiyappan is regarded, by orthodox Hindus, as the son of Śiva and Viṣṇu, who assumed the alluring female form of Mohinī to lure away the demons when the Elixir of Immortality (*aṃrta*) was extracted from the churned Ocean of Milk. Aiyappan's core myth, however, tells of a baby boy who was found mysteriously in the forest, and who as a youth was sent on a perilous journey, intended to kill him, to retrieve tiger's milk. He returned victoriously riding the tiger and revealed himself to be the divinity Aiyappan.

Pilgrims don a black cloth lower garment (*luṅgi*), eat a simple diet of fruit and grain, and abstain from shaving, sex, and alcohol. Then, with periodic loud shouts, calling upon Aiyappan, they conduct their journey to various shrines, and into the mountain forests inhabited by tigers and wild elephants. At the main temple, the destination of their strenuous pilgrimage, they smash a coconut that they have been carrying on one of eighteen steps, ideally repeating this journey annually, to complete the rite on all eighteen of the steps. By enduring the challenges of the forest ordeal and encountering the dangerous power of the wilderness, they emerge transformed, figuratively and experientially united with Aiyappan himself.

Discussion questions

1. If it is regarded as poor taste to request favors from deities, why do you think it is so common for people to do so?
2. Do you think that the term "orthodoxy" is a problematic one, especially in terms of the "Great Tradition," and if so why?

3. Even the most rudimentary temples often incorporate the dual symbolism of the male and female principles, why do you think this is the case?
4. In what ways did Hindu *bhakti* ideology begin to embrace women and lower-caste participation?
5. In what ways does domestic worship differ from temple worship, and in what ways are they similar?
6. Who is allowed to perform the rites of worship at homes and in temples, and what qualifications, if any, must they have?

Key points in this chapter

- Hinduism's developing *bhakti* ideology embraced women and lower-caste participation. *Bhakti*'s penetration into the orthodox tradition was gradual.
- *Pūjā* is a ritualized form of devotional worship (*bhakti*). The crucial feature of *pūjā* is intimate relationship with the divine.
- Deities are regarded as continuously abiding in the abodes where they have been installed.
- A Hindu temple is regarded as the abode of a deity. It integrates male and female symbolism, along with presenting the motif of ascent or a spiral movement to the source of creation.
- *Pūjā* forges a path (*marga*) that connects the devotee and deity. Its actions symbolically parallel the yogic reintegration of the elements of created reality.
- Through *pūjā* the devotee is progressively purified and the deity rendered more substantial, so that each is moved along opposite trajectories of the same path to a meeting point. This event of mutual perception is *darśana*.
- Religious institutions, such as temples, served as the primary centers of learning and culture in ancient India.
- Pilgrimage (*yātra*) is generally an optional practice whose spiritual benefits are often enhanced by degree of ordeal it presents.

Further reading

On temples

Aiyer, V. G. Ramakrishna (1946) *The Economy of a South Indian Temple*. Annamalai: Annamalai University.

Bennett, P. (1993) *The Path of Grace: Social Organization and Temple Worship in a Vaisnava Sect*. Delhi: Hindustan Publishing.

Boner, A., S. R. Sarma, and R. P. Das (1972) *New Light on the Sun Temple of Konārak: Four Unpublished Manuscripts relating to Construction, History, and Ritual of this Temple*. Varanasi: Chowkhamba Sanskrit Series Office.

Kramrisch, Stella (1946) *The Hindu Temple*, 2 vols. Calcutta: University of Calcutta.

Meister, M. W. and M. Dhaky (eds) (1983–91) *Encyclopedia of Indian Temple Architecture*. Vols. I (2 parts) and II (2 parts). Princeton, NJ: Princeton University Press and Delhi: Oxford University Press.

Michell, George (1977) *The Hindu Temple: An Introduction to its Meaning and Forms*. New York: Harper and Row.

Srikant (2002) *Power in Temples: a Modern Perspective*. Payyanur: Integral Books.

Younger, Paul (1995) *The Home of the Dancing Śivaṉ: The Traditions of the Hindu Temple in Citambaram*. New York: Oxford University Press.

On pilgrimage and festivals

Ayyar, P. V. Jagadissa (1921) *South Indian Festivities*. Madras: Higginbothams.

Babb, Lawrence (1975) *The Divine Hierarchy*. New York: Columbia University Press.

Bhardwaj, Surinder Mohan (1973) *Hindu Places of Pilgrimage: A Study in Cultural Geography*. Berkeley, CA: University of California Press.

Daniel, E. Valentine (1984) *Fluid Signs: Being a Person in the Tamil Way*. Berkeley: University of California Press.

Eck, Diana L. (1983) *Banaras: City of Light*. Princeton, NJ: Princeton University Press.

Erndl, Kathleen M. (1993) *Victory to the Mother: The Hindu Goddess of Northwest India in Myth, Ritual, and Symbol*. New York: Oxford University Press.

Feldhaus, Anne (1984) *The Deeds of God in Ṛddhipur*. New York: Oxford University Press.

Gold, Anne Grodzins (1988) *Fruitful Journeys: The Ways of Rajasthani Pilgrims*. Prospect Hills, IL: Waveland Press.

Haberman, David, L. (1994) *Journey through the Twelve Forests: An Encounter with Krishna*. New York: Oxford University Press.

Hebner, J., and D. Osborn (1990) *Kumbha Mela: The World's Largest Act of Faith*. La Jolla, CA: Entourage Publishing.

Mokashi, D. B. (1987) *Palkhi: An Indian Pilgrimage*. Philip Engbloom (trans.). Albany, NY: State University of New York Press.

Morinis, E. A. (1984) *Pilgrimage in the Hindu Tradition: A Case Study of West Bengal*. South Asian Studies Series. New York: Oxford University Press.

Roy, D. K., and J. Devi (1955) *Kumbha: India's Ageless Festival*. Bombay: Bharatiya Vidya Bhavan.

Sax, William S. (1991) *Mountain Goddess: Gender and Politics in a Himalayan Pilgrimage*. New York: Oxford University Press.
Van der Veer, P. (1988) *Gods on Earth: The Management of Religious Experience and Identity in a North Indian Pilgrimage Center*. London: Athlone Press.
Welborn, G. and G. E. Yocum (eds) (1985) *Religious Festivals in South India and Sri Lanka*. Delhi: Manohar.
Zelliott, E. and M. Bernsten (eds) (1988) *Essays on Religion in Maharashtra*. Albany, NY: State University of New York Press.

On iconography and symbols

Bahattacharya, B. (1975) *Śaivism and the Phallic World*, 2 vols. New Delhi: Oxford University Press.
Banerjea. J. N. (1956) *The Development of Hindu Iconography*. Calcutta: University of Calcutta.
Coomaraswamy, Ananda (1956) *The Dance of Śiva*. Bombay: Asia Publishing House.
Harlan, Lindsey (2003) *The Goddesses' Henchmen: Gender in Indian Hero Worship*. Oxford: Oxford University Press.
Kramrisch, Stella (1981) *Indian Sculpture*. Reprint. Delhi: Motilal Banarsidass.
O'Flaherty, W. (1981) *Sexual Metaphors and Animal Symbols in Indian Mythology*. Delhi: Motilal Banarsidass.
Pal, P. (1981) *Hindu Religion and Iconology*. Los Angeles, CA: Vichitra Press.
Rao, T. A. Gopinath (1968) *Elements of Hindu Iconography*, 4 vols. Reprint. New York: Paragon.
Sivaramamurti, C. (1960) *Indian Bronzes*. Bombay: Taraporevala.
— (1974) *Nataraja in Art, Thought and Literature*. New Delhi: National Museum.
Zimmer, Hans (1963) *Myths and Symbols in Indian Art and Civilization*. New York: Harper & Row.

History and culture in the classical period

Auboyer, J. (1965) *Daily Life in Ancient India from Approximately 200 B.C. to A.D. 700*. New York: Macmillan.
Banerjee, G. N. (1961) *Hellenism in Ancient India*. Delhi: Munshi Ram Manohalal.
Hardy, Friedhelm (1983) *The Religious Culture of India: Power, Love and Wisdom*. Cambridge: Cambridge University Press.
Siegel, L. (1983) *Fires of Love – Waters of Peace: Passion and Renunciation in Indian Culture*. Honolulu, HI: University of Hawaii Press.

On Hindu art

Bhattacharyya, T. (1963) *The Canons of Indian Art: A Study of Vāstuvidyā*. Calcutta: Firma K. L. Mukhopadhyay.

Burton, T. P. (1992) *Hindu Art*. London: British Museum Press.

Bussabarger, R. F. and B. D. Robins (1968) *The Everyday Art of India*. New York: Dover.

Goetz, H. (1964) *The Art of India*. New York: Crown Publishers.

Kramrisch, Stella (1954) *The Art of India: Traditions of Indian Sculpture, Painting and Architecture*. London: Phaidon.

Michell, George (2000) *Hindu Art and Architecture*. London: Thames & Hudson.

Rowland, B. (1967) *The Art and Architecture of India: Buddhist, Hindu, Jain*. Baltimore, MD: Penguin Books.

Swarup, B. (1958) *Theory of Indian Music*. Allahabad: Swamy Brothers.

Zimmer, Hans (1955) *The Art of Indian Asia*, 2 vols. New York: Bollingen Foundation.

— (1984) *Artistic Form and Yoga in the Sacred Images of India*. G. Chapple and J.B. Lawson (trans.). Princeton, NJ: Princeton University Press.

On worship rituals

Bühnemann, Gudrun (1988) *Pūjā: A Study in Smārta Ritual*. Vienna: Gerold.

Case, M. H. (2000) *Seeing Krishna: The Religious World of a Brahman Family in Vrindaban*. New York: Oxford University Press.

Davis, Richard M. (1991) *Ritual in an Oscillating Universe: Worshiping Śiva in Medieval India*. Princeton, NJ: Princeton University Press.

Dehejia, V. (1988) *Slaves of the Lord*. Delhi: Munishiram Manoharlal.

Diehl, C. G. (1956) *Instrument and Purpose: Studies on Rites and Rituals in South India*. Lund: CWK Gleerup.

Eck, Diana (1985) *Darśan: Seeing the Divine Image in India*. Chambersburg: Anima Books.

Fuller, Christopher J. (1984) *Servants of the Goddess: The Priests of a South Indian Temple*. Cambridge: Cambridge University Press.

— (2003) *The Renewal of the Priesthood: Modernity and Traditionalism in a South Indian Temple*. Princeton: Princeton University Press.

Ghosha, Pratapchandra (1871) *Durga Puja, with Notes and Illustrations*. Calcutta: Hindoo Patriot Press.

Harman, William (1989) *The Sacred Marriage of a Hindu Goddess*. Bloomington, IN: Indiana University Press.

Huyler, S. P. (1999) *Meeting God: Elements of Hindu Devotion*. New Haven, CT: Yale University Press.

Marglin, F. A. (1985) *Wives of the God-King: The Rituals of the Devadasis of Puri*. Delhi: Oxford University Press.

McDaniel, June (2004) *Offering Flowers, Feeding Skulls: Popular Goddess Worship in West Bengal*. Oxford: Oxford University Press.

Michaels, Axel, et al (eds.) (1996) *Wild Goddesses in India and Nepal*. Bern: Peter Lang.

Orr, Leslie C. (2000) *Donors, Devotees, and Daughters of God: Temple Women of Medieval Tamil Nadu*. New York: Oxford University Press.

Östör, Àkos. (1980) *The Play of the Gods: Locality, Ideology, Structure and Time in the Festivals of a Bengali Town*. Chicago, IL: University of Chicago Press.

Pandeya, L. P. (1972) *Sun Worship in Ancient India*. Delhi: Motilal Banarsidass.

Pocock, D. (1973) *Body, Mind and Wealth: A Study of Belief and Practice in an Indian Village*. Oxford: Blackwell Publishing.

Preston, James J. (1980) *Cult of the Goddess: Social and Religious Change in a Hindu Temple*. Prospect Heights, IL: Waveland Press.

Rodrigues, Hillary P. (2003) *Ritual Worship of the Great Goddess: The Liturgy of the Durgā Pūjā with Interpretations*. Albany, NY: State University of New York Press.

Sharma, Arvind (ed.) (2005) *Goddesses and Women in the Indic Religious Tradition*. Leiden: E. J. Brill.

Van Kooij, K. R. (1972) *Worship of the Goddess according to the Kākikāpurāṇa*. Leiden: E. J. Brill.

Waghorne, J. P. and N. Cutler (eds) (1985) *Gods of Flesh/Gods of Stone: The Embodiment of Divinity in India*. Chambersburg: Anima Publications.

12 *Vedānta*

In this chapter

The character of Hinduism is evident in the speculative philosophy of the Upaniṣads developed in subsequent centuries into what is known as Vedānta philosophy. Vedānta has numerous schools. Each is generally identified by its most influential proponent or by the way it characterizes the relationship between a person's true nature and Absolute Reality. In this chapter the three most influential schools of Vedānta are examined.

Main topics covered

- Śaṅkara's radical non-dualism
- Rāmānuja's qualified non-dualism
- Madhva's dualism

Vedānta is traditionally classified as one of the six orthodox religio-philosophical systems or *darśanas*. It is also known as Uttara Mīmāṃsā (Investigation of the Latter), which, as its name implies, reflects its concern with interpretation of the latter (*anta*) portions of the Veda. Thus Vedānta focuses on the study and understanding of the Upaniṣads. However, since the Upaniṣads are texts of inquiry into the nature of Absolute Reality or Brahman, and the true Self, Ātman, and the relationship between them, Vedānta is clearly a school of speculative philosophy, unlike its counterpart, Pūrva Mīmāṃsā, which has an intrinsically theological agenda. Besides the Upaniṣads, Vedānta thinkers ground their philosophy on two other foundational texts. These are Bādarāyaṇa's *Vedānta Sūtra* (also known as the *Brahma Sūtra*), and the *Bhagavad Gītā*. Bādarāyaṇa's text (c. second century CE) is akin to a summary and systematic presentation of the essential philosophical teachings of the principal Upaniṣads.

Śaṅkara's radical non-dualism

Śaṅkara is probably the most highly regarded Hindu philosopher. His life story has become enveloped in legend, and there is no consensus on his date of birth. He was a Brahmin, from the state of Kerala, who is believed to have lived in the eighth or nineth century BCE, and to have died at the age of thirty-two. Despite his short life span, his legacy is remarkable. In addition to his doctrinal contributions, Śaṅkara (or his students) is reputed to have founded the monastic or *maṭha* system for Hindu renouncers. Skilled in traditional Vedic learning, he did not marry, but became a *saṃnyāsin*. He is reputed to have traveled extensively throughout India, covering its length and breadth, debating with rival philosophers and always emerging victorious. The primary *maṭhas* that were established grew in number from the original four, and each became a renowned center of learning. They still endure today. Despite Hinduism's diversity, the leaders of these *maṭhas*, who are known as Śaṅkarācaryas, now wield substantial influence in dictating the norms of Hindu orthodoxy. Śaṅkara wrote commentaries on several Upaniṣads, the *Bhagavad Gītā*, and the *Brahma Sūtra*. Numerous other works, probably composed by his students, are also attributed to him.

Śaṅkara's philosophy is known as Advaita Vedānta, or radical non-dualism. It is non-dualistic (*advaita*), because it proposes that there is only one thing that is absolutely real, and that is Brahman. Moreover, Brahman is the only thing in existence. Śaṅkara's philosophy is radical, because it proposes that Brahman is indivisible, and thus cannot be partitioned into qualities, components, and so on. Brahman is *nir-guṇa*, beyond or without attributes. By extension, this means that the Ātman, one's true Self, is identical with Brahman. One's innermost Self (i.e. *ātman*) is not a part of Brahman, because Brahman is not composed of parts. It *is* Brahman, because Brahman is all there is. The reason this assertion seems counterintuitive to our day to day experience of a personal self, and our perception of what appears to be a world full of various separate things, is that we are under the sway of Māyā. Śaṅkara equates Māyā with ignorance (*avidyā, ajñāna*), and explains that Māyā is not different from Brahman. Just as the burning power of fire derives from fire itself, Māyā is the effulgence of Brahman. Māyā is the creative power through which Brahman, like a great magician, conjures up the world of seeming multiplicity and separate selves.

In order to counter arguments that Māyā then appears to be an attribute or quality of Brahman, Śaṅkara offers the analogy of a rope mistaken for a snake. As long as the illusion persists, it creates effects, such as fear or fascination. However, once the illusion is penetrated, the illusory snake vanishes, revealing the substrate upon which it was superimposed. Māyā's illusions are superimposed on Brahman, and their capacity to delude vanishes when one has attained liberating knowledge (*vidyā, jñāna*). This is *mokṣa*, the realization of one's true nature as Brahman. Māyā is therefore not fully real (i.e. existent), because its illusions are grounded in ignorance of Brahman, and these vanish with Self-realization. But Māyā's illusions are not fully unreal, since they have the power to cause us to feel and act, which something that is non-existent could not do. As the ground of all conceptions, Māyā is itself inexplicable. When one is free from the deluding power of Māyā, one recognizes oneself as Brahman and is liberated from Brahman's magical creative power of Māyā.

All conceptions about the Absolute Brahman (i.e. Parabrahman or Nirguṇa Brahman) are the workings of Māyā, Brahman's creative power, which generates our thoughts and imaginings. Thus, when we apply these imaginings to Brahman, it is understood as God, and is accorded various capacities. Śaṅkara calls this Saguṇa Brahman (Brahman with attributes) or Īśvara (The Lord). Īśvara presides over the world and is the object of religious devotion and activities. If one were to distill the qualities (*guṇa*) of Brahman to their essentials, they would be: *sat* (being or existence), *cit* (consciousness), and *ānanda* (bliss). It is not that things exist because they are God's creation, for this evokes a sense of a God different from creation. God, or the Lord, is "being" itself. It is not that things have consciousness because they are God's creation. God is "consciousness" itself. And one does not experience bliss because of God's power. Īśvara is "bliss" itself. And yet, these, too, are projections of qualities onto the nature of the Absolute, which have the mark of Māyā.

Śaṅkara upholds the path of transcendental knowledge (*jñāna marga*), as the ultimate means through which ignorance is removed and liberation attained. Since any quality that one predicates upon Brahman is a distorting limitation on its essential nature, Advaita Vedānta promotes the approach of negation, known as *neti-neti* (not "this," not "that"). This *via negativa* plays a part in why the philosophy is called non-dualism (*advaita*), rather than monism. Monism is a philosophical standpoint that makes the positive assertion of "one-ness." However, such a positive assertion inevitably triggers the opposing conceptual response of "not-one," which then exists in a dualistic tension with the concept of "one-ness." Non-dualism is a standpoint that negates any plurality or duality, especially that generated by any kind of conceptual thought.

For many centuries, the renouncer traditions that were grounded in philosophical inquiry had been dominated by heterodox *darśanas*, particularly Buddhism. Hinduism had been under the sway of *bhakti* approaches. Śaṅkara's Advaita provided a *darśana* that blended some of the most appealing dimensions of Buddhism (e.g. monasticism) and Buddhist philosophy with traditional Hinduism, reinvigorating the latter. Nirguṇa Brahman is only marginally different from the Buddhist conception of Emptiness (*śūnyata*), and Śaṅkara's concept of Īśvara allowed a place for Hinduism's *bhakti* and *karma-marga* approaches. The ever-malleable Hindu orthodoxy embraced these ideas.

Rāmānuja's qualified non-dualism

Rāmānuja was born near the South Indian city of Chennai (Madras) in the eleventh or twelfth century. Initially trained in Śaṅkara's Advaita philosophy, he eventually gravitated towards a more theistic and devotionally based approach to religion, and joined the Śrī-Vaiṣṇava tradition centered at the great temple of Śrīraṅgam. He was deeply influenced by the *bhakti*-oriented sentiments of the Ālvārs as mediated by his teachers. His most important work is the *Śrī Bhāṣya*, a commentary on the *Vedānta Sūtra*. Rāmānuja's philosophy is known as Viśiṣṭādvaita (Qualified Non-Dualism). It is non-dualistic (*advaita*) because, like Śaṅkara's philosophy, it upholds that there is only one Absolute Reality, and that is Brahman. However, it is qualified (*viśiṣṭa*) because, according to Rāmānuja, it is meaningless to comprehend, relate to, or speak about a Nirguṇa Brahman. Thus Māyā is real, and Brahman is Saguṇa, or possessing qualities. Thus Brahman is Īśvara, and may be called Nārāyaṇa (i.e. Viṣṇu) together with his consort, Śrī (i.e. Lakṣmī).

Ātmans (or *jīvas*) are not identical with Brahman, but modes or aspects of Brahman, wholly dependent upon the Lord. Just as a blue lotus possesses such modes as "flower-ness," "lotus-ness," and "blue-ness," so too, our innermost core shares some intrinsic qualities with Brahman. Upon liberation (*mokṣa*), the individual Self (*ātman*) is no longer subject to the limitations brought about through illusion and *karma*. It expands to its fullest extent, but retains its distinctness, allowing it to share, now with perfect wisdom and love, a profound communion with the Lord.

Although it is important to tread the paths of action (*karma*), which destroys karmic seeds, and knowledge (*jñāna*), which is typically understood as the study of Vedānta, Rāmānuja upholds *bhakti* as the highest path. Moreover, as a crucial concept in Rāmānuja's approach, it is only complete surrender (*prapatti*) to the Divine that is the ultimate expression of loving devotion. Ultimately, it is the Lord's decision to liberate a being, which is done through the descent of his grace, the goddess Śrī.

A few centuries after Rāmānuja, the Śrī Vaiṣṇava tradition, to which he belonged, split into two branches. These are the Vadagalai or Northern School, centered at the temple of Kañcīpuram, and the Teṅgalai or Southern School, centered at Śrīraṅgam. They primarily differ in perspectives on how one ought to appropriate the Lord's liberating grace. The Vadagalai School is known as the "monkey school," because it proposes an active surrender on the part of the devotee. Just as a baby monkey clings with all its might to its mother in order to be carried to safety, Vadagalai theology emphasizes the soul's co-operation with the Lord in the process of liberation. Devotees should engage in various types of prescribed religious activities in order to be freed from *karma* and obtain grace. By contrast, Teṅgalai theology questions the presumption that human action should participate in actualizing God's grace. Thus it is categorized as the "cat (or kitten) school," because, without any effort on its part, a kitten is picked up by the scruff of its neck and moved to safety by the mother cat.

To attempt to "do" something in order to surrender is audacious, since the Lord has supreme agency and prerogative.

The Viśiṣṭādvaita philosophy, grounded as it is in a *bhakti*-based theism, synchronizes much more closely with the actual beliefs and worship practices of the majority of Hindus, than does Śaṅkara's radical non-dualism. This does not mean that the majority of Hindus "follow" Viśiṣṭādvaita philosophy, but that the philosophy offers compelling rationales for why they might think and act as they do. Rāmānuja and Śrī Vaiṣṇavism gave theism, and the chaotically expressed theologies of feeling, articulated in the passionate sentiments of the Ālvārs and other such *bhakti* approaches, a substantial and systematic philosophical foundation. It fused these with the speculative Vedic tradition of the Upaniṣads in ways that heightened their legitimacy as credible articulations of Hindu orthodoxy.

Madhva's dualism

Madhva (1238–1317) was born near Udipi, in the region of the South Indian state of Karnataka. He was a prolific writer, producing many commentaries on the classic Vedānta foundational texts, and on the *Bhāgavata Purāṇa* and the *Mahābhārata*. Madhva's philosophy is known as Dvaita or dualism. Actually it postulates the existence of three types of entities: Brahman (Īśvara), souls (*jīvātman*), and matter (*prakṛti*). *Jīvas* and matter are dependent on Brahman for existence, but Brahman is totally independent (*svatantra*). Brahman is Saguṇa, and thus may be called Viṣṇu. The state of liberation (*mokṣa*) is attained when one fully understands the differences between: 1) Īśvara and *jīvātman*, 2) various *jīvātmans*, 3) *jīvātman* and *prakṛti*, 4) Īśvara and *prakṛti*, and 5) various phenomena of *prakṛti*.

Thus Madhva's philosophy is highly "realistic" since it has no place for an illusory reality generated by Māyā. Madhva's philosophy contains certain distinctive characteristics. For instance, although each soul is unique, souls may be categorized. Some will attain *mokṣa*. Others will be reborn continuously. Yet others will remain damned for eternity in hells. This is because they have intrinsic propensities based on their intrinsic constitution. Liberation is ultimately the result of God's grace (*prasāda*). However, *bhakti*, a renouncing attitude, and scriptural study are nonetheless worthwhile practices. A fascinating feature of Madhva's philosophy is that because each soul is unique, should it achieve *mokṣa*, the nature of its realization will also be unique. It will experience a distinctive configuration of consciousness that is but a fragment of God's infinite potential.

Key points in this chapter

- Vedānta is classified as one of the six orthodox religio-philosophical systems or *darśanas*, and focuses on the study and understanding of the Upaniṣads.
- Vedānta is concerned with speculative philosophy, unlike its counterpart, Pūrva Mīmāṃsā, which has an intrinsically theological agenda.
- Besides the Upaniṣads, Vedānta bases its philosophy on Bādarāyaṇa's *Vedānta Sūtra*, and the *Bhagavad Gītā*.
- Śaṅkara is probably the most highly regarded Hindu philosopher, whose philosophy is known as Advaita Vedānta, or radical non-dualism.
- Rāmānuja's philosophy is known as Qualified Non-Dualism, "qualified" since it assigns qualities to Brahman.
- Madhva's philosophy, known as Dvaita or dualism, is highly "realistic" having no place for an illusory reality created by Māyā.

Discussion questions

1. Why do you think Śaṅkara regards the path of transcendental knowledge (*jñāna marga*) as the ultimate means for the removal of ignorance and the attainment of liberation?
2. Why do you think Rāmānuja thinks it is meaningless to comprehend, relate to, or speak about a Nirguṇa Brahman? Do you agree with him, and why?
3. If it is ultimately the Lord's decision to liberate a being, done through the descent of his grace, the goddess Śrī, then what do you think might be the rationales for following a path such as *bhakti*?
4. In what ways does the Viśiṣṭādvaita philosophy synchronize more closely with the actual beliefs and worship practices of the majority of Hindus, than does Śaṅkara's radical non-dualism?
5. Who is Śaṅkara, what is his philosophy, and why is he important to the tradition of Vedānta?
6. How does Śaṅkara's philosophy of non-dualism differ from that of Rāmānuja's?

Further reading

General works on Vedānta and Vedāntic topics

Arapura, J. G. (1986) *Hermeneutical Essays on Vedāntic Topics*. Delhi: Motilal Banarsidass.

Atreya, B. L. (1936) *The Philosophy of Yogavāsiṣṭha*. Adyar: Adyar Library.

Bhattacharya, K. C. (1909) *Studies in Vedāntism*. Calcutta: University of Calcutta.

Devanandan, P. D. (1954) *The Concept of Māyā*. Calcutta: YMCA Publishing House.

Granoff, P. (1978) *Philosophy and Argument in Late Vedānta*. Boston, MA: Reidel.

Radhakrishnan, S. (1961) *The Brahmasūtra*. London: Allen & Unwin.

On Advaita Vedānta and Śaṅkara

Balasubramanian, R. (1976) *Advaita Vedānta*. Madras: University of Madras.

Bhagavat, H. R. (ed.) (1952) *Minor Works of Śaṅkarācārya*, Poona Oriental Series No. 8. Poona: Oriental Book Agency.

Das, R. V. (1968) *Introduction to Śaṅkara*. Calcutta: Punthi Pustak.

Deutsch, E. (1969) *Advaita Vedānta: A Philosophical Reconstruction*. Honolulu, HI: University of Hawaii.

Deutsch, E. and J. A. B. van Buitenen (1971) *A Source Book of Advaita Vedanta*. Honolulu, HI: University of Hawaii.

Halbfass, W. (1983) *Human Reason and Vedic Revelation in the Philosophy of Śaṅkara*. Reinbeck: Verlag für Orientalistische Fachpublikation.

Indich, W. M. (1980) *Consciousness in Advaita Vedānta*. Delhi: Motilal Banarasidass.

Isayeva, Natalia (1993) *Shankara and Indian Philosophy*. Albany, NY: State University of New York Press.

Nikhilananda, Swami (trans.) (1962) *Ātmabodha*. Mylapore: Ramakrishna Math.

O'Neil, L. T. (1980) *Māyā in Śaṅkara: Measuring the Immeasurable*. Delhi: Motilal Banarsidass.

Thibault, George (trans.) (1962) *The Vedāntasūtras of Bādarāyana with the Commentary by Śaṅkara*, 2 vols. Sacred Books of the East, vols. 34 and 38. Reprint. New York: Dover.

On monks and the Śaṅkarācarya tradition

Cenker, W. (1983) *A Tradition of Teachers: Śaṅkara and the Jadgdgurus Today*. Delhi: Motilal Banarsidass.

Creel, Austin B., and V. Narayanan (1990) *Monastic Life in the Christian and Hindu Tradition*. Lewiston, NY: Edwin Mellen Press.

Miller, D. M., and Dorothy C. Wertz (1976) *Hindu Monastic Life: The Monks and Monasteries of Bhubaneśwar*. Montreal: McGill-Queen's University Press.

On Viśiṣṭādvaita and Ramānuja

Balasubramanian, R. (1978) *Some Problems in the Epistemology and Metaphysics of Rāmānuja*. Madras: University of Madras.

Bharadwaj, Krishna Datta (1958) *The Philosophy of Rāmānuja*. New Delhi: Sir Sankar Lall Charitable Trust Society.

van Buitenen, J. A. B. (1965) *Rāmānuja on the Bhagavadgītā*. Delhi: Motilal Banarsidass.

Carman, John B. (1974) *The Theology of Rāmānuja: An Essay in Interreligious Understanding*. New Haven, CT: Yale University Press.

Govindacharya, Alkondavilli (1906) *The Life of Rāmānuja*. Madras: C. N. Press.

Sharma, A. (1978) *Viśiṣṭāḍvaita Vedānta: A Study*. New Delhi: Heritage Press.

Thibault, George (trans.) (1904) *Vedāntasūtras with Rāmānuja's Commentary*. In Sacred Books of the East, F. Max Müller (gen. ed.), vol 48.

Yamunacarya, M. (1963) *Rāmānuja's Teachings in his own Words*. Bombay: Bharatiya Vidya Bhavan.

On Dvaita and Madhva

Puthiadan, I. (1985) *Viṣṇu the Ever Free: A Study of the Madhva Concept of God*. Madurai: Dialogue Publications.

Rao, S. S. (trans.) (1936) *Vedāntasūtras with the Commentary of Madhva*. Tirupati: Sir Vyasa Press.

Sharma, B. N. K. (1960–61) *A History of Dvaita School of Vedānta and its Literature*, 2 vols. Bombay: Booksellers Publishing Co.

— (1961) *Madhva's Teaching in His Own Words*. Bombay: Bhavan's Book University.

— (1962) *Philosophy of Śrī Madhvācārya*. Bombay: Bharatiya Vidya Bhavan.

13 *Tantra*

In this chapter

Another challenge confronting Hindu orthodoxy came by way of Tantra, a complex assortment of ritual procedures oriented towards manipulating cosmic powers. Tantra's ritual actions were also related to various philosophical systems. Here, we explore the roots of Tantra and some of its key features. Some influential tantric schools, such as those of Kashmir Śaivism and its non-dual metaphysics, in particular, are examined. Pervasive tantric practices and symbols, such as Kuṇḍalinī yoga and *yantras,* as well as the crucial roles of goddesses and women, are also introduced in this section.

Main topics covered

- The origins of Tantra
- Characteristic elements of Hindu Tantra
- Śaivism in Kashmir
- Non-dualistic tantric philosophy
- Kuṇḍalinī yoga
- The Left Hand Path
- Goddesses and women in Tantra
- Symbolism of tantric *mantras* and *yantras*

The origins of Tantra

Tantra derives from a wide constellation of beliefs and practices that mostly belonged to the non-Vedic religious traditions of the Indian subcontinent. Tantra may date back to the period of the Indus Valley Civilization which, together with the religions of chthonic tribes, form part of its source. Since the performance of Vedic rites were restricted to Brahmin males, who constituted a minority, the majority of the populace of the subcontinent (e.g. other *varṇas,* those outside the *varṇa* system, and women) certainly engaged in their own modes of religious practice. As orthodoxy opened itself to asceticism and *bhakti* through a progressive democratization, other beliefs and practices of these once marginalized groups began to bleed into the Sanskritic tradition. Earlier than the sixth or seventh centuries CE we have evidence of Buddhist texts that refer to themselves as Tantras. They distinguish themselves from the orthodox Sūtra tradition. Although Hindu Tantras do not appear until the ninth or tenth century, the content of the Buddhist Tantras appears to have Hindu, especially Śaiva, origins. Most of these were originally composed in Sanskrit, and many Buddhist Tantras have been preserved in Tibetan translations. Some groups of tantric texts are called Āgamas or Saṃhitās.

The Hindu Tantras are typically critical of Vedic tradition, which is portrayed as inferior or incomplete. The tantric revelations claim to reflect a more sophisticated understanding of Vedic teachings, or that these merely form the foundation for the higher tantric truths. Although orthodoxy initially rejected tantric teachings, by the eleventh century tantric practices had permeated the entire Hindu world (except for the most elite Vedic adherents). Although the language of tantric texts sets up a dichotomy with Vedic tradition, Tantra is not "different" from Hinduism, anymore than Vedism is "authentic" Hinduism.

The word *tantra* means "loom" or "organizational grid." This is reasonable because the Tantras are texts that attempt to weave a large array of seemingly disparate beliefs and practices into a meaningful scheme. Ritual practices, culled from techniques for healing, manipulation of the natural and supernatural worlds, self-empowerment, and self-transmutation form the core of tantric texts. It is therefore not unusual that the assistant who aids the chief ritualist in the performance of an elaborate rite, often merely by holding his finger at the proper place in the ritual manual, is known as the *tantradhāraka*. However, when a novice performs such rites, the *tantradhāraka* is his accomplished master. The master, like the novice, holds (*dhāra*) the tantric ritual manual for his student's benefit, but, in reality, knows and holds together (*dhāra*) all the threads (i.e. the entire organizational schema (*tantra*)) of the complex rite.

Tantra is an approach to the acquisition of religious "truth," grounded in practices (*cārya*). These practices may involve internal body–mind techniques (*sādhana*) or external ritual action (*kriyā*). Thus the tantric approach is not exclusively Hindu, for it has appealed to segments of most religious groups on the Indian subcontinent. There is also Buddhist and Jain tantrism, and, arguably, Christian and Jewish tantrism burgeoning in the West.

Characteristic elements of Hindu Tantra

The Hindu tantric texts consider themselves to be revealed teachings delivered by Śiva, Viṣṇu or Devī. Paralleling the Upaniṣadic dialogues between student and teacher, the Tantras are often framed as dialogues between God and Goddess, Śiva

Figure 13.1 An experienced Bengali ritualist performs an elaborate tantric *pūjā* assisted by a novice *tantradhāraka*

(or Viṣṇu) and Pārvatī (or Lakṣmī). She asks questions, and he replies. In Śākta Tantras, Śiva asks the questions and Devī provides the answers. The oft-depicted images of Śiva and Pārvatī seated beside each other, in which she is nestled up next to him, sometimes on his lap, evoke the setting of the teaching scenario of these tantric texts. The gods, who are creators of the cosmos, inquire of each other into the meaning of existence, which is an exploration of their own natures.

Hindu Tantra, although wide-ranging in its concerns, has some distinctive characteristics. It typically involves graded teachings passed from teachers (*guru*) to student practitioners (*sādhaka*) through secret initiations (*dīkṣā*). The ideology of secrecy is important since it provides a protective framework within which tantric practitioners may work without attracting undue criticism from orthodoxy. This is because Tantra typically strives for a holistic understanding of reality, requiring the *sādhaka* to transcend traditional boundaries of purity and pollution, or auspiciousness and inauspiciousness. This places tantric rites and attitudes in direct conflict with orthodox values. Another central concern in Tantra is the acquisition of supernormal powers (*siddhi*). Although it is not considered a tantric text, a substantial portion of Patañjali's *Yoga Sūtra* deals with the supernormal powers that are produced through yogic practice. These *siddhis* are regarded as validations of one's spiritual attainments, and enable certain tantrics to serve as magicians, diviners, exorcists, and healers. Highly accomplished tantrics are known as *siddhas*. However, such access to *siddhis* may cause non-tantrics to view tantric practitioners with fear and suspicion, as well as awe.

Tantra homologizes the human body to the cosmos, often seeing the individual as a microcosm that mirrors or even "contains" the Totality. Thus body–mind practices and the manipulation of matter and energy serve the purpose of fully realizing one's relationship to the Absolute. The Absolute is generally regarded as expressing itself through male and female principles (e.g. Śiva and Śakti), which are intrinsically present at various grades of manifestation in all things. Thus sexual representations, invoking the imagery of uniting these male and female polarities, are endemic in tantric literature, ritual, and symbolic art. The feminine component, in its aspects both as goddesses and women, figures significantly in Tantra, since it embodies the dynamic dimension of the polarity. The feminine is the power (*śakti*) through which the cosmos is brought into manifestation, and the energy through which the *sādhaka* may attain *siddhis* as well as liberation. Tantric body–mind practices involve mastery of sacred gestures (*mūdra*), elaborate visualizations of deities, the awakening of latent cosmic energies within the body (e.g. Kuṇḍalinī yoga), and may include fierce forms of asceticism (such as over-night meditations in cremation grounds) or unconventional rites (such as ritual sexual intercourse). Energy-matter manipulations often involve the production of sacred sonic vibrations (*mantra*), the application of sacred geometry in the construction of two-dimensional cosmographs (*yantra, maṇḍala*), or three-dimensional ones, such as temples (*maṇḍapa*), or divine images (*mūrti*). The techniques of invoking, worshipping, and dismissing divine presences in these forms (i.e. *pūjā*) are also integral to Tantra.

Śaivism in Kashmir

The ascendancy of Tantra into mainstream Brahminic religion is particularly interesting in the case of Śaivism in the Himalayan kingdom of Kashmir, now part of the North Indian state of Jammu and Kashmir. The beliefs and practices of the numerous Śaiva sects of the region began to be consolidated in the late ninth century CE. Those various sects embraced a common set of authoritative scriptures known as the Śaiva Āgamas. Outstanding mystic-thinkers emerged, who symbolically wove, on the loom of Tantra, philosophies extracted from this shared body of scriptural texts. However, while doing so, they simultaneously wrought their own compelling metaphysical systems. Two of the main traditions that emerged were the Śaiva Siddhānta and Trika Śaivism. Śaiva Siddhānta was a dualistic philosophy based on three fundamental realities: the Lord (*pati*), namely Śiva, the beast (*paśu*), namely the soul in bondage, and the noose (*pāśa*), namely the factors of bondage. Trika Śaivism, by contrast, was non-dualistic. Its greatest exponent was the sage Abhinavagupta (c. mid tenth to eleventh centuries CE) whose*Tantrāloka* (*Light on Tantra*) is one of the most important treatises of Tantric Hinduism.

Both systems adapted themselves to orthodox Brahminic values, but did so differently. Śaiva Siddhānta accepted Brahminic valorizations of purity and pollution, the *varṇa* system, and ritual worship by qualified Brahmin priests. It eventually faded from Kashmir but had spread to South India, where it was influenced by the *bhakti* traditions of the Śaiva poet-saints, the Nāyanārs, and still endures to the present day, particularly in the Śiva-worshipping temple traditions in Tamil Nadu. The non-dual Trika systems, however, allowed seemingly orthodox householders to participate in heterodox and transgressive practices within the confines of the ritual community's arena. They emphasized the attainment of liberative understanding through covertly practiced body–mind rites, over external, formal, and public, orthodox ritual practices. These non-dual systems suffered virtual extinction in the wake of Islam's ascendancy in Kashmir by the twelfth century, but the philosophical wing of the tradition appears to have endured among some families. However, they had influenced tantric practices in Nepal, Bengal, Kerala, and the South Indian Śrī Vidyā cult dedicated to the goddess Lalitā Tripurasundarī.

Non-dualistic tantric philosophy

According to the dominant metaphysics of Kashmir Śaivism, Ultimate Reality, although beyond conceptualization, is often called Parama-śiva (Supreme Śiva) or Parameśvara (Supreme Lord), whose nature is pure Consciousness. The philosophy is non-dualistic because Parama-śiva, the Absolute, is all there is. Abhinavagupta is credited with a simplified articulation of its essential teachings for his delicately-minded students in the *Bodhapañcadaśikā* (*Fifteen [Verses] on Consciousness*) (BPD 16). A crucial feature of the non-dualistic metaphysics presented in that text is the relationship between awakened consciousness and consciousness in bondage. Unlike dualistic systems, the soul (*paśu*) in bondage is not different from the Lord (*pati*). Since the Absolute is free from all limitations, it is free to limit itself. This limitation, or contraction, is the process of production of the multiform universe, with its variety of individual beings. The world (i.e. the creation, the universe) is made manifest through the power (*śakti*) of Śiva, which in the very instance of its manifestation generates the dualism of "the produced" and "the producer." This dualism is Śiva and Śakti, which are naturally never separate and which exist in every aspect of creation (BPD 3). Śiva, here, is not Parama-śiva, but correlates to Śakti. The entire creation emerges from Parama-śiva, as a reflection, out of the Absolute's unconditional freedom, sportive playfulness, and independence to act (BPD 6, 7). This emergence is fundamentally intended for the playful purpose of Self-recognition. Intrinsic to its limitation is the Absolute's concealment of itself from itself, through the power of Māyā, the obscuring potency of Śakti. Māyā conceals the Absolute through such agencies as: partitioning the whole (*kalā*), knowledge (*vidyā*), enchantment (*rāga*), time (*kāla*), and process (*niyati*). This leads to the manifestation of the world as it is known and experienced by most people.

Kashmir Śaivism typically accepts the *tattva* scheme found in Sāṅkhya metaphysics and Vedānta systems, but subordinates or "over-codes" them to various categories of the highest and most subtle manifestations of Supreme Consciousness belonging to its own scheme. Thus Sāṅkhya's scheme of Puruṣa and Prakṛti are not the ultimate realities, but gross manifestations emerging through Māyā's agency. Unlike Śaṅkara's Advaita Vedānta, where the manifestations of Māyā are not fully real, in this form of Trika Śaivism the world as emitted by the Absolute is real. Thus the philosophy is, albeit clumsily, sometimes labeled "realistic idealism." It is "idealistic" because the nature of the Absolute is expressed as Consciousness alone. It is "realistic" because the phenomenal world is not an illusion, but a manifestation of the Absolute. Even though reality may be misapprehended, this ignorance is also very much the activity of the Absolute, and thus all aspects of existence are "real" phenomena. There is no portion of phenomenal reality that is not a reflection of the Absolute, which is why when the Absolute is truly apprehended through any means or form, it is held to be recognized in its other forms of expression as well (BPD 8).

Figure 13.2 A stone image (*mūrti*) of Śiva's terrifying aspect as Bhairava (Bhaktapur, Nepal)

Until liberation (*mokṣa*), the world as experienced is *saṃsāra*, a partially understood or misunderstood reality, which can make existence appear terrifying. Perhaps this is why Parama-śiva, when spoken of in its totality of creation, preservation, destruction, concealment, and revelation, is known as Bhairava (The Terrifying). Bhairava is the bringer of terror, as well as the destroyer of all illusion. According to the teachings of non-dual Kashmir Śaivism, one may be able to attain liberation in this lifetime (*jīvanmukti*) directly through divine grace, or by the *guru*'s approach, or through the study of appropriate sacred texts. Liberation consists in knowing oneself as that Supreme Śiva, pure Consciousness, in the fullness of its manifestation, namely, the perennial vibratory pulsation between bondage and liberation, creation and destruction (BPD 12, 13). One has come to recognize oneself as Bhairava, who holds the trident that symbolizes the tripartite power (*śakti*) of will (*icchā*), action (*kriyā*), and knowledge (*jñāna*) (BPD 15). *Icchā-śakti* is the will to become limited as well as the will to be liberated from limitation; *kriyā-śakti* is the action that leads to the diversified creation, as well as the capacity to reintegrate the plurality; and *jñāna-śakti* is the transcendental knowledge of the oscillation of concealment and revelation in the endless play of the Absolute.

Kuṇḍalinī yoga

One the many spiritual practices linked with Tantra is Kuṇḍalinī yoga. It entails awakening a dormant energy that resides at the base of a key channel within the body. Hindu psycho-physiology envisions the body as being composed of numerous sheaths. Thus a subtle body exists vaguely superimposed on the visible physical body. This subtle body (*sūkṣma-sarīra*) contains tens, if not hundreds of thousands of pathways through which vital energy (*prāṇa*) flows. The three most important of these pathways (*nāḍī*) are the *suṣumnā*, the central channel, which is flanked by two other *nāḍīs*, the *iḍā* and the *piṅgalā*. These *nāḍīs* intersect each other at certain energy centers located along the *suṣumnā*. There are seven well-recognized energy centers or vortices (*cakra*). The lowest *cakra* is the *mūlādhāra* (root-support), located approximately at the perineum of the physical body. One might imagine that Śakti in its most limited state of manifestation resides, as if dormant, in the *mūlādhāra cakra*. It is sometimes likened to a coiled serpent. Through various purification and activation techniques derived from Haṭha yoga practice, the *kuṇḍalinī* energy is awakened and induced to move upward through the central channel, the *suṣumnā nāḍī*. As it does so, it opens the otherwise closed channel and activates the various energy vortices, or *cakras*, along its route. The activation of each of these *cakras* allows for the unrestricted flow of vital energy, or *prāṇa*, through the innumerable channels (*nāḍī*) that emanate from that *cakra*, into various parts of the subtle body. Each such *cakra* activation is believed to confer various powers on the practitioner.

To induce the flow of *kuṇḍalinī* into the various *cakras*, complex meditative visualizations may be performed. Each *cakra* is visualized within its appropriate location as a lotus of a certain color, with a particular number of petals, associated with a particular deity, a mantric seed syllable (*bīja*), an element, a cosmogram (*yantra*), and so on. The second *cakra* encountered by the *kuṇḍalinī* energy as it leaves the root-support is the *svādhiṣṭhāna* (one's own place), approximately located at the genitals. It is an important *cakra* because it activates the passions, especially sexual desire. In many tantric formulations, it is the energy of desire that stokes both the Absolute's impulse for creation and its impulse for annihilation or liberation. Through Kuṇḍalinī yoga, one is inverting the process of creation, enfolding Śakti's energetic manifestations progressively into more subtle vibratory states. The *manipūra* (jewel city) *cakra* is located just below the navel. These three lower *cakras* are sometimes identified with the lower levels of material manifestation, namely the bodily functions, sensual urges, and the five senses, while the next three are regarded as corresponding to higher, more subtle manifestations of divine power, namely the inner faculties of thought, and the powers of discrimination. The *anāhata* (unstruck) is at the heart. The *viśuddha* (absolutely pure) is approximately at the throat. The *ājñā* (command) *cakra* is located in the middle of the forehead, typically at the site of the "third" or "wisdom eye." Its activation implicitly links it with the acquisition of a wide variety of supernormal psychic powers.

As *kuṇḍalinī* moves upward, practitioners are expected to gain more understanding of their true nature. Finally, the *kuṇḍalinī śakti* is induced to attain its final abode when it reaches the *sahasrāra* (thousand-fold) *cakra*, envisioned as a thousand-petalled lotus pointing downward, and located approximately at the crown of the head. Here Śiva is said to reside. In the sexual language and symbolism of Tantra, the goddess Kuṇḍalinī is sometimes described as uniting with Śiva in a sort of cosmic erotic union, resulting in an unsurpassable, unending bliss. A nectar of immortality (*amṛta*), generated by their sexual union, is said to flow downward, its taste transforming the spiritual practitioner for ever. Attainment of this state is *mokṣa*.

Kuṇḍalinī yoga illustrates the tantric homology drawn between the microcosm of the spiritual practitioner's (*sādhaka*) body, and the macrocosm. The divine energy, awakened through psycho-physical techniques within one's being, effectively reverses the process through which the entire creation becomes manifest. *Mantra* sounds, *maṇḍala* constructions, meditative visualizations, and so on, are meshed together in the service of the spiritual goal of Self-realization. However, the tantric concern with the acquisition of supernormal powers is also evident. The sexual symbolism evident in Tantra is also vivid, as is the metaphysics of reintegration through the union of Śiva and Śakti.

The Left Hand Path

Tantra's permeation into virtually all aspects of Hinduism reflects its malleability and adaptability. However, its most unconventional practices were sometimes said to be only suited for those with truly "heroic" or "divine" temperaments. While others modified the degree of their engagement with the "marginalized" dimensions of reality, heroes (*vīra*) were expected to embrace these in their efforts to unite with the Absolute. Thus Tantra developed a distinction between its conventional configurations, known as the Right Hand Path, and its transgressive approaches, referred to as the Left Hand Path (*vāmamarga*). Actual utilization of certain substances/practices, considered "impure" by orthodoxy, is the mark of the Left Hand Tantra. These substances were referred to as the "five Ms" (*pañca-makāra*), because their Sanskrit terms begin with the letter "m." Although there are textual references to them, the actual nature of the substances and the methods of their use are still somewhat unclear. They are: *māṃsa* (flesh), *matsya* (fish), *madya* (liquor), *mudrā* (parched grain, sacred gestures or female sexual partner), and *maithuna* (sexual union).

Although most persons with Western value systems may not fully appreciate the transgressive nature of these items, when one considers the strict conventions of purity and pollution found among orthodox Brahmins, the "five Ms" are startlingly transgressive. The food substances are tamasic (impure) or rajasic (passion inducing), and not sattvic (pure). Furthermore, certain tantric texts uplifted such utterly anti-orthodox forms of *maithuna* as union with a woman who was not one's wife, who belonged to the lowest classes, and who might even be menstruating at the time. By ritually embracing the polluted or "left-hand" aspects of life, tantrics sought to move beyond the dualisms that characterize spiritual ignorance and bondage. The Absolute, the source of all creation, was freed from such distinctions, and it was therefore incumbent on the tantric practitioner to embody the non-dual nature of the divine. Abhinavagupta, the renowned exponent of tantra, called the use of meat, intoxicants, and coitus, genuine spirituality (*brahmacarya*). Right Hand Tantrics, by contrast, may acknowledge these rites, but participate in them with visualizations or ritual substitutions, such as drinking milk instead of liquor. Many were critical of Left Hand Tantra, which when abused or misunderstood, appeared to be merely promoting a lifestyle of sensual indulgence and licentiousness in the guise of religion.

Goddesses and women in Tantra

Goddesses and women play a vital role in Tantra. Since Śakti is the expression of the Absolute, the means of its manifestation, and the means of its transcendence, a wide variety of goddesses as various aspects of Śakti are the focus of tantric worship. In many forms of Tantra, particularly those designated as Śākta Tantra, the Great Goddess is identified as the Supreme Reality. She is Ādi-Śakti (Primal Power), or Parama Śakti (Supreme Śakti). Every woman, regardless of her caste, embodies the feminine principle, and thus women are the objects of worship. They are each goddesses. For male tantrics, it was often regarded as indispensable to have the assistance of a female partner, whose *śakti* empowered his own spiritual progress. "Without Śakti, Śiva is a corpse" is an oft-cited expression with many shades of meaning in Tantra. It indicates the crucial role that women play in vitalizing the efforts of the male tantric practitioner. Ideally, the female tantric practitioner strives to understand her own divinity as a manifestation of the supreme feminine principle, just as the male strives to understand his divine nature. They respectively become Pārvatī and Śiva, or Lakṣmī and Viṣṇu. And through their union, each may transcend their gendered identities and come to know themselves as the Absolute.

Although Tantra may uplift women in its principles, it is difficult to know to what degree their actual lives were transformed during the period when Tantra was flourishing in the Hindu world. The Dharma Śāstras certainly portrayed women as inferior to men, and those texts articulated and reinforced the orthodox attitude. Tantric texts certainly voice something different. Nevertheless, women from the lower classes may have been "exploited" for the benefit of male tantric practitioners. However, it is also possible that women were actually empowered by Tantra, choosing to participate in its belief systems and practices because it provided them with honorable roles and status. Certain female tantrics were, indeed, credited with important achievements, and were sought out for initiations by male adepts.

Symbolism of tantric mantras *and* yantras

Tantric symbolism can be enigmatic. Therefore, tantric rites and teachings often need the aid of a qualified mentor (*guru*) to enable students to understand the significance of its symbols. One pervasive feature of Tantra is its use of sacred diagrams known as *yantras* or *maṇḍalas*. The term *maṇḍala* (Sphere [of Influence]) is more frequently encountered in tantric Buddhism, which developed particularly complex designs. *Yantras* are "tools" or "instruments" designed to hold fast or embody a divine power. *Yantras* may be designs drawn on paper, fashioned out of stone or metal, or rendered in other media. They may be visualized three-dimensionally. Both temples (*maṇḍapa*) and anthropomorphic images (*mūrti*) are elaborations upon the more rudimentary forms expressed in a *yantra*. However, this does not mean that the *yantra*

Figure 13.3 A copper *yantra* embedded in a temple floor, strewn with flower petals, rice and other offerings (Nepal)

is an inferior expression of divinity. If anything it may be superior. In many tantric temples, the "true" icon of the deity is a *yantra*, embedded within the temple's inner sanctum, invisible and inaccessible to all. The image (*mūrti*) viewed by most people, and ministered to by the chief priest, is often the secondary image. One might also understand the entire temple to be a manifest form of the divinity, a yantric tool that establishes the deity in a particular location for the benefit of the devotees.

A *yantra* typically consists of a central point known as a *bindu*. This represents the movement of the transcendent into the sphere of manifestation. It is undifferentiated. Occasionally, the seed syllable (*bīja mantra*) of the deity, whose *yantra* it is, might be inscribed below the *bindu*. Just as the seed syllable, if voiced, may "sprout" into more elaborate articulations of the nature of the deity through the recitation of the deity's name, or names, or through meditative visualization verses (*dhyāna śloka*) articulating the deity's form, the *bindu* expands, multiplies, and divides. An ascending triangle is often the sign (*liṅga*) to express the male principle, while a descending triangle encapsulates the female principle (*yoni*). Certain goddess *yantras*, such as the Kālī Yantra are often made up exclusively of descending triangles. The well-known Śrī Yantra is made up of five descending and four ascending triangles intersecting with each other in a particular configuration, mostly understood as the union of male and female principles. The entire configuration is surrounded by a circle from which lotus petals emerge. Just as a drop of water falls onto the surface of a pond, causing circular ripples that emanate outward, the petals could be understood as the outward radiation of creation, the blossoming of the sprouted seed (*bīja*). The Śrī Yantra has two such circles with eight and sixteen petals respectively. The entire yantric diagram may be surrounded by a square, perforated by "gates" that resemble entryways to a city. Thus the *yantra* is an abode of a deity.

The ritual construction of a *yantra*, and, by extension, of more elaborate expressions such as temples and *mūrtis*, are means of bringing a deity into manifestation and establishing it in a definable space. Sacred sound intersects with sacred geometry as the adept utters the *mantras* necessary to enliven the divine presence in the *yantra*. In this fashion a temple is consecrated, and in *mūrti* worship, the adept "brings the

Key points in this chapter

- Tantra derives mostly from the non-Vedic religious traditions of the Indian subcontinent, and may date back to the period of the Indus Valley Civilization.
- Buddhist Tantras appear to have Hindu, especially Śaiva, origins.
- Hindu Tantras are typically critical of Vedic tradition, but by the eleventh century tantric practices had permeated most of the Hindu world.
- Tantras attempt to weave seemingly disparate beliefs and practices into a meaningful scheme.
- Tantra is an approach to the acquisition of religious "truth," grounded in practices (*cārya*), and homologizes the human body to the cosmos.
- Śaiva Siddhānta and Trika Śaivism emerge from Kashmir Śaivism.
- Kashmir Śaivism incorporates the *tattva* schemes of Sāṅkhya and Vedānta systems, and subordinates these within its own framework.
- One of the many spiritual practices linked with tantra is Kuṇḍalinī yoga.
- Tantra distinguishes between the Right Hand Path and the Left Hand Path (*vāmamarga*).
- Tantra seeks to transcend the dualisms that characterize spiritual ignorance and bondage.
- Goddesses and women play a vital role in tantra.
- A *guru* is often required by students in order to understand tantric symbolism.

image to life." In the worship rites of the *yantra,* the adept then reverses the process, crossing the threshold into the divine abode, and through a spiral movement of worship first focused on the lotus petals (each of which is sometimes associated with other subsidiary deities), gradually approaches the center. Devotees follow a similar process in their circumambulatory approach to the inner sanctum of a temple.

Discussion questions

1. Why does Tantra strive to transcend traditional boundaries of purity and pollution, auspiciousness and inauspiciousness, and how is this viewed within the orthodox tradition?
2. Why do you think the ideology of secrecy is so important to the tradition of Tantra, and do you think this ideology is helpful or a hindrance to the tradition?
3. For what reasons do you think Kashmir Śaivism accepts the *tattva* scheme found in Sāṅkhya and Vedānta systems, and yet subordinates them to their own categories? Why accept the *tattva* scheme at all?
4. What is a *yantra,* and why is it important to Tantra?
5. How did Tantra originate, and what are some of the key characteristics of this tradition?
6. What is Kuṇḍalinī yoga, and how does it relate to the tantric tradition?
7. Explain the metaphysics of non-dual Kashmir Śaivism.

Further reading

General studies on Tantra

Banerji, S. C. (1977) *Tantra in Bengal: A Study of Its Origin, Development and Influence.* Calcutta: Naya Prokash.

— (1992) *New Light on Tantra.* Calcutta: Puthi Pustak.

Basu, M. (1986) *Fundamentals of the Philosophy of Tantras.* Calcutta: Mira Basu.

Bharati, Agehananda (L. Fischer) (1965) *The Tantric Tradition.* London: Rider and Company.

Bhattacharya, B. (1988) *The World of Tantra.* New Delhi: Munshiram Mahoharlal.

Bhattacharyya, N. N. (1982) *History of the Tantric Religion.* Delhi: Manohar.

Bose, D. N. (1956) *Tantras: Their Philosophy and Occult Secrets.* Calcutta: Oriental Publishing Co.

Chakravarti, C. (1963) *Tantras: Studies on Their Religion and Literature.* Calcutta: Punthi Pustak.

Chattopadhyaya, S. (1978) *Reflections on the Tantras.* Delhi: Motilal Banarsidass.

Feuerstein, Georg (1998) *Tantra: The Path of Ecstasy.* Boston, MA: Shambala.

Goudriaan, T., and S. Gupta (1981) *Hindu Tantric and Śākta Literature*. History of Indian Literature 2, fasc. 2. Wiesbaden: Otto Harrassowitz.
Günther, H. V. (1976) *Yuganādha: The Tantric View of Life*. Reprint. Boulder, CO: Shambala.
Gupta, S., D. J. Hoens, and T. Goudriaan (1979) *Hindu Tantrism*. Handbuch der Orientalistik. B. Spuler (gen. ed.). Leiden: Brill.
Nagaswamy, R. (1982) *Tantric Cult of South India*. Delhi: Agam Kala Prakashan.
Strickmann, M. (ed.) (1981) *Tantric and Taoist Studies in Honor of R. A. Stein*. Brussels: Institut Belge des Hautes Édudes Chinoises.
Urban, Hugh B. (2003) *Tantra: Sex, Secrecy, Politics, and Power in the Study of Religion*. Berkeley, CA: University of California Press.
White, David Gordon (ed.) (2000) *Tantra in Practice*. Princeton, NJ: Princeton University Press.
— (2003) *Kiss of the Yoginī*. Chicago, IL: University of Chicago Press.
Woodroffe, John (Arthur Avalon) (1960) *Principles of Tantra*. Madras: Ganesh & Co.
— (1963) *Introduction to Tantra Śāstra*. Madras: Ganesh & Co.
— (1963) *Mahānirvāṇatantra: The Great Liberation*. Madras: Ganesh & Co.

On Kashmir Śaivism

Alper, H. P. "Śiva and the Ubiquity of Consciousness," *Journal of Indian Philosophy* (1976): pp. 345–407.
Chetananda, Swami (1983) *Dynamic Stillness*, Vol 1. *The Practice of Trika Yoga*. Cambridge, MA: Rudra Press.
— (1991) *Dynamic Stillness*, Vol 2. *The Fulfillment of Trika Yoga*. Cambridge, MA: Rudra Press.
Dyczkowski, M. S. G. (1987) *The Doctrine of Vibration*. Albany, NY: State University of New York Press.
— (1988) *The Canon of the Śaivāgama and the Kubjikā Tantras of the Western Kaula Tradition*. Albany, NY: State University of New York Press.
— (1992) *The Stanzas on Vibration*. Albany, NY: State University of New York Press.
Flood, Gavin D. (1993) *Body and Cosmology in Kashmir Śaivism*. San Francisco, CA: Mellen Research University Press.
Gnoli, R. (1956) *The Aesthetic Experience according to Abhinavagupta*. Rome: Is MEO.
Hughes, John (1994) *Self-Realization in Kashmir Shaivism: The Oral Teachings of Swami Laksmanjoo*. Albany, NY: State University of New York Press.
Lakshman Jee, Swami (1988) *Kashmir Śaivism: The Secret Supreme*. Albany, NY: Universal Śaiva Trust.

Muller-Ortega, Paul (1989) *The Triadic Heart of Śiva: Kaula Tantrism of Abhinavagupta in the Non-Dual Shaivism of Kashmir.* Albany, NY: State University of New York Press.

Pandey, K. C. (1963) *Abhinavagupta: An Historical and Philosophical Study.* Varanasi: Chowkhamba.

Rastogi, N. (1981) *Krama Tantricism of Kashmir: Historical and General Sources.* Vol. I. Delhi: Motilal Banarsidass.

Sanderson, Alexis (1988) "Saivism and the Tantric Traditions." In S. Sutherland *et al.* (eds) *The World's Religions.* London: Routledge, pp. 660–704.

Sensharma, Deba Brata (1990) *The Philosophy of Sādhanā, with Special Reference to the Trika Philosophy of Kashmir.* Albany, NY: State University of New York Press.

Singh, Jaideva (1979) *Śiva Sūtras: The Yoga of Supreme Identity.* Delhi: Motilal Banarsidass.

— (1980) *Spanda-Kārikās: The Divine Creative Pulsation.* Delhi: Motilal Banarsidass.

— (1991) *The Yoga of Delight, Wonder, and Astonishment.* Albany, NY: State University of New York Press.

— (1992) *The Yoga of Vibration and Divine Pulsation.* Albany, NY: State University of New York Press.

— (1998) (ed. and trans.) *Pratyābhijñādṛdayam: The Secret of Self-Recognition.*. Delhi: Motilal Banarsidass.

Singh, Jaideva, Swami Lakshmanjee, and Bettina Bäumer (1988) *Abhinavagupta, Parātrītriśikā-Vivarana: The Secret of Tantric Mysticism.* Delhi: Motilal Banarsidass.

On Śākta tantrism

Brooks, D. R. (1992) *Auspicious Wisdom: The Texts and Traditions of Śrīvidyā Śākta Tantrism in South India.* Albany, NY: State University of New York Press.

Gupta, Sanjukta (trans.) (1972) *Lakshmi Tantra: A Pañcarātra Text.* Leiden: E. J. Brill.

Kinsley, David (1997) *Tantric Visions of the Divine Feminine: The Ten Mahāvidyās.* Berkeley, CA: University of California Press.

Tigunait, Rajmani (1998) *Śaktism: The Power in Tantra.* Honesdale, PA: The Himalayan International Institute.

Van Lysebeth, André (1995) *Tantra: The Cult of the Feminine.* York Beach, ME: Samuel Weiser.

On Kuṇḍalinī, yantra, tantric art, practices, and powers

Khanna, Madhu (1979) *Yantra: The Tantric Symbol of Cosmic Unity*. London: Thames and Hudson.

Krishna, Gopi (1975) *The Awakening of Kuṇḍalinī*. New York: E. P. Dutton.

Mookerjee, Ajit (1971) *Tantra Art: Its Philosophy and Physics*. Basel: Ravi Kumar.

Mookerjee, A., and M. Khanna (1977) *The Tantric Way: Art-Science-Ritual*. London: Thames & Hudson.

Potte, P. H. (1966) *Yoga and Yantra: Their Interrelation and Their Significance for Indian Archeology*. The Hague: E. J. Brill.

Rao, S. K. R. (1982) *Śrī-Cakra: Its Yantra, Mantra and Tantra*. Bangalore: Kalpatharu Research Academy.

— (1988) *The Yantras*. Delhi: Sri Satguru.

Rawson, Philip (1973) *Tantra: The Indian Cult of Ecstasy*. New York: Avon Books.

— (1978) *The Art of Tantra*. London: Thames and Hudson.

Silburn, Lilian (1998) *Kuṇḍalinī: Energy from the Depths*. Albany, NY: State University of New York Press.

Svoboda, Robert E. (1986) *Aghora: At the Left Hand of God*. Albuquerque, NM: Brotherhood of Life.

White, David Gordon (1996) *The Alchemical Body: Siddha Traditions in Medieval India*. Chicago,IL: University of Chicago Press.

Woodroffe, John (1973) *The Serpent Power*. Madras. Ganesh & Co.

Zvelebil, Kamil V. (1996) *The Siddha Quest for Immortality*. Oxford: Mandrake.

14 *Reform and revitalization*

In this chapter

The arrival of Islam and Christianity through colonization had significant effects on Hinduism. After brief historical surveys of these processes within Hindu India, Hinduism's various responses are illustrated through the use of case studies. Hinduism itself underwent numerous changes, either by reforming practices that were deemed unacceptable or by redefining itself through attempts to return to an idealized past. New religious approaches emerged, some of which extracted common features perceived within Islam, Christianity, and Hinduism. Hinduism was also co-opted into political causes, at first in defense against the ideological onslaught of colonizing values, and later in efforts to secure national independence. In effect, despite the pressures that Hinduism faced from colonial rule for over half a millennia, its creative transformations and reforms provided it with a valuable revitalization.

Main topics covered

- Some early critiques of Hinduism and its responses
- Islam in India (a brief history)
- Hinduism under Islam
- Religious syncretism (e.g. *bhakti*, Sufism, Tantra) in North India
- The British in India (a brief history)
- Hindu responses to Christianity
- Related developments
- Hinduism in universalistic religion
- Hinduism and humanism
- Hinduism and politics

Some early critiques of Hinduism and its responses

The story of Hinduism reveals its success at creatively modifying itself through adaptive responses to internal and external forces. It is worth being reminded that Hinduism is a relatively "new" catchall term that refers to both the rich assortment of practices and beliefs of various peoples both on the Indian subcontinent and the worldwide diaspora. So the pre-Islamic and pre-British critiques of Hinduism that are discussed here were to a certain extent "internal" ones. They were the voices of various philosophical perspectives and sectarian traditions in debate with each other, each attempting to assert what it deemed to be the truth about the human condition, and how one should live meaningfully in accord with it.

The Buddhist and Jain *darśanas,* for instance, were critical of Brahminic standpoints that only Brahmin males were entitled to perform religious rituals and study religious teachings. These religious philosophies also criticized the revelatory authority granted to the Vedas. Buddhism attempted to redefine a true "Brahmin" or "Āryan" as one who embodied an "enlightened" life-style and not merely one born into the Brahmin *varṇa.* It encouraged renunciation at any age for men and women. Both Buddhism and Jainism were critical of animal sacrifice as necessary dimensions of religious ritual.

The response from orthodox Brahminism to these critiques was varied. Vaiṣṇavism, in particular, began to espouse non-violence and progressively promoted vegetarianism. Inclusion of the Buddha into certain schemes of Viṣṇu's *avatāras* reveals trends towards incorporating Buddhism within the Vaiṣṇava fold. Brahminic orthodoxy confronted the call to renunciation by weaving it into the scheme of life stages, valorizing both the householder's way of life and the renouncer's. Ultimately, however, the critiques of Buddhism and Jainism proved too incompatible with the vested interests of orthodoxy and they were designated as heterodox *darśanas.*

The pressure for inclusion from disenfranchised groups, such as women, the lower classes, and the classless was accommodated in the *bhakti*-based traditions. Through *bhakti* everyone could envision the divine as they desired, and worship the divine in their own way. However, orthodoxy responded by encouraging the use of appropriate rituals conducted by Brahmin priests as an elite expression of devotion. *Bhakti,* by promoting the householder's way of life as an appropriate pathway to liberation, served the interests of the orthoprax priesthood, whose livelihood depended on the structures and rites of social life. Tantra voiced a critique of religious elitism and a social reality that was oppressive in its restrictions. Orthodoxy responded by incorporating certain aspects of Tantra into its practices, such as enhancing the place of goddesses within the pantheon of worship. It allowed, within the secret confines of particular communities, for periodic excursions in ritual contexts into the "unrestricted," as a sort of pressure valve to release the tensions of the social order. Festivals such as Holi, in which caste restrictions are temporarily annulled in an anarchic and sensually charged atmosphere, are visible manifestations of such adaptations. Narrative traditions, such as the Epics and the Purāṇas, as well as plays and folk theatrical performances, allowed individuals to experience, vicariously, the antinomian lives of gods and goddesses, demons and spirits, and men and women who either followed tradition or broke with it. They offered portrayals of the Brahmin priest as buffoon, only interested in getting invitations to rituals so that he might gorge himself on food, of tantric practitioners as womanizing drunks, and of gods who seduce and women who are seduced. While these media offer certain critiques of the religious order, and may thus encourage reform, they also function cathartically, allowing for attenuated or periodic expressions of criticism and not necessarily much else.

Islam in India (a brief history)

On the eve of India's colonization there were already social, economic, and political changes afoot on the subcontinent that were catalyzed by the arrival of foreign rulers. The Umayyad Islamic Caliphate, whose capital was Damascus, had expanded to establish a kingdom in the lower Indus River valley as early as 711 BCE. These were Arabic-speaking Muslims, many of whom also traded along India's Malabar coast. However, Islam's major push into the subcontinent began with the Turkish ruler Mahmud of Ghazni, who had his Afghan armies move into northwest India. By the time of his assassination in 1206, he had established a Turko-Afghan state bordering on Delhi. His successor, Qutb u'd-din Aibak, conquered Delhi, making it his capital, and became the first in a series of Delhi Sultans, Turko-Afghan rulers whose empire eventually stretched from the Punjab to Bengal.

It may be misleading to characterize the region of this empire as under "Muslim" or "Islamic" rule, because the ruling styles of the Hindu and Muslim kingdoms of these states were fairly similar. Furthermore, it conveys the sense that obligatory mass conversions to Islam had occurred, which current historical analyses reject. From studies in regions where Islamic populations grew, such as western Punjab and Bengal, conversion was often driven by desires for upward mobility through intermarriage, and by the teachings of charismatic religious leaders. Historians also reject a prevailing popular view of systematic wholesale destruction of non-Muslim holy places, such as Buddhist monasteries and Hindu temples. While some such places were definitely sacked for their wealth, and many religious centers were destroyed by zealous Muslim rulers, such as Firuz Tughluq (fourteenth century CE), Islam and non-Islamic spiritual and philosophical life generally coexisted and interacted peacefully. An extremely influential mode of Islamic religion bequeathed to North India during the Delhi Sultanate was Sufism. Sufi religious orders, such as the Chishti and Naqshbandi, prospered in the north, as did the Hindu *bhakti* traditions, which mutually influenced each other.

In 1526, Babar, a descendent of Timur (Tamerlane), overthrew the Delhi-based kingdom and became the first of the Mughal (i.e. Mongol, since Timur was a descendent of Genghis Khan) rulers of India. Babar's rule lasted for only four years, but he was succeeded by a series of Mughal rulers, such as Akbar and Shah Jahan, who left indelible imprints on Indian civil governance and architecture. Akbar, who inherited the throne when he was only fourteen, is remembered for his broad religious interests. He patronized the construction of Hindu temples, had the Hindu Epics translated into Persian, the language of the ruling elite during the Delhi Sultanate and the Mughal Empire, and abolished the special taxes levied on non-Muslims. Shah Jahan constructed the Taj Mahal, a mausoleum for his wife, Mumtaz, which in design and execution was an unparalleled expression of imperial majesty capable of rendering a divine paradise on earth. By the sixteenth century, with the exception of the Hindu empire of Vijayanagara in the south and a few Rajput kingdoms, India mainly had Muslim rulers. Of course, most of these rulers had Hindu viceroys, generals, and so on. Shah Jahan's successor, Aurangzeb, was far less pluralistic than his predecessors. He revived the tax on non-Muslims and destroyed Hindu temples in Mathurā, Banāras, and Rajasthan. His rule was plagued by insurgencies, particularly those of the Marathas in the south, lead by Shivaji Bhonsle (1630–1680).

Certain *zamīndārs*, who were local regional landlords, lineage heads, and chieftains, who had been granted political authority and who grew wealthy during Mughal rule, began to consolidate their power and build armies. Princely states that served as vassals to the Mughals also began to challenge imperial authority. These were not particularly unified Hindu rebellions against Muslim rulership, but regional quests for independence and power. Mughal power continued to decline as western colonialism spread to India. In 1857, the last of the emperors, Bahadur Shah Zafar, was arrested and imprisoned, bringing an end to Mughal rule and initiating a period of British hegemony until Indian Independence in 1947.

Hinduism under Islam

Since Islam is grounded in affirming its creed that Allah is the only god, whose message is conveyed by Muhammad in the *Qur'ān*, there were obvious confrontations with the religious beliefs of the people of the Indian subcontinent. The Persian speakers of the Delhi Sultanate had initially used the term "Hindu" to designate the people of India, but by the fourteenth century it had begun to be applied to all non-Muslims in India. Thus "Hindu" began to be used as both a socio-cultural category for the residents of the region, and as a religious category for those who did not follow Islam, so that "Hindu" is a default category for an assemblage of religious traditions. The assemblage was further narrowed as the British later extracted Buddhists, Jains, Parsis, Jews, Sikhs, and any other group with a well characterized religious label from being designated as "Hindus." Therefore, the religious beliefs and practices of "Hindus" are characteristically diverse, since they do not derive from teachings of a single founder, or base themselves on a unique revelation articulated in a particular scripture, or adhere to an authoritative theology that is supervised by an acknowledged body of official interpreters. It is this characteristic variety that was particularly problematic to Islamic theology.

The Hindu tolerance of innumerable conceptions of and approaches to God, and its acceptance of limitless creative expressions for the forms of God are particularly at odds with Muslim beliefs. Islam is a dualistic and theistic religious system, and although Hinduism accepts such conceptions, it also includes non-dualistic and non-theistic formulations of reality. Islamic teachings forbid the use of human or animal imagery in religious art. Hindu iconographic depictions of anthropomorphic deities, and even animal deities, such as Nandi, Hanumān, and Gaṇeśa, not to mention tantric erotic imagery on temples were all little short of abominations to most Islamic purists. The recent destruction of the megalithic Buddha statues in Bamiyan, Afghanistan is perhaps illustrative of such Islamic attitudes. The statues had endured for centuries under moderate Islamic regimes. However, although they were no longer objects of worship, the giant statues were destroyed on religious principles by the Taliban rulers in accord with their interpretations of Islamic teachings. From similar attitudes, Hindu icons were destroyed or defaced. Temple images often had their noses smashed, or limbs shattered, rendering them unworthy of worship.

Islam also promotes a spiritual egalitarianism that conflicted with the Hindu caste system. In reality, however, Muslim states maintained various forms of hierarchy between men and women, socio-economic groups and so on. It was initially thought that lower-caste Hindus had converted to Islam in large numbers in order to escape from the oppressive hierarchy of the caste system. But it appears that the largest number of converts to Islam occurred in regions where Buddhism had flourished, such as Western Punjab and Bengal, and not where Hindu orthodoxy was most vibrant. However, this could also indicate the resilience of Brahminic hegemony. While socio-political and religious agendas impede scholarly efforts to articulate the processes of Hindu-Muslim interaction effectively, it is evident that there were grave incompatibilities between Islam and Hinduism. Hindus began to regard Muslims almost like a separate caste, and thus disapproved of intermarriage.

Religious syncretism (e.g. bhakti, *Sufism, Tantra) in North India*

New articulations of religion began to appear in North India as Muslims and Hindus interacted with each other. It had been erroneously postulated that the *bhakti* traditions of India emerged as the result of Muslim or Christian influences. *Bhakti*, as prefigured in the *Śvetāśvatara Upaniṣad* and articulated in the *Bhagavad Gītā*, pre-date the rise of Christianity. The South Indian *bhakti* poets (i.e. the Ālvārs and Nāyanārs) were producing their work before the arrival of Muhammad. As India began to fall under the reign of Muslim rulers, Hindu vassals began to mimic the life-styles of the ruling elites. As a result, sexual conservatism, the seclusion of women, drastic interventions to prevent intermarriage, and so on, were bolstered among these groups. However, Hindus who had converted to Islam fused their own beliefs and cultural values with their newly adopted religion. Many strove to recognize a fundamental unity between their great gods and Allah.

Illustrative of liberal Muslim approaches, the Mughal emperor Akbar attempted to establish a new universal religion, known as the "divine faith," which syncretized the teachings of many of the religions in his empire. Muslim mystics, known as Sufis, drew from the passionate sentiments of Hindu *bhakti* poets and from the rigorous ascetic practices of Hindu *yogis*, while influencing both these strands with their own approaches. However, backlashes from orthodox Muslim leaders also led to reversals and efforts to restore the original purity of Islam in the latter centuries of Mughal rule.

Case study: Kabīr

Kabīr was born in Banāras at the beginning of the fifteenth century into a weaver *jāti*. Although members of his caste had recently converted to Islam, he was probably influenced by meditative and devotional teachings learned from a Hindu *guru*. Although regarded by his followers as illiterate, he composed poetry of startling power, emphasizing the value of such oral teachings by a master that might lead one to a spontaneous (*sahaja*) awakening to Truth. He advocated use of the *mantra* Rāma, not so much in reference to Viṣṇu or his *avatāra*, but as a meditative focus leading to God-realization. Although he enraged both Hindu and Muslim during his life, since his death both religions have attempted to claim him as their own. Many hundred of his verses are included in the Sikh sacred scripture. Interestingly, Kabīr promoted no particular religion, and criticized the foolishness found among religious believers in all traditions. He also encouraged independence in the spiritual path, not desiring to create a tradition centered on following him blindly. One of his poems runs something like this:

> Oh seeker, where are all you looking for me?
> I am right with you.
> I am not to be found in mosques, temples, the Ka'bah, or Kailāsa,
> Nor am I found through rituals, prayers, austerities, or dispassion.
> If you just look with sincerity, you will see me in an instant:
>   this very instant!
> Kabīr says: "Holy one! Know that the Lord is the essence of breath itself."

Case study: the Bauls

It is quite likely that tantric practices in Hinduism, which were flourishing in India from the ninth century CE, were forced into greater secrecy with the arrival of Islam. Whatever the complex factors may have been that fuelled its decline throughout North India, in Bengal, Tantra, which appears to have flourished during the Pala Dynasty (eighth to twelfth centuries, CE), seems to have receded into the underground until the sixteenth century, when it experienced a revival. Certain tantric traditions, such as the Sahaja or Sahajiya ("Congenital" or "Coexisting") movement, which was an amalgam of Śākta, Śaiva, and Vaiṣṇava devotionalism, with philosophical notions and meditative practices drawn from Buddhism and the yogic Nāth traditions, endured throughout these centuries of decline. They reflect syncretic and synthetic processes at work.

The Bauls are groups on the margins of Bengali society, who are characterized by their mendicant life-style and music. Their groups include both male and female practitioners, and their style of worship may be characterized as a sort of tantric Sahajiya Vaiṣṇavism. To the Bauls, "*sahaja*" is the Divine Beloved, who resides intrinsically (i.e. congenitally) within a "person of the heart." To merge with this inner Self is their goal. The Bauls' emphasis on dancing and singing, as outpourings of the heart, suggests influences from Bengali Vaiṣṇava and Sufi mystical traditions. Bauls view the entire creation as a visible expression of God's love, and human beings are the culmination of that creation. In one who has become a "person of the heart," God and human being are perfectly united. The mystery of the Infinite expressing itself through the finitude of human existence is a favorite theme in Baul songs. Bauls also use the symbol of a mysterious divine bird whose occasional appearance and sweetness of song thrusts the lover into a realization of his relationship with the Beloved.

Case study: Guru Nanak

Nanak (1469–1539) was born in the Punjab, and became the married father of two sons. However, he had a religious temperament which gravitated more towards devotional singing than scholarly study. After a mystical experience near the age of thirty, he gave up his material possessions, and responded to a calling to teach about his realization, proclaiming "There is no Hindu; there is no Muslim." Versions of his life story indicate that he traveled extensively through India, eastward via Banāras to Assam, south to Tamil Nadu and Sri Lanka, and westward through Persia to Baghdad, even to Mecca and its Ka'bah. He eventually returned to the Punjab and gathered a group of disciples who meditated and sang devotional songs together. Before his death, Nanak appointed a successor, which led to a lineage of ten esteemed teachers, given the title "Guru." Nanak is regarded as the first of these Gurus, and the founder of the Sikh ("Disciple") religion. Today, Sikhs constitute about twenty million people worldwide.

Although Sikhism has developed its own religious rituals and traditions, Nanak was highly critical of rituals. His teachings are evident in the over nine hundred poems attributed to him and gathered in the *Guru Granth Sahib* (*Honorable Book of the Teachers*). During his travels, Nanak is reputed to have met Kabīr, some of whose poetry is also included in the *Guru Granth*. Like Kabīr, Nanak was against the empty rituals in religions, as well as extremes in renunciation, and favored the householder's way of life characterized by an inner piety. Influenced by both Hindu and Muslim ideas, Nanak promoted worship of God as formless, free from iconic representations. God's essence is present in the "true name," the spiritual teacher, the scriptures, and the community, all of which are the Guru. The goal in life is the release from *saṃsāra* through the attainment of liberation (*mokṣa*).

After Nanak, Sikhism grew and found itself progressively enmeshed in political involvements, and the Sikh Gurus became akin to rulers of a princely state. By the time of the last Sikh Guru, Gobind Singh, the socio-political character of the movement was crystallized through his creation of the *khālsā*, an inner circle of religious warriors. Khālsā Sikh males wear the "five Ks," five items that begin with the Punjabi letter "k." The first of these is *kes*, which indicates that Sikhs should not cut the hair on their head or their beards. Their long hair is kept neatly bound in a turban. Amusingly, the long-bearded and turbaned Sikh forms the pervasive image of the "Hindu" for many Westerners, although Sikhs have for many centuries been regarded as constituting a distinct religion. Although the Sikh turban is distinctive in the ways in which it is tied, turbans are worn by many peoples of Central and South Asia, particularly in the northwest of the Indian subcontinent (e.g. Gujarat, Rajasthan), Pakistan, and Afghanistan. However, the vast majority of Hindus do not wear turbans. The other items worn by Khālsā Sikhs are a special type of underwear (*kachh*), a steel bangle (*kaṛā*), a dagger (*kirpān*), and a comb (*kaṅgha*).

The British in India (a brief history)

In 1600, Queen Elizabeth I initiated the formation of what would become the British East India Trading Company, which established fortified trading posts on various points of the subcontinent, such as Fort St George (Chennai), and on the backwaters of Bengal, which developed into Calcutta (Kolkata). They were in competition with other colonial powers, such as the Dutch, French, Portuguese, Danes, and Austrians. Spices, opium, tea, and cotton were of particular interest and the East India Company expanded into the interior acquiring territory, setting up forms of governance, and policing the land with a military presence.

In the late eighteenth century the British government took over the rule of Indian territories from the Company, setting up Warren Hastings (1773–1785) as the first

Governor-General of India, an official beginning to the period of the British Rāj (rule). English replaced Persian as the official language of government. In 1857, the Sepoys, mainly Muslim Indian soldiers in the British army, launched a rebellion by joining forces with the Mughal emperor. It was the first significant act of defiance against British rule, and has been subsequently glamorized as a war of independence. By the early nineteenth century, Christian missionaries were granted permission to proselytize freely in India. The British began to distinguish various "religions" from the rubric of Hinduism, and in order to facilitate administration, began to give particular emphasis to particular Hindu legal codices, such as the *Laws of Manu*. It was not particularly in British interests to foster inter-religious dialogue between Hinduism and Islam.

In 1885, the Indian National Congress, a political party many of whose members were Western-educated Indian elites, was formed. When the British governor-general, Lord Curzon, arbitrarily partitioned the region of Bengal into two states (West Bengal with its capital of Calcutta, also the capital of India, and East Bengal and Assam), educated middle-class Bengalis were angered. Not only was their beloved homeland of Bengal divided, but Bengali Hindus were no longer the majority population in West Bengal, which also included the states of Bihar and Orissa. And Muslims thus formed the majority in East Bengal. The Indian National Congress launched a nation-wide campaign to boycott British goods, and this led to their progressive development as a national political party, which attracted such notables as Mahatma Gandhi and Jawarharlal Nehru. Muslims, who were never successfully embraced by the Congress Party, formed their own party, the All-India Muslim League, in 1906. In 1919, after World War I, the British passed legislation to severely curtail political activism, which precipitated reactions such as protest marches and strikes from figures such as Gandhi. When a group of Hindus had gathered in a garden in Punjab to celebrate a festival, unaware of a government-legislated curfew, the British military commander ordered his troops to fire systematically on the crowd. Three hundred and seventy-nine people were killed and over a thousand injured in an assault in which almost every bullet was shot purposefully at its targets.

The Jallianwala Bagh massacre was a pivotal event, marking the end of positive sentiments towards Britain by the majority of Indians. Thereafter, the push for self-rule (*svarāj*), namely independence from Britain, gained greater momentum, culminating in success on August 15, 1947. To the detriment of the nation's unity, the Congress Party had continued to alienate the Muslim League, which was led by the charismatic Muhammad Ali Jinnah. Hindu–Muslim riots were widespread. Jinnah had long pressed for dividing the nation, and on the eve of independence, to avoid a civil war in the aftermath of Britain's departure, Lord Mountbatten, British India's last governor-general, authorized the country's partition into the sovereign nations of Pakistan and India. Jawaharlal Nehru became India's first prime minister.

Partition led to one of history's greatest mass migrations (an estimated twelve million people) as Muslims moved into Pakistan, and Hindus and Sikhs from the region of Pakistan moved into India. Systematic murderous raids by various factions, particularly in the divided state of Punjab, resulted in the massacre of as many as a million persons. "Ethnic cleansing" led to Pakistani Punjab becoming almost completely Muslim, and Indian Punjab becoming about 95 per cent Hindu or Sikh. Similar shifts took place in East Pakistan (formerly East Bengal) and West Bengal. Since princely states could choose which nation they wished to join, the Hindu king of Kashmir opted to join India, despite the fact that the majority of his subjects were Muslims. Pakistan assumed that Kashmir would be ceded to her. Since independence, disputes between India and Pakistan over the territory of Kashmir have fuelled wars and regional conflicts between the two countries. They have also exacerbated tensions between Hindus and the many Muslims who still live in India.

Hindu responses to Christianity

After Christian missionaries were given freedom to operate throughout India in the early nineteenth century, Hindus were exposed to Christian theologies and were forced to confront Christian critiques of their beliefs. This led to a variety of social reforms as well as the development of new theologies. However, unlike Islam, which constituted about a quarter of the population of India by the beginning of the twentieth century (and about 12–15 per cent today), Christianity never had dramatically large numbers. At the height of its power, Britain had fewer than a hundred thousand administrators and soldiers governing an Indian population of over two hundred and fifty million. Nevertheless, Britain's impact on India was immense, particularly in the creation of roads, railways, telegraph lines, and an administrative infrastructure. Today, Christians form about 2.5 per cent of the population (about twenty-five million).

Liberal thinkers, with attitudes shaped by the eighteenth century anti-religious Enlightenment notions, were often more sympathetic to many Hindu ideas than to Christian ones. Some romanticized the Hindu, particularly the Brahmin, who was viewed as a pious custodian of timeless wisdom. Others saw a need for social reform in Indian society, particularly through education. However, the evangelical stance often saw Hindus as irredeemably degenerate, and whose only salvation was through conversion to Christianity. In the cases of the Brāhmo Samāj, the Ārya Samāj, and the Ramakrishna Mission discussed below, we see but a few telling instances of the effects of Christianity, European values, and colonialism in general, upon Hinduism.

Case study: Ram Mohan Roy and the Brāhmo Samāj

Ram Mohan Roy (1772–1833) (also spelled Rammohun Ray) was a highly educated Bengali, from a wealthy Vaiṣṇava family. He mastered Arabic, Persian, Sanskrit and English, and read extensively in Islamic, Christian, and Hindu traditions. For some years he worked for the East India Company and its officers. He founded Bengali and Persian newspapers and published well received books. Ram Mohan Roy may have been influenced by the ideas of Unitarian Deists, with whom he corresponded. They believed that God's existence could be arrived at through the application of reason, and Roy thus envisioned a religion that fused the ancient teachings of Hinduism with such western rationality. In Upaniṣadic monism he saw teachings that meshed with Christian monotheism and the Islamic disdain for idolatry. However, he did not concede to Christian claims for Christ's divinity. In 1828, he founded the Brāhmo Samāj (Society of the Absolute), the first modern Hindu reform movement. Its essential purpose was to re-envision Hinduism in a manner that would free it from its Purāṇic accretions, such as rituals of image worship in temples.

The Society supported the advancement of English education, but also promoted broadening the curriculum of instruction to include the sciences and philosophy. They also advanced the cause for the abolition of *satī* and pressed to uplift the status of women. The Brāhmo Samāj attracted upper-class educated Hindus who were disenfranchised from the highest participation in Hindu religious practices because they did not belong to the purest Brahmin lineages. In spite of its Christian and Islamic leanings, the Brāhmo Samāj was a Hindu movement, and its moderate stance allowed it to cull influential members from the Bengali intelligentsia who might otherwise have converted to Christianity to improve their socio-political status. Roy's successors managed to expand the movement in size, and campaigned against the efforts of Christian missionaries. The Brāhmo Samāj's emphasis on the Upaniṣads had reintroduced many Hindu intellectuals to the teachings of the Vedas. However, Debendranath Tagore, who assumed the leadership after Roy, distanced the organization from its initial notions that the Vedas held infallible truth. He was followed by Keshab Chandra Sen (Keshava Chandra Sena), a non-Brahmin, who made the organization pan-Indian, but introduced certain practices, such as devotional singing, that were popular among Bengali Hindus. However, certain members who wanted to move away from all such distinctively Hindu features, including reading from Sanskrit texts, separated from Sen's organization. Further offshoots followed. Despite its influence in the early period of modern Hindu reform, the Brāhmo Samāj, which still exists, is relatively insignificant. However, its resonances are found in such organizations as the Vedānta Societies founded by Swami Vivekānanda.

Case study: Dayānanda Sarasvati

While Ram Mohan Roy's approach to reform was to synthesize a new tradition that drew from the common heritage, but which favored Western science and its values, Dayānanda Sarasvati's approach was to encourage a return to fundamentals. A Gujarati Brahmin with a traditional Sanskritic education and no knowledge of English, Dayānanda Sarasvati (1824–1883) rejected the Hinduism of the Purāṇas and Tantras, deeming them to be the compositions of self-serving men. He rejected polytheism, image worship, and the concept of the *avatāras,* but upheld the Vedas as the basis of all truth. In 1875, Dayānanda founded the Ārya Samāj (Society of Noble Ones), which, like the Brāhmo Samāj, was opposed to existing Hindu practices such as caste restrictions and child-marriage. The Society also promoted widows' rights to remarriage, and the education of women. The Arya Samāj's attitude to the Vedas was that they were the receptacle of all truth, and thus every enunciation of legitimate Hinduism should be traceable back to those texts. In fact, Dayānanda seemed to believe that even modern scientific theories and principles were prefigured in the Vedas. This attitude is still widespread among segments of the orthodox Hindu population.

The organization's popular appeal was surprising to intellectuals, and it became a powerful force in the development of Indian nationalism. It had adopted a stance of pride in India's religious heritage, although it had discarded over a millennium's worth of contributions by post-Vedic Hinduism and had embraced non-Hindu criticisms of polytheism and image worship. Today, the Ārya Samāj is still widespread throughout India, and has chapters worldwide. Its reformist attitudes have extremist tendencies linking it with aspects of militant Hindu fundamentalism.

Case study: Ramakrishna Paramahamsa and the Ramakrishna Order

Ramakrishna Paramahamsa (1836–1886) was a priest at the Kālī temple of Dakshineshwar not far from Kolkata (Calcutta), in the state of Bengal. Although he had little formal education, Ramakrishna embodied such a mystical piety and charisma that many educated Hindus were drawn to his teachings. One of these was Keshab Chandra Sen, who then led the Brāhmo Samāj. Ramakrishna's most influential disciple was Swami Vivekānanda, who would carry his teachings and reputation to the West. In the course of his life Ramakrishna was mentored by two significant teachers. One was a female tantric, who recognized that his unconventional behavior was based on a spiritual thirst, and the other was a master of non-dual Vedānta.

Ramakrishna's modes of behavior were so unconventional that many thought he was insane. He was known to enter into trance-like *samādhis,* ecstatic states in which he longed for or received visions of the Goddess. He sometimes dressed in women's clothing identifying with the Goddess herself, or as Rādhā in her divine passion for Kṛṣṇa. On occasion he would unconsciously eat from the plate of Kālī's food offerings, which naturally affronted certain devotees. However, such suspicions of insanity or blasphemy might quickly dissolve as his disciples listened to his often lengthy discourses. As he learned the teachings of various religions, Ramakrishna adopted the stance of each of those traditions, apparently having visions of Muhammad and Jesus. Although married, he remained celibate, worshipping his wife as an embodiment of the Divine Mother.

In Hindu mythic thought, a swan (*haṃsa*) is believed to be able to imbibe pure milk although it is mixed with water, symbolizing the capacity to extract from the heaps of scripture and religious teachings precisely what is precious. In this regard, Ramakrishna lived up to his title of Paramahamsa (Supreme Swan). Ramakrishna had been influenced by a spectrum of religions (e.g. Islam, Christianity) and approaches (e.g. Tantra, Vedānta) that circulated in Bengal in the late nineteenth century, and was able to integrate the teachings of each within his own understanding of spiritual truth. He offered visible proof that it was possible to find within what appeared to be myriad religious perspectives, each vying for its own adherents, an underlying theme of unity, which is so characteristic of the Hindu tradition. He restored to Hindus a confidence that their tradition was still fertile, and capable of producing a religious genius the likes of the Tamil poet-saints. It is little wonder that a contemporary Western scholar's analysis that Ramakrishna's mystical experiences were fuelled by suppressed homo-eroticism has fuelled much controversy. It has elicited cries by many Hindus as another instance of misinterpretation or defamation of their religious tradition and its saints by non-Hindus.

Ramakrishna's disciples banded together after his death to form an organization in 1897 known as the Ramakrishna Order. The organization emphasizes service to humanity as an important expression of religious activity. It has two wings, one with a monastic focus, the Ramakrishna Math, and the other, the Ramakrishna Mission, focused on social service. Today they have about two thousand information chapters worldwide, with a hundred and fifty major centers run by a total of a thousand monks. Within India, the Ramakrishna Mission has created schools, colleges, hospitals, dispensaries, homes for the aged, and orphanages. It is one of the most highly respected organizations of its kind within India.

Related developments

Swami Abhishiktananda/Henri Le Saux (1910–1973) was a French Benedictine monk who traveled to India shortly after its achievement of independence. He established a Christian *āśrama* named Shantivanam, in the state of Tamil Nadu. He adopted the name Swami Abhishiktananda (Bliss of the Anointed One) and took on the robes of a Hindu *saṃnyāsin*. After a pivotal meeting with Ramaṇa Mahāṛṣi, Abhishiktananda became the disciple of a Hindu *guru*, and spent many years in contemplation at Mount Arunachala, where Ramaṇa Mahāṛṣi had himself meditated. He eventually left Shantivanam in the hands of Father Bede Griffiths and set out for wanderings and contemplative retreats in the Himalayas. Bede Griffiths (1906–1993) was an English Benedictine monk who arrived in India in 1955. After spending more than a decade at a Christian *āśrama* in the state of Kerala, he visited Shantivanam, took up residence there, and eventually headed the institution. Shantivanam became a well-known center of Christian–Hindu dialogue.

Swami Abhishiktananda and Father Bede Griffiths are representatives of contemporary voices from deep within the heart of Christian mysticism, which have found common ground with the spiritual quest at the core of Hindu renunciation. Other influential figures continue this tradition of seeking for, finding, and then demonstrating to others the shared yearnings and experiences behind the Hindu and Christian search for the Divine. Noteworthy among these is Raimon (Raimundo) Panikkar (1918–), a Catholic priest born to a Hindu father and a Spanish Catholic mother. He is a blend of scientist, scholar, and theologian. Panikkar studied and taught in major universities in Spain, India, and the United States, and makes ongoing contributions to further the enterprise of intercultural and inter-religious understanding through sincerely motivated dialogue.

Hinduism in universalistic religion

While Hinduism evolved in response to the inflow of non-Indian perspectives to which it was exposed, there were also developments in which its teachings contributed to the formulations of religious systems that were global in sweep and influence. These "universalistic religions" were not primarily addressed to Hindus in attempts to attract them to a reconfigured Hinduism, but were addressed to a world audience. Centered in India, and drawing heavily from the South Asian religious heritage, they attracted many non-Hindus to their ranks. Two exemplars of these movements are the Theosophical Society and the Śrī Aurobindo Society.

Case study: the Theosophical Society

The Theosophical Society was formed by Madame Helena Petrovna Blavatsky and Colonel Henry Steele Olcott in 1875 in New York City, but shifted its headquarters to Adyar, on the outskirts of Chennai (Madras) in 1882. Madame Blavatsky was a Russian, whose religious influences were wide-ranging, including neo-Platonic thought, Tibetan Buddhism, and western occultism. Colonel Olcott, a retired soldier who fought in the Civil War, was the first prominent European American to convert to Buddhism. After initial involvements with the spiritualist movement in the United States, Blavatsky and Olcott moved to India and took up the cause of promoting Eastern religious values with a passion. Olcott was highly influential in the Buddhist revival in Sri Lanka. Theosophy (Wisdom of God) holds as its motto, "There is no religion higher than truth" and culls its teachings from all religious traditions, stripped of what are discerned as their "superstitious" accretions. It therefore encourages the study of comparative religion, philosophy, and science, without discrimination based on race, gender, caste, or creed, with an aim to uncover the laws of the natural world and the latent powers of human beings.

Theosophy developed its own tenets, envisioning a progressive spiritual evolution of humanity, through the periodic arrival of great teachers, known as *jagadgurus* (world teachers). The effort is to move humanity towards a Universal Brotherhood based on understanding the unity of all life, which shares in the divine consciousness that is God. A highly influential leader, who succeeded Madame Blavatsky, was Annie Besant, whose interests in social reform turned her to the broader agenda of transformation of the human spirit. Under her leadership, the Society expanded dramatically, so that at its fiftieth jubilee celebration, in 1925, it claimed more than 40,000 members, with over 1500 lodges worldwide. Many of its members were people of wealth and influence in Indian, European, and American society. Annie Besant worked on behalf of Indian nationalism. The Society still enjoys an honored place in India for these efforts, as well as those that encourage religious tolerance and highlight the value of Asian spiritual teachings. The Theosophical Society undertook the translation of numerous Asian religious scriptures, and continues to popularize the teachings of these traditions, although within its own interpretive framework. Mahatma Gandhi was among the many luminaries influenced by the teachings of Theosophy. However, he felt the intellectual appeal of the organization and its teachings led many to neglect the practical implications of its conception of universal brotherhood through engaged social action. The Theosophical Society now has an estimated membership of 30,000 with 140 major lodges worldwide.

Case study: Śrī Aurobindo and Integral yoga

Aurobindo Ghose (1872–1950) was a Bengali intellectual who was sent to England for his studies at the age of seven. At twenty-one, after studies at Cambridge, to which he had secured a scholarship, he returned to India and got involved in the struggle for independence. His political approach was an activism that did not discourage the use of violence, and he was imprisoned for a year on charges of sedition of which he was later acquitted. During his time in jail, he pursued his spiritual interests in *yoga* and Tantra, and underwent a life-altering change. In 1910, he took refuge from British authorities in the French colony of Pondicherry on India's southeast coast, and there eventually established an *āśrama* (hermitage) that endures to the present day. Ten years later he was joined by a Turko-Egyptian Frenchwoman, named Mira

Alfassa, who was his companion and co-leader of the organization. By 1926, when the *āśrama* was officially founded, Aurobindo had, for the most part, totally secluded himself within a wing of the main building, and Mira Alfassa, who came to be known as The Mother, essentially ran the organization until her death in 1973.

Aurobindo's philosophy is based on an evolutionary conception of the cosmos, in which pure Being or Consciousness is in the process of infusing material creation. This has resulted first in the emergence of life, and subsequently in the emergence of mind in more advanced life forms. However, the process must continue, now through the active will of human beings. The approach he offers is known as Integral yoga, a process through which Consciousness may be released from its bondage. With the aid of an experienced Master, and drawing upon a variety of techniques derived from ancient traditions, the soul can progressively evolve into its fullest spiritual, supermental expression. This evolutionary path may also be envisaged as a descent of Divine Consciousness into the lower levels of its manifestations, through the supermind, mind, life and matter.

Aurobindo's influences may be felt in the Human Potential Movement, one of whose major contributors, Michael Murphy, founder of the Esalen Institute at Big Sur, California, spent over a year at the Aurobindo *āśrama*. The Mother spearheaded the beginning of a utopian community, Auroville, based on Aurobindo's ideas of universal harmony and evolution through the integration of research into the inner world of spirit and the material world around us. It currently has about 1700 residents from thirty-five countries.

Hinduism and humanism

Although Hinduism's renewal took various religious manifestations, its trans-theistic heritage also meshed with European enlightenment thinking, and specifically with humanism. Although the term is somewhat vague and can range from hard-line secular to liberal religious humanism, humanism's focus is on human beings, and their creative expressions and potential.

Case study: Rabindranath Tagore

Rabindranath Tagore (1861–1941) was the son of Debendranath Tagore, leader of the Brāhmo Samāj, and thus the scion of a wealthy Bengali family deeply immersed in the Hindu reform movement. A naturally creative young man, Tagore grew into a prolific author of books, poetry, plays, and songs, mostly composed in vernacular Bengali. He founded a school for children, known as Viśva Bharati, at Shantiniketan, not far from Calcutta, which later became a university. The emphasis was on nurturing a close relationship between people and nature through simple harmonious interaction. Classes were held in the open air under the shade of trees.

Creative arts, such as drama and painting, were intrinsic to the curriculum. The institution's current mandate is to learn from the combined cultural heritage of humanity, but to not lose Asia's distinctive traditions in the process. Its objective is to foster world peace through mutual understanding conducted in a spirit of goodwill and cross-cultural cooperation.

Tagore's work is rooted in the Indian classical literary tradition. His personal philosophy reveals an intimate relationship with the Absolute, in an Upaniṣadic cast, with whom Tagore converses through his engagement with his everyday experience of life. His poetry collection *Gītāñjali* (*Offering of Songs*), which he translated into English, garnered the praise of Western poets such as William Butler Yeats and Ezra Pound, and Tagore was awarded the Nobel Prize for literature in 1913. Scholars have noted the influence of Indian *rāgas* and Western musicality in his compositions. By acknowledging that he was influenced by the music of the Bauls, Tagore lent to that marginalized group a new dignity. He is also credited with giving Mohandas Gandhi the title of Mahatma (Great Soul). Tagore was knighted in 1915, but yielded it in protest after the British massacre of Hindus at Jallianwala Bagh in the Punjab. One of his poetic compositions, *Jana Gana Mana Adhinayaka* (*You are the Ruler of the Minds of all People*) was eventually adopted as the Indian National Anthem.

A mere eighty years before Tagore had received the Nobel Prize, Thomas Babington Macaulay had, in his efforts to impose English as the mother tongue of all Indians, stated,

> I have no knowledge of either Sanscrit or Arabic. – But I have done what I could to form a correct estimate of their value. I have read translations of the most celebrated Arabic and Sanscrit works. I have conversed both here and at home with men distinguished by their proficiency in the Eastern tongues. I am quite ready to take the Oriental learning at the valuation of the Orientalists themselves. I have never found one among them who could deny that a single shelf of a good European library was worth the whole native literature of India and Arabia. The intrinsic superiority of the Western literature is, indeed, fully admitted by those members of the Committee who support the Oriental plan of education.
>
> It will hardly be disputed, I suppose, that the department of literature in which the Eastern writers stand highest is poetry. And I certainly never met with any Orientalist who ventured to maintain that the Arabic and Sanscrit poetry could be compared to that of the great European nations. But when we pass from works of imagination to works in which facts are recorded, and general principles investigated, the superiority of the Europeans becomes absolutely immeasurable. It is, I believe, no exaggeration to say, that all the historical information which has been collected from all the books written in the Sanscrit language is less valuable than what may be found in the most paltry abridgements used at preparatory

> schools in England. In every branch of physical or moral philosophy, the relative position of the two nations is nearly the same. (Thomas Babington Macaulay, "Minute of 2 February 1835 on Indian Education," quoted in *Macaulay, Prose and Poetry*, selected by G. M. Young (Cambridge MA: Harvard University Press, 1957), pp. 721–4 and 729.)

Macaulay's view of non-Sanskritic Indic literature was even more pejorative. It indicates the contempt that some colonialists had for Eastern literature and, in hindsight, reflects condemningly on their blind prejudice and ignorance. Thus Tagore had renewed Indians' pride in their nation's capacity to produce someone of his stature, who was recognized on the world stage for his literary accomplishments in the Bengali language.

Hinduism and politics

The relationship between religion and politics is evident both in efforts to keep them separate, or to unify them. In Hinduism's history this relationship has been acted out in the interplay between the Brahmin and *kṣatriya varṇas*, each of whom have claimed jurisdiction over one or both of the categories. Brahmins sought to be advisers to kings, who in turn patronized various deities and, on occasion, attempted to assume identifications with those divinities themselves. The dharmic ideal of righteous rule, in which government is informed by principles that serve the good of all subjects, endures in the modern period, even with the decline of monarchies and the rise of democratic political systems. The struggle for independence required strategies to unify the vast numbers of Indians who were being ruled by a relatively small number of colonial administrators and soldiers. This struggle was another factor that forged a collective sense of Hindu identity, which had previously been far more disparate. In 1915, the Indian National Congress formed the Hindu Mahāsābha (Great Association) in order to lobby government with specifically Hindu concerns, particularly in response to similar lobbying from India's Muslim factions. In the case studies that follow, we see telling examples of the successful blending of religious categories in the forging of social and cultural unity for political ends.

Case study: Bal Gangadhar Tilak

Bal Gangadhar Tilak (1856–1920) was an orthodox Brahmin from the state of Maharashtra. Attracted to the cause of Indian independence, he joined the National Congress, leading its extreme wing. British administrators called Tilak the "Father of Indian unrest," and he served many stints in jail for publishing his agitating views. On one occasion he served eighteen months in prison on sedition charges after an incident led to the assassination of a British bureaucrat in Pune, and on another occasion he was sentenced to hard labor for six years. During this latter stint in prison, he wrote a commentary on the *Bhagavad Gītā*. He was one of the early voices promoting Hindu values as part of the effort to oust the British from India and obtain self-rule (Hindi: *svarāj*). He pressed for Hindi as the official national language. Tilak mobilized Hindu sentiments by promoting large public celebrations of the festival to Gaṇeśa, on Gaṇeśa Chaturthi, which had been mostly private, family affairs. Powerful feelings of Hindu identity were aroused as people from neighborhoods gathered to view the images of Gaṇeśa on public display, and carry them to the ocean for immersion. The festival continues to be one of the largest, and most popular in Maharashtra, and like similar public festivals, such as the public Durgā Pūjā celebrations, still serves Hindu nationalistic agendas.

Many aspects of Tilak's agenda, such as a focus on indigenous industry (Hindi: *swadeshi*), the education of the masses, and the boycotting of British-made goods were further developed by Gandhi, who called Tilak the "Maker of Modern India."

Case study: Mahatma Gandhi

Mohandas Karamchand Gandhi (1869–1948) was a Gujarati from a merchant *varṇa*, who trained as a lawyer in London. After practicing law and fighting for civil liberties in South Africa for more than two decades, he returned to India in 1915 and became active in the independence movement. He started an *āśrama* in Gujarat to train disciples in the techniques of active but non-violent resistance to injustice using the "power" of "force of truth" (*satyagraha*). Influenced by Christian ethics through the writings of Leo Tolstoy, and by Henry David Thoreau's ideas of civil disobedience, Gandhi also drew upon a rich heritage of Hindu philosophical ideas in formulating his approach. Inspired by the teachings of the *Bhagavad Gītā*, which promoted action within social realities, rather than renunciation of the social order, Gandhi nevertheless attempted to maintain a life of ascetic simplicity and sexual continence in the yogic style. It was precisely this persona of the renouncer-saint that captivated the minds of the masses, giving Gandhi a stature that no other modern political leader in India has achieved.

Sometimes called Bapu, the "Father [of the Nation]," Gandhi insisted that non-violence (*ahiṃsā*) was an intrinsic feature of India's religious heritage, and made it a cornerstone of his pluralistic, inclusive approach. Gandhi's successes in India were a visible demonstration of the capacity of non-violent opposition to bring about concrete change. The *satyagraha* technique offered oppressed groups a new option for resistance. Gandhian approaches have been used by segments of the civil rights movement in the United States, in the anti-apartheid movement in South Africa, and by the women's liberation movement worldwide. Gandhi's approach has often been erroneously construed as passive, instead of active, non-violent resistance. Thus he is sometimes mistakenly portrayed as a traditional pacifist. Gandhi's approach is pacifism insofar as it is grounded in peaceful means to the achievement of a peaceful end, but it is not based on passivity or non-engagement. It is these active, engaged, confrontational, yet non-violent dimensions in his approach that have subsequently informed certain Christian liberation theologies, which have tried to overcome the paralysis of conventional religious pacifism.

Gandhi also utilized his power of asceticism to extract social responses by threatening to "fast unto death" unless policies were modified or people stopped their violent behavior. When justifying his actions, Gandhi would frequently use religious rationales. Many still ponder whether his political activism was purely the outgrowth of his religious beliefs or if he also co-opted religion in the service of a political agenda. Although he embodied the persona of a sage in the classic Indian mold, Gandhi deviated from orthodoxy in many ways. He did not embrace the caste system and fought for the equality of Untouchables, whom he referred to as Harijans (Children of God). Wherever he perceived it, he confronted evil with action, rather than attempting to transcend the good–evil dualism through the attainment of a higher state of consciousness.

Case study: Hindutva and the Bharatiya Janata Party

In 1923, Vinayak Damodar Savarkar, eventual leader of the Hindu Mahāsābha, wrote the book *Hindutva: Who is a Hindu?*, which defined "Hindu-ness" (Hindutva) as a cultural category shared by the peoples of the Indian subcontinent. Hinduism, then, (i.e. the religious dimensions) was one component of this collective culture. Hindutva was circumscribed in some measure merely by its distinctiveness from Islam and Christianity, presented as the "cultures" of India's colonizing powers. The book was a clarion call to Hindus to unite and regain their ancient homeland by installing "Hindu-ness" once again as India's dominant public-culture. While the Mahāsābha was eventually marginalized by the Indian National Congress for its excessively narrow and "communal" concerns, focused as it was on the voice of a single religious community, the concept of Hindutva seeded the ideological foundations of the RSS, the Rashtriya Swayamsevak Sangh (Community of Volunteers for the Nation).

Just as the Muslim League had pressed for the creation of a separate Muslim state, as India surged towards independence the RSS pressed for the formation of a distinctly Hindu state, in opposition to the Congress Party's notion of a secular government with religious freedom. However, they did not favor the partitioning of India, envisioning a nation in which other religions, such as the Muslims, Buddhists, and so on, recognized themselves as Hindus, under the broad cultural category of Hindutva. Although Gandhi was also opposed to Partition, which nevertheless occurred to his great disappointment, he had continued to spearhead an inclusive attitude to Indian Muslims within the new secular nation. Many Hindu nationalists felt that this focus on secularism was a betrayal of Hinduism. Gandhi was eventually assassinated by Nathuram Godse, a former member of the RSS, leading Jawaharlal Nehru, India's first Prime Minister, to outlaw the organization. Nehru was firmly committed to fashioning India into a country whose political secularism showed no partiality towards any religious denomination whatsoever.

For almost forty years, the Congress Party dominated Indian politics as Nehru's daughter, Indira Gandhi eventually succeeded him. She was assassinated in 1984, by two Sikh bodyguards who expressed the religious outrage felt against her for ordering the Indian army to storm the Golden Temple, in Amristar. The Golden Temple, the holiest Sikh shrine, had been occupied by Sikh militants involved in a violent separatist movement for an independent Punjab. She was succeeded by her son, Rajiv Gandhi (d. 1991), who was also assassinated, most likely by the Liberation Tigers of Tamil Eelam (LTTE), a separatist guerilla organization fighting for the independence of Hindu Tamil regions of northern Sri Lanka. Meanwhile, a new political party, the BJP, Bharatiya Janata Party (Party of the People of India) had formed in 1980. It had vigorous roots in the RSS and the VHP, Vishwa Hindu Parishad, (Universal Hindu Assembly), a religious organization with a distinctly political agenda. The BJP's success took flight with an issue that mobilized grass-roots Hindu sentiments, uniting disaffected Hindus from different regions of India and varying caste groups under the aegis of a powerful and ancient religious symbol of dharmic government, namely, Rām-*rājya*, the rule of the god-king Rāma.

The power of television should not be underestimated in understanding the emergence of Rāma as a symbol of such vitality. A 78-part serialized version of the *Rāmāyaṇa* was broadcast weekly on Sunday mornings on Indian National television in 1987–1988. It attracted unprecedented audiences. For some, television sets were treated as temple sanctums. Streets emptied and commercial life ground to a halt as tens of millions of viewers gathered to watch the *Rāmāyaṇa* unfold in a manner unprecedented in Hinduism's past, namely, a collectively shared and simultaneously experienced version of the myth. It was not long before national attention turned to Ayodhyā, a small town, and the mythic site of Rāma's birthplace. Local sects dedicated to Rāma worship claimed that a mosque (*masjid*) allegedly built by the Mughal emperor Babar was situated upon the site of a demolished Hindu temple marking the birthplace of Rāma. In 1990, a BJP leader began a pilgrimage campaign traversing the length of India and culminating at Ayodhyā with the intent of rousing Hindu fervor to destroy the Babari/Babri Masjid and rebuild a Hindu temple to Rāma on its ruins. Although the government stopped the destruction of the mosque in 1991 by having soldiers open fire on a descending mob, the following year a group of militants razed the mosque with hammers and pickaxes. By the late 1990s the BJP had assumed leadership of the country. Although for many this success marked a movement in the direction of the "Hindu-ification" of India, the elections of 2004 produced a surprising victory for the Congress Party, led by the late Rajiv Gandhi's

Italian-born wife and widow, Sonia. Perceptions that the BJP's agenda supports Hindu orthodoxy have alienated many from India's lowest classes. Sonia Gandhi declined the role of Prime Minister, passing it on to the former finance minister, Manmohan Singh, a Sikh. India–Pakistan relations currently appear to be on the mend. A devastating earthquake in northern Pakistan has induced the opening of border crossings between Indian and Pakistani Kashmir to permit the flow of aid. The goodwill shown during this tragedy may further the processes of reconciliation between these neighbor nations.

Hinduism's connections to politics are also evident in its conceptions of sacred geography. In the ancient myth of the goddess Satī's dismemberment one notes the identification of the land with the body of the Goddess. The Bengali author Bankim Chatterjee's poem, *Vande Mataram* (*I Praise the Mother*), composed in 1876 and revering India (or at least Bengal) as the Divine Motherland, while clearly the popular anthem of the nationalist movement, was almost chosen as the country's official National Anthem. However, only its first two verses were approved by Nehru, because in subsequent stanzas such lyrics as "Who says, Mother, you are weak? When twice seven *crore* (10,000,000) hands wield mighty swords" or "You are Durgā, Wielder of Ten Weapons," were both too militant and overtly Hindu. In the figure of the goddess Bhārat Mātā, who emerges simultaneously, enduring notions of the divinity of the earth dovetail with the modern Hindu nationalistic agenda of India as that goddess. Bhārat Mā is not merely an embodiment of sacred geography, a symbol of a fecund and nurturing Mother Earth who supports and protects all her children, but a personification of Hindu society. She is the land and its people, particularly its Hindu population, who can relate to the iconic representation of a deity, politically unified through the nation state. In temples to Bhārat Mā, the central icon is a map of India.

Case study: "Dravidian" identity

The term Dravidian was coined to reflect a group of Indian languages that did not belong to the Indo-Āryan language groups. It also refers to the people who share a common culture, and are primarily linked through their shared linguistic affiliations. There are twenty-six such Dravidian languages, which include Tamil, Malayalam, Kannada, and Telugu, spoken by South Indians, and Brahui, the language spoken on the Pakistan–Afghanistan border.

In 1916, a piece of writing known as the *Non-Brahmin Manifesto* launched what has been called the "Dravidian Movement," essentially an anti-Brahmin, anti-upper caste faction interested in promoting the interests of the lower-caste South Indians. The movement was designed to challenge the power of the upper castes to define the essence of Indian culture in terms of a Sanskritic, Vedic norm, which marginalized non-Vedic social groups. Among the expressions of this movement is the reinterpretation of Sanskritic religious literature in a new light, as containing historical evidence of the Āryan domination of "Dravidian" religion and culture. Out of these formulations come such proposals as viewing Rāvaṇa as a great Southern king, or imagining an empowered South India as a renewed kingdom of the righteous "demon" Bali. Certain disenfranchised groups chose different routes of engagement with Brahminic hegemony. B. R. Ambedkar, for instance, encouraged members of his Mahar, Untouchable community to leave Hinduism entirely and convert to Buddhism. The "Dravidian Movement," which attempted to define itself as rooted in Tamil culture, has met with limited success in engaging South Indians outside the state of Tamil Nadu.

Its political expression is particularly evident in such originally separatist, but currently non-separatist, parties as the DMK, Dravida Munnetra Kazhagam (Dravidian Progressive Federation). In its words, the DMK seeks to "revive and restore the ancient heritage of Tamil and Tamil Nadu and protect Tamil language from Hindu imperialism." Although efforts were made to include a major Dravidian language as one of the national languages of India, Hindi was chosen as the national language, with eighteen other Indic languages and English officially permitted in accord with state legislation. The DMK and its national offshoot the All-India Anna DMK (AIADMK) currently dominate Tamil Nadu politics. They seek to achieve more autonomy and state-centered decision-making power at the expense of centralized authority in Delhi, which is perceived as often promoting non-Tamil interests.

Key points in this chapter

- Hinduism has continually modified itself in response to both internal and external forces.
- Through colonization, Hinduism was exposed to Muslim and Christian critiques of its values and practices. Although some colonial efforts took the form of outright persecution, Hindu religious culture continued to endure and adapt in the face of these pressures.
- While these critiques led to the demise or marginalization of certain streams of Hindu belief and practice, they also led to the formation of new religious movements, and to internal reforms that revitalized the religion.
- Among the transformations that occurred during the period of reform was the development of religious philosophies derived from Hindu traditions that had a universal reach and appeal.
- Hinduism was and still is used to foster cultural unity and invoked on behalf of social and political ends.

Discussion questions

1. Ramakrishna Paramahamsa found an underlying unity within a variety of religions, an underlying unity that is characteristic of the Hindu tradition. Do you think that Hinduism could be generally classified as a "universalistic" religion? Why or why not?
2. Humanism's focus is on human beings, and their creative expressions and potential. In what ways might Hinduism in general be seen to take a humanistic approach, if any?
3. Discuss the relationship between the religion and politics of India. Do you think this relationship has managed to strengthen or weaken Hinduism?
4. How did Islam arrive in India, and what changes did it bring to the Indian people, and particularly to the religion of India?
5. What impact did Britain have on India, and how did this impact India's religious culture?
6. What are the Brāhmo Samāj and the Ārya Samāj, who are the important figures associated with them, and in what way are they related to Hinduism?

Further reading

Hinduism and politics

Ali, S. (1958) *The Congress Ideology and Programme*. New Delhi: People's Publishing House.

Ambedkar, B. R. (1946) *What Congress and Gandhi Have Done to the Untouchables*. Bombay: Thacker and Co.

Anderson, W. K. and S. D. Dhamle (1987) *The Brotherhood in Saffron: The Rastriya Swayamsevak Sangh and Hindu Revivalism*. Boulder, CO: Westview Press.

Appaiah, P. (2003) *Hindutva: Ideology and Politics*. New Delhi: Deep & Deep.

Athayle, D. (1921) *Life of Lokamanya Tilak*. Poona: A. Chiploonkar.

Bhave, Vinoba (1957) *Sarvodaya and Communism*. Tanjore: Sarvodaya Prachuralaya.

Brecher, M. (1959) *Nehru: A Political Biography*. London: Trübner, 1932.

Chatterjee, Bankim Chandra (1992) *Ānandamaṭh* (1882). Basanta Koomar Roy (trans.). Reprint. New Delhi: Vision Books.

Collins, L. and D. Lapierre (1975) *Freedom at Midnight*. New York: Simon and Shuster.

Hansen, Thomas B. (1999) *The Saffron Wave: Democracy and Hindu Nationalism in Modern India*. Princeton, NJ: Princeton University Press.

Hardgrave, R. L. (1965) *The Dravidian Movement*. Bombay: Popular Prakashan.

Heimsath, C. M. (1964) *Indian Nationalism and Social Reform*. Princeton, NJ: Princeton University Press.
Jaffrelot, C. (1996) *The Hindu Nationalist Movement in India*. New York: Columbia University Press.
Jaffrelot, C., and T. Hansen (eds) (1998) *The BJP and the Compulsions of Politics in India*. New Delhi: Oxford University Press.
Lele, J. K. (1995) *The Emergence of the Right*. Madras: Earthworm Books.
Malkani, K. R. (1980) *The R. S. S. Story*. New Delhi: Impex India.
Nehru, J. (1960) *The Discovery of India*. London: Meridian Books.
— (1962) *Autobiography*. New Delhi: Allied Publishers.
Savarkar, V. D. (1969) *Hindutva*. Bombay: Veer Savarkar Prakashan.
Vishva Hindu Parishad (n.d.) *The Hindu Awakening: Retrospect and Promise*. New Delhi: Vishva Hindu Parishad.
Zavos, J. (2000) *The Emergence of Hindu Nationalism in India*. New Delhi: Oxford University Press.

On Gandhi

Fischer, L. (1959) *The Life of Mahatma Gandhi*. Reprint. Bombay: Bharatiya Vidya Bhavan.
Gandhi, M. K. (1982) *An Autobiography or The Story of my Experiments with Truth*. Harmondworth: Penguin.
Tendulkar, D. G. (1952–58) *Mahātma: Life and Work of M. K. Gandhi*, 8 vols. Bombay: V. K. Jhaveri.

Reform and reformers in Hinduism

Bishop, Donald H. (ed.) (1982) *Thinkers of the Indian Renaissance*. New York: Wiley Eastern.
Collet. S. D. (1962) *The Life and Letters of Raja Rammohan Roy*. Calcutta: Sadharan Brahmo Samaj.
Crawford, S. C. (1987) *Ram Mohan Roy: Social Political and Religious Reform in Nineteenth Century India*. New York: Paragon House.
Jones, K. W. (1976) *Arya Dharm: Hindu Consciousness in 19th century Punjab*. Berkeley, CA: University of California Press.
Kaur Singh, Nikky-Guninder (1995) *The Name of My Beloved: Verses of the Sikh Gurus*. San Francisco, CA: Harper San Francisco.
Keay, F. E. (1931) *Kabīr and His Followers*. London.
Killingly, D. (1993) *Rammohun Roy in Hindu and Christian Tradition: The Teape Lectures 1990*. Newcastle upon Tyne: Grevatt and Grevatt.

Kopf, D. (1969) *British Orientalism and the Bengal Renaissance: The Dynamics of Indian Modernization, 1773–1835*. Berkeley, CA: University of California Press.

— (1979) *The Brahmo Samāj and the Shaping of the Modern Indian Mind*. Princeton, NJ: Princeton University Press.

Majumdar, J. K. (n.d.) *Raja Rammohan Roy and Progressive Movements in India, Vol. I. A Selection from Records (1774–1845)*. Calcutta: Brahmo Mission Press.

Marfati, M. I. (1979) *The Philosophy of Vallabhācārya*. Delhi: Motilal Banarasidass.

Mukta, Parita (1994) *Upholding the Common Life: the Community of Mirabai*. Delhi: Oxford University Press.

Nag, K. and D. Burman (1948) *The English Works of Raja Rammohun Roy*. Calcutta: Sadharan Brahmo Samaj.

Olson, Carl (ed.) (1897) *The Mysterious Play of Kālī: An Interpretive Study of Rāmakrishna*. Atlanta, GA: Scholar's Press.

Parekh, M. C. (1922) *The Brahmo Samāj*. Calcutta: Brahmo Samaj.

— (1926) *Brahmarshi Keshub Chander Sen*. Rajkot: Bhagavat Dharma Mission.

Rai, L. (1915) *The Ārya Samāj*. London: Longman.

Sil, N. P. (1991) *Rāmakrishna Paramahamsa, A Psychological Profile*. Leiden: E. J. Brill.

Singh, Bawa C. (1903) *Life and Teachings of Swami Dayananda*. New Delhi: Jan Gyan Prakashm.

Tagore, Rabindranath (1967) *Collected Poems and Plays*. New York: Macmillan.

Williams, R. B. (1984) *A New Face of Hinduism: The Swaminarayan Religion*. Cambridge: Cambridge University Press.

Young, R. F. (1981) *Resistant Hinduism: Sanskrit Sources on Anti-Christian Apologetics in Early Nineteenth-Century India*. Vienna: Indologisches Institut der Universität Wien.

Zelliot, E. (1992) *From Untouchable to Dalit: Essays on the Ambedkar Movement*. New Delhi: Manohar.

On Aurobindo and his teachings

Ghose, Aurobindo (1971) *Synthesis of Yoga*. Pondicherry: Sri Aurobindo Ashram.

— (1972–1975) *Sri Aurobindo*, 30 vols. Birth Centenary Library. Pondicherry: Sri Aurobindo Ashram.

— (1973) *The Life Divine*. Pondicherry: Sri Aurobindo Ashram.

Heeh, P. (1989) *Sri Aurobindo and the Mother: Glimpses of their Experiments, Experiences, and Realisations*. New Delhi: Mother's Institute of Research.

McDermott, R. (1973) *The Essential Aurobindo*. New York: Schocken Books.

Maitra, S. (1945) *An Introduction to the Philosophy of Sri Aurobindo*. Benares: Benares Hindu University.

On North Indian religious traditions

Barz, Richard (1976) *The Bhakti Sect of Vallabhācārya*. Faridabad: Thomson Press.

Gold, Daniel (1987) *The Lord as Guru: Hindu Saints in the Northern Indian Traditions*. New York: Oxford University Press.

Hawley, J. S., and M. Juergensmeyer (1988) *Songs of the Saints of North India*. New York: Oxford University Press.

Hedayetullah, M. (1978) *Kabīr: The Apostle of Hindu-Muslim Unity*. Delhi: Motilal Banarsidass.

Johnson, Linda (1994) *Daughters of the Goddess: the Women Saints of India*. St Paul, MN: Yes International.

Kripal, J. J. (1994) *Kālī's Child: The Mystical and the Erotic in the Life and Teachings of Ramakrishna*. Chicago, IL: University of Chicago Press.

Lamb, Ramdas (2002) *Rapt in the Name: The Ramnamis, Ramnam, and Untouchable Religion in Central India*. Albany, NY: State University of New York Press.

Macauliffe, M. A. (1963) *The Sikh Religion: Its Gurus, Sacred Writings and Authors*, 3 vols. Reprint. Delhi: S. Chand.

McDaniel, June (1989) *The Madness of the Saints: Ecstatic Religion in Bengal*. Chicago, IL: University of Chicago Press.

McLean, Malcolm (1998) *Devoted to the Goddess: The Life and Work of Ramprasad*. Albany, NY: State University of New York Press.

Schomer, K, and W. H. McLeod (eds) (1987) *The Sants: Studies in a Devotional Tradition of India*. Delhi: Motilal Banarsidass.

Vaudeville, C. (1957) *Kabīr Granthavālī (Dohā)*. Pondicherry: Institut Français d'Indologie.

— (1974) *Kabir*, vol. 1. Oxford: Clarendon Press.

— (1993) *A Weaver named Kabir*. Delhi: Oxford University Press.

Westcott, G. H. (1953) *Kabir and the Kabir Path*. Reprint. Calcutta: Susil Gupta.

Hinduism and Islam

Chand, T. (1963) *Influence of Islam on Indian Culture*. Allahabad: The Indian Press.

Edwardes, S. M. and H. O. O. Garrett (1962) *Mughal Rule in India*. Reprint. Delhi: S. Chand.

The British and Christianity in India

Cohn, Bernard S. (1996) *Colonialism and Its Forms of Knowledge: The British in India*. Princeton, NJ: Princeton University Press.

Gopal, R. (1963) *British Rule in India: An Assessment*. New York: Asia Publication House.

Marshall, P. J. (ed.) (1971) *The British Discovery of Hinduism in the Eighteenth Century*. European Understanding of India Series. Cambridge: Cambridge University Press.

Panikkar, Raimundo (ed. and trans.) (1977) *The Vedic Experience: Mantramañjari – An Anthology of the Vedas for Modern Man and Contemporary Celebration*. Berkeley, CA: University of California Press.

Pinch, W. (1996) *Peasants and Monks of British India*. Berkeley, CA: University of California Press.

Tod, J. (n.d.) *Annals and Antiquities of Rajasthan*, 3 vols. William Crooke (ed.) Delhi: Motilal Banarsidass.

15 *Hinduism beyond India*

In this chapter

Long before the growth in Hindu immigration beyond India, which is a relatively recent phenomenon, Hinduism had expanded well beyond the confines of the subcontinent. Among the reasons for this spread was that rulers from neighboring kingdoms often sought priestly consecrations believed capable of conferring special status on them. The aspects of Hinduism that took root in new lands developed distinctive forms as they melded with indigenous religions. Additional changes occurred in these regions from religions such as Buddhism or Islam, which arrived subsequently, modifying the styles of Hinduism there, or even supplanting it. Here we briefly explore some configurations of Hinduism in Nepal, Bali, and Southeast Asia.

Main topics covered

- Hinduism in Nepal
- Hinduism in South-east Asia
- Hinduism in Indonesia

Imagine, if you will, this scenario

You are living on a beach in Arugam Bay, Sri Lanka, in a hut rudely constructed of dried coconut palms lashed to wooden stakes, just yards away from the ocean's edge at high tide. Your dwelling's floor is the sand of the beach, and you cook your meals on a wood fire in a stone-lined pit at one end of the hut. Your lifestyle is extremely basic and idyllic. You make periodic trips to the town market to buy breadfruit, papayas, yogurt from buffalo milk, bananas, and such, and supplement your meals with seafood caught by local fishermen. You spend your days swimming in the ocean, reading, and going for long walks. You have mainly been practicing *yoga*, quite intensively, based on training you have recently received from a Tamil Hindu yogi, who had set up a small *āśrama* at Kalkudah, further up Sri Lanka's east coast.

Arugam Bay arcs to a point, a mile or more in the distance, where the waves break so famously that the site actually draws a sizeable assortment of avid surfers from around the world. Your hut is owned by Nagoorthamby, a Muslim man who lives with his wife and two young children in a more substantial mud hut some distance away. Nagoorthamby experiences occasional tensions with his Buddhist and Hindu neighbors, who live further inland from the water's edge. They feel that he has simply squatted on the public land where he has built his home, and are generally suspicious of his integrity. He, in turn, claims that most of the island's inhabitants are of low moral caliber, since Sri Lanka is a land of demons. Counting out on his fingers how one is a thief, another a liar, and so on, he cautions that only one out of five Sri Lankans should be trusted. Despite his dark appraisal of the citizenry, and the actual instances of robbery that occasionally befall the local residents, you get along well with everyone, be they Buddhists, Muslims, or Hindus, and are invited to dine with your Buddhist and Hindu neighbors on numerous occasions, and permitted to bathe daily in the fresh water from their wells.

One day, you learn about a renowned festival that has begun at Kataragama, further south on the island. Both Nagoorthamby and your Buddhist neighbors know about it, and insist that it is well worth a visit, although they themselves are unable to go. The journey there should typically be taken through Yala National Park, the abode of wild elephants, leopards, and other dangerous beasts. "If Lord Kataragama wishes you to arrive, he will offer you protection," they say, and so you and a friend journey there over several days. You arrive safely at Kataragama after dark, and after a night's sleep on a mat under a large tree, you awaken to see that pilgrims continue to stream onto the grounds of the festival site, located by a holy river, the Menik Gaṅgā.

Opting to avoid the crowds, you and your friend follow the course of the narrow babbling river to a point about a mile downstream, where a small island of rock and sand serves as an ideal, relatively isolated campsite. Large trees that line the river's banks form a protective canopy overhead. The water deepens not too far away, making it well suited for swimming, and Buddhist monks periodically arrive there to bathe. On occasion, you find yourself fighting off sizeable bands of marauding monkeys, who circle around the site, some creating distractions while others attempt to abscond with your food. The large males are quite fierce, with long canines and muscled limbs, and the younger members of the troupes are agile. As you put up a vigorous fight, using a bamboo staff as a weapon, you begin to appreciate the mythic tales of the *Rāmāyaṇa*, in which Hanumān and his monkey armies aid Rāma in his battle for Laṅkā.

The days at Kataragama definitely prove to be memorable. When you first journey back to the festival site that evening, after having established your camp, eating, and resting, you are struck by the numbers of pilgrims that have arrived since the morning. There are many villagers, but there are also city folk, and a wide assortment of *sādhus*. Suddenly a group of people passes by, dancing and crying out, "Harro, Harrah." They carry red wooden arches over their heads and on their shoulders. "They are dancing *kavadi*,'" you are informed by a distinguished gentleman, clad in white. "It is in honor of Lord Kataragama, whose wedding is being celebrated here." You look closer, and note that some of the dancers have long metal needles through their cheeks and tongues. As the days progress, you discover that numerous stalls have been erected, which pilgrims visit to have specialists insert such needles through their body parts. The stalls also equip them with the *kavadi* arches for their dancing approach to Kataragama's temple. There are also Buddhist *stūpas* on the festival site and Buddhist monks wandering about. There is a Muslim mosque nearby. Your understanding is that this is a Hindu festival, although something about its atmosphere makes you feel that it even predates Hinduism. So you are surprised to see the diversity of religions represented here, all seeming to lay claim to this deity, this sacred festival, and this site.

On subsequent days you observe men walking on sandals whose soles are upward pointing nails, and you even see instances of the iconic Indian *fakirs*, about whom you have read in travelers' tales, who sleep on beds of nails. You periodically come across various groups wheeling bamboo scaffoldings from each of which hangs an ascetic who swings from hooks inserted through the flesh of his back and the backs of his thighs. Pilgrims wave incense-filled clay pots before these ascetics as a form of veneration. Some hold up their babies, and the hook-swingers, in what appear to be trance-like states, utter prophesies to these devotees in the crowds. There are a few Westerners at the site, and you also notice some members of the Hare Kṛṣṇa movement, at that time still somewhat in its infancy. You then see that a large pyre of wood is being constructed, measuring about twenty feet long, and shoulder high. "People will walk the fire, tomorrow," you are told, and you are eager to witness this for yourself. A saffron-clad *sādhu*, with long black hair and beard, approaches you with a smile. He speaks no English, but with a sign motions you and your companion to sit with him. He pulls out a pineapple from his cloth bag, and skillfully cuts it into edible portions, sharing it with you in a disarming and memorable generosity of spirit.

Just at dusk, a procession of exquisite devotional fervor occurs. The sacred image of Lord Kataragama, concealed, is carried by a special priest out of its temple, and onto the back of an awaiting elephant. The priest wears a turban and his face is concealed by a cloth wrap. Musicians begin to play and a fire-twirler spins a large flaming baton, leading the procession and applying fire to his limbs as he walks. The *sādhu* who had earlier shared his pineapple with you is dancing in devotional ecstasy, as this wedding procession, now thronging with a crowd of worshippers, carries Kataragama to the temple of his bride to be, the beautiful tribal maiden, Valli. There is a rosy-colored hue to the light of the setting sun, and incense fills the air. Everybody's mood is infectiously joyful, for tonight Kataragama will spend the night at the temple of his bride, symbolically consummating their marriage.

The next morning you and your friend walk along the river bank in the direction of the festival site and stop at a small wayside tea shop where a bridge crosses the river. You decide to treat yourself to a breakfast snack of spicy string hoppers and *rotis*. There, you notice a couple of gentlemen dressed in white and with smart red sashes. You learn that they are local residents, and traditional fire-walkers. "You mean that you will fire-walk today?" "Yes," they reply. "We do it every year." "Do you apply anything to your feet, for protection?" "No," they reply, and offer you a glimpse of their soles, which although toughened from being frequently barefoot, look rather normal. "Do you take any medicine? Opium?" your friend asks. "Oh, no," they answer with amusement. "It is the power of faith."

The wood pyre has already been set ablaze, and burns for several hours before it is transformed into a bed of gleaming red coals, topped with a fine layer of white ash, which erupts here and there in little tongues of flame. Small rectangular pools a few inches deep are dug on either side of the long coal bed and filled with water. A man and woman, she with wild, disheveled hair, both in deep trances, are anxious to rush over the coals, but are held back by the fire-twirler, who is clad in red. He is most capable of approaching the coals, and keeps preparing the bed with beatings and proddings from a long bamboo pole. The intensity of the heat prevents you and other onlookers from getting closer than about a dozen feet. Then, at the appropriate moment, the chief temple priest first steps into the water, wets the lower portions of his red garment, which might otherwise burst into flames from the heat, and walks quickly over the coals, followed by an apparent hierarchy of other priests and the fire-twirler. The red-sashed men from the tea shop are among those who follow this group. The entranced man and woman are now released to cross the fire and they dance wildly through it. This is a signal for any others, who have courage to do so, to walk the fire. Men and women of all ages now begin to approach the coals, and after a moment's hesitation, walk briskly through the fire. Your eyes dart to the pool of water at the far end of the coal bed, where some have to douse out the flames that have ignited the lower portions of their garments. Suddenly, you notice the gentleman who first spoke to you upon your arrival. He is meditatively clapping his hands together, and as others are speeding across the coals, he walks in a slow and measured gait while muttering some half-audible prayers.

Both those who have crossed the flaming coals and the onlookers are emotionally roused by the experience. Those who have endured the ordeal appear overjoyed and empowered. Even those, like yourself, who have merely witnessed it, are somewhat awestruck. You finally approach your gentleman acquaintance whose passage through the flames was so impressively controlled. "It is to demonstrate to others the power of faith," he offers. "It is so they may witness the power of the Lord." On the journey home, you chat with an elderly woman on the crowded bus. "I have come to Kataragama many times," she tells you. "But this is the first time that I had the courage to walk the fire. Nothing happened to me, except for a small blister here on the side of my foot," she says proudly, showing it to you as a badge of courage.

You leave Kataragama wondering about the many sights you have witnessed. How ancient is the festival, which seems to predate all the religious groups that wish to lay claim to it? You wonder whether there is hope for the religious tolerance, pluralism, and harmony that seemed to exist temporarily here, in some sacred nexus of time and place, and especially on that rosy evening of Kataragama's marriage procession. Are such fierce ordeals as body piercing and fire-walking truly necessary to awaken oneself and others to the latent and mysterious powers in life? Was that the sort of fire-ordeal that Sītā underwent in Laṅkā in the *Rāmāyaṇa* myth?

Weeks have elapsed since your departure from Arugam Bay. You return to discover that someone, in an apparent act of hostility against Nagoorthamby, has burned your hut and its few material possessions to the ground. It is swiftly rebuilt by local fishermen in a matter of days. Weeks later, as you prepare to depart from Sri Lanka, you learn that the Tamil yogi, with whom you had studied, has narrowly escaped death when his *āśrama* in Kalkudah was also set ablaze. You remember him telling you that his brother had apparently been killed a few years earlier in some inter-religious feud near the island's capital, Colombo. Evoking in your imagination Hanumān's mythic burning of Laṅkā, these fires are early precursors of the flames of religious sectarian violence between Tamil Hindus and Buddhist Singhalese that will engulf the island paradise for decades to come.

Nearly three decades later a disastrous tsunami would virtually wipe out the coastal regions of Kalkudah, Arugam Bay, and Yala National Park. The wild animals of the park, harmoniously aligned with the forces of nature, would flee to higher, dry ground, and mostly survive this devastating "act of God," while tens of thousands of Hindus, Buddhists, and Muslims, some with whom you laughed, played, smoked, worked, and shared meals, would perish.

While the preceding chapters have dealt primarily with Hinduism in India, the religious traditions of Hinduism have, at various periods in history, spread beyond the confines of the subcontinent. Hinduism is not a missionary religion in character, but political conquests led to the expansion of cultural practices that were inseparable from religion. Hindu kingdoms arose in Southeast Asia and Nepal. Many of these were supplanted by Buddhism or Islam, but the vestiges of Hinduism remain in the archeological record, as well as in the character of the current dominant religions of those areas.

Figure 15.1 A Hindu ascetic suspended with hooks through his flesh swings from a bamboo scaffold and offers prophesies (Kataragama, Sri Lanka)

Hinduism in Nepal

The Himalayan country of Nepal was, until recently, the world's only multiethnic, multilingual, democratic, Hindu kingdom, with more than eighty-five per cent of its population of about twenty-eight million identifying themselves as Hindus. First inhabited by semi-legendary groups such as the Kirātas, attested to in ancient chronicles, Nepal was subsequently dominated by other "historical" dynasties, such as the Licchavis, who left behind inscriptional records. From the thirteenth to the mid-eighteenth centuries, the nation was ruled by the Malla Dynasty. In 1769, King Prithvi Narayan Shah conquered Kathmandu Valley and established the state of Nepal. From 1846 to 1951, the Rana family seized power and established a hereditary prime-minister's office, essentially ruling the country until the Shahs were restored to power with support from India. A democratic electoral system for the constitutional monarchy was also established in 1990. At the time of writing (mid-2006), the current king, Gyanendra, of the Shah Dynasty, who assumed power after a palace massacre that resulted in the death of many members of the royal family, has been stripped of political authority by the Nepalese parliament. Maoist insurgents, whose political struggle had produced a decade of violent turmoil in the country, recently joined peaceful negotiations as partners with the government in forging a new constitution. The fate of the monarchy will soon be decided by the people.

One of Nepal's most widely celebrated religious festivals is Dasain, which spans the Great Goddess's festival known as Navarātra or Navarātri in India. During

Figure 15.2 Newari Hindu virgin girls (*kumārī*) in Nepal undergo a rite of passage in which they are married to Viṣṇu in the form of a wood-apple fruit

Dasain, tens of thousands of chickens, goats, and buffaloes are ritually slain in offerings to Devī Durgā. A particularly important manifestation of the Devī is Taleju Bhavānī, a tutelary deity of the Malla kings, but whose cult was probably established in Nepal as early as the eleventh century. Taleju is still the chief protector deity of the Nepali kings, whose power is believed to derive from her. Since Taleju accepts meat and alcohol offerings, attempts by orthodoxy to move Nepali Hindus towards conventional Śāstric norms have not been successful. The sanctum of the main temple of Taleju in Kathmandu is open for only one day in the year, during Dasain, for devotees to take *darśana* of the Devī.

Nepal is also noted for its tradition of living goddesses, known as Kumārīs. These are young girls selected at ages of four or five, who are believed to be incarnate forms of Taleju. During Dasain, in Kathmandu, 108 buffaloes and goats are sacrificed in special rites to Taleju and offered to the Kumārī. That Tantric Hinduism endures in Nepal is evident in the king's relationship to the Devī, as well as in the secret nature of the rites.

Another important religious center in Kathmandu is Paśupatināth Temple, dedicated to Śiva as Lord (*nātha*) of Lord (*pati*) of Creatures (*paśu*). On the festival of Mahāśivarātri, over a hundred thousand devotees from throughout Nepal flock to the temple, among them Śaiva ascetics. The kings of Nepal from various dynasties visited this temple on such occasions. They continue to support it, because their legitimacy to rule as divine agents on earth depends on the implicit approval ceded to them by temples of such broad regional significance. The power of divine kingship derives from tacit identifications with the high gods of Hinduism, in which the king is viewed virtually as an incarnation of Śiva or Viṣṇu, and a tutelary goddess, such as Taleju, is regarded as his spouse.

Hinduism in South-east Asia

Chinese chronicles assert the existence of the kingdom of Funan, culturally influenced by India, which likely occupied a region stretching from modern day Myanmar (Burma) to Vietnam, as early as the first century CE. Funan yielded to the smaller Chenla kingdom by the sixth century CE. Artifacts dating from the seventh century from the neighboring Champa kingdom, founded in the second century CE in the region of modern day Vietnam, show definite Hindu influences.

In Cambodia

By the late eighth century, the Chenla had developed into the Khmer kingdom, whose capital eventually became the city of Angkor. Like Chenla, the Khmer kings were initially Śiva worshippers, and had established a *devarāja* cult, in which the kings (*rāja*) were considered divine (*deva*). But they had also begun to embrace Vaiṣṇavism, via an intermediary deity known as Harihara, who was a fusion of Viṣṇu (Hari) and Śiva (Hara). One of the capital cities of Jayavarman II, who founded the Khmer Empire, was known as Hariharālaya (Abode of Harihara). Brahmin priests were custodians of the ritual arts of consecrations (*abhiśeka*), which were perceived to confer grace, vigor, empowerment, and even divinity, onto those who received them. Thus Hinduism spread as local chieftains and kings sought out these special rites. Inscriptions testify to the privileged place held by important religious figures, some of whom functioned as royal priests (*rāja-purohita*).

In the early twelfth century, Suryavarman II built Angkor Wat, possibly the largest religious edifice ever built. By the thirteenth century, influences from Thailand contributed to the shift in royal patronage to Theravada Buddhism, and Angkor Wat became a Buddhist monastery by the fifteenth century. Shortly thereafter, the city was overrun by invasion, and progressively abandoned. The ruins of the city of Angkor, with its hosts of Buddhist and Hindu temples, remained thickly overgrown by tropical jungle until archeological excavations began in earnest in the late nineteenth century.

Angkor Wat was possibly a funerary temple built for Suryavarman II, and dedicated to Viṣṇu, with whom the king was identified. Some scholars estimate that it took about 70,000 laborers about thirty years to complete it. The temple soars almost seven hundred feet above ground level, more than one and a half times the height of St Peter's Basilica in Rome. Its central and surrounding peaks represent Mount Meru. In fact, the entire structural plan of Angkor is a rendition of a Vaiṣṇava model of the cosmos, with its enclosing walls representing the mountains at the edge of the world, and its surrounding moat the oceans beyond. A gallery on the first level contains more than 12,000 square feet of bas-reliefs on its sandstone walls. They depict favorite mythic themes, such as the Churning of the Ocean, and Rāma and the monkey army's battle with Rāvaṇa in Laṅkā. Reliefs of thousands of *apsaras*, celestial nymphs, sometimes in clusters of two and three, line the walls of the temple.

In Myanmar and Thailand

Hindu influences in the regions of Myanmar (Burma) and Thailand existed from the time of the Funan kingdom. Khmer Hinduism, evidenced by temples such as Wat Phu (southern Laos) and Phanom Rung (Thailand), had also revitalized Hinduism in those regions. However, Buddhism eventually became the dominant religion of Myanmar, Thailand, Laos, and Vietnam. Nevertheless, Hindu deities such as Brahmā, Indra, Garuḍa, and Gaṇeśa are still ubiquitous, especially in Thailand, primarily through their connections with Buddhism. Particular families of Thai Brahmins still conduct special *pūjās*. Most noteworthy among these are the *rājagurus*, who perform rites, such as the coronation and ploughing ceremonies, for the royal family. Thai royalty models itself on dharmic ideals derived from both Hinduism and Buddhism. The Thai capital, prior to Bangkok, was named Ayutthaya, after the mythic king Rāma's royal city. The current king of Thailand is Rama IX, the ninth king of the ruling Chakri Dynasty, who is named after the *avatāra* of Viṣṇu. The founding rulers of this dynasty composed passages included in the Thai version of the *Rāmāyaṇa*, known as the *Rāmakien*. *Rāmāyaṇa* motifs grace the walls of Buddhist temples throughout South-east Asia.

Hinduism in Indonesia

Hinduism was evident in the islands of the Indonesian archipelago by the first century CE. Hindu kings also ruled on the island of Borneo as testified by inscriptions from the fourth century CE. The Chinese pilgrim Fa-xien, writing in the mid-fifth century, tells of his stay on the island of Java, where forms of Hinduism were flourishing. Buddhism also flourished in the regions of Java and Sumatra. Buddhism and Hinduism appear to have coexisted and syncretized. The largest Buddhist monument in the world, Borobudur, was built on Java in the early ninth century. One finds Śiva temples dating from the seventh century in Java, and Prambanan, the largest Hindu temple complex in Indonesia, is also located on the island, not far from the city of Yogyakarta. Prambanan was built in the mid-ninth century, and has three main shrines (dedicated to Śiva, Viṣṇu, and Brahmā), each of which has memorable sculptural ornamentation. Islam entered Java by the thirteenth century and by the sixteenth century had dominated the religious landscape of much of Indonesia, except for the island of Bali.

Balinese Hinduism

The Hindu Mahapajit (Balinese: Majapahit) kingdom (1293–1590 CE), which had ruled Eastern Java, migrated to Bali and islands further east to escape the advance of Islam. Although 85 per cent of Indonesia's population of nearly 200 million is now Muslim, more than 90 per cent of Bali's population of 3.5 million is Hindu. Bali is an island, both literally and figuratively, of Hindu religious culture, which developed for many centuries in relative isolation from the Hinduism of India. Thus Balinese Hinduism, which had received influences from Buddhism, and which was itself superposed upon the indigenous religious traditions of the island's population, has distinctive expressions.

Almost everyone who has visited Bali has observed lines of colorfully dressed women carrying baskets teeming with fruit offerings, or has seen the Balinese making offerings of flowers and water at innumerable small shrines in household yards and throughout the countryside. The Balinese sometimes refer to their religion as Āgama Hindu Dharma (Righteous Behavior in accord with Hindu Āgamas). They have adopted the four-fold *varṇa* system of Indian Hinduism, with a number of sub-castes. The main god in Bali is Ciwa (Śiva), who is also identified in manifestation as the Sun. Ritual is of central importance, and the Balinese perform hundreds of rites (*yadnya*, from the Sanskrit *yajña*) annually. There are simple private purifications performed to rid oneself of karmic impurities, as well as public rites for collective well-being. Rites of passage include "tooth-filing," performed at the onset of puberty, in which the points of the upper canine teeth are filed to reduce, symbolically, one's animal propensities. There are rites for the ordination of priests, religious rites for a wide assortment of divine spirits both benevolent and malevolent, and a variety of temple rituals. Every family has a temple dedicated to its deified ancestors on its household premises. Every village has temples dedicated to Ciwa (Śiva), Wisnu (Viṣṇu), and Brahma (Brahmā), as well as temples of larger, regional significance. One of Bali's most important temples is at Besakih, at the foot of the volcano Mount Agung. Temple shrines are topped with multi-tiered thatched roofs, resembling the oriental pagoda design, called "*meru*" after the cosmic mountain.

The Hindu Epics are particularly important in Balinese culture. The protagonists of the *Rāmāyaṇa* and *Mahābhārata* are depicted in wood carvings and paintings, and episodes are enacted in their traditions of shadow puppetry (*wayang*) and sacred dances. In certain sacred dances, such as one that enacts the conflict between the

Figure 15.3 Dance performance in Bali enacting Hindu religious themes

female demon Rangda and the playful, lion-like Barong, dancers playing the role of the Barong's helpers are thrust into a trance by the evil Rangda and are induced to stab themselves with their daggers. However, protected by the Barong's power, their flesh is impervious to Rangda's spell. They are finally brought out of their trance through the ministrations of an attending priest, who sprinkles them with consecrated water, a pervasive element in Balinese rituals. Battles between the forces of good and evil are being fought on a cosmic scale at all times in Balinese religious philosophy. Religious rites are thus conducted regularly to honor and please the powers of good, and to propitiate the forces of evil.

Discussion questions

1. Why do you think the Hindu Epics play such an important role in Balinese religious culture?
2. What do you think was the appeal of Hindu culture that made it spread beyond the confines of the Indian subcontinent?
3. What role might geography play in shaping the religious character of a particular area? Can you use the contexts of Nepal and South-east Asia as examples?

4. Discuss the religious significance of the structure known as Angkor Wat?
5. How does Balinese Hinduism differ from Hinduism in India?
6. Discuss the processes that shape the character of Cambodian religion today.

Key points in this chapter

- Nepal is currently the world's only multi-ethnic, multilingual, democratic, Hindu kingdom.
- One of Nepal's most widely celebrated religious festivals is Dasain, celebrated in honor of Durgā, who is also identified with Taleju Bhavānī, a royal tutelary goddess.
- Nepal is also noted for its tradition of living goddesses, known as Kumārīs.
- Hinduism spread as local chieftains and kings sought out special consecration rites, believed to grant them extraordinary powers and status.
- Hindu influences are found throughout South-east Asia, even though the dominant religions of those regions have changed.
- Bali is an island that developed distinctive forms of Hindu religious culture in isolation from the Hinduism of India.

Further reading

Hinduism in Nepal

Allen, Michael (1975) *The Cult of Kumari: Virgin Worship in Nepal*. Kathmandu: Tribhuvan University.

Bennett, Lynn (1983) *Dangerous Wives and Sacred Sisters: Social and Symbolic Roles of High-Caste Women in Nepal*. New York: Columbia University Press.

Levy, Robert I. (1990) *Mesocosm: Hinduism and the Organization of a Traditional Newar City in Nepal*. Berkeley, CA: University of California Press.

Slusser, Mary Shepherd (1982) *Nepal Maṇḍala: A Cultural Study of the Kathmandu Valley*, 2 vols. Princeton, NJ: Princeton University Press.

Hinduism in Indonesia

Geertz, Clifford (1980) *Negara: The Theatre-State in Nineteenth-Century Bali*. Princeton, NJ: Princeton University Press.

Howe, Leo (2001) *Hinduism and Hierarchy in Bali*. Oxford: James Currey.

Phalgunadi, I. Gusti Putu (1991) *Evolution of Hindu Culture in Bali*. Delhi: Sundeep Prakashan.

Hinduism in South-east Asia

Kulke, Hermann (1993) *Kings and Cults: State Formation and Legitimation in India and Southeast Asia.* Delhi: Manohar Publications.

Hinduism in Sri Lanka

Obeyesekere, G. (1984) *Medusa's Hair.* Chicago, IL: University of Chicago Press.
— (1984) *The Cult of the Goddess Pattini.* Chicago, IL: University of Chicago Press.

16 *Hinduism and the West*

In this chapter

It is primarily within the last century and a half that Hinduism has spread to the West. While Hindu immigrants form the bulk of this expansion, there have been a number of religious teachers who have carried their messages to the West. Here, through a series of exemplary case studies, we examine the roles played by figures or organizations of pivotal importance. This chapter also uses certain distinctive cases to illustrate typologies of the forms in which Hinduism is being shaped for, delivered to, and experienced by the West.

Main topics covered

- Diaspora Hinduism
- Hinduism for the West
- Some contemporary teachers of Hinduism to Westerners

Over two millennia ago, Hinduism initially spread beyond the immediate confines of the Indian subcontinent through imperial expansion by Hindu monarchs and because of overtures by neighboring kingdoms desiring to expose themselves to India's religious culture. Certain Greek Sophists expressed doctrines, such as on transmigration, that paralleled Indian notions, and it is evident that some Hindu *śramaṇas* visited ancient Greece. The Persian Empire, under Darius I had already reached the banks of the Indus River by 513 BCE, linking western India to Greece. By 326 BCE, Alexander of Macedonia's eastward expansion past the Indus River had irrevocably linked Indian civilization to the West, and that Hellenic Empire was fertile soil for the intermingling of knowledge, both religious and secular. Even today, certain Hindu communities in Kashmir claim to have Greek origins. Megasthenes, a Seleucid Greek ambassador who was sent to the empire of Candragupta (Aśoka's grandfather), reported on the glories of Pataliputra, the Mauryan capital.

In the second century BCE, the Indo-Greeks from the region of Bactria (modern Afghanistan) extended their conquests after the fall of the Mauryan Empire through much of North India, including Pataliputra. The Christian Church Father, Clement of Alexandria (second century CE), expressed a familiarity with the Indian *śramaṇa* traditions, and the neo-Platonism of Plotinus (third century CE) has remarkable resonance with Upaniṣadic thought and the philosophy of Rāja Yoga. The discovery in 1945 of many apocryphal Christian scriptures, such as *The Gospel of Thomas*, at Nag Hammadi in Egypt and dated to the late fourth century CE, have fuelled renewed interest in the similarities between the Gnostic ideas they contain and Asian religious thought.

Despite the similarities among these various religious philosophies, and the provocative notion of mutual influences, it is difficult to extract convincing evidence of specific Hindu religious ideas that migrated from East to West, or vice versa. Unlike Buddhism, Christianity, and Islam, Hinduism is not intrinsically a missionary tradition, since it is so entwined with issues of caste lineages, regional affiliations and so on. Thus, its spread to further reaches of the globe has primarily occurred within the last few centuries through the migration of Hindu communities after European colonization. The Hindu diaspora has mostly gravitated to former colonies of the British Empire, and to the United Kingdom itself, although there are growing numbers of migrants to the United States and the oil rich Middle Eastern countries.

Quite remarkably, despite its lack of significant missionizing, various aspects of Hinduism have permeated the West well beyond the confines of the Hindu communities abroad. Religious movements, and in particular, certain meditative practices, have begun to be embraced in large numbers by non-Hindus worldwide.

Diaspora Hinduism

When European nations officially abolished slavery, the search for inexpensive workers led to a system of bonded labor, in which people would agree to work in various colonial outposts for a fixed duration of time. North Indian Hindus, in particular, as well as Sikhs and Muslims, went to work in sugar cane, rubber, and cocoa plantations in such places as the Caribbean islands, Fiji, South and East Africa, and northeast South America (e.g. Guyana and Surinam). Many South Indians went to Myanmar (Burma) and Malaysia. When their contracts ended, most of these laborers ended up remaining in those countries, forming sizable Hindu populations there.

Many Hindus emigrated to Britain, utilizing a right granted to all of Britain's colonial subjects. Others were recruited to fill job vacancies after the depletion of the labor force following World War II. When nationalist sentiments caused certain African countries, such as Uganda in 1972, to drive non-native Africans from their countries, tens of thousands of Hindus left for Britain and Canada. Tens of thousands of Hindus have also migrated to the Persian Gulf States, such as Dubai, Kuwait and the United Arab Emirates, where immigrant populations often outnumber the citizenry. The loosening of restrictions on immigration in Canada and the United States in recent decades has led to a marked increase in Hindus who are often elite professionals to North America, as well as to a growth in Hindu populations there through family reunification policies. North American Hindus' incomes, on average, tend to be higher than the national norm.

While certain groups of Hindus in the global diaspora are keen on cultural integration with their new home nations, many join organizations to preserve Hindu traditions to varying degrees. In small communities, Indo-Pakistani societies are religiously pluralistic, formed to preserve shared aspects of South Asian cultural heritage, such as cuisine and music. In somewhat larger communities, a Hindu temple may provide a religious center, but the diversity within Hinduism itself sometimes create tensions as members from widespread regions of the Hindu world and with differing sectarian orientations negotiate commonly acceptable worship modes. Finding Brahmin priests to preside at diasporic temples can be challenging, and there are often efforts to secure such religious professionals from India. In yet larger diasporic communities, caste distinctions become more significant, and Hindus may join caste-based organizations. Since marriage within one's caste is of central importance to most Hindus, and since marriages are mostly arranged, the affluent may send children of marriageable age back to India to find an appropriate spouse, or advertise broadly in community newspapers to secure partners closer to home. Generational conflicts, based on religious and cultural standards, are commonplace among diasporic communities as second and third generation Hindu children begin to espouse the values of their non-Hindu peers. Pre-marital sex and "love-marriages" are particular sources of tension. Some researchers have noted generational oscillations, one generation pulling away from what are regarded as old-fashioned traditions, while the next seeks to embrace and retain an endangered heritage.

Hinduism for the West

The case studies that follow offer a few salient examples of particular modes in which aspects of Hinduism have made inroads into the West.

Case study: Swami Vivekānanda and the Vedānta Society

In 1893, the World Parliament of Religions held in tandem with the World's Columbian Exposition in Chicago, attracted a number of influential figures. Among these was Annie Besant of the Theosophical Society and Swami Vivekānanda. Educated as a lawyer and a member of the Brahmo Samāj, Narendranath Dutta

(1863–1902) eventually turned to the teachings of the unconventional Hindu saint, Ramakrishna Paramahamsa, becoming his most celebrated disciple. After Ramakrishna's death, Dutta took up official renunciation and eventually assumed the name Swami Vivekānanda. During his travels from Bengal to South India, he is believed to have swum to and meditated on a large offshore rock that now bears his name, off India's southernmost tip, Kanyā Kumārī. Encouraged and supported to represent Hinduism, Vivekānanda journeyed to Chicago, where his intelligence, charisma, and eloquence made a memorable impact on his audience, most of whom were quite unfamiliar with Indian religious philosophies. Invited to speak in various venues in the United States and England after the Chicago gathering, Swami Vivekānanda then returned to India, formed the Ramakrishna Order, and dispatched teachers to the West. Vivekānanda's visit to the West is regarded as a pivotal moment in the West's burgeoning interest in Hinduism.

Ramakrishna had promoted both the attainment of liberation and work for the social welfare of humanity, holding neither one as a substitute for the other. The branches of the Ramakrishna Order in the West go by the name of the Vedānta Society, because this is the primary expression of Hinduism that was perceived to have the most universal appeal. Although Ramakrishna's personal spiritual practices spanned the spectrum from Tantra and *bhakti* to non-dual Vedānta, the Vivekānanda schools emphasize the latter approach, in resonance with the Upaniṣadic focus of the Brahmo Samāj, which had attracted Vivekānanda in his youth. Vedānta is so central to the philosophy of the Ramakrishna Order that Vivekānanda would have liked to use the term as a synonym for Hinduism. The influence of the Vedānta Society in the West was so great in the twentieth century that it is not unusual to still find introductory texts on Hinduism portraying "Hindu religion/philosophy" essentially as radical non-dualistic Vedānta in the tradition of Śaṅkara. A quote from the *Ṛg Veda* (I.164.46) that runs, *"Ekaṃ sad; vipra bahudha vadanti"* (Truth is one; sages call it variously) conveys their inclusive, tolerant spirit. The Vedānta Society exemplifies the transmission of those facets of Hinduism which have intellectual appeal and meld well with Western rationalism and Christian monotheism.

In the wake of Vivekānanda's influence, many other notable teachers arrived from India and formed various organizations in the West. Among these was the founder of the Self-Realization Fellowship, Paramahansa Yogananda, whose book *Autobiography of a Yogi* continues to be widely read. The case studies that follow highlight an assortment of such significantly influential figures.

Case study: Jiddu Krishnamurti (1895–1986)

Although he may be just as easily categorized as a Buddhist rather than a Hindu religious teacher, Jiddu Krishnamurti would certainly have rejected both such designations. Selected by Annie Besant and other Theosophists when he was a boy, Krishnamurti, who came from a South Indian Brahmin family, headed the Order of the Star, a subgroup of the Theosophical Society. Schooled in London and Paris, Krishnamurti was envisioned as becoming the physical vehicle of the next World Teacher (*jagadguru*), a sort of fusion of the Christ and the Buddha, who would initiate a teaching that would move humanity in its spiritual evolution. However, after a pivotal mystical experience, Krishnamurti disbanded the Order at the age of thirty-four, left the Theosophical Society, and promulgated his own teachings for the remainder of his life. His departure dealt a powerful blow to the Theosophical Society, which had invested much of their credibility in him as the spokesperson for Theosophist doctrines.

Krishnamurti's essential message supports the notion that a radical transformation of one's consciousness is essential to bring an end to personal psychological conflict and conflict in the world. However, religious organizations, beliefs, and teachers are impediments to one's liberation, since these construe spiritual awakening as a graded journey, which serves their interests and reinforces self-centered, egotistic modes of consciousness. Krishnamurti's criticisms of all spiritual teachers (*guru*), religious paths, scriptures, and dogmas have garnered him considerable respect, as well as marginalization. Those religious authorities who acknowledge the gist of his message, but who still promote their structured, institutional approaches tend to place him on a pedestal as having attained liberation unconventionally, or claim that his teachings are too radical for the masses.

In the years before his death Krishnamurti had some landmark conversations with the renowned physicist David Bohm, whose holistic theoretical formulations are garnering interest, especially among those seeking connections between science and spirituality. Although some have compared Krishnamurti's teachings with the *via negativa* of radical non-dual Vedānta, Krishnamurti did not endorse any scriptures, and does not promulgate blind belief in the existence of any Absolute entity (e.g. Saguṇa Brahman). He does exemplify the renouncer spirit of Hinduism, which upholds the value of liberative understanding by transcending ego-sustaining attachments to the formulations of the thinking mind.

Case study: Maharishi Mahesh Yogi (1917–) and Transcendental Meditation

Maharishi Mahesh Yogi was born in central India, and obtained a university degree in physics. After having served for many years under one of the leaders of a Śaṅkara monastery in north India, he began his own organizations which came to be known as the Transcendental Meditation (TM) movement. TM took the West by storm in the early 1970s after having attracted such high profile disciples as The Beatles. The organization claims to have taught its technique to over five million people and now runs a variety of educational centers.

Transcendental Meditation consists of *mantra* repetition, which is to be performed in two, twenty-minute sessions daily. TM is presented very clearly as not a religion, lifestyle, or philosophy, but as a simple technique that reduces stress and enhances mental tranquility, and as a result brings with it other health and even economic benefits. It has supported scientific research into the physical and psychological benefits derived from the practice of its technique. It would not be an exaggeration to acknowledge that the Transcendental Meditation movement was a major contributor to the general acceptance in the West of meditation as an effective means of stress reduction, and similar techniques are now routinely prescribed by medical professionals. TM exemplifies the promulgation of a technique derived from ancient yogic practices, but divorced from its religious and soteriological contexts. This has earned it some criticism from Hindu traditionalists. It typifies the widespread permeation of particular spiritual practices (e.g. Haṭha Yoga), with substantial pedigrees in Hindu traditions, stripped of their religious connotations. In doing so, the TM method has not been perceived as much of a threat to Western religious traditions, and it is rare to hear accusations of "brainwashing" and so on, which were commonplace during the years of its introduction to the West.

Case study: Swami Bhaktivedanta and the International Society for Kṛṣṇa Consciousness (ISKCON)

The Vedānta Society and the Transcendental Meditation Movement conveyed select aspects of Hinduism with just enough Indian cultural trappings to gain some advantages derived from their exotic, newly respectable Eastern origins. However, Swami Bhaktivedanta brought Kṛṣṇa *bhakti* to the West in a form that still hallmarks the Western stereotype of unusual Eastern religions. The Bengali born Swami Bhaktivedanta Prabhupada (1896–1977) studied chemistry at university and ran a small pharmacy before taking initiation at the age of thirty-six in the Gaudiya tradition founded by Śrī Caitanya. At the age of sixty-three, he became a *saṃnyāsin*. Encouraged by his *guru* to spread the message of Kṛṣṇa devotion to English speakers and the West, he set sail for the United States, enduring two heart attacks during the voyage, and arriving at the age of sixty-nine in New York City with seven dollars in his pocket. Undaunted by this unpromising beginning to his missionary enterprise, he began to preach in the Lower East Side of Manhattan, a nexus of the burgeoning counter-culture movement. He soon attracted disciples whose public chanting (*kīrtana*) of the Vaiṣṇava's *mahāmantra* led people to call them the Hare Kṛṣṇas. More distinctive and attention-grabbing than the ecstatic, trance-like singing and dancing was the appearance of the young devotees, who had shaved heads, wore saffron robes of renunciation, and decorated their foreheads with Vaiṣṇava sect markings. Members of the Hare Kṛṣṇa movement, which is officially known as the International Society for Kṛṣṇa Consciousness (ISKCON), were highly visible because they often button-holed passers-by on street corners or at airport arrival gates with flowers and free copies of the *Bhagavad Gītā*, translated and commented upon by Swami Bhaktivedanta.

Conversions to this movement sometimes led to backlashes by those who thought their family members were being brainwashed, and some families even hired "de-programmers" from anti-cult organizations to free their loved ones from what was perceived as a dangerous religious cult. The movement was plagued by scandals and law-suits with charges ranging from aggressive proselytizing to child molestation. Nevertheless, over the years since Swami Bhaktivedanta's death, ISKCON has become one of the most highly visible and influential societies for the propagation of Vaiṣṇava *bhakti* Hinduism in the West. Its many temples worldwide have even begun to attract Hindus from the diaspora.

Figure 16.1 Lifelike image of Swami Bhaktivedanta, founder of ISKCON, at the organization's headquarters in Britain (Watford) [Photo courtesy of Sarah Ginn]

ISKCON is an exemplar of Hinduism that has come to the West with a fairly full deck of Indian culture appended to it. Its adherents were expected to adopt the appearance and cultural aesthetics of Bengali Vaiṣṇavas along with their religious world view, which were regarded as intrinsically connected. ISKCON considers itself fully aligned with the Gaudiya Vaiṣṇava tradition, although it actually reflects a North American offshoot of the movement. Despite its seeming traditionalism, ISKCON was radical in many ways. Drawing on arguments that one's piety is the true mark of a Brahmin, Swami Bhaktivedanta began to call anyone, including women, who officially joined the organization a Brahmin (*brāhmaṇa*), ceding higher respect to those who had taken *saṃnyāsa*. This outrages many hereditary Brahmins in India. Also, in contrast with traditional Hinduism, ISKCON is unabashedly intent on proselytizing. Many devotees consider Swami Bhaktivedanta to be an *avatāra* of Śrī Caitanya.

Case study: Osho (Bhagwan Rajneesh)

Osho (1930–1990) was born to Jain parents in central India, where he studied and eventually taught philosophy at the University of Jabalpur. At the age of thirty-five, he became a religious teacher, first attracting Indian and then Western disciples to his *āśrama*, which was eventually located in Pune (Poona), in the state of Maharashtra. His organization had received wide public attention because his disciples used to wear orange clothes, symbolizing the spiritual path, and a photograph of their *guru*, who then went by the name of Bhagwan (Lord) Rajneesh, on a beaded necklace. Rajneesh had also achieved some notoriety because he approved of tantric oriented practices of co-opting sexual energy for the attainment of spiritual goals. In 1981, he moved his *āśrama* to a rural region of Oregon, in the United States. The affluence of many of his disciples led to massive financial contributions and scandalous displays of conspicuous consumerism. Rajneesh is reputed to have had over ninety Rolls Royce automobiles given to him. The *āśrama* was also rocked with allegations of assassination plots (on local citizenry), tax evasion, and political manipulation. It is generally believed these were the acts of disciples whose actions were no longer under the control of Rajneesh himself. Rajneesh then returned to India, assumed the name Osho, and re-established his *āśrama* in Pune.

Like most Eastern religious teachers, Osho emphasized the need for the attainment of enlightenment. However, he felt that human beings, particularly those from Western cultures, were so psychologically repressed that they needed to use every available method at their disposal to free themselves from their conditioning and enable them to tread the path to liberation effectively. Thus Osho's *āśrama* promotes both Eastern meditative methods, such as various *yogas*, and techniques found in the modern Western psycho-therapeutic tradition. In addition, he utilized his own meditative techniques, such as the Mystic Rose, where participants laugh for three hours daily for a week, then cry for a similar stretch of time, and finally remain with quiet awareness for the final week.

Osho exemplifies the controversial Indian *guru*, a term which, for many in the West, often conjures up the figure of a charlatan who is a purveyor of religion for personal gain. Osho's material excesses, the intrigues at his *āśrama*, and the promotion of tantric sexual techniques, have all contributed to that image. However, he also typifies the inclusive spirit found in Hindu traditions. While Krishnamurti's teachings advise extreme prudence when following religious teachers and their prescribed methods, Osho appears to endorse embracing whatever is available and suited to one's temperament. In keeping with its tantric spirit, Osho's teachings promote channeling the human thirst for joy, pleasure, and passion towards the spiritual quest. They also support the notion that enlightenment is fundamentally a return to one's original childlike innocence, which has been lost through the effects of social and religious conditioning.

Case study: T. Krishnamacharya and Haṭha Yoga

Tirumalai Krishnamacharya (1888–1988), although mostly unknown, has been one of the most influential patriarchs of *yoga* practice in the West. Born in South India, Krishnamacharya, whose family traces its lineage to Nathamuni, claimed to have had a vision of that eleventh century Ālvār saint, who taught him the lost *sūtras* of the ancient *Yoga Rahasya* (*Esoteric Teachings on Yoga*). B. K. S. Iyengar (1918–) is one of Krishnamacharya's best known disciples. Iyengar's widely read *Light on Yoga* is mainly a manual on *yoga* postures (*āsanas*), which is of principal interest to many Western practitioners of *yoga*. Various systems of yogic techniques, introduced by other disciples of Krishnamacharya, are also gaining popularity. Among these is Ashtanga Vinyasa, promoted by Pattabhi Jois, which emphasizes fluid transitions between postures, providing a vigorous cardio-vascular workout. Krishnamacharya's son, T. K. V. Desikachar, has been carrying on the tradition of his father's latter-day teachings in what is referred to as the Viniyoga approach, because it adapts yogic techniques to the needs and limitations of the practitioners. Although all the schools spawned by Krishnamacharya's teachings purport to integrate all of the Eight Limbs (*aṣṭāṅga*) presented in Patañjali's *Yoga Sūtra*, and other *yoga* treatises, the schools emphasize primarily posture and breath work, at least in the initial stages. In this regard, all these methods are most closely aligned with the Haṭha Yoga approach.

Yoga has entered the mainstream in the West and is widely practiced as a form of physical fitness exercise responding to Western pre-occupations with longevity and quality of life. As in the case of Transcendental Meditation, the liberative purposes of *yoga*, as expressed in Patañjali's *Yoga Sūtra*, are downplayed or completely ignored. Because of their differing objectives, it might be more appropriate to label the configurations of the Western practices as yogic techniques, rather than the *darśana* of Yoga, per se.

Some contemporary teachers of Hinduism to Westerners

The groups or persons discussed here are only selected because they have achieved some repute among Westerners interested in Hindu religious practices, or among Western seekers of liberation. They offer touchstones to other teachers and teachings and are illustrative of particular typologies of approaches.

Case study: Swami Sivananda Saraswati and the Divine Life Society

Swami Sivananda Saraswati (1887–1963), born in South India, was educated as a doctor and worked for many years in Malaya. After returning to India, he was ordained as a monk, and wandered the length and breadth of India. He went back to Rishikesh, at the Himalayan foothills, and began the Divine Life Society. His reputation grew through providing venues for monks to gather, and he emphasized the need for monks to care for each other. He wrote extensively, and his Society later attracted Western disciples interested in Vedānta and in his Yoga of Synthesis, a blend of *jñāna, karma,* and *bhakti* approaches. Among his disciples who went to the West were Swami Vishnudevananda, who formed *yoga* centers worldwide, headquartered in Montreal, Canada, and Swami Sivananda Radha, a female *saṃnyāsinī,* whose *āśrama* is located in British Columbia, Canada. The Divine Life Society conveys a mostly orthodox, moderately conservative Hindu ideology, typical of the organized renouncer traditions of the Śaṅkara monasteries.

Case study: Ramesh Balsekar

Ramesh Balsekar (1919–) is a British-educated former manager of the Bank of India. He was a disciple of Nisargadatta Maharaj (1897–1981), who was known as the "Bīdī Baba" because he ran a small shop selling *bīdīs,* Indian cigarettes made from low-grade tobacco rolled in leaves from the Tendu tree, not paper. Nisargadatta achieved international recognition through the publication of his book, *I Am That*. After Nisargadatta's death, Balsekar began holding *satsangs* (gatherings) at his Mumbai (Bombay) apartment in the early 1980s. Balsekar uses references to Buddhism, Taoism, and Advaita Vedānta in his teachings, which stress the illusion of a separate self as agent. The only reality is Consciousness, which acts. People's unhappiness and their search for meaning is the result of a misplaced identification with a particular configuration of events, or "happenings." By watching the unfolding of the activities of Consciousness, without attachment, one may attain Self-realization. Balsekar's students include the poet Leonard Cohen, and some disciples who have been acknowledged by Balsekar as having become realized, such as Wayne Liquorman (aka Ram Tzu), spread his teachings through seminars around the world.

Balsekar exemplifies the transnational lay religious teacher, whose message is no longer delivered exclusively in the idiom of Hinduism. He is conversant with the "perennial philosophy," a notion that similar realizations have been attained by mystics in all cultures throughout time, expressed variously and reflective of their cultural circumstances. Balsekar typifies approaches that do not endorse monastic renunciation as a mark of authenticity.

Case study: Gangaji

Gangaji (1942–) was born Antoinette Varmer in the United States. She became a disciple of the Punjabi-born, Lucknow-based Indian spiritual master, H. W. L. Poonjaji (also known as Papaji). Poonjaji (1910–1997), who attracted many western disciples, was inspired by the teachings of Sri Ramaṇa Mahāṛṣi, whom he claimed as his master. Gangaji travels around the world, conveying a message of awakening to one's true nature as "That," the source and substance of all reality.

Gangaji typifies teachers who claim Hindu spiritual lineage transmissions, but who are themselves not of Indian origin. Such lineage authorization is highly desired by many disciples, because belief in the indispensable need for and official dispensation from a living, self-realized *guru* leads many seekers to hunt out appropriate teachers and lineage holders. What such non-Indian teachers lose in their appeal as "exotic Hindu" masters, they gain in the cultural background they share with their disciples, which allows for easier communication and accessibility. They may also gain the disdain of certain groups of orthodox Hindus who feel that "authentic Hinduism" requires all purveyors of its teachings to belong to upper class *varṇas*, while all outsiders are Untouchables, by default. However, such teachers may not actually be breaching orthodox norms, since they are akin to renouncers, to whom the dharmic restrictions of *varṇa* do not apply.

Such authorized lineage holders who teach in the West eliminate the burden of arduous travels to and prolonged residence in the East for those Western disciples who are themselves seeking authorization to teach, and who are interested in eventually establishing their own organizations. Thus, they represent the frontline of burgeoning, distinctive religious institutions, rooted in Hindu teachings on liberation, abroad.

Case study: Adi Da

Born Franklin Albert Jones in New York in 1939, Adi Da studied with Swami Muktananda in India, and became a self-proclaimed awakened teacher in 1970.

Swami Muktananda (1908–1982) was the propagator of the Siddha Yoga Tradition, which has its headquarters at Ganeshpuri, not far from Mumbai (Bombay) in the state of Maharashtra. The official lineage holder currently in Muktananda's organization is a woman, Swami Chidvilasananda (or Gurumayi), whose detractors question her luxurious and mostly Western lifestyle. Adi Da has adopted various names through the years, including Bubba Free John, Da-Love Ananda, and Adi Da Samraj. He has founded a religion known as Adidam, headquartered on the Fijian island of Naitouba, where he and his closest disciples live. Adi Da's teachings emphasize a complete surrender to the *guru*, regarded as Divine, who through esoteric practices, which may include sexual interactions, might enable the disciple to gain liberation.

Adi Da exemplifies non-Hindu *gurus* whose teachings are derived from, or blended with, conceptual categories derived from Hinduism, but which are presented in forms that are unique to the teacher. Not purporting to belong to, to have derived authorization from, or to feel committed to upholding any particular tradition, the formulations of such teachers and their groups are often eclectic, controversial, and creative expressions of Hinduism at the periphery of its global expansion.

Discussion questions

1. *Yoga* has entered the mainstream in the West and is widely practiced as a form of physical fitness often excluding its enlightenment purposes as described in ancient yogic texts. Do you think that it is still appropriate for Westerners to call it *yoga*? Why or why not?
2. Gangaji claims a Hindu spiritual lineage, but is not of Indian origin. Do you think this would be looked upon more positively or negatively by Western students seeking a "Hindu" *guru*?
3. In what ways do you think Hinduism has changed as it entered the West? Do you think its movement into the West has caused Hinduism to simplify itself, or do you think it has become more complex through the process?
4. Choose two of the important figures discussed in this chapter. Explain their teachings, and how they were important in bringing Hinduism to the West.
5. Choose two of the important organizations discussed in this chapter. Describe the organizations, the individuals associated with them, and what impact each had in bringing Hinduism to the West.
6. What events took place that allowed for the spread of Hinduism to the West?

Key points in this chapter

- Hinduism, which is not intrinsically a missionary tradition, spread beyond India through imperial expansion by Hindu monarchs and due to an interest in India's religious culture.
- The migration of Hindus outside India after European colonization has spread Hinduism across the globe.
- Many Hindus in the global diaspora join organizations to preserve their religious traditions abroad.
- In 1893, Swami Vivekānanda's visit to the World Parliament of Religions marks a beginning of the modern West's exposure to Eastern religions.
- The Vedānta Society, Transcendental Meditation, ISKCON, and the Hare Kṛṣṇa movement have all greatly influenced understandings of Hinduism in the West.
- Hinduism continues to permeate Western culture through the appeal of various teachings, and the efforts of a variety of teachers.

Further reading

On the Hindu diaspora

Burghard, R. (ed.) *Hinduism in Great Britain: The Perpetuation of Religion in an Alien Cultural Milieu*. London: Tavistock.

Coward, Harold, G. et al (1998) *The South Asian Religious Diaspora in Britain, Canada, and the United States*. Albany, NY: State University of New York Press.

Eck, D. (2002) *On Common Ground: World Religions in America*. New York: Columbia University Press.

Fenton, J. Y. (1988) *Transplanting Religious Traditions: Asian Indians in America*. New York: Praeger.

Jackson, R., and E. Nesbitt (1993) *Hindu Children in Britain*. Stoke on Trent: Trentham Books.

Knott, K. (1986) *Hinduism in Leeds*. Leeds: University of Leeds Press.

Knott, K. and R. Toon (1982) *Muslims, Sikhs and Hindus in the UK: Problems in the Estimation of Religious Statistics*. Theology and Religious Studies Department, University of Leeds.

Lal, C. (1961) *Hindu America*. Bombay: Bharatiya Vidya Bhavan.

Majumdar, R. C. (1963) *Hindu Colonies in the Far East*. Calcutta: Firma K. L. Mukhopadhyay.

Rukmani, T. S. (ed.) (1999) *The Hindu Diaspora: Global Perspectives*. Montreal: Concordia University Chair in Hindu Studies.

Vertovec, S. (1992) *Hindu Trinidad*. London: Macmillan.
— (2000) *The Hindu Diaspora: Comparative Patterns*. London: Routledge.
Williams, B. (1988) *Religions of Immigrants from India and Pakistan*. Cambridge: Cambridge University Press.

On Hindu teachers and teachings in the West

Babb, Lawrence A. (1987) *Redemptive Encounters: Three Modern Styles in the Hindu Tradition*. Delhi: Oxford University Press.
Harper, M. H. (1972) *Gurus, Swamis, and Avatāras: Spiritual Masters and Their American Disciples*. Philadelphia, PA: Westminster Press.
Humes, Cynthia and T. Fortshoefel (eds) (2005) *Gurus in America*. Albany, NY: State University of New York Press.
Pechilis, Karen (ed.) (2004) *The Graceful Guru: Hindu Female Gurus in India and the United States*. Oxford: Oxford University Press.
Riepe, D. (1990) *The Philosophy of India and its Impact on American Thought*. Springfield: Charles C. Thomas.

On specific teachers and organizations

Besant, A. (1922) *Theosophy and World Problems*. Adyar: Theosophical Publishing House.
Brooks, Charles R. (1989) *The Hare Krishnas in India*. Princeton, NJ: Princeton University Press.
Dāsa Goswami, Satsvarūpa (1983) *Prabhupāda: He Built a House in which the Whole World can Live*. Los Angeles, CA: Bhaktivedanta Book Trust.
Eban, Martin (ed.) (1968) *Maharishi the Guru: The Story of Maharishi Mahesh Yogi*. Bombay: Pear Publications.
Feuerstein, G. (1990) *Holy Madness: The Shock Tactics and Radical Teaching of Crazy-Wise Adepts, Holy Fools, and Rascal Gurus*. New York: Arkana.
Gelberg, S. J. (ed.) (1983) *Hare Krishna, Hare Krishna: Five Distinguished Scholars on the Krishna Movement in the West*. New York: Grove Press.
Jayakar, Pupul (1987) *J. Krishnamurti: A Biography*. Delhi: Penguin India.
Krishnamurti, Jiddu (1954) *The First and Last Freedom*. London: V. Gollancz.
— (1976) *The Awakening of Intelligence*. New York: Avon Books.
Kundra M. R. (n.d.) *Twenty-five Years with Divinity*. India: Sai Shriram Printers.
Muktananda, Swami (1983) *Secret of the Siddhas*. South Fallsburg, NY: SYDA Foundation.
Nikhilananda, Swami (trans.) (1930) *Gospel of Sri Ramakrishna*. Calcutta.
Radha, Swami Sivananda (aka Sylvia Hellman) (1981) *Rādhā: Diary of a Woman's Search*. Porthill: Timeless Books.

Rodrigues, Hillary (1991) *Insight and Religious Mind: An Analysis of Krishnamurti's Teachings on Insight and Religious Mind*. New York: Peter Lang Publishing.
— (2003) *Krishnamurti's Insight: An Examination of his Teachings on Mind and Religion*. Varanasi: Pilgrims Publishing.
Sharma, S. R. (1961) *Swami Rama Tirtha*. Bombay: Bharatiya Vidya Bhavan.
Vivekananda, Swami (1970–1971) *Complete Works of Swami Vivekananda*, 8 vols. Calcutta: Advaita Ashrama.
Yogananda, Paramahamsa (1960) *Autobiography of a Yogi*. Bombay: Jaico.

17 *Select themes in Hinduism*

In this chapter

As the dominant religion of the world's largest democracy, Hinduism will inevitably play significant roles in a world where nations are more interconnected than ever before. Environmental issues are global concerns. Communication technologies are dramatically linking people of the planet, exposing them to each other's values and interests, and compelling each person to confront international appraisals of their religious attitudes. The face of Hinduism is already changing in response to these forces. Here, we take a snapshot of salient features of Hinduism's current profile (e.g. influential figures and values), and then point to key areas in which global pressures are most intense (e.g. caste, gender, technology) and transformations most likely.

Main topics covered

- Hinduism and ecology
- Some noteworthy figures in contemporary Hinduism
- Hinduism and modernity

Hinduism and ecology

The world-negating themes in Hinduism, which emphasize transcendence of worldly existence, might suggest a disdain for the natural world. However, Hindu tradition has numerous themes that nurture ecological awareness and reverence for the creation. The earliest strata of Hindu religious literature, the Vedic Saṃhitās, intone hymns of praise and wonder to divine forces of nature, such as Agni (Fire), and Pṛthivi (Earth). The entire cosmos is envisioned in organic terms, as the Golden Egg (Hiraṇyagarbha), or as a Cosmic Person (Puruṣa). In such myths as the goddess Satī's dismemberment, in which her body parts fall to the earth, we note an unequivocal message that the entire world is the manifest body of the Goddess, and should thus be treated with respect. Every Hindu city, town, and village has an associated goddess, understood as the "mother" (Tamil: *ammā*) of that portion of land and the living things that inhabit it and who looks after their well-being, providing nourishment and protection for her "children." Even the nation of India is envisaged as the goddess Bhārat Mātā. The crucial role that rivers play in sustaining life was recognized from Vedic times, and it is therefore not incidental that the Gaṅgā River is regarded as a goddess.

While it is rarely correct to insinuate that religious values are grounded solely in "this-worldly" concerns, it is certainly true that holding something in high, even sacred, regard can further the attention and care given to it. The sacred designations of landscapes, rivers, and social communities, provide a foundation for reverential treatment of these entities, and can serve ecological interests. Organizations working to clean the Gaṅgā River, which suffers from both industrial and organic pollution as India's urban populations grow along its banks, frequently invoke the river's sacred status to mobilize social eco-active responses.

Figure 17.1 Lithograph depicting the goddess Gaṅgā atop her crocodile mount

The sacredness of the cow is one of the most emblematic symbols in Hinduism. To visitors, the sight of old cows in the urban landscape of India, wandering the streets amid automobile traffic or ambling into temples, is particularly perplexing. India's cow population is estimated at about three hundred million. Non-vegetarians are surprised that cow slaughter is illegal in almost all of India's states and its protection is enshrined in the nation's constitution. There are thousands of cow-shelters built in various parts of the country for stray and ill cattle. Many wonder why Hindus have this relationship to the "holy cow" when there are so many malnourished people in the country.

There are many reasons why cows enjoy such reverence. The migrating, pastoral Āryans regarded their cattle as a sign of wealth. In scriptures and myths, the virtues of the cow are constantly extolled. The stories of Kṛṣṇa and his life as a cowherd is an example of an ancient, romantic, religious, and mythic ideal that is deeply ingrained in the Hindu psyche. An instructive parallel might be the mythic American West, and the cowboy's relationship to his horse. Expecting a Hindu to eat a cow would be like asking the Lone Ranger to eat his horse Silver! The Hindu cow is a maternal symbol, because it provides more sustenance for a family if kept alive than if slaughtered for its flesh. A cow is the "workhorse" of the small family farm. It can plough a field, and provides milk, yogurt, butter, and ghee, all vital nutrients for people on a vegetarian diet. Anthropological studies have shown that foraging urban cows clean up organic garbage, transforming it into valuable dung, which, besides its use as fertilizer, serves as cooking fuel, as well as an ingredient in wall and floor plaster. The cow is also a symbol of non-violence, for it is a meek animal whose relationship to human beings is regarded as mostly beneficial. Scriptural injunctions to protect the cow thus also serve, if not reflect, a visionary ecological agenda. They further ensure a binding relationship between human beings and another living creature, expanding a person's sense of connectedness to the web of life.

The concepts of reincarnation and saṃsāric transmigration through various realms imply that all living things are profoundly connected to each other, and that anyone might be reborn as an animal destined to be somebody's next meal. Vegetarianism, induced by such a world view and adhered to by many Hindus, promotes an awareness of and fundamental respect for other living creatures. It also derives from the Hindu ideal of non-violence (*ahiṃsā*), which has implicit ecological underpinnings and ramifications, because environmental depredation causes harm to life.

It is worth reiterating that these eco-friendly ideals are embedded within the discourses of Hinduism. That is, they are religious themes that may be drawn upon to advance agendas that favor the preservation of the natural environment. However, it would be naïve to assume that all Hindus actually adhere to these values rigorously. The discourses of progress, economic success, and modernization, as well as the simple imperative to survive, can be far more compelling. India, by virtue of its expanding population (currently over one billion) and its burgeoning middle-class with greater affluence than ever before, will soon face unprecedented challenges in demands for energy to fuel automobiles, industry, and consumer needs. Increases in land, water, and air pollution are inevitable. Indiscriminate logging of old-growth forests promotes soil erosion and flooding, and hydro-electric projects through dam construction threaten natural forest and farm lands and the homes of India's indigenous tribal inhabitants (*ādivāsi*). A pertinent recent example has many environmental activists focused on the Sardar Sarovar Dam, one of thirty large dams to be built along the Narmadā River. Some *ādivāsis*, threatened to be displaced, staged Gandhian *satyagraha* fasts in protest against its construction. Prefiguring this sort of environmental activism, which is grounded in Hindu moral sensibilities, including non-violence, is the example of the Chipko Movement. In the late 1970s, Chandi Prasad Bhatt led the Chipko ("hugging") movement, in which local villagers began to hug trees in the Himalayan forests to prevent loggers from cutting them down. Chipko has been effective in transforming Indian government policy, and has inspired similar forms of non-violent environmental activism around the world.

Some noteworthy figures in contemporary Hinduism

There are virtually unlimited numbers of persons that might be discussed here. The two cases that follow enjoy relatively high profiles throughout the Hindu world. These are Hindus to whom Hindus turn for spiritual inspiration and guidance.

Case study: Satya Sai Baba

Satya Sai Baba (1926–) was born in the State of Andhra Pradesh and claims to be the incarnation of the saint Sai Baba of Shirdi (*c.* 1838–1918), in Maharashtra, whose name he adopted. Sai Baba of Shirdi was a somewhat mysterious figure, believed to have been a miracle worker. He exemplifies the classic image of the *fakir*, an itinerant holy man, whose ascetic practices and reputed powers are consonant with the values of both Islamic Sufism and the Hindu *śramaṇa* tradition. Shirdi Sai Baba's simple lifestyle of poverty and unaffected camaraderie with those who visited him at his abode in an abandoned mosque attracted the respect of both Hindus and Muslims. He is reputed to have promulgated the unifying message: "Everyone's Lord is [the same] One" (Hindi: *sabka mālik ek*). After his death, he was entombed in a Hindu temple.

Satya Sai Baba's life contrasts with that of his proclaimed predecessor. He has gathered a large following in India and abroad, estimated by some to be at least twenty million, and is probably the most recognized Hindu holy man in all of India. He is particularly renowned for the apparently miraculous production of sacred ash (*vibhūti*) from his fingertips, as well as other objects, such as rings and necklaces.

His detractors recognize these as simple magician's tricks. Nevertheless, Satya Sai Baba's society, headquartered at Puttaparthi, the town of his birth, runs a vast network of social service organizations, in conformity with his message to lead a moral life and to work for the welfare of others. While devotees regard him as God in human form, a growing number of allegations accusing him of sexual molestation of juveniles continue to tarnish his image. Satya Sai Baba teaches the unity of all religious traditions, and claims that he will take up a third incarnation under the name of Prem Sai Baba.

Case study: The Śaṅkarācāryas

The Śaṅkarācāryas are the heads of various Hindu monasteries (*maṭha*), claimed to have been founded by Śaṅkara and his disciples. The four most important of these *maṭhas* are Śṛṅgerī, Dvāraka, Jyotirmath (or Badrināth), and Puri, in the south, west, north, and east of India, respectively. Another southern *maṭha* at Kāñcīpuram, also claims to have been founded by Śaṅkara. The chief preceptors (*ācārya*) of these monasteries trace their spiritual lineages back to the founder who is often referred to as Ādi Śaṅkara, to avoid misidentification with the current leaders. The high regard for non-dual Vedānta, from such notable voices as Swami Vivekānanda and subsequently by Sarvepalli Radhakrishnan, once Spalding Professor of Religion at Oxford and the second President of India, had added to the status of the Śaṅkara *maṭhas* and their leaders. Monks ordained through these orders are called Daśanāmis (Ten Names), because there were ten traditional suffixes, such as *tīrtha, puri,* or *bhārati,* added to their monastic names. They are also known as *daṇḍa-svāmis,* because of the staffs (*daṇḍa*) that they carry during the wandering lifestyle they are expected to adopt. The most renowned Śaṅkarācāryas, and their monastic centers, are the closest that Hinduism comes to having a centralized authority or cornerstone of orthodoxy.

Hinduism and modernity

As modern technologies such as television, air travel, computers and the Internet accelerate global communication, Hindu India is progressively less isolated from the cultures of the world. Hinduism finds itself in confrontation with moral and ethical issues that impinge on all of the world's religions. What follows is a moderate selection of particularly salient issues.

Casteism

One of the most disagreeable dimensions of Hinduism for many people, especially those adhering to egalitarian religious ideologies, is the hierarchical caste system, and its attitude concerning Untouchables, in particular. Although one might acknowledge the existence of class distinctions within one's own society, which derive from economic status or vestiges of aristocratic attitudes, Hinduism's religious injunctions on social divisions based on birth often have disturbing implications. It is useful to be reminded that the propagation of these distinctions initially emanated from Brahminic sources, in order to ensure the hierarchical superiority of their proponents. These distinctions were progressively accepted by the lower classes, who sought some measure of inclusion into the social and religious hierarchy. However, resistance to the class system can certainly be traced to the late Vedic period, where it is evident in the *śramaṇa* movements and in the renouncer traditions of the Upaniṣads. The history of Hinduism reveals an almost continuous interaction between the marginalized and privileged groups of Hindu society. Women and *śūdras*, as well as Untouchables, strove for greater rights to participate in religious activities, and the rise of *bhakti*, Tantra, and *pūjā*, were among the developments in response to these efforts. In most cases, Sanskritization and universalization have been important features, for it is the privileged tradition that has "approved" of the inclusion of "deities" or "practices" into its religious worldview, and articulated this acceptance in the language and media deemed suitable. Thus Tantras and Purāṇas were composed in Sanskrit. However, eventually, even works in "Prakritic" languages, such as Tulsidās' *Rāmacaritamānas*, have gained near *śrūti* status.

Efforts to achieve equality among the various castes continue to be met with resistance by factions that do not want to lose their hierarchically privileged status, and religious norms are often co-opted into arguments to preserve the status quo. For instance, in 1980, the Mandal Commission submitted a report proposing that a policy of affirmative action in government employment would uplift the socially and economically disadvantaged. The so-called "Scheduled Castes" and "Scheduled Tribes" (SC/ST), together with the "Other Backward Castes" (OBC) actually constitute over seventy per cent of India's population. It was recommended that pre-existing quotas be expanded, to allow members of these groups to compete for and fill fifty-two per cent of government civil service jobs. In 1990, the Janata Dal party, which governed India at the time, tried to implement the recommendations of the Mandal Commission, leading to a backlash from high-caste Hindus. Recognizing that their access to these coveted government positions would become much more competitive, high-caste university students organized protest marches and demonstrations, many of which ended in violent riots with the police and the destruction of government property. Dozens of upper-caste students performed self-immolations, a symbolic action with powerful religious undertones, for the dubiously honorable privilege of securing government jobs for the elite. Their actions contributed to the fall of the Janata Dal, and the rise of the Bharatiya Janata Party in Indian politics.

Gender equality

In the movements launched during the colonial period of Hinduism, reforms to rectify the inequality between men and women were initiated. Among these one may list legally outlawing *satī* (1829), permitting widows to remarry (1856), prohibiting child marriages (1929), and granting women the right to file for divorce (1955) and to have full property ownership rights (1956).

In 1961, legislation was passed to forbid the practice of dowry in India. A daughter, when married, was expected to provide her husband's family with a dowry, namely, gifts or a sum of money. Despite numerous positive portrayals of women in Hindu literature in the past, the birth of a daughter is thus viewed by many as a financial burden. Unfortunately, the practice has been such a long-standing custom that the law forbidding dowry is routinely ignored. The practice has also led to abuses, in which wives have sometimes been murdered if their families did not come through with their promised dowry. In the mid-1990s in India, about five thousand such deaths were reported nationally. Furthermore, since a son is deemed essential for the continuation of the lineage, and is also crucial for the performance of his parents' death rites, the birth of only daughters is often met with dismay. The preceding factors have contributed to the practice of infanticide of baby girls.

Technology

The industrial revolution and the current high-technology revolution have had an impact on Hinduism's expression and values. Biotechnology has allowed parents to determine the sex of an embryo, which because of religiously promulgated attitudes, has resulted in selective abortions of female embryos. Although the Dharma Śāstras would probably condemn such an action, these texts are mostly read and cited selectively, to suit particular agendas. While women typically outnumber men in most national populations, such practices have left India with alarmingly fewer women than men.

Advances in transportation systems have also affected Hinduism. Affluent Hindus from the diaspora can jet into India to attend important festivals and now expect amenities, such as suitable accommodation and meals. Pilgrims within India are capable of traveling to the remotest corners of the country much more easily, mobilizing changes in pilgrimage centers to suit their growing numbers and needs.

Media technologies, such as television, the production of audio and videotapes, as well as compact discs and DVDs, have transformed many of the features of Hinduism.

Many families have reduced their attendance at month-long evening recitals of the Purāṇas, or at public religious theatre, such as the Rām Līlās, preferring to watch television productions on such themes within the comfort of their home. Recordings of sacred Vedic chants and temple dance performances, once restricted to the ears and eyes of the select, are now accessible to anyone. Even the concept of *darśana* is changing. Film and television portrayals of deities are seen by some as equivalent to *darśana* in a temple, as evidenced in the cases of the movie about the Hindu deity Santoṣī Mā, and the airings of the *Rāmāyaṇa* series on television. Since temple performances can attract audiences that are too large to be accommodated in front of the deity, these are broadcast to various locations on the temple's premises. On occasion, the live performance is held in a location more suitable for the audience, and a television is set up for the deity's enjoyment!

Cable and satellite broadcasting, as well as the Internet, are having an unprecedented impact on Hindu values. Indians have never had such exposure to global realities, since their understanding of "others" was curtailed by their limited access to information. The affluence of Western societies, portrayals of lifestyles that depart sharply from traditional Hindu moral sensibilities, and pornography on easily accessible websites are but a few examples of the plethora of visual images that now bombard Indians, who were, until now, virtually insulated from them. Where such facilities are available, Hindu teenagers have gone almost overnight from virtually no exposure to the West, to a steady diet of MTV (an American cable television channel, primarily geared to music videos for teenage and young adult audiences). The Internet has not only spurred an economic revolution through job out-sourcing, but is transforming the face of Hinduism through cross-cultural, trans-national, inter-religious dialogue. Websites can provide information on the performance of *vratas*, replace *pañcāṅgas* by indicating when a ritual is supposed to occur, and recount the Purāṇic and local myths of a renowned pilgrimage site. The long-term implications of these changes are well beyond the scope of the most discerning predictions.

Key points in this chapter

- Hindu tradition has many themes that nurture ecological awareness and reverence for creation.
- The sacred designations of landscapes, rivers, and social communities can serve ecological interests.
- The sacredness of the cow is one of the most emblematic symbols in Hinduism.
- The concepts of reincarnation and *saṃsāra* imply that all living things are connected.

- Vegetarianism promotes a fundamental respect for other living creatures.
- Eco-friendly ideals are embedded within the discourses of Hinduism.
- Many people are offended by the hierarchical caste system that is an aspect of Hinduism.
- Many with privileged status continue to resist efforts to achieve equality among the various castes.
- During the colonial period of Hinduism, movements emerged that sought an equality between men and women.
- The high-technology revolution is affecting Hinduism's expression and values in unimaginable ways.

Discussion questions

1. Why is Satya Sai Baba so important to contemporary Hinduism?
2. The most renowned Śaṅkarācāryas, and their monastic centers, are the closest that Hinduism comes to having a centralized authority or cornerstone of orthodoxy. Do you think this is important for Hinduism? Why or why not?
3. Discuss whether you think Hinduism is changing the Western world, or whether the Western world is changing Hinduism.
4. Why is the cow considered sacred in the Hindu tradition, and how is it honored?
5. Hinduism has numerous themes that nurture ecological awareness and reverence for the creation. What are these themes and how are they established within the tradition?
6. What are some of the important moral and ethical issues Hinduism is facing with regards to modernity? Discuss these issues in detail.

Further reading

On Satya Sai Baba

Baskin, D. (1990) *Divine Memories of Sathya Sai Baba*. Prashanti Nilayam: Sri Sathya Sai Books and Publication Trust.

Krystal, P. (1985) *Sai Baba: The Ultimate Experience*. Mangalore: Sharada Press.

Ruhela, S. P., and D. Robinson (eds) (1976) *Sai Baba and His Message*. Delhi: Vikas.

Sāī Bābā, Śrī Satya (1972–1976) *Satya Sāī Speaks*, 7 vols. Kadugodi: Sri Sathya Sai Education and Publication Foundation.

Contemporary studies (village, urban, and regional Hinduism)

Baden-Powell, B. H. (1958) *The Indian Village Community*. Reprint. New Haven, CT: Yale University Press.

Balsara, J. F. (1964) *Problems of Rapid Urbanisation in India*. Bombay: Manaktala.

Beals, A. R. (1965) *Gopalpur, a South Indian Village*. New York: Holt Rinehard & Winston.

Berreman, G. D. (1963) *Hindus of the Himālayas*. Berkeley, CA: University of California Press.

Cohn, B. (1971) *India: The Social Anthropology of a Civilization*. Englewood Cliffs, NY: Prentice-Hall.

Marriott, McKim (ed.) (1955)*Village India: Studies in the Little Community*. Chicago, IL: University of Chicago Press.

Singer, M. (ed.) (1959) *Traditional India: Structure and Change*. Philadelphia, PA: American Folklore Society.

Wiser, W. H. (1963) *Behind Mud Walls 1930–60*. Berkeley, CA: University of California.

Caste issues

Anand, Mulk Raj (1956) *Untouchable*. Bombay: Jaico Publishing.

Juergensmeyer, M. (1982) *Religion and Social Vision: The Movement against Untouchability in 20th Century Punjab*. Berkeley, CA: University of California Press.

Khare, R. S. (1970) *The Changing Brahmans: Associations and Elites among the Kanya-Kubjas of North India*. Chicago, IL: University of Chicago Press.

Kothari, R. (1970) *Caste in Indian Politics*. New Delhi: Orient Longman.

General studies of contemporary Hinduism

Baird, Robert D. (ed.) (1981) *Religion in Modern India*. Delhi: Manohar.

Breckenride, C. A. and P. Van der Veer (eds) (1993) *Orientalism and the Postcolonial Predicament: Perspectives on South Asia*. Philadelphia, PA: Pennsylvania University Press.

Dalmia, V. and Stietencron, H. (eds) (1995) *Representing Hinduism: The Construction of Religious Traditions and National Identity*. New Delhi: Sage.

Edwin, D., and A. E. Driver. (1987) *Social Class in Urban India: Essays on Cognition and Structures*. Leiden: E. J. Brill.

French, H. W. and A. Sharma (1981) *Religious Ferment in Modern India*. New York: St Martin's Press.

George, A. (1986) *Social Ferment in India*. London: Athlone Press.

Inden, Ronald (1990) *Imagining India*. Oxford: Blackwell.

King, Anna S. (ed.) (2006) *Indian Religions: Renaissance and Renewal*. London: Equinox.

Larson, Gerald (1995) *India's Agony over Religion*. Albany, NY: State University of New York Press.

Marriott, McKim (ed.) (1990) *India through Hindu Categories*. New Delhi: Sage Publication.

Marty, Martin E., and R. S. Appleby (eds) (1994) *The Fundamentalism Project*. Chicago, IL: University of Chicago Press.

—— (eds) (1991) *Fundamentalisms Observed*. Chicago, IL: University of Chicago Press.

Smith, W. C. (1963) *Modern Islam in India*. Lahore: Mohammed Ashraf.

Sontheimer, G. D., and H. Kulke (eds) (1989) *Hinduism Reconsidered*. New Delhi: Mahohar.

Women's issues in modern Hinduism

Calman, Leslie J. (1992) *Toward Empowerment: Women and Movement Politics in India*. Boulder, CO: Westview Press.

Franco, F., *et al.* (2000) *The Silken Swing: The Cultural Universe of Dalit Women*. Calcutta: STREE.

Hancock, Mary (1999) *Womanhood in the Making: Domestic Ritual and Public Culture in Urban South India*. Boulder, CO: Westview Press.

Harlan, Lindsey (1992) *Religion and Rajput Women: The Ethic of Protection in Contemporary Narratives*. Berkeley, CA: University of California Press.

Llewellyn, J. E. (1998) *The Legacy of Women's Uplift in India: Contemporary Women Leaders in the Arya Samaj*. London: Sage.

Metha, Rama (1970) *The Western Educated Hindu Woman*. New York: Asia Publishing House.

Miller, Barbara D. (1981) *The Endangered Sex: Neglect of Female Children in Rural North India*. Ithaca, NY: Cornell University Press.

Mitter, Sara S. (1991) *Dharma's Daughters: Contemporary Indian Women and Hindu Culture*. New Brunswick, NJ: Rutgers University Press.

Sarkar, T. (2001) *Hindu Wife, Hindu Nation: Community, Religion, and Cultural Nationalism*. Bloomington, IN: Indiana University Press.

Sarkar, T., and U. Butalia (eds) (1995) *Women and the Hindu Right*. New Delhi: Kali for Women.

Hinduism, ecology, and ethics

Chapple, Christopher K. (1993) *Nonviolence to Animals, Earth, and Self in Asian Traditions*. Albany, NY: State University of New York Press.
Coward, Harold, G., J. J. Lipner, and K. K. Young (eds) (1991) *Hindu Ethics*. Albany, NY: State University of New York Press.
Crawford, S. Cromwell (1982) *The Evolution of Hindu Ethical Ideals*. Honolulu, HI: University of Hawaii Press.
Creel, A. B. (1977) *Dharma in Hindu Ethics*. Columbia, MO: South Asia Books.

Appendix I

A timeline of Hinduism

6000–3300 BCE	Rudimentary Indus Valley cultural groups emerging
3500 BCE	Evidence of rudimentary Indus Valley script
3300–2600 BCE	Continuous inhabitation of Indus Valley region
2600–1900 BCE	Indus Valley Civilization flourishes with common cultural features
1900–1700 BCE	Regional variations emerge in Indus Valley Civilization
1700 BCE	Evidence of writing vanishes from Indian subcontinent
1700–1300 BCE	Disappearance of distinctive Indus Valley Civilization
1500 BCE	Āryan migration begins
c. 1400 BCE	Hittite-Mittani treaty tablets mentioning some Vedic gods
1500 BCE–1000 BCE	*Ṛg Veda Saṃhitā* composed
12th–8th CENTURIES BCE	Brāhmaṇas and Āraṇyakas composed
8th CENTURY BCE	Earliest Upaniṣads composed
7th–3rd CENTURIES BCE	Grammarian Pāṇinī
6th CENTURY BCE	*Śramaṇa* movement is under way
6th–5th CENTURIES BCE	Jainism begins
513 BCE	Darius I expands the Persian Empire to the Indus River
5th–4th CENTURIES BCE	Buddhism begins
5th CENTURY BCE	Vedāṅga literature emerges
4th CENTURY BCE	Evidence of writing re-emerges *Śvetāśvatara Upaniṣad* already composed
326 BCE	Alexander the Great reaches the Indus River
322 BCE	Mauryan Dynasty under Candragupta Maurya emerges
265–238 BCE	Aśoka Maurya rules

187 BCE	Mauryan Empire falls
2nd CENTURY BCE	Indo-Greeks (Bactrians) rule North India
	Mīmāṃsā writings emerge
2nd–1st CENTURIES BCE	Grammarian Patañjali
1st CENTURY BCE	Evidence of Vāsudeva cult
4th BCE–4th cent CE	Composition of the *Rāmāyaṇa*
2nd BCE–2nd cent CE	Composition of the *Mahābhārata*
2nd BCE–3rd cent CE	Saṅgham period in South India
1st CENTURY CE	Classical Sanskrit diminishes as a spoken language
	Composition of *Tolkāppiyam*, a Tamil grammar
	Theistic worship of Viṣṇu and Kṛṣṇa already exists
	Indian influences in Funan kingdom
2nd CENTURY CE	Evidence of Skanda (Kārttikeya) worship
	Hindu kingdom in Champa (Vietnam)
	Hindu kingdoms already on island of Java
	Yoga master Patañjali composes *Yoga Sūtra*
	Pāśupata Śaiva sect emerges
	Bādārayāṇa's *Vedānta Sūtra* composed by this period
	Nyāya and Vaiśeṣika philosophies already in existence
4th CENTURY CE	Hindu consecrations in Borneo
	Earliest Purāṇas composed
	Vaikhānasa Sūtra composed
330–550 CE	Gupta Dynasty flourishes
	Hindu temple building begins in earnest
c. 400 CE	Īśvarakṛṣṇa's *Saṅkhya Kārikā*
5th CENTURY CE	Evidence of Gaṇeśa worship emerges
	Apabrahmśas, precursors to vernaculars (e.g. Hindi), grow
	Grammarian Bhartṛhari
	Śrī-Lakṣmī associated as consort of Viṣṇu
6th–7th CENTURIES CE	Great Goddess (Mahādevī) concept emerges
	Buddhist tantric texts appear
6th–11th CENTURIES CE	South Indian *bhakti* (Ālvārs and Nāyanārs) flourishes
6th–8th CENTURIES CE	Śaiva Nāyanār poet-saints
7th CENTURY CE	Islam reaches India
	Śākta Purāṇas appear
	Pallava Dynasty rock caves/temples at Mahabalipuram
	Śiva temples built in Java
8th CENTURY CE	Kailāsanātha temple built at Ellora
	Angkor becomes the capital of Khmer kingdom

7th–14th Centuries ce	Pāśupata and Kālamukha Śaiva sects flourish in South India
8th–9th Centuries ce	Śaṅkara, Advaita Vedānta philosopher
8th–12th Centuries ce	Pālā Dynasty in Bengal, Tantra flourishes
9th Century ce	Prambanan temple complex on Java
9th–10 Centuries ce	Hindu tantric texts appear
10th–11th Centuries ce	Abhinavagupta, philosopher of Kashmir Trika Śaivism
10th–12th Centuries ce	Chandella Dynasty builds temples at Khajuraho
11th Century ce	Mahmud of Ghazni annexes the Punjab
	Cola Dynasty builds Bṛhadīśvara temple in Thanjavur
	Taleju Bhavānī cult already established in Nepal
11th–12th Centuries ce	Rāmānujā, Viśiṣṭādvaita Vedānta philosopher
12th Century ce	Devanāgarī script develops
	Jayadeva writes the *Gītāgovinda*
	Jagannātha temple built at Puri
	Angkor Wat is constructed in Khmer kingdom
1106–1167 ce	Basavanna founds Liṅgayat movement
13th Century ce	Sun Temple at Konarak built
1238–1317 ce	Madhva, Dvaita Vedānta philosopher
c. 1275–1296 ce	Jñāneśvara, Maharashtrian poet
1270–1350 ce	Nāmdev, Maharashtrian poet
13th–16th Centuries ce	North India under Turko-Afghan rule (Delhi Sultanate)
1293–1590 ce	Hindu Mahapajit kingdom established in East Java
13th–18th Centuries ce	Malla Dynasty rules Nepal
14th Century ce	Earliest history book in India
	Sāyaṇa writes commentaries on Vedas and Vedic works
15th Century ce	Kabir, Banaras-born poet
1469–1539 ce	Guru Nanak, Punjabi-born founder of Sikhism
1486–1534 ce	Śrī Caitanya, Bengali *bhākta*
16th Century ce	Buddhism dies out in India
	Portuguese establish colony in India
	Eknāth, *bhakti* poet
1532–1623 ce	Tulsidās, Banāras-based *bhakti* poet
16th–19th Centuries ce	Mughal rule in India
1526 ce	Babar/Babur establishes Mughal rule
1556–1605 ce	Akbar rules
1658–1707 ce	Aurangzeb rules
1857 ce	Bahadur Shah Zafar, last Mughal emperor, ousted

17th Century ce	British and French establish colonies in India
1600 ce	British East India Company founded
c. 1568–1650 ce	Tukārām, Maharastrian *bhakti* poet
1630–1680 ce	Shivaji Bhonsle, leader of Maratha rebellion
18th Century ce	King of Jaipur performs an *aśvamedha* ritual
	Rāmprasād Sen, Bengali *bhakti* poet
1769 ce	Prithvi Narayan Shah establishes Shah Dynasty in Nepal
1773–1785 ce	Warren Hastings, first British Governor-General of India
1772–1833 ce	Ram Mohan Roy, founder of the Brāhmo Samāj
19th Century ce	Dravidian coined for the Tamil-related language groups
	Christian missionaries permitted to proselytize
1824–1883 ce	Dayānanda Sarasvati, founder of the Ārya Samāj
1829 ce	*Satī* outlawed in Bengal
1836–1886 ce	Ramakrishna Paramahamsa, Bengali temple priest/ saint
1846–1951 ce	The Rana family rules Nepal
1856 ce	Widow remarriage permitted
1856–1920 ce	Bal Gangadhar Tilak, political activist and freedom fighter
1857 ce	The Sepoy Rebellion
1861–1941 ce	Rabindranath Tagore, Bengali poet and Nobel laureate
1863–1902 ce	Swami Vivekānanda, propagates Vedānta worldwide
1869–1948 ce	Mohandas (Mahatma) Gandhi, patriarch of modern India
1872–1950 ce	Aurobindo Ghose, founder of Integral Yoga
1876 ce	*Vande Mataram* composed by Bankim Chatterjee
1879–1950 ce	Ramaṇa Mahāṛṣi, South Indian sage
1882 ce	Theosophical Society headquarters established in Adyar
1885 ce	Indian National Congress formed
1887–1963 ce	Swami Sivananda Saraswati, founder of Divine Life Society
1888–1989 ce	Tirumalai Krishnamacharya, Haṭha Yoga master
1893 ce	World Parliament of Religions held in Chicago
1895–1986 ce	Jiddu Krishnamurti rejects religious systems and paths
1896–1977 ce	Swami Bhaktivedanta Prabhupada founds ISKCON

1897–1981 CE	Nisargadatta Maharaj, non-dualistic sage
20th CENTURY CE	Buddhist revival in India
1906 CE	All-India Muslim League formed
1908–1982 CE	Swami Muktananda, propagator of the Siddha Yoga tradition
1910–1997 CE	H. W. L. Poonjaji, Hindu sage
1917–	Maharishi Mahesh Yogi, founds TM movement
1918–	B. K. S. Iyengar, Haṭha Yoga teacher
1919–	Ramesh Balsekar, Advaita sage and teacher
1923 CE	Concept of Hindutva articulated
1930–1990 CE	Osho (Bhagwan Shree Rajneesh), controversial *guru*
1939–	Adi Da (Da Free John), American-born controversial *guru*
1942–	Gangaji, American-born teacher of *mokṣa*
1947 CE	India achieves Independence. Congress Party elected
1970s	Indians expelled from Africa migrate to N. America
1975 CE	Scholars commission a performance of the *agnicayana* rite
	Film on Santoshi Mā is released
1980 CE	Bharatiya Janata Party (BJP) founded
1984 CE	Indira Gandhi assassinated
1991 CE	Rajiv Gandhi assassinated
1992 CE	Babari Masjid demolished
1998 CE	Bharatiya Janata Party forms government
2004 CE	Congress Party forms government

Appendix II

A: Pronunciation guide and general glossary

A note on pronunciation

It is crucial to remember that "uh," wherever it occurs, is pronounced as in the expression "huh" or like the "u" in "but." Also note that "aye," wherever it occurs, is pronounced as in the nautical "aye" or the optical "eye." The "oo" is sounded like the bovine "moo," and the "ee" as in the word "see." However, the "ee" and "oo" are pronounced either short or long, depending on the length of the vowel in the original word. Capitalized syllables roughly indicate where emphasis should be placed. Remember that the Sanskrit "d" as in "*deva*" is sounded somewhere between "DHEY-vuh" and "THEY-vuh." Such sounds are indicated as "D/THEY-vuh." An "aa" is pronounced as the "a" in "father." Additional guidance is found in the Preface, and in Chapter 5: The Sanskrit Language.

Adharma [uh-D/THUHR-muh]: Chaos; unrighteousness.
Advaita Vedānta [uh-DV-AYE-tuh vey-D/THAAN-tuh]: Radical non-dualism.
Āgama [AA-guh-muh]: Traditional scripture.
Agni [UHG-nee]: God of fire.
Agnicayana [UHG-nee-CHUH-yuh-nuh]: Vedic sacrificial rite to the fire-god Agni; perhaps humanity's oldest surviving religious ritual.
Ahaṅkara [uh-HUHN-kuh-ruh]: Interior component of reality (*tattva*) known as the I-maker, or ego.
Ahiṃsā [uh-HING-saa]: The value of non-harming.
Aiyappan [AYE-yuhp-puhn]: South Indian forest god; regarded, by orthodox Hindus, as the son of Śiva and Viṣṇu.
Ājñā [AAJ-nyaa]: Command; sixth internal energy vortex (*cakra*) approximately located at the site of the "third" or "wisdom eye."
Ākāśa [AA-kaa-shuh]: Space.
Ālvār [AAL-vaar]: Early South Indian *bhakti* worshippers of Viṣṇu.

Anāhata [uhn-AA-huh-thuh]: Unstruck; fourth internal vortex (*cakra*), located at the heart.

Ānanda [AA-nuhn-d/thuh]: Bliss.

Ananta [UH-nuhn-thuh]: The cosmic serpent whose name means "without end."

Aṅga [UHN-guh]: Appendages; components.

Antyeṣṭi [UHNTH-yehsh-tee]: Cremation; the final offering.

Anusvāra [uh-noo-SVAA-ruh]: The Sanskrit ṃ; sounded like the resonant ring of an iron bell.

Apsaras [UP-suh-ruhs]: Celestial nymphs.

Āratī [AAR-uh-thee]: Worship of a deity, particularly the flame offering, mostly in temples.

Ardhanarīśvara [uhr-dhuh-naa-REESH-vuh-ruh]: (The Lord who is Half Woman) A fusion of Śiva and Pārvatī as the Divine.

Artha [UHR-thuh]: The goal of skill, attainment, power or wealth.

Ārya Samāj [AAR-yuh SUH-maaj]: Organization founded by Dayānanda Sarasvati. It emphasized the Vedas as the basis of religious doctrine.

Āryan [AAR-yuhn]: Noble Ones; a cattle-herding people evident on the Indian subcontinent after 1500 BCE.

Āsana [AA-suh-nuh]: Posture.

Āśrama [AA-shruh-muh]: Hermitage; a stage in life.

Aṣṭāṅga [uhsh-TAANG-uh]: Eight limbs; components of yogic practice according to Patañjali.

Āstika [AAS-thee-kuh]: Orthodox.

Asura [UH-soo-ruh]: Titans or powerful demons.

Aśvamedha [UHSH-vuh-mey-d/thuh]: Vedic ritual known as the horse sacrifice.

Ātman [AATH-muhn]: The individual self; often used as a synonym for Brahman.

Aum [AA-OH-MM]: Om; a sacred utterance (*mantra*); Brahman as sound.

Avatāra [uh-vuh-THAA-ruh]: Incarnations; descents.

Avidyā [uh-vid/th-YAA]: Ignorance.

Āyurveda [AA-yoor-vey-d/thuh]: Medicinal tradition grounded in a complex theory of bodily science.

Babari Masjid [BAA-buh-ree MUHS-jid/th]: A sixteenth century mosque in Ayodhyā; demolished in a 1992 riot.

Balarāma [buh-luh-RAA-muh]: Also known as Saṅkarṣaṇa, deity associated with Viṣṇu, and regarded as Kṛṣṇa's brother.

Banāras [buh-NAA-ruhs]: Hindu holy city; also known as Vārāṇasī or Kāśī.

Baul [BAUL]: Marginal religious group in Bengali society, characterized by their mendicant lifestyle and devotional music.

Bhāgavata [BHAAG-vuh-thuh]: Early cult centered on deities later associated with Viṣṇu.

Bhairava [BH-AYE-ruh-vuh]: (The Terrifying) Parama-śiva in its totality.

Bhajan [BHUH-juhn]: Devotional hymns.

Bhākta [BHAAK-thuh]: Those engaged in devotional worship (*bhakti*).

Bhakti [BHUHK-thee]: Devotional worship (typically of a personal god) through action.

Bhakti marga [BHUHK-thee MUHR-guh]: Path of Loving Devotion.

Bhārat Mātā [BHAA-ruhth MAA-thaa]: Mother goddess who is the Nation of India.

Bhāratavarṣa [BHAA-ruh-thuh-vuhr-shuh]: In Hindu cosmology, the southernmost region of Jambudvipa, also known as India or Bhārata.

Bharatiya Janata Party (BJP) [BHAA-ruh-thee-yuh JUH-nuh-thuh PAAR-tee]: Indian People's Party; pro-Hindu political party.

Bhu Devī [BHOO D/THEY-vee]: Goddess Earth.

Bhūta [BHOO-thuh]: A spirit.

Bīja [BEE-juh]: Seeds; often refers to one's actions with regards to *karma*.

Bindu [BIN-d/thoo]: A drop; a central point in a *yantra*.

Brahmā [bruh-MAA]: The creator god.

Brahmacarya [BRUH-muh-CHUHR-yuh]: The way of Brahman; chastity; one of the four stages in life.

Brahman [BRUH-muhn]: Ultimate Reality; a hallowed power within sacred utterances (*mantra*) of the Vedic *ṛṣis*; the Absolute.

Brāhmaṇa [BRAAH-muh-nuh]: The priestly class (i.e., Brahmin); genre of Vedic ritual texts.

Brahmāṇḍa [bruh-MAAN-duh]: The Brahmā Egg; Hindu cosmological symbol.

Brāhmī [BRAAH-mee]: A script that developed from the Kharoṣṭhī script.

Brahmin [BRAH-min]: Class in Hindu social hierarchy, often consisting of priests and scholars of the Vedas.

Brāhmo Samāj [BRAAH-mo suh-MAAJ]: Society of the Absolute; founded by Ram Mohan Roy.

Buddhi [BUDH-d/thee]: Intelligence; the most subtle internal element (*tattva*).

Buddhism [BUDH-d/thiz-im]: Religio-philosophical tradition, developed from the teachings of Siddhārtha Gautama, the Buddha, regarded as heterodox by orthodox Hindus.

Cakra [CHUHK-ruh]: A discus; energy centers or vortices.

Caṇḍāla [CHUHN-daa-luh]: Fierce; a fifth category of the *varṇa* system; the Untouchables.

Caṇḍī [chun-DEE]: (She who is Fierce) A name for the Hindu Great Goddess.

Candra [CHUHN-d/thruh]: The moon.

Cārvāka [CHAAR-vaa-kuh]: Sweet-Voiced philosophy; also known as the Lokāyata or the Way of the Masses.
Cit [CHITH]: Consciousness.
Citta [CHIT-thuh]: The three elements that constitute mind or thought.

Dakṣiṇā [D/THUHK-shin-aa]: Monetary or material payment for *yajña* services.
Dalit [D/THAA-lith]: Oppressed; an Untouchable.
Darśana [D/THUR-shuh-nuh]: Viewpoint; perspective; philosophical school; audience with a deity.
Dāsa [D/THAA-suh]: Enemy; slave; refers to the darker-skinned peoples of India that were defeated by the Āryans; also called Dasyu; term applied to a devotee of a deity.
Dasain [D/THUH-saye-en]: One of Nepal's most widely celebrated religious festivals.
Daśanāmi [D/THUH-shuh-NAA-mee]: "Ten Names"; monks ordained through Hindu monasteries (*maṭha*).
Deva [D/THEY-vuh]: A god.
Devadāsī [D/THEY-vuh-D/THAA-see]: Servants of God; women associated with temples who danced for and served the deity.
Devanāgarī [D/THEY-vuh-NAA-guh-ree]: Script used for languages such as Sanskrit and Hindi.
Devī [D/THEY-vee]: The Hindu Great Goddess; general term for a goddess.
Dhāraṇa [D/THAA-ruh-nuh]: Concentration; one of the eight limbs of *yoga*.
Dharma [D/THUHR-muh]: Righteousness; duty; morality; law; social obligations; particular religious teachings; the deity who embodies righteousness.
Dharmaśālā [D/THUHR-muh-SHAA-laa]: Pilgrims' rest quarters.
Dhūpa [D/THOO-puh]: Incense.
Dhyāna [D/THYAA-nuh]: Meditation; one of the eight limbs of *yoga*.
Dīkṣā [D/THEEK-shaa]: Initiation rites.
Dīpa [D/THEE-puh]: A flame.
Dīpāvalī [d/thee-PAA-vuh-lee]: Row of Lights; festival which occurs in late autumn.
Dīvālī [D/THEE-vaa-lee]: Festival of Lights; also known as Dīpāvālī.
Doṣa [D/THOH-shuh]: Humors of the body according to Āyurveda.
Draviḍa [D/THRUH-vid-uh]: A Southern style of temple.
Dravidian language: Family of languages spoken primarily in southern India and northern Sri Lanka (e.g. Tamil, Telugu, Malayalam, and Kannada).
Dravidian religion: Religious beliefs and practices of the non-Āryan high cultures on the Indian subcontinent, loosely linked to the speakers of Dravidian languages.
Durgā [D/THOOR-gaa]: She who is Formidable; name of the Great Goddess.
Durgā Pūjā [D/THOOR-gaa POO-jaa]: Festival in honor of the goddess Durgā.

Dvaita Vedānta [D/THV-AYE-thuh vey-D/THAAN-thuh]: Dualistic philosophy propounding that God, souls, and matter, are separate and real.
Dvāpara Yuga [D/THVAA-puh-ruh YOO-gah]: An age lasting 2400 god (*deva*) years.
Dvija [D/THVIJ-uh]: The twice-born; a particular *varṇa* status.
Dyaus-Pitṛ [d/th-yaus PITH-uhr]: God of the Heavens; the sky god.

Fakir [FUH-keer]: Wandering holy men, often renowned for their asceticism and powers.

Gaṇa [GUH-nuh]: Śiva's cohort of spirits and demigods.
Gaṇapati [GUH-nuh-puh-thee]: Gaṇeśa, the elephant-headed god.
Gandha [GUHN-d/thuh]: A fragrant paste.
Gandharva [GUN-d/thuhr-vuh]: Celestial musicians/spiritis known for lives of pleasure.
Gaṇeśa [GUH-nay-shuh]: (Lord of the Hosts) Also known as Gaṇapati or Vināyaka; elephant-headed deity regarded as the son of Śiva and Pārvatī; eliminator of obstacles.
Garbha [GUHR-bhuh]: Embryo or womb.
Garbha-gṛha [GUHR-bhuh-GUR-huh]: Inner sanctum of a Hindu temple.
Garuḍa [GUH-roo-duh]: The king of birds; Viṣṇu's mount.
Gauḍīya Vaiṣṇava [GAU-dee-yuh V-AYESH-nuh-vuh]: A school of Vedānta centered on devotion to Kṛṣṇa and Rādhā.
Gāyā [GAA-YAA]: Pilgrimage site popular for the performance of ancestral death rites.
Gāyatrī [GAA-yuh-three]: Sacred utterance (*mantra*) believed to be the condensed essence of the Vedas.
Gopī [GO-pee]: A cowgirl.
Gopura [GOH-poo-ruh]: Impressive gateways characteristic of the Southern style of temple.
Gotra [GOH-thruh]: Family lineage.
Graha [GRUH-huh]: (Grasper) Semi-divine forces (e.g. planets) that affect human activities.
Gṛhastha [GUR-huh-sthuh]: The householder stage in life.
Guṇa [GOO-nuh]: Qualities inherent in substances in the body (e.g. blood, bone, fat) and the created world.
Guru [GOO-roo]: A teacher; particularly one who offers initiation and spiritual guidance.

Hanumān [HUH-noo-MAAN]: Monkey god and hero who aids Rāma in the *Rāmāyaṇa*.

Hare Kṛṣṇa Movement [HUH-rey KURSH-nuh]: The International Society for Kṛṣṇa Consciousness, a *bhakti* movement founded by Swami Bhaktivedanta.
Harijan [HUH-ree-juhn]: Children of God; a name given to the Untouchables by Gandhi.
Haṭha Yoga [HUHT-huh YOO-guh]: Yoga involving the performance of specific yogic postures and breathing techniques.
Hindi [HIN-d/thee]: North Indian vernacular language; a national language of India.
Hindu [HIN-d/thoo]: A practitioner of Hinduism.
Hinduism [HIN-d/thoo-iz-im]: Refers to the wide range of beliefs and practices of the majority of the people of South Asia, in particular those of India and Nepal.
Hindutva [HIN-d/thoo-tvuh]: Concept of "Hinduness," first articulated in a book by nationalist leader Veer Savarkar.
Holi [HOH-lee]: A festival in which caste restrictions are temporarily annulled, and participants douse each other with colors.
Homa [HOHM-uh]: Modern day Vedic-styled rituals of offerings into the sacred fire.

Īḍā [EE-d/thaa]: One of the three most important energy channels (*nāḍī*).
Indra [IN-d/thruh]: God of storms and lightning; the warrior-god; king of the gods.
Īśvara [EESH-vuh-ruh]: Lord; the lord of Yoga.

Jagannātha [juh-guh-NAA-thuh]: Viṣṇu/Kṛṣṇa as Lord of the World.
Jambu-dvīpa [JUHM-boo-D/THVEE-puh]: Island of the Wood-apple Trees; the innermost island in Hindu geographical cosmology.
Jāti [JAA-thee]: Birth group; subdivision within Hindu society; often referred to as a caste.
Jauhar [JAU-huhr]: Mass suicide by *kṣatriya* women through immolation.
Jina [JIN-uh]: Conqueror; title applied to Vardhamāna Mahāvira, the founder of Jainism.
Jīva [JEE-vuh]: The individual soul.
Jīvanmukti [JEE-vuhn-muhk-thee]: A Self-realized being; liberated while alive.
Jñāna Marga [J-NYAA-nuh MUHR-guh]: The Path of Transcendental Knowledge.

Kailāsa [K-AYE-laa-suh]: Śiva's mountain abode.
Kaivalya [K-AYE-vuhl-yuh]: Aloneness or "only-ness."
Kālāmukha [KAA-laa-MOO-khuh]: An offshoot of the Pāśupata Saiva sect.
Kālī [KAA-lee]: (Time/Black) Goddess representing the power of destruction.

Kali Yuga [KUHL-ee YOO-guh]: An age lasting 1200 god (*deva*) years; characterized by the rapid degeneration of the *dharma*; often mistakenly called the Kālī Yuga.

Kalki [KUHL-kee]: Viṣṇu's *avatāra,* who has yet to come.

Kalpa [KUHL-puh]: Explanations on ritual action; also, a duration of time consisting of a thousand *mahāyugas* or fourteen *manvantras.*

Kāma [KAA-muh]: Desire/Attachment; one of the appropriate goals of orthodox Hinduism; the God of Love.

Kāmākhyā [KAA-maa-khyaa]: A goddess whose abode is at Kāmarūpa.

Kāpālika [kaa-PAA-lee-kuh]: A Śaiva sect.

Karma [KUHR-muh]: Concept of causality in moral action in which good deeds are meritorious (*puṇya*), while evil or sinful deeds (*pāpa*) have painful effects.

Karma Marga [KUHR-muh MUHR-guh]: The Path of Action.

Kārttikeya [KAAR-thee-kay-yuh]: Deity born out of Śiva's seed; the war god, also known as Skanda or Kumāra.

Kaurava [KAU-ruh-vuh]: One of the hundred sons of Dhṛtarāṣṭra and Gāndhārī in the *Mahābhārata.*

Kavadi [KAA-b/vuh-d/tee]: Decorated arch carried on the shoulders in worship of Murugan; also called *Kāvaṭi.*

Ketu [KAY-thoo]: The South Node of the moon.

Kṛṣṇa [KURSH-nuh]: Pastoral deity associated with the teachings of the *Bhagavad-Gītā* and identified as an incarnation of Viṣṇu.

Kṛta Yuga [KUR-thuh YOO-guh]: Also called Satya Yuga; an age, lasting 4800 god (*deva*) years, or 1,728,000 human years.

Kṣatriya [kSHUH-three-yuh]: Warrior class; one of the upper three classes of the *varṇa* system.

Kumārī [koo-MAA-REE]: A little princess; virgin girl/goddess; in Nepal, believed to be incarnate forms of goddess Taleju.

Kumbha Mela [KOOM-bhuh MEY-laa]: Major pilgrimage gatherings, which occur every three years rotating between four locations.

Kuṇḍalinī Yoga [KOON-duh-lee-nee YOH-guh]: The path of awakening of latent cosmic energies within the body.

Kūrma [KOOR-muh]: Tortoise.

Lakṣmī [LUHK-shmee]: Goddess of wealth and fortune.

Liṅga/liṅgam [LING-uh] [LING-uhm]: A phallic emblem and symbol of Śiva.

Liṅgayat [LING-uh-yuhth]: An unorthodox Śaiva movement, also known as the Vīraśaiva.

Lokāyata [loh-KAA-yuh-tuh]: Cārvāka or Sweet-Voiced philosophy; also known as the Way of the Masses.

Mā [MAA]: Mother; also Mātā.
Mahābhūta [muh-HAA-BHOO-thuh]: The grossest component elements of reality (*tattva*).
Mahābrāhmaṇa [muh-HAA-BRAAH-muh-nuh]: Priests who preside over death rituals.
Mahādevī [muh-HAA-d/they-VEE]: The Great Goddess; also just Devī.
Mahākālī [muh-HAA-KAA-lee]: Supreme Śakti or the power associated with destruction.
Mahālakṣmī [muh-HAA-LUHK-shmee]: Supreme Śakti or the power that presides over preservation.
Mahāmantra [muh-HAA-muhn-thruh]: The great *mantra;* AUM; also, the Hare Kṛṣṇa *mantra.*
Mahārāja [muh-HAA-RAA-juh]: An emperor or great king.
Mahāsarasvatī [muh-HAA-suh-RUHS-vuh-thee]: Supreme Śakti, or seen as the power that presides over creation.
Mahāyuga [muh-HAA-yoo-guh]: A Great Age; total of the four main *yugas* (ages) lasting 12,000 god years or 4,320,000 human years.
Maheśvara [muh-HAYSH-vuh-ruh]: (Great Lord) Śiva.
Mahiṣamardinī [muh-HISH-uh-MUHR-d/thin-ee]: Crusher of the Buffalo [Demon]; a famous image of Mahādevī Durgā.
Maithuna [M-AYE-thoo-nuh]: Sexual union; coitus images.
Manas [MUH-nuhs]: Heart-mind; an interior constituent element (*tattva*).
Manasā [MUH-nuh-saa]: Snake goddess popular in Bengal; sister of Vāsuki the *nāga* king.
Manu [MUH-noo]: A divine being who presides over a *manvantra,* an age of humanity.
Manauti [muh-NAU-thee]: A promise (Hindi).
Maṇḍala [MUHN-duh-luh]: Book; a cosmograph.
Maṅgala [MUHN-guh-luh]: A category of auspiciousness.
Mantra [MUHN-thruh]: A sacred utterance.
Manvantara [muhn-VUHN-thuh-ruh]: Seventy-one *mahāyugas;* an age of humanity, presided over by a divine being known as a Manu.
Marga [MUHR-guh]: Approach; a conduit; path.
Maṭha [MUH-tuh]: Monasteries; the Hindu monastic system.
Māyā [MAA-yaa]: Illusion.
Meru [MAY-roo]: The cosmic mountain; also Sumeru; a pagoda design.
Mīmāṃsā [mee-MAANG-saa]: Interpretation; a school of philosophy.
Mīnākṣī [MEE-naak-shee]: Fish-Eyed Goddess whose abode is the temple at Madurai.
Mokṣa [MOHK-shuh]: Liberation from the cycle of birth, death, and rebirth.

Mudrā [moo-D/THRAA]: Sacred gestures; parched grain, or female sexual partner.

Mughal [MOH-ghuhl]: Muslim descendants of the Mongol emperor Genghis Khan who ruled India.

Mukti [MOOK-thee]: Freedom or release from *saṃsāra*.

Mūrti [MOOR-thee]: A deity that is embodied in a material form.

Murugan/Murukaṉ [MOO-roo-guhn]: Popular South Indian god, identified as Śiva's son.

Nāḍī [NAA-dee]: Pathways in the subtle body through which vital energy (*prāṇa*) flows.

Nāga [NAA-guh]: Serpent deities associated with fertility and underworld wealth.

Nāgara [NAA-guh-ruh]: City; the Northern style of Hindu temples.

Naivedya [N-AYE-vey-d/thyuh]: Something edible; food offering in *pūjā*.

Namaste [NUH-muhs-they]: A greeting in India.

Narasiṃha [NUH-ruh-SING-huh]: Man-lion; also Nṛsiṅgha, the Man-Lion incarnation of Viṣṇu.

Nārāyaṇa [naa-RAA-yuh-nuh]: A deity identified with Viṣṇu.

Nāstika [NAAS-thik-uh]: Heterodox.

Nāth [NAATH]: Member of a Śaivite sect that emphasizes Haṭha yoga practice for the attainment of supernormal powers (*siddhi*).

Nava-graha [nuh-vuh-GRUH-huh]: The nine graspers (*graha*): Sūrya (the Sun), Candra (the Moon), Maṅgala (Mars), Budha (Mercury), Guru or Bṛhaspati (Jupiter), Sukra (Venus), Śani (Saturn), and Rāhu and Ketu (North and South nodes of the moon).

Navarātra/Navarātrī [nuh-vuh-RAA-thruh (-three)]: A nine-night festival in honor of the Great Goddess.

Nāyanār: Member of a South Indian group of Śaiva devotees; likely responsible for the expansion of Śaiva devotion during the Middle Ages.

Nirbīja samādhi [nir-BEE-juh suh-MAA-d/thee]: Seedless *samādhi*; the perfection of Yoga.

Nirguṇa Brahman [NIR-goo-nuh BRUH-muhn]: Ultimate Reality beyond any attributes.

Nirvāṇa [nir-VAA-nuh]: Emancipation or freedom from *karma* and *saṃsāra*; insight into the true nature of reality and the Self.

Niṣ-kāma karma [NISH-kaa-muh KUHR-muh]: Action without attachment.

Niyama [NEE-yuh-muh]: Observances; One of the eight limbs of *yoga*.

Nyāya [NYAA-yuh]: Logical reasoning; orthodox school of philosophy, dealing with logic and epistemology.

Pañca-makāra [PUHN-chuh-muh-KAA-ruh]: The five Ms of the Left Hand Tantra.
Pañcarātra [PUHN-chuh-RAA-thruh]: A Vaiṣṇava Tantric system.
Pāṇḍava [PAAN-duh-vuh]: The five "sons of Pāṇḍu" from the *Mahābhārata* epic.
Paṇḍita [PUHN-dee-tuh]: Vedic scholar; a learned man or pundit.
Paramahamsa [PUH-ruh-muh-HUHNG-suh]: (Supreme Swan) Title given to Hindu saints.
Paraśurāma [PUH-ruh-shoo-RAA-muh]: (Rama with Axe) Brahmin warrior *avatāra* of Viṣṇu.
Pārvatī [PAAR-vuh-thee]: (She of the Mountains) Wife of Śiva; an incarnation of Satī.
Pāśa [PAA-shuh]: Noose; that which keeps souls in bondage in Śaiva Siddhānta philosophy.
Paśu [PUH-shoo]: Beast; soul; one of three real and eternal entities in Śaiva Siddhānta.
Pāśupata [PAA-shoo-PUH-thuh]: The earliest of the known Śaiva sects.
Paśupati [PUH-shoo-PUH-thee]: (Lord of Animals) The god Śiva.
Pati [PUH-thee]: Lord; husband; one of three real and eternal entities in Śaiva Siddhānta.
Pativrata [PUH-thee-vruh-thuh]: Ongoing ascetic dedication to one's husband (*pati*).
Piṅgala [PIN-guh-luh]: One of the body's three central energy channels (*nāḍī*).
Pīṭha [PEET-huh]: A seat; a sacred site, particularly of the Devī.
Pitṛ-loka [PITH-ur-LOH-kuh]: The world of the ancestors; the atmosphere (*bhuvaḥ*).
Prahlāda [pruh-LAA-d/thuh]: Righteous demon lad, rescued by Viṣṇu.
Prajāpati [pruh-JAA-puh-thee]: (Lord of Creatures) Creator God in the Vedas.
Prakṛti [PRUHK-ur-thee]: Nature or materiality in Sāṅkhya philosophy.
Pralaya [PRUH-luh-yuh]: A period of cosmic dissolution.
Prāṇa [PRAA-nuh]: The vital energy.
Pranava [PRUH-nuh-vuh]: Aum; vibratory hum produced from use of the *mantra* Aum.
Prāṇāyāma [praa-NAA-yaa-muh]: Regulation of the vital energy (*prāṇa*).
Prapatti [PRUH-puht-thee]: Surrender; a supreme expression of *bhakti*.
Prasāda [pruh-SAA-d/thuh]: Rendered immaculate or blessed.
Pratyahara [PRUH-thyuh-huh-ruh]: Sense withdrawal; one of the eight limbs of *yoga*.
Preta [PREY-thuh]: Ghost; a being who has departed from this life.
Pṛthivī [PUR-thiv-ee]: The earth goddess.
Pūjā [POO-jaa]: Hindu devotional worship.
Pūjāri [poo-JAA-ree]: A priest who conducts the rites of worship at a temple.

Purohita [poo-ROH-hith-uh]: A priest who performs worship at household shrines and temples.
Puruṣa [POO-roo-shuh]: Being/person; pure, or supreme consciousness; the true Self.
Puruṣārtha [poo-roo-SHAAR-thuh]: The four goals of life.
Pūrva Mīmāṃsā [POOR-vuh mee-MAANG-saa]: (Investigation of the Primary) A theological school based on Vedic interpretation.
Puṣpa [POOSH-puh]: Fresh flowers.

Rādhā [RAA-d/thaa]: Kṛṣṇa's lover.
Rāga [RAA-guh]: Enchantment; type of Indian classical music composition.
Rāhu [RAA-hoo]: North Node of the moon; a demon beheaded by Viṣṇu's discus.
Rāja Yoga [RAA-juh YOH-guh]: Royal Yoga; Patañjali's Yoga.
Rajas [RUH-juhs]: The quality (*guṇa*) in nature of passion or energy.
Rākṣasa [RAAK-shuh-suh]: A demon.
Rāma [RAA-muh]: Hindu prince and hero of the epic *Rāmāyaṇa*.
Rāmānandi [raa-MAA-nuhn-d/thee]: A sect in North India dedicated to Rāma.
Rāmlīla [RAAM-lee-luh]: Popular *Rāmāyaṇa* festivals staged in North India.
Rām-rājya [RAAM-RAAJ-yuh]: The rule of the god-king Rāma.
Rātra [RAA-thruh]: Night; also called *rātri* [RAA-three].
Rāvaṇa [RAA-vuh-nuh]: Ten-headed demon king in the epic *Rāmāyaṇa*.
Ṛṣi [UR-shee]: Semi-divine perceivers.
Ṛta [UR-thuh]: The right way; the cosmic order.
Rudra [ROO-d/thruh]: (Howler) Deity mentioned in *Ṛg Veda* hymns; later identified with Śiva.

Sabīja [suh-BEE-juh]: With seed; capable of producing effects.
Sādhana [SAA-dhuh-nuh]: Spiritual practice.
Sādhu [SAA-d/thoo]: Holy man; often applied to anyone who has renounced the world.
Saguṇa [SAA-goo-nuh]: Possessing qualities.
Saguṇa Brahman [SAA-goo-nuh BRUH-muhn]: Ultimate Reality assigned with attributes.
Sahajiya [suh-HUH-jee-yuh]: Congenital; coexisting; a Bengali tantric tradition.
Sahasrāra [suh-huhs-RAA-ruh]: Thousand-fold; the seventh interior energy vortex (*cakra*) located approximately at the crown of the head.
Śaiva [SH-AYE-vuh]: Śiva-centered groups, such as the Śaiva-siddhānta school in southern India, as well as the sophisticated philosophies of Trika Śaivism.
Śaiva-siddhānta [SH-AYE-vuh sid-D/THAAN-thuh]: A dualistic Śaiva tantric philosophy.
Śākta [SHAAK-thuh]: Hindu sect that holds Śakti or Devī pre-eminent.

Śakti [SHUHK-thee]: The power that animates the cosmos; the feminine aspect of the Divine.
Śālagrāma [SHAA-luh-GRAA-muh]: Spherical ammonite fossils, which are believed to be forms of Viṣṇu.
Samādhi [suh-MAA-d/thee]: Contemplative absorption; one of the eight limbs of *yoga;* entombment structures for Self-realized *saṃnyāsins.*
Saṃhitā [suhng-HITH-aa]: Joined/collected; hymn collections.
Saṃnyāsa [suhng-NYAA-suh]: Renunciation; the final stage in life prescribed by orthodoxy.
Saṃsāra [suhng-SAA-ruh]: To flow together; to wander; the cycle of repeated rebirths.
Saṃskāra [suhng-SKAA-ruh]: Life cycle rites; karmic dispositions.
Śaṅkarācārya [SHUHN-kuh-RAA-chaar-yuh]: Heads of various Hindu monasteries (*maṭha*), claimed to have been founded by Śaṅkara and his disciples.
Saṅkarṣaṇa [suhm-KUHR-shuh-nuh]: A deity later associated with Viṣṇu; Balarāma.
Sāṅkhya [SAAN-khyuh]: Indian philosophical school of dualistic realism.
Sanskritization: South Asian process of adoption of specific upper class values and practices by lower class citizens.
Santoshi Mā [SUHN-tho-shee MAA]: Goddess of contentment and compassion.
Sarasvatī [suh-RUHS-vuh-thee]: (She who is Full of Juice) Vedic river goddess later associated with Vāc and creative activity.
Sat [SUHTH]: Being; existence.
Satī [SUH-thee]: Śiva's wife; a ritual in which a woman immolates herself on her dead husband's funeral pyre.
Sattva [SUHTH-vuh]: Purity; luminosity; a fundamental quality (*guṇa*) of Nature.
Satya Yuga [SUHTH-yuh YOO-guh]: The Kṛta Yuga.
Satyagraha [SUHTH-yuh-GRUH-huh]: Holding fast to truth, a term coined by Gandhi.
Saubhagya [sau-BHUHG-yuh]: Auspiciousness as it relates to married women and their concerns.
Siddha [SID-d/thuh]: A great yogic adept; highly accomplished tantrics.
Siddhi [SID-d/thee]: Supernormal powers.
Śikhara [SHIK-huh-ruh]: A temple spire characteristic of the Northern style of temple.
Śiṣya [SHISH-yuh]: A disciple; first of the stages in life prescribed by orthodoxy.
Śītalā [SHEE-thuh-laa]: (She who is Cool) The smallpox goddess.
Śiva [SHIV-uh]: (Auspicious) Lord of the *yogis,* the Ultimate Reality.

Skanda [SKUHN-d/thuh]: War god regarded as the son of Śiva; also known as Kumāra and Kārttikeya.

Smārta Brahmin [SMAA-thuh]: Orthodox Brahmins who worship at the shrines of five major deities.

Smṛti [SMUR-thee]: Traditional; literature thought to have been composed by human beings and passed down as tradition through the generations; contrasts with *śruti*.

Soma [SOH-muh]: A sacred plant; the moon; intoxicating beverage made from the Soma plant.

Sphoṭa [SP-HOH-tuh]: Bursting forth; refers to how meaning is conveyed through sound.

Śrāddha [SHRAAD-d/thuh]: Funerary rites.

Śramaṇa [SHRUH-muh-nuh]: Wandering philosophers.

Śrī [SHREE]: The Goddess of Prosperity; Lakṣmī.

Śrī-Lakṣmī [SHREE LUHK-shmee]: Goddess of good fortune; consort of Viṣṇu.

Śrī Vaiṣṇava [SHREE V-AYE-shnuh-vuh]: A South Indian theistic sect of worshippers of Viṣṇu and the goddess Śrī or Lakṣmī.

Śruti [SHROO-thee]: Texts that are considered to have been divinely perceived or revealed to the *ṛṣis*.

Śūdra [SHOO-d/thruh]: The Servant class; the lowest class in the *varṇa* system.

Sūrya [SOOR-yuh]: The Sun god.

Suṣumnā [soo-SHOOM-naa]: The central vital energy pathway (*nāḍī*) of the subtle body.

Sūtra [SOO-thruh]: Aphoristic verses.

Svādhiṣṭhāna [SVAA-d/thish-THAA-nuh]: (One's own place) The second energy vortex (*cakra*) of the subtle body.

Taleju Bhavānī [THUH-lay-joo bhuh-VAA-nee]: A manifestation of Devī Durgā and the chief protector deity of the Nepali kings.

Tamas [THUH-muhs]: Dark; heavy; opaque; a fundamental quality (*guṇa*) of nature.

Tantra [THUHN-thruh]: Schema; method; also known as Āgama; ritual texts; unorthodox, esoteric Hindu beliefs and practices grounded in ritual practice.

Tantradhāraka [THUHN-thruh-D/THUH-ruh-kuh]: Holder of the schema; an assistant/mentor to a tantric ritualist.

Tapas [THUH-puhs]: A purifying inner heat; identified with ascetic practice.

Tattva [THUHT-vuh]: Components; Elements of Prakṛti's evolutionary manifestation.

Tīrṭha [THEERT-huh]: A ford or crossing place.

Tretā Yuga [THREY-thaa YOO-guh]: An age lasting 3600 god (*deva*) years.

Trika Śaiva [THREE-kuh SH-AYE-vuh]: A branch of Kashmir Śaivism; Trika refers to the triad of God, souls, and bonds, with which the philosophy deals.
Tri-loka [THREE-loh-kuh]: The triple world system consisting of the world of the gods, the world of the ancestors, and the human world.
Trimūrti [THREE-moor-thee]: Three forms of a supreme divinity.

Upanayana [OO-puh-NUH-yuh-nuh]: The Investiture with the Sacred Thread rite of passage (*saṃskāra*).
Upāṅga [oo-PAANG-uh]: The secondary appendages to the Vedas.
Uṣas [OO-shuhs]: The Goddess Dawn.
Uttara Mīmāṃsā [OO-thuh-ruh mee-MAANG-saa]: Investigation of the Latter; another name for Vedānta philosophy.

Vāc [VAACH]: Goddess of speech; also Vāgdevī.
Vāhana [VAA-huh-nuh]: A mount; vehicle.
Vaikhānasa [v-aye-KHAA-nuh-suh]: An orthodox sect of Vaiṣṇavas.
Varāha [vuh-RAA-huh]: Viṣṇu's wild boar incarnation.
Vārkarī [VAAR-kaa-ree]: (Pilgrim) Followers of the tradition founded by Namdev.
Varuṇa [VUH-roo-nuh]: God of the waters.
Vaiśeṣika [v-aye-SHEY-shik-uh]: Particularities; one of the six orthodox schools of Indian philosophy; founded by Kaṇāda, it constitutes a proto-science of matter.
Vaiṣṇava [V-AYESH-nuh-vuh]: Viṣṇu-centered sects such as those founded by Rāmānuja, Madhva, and Śrī Caitanya.
Vaiśya [V-AYE-shyuh]: The merchant class; one of the upper three classes of the *varṇa* system.
Vanaprastha [VUH-nuh-PRUH-sthuh]: The forest-dweller stage of life prescribed by orthodoxy.
Varṇa [VUHR-nuh]: Color; Hindu class system, which confers a privileged status to the upper three classes of Priests (Brahmins, *brāhmaṇa*), Warriors (*kṣatriya*), and Merchants (*vaiśya*), over the lower Servant (*śūdra*) class.
Varṇāśramadharma [vuhr-NAASH-ruh-muh-D/THUR-muh]: A system laid out in the Dharma Śāstras regarding stages of life and social obligations based on class status.
Vāyu [VAA-yoo]: The wind god.
Veda [VEY-d/thuh]: Knowledge.
Vedāṅga [vey-D/THAANG-guh]: Limbs or appendages of the Vedas, namely: phonetics (*śikṣa*), prosody (*chandas*), grammar (*vyākarana*), etymology (*nirukta*), astronomy (*jyotiṣa*), and ceremonial (*kalpa*).

Vedānta: Often refers to the Upaniṣads and the interpretation of their teachings since they form the end or concluding sections (*anta*) of revealed Vedic literature.
Vicāra [vee-CHAA-ruh]: The meditative technique of inquiry.
Vidyā [vid/th-YAA]: Liberating knowledge; also referred to as *jñāna*.
Vīraśaiva [VEE-ruh-SH-AYE-vuh]: Heroic Followers of Śiva; a sect founded by Basava; also known as Liṅgayats.
Viśiṣṭādvaita Vedānta [vi-shish-TAADH-v-aye-thuh vey-D/THAAN-thuh]: The theistic philosophy of qualified non-dualism.
Viṣṇu [VISH-noo]: All-pervading Lord who creates and defends *dharma*.
Viṭhobā [vee-TOH-baa]: A pastoral deity whose main temple is located at Pandharpur, in Maharashtra.
Vivāha [VEE-vaa-huh]: Marriage.
Vrata [VRUH-thuh]: Vowed ascetic observances.

Yajamāna [yuh-juh-MAA-nuh]: The patron of Vedic rites.
Yajña [YUHJ-nyuh]: Vedic sacrificial rites.
Yajñopavita [YUHJ-nyoh-PUH-vith-uh]: The sacred thread; *janëu* (Hindi); symbol of the twice-born classes.
Yakṣa [YUHK-shuh]: Male nature sprites; female is Yakṣī [YUHK-shee].
Yama [YUH-muh]: Restraints; one of the eight limbs of *yoga*; the Lord of Death, also known as Dharma-rāja.
Yantra [YUHN-thruh]: Instrument; a cosmological diagram.
Yātra [YAA-thruh]: Pilgrimage.
Yoga [YOH-guh]: Union; *mokṣa*; a spiritual path to Self-realization and its goal.
Yogi [YOH-gee]: One who follows a disciplined path to liberation; also *yogin*.
Yoni [YOH-nee]: The female reproductive organ; vulva.
Yuga [YOO-guh]: Age; eon.

Zamīndār [zuh-meen-D/THAAR]: Local regional landlords, lineage heads, and chieftains, given political authority during Mughal rule.

B: Pronunciation guide and glossary of people's names

A note on pronunciation

It is crucial to remember that "uh," wherever it occurs, is pronounced as in the expression "huh" or like the "u" in "but." Also note that "aye," wherever it occurs, is pronounced as in the nautical "aye" or the optical "eye." The "oo" is sounded like the bovine "moo," and the "ee" as in the word "see." However, the "ee" and "oo" are pronounced either short or long, depending on the length of the vowel in the original word. Capitalized syllables roughly indicate where emphasis should be placed. Remember that the Sanskrit "d" as in "*deva*" is sounded somewhere between "DHEY-vuh" and "THEY-vuh." Such sounds are indicated as "D/THEY-vuh." An "aa" is pronounced as the "a" in "father." Additional guidance is found in the Preface, and in Chapter 5: The Sanskrit Language.

Abhinavagupta [uh-BHEE-nuh-vuh-GOOP-thuh]: Most renowned philosopher of Trika Śaivism.
Akbar [UHK-buhr]: Mughal emperor who ruled from 1556 to 1605 CE.
Ānandamayī Mā [AA-nuhn-d/thuh-muh-YEE MAA]: A contemporary female Bengali saint.
Aniruddha [uh-nee-ROO-d/thuh]: Kṛṣṇa's grandson; an emanation in Pañcarātra philosophy.
Āṇṭāḷ [AAN-taal]: Renowned female Ālvār, a devotee of Viṣṇu.
Appar [uh-PUHR]: One of the most renowned Nāyanārs.
Arjuna [UHR-joo-nuh]: A *kṣatriya* hero in the *Mahābhārata* epic.
Aśoka [uh-SHOK-uh]: Grandson of Candragupta and a convert to Buddhism; he expanded the Mauryan empire to its maximum size; ruled 265–238 BCE.
Aurangzeb [au-RUHNG-zeb]: Mughal emperor who ruled from 1658 to 1707 CE, and under whom Hinduism experienced persecution.
Aurobindo Ghose [AU-roh-BIN-d/thoh GHOHS]: (1872–1950 CE) Founder of Integral Yoga.

Babar [BAA-buhr]: Establisher of Mughal rule; also Babur.
Bādārayāṇa [BAA-d/thaa-RAA-yuh-nuh]: Author of the *Vedānta Sutra*.
Bahadur Shah Zafar [BUH-huh-d/thoor SHAAH ZUH-fuhr]: The last Mughal emperor.
Balabhadra [BUH-luh-BHUH-d/thruh]: Kṛṣṇa's brother; Balarāma.
Bal Gangadhar Tilak [BUHL GUHN-guh-d/thuhr THEE-luhk]: (1856–1920 CE) Political activist and freedom fighter.
Bankim Chatterjee [BUHN-kim CHUH-thur-jee]: Bengali author who composed *Vande Mataram*.

Basava [BUH-suh-vuh]: Founder of the Vīraśaiva or Liṅgayat sect; also Basavanna [BUH-suh-VUH-nuh].

Bede Griffiths (1906–1993): English Benedictine monk who fused Christian and Hindu monasticism.

Bharata [BHUH-ruh-thuh]: The son of Kaikeyī in the epic *Rāmāyaṇa*; ancestral king whose descendants are the characters in the *Mahābhārata* epic (different from the *Rāmāyaṇa* prince).

Bhartṛhari [BHUHR-tur-HUH-ree]: (570–651? CE) Grammarian, philosopher, and poet; wrote the grammar treatise entitled *Vākyapadīya*.

Bhīma [BHEE-muh]: Pāṇḍava hero; son of Kuntī and Vāyu having vast proportions, appetite, and strength.

Bhīṣma [BHEESH-muh]: A powerful warrior and grandfather figure in the *Mahābhārata* epic.

B. K. S. Iyengar [ee-YEHN-guhr]: (1918–) Haṭha Yoga teacher, and founder of an influential style of *yoga*.

B. R. Ambedkar [uhm-BEYDH-kuhr]: Prominent Indian Untouchable leader from the early twentieth century.

Buddha [BOO-d/thuh]: The Awakened One; title of Siddhartha Gautama, founder of Buddhism.

Candragupta Maurya [CHUHN-d/thruh-GOOP-thuh MAUR-yuh]: Founder of the Mauryan (Peacock) Dynasty which emerged on the Indian subcontinent in 322 BCE.

Chandi Prasad Bhatt [CHUHN-dee pruh-SAAD/TH BHUHT]: Leader of the Chipko ("hugging") movement.

Dakṣa [D/THUHK-shuh]: Father of Satī; identified with Prajāpati.

Darius I [duh-R-AYE-us][DA-ree-us]: Darius the Great; emperor of Persia from 521 to 425 BCE, he expanded the Persian Empire to the Indus River.

Daśaratha [DUH-shuh-ruh-thuh]: Father of Prince Rāma in the *Rāmāyaṇa*.

Dayānanda Sarasvati [d/thuh-YAA-nuhn-d/thuh suh-RUHS-vuh-thee] (1824–1883 CE) Founder of the Ārya Samāj (Society of Noble Ones).

Debendranath Tagore [d/they-BEYN-d/thruh-NAATH thuh-GOHR]: Ram Mohan Roy's successor; leader of the Brāhmo Samāj; father of Rabindranath Tagore.

Dhṛtarāṣṭra [D/THUHR-thuh-RAASH-thruh]: Father of the Kaurava princes in the *Mahābhārata*.

Draupadī [D/THRAU-puh-d/thee]: The princess wife of the five Paṇḍava brothers in the *Mahābhārata*.

Duḥśāsana [D/THOO-huh-SHAA-suh-nuh]: Duryodana's younger brother in the *Mahābhārata*.

Duryodhana [d/thoor-YOH-d/thuh-nuh]: The eldest son of Gāndhārī and Dhṛtarāṣṭra in the *Mahābhārata.*

Eknāth [ey-k-NAATH]: A *bhakti* poet and saint of Maharashtra; wrote a masterful commentary on a portion of the *Bhāgavata Purāṇa.*

Fa-xien [FAA-SHEE-en]: Chinese pilgrim whose mid-fifth-century writings tell of his stay on the island of Java.

Gāndhārī [GAAN-d/thaa-ree]: Dhṛtarāṣṭra's wife in the *Mahābhārata.*
Gangaji [GUHN-gaa-jee] (1942–): American-born spiritual teacher.
Gorakhnātha [GO-ruhkh-NAATH]: Founder of a Śaivite sect known as the Nāths; traditionally attributed with the authorship of the first treatise on Haṭha Yoga; also Gorakṣanātha, and Gorakhnāth (Hindi).
Guru Nanak [GOO-roo NUH-nuhk]: Punjabi-born founder of Sikhism.

H. W. L. Poonjaji [POON-jaa-jee]: (1910–1997 CE) A Hindu sage also known as Pāpājī.

Indira Gandhi [in-D/THEE-ruh GAAN-d/thee]: (1917–1984) Female Prime Minister of India; daughter of Nehru.

Janaka [JUH-nuh-kuh]: King in the epic *Rāmāyaṇa* and Sītā's father.
Jaṭāyu [juh-TAA-yoo]: The vulture king and ally of Rāma in the epic *Rāmāyaṇa.*
Jawarharlal Nehru [juh-VAA-huhr-luhl NEYH-roo]: India's first prime minister.
Jayadeva [JUH-yuh-D/THEY-vuh]: Author of the lyrical poem *Gītāgovinda.*
Jayavarman II [JUH-yuh-VUHR-muhn]: Founder of the Khmer Empire.
Jiddu Krishnamurti [JID-d/thoo KRISH-nuh-MOOR-thee]: (1895–1986) Former Theosophist, promoted as the World Teacher, a role he abandoned to advocate self-reliance in the search for truth.
Jñāneśvara [jnyaa-NEYSH-vuh-ruh]: Maharashtrian religious poet.

Kabir [kuh-BEER]: (1440–1518) Banaras-born mystic poet who favored a monistic philosophy viewing all of humanity as one.
Kaikeyī [k-aye-KAY-yee]: King Daśaratha's wife and mother of Bharata in the *Ramāyaṇa.*
Kalidāsa [KUH-lee-D/THAA-suh]: One of India's greatest playwrights and Sanskrit poets.
Kaṃsa [KUHNG-suh]: Mythic king of Mathurā killed by Kṛṣṇa.
Kaṇāda [kuh-NAA-d/thuh]: The likely author of the *Vaiśeṣika Sūtra.*

Kapila [KUH-pee-luh]: The origins of Sāṅkhya are attributed to this semi-legendary sage.
Karṇa [KUHR-nuh]: The golden armored son of Sūrya and Kuntī in the *Mahābhārata*.
Kausalya [KAU-suh-lyuh]: King Daśaratha's wife, and Rāma's mother in the *Ramāyaṇa*; also Kauśalya.
Keshab Chandra Sen [KAY-shuhb CHUHN-d/thruh SEYN]: One of Ram Mohan Roy's successors; also called Keshava Chandra Sena.
Kuntī [KOON-thee]: Mother of the Pāṇḍava heroes in the *Mahābhārata*.

Lakṣmana [LUHKSH-muh-nuh]: One of the twins born to Queen Sumitrā in the *Rāmāyaṇa*; Rāma's younger brother and inseparable companion.
Lakulīśa [luh-KOO-lee-shuh]: (Lord of the Club) Founder of the Pāśupatas.

Madhva [MUHD-vuh]: A Dvaita Vedānta philosopher.
Mādrī [MAA-d/three]: A wife of King Pāṇḍu; mother of Nakula and Sahadeva.
Mahādevyakka [muh-HAA-d/they-VYUHK-kuh]: A female Vīraśaiva poet and saint.
Maharishi Mahesh Yogi [muh-HAA-REE-shee muh-HEYSH YOH-gee]: (1917–) Founder of the (Transcendental Meditation™) movement.
Mahmud of Ghazni [MAAH-mood/th of GHUHZ-nee]: Ruler of the Ghaznavid Dynasty from 999 to 1030 CE.
Maitreyī [M-AYE-trey-yee]: Upaniṣadic female teacher and wife of Yajñavalkya.
Manmohan Singh [MUHN-moh-huhn SINGH]: Prime Minister of India as of 2004.
Māṇikkavācakar [MAA-nee-kuh-VAA-chuh-kuhr]: Śaiva *bhakti* poet; often regarded as a sixty-fourth Nāyanār; his poetry is located in the *Tiruvācakam*.
Mīrabai [MEE-ruh-b-aye]: A female *bhakti* poet saint of the northern Sant tradition.
Mohandas Gandhi [moh-HUHN-d/thuhs GAAN-d/thee]: (1869–1948 CE) Leader of India's independence movement, and proponent of the philosophy of *ahiṃsā* or non-violence; also known as Mahatma (Great Soul) Gandhi.
Muhammad [muh-HUHM-muhd/th]: The Prophet of Islam.
Muhammad Ali Jinnah [muh-HUHM-muhd/th AA-lee JIN-nuh]: Leader of the Muslim League.

Nāmdev [NAAM-d/theyv]: Maharashtrian poet and Jñāneśvara's disciple.
Nammālvār [nuhm-MAAL-vaar]: An Ālvār and author of the *Tiruvāymoli*.
Nāthamuni [NAA-thuh-MOO-nee]: Collected the poems of the Ālvārs into the *Nālāyira Divyaprabandham*.

Nisargadatta Maharaj [nee-SUHR-guh-D/THUH-tuh muh-HAA-RAAJ]: (1897–1981 CE) A non-dualistic sage; composer of *I am That*.

Osho [OH-shoh]: (1930–1990 CE) A controversial *guru*, also known as Bhagwan Shree Rajneesh.

Pāṇinī [PAA-nin-EE]: An early renowned Sanskrit grammarian.

Patañjali [puh-THUHN-juh-lee]: A Sanskrit grammarian; author of the *Yoga Sūtra*.

Pattabhi Jois [PUH-thuh-bhee JOH-ees]: Yoga teacher and student of Krishnamacharya.

Pradyumna [PRUH-d/thyoom-nuh]: Kṛṣṇa's son; an emanation in Pañcarātra philosophy.

Prahlāda [pruh-LAA-d/thuh]: The demon Hiraṇyakaśipu's dharmic son.

Rabindranath Tagore [ruh-BIN-d/thruh-NAATH thuh-GOHR]: (1861–1941) Bengali poet and Nobel laureate; son of Debendranath Tagore, leader of the Brāhmo Samāj.

Rājarāja I [RAA-juh-RAA-juh]: The greatest of the kings of the Cola Dynasty.

Rajiv Gandhi [RAA-jeev GAAN-d/thee]: (1944–1991) Son of Indira Gandhi and Prime Minister of India from 1984 to 1989; assassinated in 1991 CE.

Rāma [RAA-muh]: Hero of the epic *Ramāyaṇa*.

Ramakrishna Paramahamsa [RAA-muh-KRISH-nuh PUH-ruh-muh-HUHNG-suh]: (1836–1886 CE) Bengali temple priest/saint who taught Advaita Vedānta and worshipped the goddess Kālī.

Ramaṇa Mahāṛṣi [RUH-muh-nuh muh-HAAR-shee]: (1879–1950 CE) South Indian mystic and proponent of Advaita Vedānta who taught the practice of Self-inquiry (*ātma-vicāra*).

Rāmānuja [raa-MAAN-noo-juh]: (eleventh to twelfth centuries CE) Vedānta philosopher associated with Qualified Non-Dualism.

Ramesh Balsekar [ruh-MEYSH BUHL-say-kuhr]: (1919–) Advaita sage and teacher; disciple of Nisargadatta Maharaj.

Ram Mohan Roy [RAAM MOH-huhn ROY]: (1772–1833 CE) Founder of the Brāhmo Samāj, a reform movement in India; fostered the abolishment of *satī*.

Rāmprasād Sen [RAAM-pruh-SAAD/TH SEYN]: (eighteenth century CE) Bengali songwriter and *bhakti* poet; devotee of Kālī.

Rāvaṇa [RAA-vuh-nuh]: The ten-headed demon in the *Rāmāyaṇa*; slain by Rāma.

Sai Baba of Shirdi [S-AYE BAA-baa]: (*c.* 1838–1918) Humble but renowned Maharashtrian saint.

Śakuni [SHUH-koo-nee]: Duryodhana's dice-playing uncle in the *Mahābhārata*.

Sambandar [SUHM-buhn-d/thuhr]: One of the three most renowned Nāyanārs; also Campantar.

Śaṅkara [SHUHN-kuh-ruh]: Hindu Advaita Vedanta philosopher.

Saṅkarṣaṇa [suhn-KUHR-shuh-nuh]: Kṛṣṇa's elder brother, also known as Balarāma.

Sarvepalli Radhakrishnan [SAAR-vey-PAA-lee RAA-d/thaa-KRISH-nuhn]: Once Spalding Professor of Religion at Oxford and the second President of India.

Satya Sai Baba [SUHTH-yuh S-AYE BAA-baa]: (1926–) Self-proclaimed incarnation of the saint Sai Baba of Shirdi (*c*. 1838–1918), and known for his magical feats.

Satyavan [SUHT-yuh-vuhn]: Mythical Hindu prince taken by Yama, the Lord of Death.

Sāvitrī [SAA-vith-ree]: In Hindu myth, her dedication won her husband back from Yama, the Lord of Death.

Sāyaṇa [SAA-yuh-nuh]: Fourteenth-century writer of commentaries on Vedas and Vedic works.

Shah Jahan [SHAAH juh-HUHN]: Mughal ruler who constructed the Taj Mahal.

Shivaji Bhonsle [shiv-AA-jee BHON-sley]: Leader of the Maratha rebellion.

Siddhārtha Gautama [SID-d/thaar-thuh GAU-thuh-muh]: Original name of the Buddha before he gained enlightenment.

Sītā [SEE-thaa]: Wife of Rāma, and heroine of the epic *Rāmāyaṇa*.

Sonia Gandhi [SOH-nee-yuh GAAN-d/thee]: Rajiv Gandhi's Italian-born wife and widow and leader of the 2004 Congress Party.

Sri Aurobindo [SHREE AU-roh-BIN-d/thoh]: Political activist turned philosopher-saint, and creator of Integral Yoga.

Śrī Caitanya [SHREE ch-aye-THUHN-yuh]: (1486–1533 CE) Bengali *bhakti* saint who worshipped God in the form of Rādhā-Kṛṣṇa.

Subhadrā [SOO-bhuh-D/THRAA]: Kṛṣṇa's sister and wife of Arjuna in the *Mahābhārata*.

Sugrīva [soo-GREE-vuh]: Monkey king of Kiṣkindhā in the *Ramāyaṇa*.

Sundarar [SOON-d/thuh-ruhr]: One of the three most renowned Nāyanārs; also called Cuntarar.

Śūrpaṇakhā [SHOOR-puh-nuh-KHAA]: Shape-shifting demoness in the *Ramāyaṇa*.

Suryavarman II [SOOR-yuh-VUHR-muhn]: Hindu emperor, Khmer ruler, and builder of Angkor Wat.

Śvetaketu [SHVEY-thuh-KAY-thoo]: Student in the *Chāndogya Upanisad* who receives valuable lessons from his father.

Swami Abhishiktananda [SVAA-mee uh-bhee-SHIK-THAA-nuhn-d/thuh] (1910–1973) French Benedictine monk (originally Henri Le Saux), disciple of a Hindu *guru*, and founder of Shantivanam.

Swami Bhaktivedanta Prabhupada [SVAA-mee BHUHK-thee-vey-D/THAAN-thuh pruh-bhoo-PAA-d/thuh]: (1896–1977 CE) Vaiṣṇava renouncer; founder of the International Society for Kṛṣṇa Consciousness (ISKCON).

Swami Chidvilasananda [SVAA-mee CHID-vee-LAA-SAA-nuhn-d/thuh]: Female lineage holder in Swami Muktananda's organization; also known as Gurumayi.

Swami Muktananda [SVAA-mee mook-THAA-nuhn-d/thuh]: (1908–1982 CE) Propagator of the Siddha Yoga tradition.

Swami Sivananda Radha [SVAA-mee shiv-AA-nuhn-dhuh]: A *saṃnyāsinī* disciple of Swami Sivananda; her *āśrama* is located in British Columbia, Canada.

Swami Sivananda Saraswati [SVAA-mee shiv-AA-nuhn-dhuh]: (1887–1963 CE) Founder of The Divine Life Society.

Swami Vishnudevananda [SVAA-mee VISH-noo-d/they-VAA-nuhn-d/thuh]: Disciple of Swami Sivananda Saraswati who formed *yoga* centers worldwide.

Swami Vivekānanda [SVAA-mee vee-VEYK-AA-nuhn-d/thuh]: (1863–1902 CE) Disciple of Ramakrishna Paramahamsa and propagator of Vedānta worldwide.

Tagore: see Rabindranath Tagore.

Tirumalai Krishnamacharya [THIR-oo-muh-L-AYE KRISH-nuh-MAA-chuh-ryuh]: (1888–1988 CE) Haṭha Yoga master; one of the most influential patriarchs of *yoga* practice in the West.

T. K. V. Desikachar [D/THEY-see-KAA-chuhr]: Yoga master and son of Tirumalai Krishnamacharya.

Tukārām [THOO-kaa-RAAM]: Maharastrian *bhakti* poet and devotee of Kṛṣṇa.

Tulsidās [THOO-luh-see-D/THAAS]: Banāras-based *bhakti* poet and philosopher.

Uddālaka [oo-D/THAA-luh-kuh]: Śvetaketu's father and teacher in the *Chāndogya Upaniṣad.*

Vālin [VAA-lin]: Monkey king; brother to Sugrīva in the *Rāmāyaṇa*; also Vāli.

Vālmīki [VAAL-mee-kee]: Attributed author of the oldest version of the *Rāmāyaṇa.*

Vande Mataram [VAAN-d/they MAA-thuh-ruhm]: India's national song, considered a call for freedom during India's British occupation; composed by Bankim Chatterjee in 1876 CE.

Vardhamāna Mahāvīra [VAAR-d/thuh-MAA-nuh muh-HAA-VEE-ruh]: (599–527 BCE) Founder of Jainism; also called The Jina.

Vibhīṣaṇa [vi-BHEE-shuh-nuh]: A dharmic brother of the demon Rāvaṇa in the *Rāmāyaṇa*.

Viśvāmitra [vish-VAA-mith-ruh]: A *ṛṣi* who taught Rāma and Lakṣmana in the *Rāmāyaṇa*.

Vyāsa [VYAA-suh]: A *ṛṣi;* mythic author of the *Mahābhārata;* a historic author of a commentary on the *Yoga Sūtra*.

Yajñavalkya [YUHJ-nyuh-VUHL-kyuh]: A sage mentioned in the Upaniṣads.

Yaśodā [yuh-SHOH-d/thaa]: The cowherd foster-mother of Kṛṣṇa.

Yudhiṣṭhira [yoo-D/THISHT-hir-uh]: Firm in battle; a dharmic king and eldest of the Pāṇḍava brothers in the Hindu epic the *Mahābhārata*.

C: *Pronunciation guide and glossary of place names*

A note on pronunciation

It is crucial to remember that "uh," wherever it occurs, is pronounced as in the expression "huh" or like the "u" in "but." Also note that "aye," wherever it occurs, is pronounced as in the nautical "aye" or the optical "eye." The "oo" is sounded like the bovine "moo," and the "ee" as in the word "see." However, the "ee" and "oo" are pronounced either short or long, depending on the length of the vowel in the original word. Capitalized syllables roughly indicate where emphasis should be placed. Remember that the Sanskrit "d" as in "*deva*" is sounded somewhere between "DHEY-vuh" and "THEY-vuh." Such sounds are indicated as "D/THEY-vuh." An "aa" is pronounced as the "a" in "father." Additional guidance is found in the Preface, and in Chapter 5: The Sanskrit Language.

Also: I have indicated Indic pronunciations in certain cases. Thus, for instance, I write NEY-paal instead of nuh-PAUL for the country of Nepal, and D/THEY-lee instead of DEL-ee for the city of Delhi.

Afghanistan [uhf-GHAA-nis-THAAN]: South central Asian country that borders Pakistan and Iran.

Andhra Pradesh [UHN-d/thruh pruh-D/THEYSH]: State located in the southeast of India.

Angkor [UHNG-kor]: Ancient city in Cambodia; home to a number of capital cities of the Khmer empire from the ninth to the fifteenth centuries CE.

Angkor Wat [UHNG-kor WAAT]: Temple at Angkor, Cambodia; originally built for King Suryavarman II in the early twelfth century and dedicated to Viṣṇu; later used by Theravada Buddhists.

Arunachala [uh-ROO-nuh-CHUH-luh]: A hill sacred to Śiva, near Tiruvannamalai.

Assam [UHS-suhm]: Northeast Indian state where Kāmakhyā temple is located.
Ayodhyā [uh-YOH-d/thyaa]: City in North India; Rāma's legendary birthplace.
Ayutthaya [uh-YOOT-thuh-YAA]: Thailand's ancient capital named after Rāma's capital, Ayodhyā.

Babari Masjid [BUH-buh-ree MUHS-jid/th]: Mosque reputedly built by the Mughal emperor Babar in Ayodhyā.
Badrinath [BUHD-ree-NAATH]: Himalayan temple dedicated to Viṣṇu near a source of the Gaṅgā.
Baijnāth [b-ayej-NAATH]: Town in the Kumaon Himalayas and site of a temple to Pārvatī.
Bali [BAA-lee]: Hindu island in Indonesia.
Banāras [buh-NAA-ruhs]: Vārānasī; Hindu holy city on the banks of the river Gaṅgā.
Bangladesh [BUHN-gluh-D/THEYSH]: Country that constitutes the eastern part of the ancient region of Bengal.
Bengal [BEYN-guhl]: A north eastern region of South Asia; presently separated into the independent country of Bangladesh and the Indian state of West Bengal.
Besakih [bey-SAA-kee]: Renowned Balinese temple at the foot of the volcano Mount Agung.
Bihar [bee-HAAR]: East Indian state where the cities of Gāyā and Bodh-gāyā are located.
Black Pagoda: Temple to the sun god Sūrya at Konārka (Konarak) in the state of Orissa.
Borobudur [BOH-roh-buh-D/THUHR]: Largest Buddhist monument in the world; built on Java in the early ninth century.
Bṛhadīśvara [BUR-huh-D/THEESH-vuh-ruh]: Renowned Hindu temple at Thanjavur in the Indian state of Tamil Nadu.
Burma: Country in mainland Southeast Asia; now known as Myanmar.

Cambodia: Southeast Asian country where Angkor Wat is located.
Cera [CHEY-ruh]: Ancient South Indian kingdom occupying a thin strip of India's southwestern coast, around modern Kerala.
Chennai [CHEY-n-aye]: Southeastern city in India formerly known as Madras.
Cidambaram [CHID/TH-uhm-buh-ruhm]: Vast Śiva temple in South India.
Cola [CHOH-luh]: A major South Indian kingdom.

Dakṣineśvar [D/THUHK-shee-NEYSH-vuhr]: Town near Kolkata (Calcutta), in the state of Bengal made famous by Ramakrishna Paramahamsa; also Dakshineshwar.

Delhi [D/THEY-lee]: The capital of India; also New Delhi.

Durgā Kuṇḍa [D/THUHR-gaa KOON-duh]: Pond and temple in Banāras dedicated to Durgā.

Dvāraka [D/THVAA-ruh-kuh]: Kṛṣṇa's mythic home kingdom in the *Mahābhārata*; a *maṭha* claimed to have been founded by Śaṅkara and his disciples.

Elephanta Caves: Site of rock-cut temples on an island off the coast of Mumbai.

Ellora [el-LOH-ruh]: Site in the Indian state of Maharashtra famous for its rock-cut Buddhist and Hindu caves.

Gaṅgā [GUHN-gaa]: The Ganges River, believed to be a living goddess (Ma Gaṅgā), and venerated by most Hindus.

Gāyā [GAA-yaa]: Pilgrimage site in the Indian state of Bihar.

Ghaggar-Hakra River [GHUH-guhr-HUH-kruh]: Identified with the mythic Sarasvati, it is a seasonal river that runs through the Indian states of Punjab, Haryana, and into Rajasthan.

Golden Temple: Holiest Sikh shrine, located in Amritsar.

Govardhana [goh-VUHR-d/thuh-nuh]: Mountain supported by Kṛṣṇa in Hindu myth.

Gujarat [GOO-juh-RAATH]: Westernmost state of India.

Harappa [HUH-ruh-puh]: One of the largest cities of the Indus Valley Civilization.

Haridvar [HUH-ree-D/THVAAR]: Holy city at the Himalayan foothills where the Gaṅgā meets the plains.

Himalaya [him-AA-luh-yuh]: World's highest mountain range; separates the Indian subcontinent from the Tibetan Plateau.

Indonesia: Located in the Malay Archipelago (a large group of islands positioned between Indochina and Australia); the fourth most populated nation in the world.

Indus River [IN-d/thuhs]: Also known as the Sindhu, it originates in Tibet, flowing from the Himalayas through Kashmir and then south into Pakistan.

Indus Valley Civilization: Located on the banks of the lower Indus River and the Ghaggar-Hakra River; also known as the Harappan Civilization.

Jagannātha [JUH-guh-NAA-thuh]: Temple in the city of Puri, Orissa renowned for its chariot festival.

Jallianwala Bagh [JUH-lee-aan-VAA-luh BHAAG]: Garden in the Punjab; site of a British massacre of Hindus.

Jammu and Kashmir [JUHM-moo, KAASH-meer]: Northernmost state of India.

Java [JAA-vaa]: Part of Indonesia, the most populated island in the world; site of the Hindu temple complex of Prambanan.

Jyotirmath [JYOH-thir-MUHT]: Monastery (*maṭha*) claimed to have been founded by Śaṅkara; also known as Badrināth.

Ka'bah [KAA-baah]: Most revered Muslim shrine, located in Mecca (Makkah), Saudi Arabia.

Kailāsanātha [k-aye-LAA-suh-NAA-thuh]: Massive rock-cut temple dedicated to Śiva in Ellora.

Kālīghat temple [KAA-lee-GHAAT]: Renowned Kālī temple in Kolkata (Calcutta).

Kāmarūpa [KAA-muh-ROO-puh]: Site of a renowned goddess temple in the state of Assam.

Kāñcīpuram [KAAN-chee-POO-ruhm]: Renowned temple city in South India.

Kandāriya Mahādeva [kuhn-D/THAA-ree-yuh muh-HAA-D/THEY-vuh]: (Great God of the Crag Cave) Temple dedicated to Śiva in Khajuraho.

Kanyā Kumārī [KUHN-yaa koo-MAA-ree]: Southernmost tip of India; formerly known as Cape Comorin.

Karnataka [kuhr-NUH-thuh-kuh]: A southern Indian state.

Kashmir [KUHSH-meer]: Region in the northern area of the Indian subcontinent.

Kāśī [KAA-shee]: Luminous; another name for Banāras.

Kathmandu Valley [KUHT-muhn-doo]: In the country of Nepal, conquered in 1769 by King Prithvi Narayan Shah.

Kedarnāth [KEY-d/thuhr-NAATH]: Śaiva pilgrimage site near a source of the Gaṅgā in the Himalayas.

Kerala [KAY-ruh-luh]: State located on the southwestern coast of India.

Khajuraho [KHUH-joo-RAA-hoh]: City in the Indian state of Madhya Pradesh, renowned for its large group of medieval Hindu temples and their erotic sculpture.

Khmer Empire [khmey-r]: Developed from the kingdom of Chenla; known for its capital Angkor.

Kolhapur [KOH-huh-POO-r]: City in Maharashtra state; site of a renowned Lakṣmī temple.

Konarak [KOH-nuh-ruhk]: Town in the state of Orissa, renowned for its ancient Sun temple.

Laṅkā [LUHN-kaa]: Abode of the *Rāmāyaṇa*'s demon king Rāvaṇa.

Madhya Pradesh [MUH-d/thyuh pruh-D/THEYSH]: A state in central India.
Madurai [MUH-d/thoo-R-AYE]: City in South India renowned for its Mīnākṣī temple.
Mahapajit kingdom [muh-HAA-puh-JEETH]: Javanese maritime empire that ruled over the minor kingdoms of Indonesia and Malaya from approximately 1300 to the early sixteenth century.
Maharashtra [muh-HAA-RAASH-thruh]: West-central Indian state
Mathurā [MUH-thoo-RAA]: Town regarded as the birthplace of Kṛṣṇa.
Mohenjodaro [moh-HEN-joh-D/THAA-roh]: Large unearthed city in the lower Indus Valley.
Mount Agung [AA-goong]: Sacred volcano in Bali.
Mount Govardhana [goh-VUHR-d/thuh-nuh]: In a Hindu myth, Kṛṣṇa supported this mountain with his finger.
Mount Kailāsa [k-aye-LAA-suh]: Śiva's abode in the Himalayas.
Mount Mandara [MUHN-d/thuh-ruh]: Mythical mountain used to churn the milk ocean.
Mount Meru [MAY-roo]: Cosmic mountain at the center of the world; also called Sumeru.
Mumbai [MOOM-b-aye]: Capital of the state of Maharashtra; formerly known as Bombay.
Myanmar [MYUHN-maar]: Country bordering on India and Thailand; formerly known as Burma.

Nagaland [NAA-gaa-land]: A state in north-eastern India.
Narmada River [NAAR-muh-D/THAA]: Located in central India; divides India into North and South.
Nepal [NEY-paal]: Hindu kingdom in the Himalayan foothills.
New Delhi [D/THEY-lee]: The capital of India; situated in the northern state of Uttar Pradesh.

Orissa [oh-RIS-suh]: State positioned along the mid-east coast of India.

Pakistan [PAA-kis-THAAN]: Muslim country partitioned from India at the end of British rule.
Pandharpur [puh-DHUHR-poo-r]: Famous pilgrimage destination in Maharashtra state.
Pāṇḍya [PAAN-dyuh]: Ancient South Indian kingdom.
Paśupatināth Temple [PUH-shoo-puh-thee-NAATH]: Located in Kathmandu.
Persia: Vast empire that surfaced during the sixth century BCE under the Achaemenid Dynasty; modern day Iran.

Pondicheri [PON-d/thee-CHEY-ree]: A Union Territory in Southern India; also called Puduchcheri.

Prambanan [pruhm-BAA-nuhn]: Largest Hindu temple complex in Indonesia.

Prayāg [pruh-YAAG]: City at the confluence of the Gaṅgā and Yamunā rivers; also called Allahabad; renowned as the site of the largest Kumbh Mela.

Punjab [puhn-JAAB]: Northwest Indian state with a large Sikh population.

Puri [POO-ree]: City located in the state of Orissa, India, renowned for the legendary Jagannath temple and for a monastery founded by Śaṅkara.

Pushkar [POOSH-kuhr]: Town and holy lake in the state of Rajasthan renowned for its Brahmā temple.

Rajasthan [RAA-juhs-THAAN]: Northwestern Indian state.

Rāmeśvaram [raa-MEYSH-vuh-ruhm]: City near India's southernmost tip.

Rām Janma Bhumi [RAAM JUHN-muh BHOO-mee]: Reputed site of Rāma's birthplace; former site of the Babari Masjid; name of a proposed Hindu temple.

Rishikesh [RISH-ee-KAYSH]: Holy city located along the Gaṅgā in the foothills of the Himalayas.

Sabarimalai [SUH-buh-ree-muh-L-AYE]: Pilgrimage site in the state of Kerala.

Sarasvatī River [suh-RUHS-vuh-thee]: Mentioned in ancient Vedic texts; may be the present-day Ghaggar-Hakra River.

Sri Lanka [SHREE LUHN-kaa]: Island nation situated just off India's most southern edge; formerly known as Ceylon.

Śrīraṅgam [SHREE-ruhn-guhm]: Largest temple complex in all of India, located in Tamil Nadu.

Śṛṅgerī [SHURN-gey-ree]: Monastery (*maṭha*) reputedly founded by Śaṅkara.

Taj Mahal [THAAJ muh-HAAL]: Tomb in Agra, India, built by the Mughal emperor Shah Jahan for his wife, Mumtaz.

Tamil Nadu [THAA-mil NAA-d/thoo]: State at the southern tip of India.

Thanjavur [thuhn-JAA-vuhr]: City in the Indian state of Tamil Nadu renowned for its Bṛhadīśvara Temple.

Tirupati [THIR-oo-puh-thee]: Wealthiest temple in India, located in Andhra Pradesh state.

Tiruvannamalai [THIR-oo-VUHN-nuh-muh-l-aye]: Town in Tamil Nadu state, known for its Arunchaleśvara Temple.

Udaipur [oo-D/TH-AYE-poo-r]: City in the Indian state of Rajasthan renowned for its royal palace.

Uttar Pradesh [OO-thuhr pruh-D/THEYSH]: Northern and most populated state in India.

Vaikuṇṭha [v-aye-KOON-tuh]: The mythic abode of Viṣṇu.
Vaitarni [v-aye-THAAR-nee]: Foul river believed to separate the god of death's realm from the earthly realm.
Vārāṇasī [vaa-RAA-nuh-SEE]: Hindu holy city in north India, on the banks of the Gaṅgā River, and particularly dedicated to the god Śiva; also Banāras, or Kāśī.
Vijayanagara [vee-JUH-yuh-NUH-guh-ruh]: Last of the great Indian Hindu kingdoms, located in state of Karnataka.
Vindhya Mountains [VIN-d/thyuh]: A range in central India dividing the Indian subcontinent into north and south.
Vṛndāvana [vurn-D/THAA-vuh-nuh]: The forested region where Kṛṣṇa grew up as a humble cowherd (*go-pala*).

Yamunā River [YUH-moo-naa]: A river located in Northern India.

D: Pronunciation guide and glossary of texts

A note on pronunciation

It is crucial to remember that "uh," wherever it occurs, is pronounced as in the expression "huh" or like the "u" in "but." Also note that "aye," wherever it occurs, is pronounced as in the nautical "aye" or the optical "eye." The "oo" is sounded like the bovine "moo," and the "ee" as in the word "see." However, the "ee" and "oo" are pronounced either short or long, depending on the length of the vowel in the original word. Capitalized syllables roughly indicate where emphasis should be placed. Remember that the Sanskrit "d" as in "*deva*" is sounded somewhere between "DHEY-vuh" and "THEY-vuh." Such sounds are indicated as "D/THEY-vuh." An "aa" is pronounced as the "a" in "father." Additional guidance is found in the Preface, and in Chapter 5: The Sanskrit Language.

Āgama [AA-guh-muh]: (Scripture) Texts dedicated to Viṣṇu, Śiva, or Devī.
Aitareya Āraṇyaka [AYE-tuh-ray-yuh AA-ruhn-yuh-kuh]: One of the Wilderness Texts.
Anaṅga Raṅga [uh-NUHNG-uh RUHNG-uh]: Text in the Kāma Śāstra literature dealing with human sexuality.
Āraṇyaka [aa-RUHN-yuh-kuh]: Wilderness Text; genre of Vedic literature providing mysterious explanations of sacrificial rites.
Artha Śāstra [UHR-thuh SHAAS-thruh]: A treatise on *artha;* believed authored by Kautilya.
Aṣṭādhyāyī [uh-SHTAA-dhyaa-yee]: (*Eight Chapters*) Grammar text composed by Pāṇinī.

Atharva Veda [uh-THUHR-vuh VEY-d/thuh]: The fourth Vedic Saṃhitā, a collection of hymns with magical prescriptions.

Bhagavad Gītā [BHUH-guh-vuhdh GEE-thaa]: (*Song of the Lord*) Part of the *Mahābhārata,* it is an instructive poetic conversation between Kṛṣṇa and warrior-prince Arjuna.

Bhāgavata Purāṇa [BHAA-guh-vuh-thuh poo-RAA-nuh]: A Vaiṣṇava *purāṇa.*

Bodhapañcadaśikā [BO-dhuh-puhn-chuh-DUH-shik-uh: (*Fifteen [Verses] on Consciousness*) Concise Kashmir Śaivism text attributed to Abhinavagupta.

Brāhmaṇa [BRAA-muh-nuh]: Vedic texts dealing with sacrificial rites.

Bṛhadāraṇyaka Upaniṣad [BUR-huhdh-AA-ruhn-yuh-kuh oo-PUH-nish-uhdh]: An Upaniṣad that bridges the textual genres of the Āraṇyakas and Upaniṣads.

Caraka Saṃhitā [CHUH-ruh-kuh SUHNG-hith-aa]: Ancient authoritative Āyurveda treatise.

Chāndogya Upaniṣad [CHAAN-d/thoh-gyuh oo-PUH-nish-uhdh]: Early Upaniṣad associated with the *Sāma Veda.*

Devī-Bhāgavata Purāṇa [D/THEY-vee BHAA-guh-vuh-thuh]: A Śākta *upa-purāṇa.*

Devī Māhātmya [D/THEY-vee maa-HAAT-myuh]: (*Glorification of the Great Goddess*) Text articulating the conception of a Great Goddess; also known as the *Durgā Saptaśatī.*

Devī Sūkta [D/THEY-vee SOOK-thuh]: A *Ṛg Veda* hymn, sung by the goddess Vāc to herself.

Dharma Śāstra [D/THUHR-muh SHAAS-thruh]: Legal treatises (*śāstra*) that deal specifically with *dharma.*

Dharma Sūtra [D/THUHR-muh SOO-thruh]: Part of the Kalpa Sūtras dealing with moral prescriptions for householders.

Epic of King Gesar [GAY-suhr]: A Tibetan oral epic; possibly the world's longest text.

Gītā [GEE-thaa]: The *Bhagavad Gītā.*

Gītāgovinda [GEE-thaa-go-vin-dhuh]: A poem written by Jayadeva, celebrating the love between Kṛṣṇa and Radha.

Gītāñjali [gee-THAAN-juh-lee]:(*Offering of Songs*) A poetry collection by Tagore.

Gorakṣa-śataka [GOH-ruhk-shuh-SHUH-thuh-kuh]: (*Hundred Verses by Gorakṣa*) An influential Haṭha Yoga text.

Gṛhya Sūtra [GUR-hyuh SOO-thruh]: Part of the Kalpa Sūtras dealing with life cycle rites (*saṃskāra*) and household rituals.

Guru Granth Sahib [GOO-roo GRUHNTH SA-hib]: (*Honorable Book of the Teachers*) Sacred Book of the Sikhs, containing poems by Kabīr and the Sikh Gurus.

Harivaṃśa [HUH-ree-vuhm-shuh]: (*Dynasty of Viṣṇu/Hari [i.e., Kṛṣṇa]*) An appendix to the *Mahābhārata*.

Haṭha Yoga Pradīpika [HUH-tuh YO-guh pruh-d/thee-pik-uh]: Fifteenth-century Yoga treatise.

Itihāsa [ITHI-haa-suh]: The Epics.

Jñāneśvarī [jnyaa-NEYSH-vuh-ree]: Commentary on the *Bhagavad Gītā* written by Jñāneśvara.

Kalpa Sūtra [KUHL-puh SOO-thruh]: Literature appended to the Vedas containing explanations of ritual action.

Kāma Śāstra [KAA-muh SHAAS-thruh]: Literature regarding love and sexual pleasure.

Kāma Sūtra [KAA-muh SOO-thruh]: Text in the Kāma Śāstra literature dealing with sexual relationships.

Laws of Manu [MUH-noo]: Influential Dharma Śāstra text.

Liṅga Purāṇa [LING-uh poo-RAA-nuh]: A Śaiva *purāṇa*.

Mahābhārata [muh-HAA-BHAA-ruh-thuh]: A major Hindu epic, dealing with a conflict of kingly succession.

Mahābhāṣya [muh-HAA-bhaash-yuh]: A commentary (*bhāṣya*) on Pāṇinī's grammar.

Mahāpurāṇa [muh-HAA-poo-RAA-nuh]: The eighteen or so major Purāṇas.

Mānava Dharmaśāstra [MAA-nuh-vuh D/THUR-muh SHAAS-thruh]: (*Laws of Manu*) An influential Dharma Śāstra.

Manu Smṛti [MUH-noo SMUR-thee]: A term sometimes used for the *Mānava Dharmaśāstra* (*Laws of Manu*).

Mārkaṇḍeya Purāṇa [MAAR-kuhn-dey-yuh poo-RAA-nuh]: A Śākta *purāṇa*.

Matsya Purāṇa [MUHT-syuh poo-RAA-nuh]: A Vaiṣṇava *purāṇa*.

Nālāyira Divyaprabandham [naa-LAA-yir-uh DIV-yuh-PRUH-buhn-d/thum]: (*Four Thousand Divine Literary Works*) Poems of the Ālvārs collated by Nāthamuni.

Nyāya-sūtra [NYAA-yuh SOO-thruh]: (*Aphorisms on Inquiry*) Seminal text of the Nyāya philosophical school.

Pañcarātra Saṃhitā [PUHN-chuh-raa-thruh SUHNG-hith-aa]: Main texts of the Pañcarātra sect.

Periya Purāṇa [PEY-ree-yuh poo-RAA-nuh]: South Indian text with stories of the Nāyanārs.

Purāṇa [poo-RAA-nuh]: Genre of religious literature consisting of ancient myths.

Puruṣa Sūkta [POO-roo-shuh SOOK-thuh]: Ṛg Vedic hymn that describes the cosmos as a giant being/person (*puruṣa*).

Pūrvā Mīmāṃsā Sūtra [POOR-vaa MEE-maang-saa SOO-thruh]: Mīmāṃsā philosophy foundational text.

Rāmacaritamanas [RAA-muh-CHUH-ree-thuh-muh-nuhs]: (*Ocean of the Deeds of Rāma*) A sixteenth-century telling of the *Rāmāyaṇa* by Tulsidās.

Rāmakien [RAA-muh-kee-en]: Thai version of the *Rāmāyaṇa*.

Rāmāyaṇa [raa-MAA-yuh-nuh]: Major Hindu epic dealing with the adventures of the divine prince Rāma.

Ṛg Veda Saṃhitā [URG VEY-d/thuh SUHNG-hit-aa]: Earliest of the Vedic hymn collections.

Śaiva Āgama [SH-AYE-vuh AA-guh-muh]: Authoritative texts of Kashmir Śaivism.

Śākta Purāṇa [SHAAK-thuh poo-RAA-nuh]: Goddess-centered *purāṇas*.

Śākta Tantra [SHAAK-thuh THUHN-thruh]: Tantras holding Devī preeminent.

Sāma Veda Saṃhitā [SAA-muh VEY-d/thuh SUHNG-hit-aa]: An assortment of hymns, mostly borrowed from the *Ṛg Veda,* and sung to various tunes.

Sāṅkhya Kārikā [SAAN-khyuh KAA-rik-aa]: Earliest authoritative book on Sāṅkhya philosophy.

Śāstra [SHAAS-thruh]: Treatise; knowledge/education.

Śatapatha Brāhmaṇa [SHUH-thuh-puh-thuh BRAAH-muh-nuh]: Ritual text belonging to the *White Yajur Veda* school.

Śatarudriya [SHUH-thuh-roo-d/three-yuh]: (*One Hundred [verses] concerning Rudra*) A *Yajur Veda* hymn.

Śilpa Śāstra [SHIL-puh SHAAS-thruh]: Treatises on image and temple construction.

Śiva Purāṇa [SHIV-uh poo-RAA-nuh]: A Śaiva-oriented *purāṇa*.

Śrauta Sūtra [SHRAU-thuh SOO-thruh]: Part of the Kalpa Sūtras concerning elaborate public rites.

Śrī Bhāṣya [SHREE BHAA-shyuh]: Rāmānuja's commentary on the *Vedānta Sūtra.*

Śrī Sūkta [SHREE SOOK-thuh]: Goddess-centered hymn within a *Ṛg Veda* appendix.

Śulva Sūtra [SHOOL-vuh SOO-thruh]: Part of the Kalpa Sūtras concerning the measurement and construction of ritual spaces.

Suśruta Saṃhitā [SOO-shroo-thuh SUHNG-hith-aa]: A treatise on Āyurveda.

Śvetāśvatara Upaniṣad [shvey-TAASH-vuh-tuh-ruh OO-puh-nish-uhdh]: Śaiva-centered Upaniṣad, with an early *bhakti* orientation.

Taittirīya Saṃhitā [TH-AYE-thir-ee-yuh SUHNG-hith-aa]: The *Black Yajur Veda.*

Tantra [THUHN-thruh]: Esoteric scriptures, considered unorthodox.

Tantrāloka [thuhn-THRAA-loh-kuh]: (*Light on Tantra*) Seminal treatise of Tantric Hinduism.

Tēvāram [THEY-vaa-ruhm]: Contains the writings of three of the most renowned Nāyanārs.

Tirumurai [THIR-oo-moor-aye]: Collection of eleven books of the poetry of the Nāyanārs.

Tiruvācakam [THIR-oo-VAA-chuh-kuhm]: A book in the *Tirumurai.*

Tiruvāymoli [THIR-oo-VA-AYE-moh-lee]: (*Venerable Ten*) Text containing a thousand hymns composed by Nammālvār.

Tolkāppiyam [thol-KAAP-pee-yuhm]: Early grammar text of literary Tamil named after its author.

Upaniṣad [oo-PUH-nish-uhdh]: The last segment of Vedic literature consisting of poetic verses concerning spiritual and philosophical matters.

Upapurāṇa [oo-puh-poo-RAA-nuh]: Lesser *purāṇas.*

Upaveda [oo-puh-VEY-d/thuh]: A body of literature that is supplemental to the Vedas.

Vāgbhaṭa Saṃhitā [VAAG-bhuh-tuh SUHNG-hith-aa]: An Āyurveda treatise.

Vaikhānasa Saṃhitā [v-aye-KHAA-nuh-suh SUHNG-hith-aa]: The scriptures of the Vaikhānasas.

Vaiśeṣika Sūtra [v-aye-SHEY-shik-uh SOO-thruh]: (*Aphorisms on Particularities*) Treatise on Vaiśeṣika philosophy.

Vājasaneyī Saṃhitā [VAA-juh-suh-ney-yee SUHNG-hith-aa]: *The White Yajur Veda.*

Veda (VEY-d/thuh): Sacred oral literature of the Āryans held to have been divinely revealed.

Vedānta-sūtra [VEY-d/thaan-thuh SOO-thruh]: Also called *Brahma-Sūtra;* early systematization of Upaniṣadic teachings composed by Bādarāyaṇa.
Viṣṇu Purāṇa [VISH-noo poo-RAA-nuh]: A Vaiṣṇava-oriented *purāṇa.*

Yājñavalkya Smṛti [YAAJ-nyuh-vuhl-kyuh SMUR-thee]: A Dharma Śāstra text.
Yajur Veda Saṃhita [YUH-joor VEY-d/thuh SUHNG-hith-aa]: Scripture of verses from the *Ṛg Veda;* it exists in two recensions, known as the *Black* and the *White Yajur Vedas.*
Yoga Sūtra [YOH-guh SOO-thruh]: Seminal early text on Rājā Yoga philosophy attributed to Patañjali.

Further reading

Introductory textbooks

A number of excellent textbooks, introductory treatments, and encyclopedic surveys of Hinduism are available, which instructors or students may profitably consult. They vary widely in content and style with regard to their intended audience. I am indebted to many of them for what they have taught me. Some are listed below.

Bhaskarananda, Swami (2002) *The Essentials of Hinduism: A Comprehensive Overview of the World's Oldest Religion*. Seattle, WA: Viveka Press.

Biardeau, Madeleine (1992) *Hinduism: The Anthropology of a Civilization*. Richard Nice (trans.). Delhi: Oxford University Press.

Chaudhuri, N. C. (1979) *Hinduism*. London: Chatto & Windus.

Falk, Nancy Auer (2006) *Living Hinduisms: An Explorer's Guide*. Belmont, CA: Wadsworth.

Flood, Gavin (1996) *An Introduction to Hinduism*. Cambridge: Cambridge University Press.

Flood, Gavin (ed.) (2003) *The Blackwell Companion to Hinduism*. Oxford: Blackwell Publishing.

Fuller, Christopher J. (2004) *The Camphor Flame: Popular Hinduism and Society in India* (Revised and Expanded). Princeton, NJ: Princeton University Press.

Hopkins, Thomas J. (1971) *The Hindu Religious Tradition*. Belmont, CA: Wadsworth.

Johnsen, Linda (2002) *A Complete Idiot's Guide to Hinduism*. Indianapolis, IN: Alpha Books.

Kinsley, David R. (1993) *Hinduism: A Cultural Perspective*. Englewood Cliffs, NJ: Prentice Hall, Inc.

Klostermaier, Klaus, K. (1989) *A Survey of Hinduism*. Albany, NY: State University of New York Press.

Knipe, David M. (1991) *Hinduism: Experiments in the Sacred*. New York: Harper Collins.

Knott, Kim (2000) *Hinduism: A Very Short Introduction*. Oxford: Oxford University Press.

Lipner, Julius (1994) *Hindus: Their Religious Beliefs and Practices*. New York: Routledge.

Michaels, Axel (2004) *Hinduism*. Barbara Harshav (trans.). Princeton, NJ: Princeton University Press.

Narayanan, Vasudha (2004) *Hinduism*. New York: Oxford University Press.

Shattuck, Cybelle (1999) *Hinduism*. Upper Saddle River, NJ: Prentice-Hall, Inc.

Walker, Benjamin (1968) *The Hindu World: An Encyclopedic Survey of Hinduism*, 2 vols. New York: Praeger.

Younger, Paul (1972) *Introduction to Indian Religious Thought*. Philadelphia, PA: Westminster Press.

Zaehner, R. C. (1962) *Hinduism*. Oxford: Oxford University Press.

Sourcebooks and readers

deBary, William Theodore (ed.) (1958) *The Sources of Indian Tradition*, 2 vols. New York: Columbia University Press.

Embree, Ainslie T (ed.) (1972) *The Hindu Tradition: Readings in Oriental Thought*. New York: Vintage Books.

Goodall, Dominic (ed. and trans.) (1996) *Hindu Scriptures*. Berkeley, CA: University of California Press.

O'Flaherty, Wendy Doniger (ed. and trans.) (1988) *Textual Sources for the Study of Hinduism*. Manchester: Manchester University Press.

Radhakrishnan, Sarvepalli and Charles A. Moore (1957) *A Source Book in Indian Philosophy*. Princeton, NJ: Princeton University Press.

Renou, Louis (1962) *Hinduism*. New York: George Braziller.

Index

Abhinavagupta 265
Abhishiktananda, Swami (Henri Le Saux) (1910–1973) 285–6
Absolute Brahman 251
Adi Da Samraj *see* Jones, Albert (Adi Da)
Adidam 325
Advaita Vedānta (radical non-dualism) 250
Āgama Hindu Dharma 310
Āgamas 38
Aiyappan 243
Akbar, emperor 19
Alexander the Great 17, 107, 314
All-India Anna DMK (AIDMK) 295
All-India Muslim League 281
Ālvārs 19, 166–7, 277
Angkor Wat 238–9, 308–9
antyeṣṭi (Final Sacrifice/Cremation) 77, 86–9
Āpastamba 56
Aramaic 107
Āraṇyakas 17, 33–4, 38, 76
art 240; *devadāsī* 241; *pūjāri* 240
Ārya Samāj 20, 282, 284, 296
Āryans 12; Cultural Diffusion Hypothesis 14; Indo-European Imigration Thesis 12–14; influences 14–16
Ashtanga Vinyasa 322
Aśoka, emperor 17–18, 107, 121, 165, 314
Aṣṭādhyāyī 109
astrology 39–40
Atharva Veda 17, 26, 37, 174
ātman 36–7
Aum (Om) 111–13, 127, 213
Aurangzeb, emperor 19
Aurobindo Ghose, Śri (1872–1950) 126, 287–8
auspiciousness (*saubhagya*) 70–2, 96–7
Āyurveda 40–1

Bali 310–11
Balsekar, Ramesh (1919–) 323–4
Baluchistan 10, 17–18
Banāras 86–7, 121
Basavanna (1106–1167) 176
Bauls 279
Besant, Annie 316
Bhagavad Gītā 38, 86, 126, 227, 249; and the Ālvārs/Nāyanārs 166–7; background 154–7; Bhakti yoga 162–5; Jñāna yoga 158–60; Karma yoga 160–2; and rise of devotionalism 165–6; and South Indian Hinduism 165–6; three *yogas* 158
bhakti theism 189–90, 225–6, 277–8
Bhakti yoga 162–5
Bhaktivedanta Prabhupada, Swami (1896–1977) 319–21
Bharatiya Janata Party (Party of the People of India) (BJP) 293–4
Bhartṛhari (c.fifth century CE) 110
Bhū Devī 200, 207
'Bidi Baba' see Nisargadatta Maharaj (1897–1981)
Black Pagoda 237

Black Yajur Veda 25
Blavatsky, Madame (Helena Petrovna) 286
Borobudur 309
Brahmā 30, 46, 82, 191–2, 199–201, 207, 310
Brahma Sūtra see Vedānta Sūtra
brahman 36–7
Brāhmaṇas 17, 28, 38
Brāhmī script 107–8
Brāhmo Samāj 283
Bṛhadāraṇyaka Upaniṣad 36, 213
Bubba Free John *see* Jones, Albert (Adi Da)
the Buddha *see* Siddhārtha Gautama
Buddhism 17, 77, 121–2, 309

Caitanya, Śri (1486–1533) 164–5, 180
calendar 47–8
Cambodia 308–9
caṇḍāla see Untouchables
Candragupta Maurya 17
Caraka Samhitā 40
Cārvāka 122–3
caste system 60–5, 334
cave temples 19
Chakri Dynasty 309
Chandella Dynasty 236
Chāndogya Upaniṣad 36
Chatterjee, Bankim 294
childbirth 84–6
Chopra, Deepak 41
Christianity 20, 273, 277, 282–5
class system (*varṇa*) 57–60; behaviour 58–9; dissents/tensions 59–60; duties of a king 59; skin-complexion theory 58
Classical Sanskrit 108, 109
Clement of Alexandria 315
Cohen, Leonard 324
cows 331
Cremation *see antyeṣṭi*(Final Sacrifice/ Cremation)
Cultural Diffusion Hypothesis 14

Da-Love Ananda *see* Jones, Albert (Adi Da)
Darius I 314
darśana 230–4
Dasain festival 306–7
Dāsas 12
Dasyus 12
Dayānanda Sarasvati (1824–83) 284
death 86–9
deities 11–12, 14, 15, 18, 18–19, 25, 46, 70, 72, 157, 188; goddesses 181–3, 215, 266, 329–30; numbers/variety of 213–17; Śaiva 192–8; Śākta 205–12; Vaiśṇava 199–205; Vedic 26–7, 190–2
demons 213
Desikachar, T.K.V. 322
devadāsī (servants of God) 241
Devī Durgā (goddess) 307
Devī Māhātmya 181–2, 211
devotionalism 165–6
dharma (righteous social engagement) 4–5, 27, 55–6, 77
Dharma Śāstras 45, 56–7, 120
Dharma Sūtras 39
dīkṣā 77
Dīvālī209
Dravida Munnetra Kazhagam (Dravidian Progressive Federation) (DMK) 295
Dravidian Movement 294–5
Dravidian (Southern) culture 12–13, 16
Durgā Pūjā festival 72

East India Company 20, 280
ecology 329–32
Epics 136–7, 149–50, 214, 310–11, *see also Mahābhārata; Rāmāyaṇa*

Fa-xien 309

Gandhi, Indira 293
Gandhi, Mohandas Karamchand (Mahatma Gandhi) (1869–1948) 161–2, 281, 289, 291–2
Gandhi, Rajiv 293
Gandhi, Sonia 294
Gaṅeśa (elephant-headed god) 15, 19, 196–7, 309

Gaṅgā (Ganges) River 1, 89, 330
Gangaji (1942–) 324
Garuda 200, 309
Gaudiya Vaiṣṇava 179–80
Gautama, Siddhārtha (the Buddha) 17, 56, 121–2
Gāyatrī 80
Genghis Khan 19
Ghaggar-Hakra River 9
Gnostics 315
goals/aims of life (*puruṣārtha*) 89, 157
Golden Temple (Amritsar) 293
Gorakṣanātha 176
The Gospel of Thomas 315
Great Tradition 15, 226
Gṛhya Sūtras 39
Griffiths, Father Bede (1906–1993) 286
Gupta Dynasty 18–19, 234
guru 77
Gyanendra, king 306

Hanumān 15, 140–1, 150, 202, 277, 302
Harappa 8
Haridvāra 242
Hariharālaya 308
Haṭha Yoga 322–3
Havik Brahmins (Mysore) 67–70
Hindu Calendar 47
Hindu/s 1; definition 4; geographical distribution of 5
Hinduism, and Christianity 282–5; contemporary figures in 332–3; contemporary teachers 323–5; definition 4–5; diaspora 315–16; diversity/complexity of 1–3; early critiques/responses 274–5; and ecology 329–32; history of 17–21; and humanism 288–90; in Indonesia 309–11; and Islam 276–7; and modernity 333–6; in Nepal 306–8; and politics 290–5; religious components of 15–16; scenario 301–5; in Southeast Asia 308–9; in universalistic religion 286–8; and the West 314–15, 316–23
Hindutva: Who is a Hindu? 292
householders 91–3, 157
humanism 288–90
inauspiciousness 70–2
India 4, 5–6; British in 280–2
Indian National Congress party 281
Indo-European Migration Thesis 12–14
Indonesia 309–10
Indra 25
Indus Valley Civilization 8–10, 107, 125–6, 180, 257; and the Āryans 12; religion of 10–12
Integral yoga 126, 287–8
International Society for Kṛṣṇa Consciousness (ISKCON) 180, 320–1
Investiture with Sacred Thread (*upanayana*) 78–80
Islam 19; and Hinduism 276–7; historical background 275–6
Iyengar, B.K.S. (1918–) 322

Jagannātha temple 237
Jai Santoshi Mā (film, 1975) 215
Jainism 17, 77, 121
Jallianwala Bagh massacre 281
Jana Gana Mana Adhinayaka (You are the Ruler of the Minds of all People) 289
Janata Dal party 334
jātis (birth-group) 57; circumscription of 61–2; as closed communities 62; coexist/overlap with *varṇa* 60–1; complexity of system 62–4; occupational diversification 65; origin 61; stratification of 64–5
Jayavarman II, king 308
Jinnah, Muhammad Ali 281
Jñāna yoga 158–60
Jñāneṣvara (c1275–1296 CE) 179
Jones, Albert (Adi Da) 324–5

Kabīr (fifteenth century) 278
Kailāsanātha temple 237–8
Kālī (goddess) 209–11
Kalidāsa 18–19

Kalpa Sūtras 39, 56
Kāpālikas 174–5
karma 50–1, 57
Karma yoga 160–2
Kārttikeya *see* Skanda
Kashmir 260–1
Katha Upaniṣad 36
Keshab Chandra Sen 284
Kharoṣṭhī script 107
Khmer Empire 308
Krishnamacharya, Tirumalai 322–3
Krishnamurti, Jiddu (1895–1986) 318
Kriyā yoga 126
Kṛṣṇa 203–5
Kubera 217
Kumbha Melas 242
Kuṇḍalinī Yoga 126, 263–4
Kuṣāṇas 18

Lakṣmī see Śri Lakṣmī
Law Books *see* Dharma Śāstras
Lāya yoga 126
Left Hand Tantra 265
lesser Upaniṣads 38
Liberation Tigers of Tamil Eelam (LTTE) 293
Liquorman, Wayne (aka Ram Tzu) 324
Little Tradition 15, 225, 226

Macaulay, Thomas Babington 289–90
Madhva (1238–1317) 20, 253
Mahābhārata 18, 108, 144–9, 174, 310
Mahābhāṣya 109
Mahādevī Durgā (goddess) 211–12
Mahapajit (Majapahit) kingdom 310
Maharishi Mahesh Yogi (1917–) 318–19
Mahāsābha 292
Mahāśivarātri festival 193, 307–8
Mahāvīra, Vardhamāna 121
Mahmud of Ghazni 19
Malla Dynasty 306
Manasā (snake goddess) 216
Mānava Dharmastra (Laws of Manu) 56
Mandal Commission (1980) 334
mantra 36, 80, 111–12, 266–8
Marathas 61
Mariyamman (goddess) 215–16
marriage (*vivāha*) 61, 72, 77, 801; categories of 82; lineage/male-heir function 82–3; love-based 82; *pativrata* ideal 97–9; polygamous 81; ritual 83–4; selection of bride 81
Mātṛkās 217
Mauryan (Peacock) Dynasty 17–18, 315
Mīmāṃsā (Interpretation) *darśana* 131–2
Mitra 25
Mohenjodaro 8, 9, 12
mokṣa (liberation) 52–3, 77
Mountbatten, Lord Louis 281
Mughals 19–20
Muktananda, Swami (1908–1982) 324–5
Murugan 166, 190, 198
Muslim League 292
Myanmar (Burma) 309

Nāda yoga 126
Nāgas (serpents) 216
Nālāyira Divyaprabandham (Four Thousand Divine Literary Works) 166
Nāmdev (1270–1350) 179–80
Nanak, Guru (1469–1539) 279–80
Nāth sect 176
Navarātra (Nine Nights) festival 72, 97, 306–7
Nāyanārs 19, 166–7, 175, 278
Nehru, Jawaharlal 20, 281, 293
Nepal 306–8
nirvāṇa 121
Nisargadatta Maharaj (1897–1981) 323
non-dualism, qualified 252–3; radical 250–1
Nyāya *darśana* 128–30

Olcott, Colonel Henry Steele 286
Om *see* Aum
orthodoxy 225–6
Osho (Bhagwan Rajneesh) (1930–1990) 321–2

Pallava Dynasty 19
Pañcarātra sect 178–9
Pāṇinī (seventh–third centuries BCE) 109
Paramahansa Yogananda 317
Pārvatī *see* Satī/Pārvatī
Pāśupatas 174
Paśupatināth Temple 307
Patañjali (second-first century BCE) 109, 125, 322
Pattabhi Jois 322
philosophy, heterodox 21–3; orthodox 23–32; orthodox vs heterodox schools 120; scenario 115–19; wandering philosophers 119
pilgrimage 242–3
Plotinus 18
politics 290–4
pollution 265; ritual 66–70
Pound, Ezra 289
Prambanan Temple 309–10
Prithvi Narayan Shah 306
Pūjā 227–9
pūjāri (priest) 240
Purāṇas 45, 188–90, 214
Puranic period 50
purity 265; ritual 66–70
Puruṣottama, King 17
Pythagoras 18

Rāja Yoga 315
Rāma 72
Rama IX, king 309
Ramakrishna Order 285
Ramakrishna Paramahamsa (1836–1886) 284–5, 317
Ramaṇa Mahāṛṣi (1879–1950) 159–60
Rāmānuja 20, 252–3
Rāmāyaṇa 18, 56, 86, 100, 108, 136–43, 217, 293, 310
Rana family 306
Raṅganāthaswami temple 238
Rashtriya Swayamsevak Sangh (RSS) (Community of Volunteers for the nation) 292–3
reincarnation 50–1, 331
renouncers 157, 251
Rg Veda 25, 37, 48–9, 55, 57, 180
Rg Veda Samhitā 17
rites of passage (*samskāra*) 51, 77; conception/childbirth 84–6; death/cremation 86–9; educational 80, *see also* Cremation (*antyeṣṭi*); Investiture with Sacred Thread (*upanayana*); Marriage (*vivāha*)
ritual, Balinese 310; marriage 83–4; pollution 66–70; purity 66–70
Roop Kanwar 100
Roy, Ram Mohan (1772–1833) 283
ṛta 27

Sai Baba of Shirdi (1838–1918) 332
Śaiva Āgamas 260
Śaiva Siddhānta 175–6, 260
Śaivism 260–1; origins/development 172–4; schools 174–6
Śāka-Parthians 18
Śāktism, modes of 181–3; *Rg Veda* 180; origins/development 180–1
Sāma Veda 17, 25, 37
Samāvartana (Returning Home) 80
samskāra see rites of passage
sanātana dharma 5
Saṅgham period 165–6
Śaṅkara 250–1
the Śaṅkarācāryas 333
Sāṅkhya 123–5
Sanskrit 13, 289–90; *Aṣṭādhyāyī* 109; historical background 107–9; *mantra*/theology of sound 111–12; scenario 105–7; *sphoṭa* theory 109–11; structure of alphabet 110
Sanskritization 15
Santoshi Mā (goddess) 215, 216
Sarasvatī (goddess) 205–7
sati (immolation while alive) 99–100
Satī/Pārvatī (goddess) 193–6
Satya Sai Baba (1926–) 332–3
Savarkar, Vinayak Damodar 292

Self-realization 157
Self-Realization Fellowship 317
Shah dynasty 306
Shivaji Bhonsle 61
Sikhism 20
Sītā 56 138–43, 150–1, 208, 305
Śitalā (goddess) 215–16
Śiva 11–12, 14, 19, 172–6, 192–3, 307–8
Sivananda Saraswati, Swami (1887–1963) 323
Skanda/Kārttikeya (son of Śiva) 19, 198
Smārta Brahmins 174, 190, 197, 214
smṛti 37–8
Soma 33
sphoṭa theory of language 109–11
śrāddha rites 87–8
śramaṇa movements 77, 190
Śri Bhāśya 252
Śrī Caitanya 20
Śri Lakṣmī (goddess) 207–9
Sri Lanka 5
Śri Veṅkaṭeśvara temple 242–3
śruti 37–8
stages of life, four, *gṛhastha* (householder) 91–3; *saṃnyāsa* (renouncer) 93–4; *śiṣya* (student) 89–90; *vanaprastha* (retirement) 93
śūdra 57–8, 61–2, 65–8, 166,334
Śuṅga Dynasty 18
Sūrya 19
Suryavarman II, emperor 50, 308
Suśruta Saṃhitā 40
sūtras 38
Śvetāśvatara Upaniṣad 15, 162, 277

Tagore, Debendranath 283
Tagore, Rabindranath (1861–1941) 288–90
Taleju 307
Tantra 26, 38; characteristic elements 258–60; and goddesses/women 266; and Kuṇḍalinī yoga 263–4; Left Hand Path 265; non-dualistic 261–3; origins 257–8; and Śaivism 260–1; symbolism of *mantras/yantras* 266–8
Tantrāloka (Light on Tantra) 260
Tantric 15
Tantrism 126
technology, biotechnology 335; cable/satellite 336; media 335–6; transportation 335
temples, Hindu 234–6; images in 237; Indonesia 309–10; inner sanctum 231, 235–6; Northern (Nāgara) style 234–5, 236–8; noteworthy 236–9; rock-cut 237–8; sexual imagery on 236–7; Southern (Dravida) style 234, 235, 238; and worship 230–4
Thailand 309
theistic sects *see* Śaivism; Śāktism; Vaiṣṇavism
Theosophical Society 286–7
Thoreau, David 291
Tilak, Bal Gangadhar (1856–1920) 290–1
time 45–6, 72
Tolkāppiyam 15
Tolstoy, Leo 291
transcendental knowledge 251
Trika Śaivism 260
Tulsidās 150, 202, 321

universalization 15
universe 48–50
Untouchables (*caṇḍāla*) 58, 65–6, 334
upanayana see Investiture with Sacred Thread
Upāṅgas 39
Upaniṣadic period 77
Upaniṣads 17, 34–6, 49, 249
Upavedas 40

Vāgbhaṭa 40
Vaikhānasas sect 179
Vaiṣeṣika *darśana* 128, 130
Vaiṣṇavism, origns/development 177–8; schools 178–80
Vākyapadīya (On Sentence and Word) 110

Vande Mataram (I Praise the Mother) 294
Vārānasī (Banāras) 1
Vardhamāna (Mahāvīra, Jina the Conqueror) 17
varṇa see class system
Varuṇa 25
Vedāṇgas 38–9
Vedānta 131–2, 249
Vedānta Society 283, 317
Vedānta Sūtra (Brahma Sūtra) 249
Vedārambha (Beginning of Vedic Knowledge) 80
Vedas 4, 12, 14, 15, 17
Vedic 15, 16
Vedic deities 26–7
Vedic literature, other 38–9; religious 37–8
Vedic rituals (*yajṇa*) 28–33; *agnicayana* 31–3; horse sacrifice (*aśvamedha*) 30–1
Vedic Samhitās 25–6
Vedic Sanskrit 25, 108
Vedāṅgas 56
Vidyārambha (Beginning of Study) 80
Viniyoga 322
Vīraśaiva sect 176
Vishnudevananda, Swami 323
Vishwa Hindu Parishad (Universal Hindu Assembly) (VHP) 293
Viṣiṣṭādvaita (qualified non-dualism) 252
Viṣṇu 19, 199–200; *avatāras* 200; Balarāma (Buddha) *avatāra* 203; Boar *avatāra* 201; Dwarf *avatāra* 202; Fish *avatāra* 200–1; Kalki *avatāra* 203; Man-Lion *avatāra* 201; Rāma *avatāra* 202–3; Rāma with Axe *avatāra* 202; Tortoise *avatāra* 201
Viṣṇu (Vāsudeva) 18
Vivekānanda, Swami (Narendranath Dutta) (1863–1902) 283, 316–17
vowed ascetic observances (*vrata*) 96–7
Vyāsa 125

White Yajur Veda 25
women 94–6, 334; and gender equality 335; and marriage 97–9; and *satī* 99–100; and *Tantra* 266; and vowed ascetic observance/auspiciousness 96–7; and widowhood 100–1
World Parliament of Religions (1893) 316
worship, domestic 227–9; scenario 222–4; temple 230–4

yajña 28–33
Yājñavalkya Smṛti 56
Yajur Veda 17, 25, 37
Yakṣas 216–17
yantra 266–8
Yeats, William Butler 289
Yoga 125–6; eight limbs of 127–8; Patañjali's *Yoga Sūtra* 126–7; *yogi* 128
Yoga Rahasya (Esoteric Teachings on Yoga) 322
Yoga Sūtra 111, 125, 126–7, 322
Yoga of Synthesis 323
yugas 46, 189

Hindus

Their religious beliefs and practices

Julius Lipner

'This is quite simply the best book I have read on Hinduism in a long time.'
Girish Karnad, *The Book Review*

'This book is a landmark in the Western study of Hinduism.'
Arvind Sharma, *Religion*

'Julius Lipner's book is a scholarly but at the same time very readable guide to Hinduism – a religion which is all too often misunderstood and misrepresented.'
Mark Tully, writer and commentator on India and former BBC Delhi Correspondent

Hindus offers us a major study of religious Hinduism. Julius Lipner explains the evolution and multidimensional nature of the religion in a clear and direct fashion. Covering history, belief and practice, he combines factual information with explanation and analysis, and illustrates the material with vivid stories and entertaining asides.

Library of Religious Beliefs and Practices
Series editors: John Hinnells and Ninian Smart

ISBN10: 0-415-05181-9 (hbk) ISBN13: 978-0-415-05181-1 (hbk)
ISBN10: 0-415-05182-7 (pbk) ISBN13: 978-0-415-05182-8 (pbk)

Related titles from Routledge

Introducing Buddhism

Charles S. Prebish and Damien Keown

'An up-to-date textbook for beginners as well as advanced students of Buddhism. Its clear structure helps beginners getting oriented in the complex field of Buddhism, and its respective chapters are rich in detailed information for students who already have some basic knowledge. Instructors and students alike will appreciate its didactic tools. I have used this book in my classes, with great success.'

Oliver Freiberger, University of Texas at Austin

Introducing Buddhism is the ideal resource for all students beginning the study of this fascinating religion. Damien Keown and Charles S. Prebish, two of today's leading Buddhist scholars, explain the key teachings of Buddhism, and trace the historical development and spread of the religion from its beginnings down to the present day. A chapter is devoted to each of the major regions where Buddhism has flourished: India, South East Asia, East Asia and Tibet. In addition to this regional focus, the introduction takes contemporary concerns into account, covering important and relevant topics such as Engaged Buddhism, Buddhist Ethics and Buddhism and the Western World, as well as a chapter devoted to Meditation.

Introducing Buddhism also includes illustrations, lively quotations from original sources, learning goals, summary boxes, questions for discussion, and suggestions for further reading, to aid study and revision.

ISBN10: 0-415-39234-9 (hbk)
ISBN10: 0-415-39235-7 (pbk)

ISBN13: 978-0-415-39234-1 (hbk)
ISBN13: 978-0-415-39235-8 (pbk)

Related titles from Routledge

Religions of South Asia

Edited by Sushil Mittal and Gene R. Thursby

South Asia is home to many of the world's most vibrant religious faiths. It is also one of the most dynamic and historically rich regions on earth, where changing political and social structures have caused religions to interact and hybridize in unique ways. This textbook introduces the contemporary religions of South Asia, from the indigenous religions such as the Hindu, Jain, Buddhist and Sikh traditions, to incoming influences such as Christianity, Judaism and Islam. In ten chapters, it surveys the nine leading belief systems of South Asia and explains their history, practices, values and worldviews. A final chapter helps students relate what they have learnt to religious theory, paving the way for future study.

Entirely written by leading experts, ***Religions of South Asia*** combines solid scholarship with clear and lively writing to provide students with an accessible and comprehensive introduction. All chapters are specially designed to aid cross-religious comparison, following a standard format covering set topics and issues; the book reveals to students the core principles of each faith, compares it to neighboring traditions, and its particular place in South Asian history and society. It is a perfect resource for all students of South Asia's diverse and fascinating faiths.

ISBN10: 0-415-22390-3 (hbk)
ISBN10: 0-415-22391-1 (pbk)

ISBN13: 978-0-415-22390-4 (hbk)
ISBN13: 978-0-415-22391-1 (pbk)